OPERATIONS MANAGEMENT

Continuous Improvement

THE IRWIN SERIES IN PRODUCTION OPERATIONS MANAGEMENT

Aquilano and Chase, *Fundamentals of Operations Management, First Edition*
Chase and Aquilano, *Production and Operations Management, Sixth Edition*
Berry et al., *ITEK, Inc., First Edition*
Hill, *Manufacturing Strategy: Text & Cases, Second Edition*
Klein, *Revitalizing Manufacturing: Text & Cases, First Edition*
Lambert and Stock, *Strategic Logistics Management, Third Edition*
Leenders, Fearon, and England, *Purchasing and Materials Management, Ninth Edition*
Lotfi and Pegels, *Decision Support Systems For Production & Operations Management for Use with IBM PC, Second Edition*
Nahmias, *Production and Operations Analysis, Second Edition*
Niebel, *Motion and Time Study, Eighth Edition*
Sasser, Clark, Garvin, Graham, Jaikumar, and Maister, *Cases In Operations Management: Analysis & Action, First Edition*
Schonberger and Knod, *Operations Management: Continuous Improvement, Fifth Edition*
Stevenson, *Production/Operations Management, Fourth Edition*
Vollmann, Berry, and Whybark, *Manufacturing Planning & Control Systems, Third Edition*
Whybark, *International Operations Management: A Selection of Imede Cases, First Edition*

THE IRWIN SERIES IN STATISTICS

Aczel, *Complete Business Statistics, Second Edition*
Duncan, *Quality Control & Industrial Statistics, Fifth Edition*
Emory and Cooper, *Business Research Methods, Fourth Edition*
Gitlow, Gitlow, Oppenheim, and Oppenheim, *Tools and Methods For the Improvement of Quality, First Edition*
Hall and Adelman, *Computerized Business Statistics, Second Edition*
Hanke and Reitsch, *Understanding Business Statistics, Second Edition*
Mason and Lind, *Statistical Techniques in Business and Economics, Eighth Edition*
Neter, Wasserman, and Kutner, *Applied Linear Statistical Models, Third Edition*
Neter, Wasserman, and Kutner, *Applied Linear Regression Models, Second Edition*
Siegel, *Practical Business Statistics, Second Edition*
Webster, *Applied Statistics For Business and Economics, First Edition*
Wilson and Keating, *Business Forecasting, Second Edition*

THE IRWIN SERIES IN QUANTITATIVE METHODS AND MANAGEMENT SCIENCE

Bierman, Bonini, and Hausman, *Quantitative Analysis For Business Decisions, Eighth Edition*
Knowles, *Management Science: Building and Using Models, First Edition*
Lotfi and Pegels, *Decision Support Systems For Management Science & Operations Research, Second Edition*
Stevenson, *Introduction to Management Science, Second Edition*
Turban and Meredith, *Fundamentals of Management Science, Sixth Edition*

OPERATIONS MANAGEMENT

Continuous Improvement

Richard J. Schonberger
University of Washington
and
Schonberger & Associates, Inc.

Edward M. Knod, Jr.
Western Illinois University

IRWIN

Burr Ridge, Illinois
Boston, Massachusetts
Sydney, Australia

The cover photo is the sign on a Japanese paint shop. Kanban, from the Japanese, means ''card'' or ''visible record.'' An ancient meaning of kanban is shop sign. The colorful artistic sign conveys simple, accurate information about a shop's product or service to the passing shopper. A kanban card in operations management tells what and how much to provide to the customer.

© RICHARD D. IRWIN, INC., 1981, 1985, 1988, 1991, and 1994

Senior sponsoring editor:	Richard T. Hercher, Jr.
Developmental editor:	Gail Korosa
Marketing manager:	Robb Linsky
Project editor:	Stephanie M. Britt
Production manager:	Irene H. Sotiroff
Art coordinator:	Mark Malloy
Designer:	Larry J. Cope
Cover designer:	Crispin Prebys
Compositor:	Carlisle Communications, Ltd.
Typeface:	10/12 Palatino
Printer:	Von Hoffman Press

Library of Congress Cataloging-in-Publication Data

Schonberger, Richard J.
    Operations management : continuous improvement / Richard J.
Schonberger and Edward M. Knod, Jr. — 5th ed., Continuous
improvement instructor's ed.
        p.   cm.
    Includes bibliographical references and index.
    ISBN 0-256-11218-5. — ISBN 0-256-13780-3 (instructor's ed.) — ISBN 0-256-15602-6 (international ed.)
    1. Production management. I. Knod, Edward M. II. Title.
TS15.S3244   1994   93–10644
658.5 — dc20

Printed in the United States of America
1 2 3 4 5 6 7 8 9 0   VH   0 9 8 7 6 5 4 3

Every member of every organization serves somebody else: the customer at the next process. We earn our pay and much of our job-related satisfaction from serving that customer well, with consistently high and ever-improving quality. Effective operations management (OM) aims squarely at this customer-serving objective.

Operations Management is intended as an introductory textbook, suitable for majors or nonmajors, undergraduate or graduate. In addition, practicing operations managers and associates may find it useful as a general guidebook and basic reference.

Achieving the objective requires engaging, coordinating, and continually upgrading the operating resources of the organization: data, equipment, tools, space, materials, and especially people. Effective OM harnesses the talents of front-line employees, technicians, experts, supervisors, and upper-level managers. Their individual skills—as designers, schedulers, equipment operators, planners, and so on—are important, but that is not enough. Individuals can get fixated on their narrow role, to the neglect of the whole product or service and its user, the final customer.

Therefore, in this text, we emphasize people operating in teams for improved delivery of goods and services to customers. The full power of this approach requires team membership that crosses organizational and company boundaries, heavy reliance on process data and data analysis, and local responsibility for results.

These themes—customer-focused, team-driven, data-based continuous improvement—are centerpieces of the worldwide total quality management (TQM) movement. While some companies are well along the TQM path, others are not. Therefore, we must present both conventional and TQM-enhanced concepts. At the same time, we make an effort to note which conventional OM concepts still work well, which do not, and why.

With other supplementary study materials or readings, this book could serve as a TQM textbook. Six chapters—1, 2, 3, 4, 7, 8, and 18—provide a strong TQM foundation. Additional TQM-oriented topics may be found in parts of Chapters 9, 10, 11, 15, 16, and 17.

Part of continuous improvement is preventing things from going wrong, which greatly simplifies operations management. Unexpected stoppages, delays, and slowdowns are avoided, making planning easier and cutting out corrective actions that disruptively ripple through the organization. The simplification theme, found throughout the book, cuts both ways: Simplify to reduce mistakes. Reduce mistakes to make work life simpler.

This should not imply that OM is itself simple and easy to master. Even in small organizations, managing operations is complex because it involves coordination of diverse resources, processes, suppliers, and customer demands.

The relevance of operations management to you may be quite direct. If you are an employee—or even a volunteer in a service capacity—as well as a student, you are an operations manager. You have some responsibility for planning and controlling your operation. At the very least, these studies should give you ideas on how to improve an operation and your role in it.

We owe special thanks to a select group of experts who reviewed our manuscript and whose astute advice was mostly incorporated. They include: S. Keith Adams, Iowa State

University; Karen Brown, Seattle University; James J. Browne, New York University; James P. Gilbert, University of Georgia; James R. Gross, University of Wisconsin, (Oshkosh); Ray M. Haynes, California Polytechnic State University; John J. Lawrence, The University of Idaho; and Victor E. Sower, Sam Houston State University.

We are appreciative as well of the specialized advice and information provided by H. Thomas Johnson, Portland State University, Steve Kline, Western Illinois University; consultant Thomas Billesbach; Taeho Park, San Jose State University, for checking the calculations in examples and problems; and Steve Replogle and Farhad Moeeni, both of Arkansas State University, who prepared the Study Guide. Steve Replogle also provided the transparency masters on disks. Finally, we thank our publication team headed by Richard Hercher, Sr. Sponsoring Editor, and Gail Korosa, developmental editor, for their pioneering efforts to bring real teamwork into this complex business of transforming ill-formed ideas and rough drafts into a complete learning package.

Richard J. Schonberger
Edward M. Knod, Jr.

When you study operations management, or OM, keep in mind that there are two separate ideas about what we mean by the word operations. First, and generally, operations refers to harnessing resources to provide a service or produce something. As such, operations belong to no specific part of an organization; they are part of every kind of organized activity and touch your life as customer or provider of those operations.

Within this first context, the relevance of operations management to you is quite direct. Whether as an employee—even a volunteer in a service capacity—or as a student, you are an operations manager. You have some responsibility for planning and controlling the things you do and for the results of those activities. At the very least, your OM studies should give you ideas on how to improve your operation and others connected to it.

The second and narrower meaning refers to operations as one or more departments or functional areas within organizations. Historically, operations areas have housed value-adding activities where certain resources are transformed into goods and services. Within this context, your study of OM will provide insights on the interdependencies between operations and other areas—marketing, accounting, product design, human resources, and information systems. These insights are valuable even to people on the lowest rungs of the organizational ladder; they can make or break a career for those aspiring to climb up the ladder. Chapter 18 elaborates on these matters of possible personal interest to you and your career.

In your study of OM, you'll need to keep both meanings in focus. Beyond the impact on yourself, however, there is a bigger picture to consider. Effective OM blends the interests of customer, employee, and manager, along with those of the public, stockholders, and other stakeholders. Diverse resources, changing technologies, and hard-to-predict demands add to the challenge. Human ingenuity, diligence, and the right management tools, are required to blend all the interests properly.

Your OM studies, therefore, will involve a certain amount of complexity and an array of management tools and techniques. These have their soft side (guidelines, procedures, and flowcharts), and their hard side (formulas and management science models).

As you study each succeeding chapter, you will repeatedly encounter some of the core topics—quality, quick response, cellular organization of people and facilities, and so on. These topics are multifaceted. Poorly managed organizations often make the deadly mistake of trying to manage quality, for example, out of a single department using a far too limited set of concepts and tools.

Special features designed to provide relevance, interest, and help in your studies include:

- Margin notes that highlight a major point, define a term, or add an insight.
- Key-word listings at the end of each chapter, collected into a glossary at the end of the book.
- Boxed presentations of real-life applications.
- Photos of successful implementations.
- Examples illustrating complex concepts and calculations.
- End-of-chapter solved problems.
- An appendix containing more complete answers to selected problems and exercises.
- Contrast boxes comparing conventional concepts with newer ideas.
- Special margin notes in every chapter to connect a point back to the principles of operations management from Chapter 1.
- A large, thorough index.
- A study guide covering key topics.

Good luck in your OM studies. Please let your instructor know what you like and don't like about the fifth edition. We value your opinion, passed on to us through the instructor. Continuous improvement is our objective, too.

R. J. S.
E. M. K.

CONTENTS IN BRIEF

C O N T E N T S

INTRODUCTION TO OPERATIONS MANAGEMENT

I

The operating end of a business is where services are provided and products are made, where most of the firm's money is spent and earned, and where most of the people work. How best to manage the factors of operations is the central issue of this book. The following two-chapter introduction provides an overview and details the key issues.

Chapter 1 sets forth the theme of the book: Teaming up in the cause of continually improving service to customers is a strategically important, overriding goal of operations management. The chapter provides a set of principles that will help operations associates accomplish this never-ending goal. Chapter 2 focuses on achieving a serious commitment to continuous improvement of quality—customers' number one concern—as part of the fabric of operations management.

1 CUSTOMERS, COMPETITIVE STRATEGIES, PRINCIPLES

Chapter Outline

High public awareness of such issues as competitiveness, globalization, international balance of payments, and national quality awards has put operations management (OM) and operations people in the spotlight. The result has been the emergence of two opposing images of OM. One is of chaotic, high-cost, wasteful operations that alienate both customers and employees—an image that foretells layoffs, plant closings, and bankruptcies. The other image is one of continuing improvement that is customer centered, employee driven, and nourished by fresh ideas, concepts, and techniques. That is the image of a world-class organization, capable of competing globally if that opportunity exists.

In this book, we emphasize the latter image and concentrate on making that image a reality. In other words, we will not be content with presenting alternative approaches to a topic or problem. Rather, we will state our preferences clearly, even when they are different from practices widely in use. We will begin with a few observations about the meaning of operations management and current thinking about it.

Operations and Operations Management

All organizations have operations:

A manufacturing company may conduct operations in a foundry, mill, or factory.

Hospital operations occur in surgical suites, admitting offices, and examining rooms.

EXHIBIT 1–1   The Focus of Operations Management

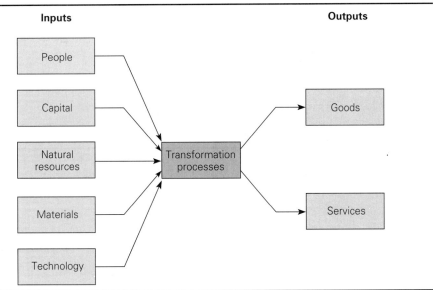

Banks and public accounting firms operate out of offices.

Restaurant operations take place on grills, chopping blocks, serving tables, and take-out counters.

Builders operate in meeting rooms where proposals are prepared and at construction sites.

University operations take place in classrooms, research labs, theaters, and athletic fields.

Supermarkets and other retailers perform operations from the back dock through shopping aisles and past cashier stations.

The common thread in each of these examples is the focus on transformation of resources into goods and services. In **operations**, inputs—knowledge and skills of people, capital, natural resources, materials, and technology—are transformed into outputs (see Exhibit 1–1).

Our interest is in the management of operations, or **operations management (OM)**, including the usual management cycle of planning, implementing, and monitoring/controlling. Beyond that, however, modern OM places special emphasis on *people* dedicated to repeating the plan-implement-monitor cycle rapidly, with the aim of fast-paced **continuous improvement**.

Some of the fresh ideas concerning OM began to emerge during the 1980s and include the following:

- The driving force for operations management must be an overriding goal of continually improving service to customers, where *customer* means the next process as well as the final, external user.

- Broad principles have been developed to guide OM associates along the path of continual improvement.

- The critical mechanism for translating the goals and principles into action is total involvement of the work force, ideally in action teams and other partnership arrangements.
- Because effective OM requires the entire work force to be involved in continual improvement, the term *operations manager* includes everybody, not just those with *manager* in their title.
- Since there is an operations element in every function of the enterprise, all people in all jobs in every department of the organization should team up for improvement of their own operations management elements. In other words, OM deals with how the functions of the business and the jobs and skills of people are performed and managed.
- Quality is the standard, and it applies to both outputs and transformation processes.

We will expand on these ideas in the remainder of Part I. The first five are addressed in this chapter, and the last one is treated in Chapter 2.

Teaming Up with Customers

We are all familiar with the supplier-to-customer connection in the retail setting. We've all been customers, with needs and expectations about how those needs should be met. We convey our feelings in the form of requirements when we purchase goods and services (or gripes when our needs are poorly met). In a bank, hardware store, or optometrist's office, face-to-face meetings and real-time discussions generally result in a more satisfying relationship. The oft-heard question "May I help you?" is a comforting reminder that the supplier-customer connection is a close one.

Maintaining a close supplier-customer connection is important for retailers and for salespeople in general. However, the value of close connections applies equally to every operation leading to the final customer.

Disconnections Spell Trouble

What happens when supplier and customer are disconnected? Consider design work, for example. Not only is the final customer not around during the design stage, but designing takes place weeks or months before pilot tests are begun or prototypes are completed. In addition, it may be years before a retail customer tries out a new design, and production may have taken place across a continent or an ocean. Whether we speak of goods or services, time-and-distance separation in the supplier-customer connection invites trouble.

Further, there seems to be a human tendency to react to these kinds of problems by pulling back from, instead of reaching out, to the customer. Even grocery store clerks, almost eyeball to eyeball with customers, are susceptible:

Question: "What's your job?"
Answer: "I run the cash register and sack groceries."
Question: "But isn't your job to serve the customer?"
Answer: "I suppose so, but my job description doesn't say that."

In grocery stores, where the supplier-customer relationship is immediate, the operations management system is hard pressed to maintain a customer focus. In manufacturing, where time and distance make it much easier to stay in the background, the operations management challenge is enlarged. The almost certain consequences of inadequate contact with customers are obvious: lost orders and contracts, declining revenue, closed plants, loss of jobs, and economic decline.

𝒞ontrast

Classifying People

Them versus Us	**We**
Common *people* terminology: Managers and professionals versus workers. Salaried versus wage earners. Skilled versus unskilled. Exempts (from U.S. Wage and Hour Law) versus nonexempts.	Uncommon alternative: Some firms call all employees associates; they banish words implying that a manager class has charge of improvements and a worker class carries them out.

Against that bleak backdrop, there nevertheless is cause for cheer. For one thing, industry has come up with a potent new concept of the **customer**: The customer is the next process, or where the work goes next.[1]

The next-process concept has its roots in the worldwide quality movement, and it has caught the attention not only of managers but also of front-line and indirect associates in many major companies. As part of training in quality improvement, these companies are telling test equipment operators that their customer is the packer who packs what was just tested, and foundry people that their customer is the milling machine operator who mills the casting from the foundry. A buyer's customer is the associate in the department to whom the purchased item goes; a cost accountant's customer is the manager who uses the accounting information to make a decision, and a product designer's customer is operations—where the design will be produced or the service provided. Thus, the next-process concept makes it clear that every employee, not just the salesperson, has a customer. It is also clear that throughout the organization, people not only have customers, they are customers. Let's turn our attention to what customers want.

Connecting with the Customer

In this book we use the terms *associate, employee,* and *manager*—plus specialized terms such as *assembler, direct labor,* and *front-liner.* The term *worker* was abolished from this book's second edition—and hasn't been used since except when quoting someone else.

Customers' actual wants are likely to be somewhat different from the provider's interpretation of those wants. The customer's requirement, which tends to be poorly stated or stated incompletely, may have these three components:

1. A statement of recognized need.
2. The expected manner in which that need should be met.
3. Some idea of the benefits of having the need met.[2]

The requirement is a recipient's or customer's view of a good or service. A specification, on the other hand, is the provider's or supplier's view. The ''spec'' is the provider's target, which must reflect, as closely as possible, the customer's actual requirements. A close partnership with the customer helps create good specifications, increasing the supplier's ability to fulfill the customer's needs.

A Short List of Basic Customer Wants

---

[1]This phrase is attributed to the late Kaoru Ishikawa, a Japanese authority on quality.
[2]Gabriel A. Pall, *Quality Process Management* (Englewood Cliffs, N.J.: Prentice-Hall, 1987), pp. 18–19 (TS157.P35).

EXHIBIT 1–2   General Customer Requirements

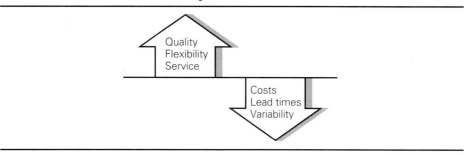

What else do customers want? As consumers, our personal requirements are constantly changing, and the same is true for businesses and industrial consumers. Although these personal and business requirements can be stated in great detail, the number of persistent general requirements appears to be small (see Exhibit 1–2), and they seem to apply universally, regardless of person or organization, company or industry, service or good.

Customers have six requirements of their providers:

1. High levels of quality.
2. A high degree of flexibility (to change such things as volume, specifications, and products).
3. High levels of service.
4. Low costs.
5. Short lead times for getting new and better innovations to market, as well as processing ongoing demands.
6. Little or no variability (deviation from target).

The six customer requirements dictate, to some extent, the topics and concepts presented in this book, for a well-conceived operations management system must attempt to provide goods and services that meet all six of these attributes.

Be careful not to view Exhibit 1–2 as potential trade-offs. Customers don't. For example, as customers, we don't want to settle for either high quality or low costs, or for increased flexibility or shorter lead times; we require that all of these needs be met. Nevertheless, until recently, the trade-off viewpoint prevailed.

In general, updated thinking regarding trade-offs may be summed up as follows: (1) weak companies suffer from trade-offs that appear to be clear opposites, (2) improving companies develop immunities to some of the trade-offs that once plagued them; and (3) world-class companies recognized for excellence in providing all six customer wants have largely eliminated trade-off obstacles.

"The company that is satisfied with its progress will soon find that its customers are not." Company philosophy, Motorola Corp.

An equally important point about Exhibit 1–2 is that it is not a static list; the arrows are meaningful. They signify that customers want—and expect—improvement along all six dimensions.

An organizational commitment with wide-ranging effects, such as continuing improvement in meeting customer needs, is called a strategy. Next, we consider operations strategies and their relationship to business strategies.

Exhibit 1–3   Basic or Generic (Line) Functions

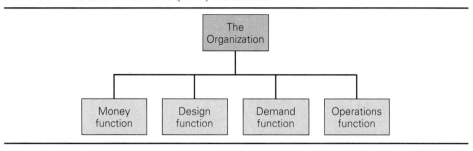

Operations Strategy

In the formation of any organizational strategy, three key elements must be taken into account: the company itself, the customers, and the competitors.[3] These three strategic elements apply not just to businesses but to any organization—including churches, charities, and government agencies. Such nonbusiness entities have their own kinds of customers and competitors. They compete with one another (and sometimes with profit-making businesses as well) for funding, client allegiance, volunteers, and so forth.

Managers should strive to develop a balanced perspective on the three elements. Strategy itself is necessary because of competition, and successful strategy ensures that company strengths match customer requirements. In short, getting well acquainted with the customer and the competition has strategic implications for the company.

Competitor:
Another organization vying with yours for sales and customers as well as for employees, permits, funding, supplier loyalty, and so on.

Integrated Business Strategy

Whether private or public, manufacturing or service, all organizations have four basic functions that must be managed: money, design, demand, and operations (see Exhibit 1–3). These are known as line functions. As organizations begin to grow, line functions tend to become the first departments, such as the departments of finance, research and development, marketing, and operations, or maybe accounting, design, sales, and production.

To accomplish its aims, the business team must plan strategy in all four line functions. A comprehensive strategic business plan deals with issues affecting the whole organization: employees, markets, location, line of products and services, customers, capital and financing, profitability, competition, public image, and so forth.

If formulated correctly, the four functional strategies of the overall plan are mutually reinforcing and compatible. All too often, however, that has not been the case. In larger firms especially, planners have tended to develop careful and thorough strategies for finance, design, and marketing, but have paid scant attention to operations.[4] A firm lacking proper OM strategy is like an anchored ship. Finance, design, and marketing may set the rudder and expect the ship to steam off, but with anchor set, the ship won't move, or moves reluctantly, dragging its burden.

---

[3]Kenichi Ohmae, *The Mind of the Strategist: Business Planning for Competitive Advantage* (New York: Penguin Books, 1983), chap. 8 (HD31.0485).

[4]Elwood Buffa, *Meeting the Competitive Challenge: Manufacturing Strategy for U.S. Companies* (Homewood, Ill.: Dow Jones–Irwin, 1984), chap. 1.

OM strategies should be consistent with the business plan, but with a narrower focus:

- *Capacity* (operating resources): front-line and support people, information, equipment and tools, materials, location (space). Capacity strategies deal with such matters as when and where to add or remove a unit of capacity, skills and flexibility of the work force, and whether to make or buy.
- *Products, processes, methods, and systems:* Strategies might include level of investment in product and process development, standardization, and manual versus automated information processes.
- *Outputs:* Quality, cost, lead time, flexibility, variation, and service.

Strategic issues arise throughout the book. For now, let's consider two brief examples of OM's role in strategic planning, one for a single firm and another comparing two firms.

1. *Fitness, Inc.* Executives at Fitness have decided on a business strategy that includes maintaining market share for its chain of exercise businesses. Operations managers translate that business strategy into an operations strategy of developing two new fitness-related services, which will maintain high utilization of staff and space, as substitutes for two other services that are declining in popularity.

2. *Companies A and B.* Two companies, both manufacturers of shoelace extenders, have the same dominant business strategy: rapid customer service. At Company A, operators have trouble changing machines over from extenders for 18-inch laces to the 24- or 28-inch sizes. Much downtime and defective output occur during and after changeovers. Also, Company A always seems to be out of the size and style that customers want most. To try to achieve its business objective of quick response, Company A's operations managers have agreed on a strategy of larger inventories, based on forecasts. Unfortunately, the forecasts are not very accurate and the large stock is high in defects, adding to company—and customer—woe.

Company B, on the other hand, has none of these deficiencies. Its operating team follows an operations strategy of methods improvements to reduce changeover times, frequent runs of each size and style in small quantities that closely match actual sales, and process-control charting that keeps output quality high.

Although the business strategy is the same at both companies, Company B's operations strategy will provide superior customer service and overall success.

At times it seems that whole industries, or at least large segments, get into messes like Company A's. Big integrated steel manufacturers are an example.[5]

Although some integrated mills (all steps, from raw ore to finished sheet or bar, are in one mill) have recently shifted strategies and become strong, most North America mills were in precipitous decline by the late 1970s. At the same time another segment of the steel industry, the minimills, was thriving (minimills start with scrap iron rather than ore.) Were their operations strategies very different from those of the larger, integrated producers? Indeed they were. For one thing, the minimills recognized the importance of developing distinctive competency.

Distinctive Competency

After a series of biological experiments in 1934, Professor G. F. Gause of Moscow University postulated his principle of competitive exclusion: No two species that make their living the same way can coexist.[6] Thus, a key element of business strategy will be the firm's efforts to distinguish itself from its competitors.

---

[5]John P. Hoerr, *And The Wolf Finally Came: The Decline of the American Steel Industry* (Pittsburgh: The University of Pittsburgh Press, 1988) (HD9517.M85H64).

[6]Cited in Bruce D. Henderson, "The Origin of Strategy," *Harvard Business Review,* November–December 1989, pp. 139–43.

Consider a town with three hospitals. The average citizen may see little difference among them. But an administrator or board member at one of the hospitals might explain, "We are the only hospital in the city with a fully certified burn center," or perhaps, "We have the only neonatal care unit in the entire region." What is being highlighted is the hospital's distinctive competency.

Distinctive competency: A strength that sets the organization apart from its competition.

Distinctive competencies might be obvious to customers; fast service, very clean premises, and superior quality are examples. But less obvious factors also qualify, things like expert maintenance, low operating costs, and effective research and development. All of these might help a firm satisfy one or more of the six customer requirements in some special or unique way. This ability allows the firm, as Professor Gause put it, to make its living a little differently from its competitors to achieve success and survival.

It is usually easier to develop and maintain distinctive competencies when strategy is focused on doing a few things well and thus avoiding the ills of too much diversity. Shouldice Hospital near Toronto, which treats only hernia patients, is an example. Facility layout, medical staff, cafeteria, surgery and recovery rooms, and lounges all cater to that type of patient. By doing numerous hernia repairs each year, and no other surgeries, Shouldice doctors have become proficient. The narrow focus allows nurses to give better care to a greater number of patients, avoids the need for expensive equipment that diversified hospitals must have, and, most important, results in higher-quality care. As measured by number of patients needing repeat hernia treatment, Shouldice is 10 times more effective than other hospitals.[7]

When a company is unable to sustain any distinctive competencies, it goes under. But when a company can be distinctively competent in several ways, it wows the world. Walt Disney Co., Hewlett-Packard, McDonald's, United Parcel Service, and Toyota are examples. All five have dependably high quality. UPS and Toyota have very low production costs. Hewlett-Packard has fanatically dedicated employees. Disney offers customer service unparalleled in its industry. Toyota, McDonald's, and UPS have very efficient process control, which leads to product and service uniformity. McDonald's provides very fast response to customer orders. Toyota is extremely flexible, well known for its ability to rapidly change machines and production lines from one component or car model to another.

Developing distinctive competencies helps retain customers and invites new business. Companies develop distinctive competencies partly by strategic design, but outside forces, considered next, play a role, too.

Regional and Global Influences

Until recently, most of the world's businesses operated in relatively small, dissimilar, protected markets. It took hard work and patient money to set up a business in another country.

Today, deregulation and privatization have gained a foothold throughout the former Soviet bloc and in India, Indonesia, China, Mexico, Argentina, and several other countries. The countries of Western Europe are adopting uniform economic laws and policies, and several are selling off government-owned businesses (e.g., airlines) and further deregulating. North America is working on a trade pact. Central and South American countries may be added, forming a much larger mass market.

In sum, the world is becoming both more uniform economically and more wide open to business expansion, relocation, alliances, and partnerships. Many of the world's businesses may not be immediately affected, but thousands of others are exposed and

[7]William H. Davidow and Bro Uttal, "Service Companies: Focus or Falter," *Harvard Business Review,* July–August 1989, pp. 77–85.

ontrast

Takeover versus Investment

We Win, You Lose

Strategy: Take over a weak business (with other people's money) and make it strong (and us rich) by mass shutdowns and layoffs of its weakest elements. (It's legal, yes, but is it ethical?)

Win-Win

Strategy: For a weak business, invest not just (or mainly) money but also training and help in implementing customer-centered quality, efficiency, and continuous improvement.

---

vulnerable. For them, the 1990s will be a watershed decade. Companies that learn how to deliver quality efficiently and to achieve continuous improvement should find rich opportunities. But no-change businesses may get trampled.

The emphasis here is on how global competition affects business opportunities, not on the results of competition on nations and national economies. As Michael Porter points out:

> There has been no shortage of explanations for why some nations are competitive and others are not. Yet these explanations are often conflicting, and there is no generally accepted theory. It is far from clear what the term "competitive" means when referring to a nation.[8]

The important issue, Porter contends, "is to explain why firms based in a nation are able to compete successfully against foreign rivals in particular segments and industries."[9] In keeping with this view, we will refer occasionally to leading companies in, say, Japan or Germany, but we will not try to unravel the factors that make nations economically successful.

The strategic factors that best describe competitive success for any company—quality, efficiency, continuous improvement—go to the heart of operations management. It should be understood that some paths to wealth, such as buying companies and milking them dry, that were exploited in recent decades and that have been criticized on ethical grounds, are riskier today. Moreover, a tired, run-down state-owned hotel chain in Hungary or Lithuania needs more than Western money. It needs customer- and quality-centered operations management. This kind of help cures basic weaknesses, thereby protecting the investor, and it helps preserve and strengthen the business and the jobs and skills of its associates. When a management action yields a good result for each party, business people call it a win-win situation.

Continuous Improvement as Strategy

Much that is in this book was absent from the OM field just a few years ago. Vigorous international competition has generated a lot of the newer concepts and methods. These changes are best captured in the term *continuous improvement*.

If continuous improvement is confined to the ranks of management and technical experts, it is a weak strategy. It must be woven into the fabric of everyday work of all employees. Moreover, to be strategically effective, continuous improvement must

---

[8]Michael E. Porter, *The Competitive Advantage of Nations* (New York: The Free Press, 1990), p. 3.
[9]Ibid., p. 10.

$\mathscr{I}$nto $\mathscr{P}$ractice

Lean Production

[It] is ''lean'' because it uses less of everything . . . half the human effort in the factory, half the manufacturing space, half the investment in tools, half the engineering hours to develop a new product in half the time. Also, it requires keeping far less than half the needed inventory on site, results in many fewer defects, and produces a greater and ever growing variety of products.

SOURCE: James P. Womack, Daniel T. Jones, and Daniel Roos, *The Machine That Changed the World* (New York: Rawson Associates, 1990), p. 13.

encompass the requirements of customers, the attributes of competitors, and the organization's internal capacities and capabilities.

Continuous improvement got its start in operations, first in leading Japanese export companies, then in competing companies elsewhere in the world. The idea has always been to continually, and incrementally change and improve *everything:* equipment, procedures, employee skills, throughput time, quality, supplier relations, product and service designs, and so on.

> The Japanese term for continuous improvement, *kaizen,* has been adopted in a few Western firms.

Since this idea, and many supporting techniques, were perfected first at Toyota, they have been called the **Toyota production system**. In an MIT study of worldwide automobile assembly, the system was labeled **lean production**. This approach is so powerful that it seems to have become the strategic leading edge in some companies. This occurred first within Japan's manufacturing sector, where furious competition reduced the number of motorcycle makers from over 1,000 to a handful. Similar outcomes occurred in many other industries, which resulted in a few very strong companies that turned their sights first to the United States, the world's largest market.

The pattern has repeated itself in other countries in response to competition, plus widespread transfer of knowledge on how to generate continuous improvement. By the mid-1980s (according to one survey of superior manufacturers in the United States, Japan, and Western Europe) strategic focus in Japanese and American industry had evolved and become much alike, while Western Europe's remained conventional. The survey is summarized in Exhibit 1–4. We see that 8 out of 10 strategically important performance measures are common to the Japanese and United States lists. The inventory and lead time items on those lists reflect competitive pressures for tighter linkages with customers and suppliers, which can lead to dramatic improvements in competitiveness. The Western European list was more internally directed.

> Manufacturing productivity increases, from 1982 to 1990, ''were terrific . . . [rising] at a 4.5% annual rate.''
> *Fortune,* April 22, 1991

The first and fifth items on the European list may seem customer oriented. In practice, however, outgoing quality (first item) is usually associated with internal inspectors sorting out bad products, a wasteful and costly way of getting quality. Thus, it fails to meet customers' needs for high quality at low cost. Also, on-time deliveries (fifth item) typically refers to being on time against internally set schedules rather than to external customer needs.

> ''Inventories throughout the economy are low not only for the onset of a recession, but they are about as low as they have ever been.''
> *The Wall Street Journal,* November 19, 1990

Exhibit 1–4 is a snapshot taken during the middle of the last decade. Since then, many of Western Europe's leading manufacturers have adopted the strategies of leading United States and Japanese producers. Today, also, we find similar strategies in top-notch companies in many of the world's developing countries.

EXHIBIT 1–4   **Top 10 Strategic Measures in Successful Industrial Firms—United States, Japan, and Western Europe**

United States and Japan		Western Europe
Incoming quality		Outgoing quality
Inventory accuracy		Unit manufacturing cost
Direct labor productivity	•	Unit material cost
Manufacturing lead time		Unit overhead cost
Supplier lead time		On-time deliveries
Work-in-process inventory turnover		Incoming quality
Material yield		Direct labor productivity
Indirect labor productivity		Material yield
		Unit labor cost
		Forecast accuracy

United States Only	Japan Only	Common to United States and Western Europe
Machine setup time	Finished goods inventory turnover	Outgoing quality
	Absenteeism	

SOURCE: Jeffrey G. Miller et al., *Closing the Competitive Gap—The International Report of the Manufacturing Futures Project* (Boston University Manufacturing Round Table, 1988).

Example: MIT's international automotive study cited Ford's assembly plant in Hermosillo, Mexico, as the world's most efficient.[10]

Example: Eicher Tractors Ltd., operating nine factories in India, intensively trains its work force. In Eicher's Faridabad tractor assembly plant, evidence of visual process controls can be seen everywhere (see photos). Output incentive payments have been abolished in favor of producing just in time for use at the next process. Improvement projects are under way in support departments as well as in the factory. In personal transportation, drivers are assuming ownership of vehicle maintenance and have teamed up on a parking lot improvement project. In the finance department, an improvement team has cut the time to issue stock certificates (to investors) from three months to one week.

Eicher Tractor's application of continuous improvement in the back office is a natural extension of doing it in the plant. The same thing has been taking place in the offices of leading manufacturers globally.

At the same time, continuous improvement is becoming a competitive force among leading organizations in services. Manufacturers have several names for this strategy (e.g., lean, world-class, or Toyota system), but the service industries tend to favor a single term, **total quality management (TQM).** While TQM can take on a narrow definition, it is also used broadly, encompassing organization-wide continuous improvement in meeting customers' requirements.

In other words, continuous improvement has achieved prominence as an OM strategy (as well as a business strategy) in services as well as in manufacturing. It is easy to cite differences between goods makers and service providers (e.g., goods are inventoriable), but it may be more useful to show how similar the two sectors are. The similarities stand out when we closely examine basic operating principles, supportive of the continuous improvement strategy, that seem to apply equally to both sectors.

---

[10]James P. Womack, Daniel T. Jones, and Daniel Roos, *The Machine That Changed the World* (New York: Rawson Associates, 1990), p. 13.

Process specification sheets, mostly operator prepared, are posted in each work area at the Faridabad assembly plant of Eicher Tractor Ltd. in India. The specs sheets include operating procedures and are an aid to process control, process improvement, and cross-training.

Top: Close-up of specs sheets.

Bottom: Assembly team in white gloves; specs sheets above parts trays at either side.

Principles of OM—As Strategy

Many diverse organizations, in both goods and services, are adopting similar operations management strategies. This fact suggests, not only that attitudes have changed fundamentally, but also that certain basic principles may serve as guides for implementing OM strategies.

Exhibit 1–5 is a 16-point set of the principles of OM, that is, the principles of employee- and team-driven, customer-centered continuous improvement in operations management. These principles serve as a strategic foundation for any organization, just as running and blocking are fundamentals for any team in a variety of sports. Operations strategy in the firm is comparable to a sports team's game plan. In each case, execution of the plan depends on strength in the fundamentals.

The 16 principles are in two broad groups and seven categories. The first group, formulation of operations strategy, must account for customers, the company, and competitors if the OM strategy is to be complete. The second group, implementation, includes the other four categories, which are the building blocks of strategic support for the first group.

The principles have a commonsense ring. Nevertheless, numerous companies take a different path—sometimes an opposite one—as we discuss below.

Contrast

Strategy

Conventional Wisdom

Strategy is something done by senior executives, often with advice from highly paid consultants.

Strategy permeates the organization through level-by-level, top-down planning.

New Thinking

Much of strategic management can be reduced to basic principles.

Widely shared information and involvement in strategic planning fosters unified purpose and eases implementation of strategies.

Exhibit 1–5   Principles of Operations Management

Operations Strategy—Formulation

Customers:
1. Get to know and team up with the next and final customer.
2. Become dedicated to continual, rapid improvement in quality, cost, lead time, flexibility, variability, and service.

Company:
3. Achieve unified purpose via shared information and team involvement in planning and implementation of change.

Competitors:
4. Get to know the competition and the world-class leaders.

Operations Strategy—Implementation

Design and organization:
5. Cut the number of product or service components or operations and the number of suppliers to a few good ones.
6. Organize resources into multiple "chains of customers," each focused on a product, service, or customer family; create cells, flow lines, and "plants-in-a-plant."

Capacity:
7. Continually invest in human resources through cross-training (for mastery of multiple skills), education, job and career-path rotation, and improved health, safety, and security.
8. Maintain and improve present equipment and human work before thinking about new equipment; automate incrementally when process variability cannot otherwise be reduced.
9. Look for simple, flexible, movable, low-cost equipment that can be acquired in multiple copies—each assignable to focused cells, flow lines, and plants-in-a-plant.

Processing:
10. Make it easier to make/provide goods or services without error or process variation.
11. Cut flow time (wait time), distance, and inventory all along the chain of customers.
12. Cut setup, changeover, get-ready, and startup times.
13. Operate at the customer's rate of use (or a smoothed representation of it); decrease cycle interval and lot size.

Problem solving and control:
14. Record and *own* quality, process, and problem data at the workplace.
15. Ensure that front-line improvement teams get first chance at problem solving—before staff experts.
16. Cut transactions and reporting; control causes, not symptoms.

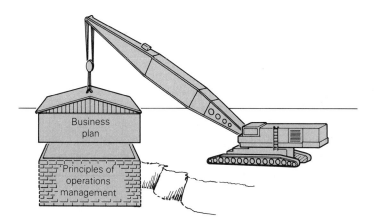

1. Get to Know and Team Up with the Next and Final Customer.   The customer, whether final consumer or next process, is the object of the first and most important principle. The remaining principles, which follow from this one, concern *how* to serve the customer better.

Getting to know and teaming up with the customer often requires breaking barriers—for example, departmental walls. Teaming up can mean moving associates out of functional departments and into teams and cells, that is, organizing associates by how the work flows. If that isn't practical, then organize cross-functional improvement teams. Although these teams do not ''live'' together, they meet periodically to solve problems.

Geography is often a barrier (e.g., a customer is located miles away). But responses to such barriers can be very creative. For example, Globe Metallurgical, supplier of additives to steel mills and foundries, buses its factory associates to customer plants where they get to know their counterparts. This facilitates quick, easy communication, associate to associate, when the customer has a problem, or when Globe people have questions about customer needs. Globe's strong customer focus contributed to its being named the first (1988) recipient of the Malcolm Baldrige quality prize in the small business category.

A metal foundry makes castings by pouring hot metal into a mold, letting it set, and breaking the mold.

2. Become Dedicated to Continual, Rapid Improvement in Quality, Cost, Lead Time, Flexibility, Variability, and Service.   A decade ago the slow pace of economic improvement (or lack of it) prompted journalists to declare a productivity crisis. The situation could just as well have been called a quality crisis—where quality is broadly defined as improved delivery of all of the customers' requirements. This principle aims squarely at resolving that crisis by prescribing a customer-oriented agenda suitable for any business. Still, each business is unique, and the next two principles aim at tailoring OM strategy to the particular organization and its competitive environment.

3. Achieve Unified Purpose via Shared Information and Team Involvement in Planning and Implementation of Change.   Information must be shared throughout the organization if employee-driven continuous improvement is to occur. Few companies apply this principle as effectively as Zytec, a producer of power supplies for computing equipment and a 1991 Baldrige quality prize winner. In developing its five-year strategic plan, Zytec involves 20 percent of its work force, from all corners of the firm; it even has a few key suppliers and customers comment on the plan. Then, every employee and team has a role in translating the plan into action elements with measurable yearly goals.[11]

---

[11]Karen Bemowski, ''Three Electronics Firms Win 1991 Baldrige Award,'' *Quality Progress*, November 1991, pp. 39–41.

4. Get to Know the Competition and the World-Class Leaders. In many firms, getting to know the competition has been viewed as a sales and marketing function, useful for competitive pricing, product positioning, and promotion. But for superior companies, that approach is insufficient. Operations management associates cannot be effective without competitive information. They need to learn about competitors' designs, capacities, skill base, and supplier/customer linkages—as well as costs, quality, flexibility, and lead times.

Benchmarking was developed by Xerox Corporation, whose first benchmarking study took place in 1979. Benchmarking was quickly adopted by many other companies.

Old-style competitive analysis is limited to sampling competitors' services and acquiring and "reverse-engineering" their products; continuous improvement requires that and much more. Blue-chip companies conduct benchmarking studies, in which they gather data and exchange visits with other companies, often in totally different industries. They seek to discover the best practices, not just the best services and products. A number of manufacturers have benchmarked Federal Express in order to learn better ways of handling freight.

Failure to learn about the strengths of the competition or about the best performance in any industry (e.g., the ability to deliver better quality or offer quicker response) leads to complacency and decline. But obtaining and using such information helps motivate a company's people to make necessary improvements, which are stated as principles 5 through 16.

5. Cut the Number of Product or Service Components or Operations and Number of Suppliers to a Few Good Ones. Having too many components of a product or service or too many suppliers makes it difficult to do justice to any of them. Reducing the number of product components has become a centerpiece of continuous improvement in many top-flight manufacturing companies. Cutting down on the number of suppliers (of component parts or services) is closely related, and it is becoming common practice in both manufacturing and service organizations.

This principle, the first of two in the design and organization category, pertains to things; the next deals with people.

6. Organize Resources into Multiple Chains of Customers, Each Focused on a Product, Service, or Customer Family; Create Cells, Flow Lines, and Plants-in-a-Plant. This principle addresses problems implicit in familiar bureaucratic statements like, "This office is responsible for issuing the permit," or "Our department processes those forms." Department-to-department work flows can be impersonal and invite finger pointing—at the other department—when things go wrong.

To ensure good coordination, error prevention, and continuous improvement, the customer at the next process should be known and familiar, a real partner or team member. Also, a dependable work flow path is needed. These are among the reasons why some insurance companies, for example, are breaking up underwriting and claims-processing departments and reorganizing into multifunctional teams, and why factories and their support offices are organizing focused cells by the way the paperwork and production flows.

7. Continually Invest in Human Resources through Cross-Training (for Mastery of Multiple Skills), Education, Job and Career-Path Rotation, and Improved Health, Safety, and Security. Capacity is high in cost and has long-term impact. That goes not only for physical capacity, treated in principles 8 and 9, but also for human resource capacity.

The human resource department is not responsible for human resource management; it is just the overseer. Since human resources are involved in formulating OM strategy and are the driving force for formulating and carrying it out, as well as a key element of capacity, it is necessary to put increased emphasis on development of human resources.

Old practices: Divide work into jobs so small and simple that any unskilled person, paid minimum wage, could master it the first day. Assign managers, experts, and professionals to a single career track and keep them there for life so they can really learn the business.

Continuous improvement: Each associate continually masters more job and job support skills, problem-solving techniques, and self (team) management. Through job switching, associates learn the impact of job A on job B; they discover their collective impact on the whole service or product, as well as their effect on customer satisfaction; and they understand their contribution to employee health, safety, and security. Managers and professionals require occasional career-path switching to gain a broader outlook, to increase their value to the company, and to achieve greater personal career security.

8. Maintain and Improve Present Equipment and Human Work before Thinking about New Equipment; Automate Incrementally When Process Variability Cannot Otherwise Be Reduced.   People are variable, and variability stands in the way of serving the customer. Progress will therefore require new equipment and automation. The easy, cheap way to achieve progress is for associates to tighten up their slack habits and bad practices. This defers the cost and complexity of automation. It also avoids succumbing to the glamour of automation and the tendency to automate for the wrong reasons. For example:

- ''Replace run-down, poorly maintained present equipment, and cope with quality variation.'' Automation actually requires a higher degree of attention to equipment care and maintenance and better process controls on qualilty.
- ''Become more flexible.'' But the most flexible resource is the human resource, not flexible automation.
- ''Invest retained earnings.'' Investing retained earnings in automation sometimes makes sense, but investing in the company's existing human and physical infrastructure is always a good choice.
- ''Eliminate the 'labor problem.' '' Automation causes major work force changes and potentially even greater labor problems. Labor problems (which often are management problems) are best solved before piling on other major changes.

9. Look for Simple, Flexible, Movable, Low-Cost Equipment that Can Be Acquired in Multiple Copies—Each Assignable to Focused Cells, Flow Lines, and Plants-in-a-Plant.   How is growing demand to be served? The common tendency is to speed up the existing process: to add more people or to replace a small machine with a bigger, faster, costlier one.

Companies that have followed such practices for several generations of growth may find themselves with serious capacity obstacles. Their single, fast process is not divisible into focused units; it can process only one model at a time in huge amounts, which usually will be out of phase with actual customer demand patterns; it may be in the wrong location and too costly to move.

This plurality principle is the antidote to these problems. Planning in multiple-capacity units allows growth to occur at the same time as the firm is becoming product/customer focused. Moreover, focusing equipment and operating teams on narrow families of products/customers helps large and growing companies act like small, customer-service-minded ones.

10. Make it Easier to Make/Provide Goods or Services without Error or Process Variation.   This and the next three principles involve the processing itself—the transformation of resources into goods and services. This broad principle might be abbreviated as: do it right the first time. It enlists concepts and practices stretching from designing for quality, to partnering up with suppliers and customers for quality, to controlling processes for quality, to collecting and analyzing data for removal of the sources of poor quality.

This approach replaces poor but conventional practices in which causes of good and bad quality were not treated. Instead, companies had sizable inspection staffs for sorting bad output from good, typically in late processing stages. Usually, plenty of bad results still slipped through, which were dealt with in special rework or complaint departments.

11. Cut Flow Time (Wait Time), Distance, and Inventory All Along the Chain of Customers.   This and the next two principles are closely associated with just-in-time operations, which shorten **throughput time** and improve responsiveness to customers.

The chain of customers from (and within) factories to distribution warehouses to retail storerooms and display counters is typically choked with work-in-process and pipeline inventories. It's a long, loose chain full of waste and delay. A change in the demand patterns takes considerable time to run through, and the customer often will not wait. Discovery of mistakes is also slow, and the mistakes can pile up before they are noted. By the time they are discovered, their causes may be unclear because the trail is cold. Removing excess inventory at each stage has the potential to enable delivery while the customer is still interested, and thus to increase sales and market share. It can also cut operating costs associated with the delays for extra handling and transport, extra shipping documents, excess scrap and rework, and other related wastes.

One way to speed up the flow and take out wastes is simply to limit the queues (cut the inventories) in front of each process. For example, strive to keep in-baskets and waiting lines empty. This allows each job or customer to be processed without delay. Often it is possible to get the desired results by moving process stages closer together—shortening the flow path—which at the same time reduces in-process inventories and cuts flow time.

12. Cut Setup, Changeover, Get-Ready, and Startup Times.   This principle deals with preparation-to-serve delays of all kinds. For example, if you want to run a program on your personal computer, you must first get set up. You have to boot the disk, which, on your older model, takes 39 seconds. Then you make a menu selection (29 seconds), instruct the computer to read disk drive A (10 seconds), and call the desired program into memory (22 seconds). After a total of 1 minute and 40 seconds of setup, you are ready to perform useful work. Not so long, perhaps, but what if you need to switch from a word-processing program to a spreadsheet? Would you have to go through another setup (reboot)? And then perhaps another, to use a data base program?

Setup, changeover, get-ready, or *startup time*: The time to switch from useful output in one mode to useful output in the second.

Excess setup time on a computer can be a mild annoyance, or it can seriously detract from someone's productivity. Or, if a client is waiting for the computer to process something, it's a serious problem of poor service.

In manufacturing, machine setup and production-line changeovers can eat up enormous amounts of costly capacity and render the company unable to change quickly from one product model to another as customer demand patterns change. As just-in-time methods have come into use, many manufacturers have become aggressive about cutting equipment setup times. For example, at Pepsi's bottling plants, bottle size changeovers have been reduced from 90 minutes to 20 minutes.

However, the problem of long preparation time does not have to involve a machine. A customer may fume while a clerk hunts for an order book or a nurse opens cabinets looking for a roll of tape. Such examples of unpreparedness are commonplace and usually easy to fix. Systematic procedures for attacking these problems have migrated from the manufacturing sector to a growing number of service organizations.

13. Operate at the Customer's Rate of Use (or a Smoothed Representation of It); Decrease Cycle Interval and Lot Size.   That is: Don't go as fast as you can go, only to see the work pile up in front of your customer at the next process. Don't invest in equipment that runs many times faster than the work can be processed downstream. And don't save up large piles of work before sending it on to the next process. Although those practices are common in typically disconnected companies, they are wasteful and stretch out the response time. Customers may not be willing to wait.

14. Record and Own Quality, Process, and Problem Data at the Workplace. Problem-solving and control, the topic of the last three principles, are ineffective if problem-solving *data* ends up in the wrong place. A common mistake is sending quality, process, and problem data from the front lines to experts in back offices. That leaves front-line associates (the majority of company employees) out of the problem-solving, control, and process ownership loop. Data is what gets them back in.

15. Ensure that Front-Line Improvement Teams Get First Chance at Problem Solving—Before Staff Experts.   This principle follows from the previous one: Front-liners can do little about quality and problems without process data, but they can do plenty when they have the data, especially in teams in which knowledge, skills, and ideas are readily shared. Staff experts may have more problem-solving skills, but they have less understanding of the processes where problems occur. Also, staff people are not only expensive and relatively scarce, they are often tied up in other projects. This leaves little time for solving ongoing process problems and on-the-spot emergencies, which are the natural responsibility of front-line associates.

16. Cut Transactions and Reporting: Control Causes, Not Symptoms.   Transactions and reports often deal with symptoms (e.g., our warranty costs are too high, too much overtime last month, etc.). But effective quality control and production control replace transactions and reports (as much as possible) with process data—categorized and detailed as to causes. Those data fuel the continuous improvement effort and need not end up in a report. In fact, in the continuous process-improvement mode, by the time a report of a problem comes out, a team of associates would probably already be working on it—or may already have solved it.

The 16 principles may serve *as* strategy, but they do not cover the whole strategic waterfront. For example, they cannot directly guide a decision on where to locate a warehouse or set up a branch office, or if or when to do this. Complex issues like these simply involve too many variables, and executive-level strategic planning will still be required. But it should follow principle number 3, enlisting the broadest possible involvement in the effort.

Operations Managers

The 16 principles of operations management tell what to strive for and how to manage operations effectively. They provide guidance for the entire work force, who, taken collectively, are the actual operations managers. They include:

1. *The associates who make the product or provide the service.* In any enterprise, every employee is a manager of the immediate workplace, which consists of materials, tools, equipment, space, and information.[12] In the best companies, every employee is

---

[12]M. Scott Myers, *Every Employee a Manager*, 3rd ed. (San Diego: University Associates, Inc., 1991).

*P*RINCIPLE 15:

Associates get first
chance at problem
solving.

teamed up with others in a work flow relationship and periodically joins a special project team. Their role—meeting current demand exactly and managing and improving processes and products—involves data collection, problem solving, process control, and ever better service to the customer.

2. *First-line supervisors.* Their proper role involves little traditional supervising; rather, they are coordinating mixtures of human and physical resources in the cause of customer satisfaction and continuing improvement.

3. *Upper-level managers, such as department heads and general managers or foremen.* One of their more important tasks is to manage the training, reward, and recognition system to bring out the potential of line associates to become involved in improvement. Good managers are teachers. Another role is to serve as focal points for coordinating the support staff of experts, whose skills back up the direct efforts of line employees to solve problems and make improvements.

4. *Staff experts.* These include designers, buyers, hirers, trainers, industrial engineers, manufacturing engineers, schedulers, maintenance technicians, management accountants, inspectors, programmers, and analysts. Most organizations overrely on staff experts, because line associates' capacities have not been solidly tapped. Still, staff expertise will always be needed. The role of staff people is to plan for change, respond expertly to problems, and serve on improvement teams.

Summary

The operations end of a business is where resources are transformed into goods and services. Proper management of operations demands that close provider-customer connections be maintained. Separation in time or distance invites trouble in the form of poor feedback and misunderstandings. Every employee has a customer; it is the next process or where the work goes next.

Customer requirements or needs include expectations about how those needs will be met. Customer requirements include increasing quality, flexibility (to change volumes or models), and service, and decreasing costs, lead times (elapsed time to design, make or serve, and deliver), and variability.

An effective OM strategy ties in with other company strategies and has the firm's customers, competitors, and the firm itself as its components. While every organization needs to carve out its own distinctive competency, worldwide competitive pressures tend to push every firm toward a roughly similar OM strategy. It is one in which all associates team up for continuous improvement. Although strategic commonality in OM affected manufacturing first (emerging from the just-in-time/total quality crusade), the service sector has also taken up the cause, generally calling it total quality management.

The goods and services sectors are now on the same strategic course, with an underlying strategic foundation consisting of 16 basic principles of operations management: get to know the customer; be dedicated to continual, rapid improvement in the six basic customer wants; achieve unified purpose; know the competition and the world's best performers; cut the number of components and suppliers; organize multiple focused chains of customers; develop and broaden human skills; maintain and improve present resources and employ them to reduce variability before investing in new or automated equipment; seek plural, low-cost units of equipment that are movable into focused capacity units; make it easy to reduce error and variation; cut flow time, distance, and inventory; cut setup or other readiness times; operate at the customer's use rate and decrease cycle interval and lot size; record and own operating data at the work place; give line associates the first chance at problem-solving; and cut the need for transactions and reports by controlling causes.

Using OM strategic principles, every employee acts as a manager.

Key Words

Note: Key words are listed in their order of appearance in the chapter. They are collected into a glossary at the end of the book, which provides short definitions.

Operations   3
Operations management (OM)   3
Continuous improvement   3
Customer   5
Distinctive competency   9

Toyota production system   11
Lean production   11
Total quality management (TQM)   12
Throughput time   18

For Further Reference

This section at the end of each chapter provides limited help for further research. (It does not necessarily list books cited within the chapter.) The book lists are intended to lead you to the parts of the library that hold material on a given topic. Thus, a list might include one book with a management (HD) Library of Congress call number, one with an industrial engineering (T or TA) number, one with a management accounting (HF) number, and so forth. That will guide you to the right shelf, where there are likely to be other books on the same topic. (Library of Congress numbers are given only for more recent books, many of which have the number printed on the copyright page.) Magazines, journals, and professional societies useful for people interested in operations management are also included.

Books

Myers, M. Scott. *Every Employee a Manager*. 3d ed. San Diego: University Associates, 1991 (HF5549.M93).

Ohmae, Kenichi. *The Borderless World: Power and Strategy in the Interlinked Economy*. New York: Harper Business, 1990 (HF3838.D44043).

Porter, Michael. *The Competitive Advantage of Nations*. New York: The Free Press, 1990 (HD3611.P654).

Schonberger, Richard J. *Building a Chain of Customers: Linking Business Functions to Create the World Class Company*. New York: The Free Press, 1990 (HD58.9.S36).

Periodicals/Societies

Business Periodicals Index, an index of articles published in a limited number of business magazines and journals.

Engineering Index, an index of articles published on engineering in a large number of periodicals.

Interfaces (Institute for Management Science), a journal aimed at the interface between the management scientist and the practitioner.

Journal of Operations Management. American Production and Inventory Control Society.

National Productivity Review.

Operations Management Review (Operations Management Society).

Target (Association for Manufacturing Excellence).

Review Questions

1. What does the word *transformation* mean in connection with operations management?
2. What is the likely fate of an organization that has no distinctive competencies? Why?
3. What organizational obstacles sometimes stand in the way of relating to one's customer?
4. What is profound about this sentence: "The customer is the next process"?
5. What is a requirement? A specification? What is the relationship between the two?

6. What are the six basic customer wants?

7. What is the world-class approach to trade-offs?

8. Why must operations be carried out in harmony with the rest of the organization?

9. OM strategy must account for customers, competitors, and the company itself in profit-making firms. What about nonprofit organizations?

10. How do the principles of operations management relate to a company's business plan?

11. Can the same set of principles of OM apply to services as well as goods producers? Explain.

12. Which principles of operations management most directly pertain to production costs?

13. Which principles of operations management most directly pertain to flexibility?

14. Identify the four types of operations managers and explain the role(s) of each type.

Problems and Exercises

Note: Some problems and exercises in this book have answers that are based almost solely on text materials. Others require thought and judgment that go beyond the book; in those cases, you should include reasons, assumptions, and outside sources of information. Answers to selected items are in Appendix D.

1. For each of the employee positions below, give an example of a next-process customer. Also give an example in which the listed employee would be the next-process customer.
    a. Assembler on a production line making kitchen cutlery.
    b. Product design engineer in a toy-manufacturing plant.
    c. Data processing manager in a bank.
    d. Employee benefits counselor in a large law firm.
    e. Cost accountant for a department store chain.
    f. Economist employed by the Federal Reserve Board.

2. What are the distinctive competencies of the following organizations? Discuss.
    a. Holiday Inn.
    b. U.S. Marines.
    c. Boeing.
    d. Procter & Gamble.

3. How does competition affect operations management? Consider, for example, some of the most successful firms in the highly competitive fast-food, lodging, and grocery industries. What do the successful firms do in operations management that their less successful competitors (maybe some that went under!) do not?

4. Think of three diverse examples of nonprofit organizations. For each, describe what its four line management functions (money, design, demand, and operations management) would consist of.

5. Most of the equipment (automatic screw machines, grinding machines, boring machines, etc.) is old and badly run down at North American Bearing Company. That leads to problems in holding tolerances and meeting specifications.
    a. What strategy do you recommend for correcting the situation? Refer to the relevant principles of operations management in your answer.
    b. Suggest a long-term strategy for continual improvement so that North American Bearing does not experience such problems in the future.

6. What are two examples of North American companies that generally have been successful in achieving both cost leadership and quality leadership? Discuss.

7. The following functions or departments are found in most businesses: human resources, sales, design, and management (cost) accounting.
    a. Why should professionals in each of those departments have a thorough understanding of the operating end of the business?

      b. Describe a company program that will achieve the right amount of exposure of people in those four departments to operations.

8. Many of the fastest-growing Western companies have assembled professional staffs composed of the top graduates from the best universities. Those professionals are innovative, competitive, and hard driving. Sometimes they get so absorbed in new, exciting projects that they hesitate to take vacations or develop their personal lives. Those same companies, for all their success, have often done poorly at getting operating-level employees involved in process improvements.

    Explain this paradox. What corrective actions are needed? (Note: Prestigious companies in Japan, like Hitachi and the trading companies, also hire the cream of the crop from universities, yet their operating employees are usually highly involved.)

9. One element of First City Bank's operations strategy is the opening of 15 new cash transaction machines in locations around the area.

      a. What business strategy does this operations strategy most likely support? Express that business strategy in one sentence.

      b. With which principle of operations management does this strategy seem most consistent? Explain.

10. Classic Wooden Toy Company's business strategy includes "responding more quickly to changes in sales patterns for our different toy models." Develop an operations strategy to support that business strategy, taking care not to violate the principles of operations management. Explain your answer.

11. The food and restaurant division of a city health department is under pressure from the department director to improve its performance. The local newspaper has been running a series of exposés on filth in some popular restaurants. The stories have criticized the health department for (*a*) infrequent inspections and (*b*) long delays in responding to written and telephone complaints about certain restaurants. The division, consisting of 5 inspectors, 20 clerical employees, and 5 managerial and supervisory employees, claims that it does not have enough staff and budget to be thorough and quick to respond, as well as make frequent visits. Select four principles of operations management that might help the division. Explain your choices.

12. In the 1960s, companywide job announcements at Deere & Company's headquarters were regularly posted on bulletin boards in the information systems department. The department's policy was to encourage computer programmers and analysts to apply for jobs in marketing, production, and so forth. Is that policy outdated or up-to-date? Does it support or inhibit service to the customer? Does it relate to any of the 16 principles of OM? Discuss.

13. Arbor Nurseries, Inc., does a large business in planting trees for real estate developers, who invariably want service "right now." Which four principles of operations management must Arbor heed in order to be responsive to this customer want? Discuss.

14. At one Seagate plant, which manufactures disk drive products, automatic process-monitoring devices capture data from the assembly processes and put them into a computer system. Operators in the work centers plot summarized data (taken from computer terminals) by hand onto visual display charts, even though the computer system has full capability to print out impressive charts with color graphics. Why not use the color graphics? What principle of operations management seems to be the basis for this Seagate practice?

15. What organization that you have dealt with as a customer or client seems best at following principle number 11 — cutting flow time and travel distance for you (as client) or for your order? How is this done? (You may need to conduct a small investigation to answer this.)

16. What organization that you have dealt with as a customer or client seems best at following principle number 12 — being able to switch quickly from one kind of work (or customer) to another without long changeover delays? How is this done? (You may need to conduct a small investigation to answer this.)

17. In your experience as an employee or volunteer, you undoubtedly have encountered annoyance over delays and high error and rework rates. To what extent do these problems seem to be related to separation into departmental specialities (needed expertise in other departments)? Suggest a solution, specific to your experience, using concepts from the chapter.

2 THE QUALITY IMPERATIVE

Chapter Outline

Quality: A Broad View

Quality Heritage
  W. Edwards Deming
  Joseph M. Juran
  Armand V. Feigenbaum
  Kaoru Ishikawa
  Philip B. Crosby
  Genichi Taguchi

From Artisanship to Total Quality
Management
  Quality Assurance
  TQM and Competitiveness
  Cost of Quality

Benchmarking

Quality Certifications, Registrations,
and Awards
  Supplier Certification
  ISO 9000 Series Standards
  Quality Awards

Employee-Driven Quality
  Time Out for Training
  Getting Organized—Team Formats
  Local Ownership—of Control,
  Improvement, and Results

Supplement: Quality Awards

Members of the 217-person student body of Mt. Edgecumbe High School in Sitka, Alaska, have been on the speaking circuit. At the invitation of blue-chip companies, they have traveled the continent telling their story of continuous quality improvement at company management meetings.

Mt. Edgecumbe, a state-run public boarding school mostly for native Alaskan students, is the world's first high school to embrace the tools of total quality—or as they call it, the continuous improvement process. Students spend 90 minutes weekly in quality improvement training and problem solving, track their own performance, study each other's learning methods, and team up with faculty and staff on improvement projects.

Principle 15:

Involve associates in
problem solving.

It has taken awhile, but quality has finally been elevated from an intangible concept (''I know it when I see it'') to a set of teachable practices that serves as the centerpiece of good management (even in high schools) and as an imperative for global competitiveness. From cover stories of news magazines to newly minted courses in colleges, quality management has been grabbing our attention.[1]

Quality is no longer treated as a specialty (''Quality? Third door on your left, Inspection Department.''). Instead, it is everybody's business—collectively as a competitive requirement; jointly, in improvement teams, for continual improvement; and singly

---

[1]See, for example, *Business Week,* October 25, 1991, an issue dedicated to ''The Quality Imperative.''

in the performance of one's job. Besides involving everybody, today's quality emphasis includes the quality of every process because process quality determines the output quality of goods and services.

In this chapter, we discuss the breadth and complexity of quality, as well as its roots—the efforts of the quality pioneers and the progression of quality assurance from artisanship to total quality management (TQM). Remaining chapter topics include the competitive importance of quality; the role of benchmarking and quality certifications and awards; and TQM's grounding in human commitment, teamwork, training, and local "ownership."

Quality: A Broad View

Quality is a complex concept. Brief, focused definitions (e.g., fitness for use and conformance to requirements) have remained popular. For some purposes, however, there is value in expanding the definition of quality into more specific measures or dimensions. Two itemized lists are given in Exhibit 2–1. The first list is service oriented, while the second is broader and incorporates product quality as well. Despite differences in terminology or definitions, both lists are intended to reflect how *customers* think about quality.

The breadth of these lists suggests the following:

1. Since quality is complex, it requires diverse implementation measures.

2. The implementation measures should be targeted to the specific customer's current concerns, which may shift over time. A customer's top concern may be reliability

---

Exhibit 2–1   Dimensions of Quality

---

10 Dimensions of Service Quality*

Reliability—consistency of performance and dependability.
Responsiveness—willingness or readiness to provide service; timeliness.
Competence—possession of the skills and knowledge required to perform the service.
Access—approachability and ease of contact.
Courtesy—politeness, respect, consideration for property, clean and neat appearance.
Communication—educating and informing customers in language they can understand; listening to customers.
Credibility—trustworthiness, believability; having customer's best interest at heart.
Security—freedom from danger, risk, or doubt.
Understanding—making an effort to understand the customer's needs; learning the specific requirements; providing individualized attention; recognizing the regular customer.
Tangibles—the physical evidence of service (facilities, tools, equipment)

8 Dimensions of Quality†

Performance—primary operating characteristics.
Features—little extras.
Reliability—probability of successful operation (nonfailure) within a given time span.
Conformance—meeting preestablished standards.
Durability—length of usefulness, economically and technically.
Serviceability—speed, courtesy, competence, and ease of repair.
Aesthetics—pleasing to the senses.
Perceived quality—indirect evaluations of quality (e.g., reputation).

---

*Adapted from Carol A. King, "A Framework for a Service Quality Assurance System," *Quality Progress,* September 1987, pp. 27–32.

†Adapted from David A. Garvin, *Managing Quality: The Strategic and Competitive Edge* (New York: The Free Press, 1988), p. 49ff.

$\mathscr{C}$ontrast

Quality and Speed

Old View	New View*
Good quality takes time. Speed (e.g., shorter cycle times) makes poor quality.	"It may sound absurd, but perhaps the surest way to improve quality is speed—by cutting the cycle time from inception to delivery, be the product a car, a piece of research, or an insurance claim."
	James F. Swallow, vice president
	A. T. Kearney (consultants)

*Source: Otis Port and John Carey, "Questing for the Best," *Business Week,* October 25, 1991, p. 8–16.

(e.g., mean time between failures or mean time to repair); later, that customer may want, *in addition to reliability,* improved after-sale service.

3. Quality requires continuing improvement. If a product or service has excellent reliability and after-sale service, the next step is achieving excellence in another dimension—perhaps aesthetics. Continually adding to the dimensions of quality excellence can broaden a product's appeal to existing customers and gain the interest of new kinds of customers as well.

4. Quality is whatever the customer wants.

The fourth point, which has long been gospel in the community of quality experts, allows continuing evolution of listings of quality dimensions. It easily admits the six general requirements of all customers, listed in Chapter 1 and emphasized throughout the book: continual improvement of quality per se, cost, lead time, flexibility, variability, and service.

In fact, at about the same time as some leading Western companies were fashioning their total quality management agenda in the early 1980s, others were placing equal, or greater, emphasis on just-in-time (JIT). From the start JIT had a strong quality improvement component, in addition to its main emphasis on lead-time reduction; quality and JIT were considered to be mutually reinforcing. Although some people differentiate between TQM and JIT, the growing tendency is to see them as mostly the same and as part of the same movement: delivering what the customer wants. The quality movement was inspired by the work of several prominent people, whose contributions are presented next.

Quality Heritage

The emergence of a quality imperative is rooted in the experiences, research and writings, and teachings of several pioneers and leaders of the quality movement. They and the few audiences they could find during the three decades following World War II are owed a great debt for sustaining the quality movement through some lean years. As the concept of total quality continues to evolve, the contributions of others will certainly come to

---

EXHIBIT 2–2   Deming's 14 Points

---

1. Create constancy of purpose toward improvement of product and service with a plan to become competitive and to stay in business. Decide whom top management is responsible to.
2. Adopt the new philosophy. We are in a new economic age. We can no longer live with commonly accepted levels of delays, mistakes, defective materials, and defective workmanship.
3. Cease dependence on mass inspection. Require, instead, statistical evidence that quality is built in. (Prevent defects rather than detect defects.)
4. End the practice of awarding business on the basis of price tag. Instead, depend on meaningful measures of quality, along with price. Eliminate suppliers that cannot qualify with statistical evidence of quality.
5. Find problems. It is management's job to work continually on the system (design, incoming materials, composition of material, maintenance, improvement of machine, training, supervision, retraining).
6. Institute modern methods of training on the job.
7. The responsibility of foremen must be changed from sheer numbers to quality . . . [which] will automatically improve productivity. Management must prepare to take immediate action on reports from foremen concerning barriers such as inherited defects, machines not maintained, poor tools, fuzzy operational definitions.
8. Drive out fear, so that everyone may work effectively for the company.
9. Break down barriers between departments. People in research, design, sales, and production must work as a team, to foresee problems of production that may be encountered with various materials and specifications.
10. Eliminate numerical goals, posters, and slogans for the work force, asking for new levels of productivity without providing methods.
11. Eliminate work standards that prescribe numerical quotas.
12. Remove barriers that stand between the hourly worker and his or her right to pride of workmanship.
13. Institute a vigorous program of education and retraining.
14. Create a structure in top management that will push every day on the above 13 points.

SOURCE: Adapted from W. Edwards Deming, *Quality Productivity, and Competitive Position* (Cambridge, Mass.: MIT, Center for Advanced Engineering Study, 1982), pp. 16–17.

the forefront, but for now, the work of six pioneers stands out: W. Edwards Deming, Joseph M. Juran, Armand V. Feigenbaum, Kaoru Ishikawa, Philip B. Crosby, and Genichi Taguchi. Though known as "quality gurus," their thinking and influence is not limited to the management of quality alone. They all speak of companywide integration of purpose and high regard for the human element, as individuals and as vital components of teams dedicated to continuing improvement.

Although relatively unknown in his native country, W. Edwards Deming has been a *W. Edwards Deming* Japanese hero for some 40 years. He began to gain recognition in the United States for his contributions to quality management on June 24, 1980, when NBC broadcast "If Japan Can . . . Why Can't We?" That documentary highlights Deming's role in Japan's industrial ascendancy.

Japan named its top national prize for contributions to quality after Deming and first awarded the Deming Prize in 1951 (See supplement to Chapter 2). Deming continued to travel to Japan over the next three decades, sharing his concepts on data-based quality, developing a competitive edge, and management's role in these areas in general.[2]

In recent years, Deming has traveled extensively, acquainting Western industry with his "14 points" for management (see Exhibit 2–2). He believes that while quality is

---

[2]America's "discovery" of Deming has been traced to Clare Crawford-Mason, a television producer. Working on a documentary on the decline of American industry in the 1970s, Crawford-Mason heard of Deming's work in Japan and pursued her journalistic instincts. See Mary Walton, *The Deming Management Method* (New York: Dodd, Mead, 1986), chap. 1 (HD38.W36).

everyone's job, management must lead the effort. Further, he states that his 14 points apply to both small and large organizations and in the service sector as well as in manufacturing.

Deming is an ardent proponent of training. He argues that doing your best simply isn't good enough until you know what you're doing. According to Deming, there is no substitute for knowledge. Classic Deming may be seen in the following excerpt from one of his (self-reported) communications to one organization's management:

> This report is written at your request after study of some of the problems that you have been having with production, high costs, and variable quality, which altogether, as I understand you, have been the cause of considerable worry to you about your competitive position. . . . My opening point is that no permanent impact has ever been accomplished in improvement of quality unless the top management carries out their responsibilities. These responsibilities never cease: they continue forever. No short-cut has ever been discovered. Failure of your own management to accept and act on their responsibilities for quality is, in my opinion, the prime cause of your trouble.[3]

As a statistician, Deming is an ardent proponent of the use of process data to make decisions and solve problems: use analysis if the data exist; if not, use experimentation and data collection. He follows an orderly approach to continual improvement known as the **Plan-Do-Check-Act (PDCA) cycle,** which is among the best-known tools in the TQM arsenal. One form is shown in Exhibit 2–3.

Joseph M. Juran

Like Deming, Joseph M. Juran was a pioneer of quality education in Japan. He has also been known in the Western world for his textbooks and as editor-in-chief of *The Quality Control Handbook.* Like Deming, however, Juran was largely ignored by American management until the 1980s.

Juran's research has shown that over 80 percent of quality defects are *management controllable* and it is therefore management that most needs change. He published *Managerial Breakthrough* in 1964 as a guide for the solution of chronic quality problems.[4] The

Deming is known for his ''rough'' style in his seminars. He won't let managers off the hook if he senses that they lack sufficient commitment to quality.

The PDCA cycle is referred to as the Deming cycle by many, perhaps because he is largely responsible for its popularity. Deming, however, gives credit for its creation to his mentor, Walter Shewhart, who also developed the control chart.

Exhibit 2–3   The Plan-Do-Check-Act Cycle for Continuing Improvement

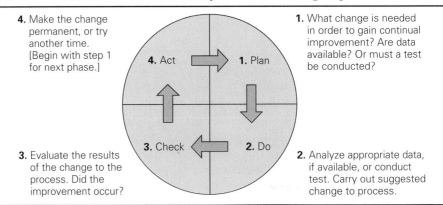

4. Make the change permanent, or try another time. [Begin with step 1 for next phase.]

1. What change is needed in order to gain continual improvement? Are data available? Or must a test be conducted?

3. Evaluate the results of the change to the process. Did the improvement occur?

2. Analyze appropriate data, if available, or conduct test. Carry out suggested change to process.

4. Act   1. Plan

3. Check   2. Do

---

[3]W. Edwards Deming, *Quality, Productivity, and Competitive Position* (Cambridge, Mass.: MIT Center for Advanced Engineering Study, 1982), p. 316.

[4]J. M. Juran, *Managerial Breakthrough* (New York: McGraw-Hill, 1964).

breakthrough procedure is designed to gain and maintain improvements in quality. The sequence is as follows:

1. Convince others that a breakthrough is needed.
2. Identify the *vital few* projects (involves Pareto analyses, discussed in Chapter 4).
3. Organize for a breakthrough in knowledge.
4. Conduct an analysis to discover the cause(s) of the problem.
5. Determine the effect of the proposed changes on the people involved, and find ways to overcome resistance to these changes.
6. Take action to institute the changes, including training of all personnel involved.
7. Institute appropriate controls that will hold the new, improved quality level but not restrict continued improvement—perhaps through another breakthrough sequence.[5]

Juran's now-classic definition of quality is *fitness for use*. He intends those words to apply broadly, to include such properties as reliability, maintainability, and producibility; also, in certain situations, service response time, service availability, and price.

Juran defines quality management in terms of the *quality trilogy,* which consists of:

Quality planning.
Quality control.
Quality improvement.[6]

Proper quality planning results in processes capable of meeting quality goals under certain operating conditions. Quality control consists of measuring actual quality performance, comparing it with a standard, and acting on any difference. Juran believes that inherent planning deficiencies might result in chronic waste, and it is up to the control process (initially) to keep the waste from getting any worse. Finally, quality improvement is superimposed on quality control. Quality improvement means finding ways to do better than standard and breaking through to unprecedented levels of performance. The desired end results are quality levels that are even higher than planned performance levels.

Armand V. Feigenbaum is best known for originating the concept of **total quality control (TQC).** In his book *Total Quality Control* (first published in 1951 under another title), Feigenbaum explains that quality must be attended to through all stages of the industrial cycle and that

Armand V. Feigenbaum

> control must start with identification of customer quality requirements and end only when the product has been placed in the hands of a customer who remains satisfied. Total quality control guides the coordinated actions of people, machines, and information to achieve this goal.[7]

To Feigenbaum, responsibility for TQC must be shared and should not rest with the quality assurance (QA) or quality control (QC) function alone. Feigenbaum also clarified the idea of *quality costs*—costs associated with poor quality. He was among the first to argue that better quality is, in the long run, cheaper. He defines "hidden plant" as the proportion of plant capacity that exists in order to rework unsatisfactory parts. This proportion generally ranges from 15 to 40 percent of the plant's capacity.

---

[5]For a detailed presentation of this sequence, see J. M. Juran and Frank M. Gryna, Jr., *Quality Planning and Analysis,* 2nd ed. (New York: McGraw-Hill, 1980), chap. 5 (TS156.J86).

[6]J. M. Juran, "The Quality Trilogy," *Quality Progress* 19, no. 8 (August 1986), pp. 19–24.

[7]Armand V. Feigenbaum, *Total Quality Control,* 3rd ed. (New York: McGraw-Hill, 1983), p. 11 (TS156.F44).

Kaoru Ishikawa

Kaoru Ishikawa, the late Japanese quality authority, acknowledged Deming's and Juran's influence on his thinking. However, Ishikawa must be recognized for his own contributions. He was responsible for the concept and initial deployment of **quality control circles**—small groups of employees that meet regularly to plan and (often) carry out process changes to improve quality, productivity, or the work environment.

He also developed Ishikawa cause-effect charts, or "fishbone diagrams," so named because of their structural resemblance to the skeleton of a fish (discussed in Chapter 4). Like Deming, Juran, and Feigenbaum, Ishikawa also emphasizes quality as a way of management.

Ishikawa felt that there is not enough reliance on inputs to quality from nonspecialists. In 1968, he began using the term *companywide quality control (CWQC)* to differentiate this broadened approach to TQC from the more specialized view. Today the terms TQC and CWQC are used almost interchangeably.

Another significant contribution of Ishikawa is his work on taking much of the mystery out of the statistical aspects of quality assurance. Conforming to the belief that without statistical analysis there can be no quality control, Ishikawa divided statistical methods into three categories according to level of difficulty, as shown in Exhibit 2–4.

The intermediate and advanced methods are for engineers and quality specialists and are beyond the scope of our discussion. The elemental statistical method, or the *seven indispensable tools* for process control, however, are for everyone's use and should be mastered by all organization members. Ishikawa intends that to include company presidents, directors, middle managers, supervisors, and front-line employees. His experience suggests that about 95 percent of *all* problems within a company can be solved with these tools. We examine them in Chapter 4.

Philip B. Crosby

Philip B. Crosby, former corporate vice president and director of quality control at ITT Corp., is the author of the popular book *Quality Is Free: The Art of Making Quality Certain.* In his book Crosby explains that quality is not a gift but is free. What costs

---

EXHIBIT 2–4   Ishikawa's Statistical Methods

I. Elemental statistical method.
  A. Pareto analysis (vital few versus trivial many).
  B. Cause-and-effect diagram, also known as the *fishbone chart* (this, Ishikawa points out, is not a true statistical technique).
  C. Stratification.
  D. Check sheet.
  E. Histogram.
  F. Scatter diagram.
  G. Graph and Shewhart process control chart.
II. Intermediate statistical method.
  A. Theory of sampling surveys.
  B. Statistical sampling inspection.
  C. Various methods of statistical estimation and hypothesis testing.
  D. Methods of utilizing sensory tests.
  E. Methods of experiment design.
III. Advanced statistical method (using computers).
  A. Advanced experimental design.
  B. Multivariate analysis.
  C. Operations research methods.

SOURCE: Adapted from Kaoru Ishikawa, *What Is Total Quality Control? The Japanese Way,* trans. David J. Lu (Englewood Cliffs, N.J.: Prentice-Hall, 1985), chap. 12 (TS156.I8313).

money is all the things that prevent jobs from being done right the first time. When quality is made certain, an organization avoids these expenses.

Crosby proposes **zero defects** as the goal for quality. To any who find that goal too ambitious, he simply asks, "If not zero defects, then what goal would you propose?" One often-used figure is the acceptable quality level (AQL), which is used in acceptance inspection. Briefly, AQL allows a certain proportion of defective items. Crosby explains that an AQL is a commitment to produce a certain amount of imperfect material—before we start! The AQL idea is certainly out of step with a commitment to continuous improvement. Taking the consumer's view, Crosby makes his point bluntly:

> Consider the AQL you would establish on the product you buy. Would you accept an automobile that you knew in advance was 15 percent defective? 5 percent? 1 percent? One half of 1 percent? How about the nurses that care for newborn babies? Would an AQL of 3 percent on mishandling be too rigid?[8]

Crosby says that mistakes are caused by two things: lack of knowledge and lack of attention. Lack of knowledge, he argues, is measurable and can be attacked with well-known means. Lack of attention, however, is an attitude problem and must be changed by the individual. The individual, in turn, has a better chance of making the change if there exists a company commitment to zero defects. Crosby also states that while the tools of quality control are useful and available, they must be put into perspective. The important factor, he insists, is understanding and meeting a customer's requirements.[9]

Genichi Taguchi

Is it sufficient to control processes, inspect output, identify and remove defects, and rely on customer feedback? Genichi Taguchi says no. To improve quality, he argues, one must look upstream at the design stage because that is where quality begins. Quality must be designed in; it cannot be inspected in later. One facet of obtaining better design is experimentation on variables that contribute to a product's performance. Taguchi's strong belief in this approach has brought **design of experiments (DOE)** into wider use by quality experts, designers, and other members of design-build teams. Taguchi also believes that teams should aim for **robust designs**—designs that can withstand the hard-to-eliminate variabilities that occur in transformation processes or later in customer use.

Little was known of Taguchi's ideas in North America until the American Supplier Institute (formerly a Ford Motor Company training unit) began to offer courses on Taguchi methods to the general public in 1984. Taguchi's short-cut variations on conventional DOE tools are efficient, working only with those variables that are most likely to contribute to large improvements quickly. For example, suppose that a compound is being created from 15 chemicals; each chemical can be purchased from two suppliers, and there is a slight variation in chemical concentrations between the two sources. Classical experimental design, calling for a *full factorial experiment,* would need 2^{15} (or 32,768) test runs to determine the mix of suppliers that yields optimal compound performance, with all chemical interactions considered. Taguchi would use a form of *fractional factorial experiment,* referred to as an *orthogonal array,* to perform the experiment in only 16 test runs.[10] The orthogonal array is a balanced plan for experimentation. Only those design variables deemed (by experts) most likely to affect output or performance are included.

While purists have faulted Taguchi's methods on various technical grounds, advocates argue that optimal design is not the important aim. Rather, a design that is nearly

---

[8]Philip B. Crosby, *Quality Is Free: The Art of Making Quality Certain* (New York: McGraw-Hill, 1979), p. 146.

[9]Philip B. Crosby, *Let's Talk Quality* (New York: McGraw-Hill, 1989), p. 181.

[10]Ranjit Roy, *A Primer on the Taguchi Method* (New York: Van Nostrand Reinhold, 1990), pp. 31–32.

Exhibit 2–5   Taguchi's Quality Loss Function

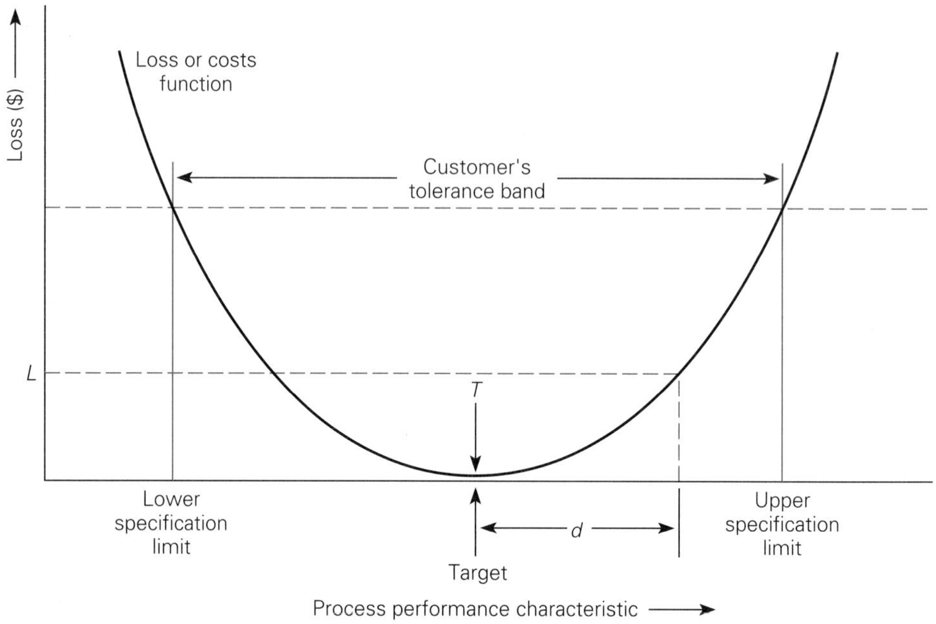

optimal *and* very quickly obtained is preferable.[11] Taguchi's approach tends to appeal to engineers—his customers—who find the presentation understandable and useable.

In addition to his work in design, Taguchi is known for development of the **quality loss function** (see Exhibit 2-5), a statement that any deviation from the target value of a quality characteristic results in extra costs to some segment of society. In fact, Taguchi defines quality in terms of the social loss, to producers or consumers, from the time a product is conceived.[12] The smaller the value of this social loss, the more desirable the product.

Briefly, Taguchi holds that unwelcome costs are associated with *any* deviation of process performance from the quality characteristic's target value. Thus, he favors going beyond zero deviation from specs to continual reduction in variability. The loss from performance variation (L) is directly related to the square of the deviation (d) of the performance characteristic from its target value (T).

Taguchi intends that the loss function remain valid at all times during a product's life. In theory, when process output performance reaches the specification limit, the customer's *economic* interest in the item is neutral; that is, the losses will exactly offset any gain from having the item.

For Taguchi, social loss must affect quality cost management decisions; that is, investments in quality improvement should be compared to savings to society rather than to the firm alone. Ultimately society will reward (or penalize) the firm for its record of societal savings; thus, Taguchi's view is meant to be sound for business.

---

[11]Robert H. Lochner, "Pros and Cons of Taguchi," *Quality Engineering* 3, no. 4 (1991), pp. 537–49.

[12]Genichi Taguchi, Elsayed A. Elsayed, and Thomas Hsiang, *Quality Engineering in Production Systems* (New York: McGraw-Hill, 1989), chap. 2.

From Artisanship to Total Quality Management

The contributions of the quality pioneers and numerous practicing advocates largely define present-day **total quality management (TQM).** To further trace TQM's development, we need to examine certain milestone concepts. We begin with artisan-based quality assurance, then move forward to note the influences of the industrial revolution and consumerism, and conclude with a look at modern quality-based competitiveness.

Notwithstanding today's high level of interest in quality, the topic is centuries old. The Code of Hammurabi, which dates from 2150 B.C., mandated death for any builder whose work resulted in the death of a customer. Other quality-related codes, often equally harsh, are found in the writings of the ancient Phoenicians, Egyptians, and Aztecs.[13] Despite the harsh codes, however, it was the artisan's pride, not fear, that contributed most significantly to supporting quality assurance for centuries to come.

Quality Assurance

Quality assurance, in the view of George Edwards of Bell Labs, who coined the term in the 1920s, requires deliberate managerial planning and action, interlocked quality activities throughout the firm, and a senior officer in charge companywide.

The Artisanship Connection.   One of Robin Hood's merry men needed a new longbow. He got in touch with the best bow maker in all of Sherwood Forest. Together, they selected the proper limb, and throughout the fabrication of the bow, the bow maker asked the archer to grasp the bow, try the draw, fire an arrow, and so forth. She took pride in her work and wanted the archer to be happy with his bow. A little carving here and shaping there, more testing, and finally the bow maker had a satisfied customer—one who would return when another new bow was needed and one who would recommend her to his friends. The provider-customer relationship was brief but close.

Today, their descendants *might* interact like their ancestors, but a more likely scenario would have the modern archer visiting a sporting goods store, where many bows would be available for trial. Today's retail transaction itself retains the provider-customer closeness of Sherwood Forest, but much is missing: Who designed the bow? Built it? Tested it? Who decided what brand of bow to stock? The missing elements constitute part of a much longer provider-customer chain. If the customer becomes unhappy, there is no single bow maker to blame. Many individuals in perhaps several companies were involved before the modern transaction occurred. As Chapter 1 pointed out, those long chains are a source of trouble in that they separate customers from providers and make the assurance of quality more difficult.

The Industrial Revolution.   Long supplier-customer chains are a product of the industrial revolution. In order for the masses to enjoy a wider array of goods, production costs had to decrease. New machines allowed production operations to be broken down into minute steps so that unskilled labor could be employed. Output increased as production costs decreased. Labor became specialized and disconnected from the big picture. Production people focused on quantity rather than quality; the reward system supported such behavior. In an attempt to stem the tide of deteriorating quality, managers resorted to the use of inspectors to check the work of line employees. Inspection, however, merely became another job specialty. Inspectors were unable to improve production quality; they could only find and remove some of the bad output after it had been produced. In many companies, quality fell apart and customers were angry.

---

[13]H. Gitlow, S. Gitlow, A. Oppenheim, and R. Oppenheim, *Tools and Methods for the Improvement of Quality* (Homewood, Ill.: Richard D. Irwin, Inc., 1989), chap. 1.

The European Community's Product Liability Directive of 1985 called for the passage of strict liability laws in each EC country.

Consumerism and Liability Laws.   Product quality and safety began to capture public attention in the mid 1960s. For example, the actions of Ralph Nader, consumer federations, action-line columns in newspapers, and investigative TV and newspaper journalists all contributed to increasing the public's interest. In 1965, the American Law Institute issued its "Restatement of the Law of Torts," which defined strict liability: making manufacturers liable for product defects even without proof of negligence.

Since the 1980s, physicians, accountants, attorneys, corporate directors, and volunteer members of civic organization boards increasingly became defendants in civil litigation. Liability insurance rates skyrocketed.

Concern for safe consumption of goods and services also led to regulatory action. In 1972, the U.S. Congress passed the Consumer Product Safety Act, which aims at preventing hazardous or defective products from reaching the consumer. Most other Western countries have followed the same pattern. Some companies extended their product warranties in the 1980s and early 1990s, but the fact of massive product recalls seemed to say that quality on the warranty paper was not quality in fact. At the same time, in affluent nations large numbers of a new and demanding type of consumer were emerging: the consumer of average means, who prefers to do without rather than pay for second best. There was a revival of neglected crafts such as handweaving, stone grinding of flour, and creation of stained-glass windows. Consumers once again sought the quality of the earlier age of the artisan.

We aren't suggesting that the bows of Robin Hood's era were superior to modern ones. As customers, we want the convenience, safety, technology, and low cost of modern goods. But we also want to know (or at least feel) that the provider of the goods or services is listening to us, cares about our needs, and will "make it right the first time."

Can we have both? That is the challenge of the quality imperative; it calls for a strong customer-oriented culture within the supply chain leading to the final consumer. Companies that can meet this challenge have an inside track in the race for competitive success.

TQM and Competitiveness

According to then IBM chairman John Akers (address at The Quality Forum VII in 1991), "IBM has two obsessions—an obsession with winning and an obsession with quality. You can't have the former unless you deliver the latter." IBM is not alone in wanting to win—and in seeing quality as a winning competitive strategy. For example, the General Accounting Office (GAO), the investigative arm of Congress, studied data from 20 finalists in the 1988 and 1989 Malcolm Baldrige National Quality Award competition to ascertain whether TQM improved performance.[14] The researchers found that the quality-minded companies experienced general improvements after beginning TQM programs (see Exhibit 2–6).

Those results complement other survey data, especially the widely quoted PIMS (Profit Impact of Market Strategy) studies, which drew data from over 2,000 businesses.[15] Exhibit 2–7 summarizes the PIMS analysis of the impact of quality on return on investment (ROI) and return on sales (ROS) results. Across the entire range of relative quality, we see a strong, positive relationship between quality and business success. ROI increases 2.7 times, from a low of 12 percent for firms in the bottom quintile of quality to a high of 32 percent for those in the top quintile, and ROS increases from a low of 5 percent for the inferior-quality group to 13 percent for the superior quintile.

---

[14]U.S. General Accounting Office, *Management Practices: U.S. Companies Improve Performance through Quality Efforts* (Gaithersburg, Md.: U.S. General Accounting Office, Report GAO/NSIAD-91-190, 1991).

[15]Robert D. Buzzell and Bradley T. Gale, *The PIMS Principles: Linking Strategy to Performance* (New York: The Free Press, 1987), pp. 107–11.

Exhibit 2-6   TQM—Impact of Quality on Performance

Market Share and Profitability

Fifteen companies supplied a total of 40 observations in this area: 34 improved, 6 got worse.

Market share—increased in 9 of 11 respondents, by an average of 13.7 percent annually.

Sales per employee—increased in all 12 respondents, by 8.6 percent.

Return on assets—increased in 7 of 9 respondents, by 1.3 percent.

Return on sales—increased in 6 of 8 respondents, by 0.4 percent.

Customer Satisfaction

Thirty observations came from 17 companies: 21 improved, 3 got worse, and 6 showed no change.

Overall customer satisfaction—increased in 12 of 14 respondents, by 2.5 percent.

Number of customer complaints—declined in 5 of 6 reporting companies, by 11.6 percent.

Customer retention—4 of 10 improved, 4 no change; slight increase averaging 1 percent.

Quality and Cost

Sixty observations came from 20 companies: 54 improved, 2 got worse, and 4 showed no change.

Reliability—improvement reported by 12 of 12 respondents, by 11.3 percent.

Delivery timeliness—improvement reported by 8 of 9 respondents, by 4.7 percent.

Order-processing time—reductions reported by 6 of 6, by 12 percent.

Errors or defects—decreases reported by 7 of 8, by 10.3 percent.

Product lead time—decreases reported by 6 of 7, by 5.8 percent.

Inventory turnover—turnover rate increases reported by 6 of 9, by 7.2 percent.

Cost savings from employee suggestions—all 9 respondents reported savings increases, ranging from $1.3 million to $116 million per year.

Employee Relations

Eighteen companies supplied 52 observations: 39 improved, 9 worsened, and 4 were no change.

Number of employee suggestions—up 16.6 percent, increased in 5 of 7 respondents.

Employee satisfaction—up 1.4 percent, increased in 8 of 9 respondents.

Attendance—above industry averages in 9 of 11 respondents, increased further in 8 of those 9.

Employee turnover—below industry averages in 10 of 11 respondents, declined further in 7.

Safety and health rates—exceed industry averages in 12 of 14 respondents, improved further in 11.

NOTE: All percentages are average annual changes measured from when the responding companies began TQM programs.

SOURCE: U.S. General Accounting Office, *Management Practices: U.S. Companies Improve Performance through Quality Efforts* (Gaithersburg, Md.: U.S. General Accounting Office, Report GAO/NSIAD-91-190, 1991).

Exhibit 2-7   Relative Quality and Rates of Return

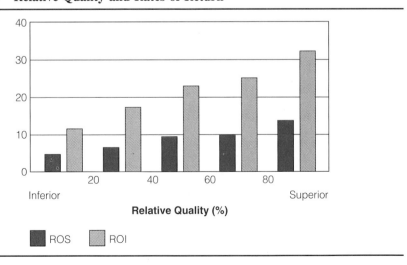

EXHIBIT 2-8   Competitive Benefits of TQM

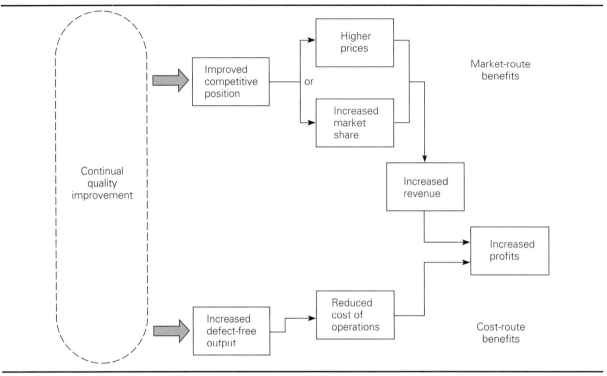

SOURCE: Adapted from Gabriel Pall, *Quality Process Management* (Englewood Cliffs, N.J.: Prentice-Hall, Inc., 1987), chap. 1.

The GAO findings and the PIMS analysis, along with other recent studies, support a conclusion that quality improvement leads to business success along two paths, market-route benefits and cost-route benefits (see Exhibit 2–8).

Along the market path, continual quality improvement generates satisfied customers, thus strengthening competitive position. That strength may be exploited by charging higher prices or by increasing market share, which both generate greater revenue. Along the cost path, quality improvement generates greater defect-free output, which cuts operating costs per unit and significantly enhances the firm's competitive position.

The cost-reduction path applies equally well to nonprofit organizations (even the market route applies in part). Those served by a quality-improving agency are more satisfied and more inclined to make donations or approve tax referendums, thus providing more revenue and resources to the agency.

Our discussion of quality and competitiveness must address one final issue: the so-called *cost of quality*.

Cost of Quality   As managers started to rely more heavily on cost accounting data as the basis for decision making, they began to ask, *How much is it costing us to ensure quality?* Four categories of quality-related costs have been identified:

Internal failure costs. Costs the provider incurs directly—prior to shipment to customers—as a result of defective output. Examples are scrap, rework, retest, downtime, and materials disposition.

External failure costs. Costs to the provider when defects are discovered after shipment to customers. Included are warranty expenses, allowances, returned material

$\mathscr{I}$nto $\mathscr{P}$ractice

Escalating Cost of Defects

The following rule of thumb has become an article of faith in the electronics industry:

- If a defective part is caught by the supplier (before leaving supplier's plant), then there is no cost to the customer (the manufacturer).
- If that defective is caught as it enters the manufacturer's plant, the cost is $0.30.
- If that part is caught at the first stage of assembly (after paperwork, handling, scheduling, and other activities that assume the part is good), the cost is $3.00.

- If that part is caught at the final test (common in electronics manufacture), the cost is $30.00.
- If that part is not discovered until after it leaves the manufacturer's plant, the cost is $300.00. It must be returned, replaced, and so on. (This figure, $300.00, *does not* include certain additional costs such as insurance, warranty, lost business, or loss of customer goodwill.)

NOTE: Raymond A. Cawsey, vice president of quality, Dickey-John Corp., confirms that these figures are "very close" to the true mark for his employer, an electronics firm.

handling, and complaint processing and resolution. In extreme cases, liability settlements and legal fees could also be included.

Appraisal costs. Costs of determining the degree of quality. They include materials inspection and testing, maintenance of test equipment, and materials and other resources consumed during inspection and testing (e.g., destructive testing of flashbulbs or food items).

Prevention costs. Costs incurred in an effort to minimize appraisal and failure costs. They include quality planning, training, new-products review, reporting, and improvement projects.

Though few firms' cost accounting systems bore expense accounts with these names, the cost-of-quality expenses did receive considerable attention in more theoretical cost-versus-quality debates. And in some instances, these concepts guided quality planning and budgeting efforts. Astute quality pioneers noted, however, that "these costs are associated solely with defective product—the costs of making, finding, repairing, or avoiding defects. The costs of making good products are not a part of quality costs."[16]

Thus, the term *cost-of-quality* itself is misleading. Taguchi (with his quality loss function) and others have correctly pointed out that the worrisome costs are those associated with *not having quality.* (See the box titled "Escalating Cost of Defects" for an example.)

Quality advocates in a number of well known firms, such as Motorola, Texas Instruments, and Xerox, used the cost-of-quality argument for shock value in the formative stages of their TQM efforts. Cost-minded senior managers were often startled to learn that "costs of *un*-quality" in their companies were 10 percent to 20 percent of annual revenue. When other arguments for managerial commitment to quality improvement programs failed, the cost-of-quality speech often got results.

Leading Japanese companies, having launched TQM by other means, had little use for cost-of-quality accounts or logic and have avoided this usage.

---

[16]J. M. Juran and Frank Gryna, *Quality Planning and Analysis,* 2nd ed. (New York: McGraw-Hill, 1980), p. 13.

Ϲontrast

Benchmarking

Keep It a Secret	**Trade It**
Our results, practices, and process knowledge are for our eyes only. Lock the doors, frown on outside visitors.	Our results, practices, and knowledge are valuable assets; so are those of other good companies. Let's trade.

Should firms that already have thriving TQM programs continue doing annual cost-of-quality audits? Probably not. Consider, for example, a process improvement that prevents defective output. In a TQM company, it's a better-than-even bet that that change has other benefits; perhaps it results in faster or better engineering, reduces cycle times, or improves safety. Is the expense of the change a cost of quality? or of engineering, production, or employee safety? Under TQM, quality is everybody's business; it's woven into the fabric of every job. So, the amount spent to achieve quality is difficult to state precisely. But even if we could find it, it isn't a cost we want to eliminate anyway.

The main value of the cost-of-quality concept was in raising consciousness about quality's competitive importance. Competitive people aim high; they want to win by giving customers the very best. Sometimes, the search for what is best carries us beyond our own company resources; beyond the industry, perhaps. In those instances, *benchmarking* comes into play.

Benchmarking

Benchmarking, developed at Xerox Corporation in the late 1970s, is the systematic search for the best practices, from whatever source, to be used in improving a company's practices.

At first, Xerox people called it competitive benchmarking. As the words suggest, it was limited to finding their direct competitors' best practices. Xerox benchmarking teams boldly contacted competing manufacturers of copiers, computers, and other Xerox products with this sort of proposal: "How about we visit you and you visit us? We'll exchange information about each other's practices and put the information to use."

Why would rivals go for such a brazen proposal? Because the two companies involved would each benefit relative to other rivals not involved. Besides, with cross-hiring of people from one company to the other, plenty of information leaks out anyway. So why not be more systematic about this search for information.

Still, in dealing with one's rivals, there will always be suspicions about the other party's openness. And why restrict benchmarking to competitors anyway? This kind of thinking caused Xerox to turn toward *non*competitive benchmarking. Xerox teams began to fan out widely in search of best practices in *any* business or nonbusiness organization.

Xerox manager Robert Camp describes in some detail how a benchmarking team from his company visited L. L. Bean, the mail-order retailer, to learn what's behind

Competitive benchmarking of *processes* is a relative of a much older technique: competitive analysis of *products*, which is a topic of Chapter 3.

*Ϸ*RINCIPLE 4:

Know the competition and world leaders.

EXHIBIT 2–9   The Benchmarking Process: Common Steps

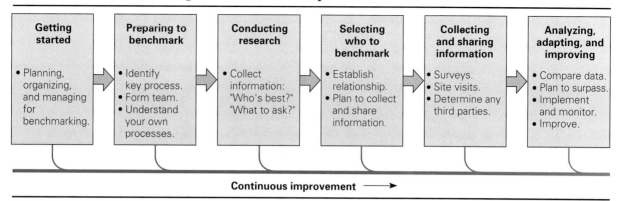

Getting started	Preparing to benchmark	Conducting research	Selecting who to benchmark	Collecting and sharing information	Analyzing, adapting, and improving
• Planning, organizing, and managing for benchmarking.	• Identify key process. • Form team. • Understand your own processes.	• Collect information: "Who's best?" "What to ask?"	• Establish relationship. • Plan to collect and share information.	• Surveys. • Site visits. • Determine any third parties.	• Compare data. • Plan to surpass. • Implement and monitor. • Improve.

Continuous improvement ⟶

SOURCE: Reprinted with permission from QUALITY (March 1992), a Capital Cities/ABC, Inc., Company.

Bean's renown for excellent customer service.[17] Other companies have followed Xerox to L. L. Bean. Another frequently benchmarked company is Federal Express, for its ability to deliver overnight.

Now, though benchmarking is only a few years old, it is well known and in wide use by major hotels, accounting firms, transportation companies, banks, manufacturing companies, and others. Marriott Hotels have benchmarked the hiring, training, and pay practices of fast-food companies because hotels hire out of the same labor pool. Corporate attorneys at Motorola have even employed benchmarking. According to Richard Weise, general counsel at Motorola, "We began to compile information on how many lawyers and paralegals it takes for each $1 billion in sales. We looked at how other law departments use tools such as computers [and] learned from them. Finally, we determined relative costs of delivering legal services domestically versus internationally."[18]

With so many firms involved in benchmarking—and trying to visit some of the same high-performance firms—the idea of putting benchmarking data into data banks arose. Thus, under the sponsorship of subscribing companies, the American Productivity and Quality Center in Houston has established an International Benchmarking Clearinghouse.

One of the Clearinghouse's early projects was to survey current benchmarking procedures. While they vary somewhat from firm to firm, most benchmarking programs use six common steps, according to the survey (see Exhibit 2–9).

As the exhibit shows, a benchmarking effort begins through planning and organization. The next step is all-important: selecting the process to be benchmarked and the team members. However, the team should not immediately set off to benchmark another company. First they need to benchmark their *own* process, in the following terms:

Metrics (which means measurements in numbers). For example, a team from accounts payable may find it takes 18 hours average elapsed time and 23 minutes of paid labor to process an invoice.

Practices. The team documents every step in the process, noting delays, sources of errors, departments and skills involved, and so forth.

> Houston's Second Baptist Church, serving 12,000 parishioners weekly, uses benchmarking (e.g., Disney World's parking and people skills) in its own customer quality program.

---

[17]Robert C. Camp, *Benchmarking: The Search for Industry Best Practices That Lead to Superior Performance* (Milwaukee: ASQC Quality Press, 1989).

[18]Ronald E. Yates, "Lawyers Not Exempt from Quality Crusade," *Chicago Tribune*, December 1, 1991.

The third step is collecting information on whom to benchmark and what questions to ask. The fourth is to gain approval and establish plans for exchange visits with firms to be benchmarked.

Fifth is the benchmarking itself, including a visit to the benchmarked firms' sites. Information sought must parallel that already gathered by the team for its own firm, namely, metrics and practices. The final step is for the benchmarking team to analyze the data, develop plans for change, and follow through.

Benchmarking has spread from North America, where it originated, to European companies and beyond. Now benchmarking teams criss-cross oceans in the continual quest for competitively valuable process knowledge. Perhaps some of the intercontinental travel will dissipate somewhat as clearinghouse information becomes more available. Still, benchmarking seems to have found a solid place in the TQM tool kit, at least in the United States, inasmuch as it is now one of the criteria used in assessments for the Malcolm Baldrige National Quality Award. That award, as well as other formal means of recognition for quality performance, is our next topic.

Quality Certifications, Registrations, and Awards

We've seen that in the third step, the benchmarking team's question is, Who's the best? The team might start by asking its own purchasing department what companies are certified high-quality suppliers and checking on who has won quality awards lately. Certified suppliers and quality award winners might have a few good practices worth investigating.

Supplier Certification

Traditional assessments of supplier performance and capability were not stringent enough for TQM-driven companies. A quality-centered approach, called supplier certification, fills the need. Certification can have several levels. For example, Upright-Ireland, a maker of custom scaffolding, uses four levels (see Exhibit 2–10). As at other companies that certify suppliers, Upright's highest level of certification (registered firm suppliers) means there's no need to inspect the supplier's goods or services; an Upright certification team is satisfied that the supplier has processes capable and under control.

Each monthly issue of *Quality,* in its "Quality Reports" section, lists recent suppliers that have been certified by certain of their customers.

Upright has only about 180 employees. But it is one of many small and medium-sized firms that have extensively implemented total quality management concepts. Three small manufacturers (Zytec Corp., Solectron Corp., and Marlow Industries)—and no large ones—were awarded Malcolm Baldrige National Quality Awards in 1991, which indicates how far TQM thinking has penetrated industry.

Receiving an important customer's highest certification is grounds for celebration at any supplier company. But someone should note that awards can also be lost if improvement does not continue. Other customers' certifications are the next challenges.

Marketers—always on the lookout for a competitive edge—quickly insert certification information into promotional materials. For example, if a company called Acme Office Supplies Co. were to receive, say, Kodak's "Quality First" certification, that might be the clincher for an Acme sales team to sign up an insurance company as a new client.

*P*RINCIPLE 5:

Reduce to a few good suppliers.

The growth of certification programs has paralleled another, related trend. Beginning in the late 1970s, a few pioneering large original-equipment manufacturers (OEMs) began to reduce the number of their suppliers. That movement has picked up steam as more companies, service as well as industrial, see the competitive advantages of dealing with

---

EXHIBIT 2–10   Supplier Certification at Upright-Ireland

Top: *Wall chart listing Upright's certified (just-in-time, with no inspection) suppliers, in four categories.*

Lower: *Color-coded bins, which some of Upright's certified suppliers refill daily. Clipboards, one for each supplier, give daily feedback information to suppliers.*

a few, good suppliers only. What suppliers do they keep? Those that can meet their quality certification requirements.

Suppliers may grumble about coercion, but those that are certified by big customers may find that effort an extra payoff when the time comes for them to seek registration to the ISO 9000 standard.

Exhibit 2–11   ISO 9000 Standards and Canadian and U.S. Equivalents

Standard		Canadian Equivalent	United States Equivalent
ISO 9000	Quality management and quality assurance standards—guidelines for selection and use	CSA Z299.0-86	ANSI/ASQC Q90
ISO 9001	Quality systems—model for quality assurance in design/development, production, installation, and servicing	CSA Z299.1-85	ANSI/ASQC Q91
ISO 9002	Quality systems—model for quality assurance in production and installation	CSA Z299.2-85	ANSI/ASQC Q92
ISO 9003	Quality systems—model for quality assurance in final inspection and test	CSA Z299.4-85	ANSI/ASQC Q93
ISO 9004	Quality management and quality system elements—guidelines	CSA Q420-87	ANSI/ASQC Q94

ISO 9000 Series Standards

In the late 1980s, countries began to prepare for the emergence of the European Community (EC). Part of the plan was to erase trade barriers among the 12 countries comprising the EC—Belgium, Denmark, France, Germany, Greece, Ireland, Italy, Luxembourg, Netherlands, Portugal, Spain, and United Kingdom—by the end of 1992, creating the world's largest free single-market arrangement, with upwards of 350 million consumers. To further the single community concept, the EC adopted **the ISO 9000 Series standard** as the governing quality documentation for all producers worldwide that might wish to deal with the EC.

ISO 9000 is actually an umbrella for five separate quality standards originally published by the International Organization for Standardization in 1987. Although there are national equivalents in many countries, the *ISO 9000* name is by far the most commonly used. Exhibit 2–11 shows the ISO 9000 series and the technically equivalent Canadian and U.S. standards.

Under the ISO 9000 scheme, a company arranges to have its *quality systems documentation and implementation* audited by an independent accredited registrar. If those systems meet the requirements of the appropriate ISO 9000 standard, the registrar grants certification and the company is registered as having met ISO 9000 supplier requirements. The registrar continues to survey the supplier and makes full reassessments every three or four years. Often, the quality system certification is a prerequisite to a specific product or service certification. Thus, the initial focus is on the company's *ongoing programs for continual quality improvement;* those must be approved before the issue turns to specific products and services. Also, as Exhibit 2–11 reveals, the particular role(s) to be played by a supplier (design, production, etc.) determines which of the contractual standards— ISO 9001, 9002, or 9003—must be met.

Registration isn't cheap. For a prospective supplier to register a small plant (200–300 employees) with a single product line, to ISO 9002 level, registrars place the cost at between $10,000 and $15,000 if the registration is obtained on the first try and no corrective action or reassessment is necessary. This does not include expenses for assessment team travel, application preparation, and subsequent reassessment. Typically, that minimum cost ideal isn't the reality. One large international corporation registered 20 of its plants at a per-plant cost of $200,000 to $300,000. When asked how his company could justify such expenditures, one manager replied, "We can't afford not to."[19]

Is registration to ISO 9000 series standards the ultimate quality performance achievement? No. As mentioned earlier, the series does *not* certify quality of goods and services, but rather registers the existence of proper quality plans, programs, documentation, and procedures. Regardless of ISO 9000 registration, however, companies may want to conduct their own more specific certification of prospective suppliers. Suppliers serious about continuous improvement will have to continue making the effort to improve quality.

Quality Awards

Some firms view company-based supplier certifications and ISO 9000 series registration as essential for maintaining good business relations with desired customers. Beyond that, some will exert the extra effort required to have a chance at a glamorous public quality award. Japan's Deming Prize, named after W. Edwards Deming and first presented in 1951, is the oldest and arguably the most internationally prestigious. In the United States, the Malcolm Baldrige National Quality Award, first presented in 1988, is the best known of these public awards. The Canadian equivalent to the Baldrige award is the Canada Awards for Business Excellence.

The Baldrige award received an extra measure of publicity when, after winning its own Baldrige in 1988, Motorola announced that it expected all of its suppliers to apply for the award. Motorola's position was that whether or not a supplier actually won, the thorough self-assessment of quality required of a Baldrige applicant would have beneficial results. (Additional material on quality awards may be found in the supplement to this chapter.)

Quality certifications and awards signify success in achieving TQM. Perhaps they also reflect a desire to reward close connections with customers. Undoubtedly, winning companies understand that the *total* in TQM means the total involvement of every associate in every department—our next topic.

Employee-Driven Quality

We have considered the roots and development of the quality imperative. We now turn to implementation, specifically, the need for broad-based human involvement and commitment. Gaining that commitment requires action on three fronts:

1. *Training.* Everyone needs training in the tools of continuous improvement, problem solving, and statistical process control; in addition, they require training in job skills, plus cross-training for an understanding of the bigger picture.
2. *Organization.* People need to be put into close contact with customers (next process) and suppliers (previous process). This calls for organization of customer-, product-, or service-focused cells, teams, and projects.
3. *Local ownership.* The management, control, and reward system needs to be realigned with the goals of employee- and team-driven, customer-centered quality and continuous improvement.

---

[19]George Q. Lofgren, "Quality System Registration: A Guide to Q90/ISO 9000 Series Registration," *Quality Progress,* May 1991, p. 37.

*C*ontrast

Management Theories

Theory X	**Theory Y**	**Theory T (for *Training*)**
Experts plan; operators do as they are told.	Listen to your people; they are intelligent and earnest.	Training provides the tools for continual employee-driven improvement; no training, little improvement.

Time Out for Training

Quality is free, Philip Crosby says. It pays its own way—but not without an up-front investment. The investment is for training, the essential catalyst for action.

Amid all the evidence that businesses have taken the quality imperative to heart, the elevated commitment of certain firms to quality-oriented training and cross-training stands out. For example:

- Univar, the largest U.S. chemical distributor, committed $2 million to TQM training and implementation.
- At Xerox, within 90 days of being hired, salespeople receive TQM training.
- At Quad/Graphics, associates spend one day per week in the classroom—a "day a week, forever," as a leader in the firm's educational program puts it.
- Banc One Mortgage in Indianapolis has reorganized into teams averaging 17 cross-trained people who work on all aspects of a loan application at once.
- Carolina Power & Light trains all service specialists in two job areas foreign to them.

*P*RINCIPLE 7:

Cross-training, mastery, education.

There are thousands more examples like these. Most come from companies—including many large, well-known ones—that had been spending virtually nothing on training front-line employees. In the past, only managers and professionals had received company-sponsored training. The view had been that training is an expense rather than an investment, one that detracts from profits, takes away time from real work, and is wasted when an employee leaves the company.

To avoid spending on training, businesses exploited the division-of-labor concept: Break the work down into its simplest elements, bundle a few elements into a job classification, and hire an unskilled person at minimum wage to do it with no training. Many companies, of course, still follow those practices—which leaves them with fewer resources (minds) for making improvements, or even for seeing what needs to be improved.

Lack of training also deters teamwork because, at least in Western cultures, people do not seem to be naturally team oriented. Athletic coaches and managers, for example, have to spend years molding lone wolves into wolf packs. In response to the demands of TQM, consultants are out in force providing team-building assistance.

Exhibit 2–12   Quality Circles: Gangs versus Teams

A. Gangs: Quality circles composed of employees from same
   department or shop.

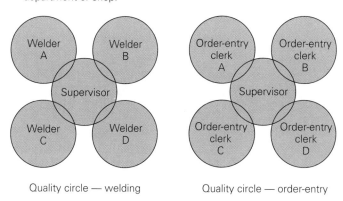

Quality circle — welding   Quality circle — order-entry

B. Teams: Quality circle composed of a chain of provider user pairs —
   formally organized into a work cell.

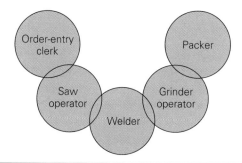

Team *organization* comes before team building. If a group of angry prisoners received team-building training, they might unite to burn down the jail. And so it is with outside businesses and agencies. The first priority is getting the right people on the team.

Quality Circles.   One useful kind of team is the quality circle (QC) (which, as was noted earlier, is an innovation of Kaoru Ishikawa in Japan, where it is called a quality control circle). In the late 1970s, Western visitors to Japan were mesmerized by the apparent potency of quality circles. Japan's QC circles contributed as many as 100 times more suggestions per employee than Western companies could elicit. In short order, quality circles were organized from Melbourne to Calcutta, Cape Town to Oslo, and Montevideo to Anchorage. The results were favorable, but not much more so than certain other programs, such as suggestion plans. It now seems clear that most quality circles were organized in a way that *avoided* a customer focus—that is, they excluded next processes (see Exhibit 2–12).

   Part A of the figure shows two examples of a quality circle composed of five people in a single department. The first consists of four welders and a supervisor, while the

Getting Organized—
Team Formats

$\mathcal{I}$nto $\mathcal{P}$ractice

Four Team Formats at Globe Metallurgical

At Globe Metallurgical (producer of additives for steel making and foundries), winner of a 1988 Baldrige Quality Prize in the small-business category, there are four kinds of teams. Within Globe, all four are frequently referred to as quality circles; the first three meet weekly, sometimes with pay and sometimes off-shift without pay:

1. Departmental teams—hourly associates from one department. The volunteer rate is about 60 percent.

2. Cross-departmental teams—appointed groups, including representation from all departments within a single plant.

3. Project teams—multidisciplinary teams assigned to specific quality improvement projects.

4. Interplant teams—hourly and salaried associates from Globe's two plant sites exchange visits quarterly.

SOURCE: Adapted from "Quality Through Consistency: Globe Metallurgical Makes Improvements Quickly," *Target,* Fall 1989, pp. 4–12.

second has four order-entry clerks and a supervisor. Those circles could meet every day and never hear a complaint about the quality of welds or errors in recording customer requirements. Also, the circles would not be inclined to discuss causes of delays in forwarding their outputs. Since their customers are not in the circles, the circles will discuss shared annoyances: room temperature, lighting, company recreation and benefits, work hours, and so forth. While all deserve to be discussed, they are only indirectly related to serving a customer. In fact, circles like these may spend much of their time complaining about the demands of customers, instead of teaming up to serve them.

Cells.   Part B of Exhibit 2–12 shows how to organize quality circles for effective process improvement. This type of circle is hard to organize because it requires moving people and equipment out of functional departments. Here an order-entry clerk is teamed up with the customer who processes the order at the first production operation: a saw operator. The order-entry terminal and the saw are moved close together. Then add more maker-customer pairs from other departments: a welder and welding equipment, a grinder and grinding equipment, and a packer and packing tools and supplies. The five operations become one, a **work cell,** or simply a **cell.**

Document processing cells and manufacturing cells are rarely organized for the purpose of creating quality circles. Rather, they are formed to quicken response times, cut out many clerical activities and transactions, eliminate bulk handling across long distances, and slash inventories along with potential rework or scrap.

While most cells are formed for these reasons, one result is the establishment of a group of associates who can scarcely avoid some quality circle behaviors. The welder who closes a seam incompletely will hear about it very soon from the grinding machine operator at the adjacent work station. The two are a team whether or not they care to be. A "bad pass" from one cell member to the next gets prompt attention.

Teams.   Ten years after the first wave of Western interest in quality circles, a new wave surged, this time generally called *teams.* As 1980s circles did, 1990s teams often employ a *facilitator,* who provides training in process analysis and improvement and may lead problem-solving team meetings. The techniques include process flowcharts, Pareto, fish-bone, run diagrams, and other process control tools (all discussed in Chapter 4). Members also study group dynamics methods, including brainstorming, nominal group techniques, role playing, multivoting, cohesiveness building, and consensus attainment as well as how to make presentations on proposed improvements. In addition, they may be empowered to interview and choose new employees and to evaluate each other's performance.

While some teams include a supervisor, others are leaderless or are coordinated by a "leadperson," industry's name for an operative who represents the group. In some companies team membership is voluntary; in others it's a part of everyone's job. Much of the new wave of interest has come from the services sector. In the 1980s, by contrast, circles and cells were of interest mainly to manufacturers, first in the plant and then in support offices.

It appears that teams in service businesses are often organized in the less effective pattern of Exhibit 2–12A (gangs). But there are notable exceptions. For example, Fidelity Investments has formed several fully staffed units (cells) to perform a complete service. One is Fidelity's "Monetary Gate" team, which, in its own corner of a single building in Texas, is able to process monetary corrections in 24 hours; formerly, corrections went back and forth among offices in dispersed cities and sometimes took months to complete.

Project Teams.   What about the many situations in which associates in the work flow are not co-located? They may be out of view, in different departments, or in different cities. That situation calls for still another kind of team: the multifunctional problem-solving, or project, team. Since most people in a work flow sequence do tend (rightly or wrongly) to be separated, this team form has an important place in total quality management.

In some situations, such as in the transportation industry, it is impossible for people to co-locate and form a cell. Chemical Lehman Tank Lines, a Pennsylvania-based petroleum hauler, creates projects across distance by sending action teams of its employees to customer sites. In an unusual twist to cross-training, Lehman even has initiated exchanges of employees with its customers. Those employees are likely to gain insights that will improve their ideas in any team format.

*𝒫*RINCIPLE 1:

Team up with customers.

In Chapter 3, we consider a related concept in teaming up for quality: the extended product or service design team, which can involve assigning component design people from a supplier company to serve on an end-product design team at a customer company. This subject arises again in the chapters on flow control (Chapter 7) and purchasing (Chapter 8).

The third essential element in achieving employee-driven quality is switching process ownership from managers to doers. If each associate and each team is expected to be the driving force in achieving continuous improvement, then everyone must feel a sense of ownership. This includes ownership of control, of improvements, and of results. It also means less control from on high and fewer levels of management reviewing improvement proposals, plus a shift toward rewarding specific results at local levels rather than general ones at high levels.

Local Ownership of Control, Improvement, and Results

*𝒫*RINCIPLE 14:

Retain local ownership of quality, data, results.

To support local ownership, managers need to be out of their offices and visible locally, where they admire control charts and process experiments, help remove obstacles, and pass out awards. When local ownership has truly taken root, the evidence is likely to include charts of all kinds—on walls, doors, and partitions—*in the workplace* rather than in managers' offices. Exhibit 2–13 shows two examples from Florida Power & Light, 1989 winner of Japan's Deming Prize (the first non-Japanese winner of the prize).

There is much more to be said about local ownership and much more to be said about total quality control. We will continue to explore these topics in detail in the remaining chapters.

EXHIBIT 2–13   **Two of the Many Quality Improvement Charts at Florida Power & Light**

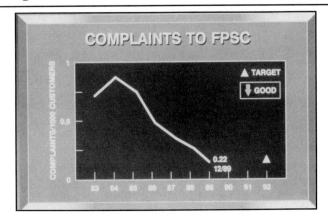

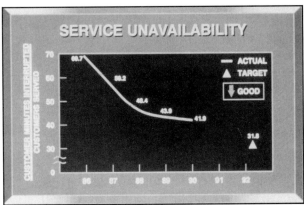

Summary

During the 1980s and early 1990s, quality evolved from a vague concept to a set of teachable practices for sound management and global competitiveness. No longer a responsibility assigned to inspectors and other specialists, quality has become everybody's business.

Customers have a multidimensional view of quality. Lists of specific dimensions of quality suggest diverse methods for providers to implement quality, shifting customer concerns, a continuous improvement mandate, and realization that quality is whatever the customer wants. Today, TQM and JIT are increasingly viewed as parts of the same customer-serving movement.

Commitment to total quality has evolved. Contributions from pioneers like Deming, Juran, Feigenbaum, Ishikawa, Crosby, and Taguchi set the stage for the modern view of total quality, and their ideas continue to guide the work of process quality improvement teams. Artisanship—pride in one's work—acted to promote quality from the time of ancient cultures until the industrial revolution weakened provider-customer connections. Ensuing quality degradation ushered in consumerism movements, changes in liability laws, and a desire for a stronger customer orientation.

Recent studies suggest a strong relationship between TQM and competitiveness. Market-route benefits include increased market share, profitability, and customer satisfaction. Cost-route benefits include better quality, lower costs, and improved employee relations. Regarding cost-of-quality, competitive companies worry more about costs associated with not having quality than they do with expenditures that enhance quality by improving processes.

Benchmarking is the systematic search for best practices that can help improvement efforts. The procedure includes start-up organization, key process identification and analysis, research on ''who's best,'' selection of benchmark targets, information collection and sharing, and adapting for continuing improvement.

Quality certifications, registrations, and awards have emerged in a big way. As large OEMs began to pare down their lists of suppliers, surviving vendors were those that achieved customer-certified status. Export-inclined companies and their suppliers have increasingly sought to become registered to the ISO 9000 standards, which are internationally recognized. Atop the award heap are the glamorous public quality awards, most notably the Deming Prize and the Malcolm Baldrige National Quality Award.

Implementation of TQM occurs through broad-based human involvement and commitment. Success demands action on three fronts: training, organization into customer-oriented teams, and realignment for local ownership of control, improvement, and results.

Key Words

For Further Reference

Books

Crosby, Philip B. *Quality is Free.* New York: McGraw-Hill, 1979.

Deming, W. Edwards. *Out of the Crisis.* Cambridge, Mass.: MIT Center for Advanced Engineering Study, 1986.

Dobyns, Lloyd, and Clare Crawford-Mason. *Quality or Else: The Revolution in World Business.* Boston: Houghton Mifflin, 1991 (HD62.15.D63).

Feigenbaum, Armand V. *Total Quality Control.* 3rd ed. rev. New York: McGraw-Hill, 1991.

Garvin, David A. *Managing Quality: The Strategic and Competitive Edge.* New York: The Free Press, 1988 (HF5415.I57.G37).

Huge, Ernest C., ed. *Total Quality: An Executive's Guide for the 1990s.* Homewood, Ill.: Dow Jones–Irwin, 1990 (TS156.H84).

Ishikawa, Kaoru. *What is Total Quality Control? The Japanese Way.* Translated by David J. Lu. Englewood Cliffs, N.J.: Prentice-Hall, 1985 (TS156.I8313).

U.S. General Accounting Office. *Management Practices: U.S. Companies Improve Performance through Quality Efforts.* Gaithersburg, Md.: U.S. General Accounting Office, Report GAO/NSIAD-91-190, 1991.

Roy, Ranjit. *A Primer on the Taguchi Method.* New York: Van Nostrand Reinhold, 1990 (TS156.R69).

Sewell, Carl, and Paul B. Brown. *Customers for Life: How to Turn That One-Time Buyer into a Lifetime Customer.* New York: Doubleday Currency, 1990 (HF5415.5.S49).

Walton, Mary. *The Deming Management Method.* New York: Dodd, Mead, 1986 (HD38.W36).

Periodicals/Societies

Quality, a Hitchcock publication.

Quality Progress (ASQC).

Quality Management Journal (ASQC).

Review Questions

1. What is the meaning of the phrase "the quality imperative"?
2. Explain why quality ought to be everybody's business, not delegated to a few specialists.
3. What is the broad view of quality? Make your answer as specific as you can.
4. List one major contribution to the evolution of the concept of total quality from each of the following: Deming, Juran, Feigenbaum, Ishikawa, Crosby, and Taguchi. What common beliefs do their teachings express?
5. What is artisanship? What has been its role in quality evolution and in development of the modern customer-oriented view of quality?
6. How was quality affected by the industrial revolution? the consumerism movement?
7. List ways in which TQM has been shown to improve performance and competitive position.
8. Explain what would be meant by the "cost of *un*-quality."
9. Why are costs of improving quality hard to isolate?
10. What is benchmarking? What are the common steps in the benchmarking procedure?
11. How does supplier certification serve as an incentive to improve quality?
12. What are the ISO 9000 series standards? Comment on the importance of ISO 9000 registration.
13. How does competition for a major quality award (e.g., The Deming Prize or the Malcolm Baldrige Award) affect applicant companies?
14. What do we mean by employee-driven quality? Explain in terms of training, organization, and ownership.
15. Name and define three types of teams one might find in world-class organizations.
16. What does local ownership mean?

Problems and Exercises

1. Interview two managers, one in the private sector and the other from the public sector. Ask the following questions:
    a. Is quality increasing or decreasing in importance in your field?
    b. Does improved quality pay? Why or why not?
   Discuss your findings.
2. "The only acceptable performance is zero defects." Discuss the application of that phrase to each of the following situations:
    a. Surgeons performing elective surgery.
    b. Machinists fabricating automobile engines.
    c. Lawyers defending accused child molesters.
    d. Grocers stocking the supermarket deli display.
    e. Investment counselors giving financial advice.
    f. Police officers apprehending a suspect.
    g. County clerks recording tax payments.
    h. Merchants selling exercise equipment.
    i. College students typing term papers.
3. How do you determine quality in products? For example, how do you distinguish a good automobile (or bar stool, topcoat, aspirin, or golf ball) from a bad one? Does the item's price influence your thinking? What are society's beliefs regarding a relationship between price and quality? Are these beliefs realistic?

4. How do you determine quality in services? For example, how do you distinguish a good lawyer (or accountant, professor, athlete, or barber) from a bad one? Does the service's price—fee charged or salary received—have any influence on your thinking? Does society pay the same attention to price when judging the quality of services as it does in the case of products? Why or why not?

5. Refer to Exhibit 2–1, "Dimensions of Quality":
   a. Explain each of King's 10 dimensions of service quality as it applies to one service of your choice.
   b. Explain each of Garvin's eight dimensions of quality as it applies to a product of your choice.

6. Apply the Plan-Do-Check-Act cycle—suggest specific actions for each of the four steps—to one of the following problems:
   a. Fellow employees (or students) are habitually late or absent from team meetings.
   b. Cashier lines at the cafeteria take too much time.
   c. Utility bills at home (house, apartment, dorm, or fraternity or sorority house) are too high.
   d. The bookstore always runs out of blank computer diskettes.
   e. Printer ribbons in the computer lab run out of ink (creating light print) too soon.

7. *John:* Hi Jane! How's it going?
   Jane: Lousy! My grandmom sent me a sweater for my birthday, but there's a flaw in the weaving. I have to mail it back to her, she has to return it to the store and hope they have another of the same style and color in my size, and then send it back to me. What a pain! She shouldn't have to go through that hassle.
   John: Yeah, I've been through that no-questions-asked returns policy too many times myself.
   a. List the members of the provider-customer chain in the above story.
   b. Where did quality break down?
   c. What social costs occurred in the above story?
   d. How might situations like the above be prevented?
   e. Is a free-returns policy high-quality service? Why or why not?

8. Acme Inc. has just installed a high efficiency motor-generator set to clean up the electrical power supply (remove unwanted fluctuations) to its precision equipment lab. Results include more accurate readings for tests, longer equipment life with less downtime, lower maintenance costs, shorter turnaround times for lab services for Acme's customers, and more accurate job scheduling due to increased equipment reliability. Is the expenditure for the motor-generator set a cost of quality? Discuss.

9. Al and Alice are co-chairs of the University Student Service Club's fundraising committee. For the past few years, fundraising has been on the decline, but Al and Alice are determined to reverse that trend. They plan to benchmark other campus organizations, and copy the successful ones. What are the pros and cons of their plan?

10. Obtain a list of the Malcolm Baldrige National Quality Award winners (the first awards were given out in 1988). Then refer to Exhibit 2–6, "TQM—Impact on Performance," for examples of performance criteria and pick two of the winners and investigate their performance since winning the award. Discuss your findings.

11. *Suzy:* Sam, they've reduced our training budget again! How can my people provide the TQM training our company needs in order to achieve preferred supplier certification from Caterpillar? And we're also trying to get ISO 9002 registration!
    Sam: I know. I talked to Betty in budgeting this morning. The feeling among the powers that be is that during the current business slump cuts have to come from soft areas—places that aren't value-adding. I guess their feeling about training is, "Adds costs but no proven value." Do you think we might present a convincing argument to change their minds?
    Write a brief essay containing arguments that Suzy and Sam could use in trying to get the training budget restored.

12. Would quality circles work well in improving performance of a hockey team? Of a group of students banding together to study? Discuss.

13. After 12 percent to 19 percent increases in tuition and other fees across the state university system, a group of concerned students, parents, and other friends of higher education formed an ad hoc group to investigate the problem of runaway college costs.
    a. Is this group a team as defined in the text? Discuss.
    b. Who (what agencies, groups, etc.) ought to be represented in the group to prevent the *gang* syndrome from taking over.

14. At Rocky Mountain Academy, the basketball and skiing coaches have decided to employ the quality circle concept. Each circle will consist of the top five athletes on the team. The coaches' purpose is to try to tap their athletes' intelligence and thereby generate ideas that will improve the teams' effectiveness. Considering what makes quality circles work well or poorly, assess the likely results of the quality circle experiment for each coach.

15. Seven bank tellers volunteered to form the bank's first quality circle. The human resources department conducted an attitude survey just before the quality circle was formed and again after it had been meeting for six months. The survey showed a dramatic improvement in morale and attitude. Further, the circle produced 38 suggestions in the six-month period. Is this quality circle well conceived? Are its results excellent, or not?

SUPPLEMENT

QUALITY AWARDS

In recent years, quality awards have received increasing attention. Managers recognize not only the marketing potential that comes with winning an award but also the positive effects on operations that result simply from having competed for one. In this supplement, we discuss some of the more popular awards to reflect the growing global emphasis that quality awards have attained in manufacturing and service sectors.

Deming Prize

Started in 1951 and named after W. Edwards Deming, the American statistician who was instrumental in helping the Japanese rebuild their war-torn economy, the Deming Prize is the grandaddy of all quality awards. Until the late 1980s, it was the only award of note. The Deming Prize is administered by the Union of Japanese Scientists and Engineers—commonly known as JUSE—and is given in two major categories: individuals for contributions to statistical theory, and companies for success in achieving companywide quality improvement. There may be multiple winners in a given year.

A notable individual winner is Genichi Taguchi, who won his first (of four) Deming Prize in 1960 for his pioneering work in experimental design. At the company level, the Deming Prize may be won by firms in any nation. Often, several years are spent preparing for the actual year-long evaluation process, with extensive documentation. For example, NEC Tohoku, Ltd., a NEC Corporation subsidiary, won the Deming Prize in 1989. The directives, plans, and reports required for its application totaled about 244,000 pages, and the presentation to JUSE judges required an additional 300 pages of data.

Some critics argue that the Deming competition causes companies to create large quality department bureaucracies and spend great sums on consultants from JUSE, but few debate the reputations for quality products enjoyed by Deming Prize recipients such as Hitachi, Nippon Steel, Nissan, Texas Instruments, and Toyota. NEC's president, Hisaei Kikuchi, has no regrets about the time and money NEC invested in the Deming competition. He feels that the effort turned his company around and put it on the road to success in the next century.

EXHIBIT S2–1   Malcolm Baldrige National Quality Award Evaluation Criteria— 1992

Category	Maximum Points
Leadership	90
Information and analysis	80
Strategic quality planning	60
Human resource development and management	150
Management of process quality	140
Quality and operational results	180
Customer focus and satisfaction	300
Total points	1,000

Malcolm Baldrige National Quality Award

In August 1987, President Reagan signed Public Law 100-107, the Malcolm Baldrige National Quality Improvement Act. Named after the late secretary of commerce, the legislation reflected growing belief that the U.S. government should take a more active role in promoting quality improvement. The act established the Malcolm Baldrige National Quality Award, to be administered by the National Institute of Standards and Technology. The award is presented annually, usually in October (National Quality Month), to no more than two winners in each of three categories: manufacturing, service, and small business. Only U.S. firms are eligible. In 1988, the first Baldrige Awards went to Motorola, Inc., the Commercial Nuclear Fuel Division of Westinghouse Electric Corporation, and Globe Metallurgical Inc. Typically, there are fewer than six annual recipients, for examiners have discretion not to give the award if applicants fail to measure up.

Hundreds of thousands of Baldrige award application forms are mailed out each year, but actual applications are far fewer (e.g., 40 in 1989, 106 in 1991, and 90 in 1992). Companies have discovered that while it is nice to win the award (increased quality, market share, profitability, and customer satisfaction are among the payoffs), substantial benefits accrue from merely conducting the thorough self-assessment required by the application process. Firms nominate themselves for the Baldrige award and must present documentary evidence of their success in having established and maintained an ongoing program of quality improvement in the application criteria areas shown in Exhibit S2–1.

As with the Deming Prize, the Baldrige has its critics. For example, some people lament the marketability of success that comes from winning the award, or feel that the Baldrige award mandate for winners to share the secret of success with other companies (even competitors) is unrealistic. Despite the criticisms, however, Baldrige winners continue to attract attention. Perhaps the greatest contribution of the Baldrige award to date, however, is the fallout in the form of other awards that closely follow its format and the widespread acceptance of its criteria by companies as guidelines for internal improvement efforts, often independent of any award application process.

RIT/*USA Today* Quality Cup

Rochester Institute of Technology (RIT) joined forces with the newspaper *USA Today* and on October 10, 1991, announced the RIT/*USA Today* Quality Cup for individuals and teams. More than 2,000 organizations requested applications for the 1992 Quality Cup with 431 eventually applying. A panel of 11 judges chosen by RIT evaluated the applications received in all of the award's five categories.

Like other quality awards, Quality Cup evaluation guidelines call for judges to review applications, conduct extensive interviews with selected finalists, and visit sites. Perhaps more than any other major quality award, the Quality Cup supports the employee-driven team focus discussed in

---

EXHIBIT S2–2 **Initial RIT/*USA Today* Quality Cup Winners**

Manufacturing: U.S. Steel Gary Works, Gary, Indiana. Five union employees at U.S. Steel's Gary Works mill saved contracts, and probably the plant, by meeting with dissatisfied customers and relaying fixes to plant management.

Service: Federal Express, Memphis, Tennessee. A team of 12 Federal Express employees—most part-timers—reorganized the minisort operation for misdirected packages, saving the company $938,000 in one 18-month period.

Small firms: L-S Electro-Galvanizing, Cleveland, Ohio. A team of 13 LSE employees implemented a quality-monitoring system for galvanizing steel, saving $2.2 million during 1991 —an amount equal to 27.5 percent of LSE's net income.

Not-for-profit: Sentara Health System, Norfolk, Virginia. A team of nine employees and managers redesigned the X-ray-testing process at Sentara Norfolk General Hospital, cutting it from an average 72.5 hours to 13.8 hours.

Government: Navy Operations Center, Patuxent River, Maryland. A team of nine employees and managers simplified and automated the travel planning process for the Naval Aviation Depot Operations Center, eliminating 85 percent of the errors, cutting required signatures from 100 to 5, and saving over two person-years of clerical work.

SOURCE: *USA Today,* April 10, 1992, Section B.

EXHIBIT S2–3 **Shingo Prize Criteria: Manufacturing Process Integration**

Cell, continuous flow, or mixed manufacturing.
Nonstock production or inventory elimination.
Concurrent or simultaneous engineering.
Quality function deployment.
Total productive maintenance.
Kanban pull system.
Quick changeover and setup reductions.
CAD/CAM and computer integrated manufacturing (CIM).

Chapter 2. Exhibit S2–2 shows the accomplishments of the initial Quality Cup winners in each category as announced in the April 10, 1992, issue of *USA Today.*

Shingo Prize

Established in 1988, The Shingo Prize for Excellence in Manufacturing recognizes American companies that excel in productivity, quality, customer satisfaction, and manufacturing processes. The annual prize is administered by Utah State University and cosponsored by the American Productivity and Quality Center, the Health Care Manufacturers Association, the National Association of Manufacturers, and Productivity, Inc.

The Shingo prize differs from the Deming, Baldrige, and RIT/*USA Today* prizes in that its roots are in the just-in-time path to quality excellence and it is limited to manufacturers. It is named after the late Shigeo Shingo, who may someday be listed among the quality pioneers in the body of the chapter. Shingo's contributions promote an integrated mix of waste elimination, lead-time reduction through JIT, quality, employee involvement, and other related concepts. One of his books, *Zero Quality Control: Source Inspection and the Poka-Yoke System,* is an innovative treatment of quality that seems likely to become a classic in TQM.

Some of the criteria that Shingo prize examiners use to judge applicants are similar to those of other quality prizes: leading, empowering, partnering, manufacturing vision and strategy, manufacturing process integration, productivity improvement, quality enhancement, and customer satisfaction. The JIT flavor is especially apparent in the category on manufacturing process integration; for this category, Exhibit S2–3 lists the kinds of evidence of integration that examiners look for when evaluating Shingo Prize applicants.

Exhibit S2–4   European Quality Award Evaluation Criteria

Category	*Weight*
Customer satisfaction	20 percent
Business results	15 percent
Processes	14 percent
Leadership	10 percent
People (employee) satisfaction	9 percent
Resources	9 percent
People management	9 percent
Policy and strategy	8 percent
Impact on society	6 percent

European Quality Award

The quality imperative truly is global. The European Quality Award, a creation of the European Foundation for Quality Management (EFQM) in partnership with the European Commission and the European Organization for Quality, was announced in Paris in October 1991. The aim is to identify the company that can best demonstrate how total quality management has contributed to customer satisfaction, employee well-being, and service to others with a stake in the company. Because EFQM emphasizes that the ultimate measure of performance is long-term success, winners of the European Quality Award—as well as the other quality awards for that matter—tend to be companies that are already advanced in TQM implementation. Exhibit S2–4 shows the nine evaluation criteria for the European Quality Award.

Application procedures roughly parallel those of the Deming Prize and the Baldrige award. Companies wishing to compete for the European Quality Award must first perform self-assessments. Judges review those assessments and select finalists. Finally, interviews and site visits are used to determine winners. Any company is eligible to apply provided at least half of its business operations are in Western Europe and have been there for at least five years.

Other Quality Awards

The five quality awards discussed above are among the better known and reflect the global nature of the quality imperative. Many other quality awards exist, however. For example, we mentioned in the chapter the Canadian equivalent to the Baldrige—Canada Awards for Business Excellence. Awards are sometimes given by a single agency to its most deserving contractors. NASA's George M. Low Trophy, for example, is presented annually to recognize outstanding achievements in quality and productivity by NASA contractors and subcontractors. The public sector is also represented. The Quality Improvement Prototype (QIP) Award, with a format similar to the Baldrige, is given by the Federal Quality Institute to federal agencies that use TQM concepts to improve service quality.

A fast-growing number of states, provinces, cities, and regions have also instituted awards for quality excellence. Examples include the Connecticut Quality Improvement Award Medallion, the Minnesota Quality Award, New York State's Excelsior Award, and the Erie Quality Award in Erie County, Pennsylvania. In addition, dozens of regional quality councils or smaller quality networks have formed to help spread the TQM message and to strengthen business competitiveness and quality in the given region. These include "Quality Valley," the Lehigh Valley in Pennsylvania, and the Texas Quality Consortium (a network of small technology-oriented companies).

Quality Awards in Perspective

Is the emphasis on quality awards a short-term phenomenon of the closing years of the 20th century? Or are quality-oriented awards permanent features of global competitiveness? Although not every award winner has continued to prosper in the years after receiving an award, most have weathered the recessionary economic forces and other broad factors that affect financial performance better than their competitors. There seems to be a sticking power to the kinds of general good business practices required to win a major quality prize.

Critics argue that the awards create a mini-industry that has become self-perpetuating. But proponents say that benefits far outweigh those concerns. Customers, they argue, are the ultimate beneficiaries. For as long as those benefits are recognized, the awards have a place in the quality movement.

Sources: Brian M. Cook, "Quality: The Pioneers Survey the Landscape," *Industry Week,* October 21, 1991, p. 68ff.

David Craig, "Some Baldrige Winners Are Losers," *USA Today,* October 10, 1991, p. 3B.

David A. Garvin, "How the Baldrige Award Really Works," *Harvard Business Review,* November–December 1991, pp. 80–93.

Chester Placek, "Baldrige Award as a Quality Model," *Quality,* February 1992, pp. 17–20.

Shigeo Shingo, *Zero Quality Control: Source Inspection and the Poka-Yoke System* (Cambridge, Mass: Productivity Press, 1985).

Brad Stratton, "A Different Look at the Baldrige Award," *Quality Progress,* February 1991, pp. 17–20.

U.S. Department of Commerce, *Award Criteria: Malcolm Baldrige National Quality Award* (Gaithersburg, Md.: National Institute of Standards and Technology, 1992).

New York Department of Economic Development, *The Governor's Excelsior Award: Quality at Work in New York State* (Albany, N.Y.: New York Department of Economic Development, 1992).

"The Quality Imperative," Business Week Special Report, *Business Week,* October 25, 1991.

"The Quest for Quality," *USA Today,* April 10, 1992, Section B.

Design and Control for Customer Satisfaction

II

Customer requirements are the driving force for operations. Seldom fully satisfied with what's available, customers keep shifting, usually elevating, their expectations. The competitive organization must respond with innovative products and services and continual improvement in the processes that create them. These design issues are addressed in Chapter 3.

A fundamental lesson for business, industry, and public and volunteer services concerns the dominating importance of quality. Chapter 4 looks at quality management from a planning and competitive standpoint and includes an assortment of techniques usable in the front lines of operations.

3

DESIGNED-IN QUALITY: PRODUCT, SERVICE, AND PROCESS PLANNING

Chapter Outline

Research and Development: Strategic Issues

Teaming Up for Effective Product-Process Design
    Concurrent Design
    Appeal and Fit
    Competitive Analysis
    Environmental Awareness

Quality Function Deployment

Design for Operations: Guidelines
    General Guidelines
    Quality Guidelines
    Operability Guidelines

Simplified Design and Robotics: An Example

Design Review, Performance Measurement, and Control

Process Technology: People and Automation in Perspective
    People and Machines
    Preautomation
    Low-Grade Process Automation
    Justifying Automation and Other Improvement Projects

Supplement: Annotated Glossary of Technology

When we encounter high quality and efficiency, it looks elegant, simple, effortless. This happens when overall excellence is designed in. High-quality design, of both products and processes, plays a critical role in operations management. When overlaid on a foundation of good design, quality by process capability and control, discussed in Chapter 4, occurs naturally.

By product design we mean the design and development of the firm's goods and services. Its close partner is process design, which is specifying the procedures, standards, equipment, supplies, tools, and training needed for producing the goods or providing the services.

Until recently, design was undermanaged and its impact on operations was underappreciated. We probably know more about poor product- and process-design practices, which are entrenched in many organizations, than we do about good ones. By contrast, superior companies agree on several positive steps in achieving effective product-process design (see Exhibit 3–1). The first step is fitting the firm's design strategy to its competitive environment. The next move is pulling people in from different functions to form design teams, which systematically collect data on customer needs and competitor's capabilities, and then act on those data while following design-for-operations guidelines. The final follow-through employs a set of relevant measures of design effectiveness.

EXHIBIT 3-1   Effective Product-Process Design

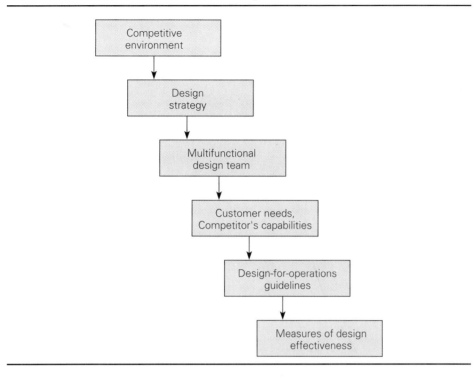

We examine these topics in the first part of this chapter. The balance of the chapter addresses special topics, including the effective uses of technology and automation. Throughout the chapter we emphasize that product design and process design must blend together seamlessly rather than being separated organizationally and in time.

Research and Development: Strategic Issues

While every organization has some sort of system for evaluating new and improved designs, overriding strategies vary widely. Some companies spend aggressively on research and development (R&D), while others spend virtually nothing. Some do in-house R&D, others farm it out.

Exhibit 3-2 lists R&D allocations, as a percentage of sales, for selected industries and countries. We can see that the top spenders (computer and medical products and services) invest about 15 times more than those at the bottom of the list. Low spenders (food, fuel, etc.) require less R&D, probably because their products are sold almost as they are obtained from nature. At just 0.9 percent, services are sold almost as they arise from human nature.

R&D spending also varies a good deal from nation to nation. With the possibility of an era of relative peace, growing opportunities for trade may nudge low-spending nations (e.g., the United States) to invest more, especially in nondefense R&D, in order to be competitive. For the same reason, perhaps top spenders will shift spending somewhat from R&D to marketing. In other words, R&D (and marketing) spending patterns may become more alike among nations.

Research pushes the boundaries of science, aiming for product or process innovations. *Development* is translating an innovation into practical product and process designs.

EXHIBIT 3–2   **R&D Expenditures**

Industries (United States, except italic)	Percentage of Annual Sales Spent on Company-financed R&D (1991)
Computer software and services	13.5
Health care: drugs and research	10.8
Computer systems design	9.9
Sweden: all-industry composite	7.2
Health care: medical products and services	6.3
Germany: all-industry composite	6.0
Leisure-time equipment (toys, sporting goods, etc.)	5.7
Data processing services	5.5
Canada: all-industry composite	5.4
Japan: all-industry composite	5.0
Non-United States: 200 nations composite	4.3
Automotive	4.3
Aerospace	3.8
United States: all-industry composite	3.6
Britain: all-industry composite	2.3
United States: nondefense composite	2.2
Housing	1.8
Service industries: composite	0.9
Containers and packaging	0.8
Fuel	0.8
Food	0.7

SOURCE: "R&D Scoreboard," *Business Week,* June 29, 1992, pp. 104–23. Obtained by *Business Week* from Standard & Poor's Compustat Services, Inc.

Knowing the average R&D commitments shown in Exhibit 3–2 might help a firm develop its own design strategy. For almost any firm, this strategy should focus on correcting two chronic weaknesses of conventional design:

1. Design is too slow. Thus, the product or service gets to market late and competitors are entrenched. A McKinsey & Company analysis shows the seriousness of being late (see Exhibit 3–3). If a company is four months late to market, potential gross profit is off 18 percent. If its design team can shave time-to-market by just one month, gross profit improves by 7.3 percent. For revenues of $25 million, that translates into $300,000 of additional gross profit; at $100 million revenue, it ups gross profit by $1.2 million.

2. Process design is neglected. This has been a common blind spot, even for Western companies known for commitment to research. They splurge on innovative new technologies, then fail to develop them into commercial successes. The best new ideas (e.g., in computer memory, metallurgy, machine control, etc.) are pioneered in one part of the world and then commercially perfected elsewhere, often in Japan.

The phenomenon is well known in government and service companies as well. A commission or legislative subcommittee will spend a year developing a new program for, say, protecting the forests or housing the poor and a law will be passed. But because the agencies that must implement the law are not involved in drafting legislation, developing the processes for implementation may take many more months. Often implementing regulations are ineffective.

Industry's reaction to these criticisms has generally been positive. Time-based competition has become a common element of company strategies to overcome slowness of design. In research, this translates into a quick time-to-market (or design-to-market) strategy.

𝒫RINCIPLE 11:

Cut flow time all along the chain of customers.

EXHIBIT 3–3   Cost of Arriving Late to Market (and Not Over Budget)

If company is late to market by:	6 mos.	5 mos.	4 mos.	3 mos.	2 mos.	1 mo.
Gross profits potential reduced:	−33%	−25%	−18%	−13%	−7%	−3%
Cut time-to-market by one month, profit improves:	+11.9%	+9.3%	+7.3%	+5.7%	+4.3%	+3.1%
For revenues of $25 million, annual gross profit increases:	+$400K	+$350K	+$300K	+$250K	+$200K	+$150K
For revenues of $100 million, annual gross profit increases:	+$1600K	+$1400K	+$1200K	+$1000K	+$800K	+$600K

SOURCE: McKinsey & Company data, cited in Joseph T. Vesey, "The New Competitors: Thinking in Terms of 'Speed-to-Market,' " *Manufacturing Engineering*, June 1991, pp. 16–24.

Regarding neglect of design, many of the same companies have raised their commitment to process design. This usually does not mean a shift in funding away from product R&D to process R&D. Rather, the commitment is to a research strategy of close linkage between product design and process design.

The remainder of this chapter details ways of carrying out an effective design strategy, with repeated emphasis on tightening the product-process design linkage and getting to market fast with high quality products that meet customers' real needs.

Teaming Up for Effective Product-Process Design

Imagine a hierarchy of chefs in a tony restaurant in which the head chef composes recipes and menus, but never works the kitchen, visits food sellers, or interacts with the serving staff. A food buyer uses the head chef's list to buy ingredients but has nothing to do with other restaurant functions. Others in the restaurant are similarly compartmentalized.

The image is, of course, ridiculous. In larger restaurants, there is a hierarchy—from head chef to sous chef and on down (and plenty of chances for misunderstanding and process variation). However, the head chef works with other key players to a very short plan-do-check-act cycle. Feedback comes quickly (e.g., carrots are tough and tasteless), so that corrective action (drop that recipe and switch to green beans) can be taken for just-arriving diners or at least for tomorrow's customers. The various chefs, servers, managers, and so on, must operate as a team, acquiring and sharing up-to-date information about what's happening. There is no time to dawdle or to pass designs and plans back and forth from department to department.

*P*RINCIPLE 1:

Team up with the next and final customer.

The last four sentences, with minor changes in terms, fittingly describe good product-process design practices for any kind of organization. Call it team design, or use fancier terms, **simultaneous engineering** or **concurrent design,** in which functional specialists execute their parts of the design as a team concurrently (at the same time) instead of in separate departments serially.

When the product's life stretches out over years (whether it's a bank savings plan or a type of disposable diaper), the design cycle tends to do the same. No urgency, no concurrency.

In some business sectors, shrinking product life cycles have pushed product-process designers into a short loop linked more closely to the do-check-act phases of continuous improvement. New generations of computer hardware, software, and peripherals—and bank savings plans and disposable diapers, too—are announced yearly or more often. Shortened life cycles are fed by high competition, technological advances, and quick compilation and communication of sales trend data.

Concurrent Design

Higher pay of product designers sets them apart. Hewlett-Packard (H-P) eliminated that barrier when, in 1985, president John Young equalized base pay for all types of H-P engineers.

$\mathscr{C}$ontrast

Design

Over-the-Wall Design	**Concurrent (Team) Design**
• Becomes common practice as organization grows and splits into functional departments.	• Tends to be common practice in very small organizations and where product redesigns occur often.
• Common, especially, in businesses with long product lives (little urgency to develop new products).	• Elevated competition has made it common in consumer electronics, cars, consumer credit, mortgage loans, and so on.
• Tends to be slow.	• Is fast and avoids problems (design rework) stemming from poor coordination and lack of shared information.
• Tends to require several costly rounds of debugging.	

But even when product life cycles are long, concurrent design has merit. Advantages include the following:

- Concurrent design gets all parties together, including customers, suppliers, and front-line associates. Designs should then be more in tune with real customer requirements, more realistic for suppliers to support, and easier for front-line associates to execute.

- Concurrent design avoids costly misunderstandings and "do-overs" in the design phase.

- Concurrent design reduces costly bugs, errors, rework, and warranty claims in production, delivery, and customer use phases. Opportunities for reducing such wastes are everywhere. For example, in a human resources department, "If a bonus system or orientation program needs to be redesigned because employees could not understand it, this is clearly 'rework.' "[1]

When a business is young or small, teaming up for good design is easy and natural. As the firm grows, people split off into specialties housed in separate departments. How specialized? One reported example is of an automotive engineer who had spent his entire career designing auto door locks:

> He was not an expert in how to make door locks, however; that was the job of the door-lock manufacturing engineer. The door-lock design engineer simply knew how they should look and work if made correctly.[2]

In manufacturing, redesign results in engineering change orders, each of which can go through many time-consuming and costly approval steps.

In that overspecialized system, product designers are accused of throwing the design "over the wall" to manufacturing—and saying, in effect, "Let's see you build that!" It's unbuildable, so manufacturing tosses it back for re-design. Round after round of design

---

[1]David E. Bowen and Edward E. Lawler III, "Total Quality-Oriented Human Resources Management," *Academy of Management Executive,* Spring 1992, pp. 29–41.

[2]James P. Womack, Daniel T. Jones, and Daniel Roos, *The Machine That Changed the World* (New York: Rawson Associates, 1990), p. 63.

Into Practice

Hallmark's "Holiday" Design Teams

Hallmark "lives or dies on new stuff—some 40,000 cards and other items a year, the work of 700 writers, artists, and designers. . . . Developing a new card had become grotesque; it took two years—longer than the road from Gettysburg to the Appomattox Court House. The company was choking on sketches, approvals, cost estimates, and proofs." But now, about half the staff will "work on cards for particular holidays. . . . A team of artists, writers, lithographers, merchandisers, bean counters, and so on,

will be assigned to each holiday. Team members are moving from all over a two-million-square-foot office building in Kansas City so they can sit together. Like a canoe on a lake, a card will flow directly from one part of the process to the next within, say, the Mother's Day team; before, it had to be portaged from one vast department to the next."

Source: Thomas A. Stewart, "The Search for the Organization of Tomorrow," *Fortune*, May 18, 1992, pp. 92–98.

235 Design/Build Teams, One Boeing Airplane

Boeing's new "fly-by-wire" commercial airplane, the 777, involved 235 design/build teams—each with members from Boeing's vaunted design group, the airlines (the customers), the mechanics who will maintain the planes, the suppliers, "and the many others who will help build it, price it, and market it."

Shin-ichi Nakagawa, leader of a group of 250 engineers from Japanese supplier companies, says Japanese companies "are familiar with teams of design and production engineers, but they haven't experienced Boeing's all-embracing teams that include customers, suppliers, and support teams."

Source: Jeremy Main, "Betting on the 21st Century Jet," *Fortune*, April 20, 1992, pp. 102–17.

Continuous Innovation at Rubbermaid

"Unlike many consumer-product companies, [Rubbermaid] does no test marketing. Instead, [it] has created entrepreneurial teams of five to seven members in each of its four dozen product categories. Each team includes a product manager, research and manufacturing engineers and finan-

cial, sales and marketing executives. The teams conceive their own products, shepherding them from the design stage to the marketplace."

Source: Valerie Reitman, "Rubbermaid Turns Up Plenty of Profit in the Mundane," *The Wall Street Journal*, March 27, 1992.

changes (often called engineering change orders) and attempts at production follow. The changes are costly and time-consuming inasmuch as they ripple through other departments, such as purchasing, finance, marketing, materials, scheduling, and human resources.

Concurrent (team) design has taken root in many companies (see examples from Hallmark, Boeing, and Rubbermaid in the accompanying box). The greatest benefits often come from getting product designers and process designers on the same team. James Lardner, vice president at Deere and Company, maintains that "we can cut capital investment for automation by 50%–60% just by getting the design and manufacturing

Into Practice

Good Designs—Not Just from Italy

" 'Smart' tools. Souped-up baseball gloves. Task-specific computers." said *Business Week*. "High-tech tires. Ergonomic wrenches. Quality Cadillacs. Bathtubs with doors. 'Floating' 52-inch TVs. If the gold winners of the 1992 Industrial Design Excellence Awards (IDEA) are harbingers . . . a product renaissance is afoot that may rival Japanese and European surges of the '70s and '80s.

"This year's 111 IDEA medalists may be the tip of the iceberg," said the article. "Devoid of decorative gewgaws and stylistic cuteness, the winners come from companies where design is an integral part of product development from the beginning." The IDEA winners included the Goodyear Tire & Rubber Co. Aquatred tire, a special-purpose Texas Instruments (TI) computer, and an Ingersoll-Rand ergonomic wrench.

"Handheld and task-specific, [the TI Audit Trading Computer] is designed to serve the toilers in the pits of the Chicago Board of Trade. TI designed it to work with a regular pen or pencil, since traders use pens and pencils to write their trades on slips of paper. The product had to be small enough to fit in the palm of a hand and rounded so that no one would get hurt in the shouting and shoving that goes on in the pits."

Ingersoll-Rand's Group Four Design Team in Avon, Connecticut, created the gold-award winning "worker-friendly wrench for automobile assembly . . . with input from Detroit assembly-line workers. Its adjustable handle and soft grip help prevent repetitive-motion injuries often associated with conventional industrial tools."

SOURCE: "Winners: The Best Product Designs of the Year," *Business Week*, June 8, 1992, pp. 52–68.

---

people together from the beginning."[3] The full concurrent-design team, however, includes marketing, finance, and other inside departments; customers, suppliers, and freight carriers; and, perhaps, community and regulatory representatives.

Appeal and Fit

In some industries, the design team needs one more type of representative: experts in **industrial design** (see box). They make the product look appealing (aesthetics) and easy for people to grasp, operate, or adapt to (*ergonomics*, also known as human factors engineering). Industrial design is burgeoning because companies see consumers rejecting products having stodgy designs, even if they are functionally excellent. According to one writer, "state-of-the-art functions, fast cycle times, high quality, and low costs are simply expected of products now. Design [i.e., industrial design] is the new differentiator."[4]

We have seen the importance of getting broad membership on the design team. Then, to get the full set of benefits, the team must systematically collect and share competitive, legal, social, and environmental information—our next topics.

Competitive Analysis

To fully do its work, the design team needs to know the competition. The trouble is, many companies have too few probes into the outside world. Competitive feedback is sparse, late, and narrow gauge—for example, limited mostly to sales totals and warranty claims.

Investigation of competitors' products is called **competitive analysis.** (In contrast, benchmarking, a newer "sibling" of competitive analysis, seeks out best processes of all kinds, rather than just competitors' products. See Chapter 2.) For services, competitive analysis usually requires going to the competitor, being served, and taking extensive notes

---

[3]Cited in presentation materials by International TechneGroup Inc., Spring 1991.
[4]Therese R. Welter, "Step Right Up," *Industry Week,* November 19, 1990, pp. 42–44.

for later use by your own service design group. Example: Warehouse stores (e.g., Circuit City, Home Depot, Sam's, and Office Club) have been expanding into new markets, which brings anxious managers of existing conventional stores in to do a competitive analysis, followed, sometimes, by redesign of their own service practices.

In manufacturing, the usual procedure is to buy a competitor's product and bring it in for thorough study, perhaps including complete disassembly, which is called *reverse engineering*. Some firms have a competitive analysis laboratory presided over by technical people. Less often, people from all over the company get involved in analyzing samples of competitors' products.

*P*RINCIPLE 4:

Get to know the competition.

On the environmental front, businesses have tended to react late rather than plan and design early. The business world's common assumption was that environmental initiatives are too costly to be in their own or their customers' direct interest.

Throughout the 1980s, however, tough pollution and recycling laws were passed, and public awareness was elevated. Reluctance sometimes changed to willing compliance, translated into planning for recycling and recovery in early design phases. The change in attitude occurred when, for example, fluids once dumped into rivers and now recycled became cash generators. Spent lubricants and chemical wash fluids turned out to be reprocessible and reusable, for less than the cost of new fluids. Recoverable metals in electronic trash and in plating acids were "gold in the trash barrel"—literally, in the case of gold-plated semiconductor leads.

Competitive one-upsmanship can be the attraction that gets environmental and social concerns on the design team's agenda. For example, a beverage company makes its competitor look bad by being the first to open up a network of can or bottle recycling centers.

Sometimes reaction to a social or environmental concern opens up a set of promising new design options. For example, in attempting to design products easily operable by disabled consumers, designers have unearthed an attractive new approach called **universal design.**[5] It often turns out that the same products (such as phones or VCRs with large buttons, easy-to-open doors, or easy-to-access information services) are popular with young and old, able and disabled. That's good news for the maker because it allows the design team to focus intensively on just a few universal designs. With fewer, more universal product variations, designers can focus on better quality. At the same time, however, the design team needs to keep an eye on the big picture.

Environmental Awareness

A Dow Chemical ethylene plant was designed to cut waste-water releases into the North Saskatchewan River from 360 gallons per minute to just 10, while also cutting energy usage 40%. Though construction cost 8% more, Dow projected full recovery in lower maintenance costs. "Growth versus the Environment," cover story, *Business Week,* May 11, 1992, pp. 66–75.

Quality Function Deployment

Quality function deployment (QFD) provides a structured way of viewing the big picture and of incorporating both product and process design concerns.[6] The structure comes from a series of matrices. The first and most important matrix spells out customer needs—the "voice of the customer"—and compares the company's and key competitors' abilities to satisfy those needs. When the matrix is filled in and "roofed over," it takes the shape of a house—the **house of quality.**

Exhibit 3–4 is a house of quality developed with the aid of the owners of a chain of dry cleaning stores. The owners might use the matrix for improving one or more of their existing stores or for planning a new one. We interpret the QFD matrix as follows:

QFD: Procedure for transforming customer requirements and competitor capabilities into provider targets, extending from product and process research to operations, marketing and distribution.

Like many quality techniques, QFD got its start in manufacturing; that may change as its uses in services (e.g., Exhibit 3–4) become better known.

---

[5]Bruce Nussbaum, "What Works for One Works for All," *Business Week,* April 20, 1992, pp. 112–13.

[6]For a critique of QFD, see Edward Knod and Ann Dietzel, "Quality Function Deployment: Potential Pitfalls," *P/OM Proceedings,* Midwest Business Administration Association, March 1992, pp. 33–40.

EXHIBIT 3–4   "House of Quality" Dry Cleaners

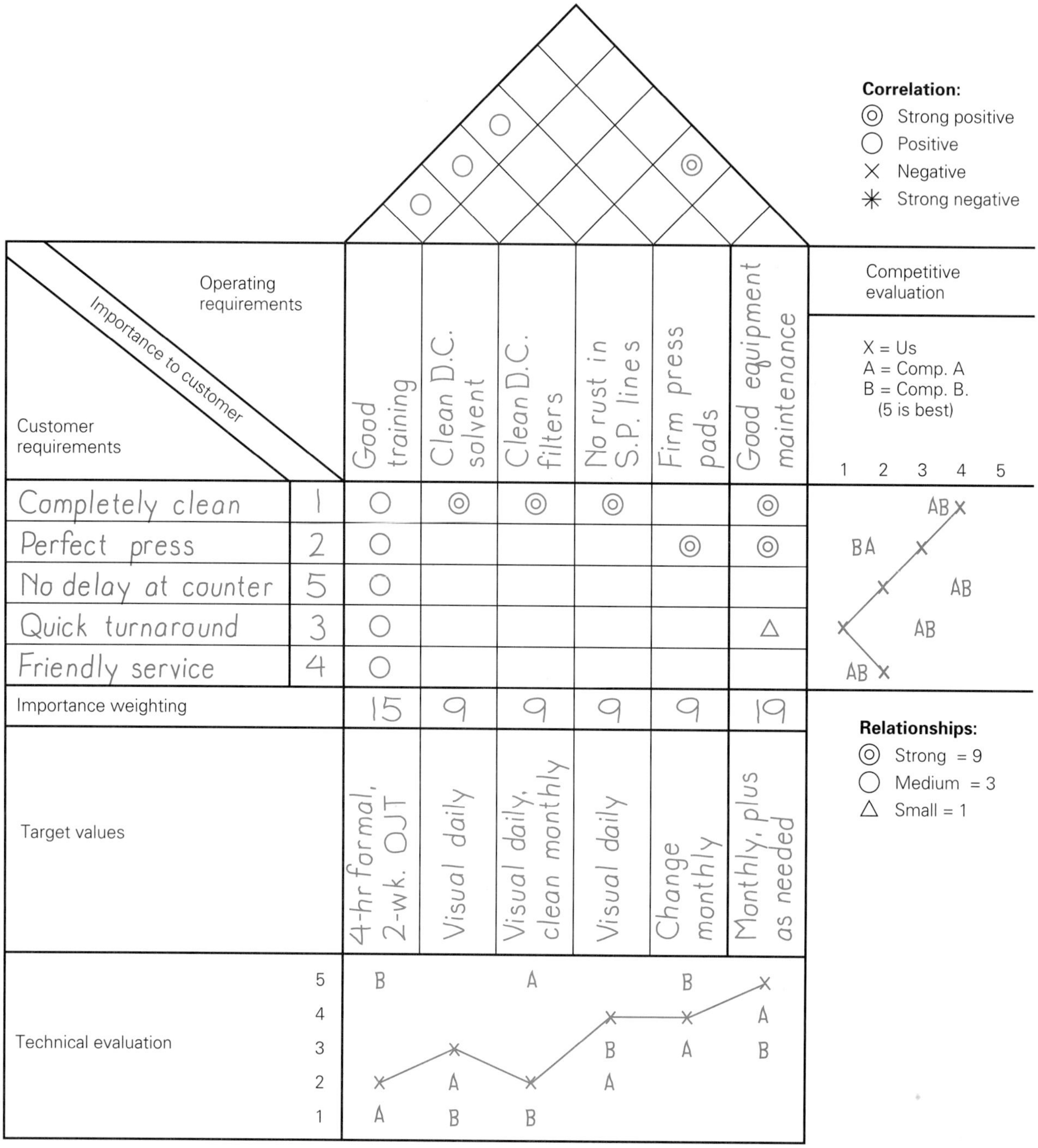

Correlation:
- ◎ Strong positive
- ○ Positive
- ✕ Negative
- ✳ Strong negative

Operating requirements

Importance to customer

Customer requirements

Operating requirements columns: Good training | Clean D.C. solvent | Clean D.C. filters | No rust in S.P. lines | Firm press pads | Good equipment maintenance

Competitive evaluation

X = Us
A = Comp. A
B = Comp. B.
(5 is best)

Customer requirements	Importance	Good training	Clean D.C. solvent	Clean D.C. filters	No rust in S.P. lines	Firm press pads	Good equipment maintenance
Completely clean	1	○	◎	◎	◎		◎
Perfect press	2	○				◎	◎
No delay at counter	5	○					
Quick turnaround	3	○					△
Friendly service	4	○					
Importance weighting		15	9	9	9	9	19

Competitive evaluation (1 2 3 4 5):
- Completely clean: AB X at 4–5
- Perfect press: BA at 2, X at 3, AB at 4
- No delay at counter: X at 2, AB at 4
- Quick turnaround: X at 1, AB at 3
- Friendly service: AB X at 1

Relationships:
- ◎ Strong = 9
- ○ Medium = 3
- △ Small = 1

Target values	Good training	Clean D.C. solvent	Clean D.C. filters	No rust in S.P. lines	Firm press pads	Good equipment maintenance
	4-hr formal, 2-wk. OJT	Visual daily	Visual daily, clean monthly	Visual daily	Change monthly	Monthly, plus as needed

Technical evaluation (5 best to 1):

Technical evaluation	Good training	Clean D.C. solvent	Clean D.C. filters	No rust in S.P. lines	Firm press pads	Good equipment maintenance
5	B		A		B	X
4				X	X	A
3		X		B	A	B
2	X	A	X	A		
1	A	B	B			

- The central portion shows what the customer wants and how to provide it.
- Symbols in the central portion show strong, medium, small, or no relationship between whats and hows. A double circle, strong, worth nine relationship points, appears six times. For example, a "perfect press" strongly depends on "firm press pads" and "good equipment maintenance," which account for two of the double circles.

$\mathcal{I}$nto $\mathcal{P}$ractice

Listening to Leading-Edge Customers

"MIT professor Eric von Hippel makes his living studying the sources of innovation. He says that sophisticated early adopters of new products, whom Hippel labels 'lead users,' can be worth their weight in gold."

While the search is for sophisticated users, the product can be as mundane as pipe hangers. Von Hippel, along with Cornelius Herstatt of the Swiss Federal Institute of Technology, helped Hilti AG, a leading European manufacturer of fastening-related products, to find lead users of pipe hangers. After surveying eight industry experts on likely developments in the next generation of pipe hangers, von Hippel and Herstatt turned their sights toward lead users.

"A random sample of 120 Hilti customers were asked, 'Do you/did you ever build and install pipe-hanging hardware of your own design?' 'Do you/did you every modify commercially available pipe-hanging hardware to better suit your needs.' "

Von Hippel and Herstatt found 74 tradesmen who installed pipe hangers. Based on in-depth interviews, that number was reduced to 22 "true pace-setters," who were culled further to 12 who seemed to have personal interests in new-product development. Finally, three design engineers from Hilti organized a three-day product-concept generation workshop with the 12 tradesmen, two of the eight industry specialists, a marketing manager, and a product manager.

"The first day, participants reviewed the specialists' findings, then broke into five subgroups to consider issues. They spent half the second day in their groups, then did generic creativity exercises. The third day, groups presented their solutions, which the entire workshop evaluated on originality, feasibility, and comprehensiveness. Then they formed a new group to explore the most promising concepts. In the end, all hands converged on a single product concept.

"But were these pace setters too far ahead of the industry? To find out, Hilti tested the workshop's idea on a dozen regular customers, not at the leading edge. Ten preferred the new product and said they'd pay up to 20 percent more for it."

SOURCE: Tom Peters, "Just Listening to Customers Isn't Enough," syndicated column appearing in *Seattle Post-Intelligencer,* May 25, 1992.

- The five customer requirements are ranked 1 to 5 in importance. "Completely clean" is the customers' number 1 concern; "no delay at counter" gets a 5.

- The ratings in each *how* column add up to an importance weighting. Good training, of medium importance for satisfying all five customer requirements, adds up to 15 points, which is second in importance to equipment maintenance, with 19 points.

- The house's roof correlates each how with each other factor. Only four of the combinations show a correlation. The double-circle indicates a strong correlation between "good equipment maintenance" and "no rust in steam-press lines," meaning that steam-press components are subject to rust and thus must be cleaned out or replaced regularly.

- Target values, in the "basement" of the house, give a specific numeric target for each how: Change press pads monthly to keep them firm.

- The house's "sub-basement" and right wing show comparisons of the company and key competitors. We see at the bottom that the company is slightly better than competitors A and B in keeping solvent clean, in avoiding rust, and in maintenance. Ratings in the right wing show that both competitors are better in counter delays and quick turnaround.

The tough part for the design team is accumulating good data to enter into the matrix. Data sources may include focus groups, surveys, studies, comparison shopping, competitive analysis, public information, calculations, and reckoning. The emphasis is on relevant data, which may require tapping the minds of leading-edge customers (see box, Listening to Leading-Edge Customers). QFD is (with good data) a structured, inclusive approach that helps keep the design team from overlooking something important.

EXHIBIT 3–5   QFD Overview

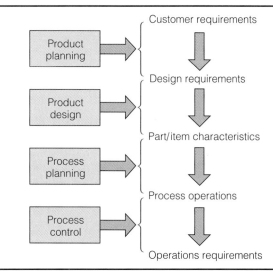

The design team uses the basic house of quality in the product-planning stage. More detailed matrices may be developed for three remaining stages of design, that is, product design, process planning, and process control planning (see Exhibit 3–5).[7] According to one report, though, only about 5 percent of QFD users go beyond the basic house.[8]

Design for Operations: Guidelines

A design team with up-to-date customer and competitive information is ready to go to work. Its work is to build quality into the product and into the process, too—and not just on paper.

Product designers can too easily overlook the realities of front-line operations: the moment of truth with an unpredictable customer, or the many sources of surprise, variation, agony, and error in operations. The design team may be able to avoid some of these pitfalls by following design-for-operations guidelines, which have evolved from the works of professors Geoffrey Boothroyd and Peter Dewhurst.[9]

In the early 1980s, Boothroyd and Dewhurst (originally from England, now professors in engineering at the University of Rhode Island) began to publish on design for operations for manufactured products. By the 1990s, tens of thousands of design engineers had studied **design for manufacture and assembly (DFMA).**

Although the DFMA guidelines were aimed at manufacturing, they have proven to be general enough to apply well to services; thus, we use the more general term, **design for operations (DFO).** Exhibit 3–6 lists one version of DFO guidelines.

A variation on DFMA: design for environment (DFE), which AT&T Bell Laboratories incorporates into its computer-aided design software. "Growth versus the Environment," cover story, *Business Week,* May 11, 1992, pp. 66–75.

---

[7]Detailed matrices are discussed in Bob King, *Better Designs in Half the Time: Implementing QFD, Quality Function Deployment in America* (Methuen, Mass.: GOAL/QPC, 1987).

[8]Charles A. Cox, "Keys to Success in Quality Function Deployment," *APICS—The Performance Advantage,* April 1992, pp. 25–28.

[9]Geoffrey Boothroyd and Peter Dewhurst, *Design for Assembly* (Wakefield, R.I.: Boothroyd Dewhurst, Inc., 1987).

EXHIBIT 3–6   Design for Operations Guidelines

General guidelines:
1. Design to target markets and target costs.
2. Minimize number of parts and number of operations.

Quality guidelines:
3. Ensure that customer requirements are known and design to those requirements.
4. Ensure that process capabilities are known (those in your firm and of your suppliers) and design to those capabilities.
5. Use standard procedures, materials, and processes with already known and proven quality.

Operability guidelines:
6. Design multifunctional/multiuse components and service elements and modules.
7. Design for ease of joining, separating, rejoining (goods) and ease of coupling/uncoupling (services).
8. Design for one-way assembly, one-way travel (avoid backtracking and return visits).
9. Avoid special fasteners and connectors (goods) and off-line or misfit service elements.
10. Avoid fragile designs requiring extraordinary effort or attentiveness—or that otherwise tempt substandard or unsafe performance.

Two guidelines are general, in that they have wide-ranging benefits.

General Guidelines

1. Target Markets and Target Costs.   Designing to target markets and target costs reinforces the need for customer and marketing representatives to be on the design team. A target cost, carefully set based on target sales and profit, may be a basis for killing a bad project or for stimulating innovation. If it looks as if operating costs are going to exceed target cost, the first response of the design team is to search, strive, and innovate until it can find a way to meet the target. Lack of targets leaves designers to play out their own whims, which may be to see how many exotic (often costly and risky) new technologies or materials they can try out and learn about.

2. Minimize Parts and Operations.   The Boothroyd-Dewhurst methodology focuses especially on this guideline, minimizing the number of parts or, outside of manufacturing, the number of operations. For example, a data-entry terminal may be used to input client data in one operation, instead of several times in several different offices of, say, a college or a clinic.

*𝒫*RINCIPLE 5:

A few good product/service components.

Exhibit 3–7 illustrates a manufacturing example. The design team is minimizing number of parts as it designs "a better mouse." The next step, in the Boothroyd-Dewhurst method, is separately analyzing each part to ascertain the best type of material and the best manufacturing method.

The next three guidelines pertain to quality: quality requirements of the product (guideline 3), quality capabilities of internal and external processes (guideline 4), and use of standardization to make quality easier to deliver (guideline 5).

Quality Guidelines

3. Customer Requirements.   Guideline 3 calls for the design team to find out customers' precise requirements, or their best estimates of them, and to keep finding out because requirements can change during the design project. Requirements may take the form of brightness, smoothness, size, speed of service, minimal waiting time, ease of maintainability, and so on. The design team must be clear on the matter because one of its jobs is to transform requirements into specifications and tolerances.

*𝒫*RINCIPLE 10:

Eliminate error and process variation.

Exhibit 3–7   Designing a Better Mouse

DFMA team at Digital Equipment Corp. designs a better mouse (computer accessory). New design cuts screws from seven to zero, assembly adjustments from eight to zero, assembly time from 592 to 277 seconds; also cuts material costs 47 percent, package costs 59 percent.

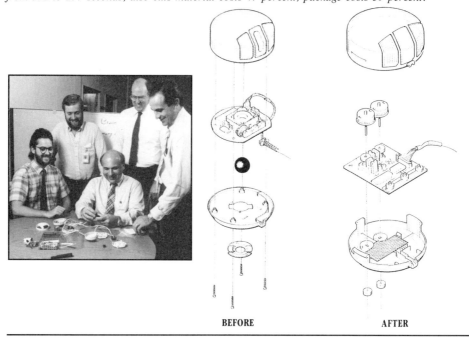

BEFORE   AFTER

Digital Equipment Corp. policy used to forbid design engineers from talking to suppliers (they had to go through purchasing); now they're required to talk to suppliers.

Since the total design—of product and process—may be split up among more than one organizational unit, it is important that designers from each unit get together on requirements. If they are kept apart, quality problems are likely. Suppliers will cite "ambiguous requirements. We followed your requirements [or specifications] and now find out you really want something else."

Such failures to communicate are not just the fault of the customer. Good suppliers, inside or outside the firm, do whatever they can to find out their customers' real requirements, avoid misunderstanding, and make their customers look good.

4. Process Capability.   Guideline 4, designing to process capability, impacts the design team in two ways. First, the team is held responsible if the design cannot easily be delivered or produced using available processes (including those of the supplier), people, equipment, facilities, and other resources. Second, in being held responsible, the design team must become familiar with process capabilities, which usually are measurable to some degree.

Capability measures might include years of experience, degree of cross-training, and educational attainment of associates; documentation of procedures; safety devices in place; equipment failure rates; and ability to achieve and hold tolerances. The latter may be measured using the process capability index, C_{pk}, which has become important in manufacturing in recent years (see Chapter 4).

5. Standard Procedures, Materials, and Processes.   The fifth guideline advises designers to favor standard procedures, materials, and processes. Related to standardization are questions about creativity, satisfying customer needs for variety, and new opportunities for global marketing. Each of these issues warrants brief discussion.

Standardization. Nonstandard designs are risky because of lack of knowledge about their performance. Xerox found this out the hard way after losing its market dominance in copiers in the 1970s. One consultant observed that, for lack of competition, the company's large staff of bright engineers developed machines with "incredibly complex technology. . . . Everything inside a Xerox machine was special. You could not go out and use a normal nut. It had to be a specially designed nut. The concept of using as many standard parts as possible was not even thought of."[10] The design complexities led to costly field service to make its copiers work properly. High costs opened the door to competition, which actually was good for Xerox.

Standardization and creativity. Now Xerox—a 1990 Malcolm Baldrige prize winner—along with many other companies, has firm policies on use of standard parts. Some apply the guideline quantitatively. For example, a copier manufacturer could set a limit of, say, 25 percent new parts in a new copier model, an opinion survey firm may limit the number of questions on a survey form, or a fast-food company may limit the number of allowable operations in a new process for delivering a new food item to a customer. While it might seem that such restrictions could stifle creativity or effectiveness, they may have the opposite effect. By not spending time designing new screws and locations for drill holes or complex multistep forms or fast-food procedures, designers may have more time to be creative or thorough on what counts and to explore new materials, technologies, and competitors' procedures.

Standardization and personalized design. Is standardization in conflict with trends toward personalized design? Not necessarily. In fact, standardization may be the only way to make personalized design profitable: carefully design a small number of standard components or workable products that can be volume-made at low cost, and have the flexibility to quickly customize them right in front of the customer.

This formula—personalization but with standard components—is the basis, for example, for Panasonic's personalized bicycle, which starts out with customer fitting in a retail store.[11] The clerk enters customer measurements, color choice, and other specs (see Exhibit 3–8A) into a computer, and a computer-aided design (CAD) routine produces a customized blueprint in three minutes.

While final assembly is still mostly manual, frame welding employs flexible automation. Racks of a limited number of frame models surround the automation equipment and are selected following the customer's specs. The frame models are somewhat standardized, which holds down production costs (perhaps by making each model using dedicated equipment); the same applies to many smaller standardized bicycle parts.

Customer-run greeting card machines follow much the same formula (see Exhibit 3–8B). A large variety of customer choices are possible from a few standardized components (plain card, envelope, and inks). According to American Greetings Corp. president Edward Fruchtenbaum, the CreataCard machine is the "ultimate combination of just-in-time manufacturing and micro-marketing."[12]

Standardization and globalization. Taken in conjunction with guideline 2 (minimize parts and operations) this guideline has strategic implications. As goods and services are designed with fewer, more standardized components and operations, costs go down and quality becomes more dependable. In turn, this increases their appeal, sometimes to the point where people around the globe know about and want the item—be it a Big Mac, a pair of Nikes, or an American Express card.

---

[10]Gary Jacobson and John Hillkirk, *Xerox: American Samurai* (New York: Macmillan, 1986), pp. 178–79.
[11]Susan Moffat, "Japan's New Personalized Production," *Fortune,* October 22, 1990, pp. 132–35.
[12]Joseph F. McKenna, "From JIT, with Love," *Industry Week,* August 17, 1992, pp. 45–51.

EXHIBIT 3-8   Personalized Design from Standard Components

A. 11,231,862 variations of Panasonic bicycle.
Customer fitting in retail store.

Used by permission of Matrix, Inc.

B. Personalized greeting card machines.

Used by permission of American Greetings Corp.   Copyright © by Hallmark Cards. Used with permission.

More broadly, three trends seem to be interrelated: (1) better designed goods and services (based on these design guidelines) and (2) widespread lowering of political and trade barriers create (3) markets of awesome size. One result is that companies with hot products and services must gear up for massive-volume production and service delivery (see Exhibit 3-9).

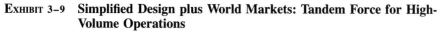

EXHIBIT 3–9   Simplified Design plus World Markets: Tandem Force for High-Volume Operations

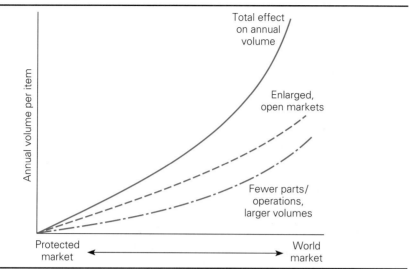

Guidelines 6 through 10 generally offer further guidance on attaining high quality. More specifically, their focus is on operability—avoiding difficulties in operations.

Operability Guidelines

6. Multifunctional/Multiuse Elements and Modules.   The do-it-yourself industry is alive and thriving. Buy some plumbing modules, shelving components, or mix-and-match clothing, and combine to taste. Good design that follows this guideline makes it possible.

Insurance companies, investment funds, health care, and other service companies do much the same thing: design a self-contained service module (e.g., payroll processing) and offer it to companies that seek ways of cutting their own overhead and getting out of service areas beyond their expertise.

7. Ease of Joining/Separating, Coupling/Uncoupling.   Push, click, snap, whirr. That's the sound of the modern keyboard, clock, or auto dashboard being assembled. It's easy, quick, and if the design team has heeded guideline 7, mostly error-free.

Are snap-together connections hard to notice? That's good—until someone needs to take off a cover for repair, or until the junked unit gets to the recycler to be separated into reusable materials. Today's designer needs extra ingenuity to make disassembly and separation as easy as push-and-snap assembly. (Yet another contemporary term: *design for disassembly,* or *DFDA.*)

A service example of this guideline is a salesperson with cellular phone and data diskette who can go to work on the road, at home, or in the sales office. This design of the sales process permits easy service coupling/uncoupling as the need arises. Many services (in hotels, airlines, restaurants, etc.) are designed so that service people can easily plug in and plug out.

8. One-Way Assembly and Travel.   Who hasn't had to stand in one line for a certain service element, wait in another line for the next element, and then later go back to the first line? Guideline 8 aims at avoiding that kind of backtracking and in manufacturing is helping to revitalize some assembly plants. For example, IBM was an early convert to designing products for layered assembly. The bottom layer may be the box itself (except for the box top). Then comes a bottom plastic cover for, say, a personal computer. Next are the inside components, then the top cover and loose accessories, and finally the top of the box. Since all assembly motions are up-and-down, IBM can equip the assembly lines with its own simple pick-and-place robots; no need for elaborate, costly robots with multiple axes of motion.

9. Avoid Special Fastening and Fitting.   This guideline avoids special steps. In manufacturing, the guideline applies especially to connectors and fasteners (*fasteners* is industry's term for bolts, washers, nuts, screws, etc.). For example, the number of screws in IBM's re-designed LaserPrinter was cut from dozens to a handful. "IBM had expected to assemble [them] by robot. Instead, engineers found that simplicity yielded yet another dividend: It turned out to be cheaper and easier to make them by hand."[13] A misfit service would include one that requires a server to leave a client to fetch a file folder or get an approval.

10. Avoid Fragile Designs.   Tendencies or temptations to take unsafe shortcuts, to be careless with sensitive equipment, to be brusque with customers, to steal, or otherwise misperform are partly avoidable by using designs that make such tendencies difficult.

One approach is to design controls into the process. Examples: design the process to maintain strict segregation of personal and business possessions, clearly labeled locations for all files and materials, easy access to backup help, and safety-guard gates to keep associates from blundering into an unsafe area.

Another approach is the use of **robust design** concepts. Examples: shatter-resistant glass, a waterproof watch, carpeting that comes clean even if smeared with black grease, and keyboards you can spill Coke on.

Simplified Design and Robotics: An Example

As firms consider process automation, operability guidelines 6 through 10 take on extra importance because nobody wants to automate wasteful processes. In striving for an easy-to-automate design, the designers sometimes get an unexpected dividend: following the guidelines can simplify processes enough to get by without spending on automation (see Example 3–1).

EXAMPLE 3–1   Design for Assembly and Robotics

Exhibit 3–10 shows an assembly diagram for a simple product. Redesign the product for ease of assembly and robotics.

Solution:

First, the design team evaluates the present method in terms of the strict and well-defined requirements for assembly by a robot. Then it simplifies the design.

Step 1: Robotic assembly. The design team specifies the following robotic assembly method. The robot starts by putting four bolts upright into four pods in a special fixture, one at a time. Then it puts a washer on each bolt. Next, the robot must position the base so the holes line up with the four bolts—a difficult alignment unless the holes are large. The robot's next tasks are to grab a bracket, position it, and secure it at each end with a washer, a lock washer, and a nut. Tightening the nuts requires that the robot return its ordinary gripper to the tool rack and fasten its "wrist" to a special nut-turning device; then, after the nuts are tight, switch back to the ordinary gripper.

Exhibit 3–11 gives the design team's estimated times for the seven tasks described (some done more than once), plus five more. Their estimate of 12 seconds for assem-

---

[13]"IBM Discovers Simple Pleasures," *Fortune*, May 21, 1991, p. 64.

EXHIBIT 3–10   Assembly Using Common Fasteners

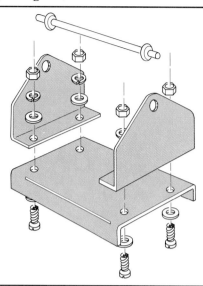

Adapted from G. Boothroyd and P. Dewhurst, ''Product Design . . . Key to Successful Robotic Assembly,'' *Assembly Engineering*, September 1986, pp. 90–93. Used with permission.

EXHIBIT 3–11   Approximate Robotic Assembly Time—Bracket-and-Spindle Assembly

Part	Repeats	Time (Seconds)	Operation
Screw	4	12	Place in fixture
Washer	4	12	Place on screw
Base	1	3	Place on screws
Bracket	1	3	Position on base
Washer	2	6	Place on screw
Lock washer	2	6	Place on screw
Nut	2	12	Secure bracket (requires tool change)
Spindle	1	3	Insert one end in bracket (needs holding)
Bracket	1	3	Position on base and locate spindle
Washer	2	6	Place on screw
Lock washer	2	6	Place on screw
Nut	2	12	Secure bracket (requires tool change)
Totals	**24**	**84**	

bling the two nuts may be optimistic. They assume that bolts or nuts have special self-alignment features so threads will engage correctly and not bind or get cross-threaded.

The robot continues by inserting the spindle into one bracket hole and then moving the second bracket to receive the spindle. Since the robot has only one hand, it cannot hold the spindle and move the second bracket into place at the same time. It must move a fixture into place to hold up the spindle momentarily. Finally, the bracket is fastened down with washers and nuts.

The complete set of tasks includes insertions in several directions, which the team agrees would require an elaborate, costly robot. The total assembly time is 84 seconds, of which 86 percent is fastening. Of the 24 parts in the assembly, 20 are just for fastening. Are all those bolts, nuts, and washers really necessary? Perhaps not. But they are common and cheap, and assembly designers routinely choose such means of fastening.

EXHIBIT 3–12   One-Piece Base and Elimination of Fasteners

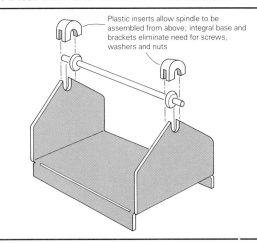

Plastic inserts allow spindle to be
assembled from above; integral base and
brackets eliminate need for screws,
washers and nuts

EXHIBIT 3–13   Design for Push-and-Snap Assembly

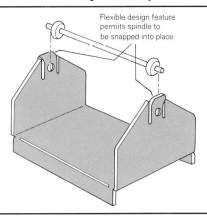

Flexible design feature
permits spindle to
be snapped into place

Step 2: Simplified design. One way to simplify the design is to look for simpler ways to fasten the brackets. But why fasten them? Isn't it possible to make the brackets and base as one piece? The team believes it is. Their new design is shown in Exhibit 3–12. In that design, plastic inserts secure the spindle; both spindle and inserts may be assembled from above, which allows use of a simpler, cheaper type of robot with no special grippers or holding fixtures. There are only four parts, and a robot could assemble them in, say, 12 seconds. That improves output and productivity by 600 percent (from 43 to 300 assemblies per hour).

There may be better solutions. If specifications permit, the team realizes, the spindle could be made from material that will bend or flex. Then a two-piece design, as in Exhibit 3–13, will be possible. Now assembly consists of just one step and one motion: Snap spindle downward into place. The simplest of robots may be used.

Now, however, the design team has made assembly so simple that using a robot begins to seem excessive. If a robot were used, the parts would have to be presented to the robot on some sort of carrier—probably loaded by hand. Clearly it is just as easy—or even easier—to do the whole assembly by hand. Save the robot budget for tasks difficult for people.

*P*RINCIPLE 8:

Automate incrementally when process variability cannot otherwise be reduced.

Design Review, Performance Measurement, and Control

Design and development is a loop. Preliminary designs are critiqued, improved, are critiqued again, improved again, and so on. This commonly continues after the design is in operations and customers are sampling the results. (We all hope we won't be the guinea pigs who continue doing the testing for the company.)

Thorough design, with extended design teams following design-for-operations guidelines, aims at removing most changes in the design phase. The addition of systematic design checking (called design review), along with measurement-based control of design performance, increases the effectiveness of this approach.

Suitable measures of design-team performance may include some that are related to the design-for-operations guidelines of Exhibit 3–6. For example, the second DFO guideline, minimizing number of parts and operations, may be directly measured by comparing the previous design's number of parts or operations with that of the current design. Trend charts may be set up to track reductions in parts and operations over time. An example of a broader measure of design performance is first-year cost of field service, repairs, returns, and warranty claims.

Besides these measures, companies that have quick time-to-market as a strategy will need a corresponding control measure in design and development. For this purpose, Hewlett-Packard dusted off an old measure, which incorporates both time and cost recovery, called breakeven time.[14] It is the total elapsed time "beginning with a scientific investigation and ending only when the profits from a new product offset the cost of its development."[15]

Thus far, our discussion of product and process design has focused on teams, practices, and controls. A special process design issue that inspires emotions ranging from excitement to dread is *automation,* our next topic.

Process Technology: People and Automation in Perspective

> You get the illusion of . . . an antitechnological mass movement . . . looming up from apparently nowhere saying, "Stop the technology. Have it somewhere else. Don't have it here." It is restrained by a thin web of logic that points out that without the factories there are no jobs or standard of living.[16]

People have made use of machines to amplify human abilities since the dawn of recorded time. When the machines take over and exercise some control, we call it automation. But yesterday's versions of automation (e.g., a simple lathe or electronic calculator) seem so common as to be unworthy of the description. Technology marches on.

And people's contributions march on, too, especially in companies that have learned to harness the whole work force for continuous improvement. Does this put a new slant on the long-standing concern for automation putting people out of work? The question bears some discussion.

Automation: Coined in 1947, by John Diebold and D. S. Harder, to define any "self-powered, self-guiding and correcting mechanism"; later extended to include whole factories and office and clerical work.

---

[14]In the second edition of this book, breakeven time was called complete recovery point: Richard J. Schonberger, *Operations Management: Productivity and Quality* (Plano, Tex.: BPI, 1985), pp. 568–69.

[15]Gene Bylinsky, "Turning R&D into Real Products," *Fortune,* July 2, 1990, pp. 72–77.

[16]Robert M. Pirsig, *Zen and the Art of Motorcycle Maintenance* (New York: William Morrow, 1974), p. 25.

*People and
Machines*

Between 1945 and 1955, U.S. industry suffered over 43,000 strikes.[17] Canada and England had similar labor strife. Japan, Germany, and other countries whose industrial capacity had been reduced to rubble during World War II had their own problems, including unemployment and politically induced labor agitation by Marxists, anarchists, and other groups.

For most of this century, industrialists have rallied around a technological solution to the labor problem. Replace labor with machines—in other words, automate. How valid is that rationale today? Consider the following;

Strikes: A relatively minor problem throughout the industrial world today. A *Wall Street Journal* headline bears this out: ''Work stoppages fall to near record lows last year.''[18]

Human relationships: From individualism and functional separation to cross-functional teams and improvement projects.

Militant labor: Transformed into an improvement engine in a growing number of companies.

Labor costs: In manufacturing, down from over 50 percent in 1855 to under 15 percent today.[19]

Labor availability: Where labor is scarce or too costly, instead of automating, a business may find competent lower-cost labor elsewhere in the world.

Causes of process variability: Instead of blaming labor, the first reaction today (in superior companies) is to look for poor equipment, materials, instructions, training, information, suppliers, and designs.

Productivity and quality: New awareness of potent ways to simplify, cut wastes, upgrade processes, and improve quality with existing equipment and enlightened teams of associates.

Though these points offer an alternative to a vigorous automation strategy, they by no means close the door to automation. There *is* still a labor problem to which machines can respond. That problem is peoples' inherent variability. It is hard for someone to perform a task the same way and in the same amount of time over and over. But variability of method harms quality, and variability of cycle time (time needed to perform a task) hinders meeting schedules and dependably serving the customer. A particular automation strategy may or may not be worthwhile. We offer below a few observations to help in making an evaluation. They consist of three axioms with three caveats:

1. *Process improvement* is an essential competitive strategy.
2. Automation is one tactic.
   Caveat 2.1: Automation is expensive. Less costly ways of improving processes ought to be sought first.
3. Humans' inherent variability makes automation more desirable.
   Caveat 3.1: Human variability has its good side, namely, flexibility to react to change.

---

[17]David F. Noble, *Forces of Production: A Social History of Industrial Automation* (New York: Alfred A. Knopf, 1984), p. 25.

[18]*The Wall Street Journal,* March 3, 1992.

[19]Patrick L. Romano, ''Management Accounting: Change Is Needed in Accounting Systems for Advanced Manufacturing Environments,'' *Nexus,* Summer 1987, pp. 12–13.

𝒞ontrast

Automation, Mindpower, Waste Reduction, Simplified Design

Viewpoints, 1980s	**Revisions, 1990s**
Prominent industrialist: "Automate, emigrate, or evaporate."	Mindpower viewpoint: Labor is a solution, not a problem.
Common viewpoint: Automate to "leapfrog" the Far Eastern competition.	Waste reduction: Don't automate the waste.
General Motors: "In Tokyo last April, GM Chairman Roger Smith declared GM's determination to finish first in the 'world-wide technology race' that he said will determine which of the world's auto companies will survive." Urban C. Lehner, "To Battle the Japanese, GM Is Pushing Boldly into Computerization," *The Wall Street Journal,* Monday, July 9, 1984.	Flexible manufacturing at GM: GM's Lordstown plant "will prepare to build a more flexible mix of new models that will have fewer parts and more standardized assembly procedures. That will mainly require changes in design and engineering." "General Motors: Open All Night," *Business Week,* June 1, 1992, pp. 82–83.

Caveat 3.2: People have one attribute that makes them superior to any machine: brainpower. Without brainpower in the workplace, further process improvement would come to a halt.

With those points in mind, we consider two alternatives to full, high-tech automation: preautomation and low-grade process automation. Following those topics are a few comments about justification of automation and process improvement. High technology is examined in the chapter supplement.

Whether a process is due for automation soon or not, **preautomation** is always a good idea. Preautomation is what must be done to make a work space friendly enough for automation. Preautomation boils down to two factors:

Preautomation

1. Close—short reach and travel distances.
2. Exact—everything in precise locations.

Regarding the first factor, if work units, containers, supplies, and tools are not close to the processor (machine), automation is still possible. Just put in a long powered conveyor. However, the wiser approach is automating over short distances using the machine's "fingers," instead of arm extenders, such as distance-spanning conveyors. Alternatively put, a company's automation capital is best spent on automating the process itself—where value is added to the product—rather than on the delays between value-added processes. Scenes of conveyors loaded with materials crisscrossing factories may dazzle the eye, but they often mask a faulty automation concept—too little attention to location.

*𝒫*RINCIPLE 11:

Cut flow distance.

This point is not limited to manufacturing. Instead of having, say, a robot carrying documents from office to office (or office to mail room to office), preautomation advises cutting office-to-office distances such that this job would be superfluous. At Microsoft Corp., for example, a team has been formed to process all transactions related to the purchase of computers. The first members of the team came from the purchasing and receiving departments. Members were later added from accounts payable and other offices. Team members have left their former departments and now sit together in the same room (a work cell), so documents can move almost hand-to-hand, thus eliminating the need for something like a robotic mail carrier.

Regarding the second preautomation factor, work units, tools, and fixtures must be exactly placed in preset positions, or else the machine's arm-hand will reach and come up empty. Nonautomated work does not seem to require much workplace precision because people are inherently flexible. Human eyes, hands, arms, legs, and feet can compensate for lack of exact positioning. Since a machine lacks that flexibility and sensory power, automation requires time and money for a campaign of workplace precision—parts boxes and tools may need to be positioned virtually with a surveyor's transit.

As many manufacturers have discovered, however, such careful positioning of parts and tools greatly improves the efficiency and work quality of people operating in the manual mode. Similarly, clerical work is greatly improved when office supplies, files, documents, and so forth are exactly placed nearby.

Actually, because the limits of human improvement will be reached sooner or later automation is unstoppable. A rational improvement approach is to move forward with preautomation, process by process. Then, at processes where human performance limits resist further improvement, look for automation possibilities. This is a problem-pull rather than a technology-push automation strategy.

Low-Grade Process Automation

In the problem-pull mode, automation may proceed step-by-step via installation of one low-grade device after another. Instead of across-the-board removal of present processes and operators, replaced by high-tech, fully automated equipment "owned" by technical experts, the operators stay and lead the effort to find the next automatic device to install. It might be an automatic page counter in an office, or an automatic tool changer in a factory. If preautomation has already taken place, so that several processes are close together, many other possibilities are likely to emerge.

For example, suppose that a saw and a drill press have been moved together as two of the machines in a work cell making aluminum screen doors. A former saw operator now runs both machines, first sawing a piece and then drilling it; saw, then drill; saw, drill. Cells allow this—one person to work more than one process in the product flow—and cells eliminate bulk handling (and trips to stockrooms) between processes.

There are other low-cost ways to improve the process. Our operator, if encouraged, may think of several, such as "How about an automatic feed on the saw? Then I could start the saw, and while the saw runs, I could clamp a sawed piece in the drill press."

The operator might also be able to recommend a machine start mechanism that will enhance safety as well as cut out manual steps. Here is an example:

Clamp a piece of aluminum to the saw's work surface, and go to the drill. With the operator at a safe distance from the saw blade and at the drill, the act of stopping the drill trips a switch to start the saw for a length cut.

Clamp a sawed piece under the drill, and go to the saw. The act of stopping the saw trips a switch to start the drill press to drill locator holes.

Repeat.

PRINCIPLE 10:

Make it easy to eliminate error and process variation.

PRINCIPLE 15:

Problem solving by frontline associates.

PRINCIPLE 8:

Automate incrementally.

Similar mechanisms may be added to all the machines in a multiple-machine cell so that one person can tend several machines in a circular route. This low-cost but potent form of low-grade automation was first perfected at Toyota and some of its key suppliers. Sometimes one operator tends as many as 15 machines.

Because automation is costly, raises the break-even point, and often breaks new ground, which is risky, company managers usually want to see careful financial justification before proceeding. Unfortunately many of the expected benefits—such as better quality and quicker throughput—are hard to describe in financial terms, and the finance committee's reaction may well be negative.

Justifying Automation and Other Improvement Projects

    Automation proponents assert that it is the only way for a high-wage society to compete and that executives should take it on faith that automation projects should go forward. In some cases, that advice has been followed and the results have been good. However, a number of industry's boldest automation projects have failed to recover the investment. Reasons include technical troubles, physical rigidity (designed not to be improved, moved, or changed), designs based on overly optimistic demand forecasts, and automation of mostly non-value-adding wastes.

    How can the odds of a successful project, whether automated or not, be improved? Some feel that worthy improvement proposals are failing to meet company investment hurdles—and unworthy ones are surviving—mainly because critical costs and benefits are left out, or are treated in an off-hand manner as intangibles. Consultant Michael O'Guin believes that economic proposal reviews usually fail to accurately account for protection of a company's market position. He presents a more thorough kind of economic justification that incorporates sales and market share, plus an overall weighting factor based on five key customer-perceived quality factors: consistency, lead time, personnel training, rate of product innovation, and sales engineering support. O'Guin's system rolls these vital competitive factors into the firm's traditional return-on-investment formulas.[20]

Summary

Elevated competitiveness has caused many companies to reassess their research and development (R&D) strategy. Quick design-to-market and built-in quality are common elements of companies' revised strategies. Both strategic aims are addressed by breaking down functional barriers and getting product designers on a team with people from marketing, finance, operations, purchasing, human resources, and others, including customer and supplier representatives.

    Teaming up permits concurrent design, which can greatly speed up the design process and avoid design rework and can also make use of broader information. The team may conduct competitive analysis of rivals' products or services, employ quality function deployment to bring in the "voice of the customer," and may try to anticipate and provide solutions to environmental and social concerns and problems that affect the design of product and process.

    To be effective the design team should be steeped in design for operations (DFO) (or design for manufacture and assembly) guidelines. The first two general guidelines include designing to a target cost, based on the market, and minimizing parts and operations, which reduces sources of error and overhead cost.

    Quality-oriented guidelines 3, 4, and 5 are designing for customer requirements (3), which requires close customer contact; measurable process capability factors (4); and standardization of

---

[20]Michael C. O'Guin, "A New Approach to Capital Justification," *P&IM Review with APICS News*, November 1989, pp. 35–36, 42.

procedures, materials, and processes, with quality already known and proven (5). Standardization of components can hold down costs and make personalized design affordable at the end-product level, where the components may be finished in numerous ways.

Guidelines 6 through 10, aiming at operability, also improve quality in that they avoid difficulties in making the product or providing the service. These guidelines call for designing for multiple functions and uses (6); ease of joining, separating, rejoining, coupling, and uncoupling (7); one-way assembly and one-way travel (8); avoidance of fasteners and connectors and misfit service elements (9); and avoidance of fragile designs that tempt incorrect performance (10).

Good design won't take place without controls. These consist of systematic design review and regular measures of design performance, including a measure for each DFO guideline and an overall measure of speed to market.

Process technology and automation, while attractive, is usually expensive. A preautomation effort, in which all implements and work units are closely and exactly placed, usually improves the current method's quality and effectiveness, thus putting off the need to spend and incur the risks of automation. Automation may then be introduced incrementally in response to real problems.

Finally, improved design management must include overhauling the approval process, up through the finance committee, to focus more on quality, quick design-to-market, and operability, and not just on obvious costs.

Key Words

Simultaneous engineering 61	House of quality 65
Concurrent design 61	Design for manufacture and assembly
Industrial design 64	(DFMA) 68
Competitive analysis 64	Design for operations (DFO) 68
Universal design 65	Robust design 74
Quality function deployment (QFD) 65	Preautomation 79

See, also, annotated glossary of technology in the chapter supplement.

For Further Reference

Books

Boothroyd, Geoffrey, and Peter Dewhurst. *Product Design for Assembly.* Wakefield, R.I.: Boothroyd Dewhurst, Inc., 1987.

King, Bob. *Better Designs in Half the Time: Implementing QFD Quality Function Deployment in America.* Methuen, Mass.: GOAL/QPC, 1987.

Schonberger, Richard J. *Building a Chain of Customers: Linking Business Functions to Create the World-Class Company.* New York: Free Press, 1990 (HD58.9.S36). See especially Chapter 10, "World-Class Product Development."

Wheelwright, Steven C., and Kim B. Clark. *Revolutionizing Product Development: Quantum Leaps in Speed, Efficiency, and Quality.* New York: Free Press, 1992 (HF5415.153.W44).

Review Questions

1. How is a company's financial commitment to R&D to be measured?
2. Contrast typical company commitments to product design versus process design.
3. How serious is the problem of being late to market? Can the design team do much about the problem? Explain.

4. What principles of operations management can help a firm avoid the over-the-wall problem in product design and development?

5. What connection, if any, should product designers have with suppliers of purchased materials or services? Explain.

6. What is the importance of, and what are the procedures for, learning about competitors' products?

7. Compare industrial design and universal design.

8. Where does the information come from for use in a quality function deployment matrix? Why is it called a house of quality?

9. Explain the meaning of design to target cost.

10. What is the link between design simplification and worldwide free trade?

11. What is the effect of ambiguous specs on quality?

12. What can the design team do to aid in protection of the environment?

13. How can the design team apply the principle "Automate incrementally when process variability cannot otherwise be reduced"?

14. Designing for layered assembly in manufacturing is like what in services? Explain with an example.

15. What can the design team do about mishaps, safety violations, accidents, and so forth?

16. How can design practices be measured?

17. What human weaknesses favor automation? What human strengths favor people over machines?

18. How does preautomation stave off the need for investing in automation?

19. What often-hidden factors should be given more emphasis in a proposal to spend capital on an improvement, whether automated or nonautomated?

Problems and Exercises

1. Shrinking product life cycles are sometimes leading to premature conclusions about shifting customer demand patterns, thus breeding "design nervousness." Is there a practical limit on how short product life cycles should go? Support your answer with examples.

2. Obtain the most recent copy of *Business Week's* annual R&D scoreboard (it is typically published in June for the preceding year). For one of the industry classifications, prepare a table similar to Exhibit 3–2. Decide who are the better R&D companies and tell why you think so.

3. For two of the following McDonald's end products and components, find out who the principle designers/developers were and how the developments took place: sauces for Chicken McNuggets, special chicken for McNuggets, fish sandwich, Egg McMuffin. How does McDonald's deal with the quality of ingredients?

4. A chess clock is housed in a molded plastic case that is closed up in the rear with two flat plastic square plates. (Chess clocks contain two identical clocks, one for each player in a timed chess game.) The three pieces are represented below, along with a sample of the special screw that goes into the eight drilled holes that fasten the clocks to the square plates. (Two other holes in the case and four holes and two half-moons in the squares are for clock adjustment. For purposes of this question, ignore them.)

   Suggest two practical design improvements based on the guidelines in Exhibit 3–6. (Mention the specific guidelines you are using as the basis for your suggestions.)

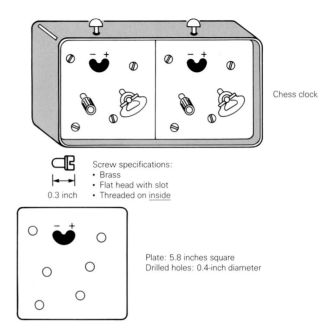

Chess clock

Screw specifications:
• Brass
• Flat head with slot
• Threaded on <u>inside</u>

0.3 inch

Plate: 5.8 inches square
Drilled holes: 0.4-inch diameter

5. Following are passages from an article on IBM's typewriter and keyboard factory:

> In the IBM Selectric System/2000 Typewriter, the new products are made with a layered design. The parts go together sequentially in one direction—from the bottom up—so that robots can do the job easily. There are many common fasteners [a limited number of different kinds], and nearly all screws were eliminated. Plastic molding offered many possibilities for more manufacturable designs.
>
> Detailed parts were combined wherever possible. Self-alignment reference points were designed for locating such things as posts and countersinks. Since robots are not efficient at finding a plug at the end of a wire, integrated packaging and solid connectors had to be used.
>
> The changes resulted in fewer parts and fewer adjustments. There are about 900 parts in the new typewriters, compared with 2,700 in the Selectric typewriter. The number of adjustments needed is down to 6 from 121 originally.[21]

   The above description indicates use of some of the 10 guidelines for effective design listed in Exhibit 3–6. Which of these guidelines can you identify in the passage? Give brief explanations where required.

6. Faceplates that cover electrical wall outlets and wall switches fasten with one or two screws. Suggest a modification that would eliminate the need for screws. Would the benefits be significant? Explain. Can you offer any arguments against redesign to eliminate screws?

7. Play the role of dietician, fashion designer, architect, or financial portfolio designer. Describe the problems you can avoid with the proper degree of interaction with your suppliers.

8. At Monitor Manufacturing Company, product development engineers operate under a strict policy of frequent interaction with customers to ensure that designs match customer requirements. Still, customers view Monitor's designs as only average. What can the problem be?

9. When Mazda first came out with a rotary (Wankel) engine, there were serious performance problems. The public virtually quit buying the car, and Mazda's existence was threatened. Survival measures included sending design engineers all over Japan to sell cars. Besides cutting costs, what design engineering problem would this practice have helped deal with?

---

[21]Mehran Sepehri, "IBM's Automated Lexington Factory Focuses on Quality and Cost Effectiveness," *Industrial Engineering,* February 1987, p. 66–74.

10. Tokyo Seating Company operates TRI-CON, a subsidiary manufacturing division in the United States. Some years ago, TRI-CON asked an American metal products company to bid on a contract to provide TRI-CON with metal seat pans for motorcycle seats. TRI-CON's request for proposal specified a steel gauge and little else. The American firm was uncomfortable with TRI-CON's minimal specifications and refused to bid. Why would TRI-CON say so little about the kind of seat pan it wanted?

11. Team or individual assignment: A partial QFD matrix is given below for a fast-food hamburger container. Your assignment is (*a*) to add the house of quality's roof, (*b*) collect real data from two fast-food hamburger restaurants and use it to complete the QFD matrix, and (*c*) draw conclusions about the excellence of the two containers.

	How			
	Design of container	Ergonomics	Insulation	Biodegradability
Hold the heat				
Container appeal				
Ease of opening/use				
Environmentally sound				

(What)

12. According to one report, Japanese automakers are talking about building networks of small market-driven factories that will allow fabrication of a car from just 37 snap-together parts. Each such factory would economically produce about 10,000 autos a year, versus a typical break-even volume of over 200,000 in today's auto plants.

    To make this prediction a reality, name and discuss the five most important design principles and guidelines that would need to be employed.

13. From your own experiences, give, and explain, an example of (*a*) robust design of a service (to reduce chances of misperformance), (*b*) design of a service to reduce or eliminate backtracking and return visits, and (*c*) easily plugged-in service modules.

14. From your own experience, give three examples of reducing the number of operations (service steps). Explain.

15. Which of the following is best suited for robotic assembly: (*a*) assembling a clock consisting of a frame, faceplate, mechanism, backplate, and three screws; (*b*) assembling a clock into a plastic box, which requires inserting a bottom liner into the bottom box piece and then placing an instruction card, clock, and top liner on top, and snapping the top box piece downward to engage with the bottom piece?

16. Which of the following are examples of preautomation? Explain each of your choices.
    a. Placing all tools in labeled bins in a designated tool room.
    b. Moving all fixtures close to the machine.
    c. Designing inserts for material-handling containers to hold parts in designated locations.
    d. Moving similar machines together into functional (process) cells.
    e. Moving unlike machines together into product cells.
    f. Moving a die or mold storage rack out of a storage area and into the machine area.
    g. Installing simple roller conveyors between machines.

17. Assume you are a manager preparing a financial justification for purchase and installation of a robot. You must include all costs and benefits regardless of their measurability. Make a complete list of all likely costs and benefits, separated into major and minor categories. Explain.

18. Find the most recent story on winners of the annual design awards in *Business Week* and the previous year's story (stories have been annual, usually in June). Write a comparison (one page or less, double-spaced) of:
    a. The kinds of companies winning awards.
    b. Source of the design expertise (e.g., outside consultant, inside design team, or both).
    c. Kinds of products winning awards.

SUPPLEMENT

ANNOTATED GLOSSARY OF TECHNOLOGY

The following is a limited list of technologies for improved management of design, operations, freight, administration, and cross-functional/company-to-company coordination. The list is representative rather than complete. Widely used abbreviations and acronyms are also included.

Automatic Guided Vehicle (AGV). Material-handling vehicle that follows painted line, embedded wire, or electronic signaling map; ranges from huge sled-like conveyances in some auto assembly plants to small mail carriers operating in hallways.

Automatic Identification. Data capture by scanning a bar code, universal product code (UPC), or radio frequency (RF) code; includes transfer of data to a computer file. Dominant applications in retail sales, with fast growing uses in shipping and receiving; applications in manufacturing are both growing (better control of in-plant flows of parts) and shrinking (replaced with simplicity of visual kanban).

Automatic Storage and Retrieval System (AS/RS). Rack storage units served by computer-guided automatic stock picker traveling horizontally (between racks) and vertically; computer keeps track of storage locations as it puts stock away for later retrieval.

Computer-Aided Design (CAD). Designing products at a computer terminal (e.g., a work station), which, among other things, can show rotatable three-dimensional views, import design modules in memory, fix up freehand light-penned drawings; in combination with local-area and wide-area computer networks (LANs and WANs), permits dispersed members of a design team, sometimes on different continents, to work on a design together.

Computer-aided Manufacturing (CAM). System in which a planner at a computer terminal can design a process (specify machines, routing, tools, fixtures, gauges, etc.) and direct the process to make the part; sometimes linked to CAD and called CAD/CAM.

Computer-integrated Manufacturing (CIM). Comprehensive system that includes designing products, components, and processes—also, perhaps, dies and molds—and carrying out the manufacturing itself; found especially in the process industries (e.g., chemicals), increasingly in high-volume assembly, and occasionally in high-mix fabrication (flexible manufacturing); can employ many of the other technologies in this listing.

Electronic Data Interchange (EDI). Data communication and transmission software using standard protocols that allow one company's computer to talk to another's, usually for conveying demand, ordering, delivery, and billing information among supplier-customer partners.

Flexible Automation. General term covering equipment that can handle high-mix operations, such as programmable equipment (e.g., robots) and numerically controlled (NC) machines.

Flexible Manufacturing Cell (FMC). Same as flexible manufacturing system (FMS), except human (instead of computer) directed.

Flexible Manufacturing System (FMS). Grouping of diverse machines (e.g., mill, lathe, grinder, and drill) for making a family of similar parts; machine loading and handling between machines is automated (conveyors or robots), and a computer directs the whole process.

Graphic Simulation. Computer routine that simulates in animation on a computer screen the workings of a moving process or product; used by design teams as an aid to communication about design alternatives.

Hard Automation. Built-in, fixed-motion (nonprogrammable) automation; relies on fixed tracks (e.g., powered conveyors), pusher bars, gears, sequencers, and so on.

Numerically Controlled (NC) Machines. Machines controlled by a digital (numeric) computer program; developed by an operator, a technician, or an engineer; may be fronted by a carousel holding several work pieces (e.g., castings, blocks of wood, or hunks of plastic), which may be loaded without human intervention when the previous job finishes; main purpose is flexible, low-volume machining, although high costs of programming sometimes lead to higher lot-size production.

Rapid Prototyping. System in which a designer at a computer terminal designs a part and directs a machine to produce a prototype of it, perhaps by stereolithography, in which laser-cut salami-like slices of plastic (sometimes, metal, wax, or ceramics) are layered and fused together into a three-dimensional representation of the part.

Robotics. Programmable machines that grasp, move, assemble, and disassemble; range from simple pick-and-place devices (suitable for simple assembly or when layered design of the item to be assembled has been achieved) to complex robots with many axes of motion (welding robots often have six axes—seven if the welder also can "walk," i.e., move on a track).

Satellite Truck Navigation. System used by some trucking companies for keeping track of truck movements and helping drivers navigate to a destination; especially for just-in-time hauling with its stringent timing requirements, sometimes to multiple pick-up and delivery locations.

Solid Modeling. Advanced computer-aided design (CAD) system in which the item under design is colored and shaded so that it looks rather like a three-dimensional view on a flat screen; the designer can turn, rotate, or zoom in on the item on the screen.

4   QUALITY CONTROL AND IMPROVEMENT

Chapter Outline

This chapter presents a set of relatively simple yet powerful tools that assist in the task of infusing a quality imperative into the work lives of every employee. We will see how associates can identify and eliminate the causes of poor quality by focusing on process analysis. Before examining these techniques, however, we need to consider the responsibility issue—that is, who does what?

Quality Improvement—At the Source

A. V. Feigenbaum wrote that the burden of proof for quality rests with the makers of the part, not with inspectors.[1] Businesses have broadened this idea and made it action

---

[1]A. V. Feigenbaum, *Total Quality Control: Engineering and Management* (New York: McGraw-Hill, 1961).

oriented: the *responsibility* for quality rests with the makers of the part or the providers of the service. Moreover, that responsibility extends from involvement in product and service design teams all the way through the transformation processes.

What should operations people do to carry out their primary responsibility for quality? Their response should consist of three parts, which repeat in a circular fashion (see Exhibit 4–1):

Actions for Total Quality

    I. *Process design and control.* Build quality into the process:
      1. Design a capable and fail-safe, or error-proof, process. **Fail-safing** is sometimes referred to by its Japanese name, *pokayoke*. The aim is to create a process that prevents a mistake from going forward or even happening at all. In machine-oriented processes, fail-safing might consist of automatic position checking of a tool or workpiece with a laser, followed by minute hydraulic adjustments to either or both. A *capable* process is one that is designed and built with certain quality objectives in mind; we consider process capability later in this chapter.
      2. If the process has not been made fail-safe, the next best response is self-inspection (which, of course, introduces chances of human error) and correction. For this to be effective, two steps are necessary:
        A. Give each employee authority to correct a mistake on the spot (placate an angry customer) or to stop production (even a whole production line) to avoid making a bad product.

EXHIBIT 4–1   Actions for Quality Operations

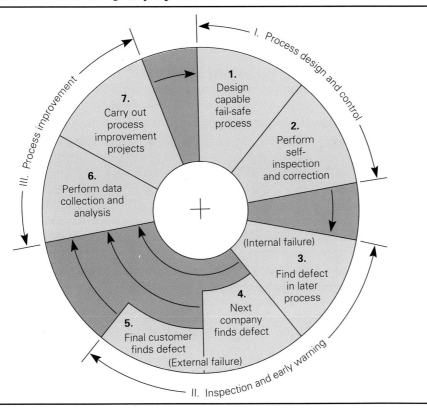

      B. Make every work group responsible for correcting its own errors and defects; avoid passing problems on to a separate rework or complaint group. Groups might also need additional authority.

  II. *Inspection and early warning.* When the process cannot be fully controlled, we're pushed into the poor practice of inspection at a later process. Since delayed detection is costly and damaging, let's not compound the error by allowing long feedback delays as well. Strive for quick and specific feedback on the problem—an early warning system tapping the following error discovery points:

    3. Inspection in a later process in the same organization.

    4. Inspection within the next company.

    5. Inspection and use by the final customer.

  Note that information from Parts II (inspection and early warning) and III (process improvement) may come from either internal or external failure, preferably the former. Also note that the external failure stages are not active steps for the provider; in them, the defect is found by the customer.

  III. *Process improvement.* Process improvement requires collection and use of data about process problems. This requires:

    6. Training supervisors and operators in how to measure quality, collect quality data, and analyze quality statistics in order to isolate causes.

    7. Formally organizing operators, supervisors, and experts into teams that carry out process improvement projects, applying data analysis and problem-solving techniques. Projects aim at making deficient processes capable and fail-safe; thus we return to step 1.

*𝒫*RINCIPLES 2 AND 15:

Dedicate to continual improvement. Involve front-line associates in problem solving.

Time-Quality Connection

Timing is a critical element in executing the activities outlined in Exhibit 4–1. Robert Galvin, Motorola's executive committee chairman, says that "one can focus on time and improve quality" and that "one can focus on quality and accomplish time."[2] The following points explain this apparent contradiction:

- *Quicker response.* Improving quality eliminates delays for rework, process adjustments, and placating customers, thus providing quicker response.

- *On-time.* Quality the first time—every time—removes a major cause of late completions and unpredictability, thereby improving on-time performance.

- *Quick feedback.* All efforts to cut out delays (the whole just-in-time, or quick-response, agenda) provide quicker feedback on causes of bad quality, allowing earlier process improvement efforts. To quote from Western Electric's classic handbook on quality control, "It is an axiom in quality control that the time to identify assignable causes is while those causes are active," and further, "delay may mean that the cause of trouble is harder to identify, and in many cases cannot be identified at all."[3] In other words, anything that reduces delays is a powerful technique for process quality improvement.

*𝒫*RINCIPLE 10:

Make quality easy to achieve.

- *Enough time for quality.* The time saved by removing delays and making quality right must not be squandered. It needs to be reinvested in training, design collaboration, inspection and on-the-spot correction, feedback and consultation with people in earlier and later processes, data collection, and improvement projects. If those activities are neglected, for example, under pressure for more output, quality

---

   [2]Lloyd Dobyns and Clare Crawford-Mason, *Quality or Else: The Revolution in World Business* (Boston: Houghton Mifflin, 1991), p. 139.

   [3]*Statistical Quality Control Handbook,* 2nd ed. (Indianapolis: AT&T Technologies, 1956), p. 217.

suffers, and a chain reaction of delays and variations results in *less* output and *slower* response.

With a quality-at-the-source orientation, a firm's front-line associates assume primary responsibility for quality. Is there still a need for inspectors and a quality assurance (QA) department? Usually there is, except in very small organizations. However, the quality movement (which is thriving, even in less-developed countries) significantly changes the role of that department, probably toward greater professionalism and breadth of responsibility.

Today, quality professionals are experiencing elevated responsibilities (see Exhibit 4–2). As they apply their unique expertise to a wider array of quality management activities, their jobs are being enriched. There is greater challenge in auditing entire quality assurance systems than in merely inspecting someone else's work. The last task listed in Exhibit 4–2 is noteworthy because quality professionals are not merely dumping duties onto line personnel. Rather, they are placing necessary quality assurance activities where they will do the most good.

Inspection cannot be completely eliminated. Quality assurance staffers usually will still need to check on service delivery and customers' reactions to it, conduct some final product tests, inspect incoming materials not yet certified at the source, and check the output of new processes or materials from new suppliers for a time. The Into Practice box details how, over the years, inspection techniques have been routinized with the aim of catching errors efficiently. In some cases, regulations (or policies) will also make it difficult to get out of the inspection mode. Nevertheless, some firms or plants have virtually eliminated inspections:

- At Kodak's copier division, the number of inspectors fell from 25 to zero.[5]
- At Kelly Air Force Base in Texas, 171 teams have been formed to focus on quality improvement. According to Rodney House, assistant to the base commander, "Inspection has always been a separate operation by certified personnel. We are now trending toward production workers' doing their own inspection and we will certify a limited number of them for it."[6]

When everyone in an organization shares responsibility for quality, the organization needs an approach that makes it easier for cross-functional teams to design and provide the quality goods and services that customers want. Process focus provides the framework.

Quality and Inspection as a Specialty

"It has become clear that by far the best way to implement quality methods is through line organizations rather than through a staff quality department. Isn't it a shame that it took us so long to understand this point?" Frank M. Gryna[4]

Exhibit 4–2   The Quality Department: Emerging Roles

- Companywide quality planning.
- Generating executive reports on quality.
- Auditing outgoing quality.
- Auditing quality practices.
- Coordinating and assisting on improvement projects.
- Training for quality.
- Consulting for quality.
- Developing new quality methodologies.
- Transferring activities to line departments.

Source: Adapted from Frank M. Gryna, "The Quality Director of the '90s," *Quality Progress,* April 1991, p. 37.

---

[4]Frank M. Gryna, "The Quality Director of the '90s," *Quality Progress,* April 1991, pp. 37–40. Dr. Gryna is co-editor of the classic *Quality Control Handbook.*

[5]William W. Davis, Dale P. Esse, and Donald L. Teringo, "Successfully Communicating Can Pay High Dividends," *Quality Progress,* July 1987, pp. 36–39.

[6]"When You Discover Things You Don't Like to Hear About," *Industry Week,* April 17, 1989, p. 54.

Into Practice

Inspection

The inspection specialty comes in several different forms:

- *100 percent inspection*. Inspector checks every unit, typically for highly critical quality characteristics, for new suppliers, and for new designs. Subject to inspector errors and fatigue unless automated.
- *Acceptance sampling*. Based on statistical sampling tables, inspector checks a random or stratified sample from a larger lot. If the sample is within the acceptable quality level (AQL), the lot passes inspection. A bad lot receives a 100 percent rectifying inspection, and bad units are replaced with good ones.
- *First-article inspection*. In low-volume operations, after the process is set up, an inspector checks the first unit; if the unit is good, the process is thought to be set up

right so that it will produce good pieces. Better: The operator (rather than an inspector) does a first- and last-article inspection; if the first and last units are good, the process probably did not change and the intervening units were good.
- *Destructive testing*. Inspector tests an item by destroying it (e.g., running a car into a wall to see how the bumper holds up); necessarily done on a sampling basis.
- *Opinion surveys*. Service clients fill out a form or answer questions about quality of a service. Open-ended questions require judgmental review; answers on, say, a 7-point numeric scale may be reduced to service-quality statistics. Willingness of clients to participate affects survey reliability.

Contrast

Quality Assurance Personnel

Inspected-In Quality	**Built-In Quality**
Quality professionals and inspectors were responsible for quality.	Front-line associates are responsible for their own process integrity and output quality.
There were never enough inspectors, so: • Parts sat around for days waiting to be declared good or bad. • Clients had to wait for an inspector to approve a service (e.g., authorize payment on a check) or review paperwork.	Quality professionals serve as expert back-up to line people, giving advice on improvement projects, training, and other quality assurance support.
	Inspectors are reassigned and carry their expertise into other line and staff work.

The Process Focus

In Chapter 1, we saw that departmentalization often prevents people from getting together to identify and solve problems. For some examples, let's eavesdrop on a meeting at Acme, Inc.:

EXHIBIT 4–3   A Transformation Process

Definition:	A unique combination of elements, conditions, or causes that collectively produces a given outcome or set of results.
Composition:	Components of a process may be classified according to the ''seven M's'':
	Materials (raw materials, components, or documents awaiting processing).
	Manpower (the human factor; better yet, *people power*).
	Methods (product and process design and operating procedures).
	Machines (tools and equipment used in the process).
	Measurement (techniques and tools used to gather process performance data).
	Maintenance (the system for providing care for process components, including training of people).
	Management (policy, work rules, and environment).
Performance:	Process performance (output, intended or incidental) depends on how the process has been designed, built or installed, operated, and maintained.

Vice president, operations: What's going on here? *All* the numbers look bad!

Shop supervisor: Tell those nitpicky inspectors to ease off. They're the *main reason* why productivity is down.

Quality inspector: Hey, we know quality isn't good. We see your people just pushing product out the door—but I blame scheduling for a schedule that isn't realistic.

Sales manager: The main reason we're losing business on replacement parts is poor record keeping in materials. The record says they have the part, then it turns out they don't.

Materials manager: The real problem is no discipline out on the floor. They take parts from stock without filling out the form, and they don't fill out scrap tickets, either.

Unfortunately, this kind of meeting is not uncommon. In too many companies, department-oriented people lack a total process focus and resort to micromanagement, with concern for but one or a few of the many outcomes of a transformation process. Low quality, high cost, and unhappy customers are the likely result.

Micromanagement: focus on a particular outcome (e.g., sales volume, training costs, course enrollment, utility expenses, etc.) without considering other results.

Processes: Description and Performance

Process management has a central role in quality control and improvement, and the word **process** has a special, broad meaning (see Exhibit 4–3).

A process is the unique set of conditions (seven M's) that creates certain outcomes. If the process is changed (deliberately or accidentally), different results (better or worse) are likely to occur. In many processes, not all of the M's are apparent. Some human services, for example, involve virtually no materials. In some cases, maintenance might be considered a part of methods. In other instances, people prefer to use category names that better fit their company or industry; *tooling* might be a category for a manufacturer, *packaging* for a warehouse, and *reservations system* for a resort. Whatever the category names, however, the aim is to describe processes in terms of all the variables that can affect process output.

Process components change over time: one data-entry person replaces another, materials come from a different supplier, a machine or its cutting tool is changed, a different maintenance schedule is started, and so on. Traditional thinking was that any change automatically created a new process that had to be restabilized before improvement could be considered. One aim of TQM, by contrast, is to make process elements easily substitutable without the burden of restabilization and with no negative impact on process performance. Fail-safe designs, training for mastery of multiple jobs, supplier certification,

Exhibit 4–4   The Normal Distribution—Shaft Diameter Output Example

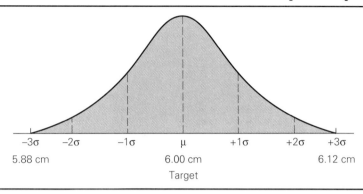

SOURCE: Adapted from Ross Johnson and William O. Winchell, *Production and Quality* (Milwaukee: American Society for Quality Control Press, 1989), p. 10.

and tool and equipment maintenance programs support that aim. But how do we know whether a substitution has changed a process? We analyze the process output.

Process Output and Quality Characteristics

In the 1920s, Western Electric's Walter Shewhart and George Edwards pioneered the use of statistical analysis of process output data. They gave us the quality (or process) control chart, discussed later in the chapter, and they showed what distributions of process output data reveal about how the process is working.

Though not all process output distributions are the same, we can gain insight from looking closer at a frequently occurring one. According to an American Society for Quality Control (ASQC) training manual:

In this book, we use *target* to refer to the intended or most desirable process output. It is the same thing as the nominal value of the specification (spec, for short).

> It has been well established that most machines and processes yield dimensions or other characteristics in the form of a normal curve [see Exhibit 4–4]. If a machine were set to turn a shaft with a target diameter of 6 cm, we know that all shafts would not be exactly the same. The precision of the machine would determine how close the variation could be held. From past experience we might know that the parts would fall in a distribution with *almost* 100 percent of the items being within ±0.12 cm of the mean value of the process output (here, equal to the target of 6.00 cm). Normal curve theory establishes that about 99.7 percent of the parts will fall within three standard deviations—3σ, or 3-sigma—of the mean. Here, three standard deviations equal 0.12 cm, thus one sigma equals 0.04 cm.[7]

If shaft diameter were designated a **quality characteristic**—a performance output of a process that is of particular interest to a customer—the maker would want to know more about how well the actual process output distribution (see Exhibit 4–4) compares to the customer's requirements for that diameter (taken up later in this chapter). Also, note that the shaft diameter distribution is centered precisely at the target. While centering on target satisfies one aim (discussed in conjunction with Taguchi's loss function in Chapter 2), there still is output variation to be concerned about.

Special and Common Causes of Variation.   Every process output distribution is subject to two kinds of variation: variation attributable to special or assignable causes, and variation attributable to natural or common causes. **Special cause variation** is created by

---

[7]Adapted from Ross Johnson and William O. Winchell, *Production and Quality* (Milwaukee: American Society for Quality Control Press, 1989), p. 10.

$\mathscr{I}$*nto* $\mathscr{P}$*ractice*

Responsibilities for the Elimination of Variation

Francis and Gerwels state that W. Edwards Deming's "enormous contribution to management theory" is his recognition "that the responsibility for improvement could be assigned according to the type of variation": those working in the system have the job of finding and eliminating special causes; those managing the system work on eliminating common causes, which are tougher to pin down and may involve spending money.*

The idea of segmenting responsibility in this way is powerful—and still new to many companies. Nevertheless, some firms have taken it even further: don't limit operating people's responsibilities to special causes; in a mature employee involvement situation, operators will have ideas for dealing with common causes as well—ideas such as changing a design, a supplier, a form, or a training procedure.

George Box gives special examples, including this one: A friend mentioned that his department secretary said, "Don't ever circulate stuff through the campus mail. They take forever to get it delivered." But Box suggests that, if campus mail really is a problem, the best way to solve it may be to make up a team of the department secretary, mail sorter, and mail deliverer.† The team might find a special cause for the delay; on the other hand, it may want to design and recommend a new system (e.g., change the delivery routes, mailing envelopes, or address designators) that eliminates a number of common causes.

---

*A. E. Francis and John M. Gerwels, "Building a Better Budget," *Quality Progress*, October 1989, pp. 70–75.

†George Box, "When Murphy Speaks—Listen," *Quality Progress*, October 1989, pp. 79–84.

(assignable to) a certain problem, for example, a machine malfunction, an incorrect tool setting, a server not following procedures, or a bad batch of raw materials. Correct the specific problem and the special variation goes away. **Common cause variation** (also called chance or random variation) is more difficult to trace; it is due to the multitude of small chance-fluctuations that occur within the process. Common variation is usually attributed to the process as a whole. It is not the fault of operating personnel, so its reduction has historically had to depend on some administrative decision to make relatively major adjustments to the process; new machines, for instance.

Since less variability is a basic customer want, a process improvement team can gauge its success by observing whether output variation falls. The general sequence is as follows:

1. Eliminate the special cause variation by correcting the problems. When a process output distribution is free of all special cause variation, that process is said to be in a state of **statistical control,** or simply in control. Removal of special causes results in a stable, predictable process output. A process that is in control still has common variation in its output, however.

2. Reduce that common variation. Required actions might include product or process redesign or some other substantial investment.

The variation elimination sequence—indeed, the discovery of the two types of process output variation—has played a key role historically in defining responsibilities among people involved in quality improvement efforts, as the accompanying box illustrates.

Variables and Attributes.   Those studying variation need process output data, which come in two forms: variables data and attributes data. **Variables data** results from

Margin notes:

Shewhart coined the term *assignable variation*. Deming, it is said, preferred to call it *special cause variation*. AT&T, where both men once worked, uses the term *unnatural variation*. All three terms refer to the same thing.

Example: Some employers send equipment operators to trade shows to help select equipment, a practice unheard of 15 years ago.

Process output data is of two types: Variables data must be measured, while attributes data is usually counted.

measuring or computing the amount of (or degree or value of) a quality characteristic. The shaft diameter distribution of Exhibit 4–4, for example, would come from measuring shaft diameters. Variables data are continuous; any value within a given output range (5.88 cm to 6.12 cm for the shaft diameters) may occur. Other examples of outputs captured as variables data are packaged weights of foods, times required for county clerks to record documents, density of pollutants, brightness in an office, loudness at a rock concert, price-earnings ratios, and grade point averages.

The other type of process data is called **attributes data,** which arises from classification and counting. Simpler than variables data, it doesn't require a measurement, just a classifying judgment: Maybe yes-or-no for friendly service; good-or-bad for a car wash; small, medium, and large for farm melons; or AAA, AA, A for debt obligations in a portfolio. A battery tester with a red zone and a green zone provides an attributes check. Similarly, we test a night light by putting it into a socket and flipping the switch. It either lights or it doesn't. A table setting in a fancy restaurant may be checked by the headwaiter. If one fork or glass is out of place, the headwaiter judges the table setting to be defective. Diameters of ball bearings could be checked by rolling them across a hole-filled surface. Those that fall through are too small; their diameters needn't be measured.

After categories have been defined so that output can be classified, employees need only count the number that fall into each category. Raw attributes data are discrete, although they may be used to compute the proportion (or percentage) of process output in each category. For example, a retail clerk checking a stock of old batteries might find 10 out of 1,000 with low voltage (in the red zone), or over a month's time, a headwaiter might find that 15 percent of tables are defective.

While attributes data are easier to collect, variables data yield more information. Example 4–1, using variables data, demonstrates some of the issues involved in studying a process—and helps show the value of focusing on processes.

EXAMPLE 4–1   Process Focus Applied

Consider a process for the production of bolts (see Exhibit 4–5). The process is made up of components from each of the seven M's and creates bolts with several quality characteristics. Customers would indicate the following:

1. *Quality characteristics important enough to receive close attention.* For a simple product like a machine bolt, customer-critical characteristics might be length, diameter, and thread depth; each would be represented by a frequency distribution. Here, we look at but one characteristic, bolt length.

2. *A desired value—and thus the maker's target—for each quality characteristic.* Here, assume customers have requested 3-inch-long bolts.

As Exhibit 4–5 shows, the output distribution of bolt lengths has a certain central tendency, or location, and an amount of variation (dispersion). Studying distribution is a simple, cheap, and effective method of understanding quite a bit about the process.

The distribution in Exhibit 4–5 reveals two useful pieces of process output information: One is whether the process is centered on 3 inches, as the customer wants, or on the high or low side. The other is the amount of variation—the less of it the better. The bolt-making machinist knows that, as shown in Exhibit 4–5, the output of this process is the input to the next. Even if it is not a problem here, bolt-length variation may cause trouble at the next (or any other downstream) process.

Unfortunately, process output distributions are not always as stable as this bolt-length distribution appears to be; stability requires work. Suppose the machinist measures bolt lengths every hour and finds them to be distributed as shown in the upper section of Exhibit 4–6, that is, centered around 2.9 inches for one hour, around 3.1 inches the next, back to 2.9, and so on. This odd pattern tells the

EXHIBIT 4-5   **The Process Focus: Contributing Variables and Performance**

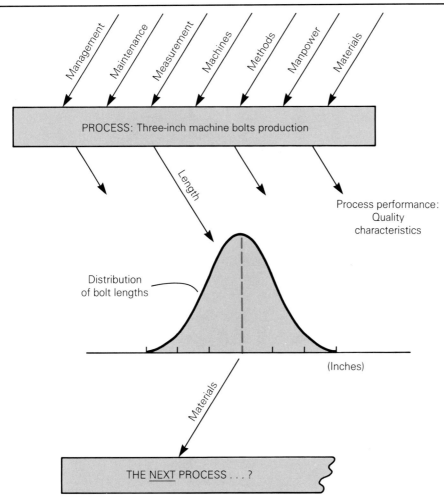

machinist to look for a special cause for the hour-to-hour variation. It may be that the machinist had been switching methods of cutting the bolt bar-stock about every hour. Suspicion falls on cutting method as the special cause.

The machinist stops switching cutting methods and focuses on the method leading to bolts averaging about 2.9 inches. The middle part of Exhibit 4–6 shows how this *new* process might appear. Continued measurement, say, for several hours, could convince the machinist that the special variation has been eliminated, resulting in a process that is in control. But process control is not enough. A larger issue remains: the bolts are still not meeting the target of 3 inches.

The machinist makes another process change: "I increased the feed of the bar-stock into the cutting tool by one-tenth of an inch by moving a stop block. That got the process centered on target." The result is process output as appears in the lowest part of Exhibit 4–6, which shows that the process is centered on target and stable across time. If there are no other special causes, the process is *in control*. Remember, the main benefit of statistical process control is predictability; as long as control is maintained, process output will be stable.

The machinist in Example 4–1 dealt with two of the three main concerns in process analysis: achieving process control and getting the process on target. But, as is clear from

Exhibit 4–6   Bolt Length Process Output

A. Two cutting methods

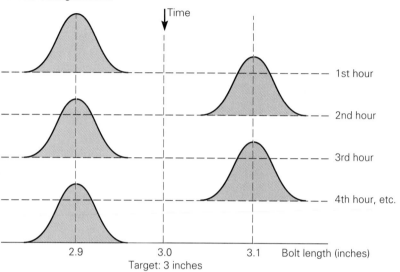

Target: 3 inches

B. Single cutting method

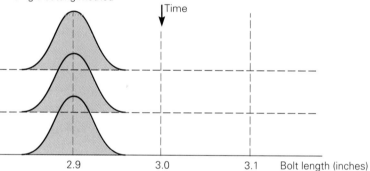

C. Single cutting method with bar-stock feed adjustment

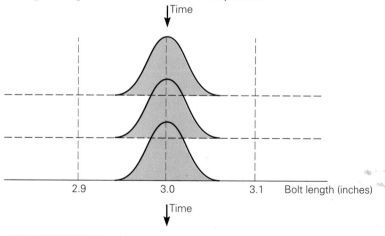

Exhibit 4–6C, the process still exhibits variation in output. Process capability analysis attacks that common variation. We reserve that topic for later in the chapter.

Also, the machinist followed a systematic approach: first, collect process output data and analyze it—what quality control people call listening to the process—make a change if necessary, and then repeat. In the simple bolt-making example, one person achieved control and (some) improvement. Usually, problems are bigger, more ill-defined, and require the efforts of teams. We look now at a systematic approach to guide those efforts.

Process Improvement Overview

In Exhibit 4–1, we saw that process improvement projects are the third part of the actions for quality operations cycle. Team-based improvement efforts can require considerable resources and therefore must be efficient, focused (not likely to go astray), and thorough (nothing overlooked).

The systematic approach to process quality improvement follows the scientific method of investigation, familiar from physical or social science studies (see Exhibit 4–7). Briefly, the sequence is to find and study a problem, generate and evaluate possible solutions, implement and review the chosen solution, then repeat for a new problem.

Plan of Attack

The scientific method provides an overall plan of attack. But process improvement teams still need a set of tools to use at each step along the way.

The quality movement has spawned a broad and continuing search for better tools to assist in process improvement programs. Many established tools are directly applicable to the task; others fit after some revision.

Tools for Process Improvement

Exhibit 4–8 lists widely accepted tools for process improvement. Those in the general category require little explanation. Team building and group interaction tools, with deep roots in the social sciences, have a new home in team-based TQM programs.

The continual improvement imperative applies to the tools of improvement as well as to processes they probe.

EXHIBIT 4–7   Scientific Method for Process Improvement

1. Identify and define the problem.
2. Study the existing situation; collect necessary data.
3. Generate possible solution alternatives.
4. Evaluate alternatives and choose the preferred one.
5. Implement the improvement and measure results.
6. Evaluate and revise if required.
7. Otherwise, return to step 1 and start again with a new problem.

EXHIBIT 4–8   Tools for Process Improvement

General Tools	Coarse-Grained Tools	Fine-Grained Tools
1. Team-building and group-interaction tools.	3. Process flowchart.	10. Run diagram.
2. Specific process/ technology tools.	4. Check sheets and histograms.	11. Process control chart.
	5. Pareto analysis.	12. Process capability analysis.
	6. Fishbone charts.	13. Precontrol analysis.
	7. Fail-safing.	
	8. Experimentation.	
	9. Scattergrams.	

The specific process and technology tools relate or apply to a certain work specialty. They might include a computer spreadsheet, stethoscope, backhoe, accident claim form, customer satisfaction survey card, or coordinate measuring machine—anything that helps improve process output.

Coarse-grained tools are used more for broad planning and analysis or where sifting through data is necessary in order to attack the most promising targets or segregate them for closer scrutiny. The fine-grained tools are for controlling and closely analyzing behavior of a single quality characteristic; they aim at the process components most responsible for the behavior of that characteristic.

Coarse-Grained Analysis and Improvement

Process improvement often begins with a study of the way materials, documents, or people flow or relate to one another, and sorting data to find promising targets of opportunity for improvement efforts. For those cases, we employ process flowcharts, check sheets and histograms, Pareto analysis, fishbone diagrams, fail-safing, experimentation, and scattergrams.

Process Flowchart   Flowcharts are useful tools in many disciplines. Their purpose in operations management, however, is to provide an improvement team with a pictorial statement of how people or things move through a series of transformations. One popular set of flowchart symbols is described in Exhibit 4–9.

Of the six flowchart symbols, only the operation symbol denotes a **value-adding transformation**—wherein value is added to an object being transformed or a valued service is being rendered. The other symbols reflect an addition of cost, not value. Thus, in process improvement, the team strives to eliminate non-value-adding steps and to

Exhibit 4–9   Flow Chart Symbols

Symbol	Name	Description
○	**Operation**	Activity that adds value to a workpiece or provides a value-adding service to a customer; usually requires a setup.
→	**Transportation**	Movement of object from one work station to another; movement of customer from one operation to another.
□	**Inspection**	Work is checked for some characteristic of quality; may call for 100 percent inspection or a sampling plan.
◇	**Decision**	Directs or alters flow of people, goods, or documents depending on status of criterion variable (e.g., yes/no, pass/fail, and so forth).
▽	**Storage**	Applies to materials or documents; may be temporary or permanent.
D	**Delay**	Time person, materials, or documents wait for next operation; in *lot* delay, wait is for other items in the lot to be processed; in *process* delay, entire lot waits for workstation or other bottleneck to clear.

Exhibit 4–10   Flowchart: Travel Authorization Process

A. Original travel authorization approval/preparation process

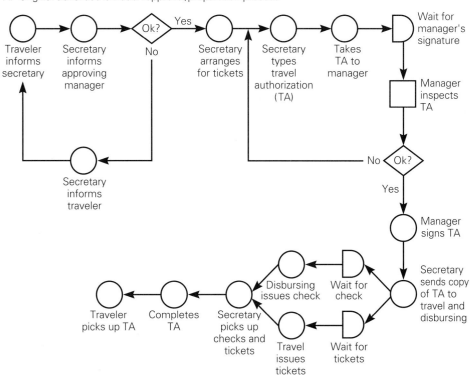

B. Improved travel authorization process

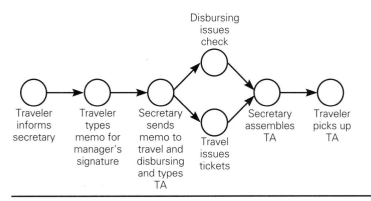

Source: Adapted from Dennis C. Kinlaw, *Continuous Improvement and Measurement for Total Quality* (Homewood, Ill.: Business One Irwin, 1992), pp. 214–15.

perfect the value-adding ones by looking for ways to perform them faster, more accurately, and more consistently. Exhibit 4–10 is a process flowchart used to describe a company's travel approval procedure, both before and after improvement. In the improved version, delays, inspections, and unnecessary operations have been eliminated. Occasionally an improvement team can complete its project using the process flowchart as the sole process analysis tool. More often, the flowchart maps the process for further analysis.

Check Sheets and Histograms

*𝒫*RINCIPLE 14:

Record process and problem data at the workplace.

Process improvement activities thrive on data, especially data collected and maintained close to the process being improved. Most useful are tools that allow for quick data collection and tell their story at a glance, which is the case for check sheets and histograms. Check sheets are the simplest of all—just make a checkmark. Busy employees needn't be delayed, yet valuable process knowledge is gained. Exhibit 4–11 is a check-sheet showing the daily occurrence of setup problems noted by operators in a five-machine work cell over a week's time. It reveals that machine A was the most trouble-prone and that Monday seems to have been a bad day for all concerned.

Those conclusions are backed up by proportions easily obtainable from the check sheet: Machine A experienced 13 out of the 35 problems (37 percent); 17 of the 35 problems (49 percent) occurred on Monday. Suppose operators had defined a setup as a "problem" if it took longer than 10 minutes. Time data, recorded in the work cell, could be presented as a histogram (a form of bar chart) with categories for values of the setup times. Exhibit 4–12 shows a histogram for the 17 setups that were defined as problems on Monday, November 18.

To create the histogram in Exhibit 4–12, operators would have measured the setup times, perhaps even in tenths of a minute (time is variables data, measured, not counted). In the histogram, however, they grouped those times into 10-minute categories; actual setup times don't appear.

The cell operators would study the histogram looking for fruitful courses of action. For example, they might note that 9 of Monday's 17 problem setups took 50 minutes or longer, and decide to focus initial improvement efforts on factors that created those worst cases.

Another tool, the Pareto chart, employs bar charting of data that naturally occur in attributes form.

Pareto Analysis[8]

Pareto analysis helps separate the vital few from the trivial many. In process improvement, Pareto analysis proceeds as follows:

1. Identify the factors affecting process variability or product quality.
2. Keep track of how often a measurable defect or nonconformity is related to each factor.
3. Plot the results on a bar chart, where length of a bar stands for (or is proportional to) the number of times the causal factor occurs. More serious causes (longest bars) are positioned to the left of less serious ones.

Exhibit 4–13 is a sample **Pareto chart** for a certain product being supplied to an important customer. The process flow (which could be shown on a process flowchart) is from raw materials, to fabrication of component parts, to subassemblies, to final assembly, to delivery. The Pareto chart shows that by far the most critical errors—about 85 percent—are made in delivering the finished product to the customer and in raw materials. The process improvers will want to focus their efforts on those two factors and save the other three for a later round of improvement. Pareto analysis often precedes—and feeds a problem to—fishbone analysis (see Exhibit 4–14), our next topic.

---

[8]The idea of giving an item the degree of attention it deserves is sometimes called the principle of parsimony (parsimony means frugality). The more general principle, widely applicable in society, is the Pareto principle, named after economist Vilfredo Pareto (1848–1923). His observation that most of the wealth is in the hands of a small percentage of the population makes it simple (frugal) to study wealth by studying just the wealthy.

EXHIBIT 4–11   Check Sheet: Machine Setup Problems

Machine ID #	Monday	Tuesday	Wednesday	Thursday	Friday	Total
			WEEK: November 18–22, 19XX			
A	✓✓✓	✓	✓✓	✓✓✓✓✓	✓✓	13
B	✓✓✓✓		✓		✓	6
C	✓✓✓	✓			✓✓	6
D	✓✓✓✓✓					5
E	✓✓	✓✓		✓		5
Total	17	4	3	6	5	35

EXHIBIT 4–12   Histogram: Machine Setup Time Requirements

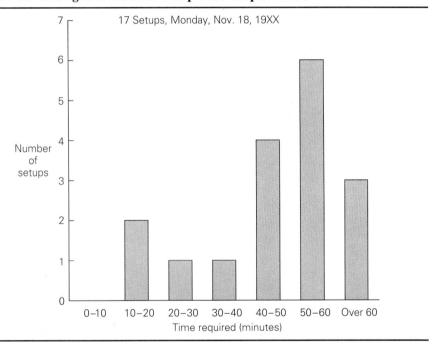

Delivery of the finished product to the customer is the most error-prone process on the Pareto chart (Exhibit 4–13). Thus, truck delivery failure becomes the spinal bone of a **fishbone chart,** so named because it looks like the skeleton of a fish.

The fishbone chart must be produced by the people who know the process: trucker, packer, material handler, material controller, dispatcher, and supervisor. The team brainstorms backwards from the target for improvement (truck delivery failures), treating that problem as an effect, then identifying its probable causes and continuing down through the "bone structure" until the most likely root causes appear as extremity bones on the chart.

Exhibit 4–15 is the full fishbone chart, as the shipping-area team might develop it. The main causes are deficiencies in trucking, packing, shipping documents, and container

Fishbone Chart

Fishbone chart is also called a cause-and-effect diagram or an Ishikawa diagram, after Kaoru Ishikawa, its developer.

EXHIBIT 4–13   **Pareto Chart: Occurrences of Errors in Providing Product to a Customer**

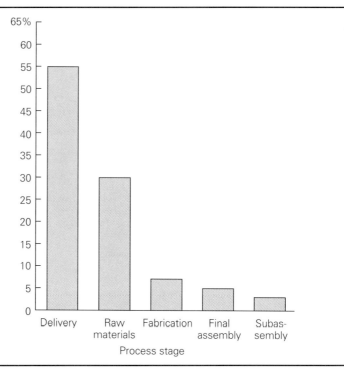

EXHIBIT 4–14   **Process Improvement Team in Action**

Improvement team at Atlanta's West Paces Ferry Hospital discusses a Pareto chart. Hospital Corporation of America, the parent company, is overseeing development of quality improvement teams in each of its hospitals.

Exhibit 4–14   (*Continued*)

The same Pareto chart just being drawn, as well as a preliminary fishbone chart.

Exhibit 4–15   Fishbone Chart—Truck Delivery Failures

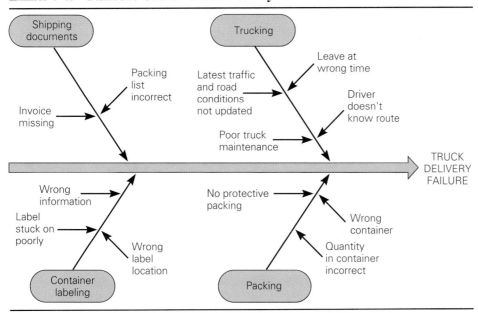

labeling. Each main cause is influenced by secondary causes. For example, trucking failure has four secondary factors, shown as small bones: rush-hour traffic and bad road conditions, poor truck maintenance, wrong departure time, and driver's failure to learn the route.

The team might post the chart in the shipping area and begin thinking about the root causes. Sometimes the mere presence of the chart (if done in enough detail) stimulates ideas for fixing root causes. But sometimes the improvement team elects to conduct further analysis—perhaps another round of Pareto and fishbone charts at a more detailed level.

What happens when the team feels that the chart breakdown is fine enough? Perhaps 50 or 100 detailed end-points (possible root causes) demand attention. The vast majority, however, will not require extensive data collection and fine-grained analysis. Rather, a simple change in procedure, equipment, materials, or design is usually the answer. For example, to ensure correct label placement, the packer decides to use a template that makes a window for the label at a measured distance from two corners of the box.

Consider, also, the sub-bone "quantity in container incorrect." If team members have been well trained, they will know about a solution that many other companies have adopted for getting the right quantity into a container: egg-crate-like partitions inside the container, serving as a simple, visual control that makes it difficult not to pack the correct quantity.

Fail-Safing

We have just seen two simple examples of fail-safing: a template to assist packer in labeling and egg-crate dividers so packers always fill the box correctly.

Fail-safing is a realistic view of people, processes, and errors. It acknowledges that people need to be protected from their natural inclinations to vary. To illustrate, if the packing crew had been trained in the fail-safing concept, they might have held a process improvement session to discuss the truck delivery failure.

> *First packer:* Anybody is going to put the label on wrong or put the wrong quantity in the container once in a while. This process is an error waiting to happen!
> *Second packer:* Yeah. Let's find a way to fail-safe it. Otherwise, people will blame us, instead of the poor process design.

This is an excellent attitude. If people are unaware that processes can and should be fail-safed, their tendency is to hide the error when it occurs to avoid the possibility of blame.

Unlike other tools of improvement, fail-safing does not depend heavily on process data. Rather, it is a mind-set that can help direct people, positively, toward fixing a process. It is best applied at the root-cause level of analysis—for example, a third- or fourth-level sub-bone of a fishbone chart. For instance:

- Leaving out parts or steps.
- Not fitting components or service elements together properly.
- Failing to follow the right process sequence.
- The process freezes up when necessary to avoid a bad result (e.g., machine stops because of excess tool wear).
- Errors cannot be passed onward (indicating the root cause has been found).

Fail-safe devices may be as simple as templates, egg-crate dividers, velcro, glue, and paint, or as fancy as limit switches, electric eyes, scales, locks, probes, timers, and scopes. Exhibit 4–16 illustrates fail-safing achieved by painting a black surface white to prevent order-fillers from leaving black disks in the previously all-black hoppers.

Experimentation

Sometimes the improvement team is stumped: flowcharts, Pareto analyses, or fishbone charts have brought too many potential causes to the surface. The team asks, "Which are the *actual* causes?" It needs help from statisticians or engineers who are seasoned veterans in the art and science of experimentation.

As noted in Chapter 2, the early 1990s witnessed renewed interest in **design of experiments (DOE)** as the quality movement progressed. The intricacies of DOE,

---

*P*RINCIPLE 10:

Make it easier to make goods without error or variation.

The statistician may reply with a phrase popular in TQM: torture the data and it will confess.

EXHIBIT 4–16   Fail-safing a Process at Microsoft-Ireland

Disk duplicating machines at Microsoft-Ireland. Production team painted black inside walls of take-up hoppers white, which fail-safed the process so that a black diskette would not be inadvertently left in the hopper when customer orders were being processed.

including Taguchi's short-cut methods, are beyond the scope of this discussion, but some comments about how they relate to process improvement are in order. The best way to incorporate experimentation into process improvement programs is to have the experts join existing quality or process improvement teams as temporary consultants; the problem should not simply be dumped on the experts while the team goes on to easier tasks. The experts don't know the process and won't have to live with any proposed solutions. In world-class organizations, increasingly, operator-owner teams are retaining control of process data for use in quick-response problem solving, so the staff experts have to travel to the shops in order to find data necessary for them to ply their trade.

Experiments are vital ingredients in process improvements, though DOE skills are not something that everyone should master. However, another experimental tool, the scatter diagram, is easy to learn and use by everyone.

A **scatter diagram**—*scattergram* for short—is used to plot process output effects against experimental changes in process inputs. The correlation coefficient (discussed in Chapter 5) may be calculated, although a rough estimate of the strength of the relationship might be clear just by looking at the scattergram. Like the experiments they typically accompany, scatter diagrams are most useful in analysis of complex processes where cause-effect relationships are unclear.

Suppose that associates producing rubber inner tubes have noted wide variation in tube strength, as revealed by overfilling the tubes with air. They run an experiment seeking ways to reduce the variation. At the previous process in their work cell, in which formed tubes are cured in ovens, they vary the curing time. Next, they test the tubes, plot curing times against tube strength on a scatter diagram, and look for a correlation.

*P*RINCIPLE 14:

Record and own process and problem data at the workplace.

Scatter (Correlation) Diagram

EXHIBIT 4–17   **Scatter Diagram—Cure Time for Inner Tubes**

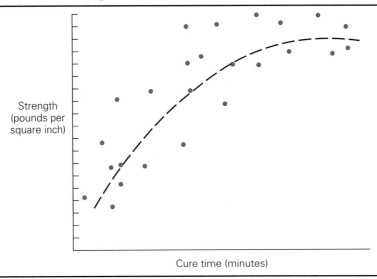

Cure time (minutes)

Exhibit 4–17 is the resulting scatter diagram. Each point represents one tube. Cure time is a point's horizontal location, and strength is its vertical location. The team's conclusions:

1. Tube strength correlates well with cure time since there is a definite clustering of points about the curving line.
2. Tube strength increases with cure time up to a point, after which further cure time does no more good and may even be harmful.

Having found one source of variation, the team presses on, looking for other factors that might correlate with tube strength.

We've considered seven course-grained tools of process analysis and improvement. They illustrate the point that most improvements should not require going beyond the coarse-grained analysis to fine-grained measurement and statistical analysis tools. Still, the fine-grained tools have their place, and it remains an important one.

Fine-Grained Analysis and Improvement

Exhibit 4–8 lists four fine-grained improvement tools that give improvement teams a closer look at the behavior of specific quality characteristics: run diagram, control chart, capability analysis, and precontrol analysis.

Run Diagram

In injection molding, hot, liquid plastic is injected into a mold containing one or more cavities in the desired shape of parts. The plastic cools and hardens forming the part.

Consider a part made in an injection-molding process. It might be a component for an electronics assembler, an appliance manufacturer, or a toy company. What sort of quality requirements might a customer have? Almost always, there will be physical dimension requirements, and those will become the specifications (specs) to which the provider makes the part. Let's assume that our part is round and has an outer diameter specification of 5.00 cm ± 0.05 cm. The 5.00 cm is the target or nominal dimension, and the plus-or-minus 0.05 cm is the tolerance. The complete outer diameter specification would be:

$$5.00 \pm 0.05 \text{ cm}$$

Parts with outer diameters in the range of 4.95 cm to 5.05 cm would meet specs. That range is referred to as the tolerance band. Specs shouldn't just happen; they should reflect customers' needs. During production (after one or more iterations of part and process design), operators will compare process output—molded parts—with the specs to determine how well the process measures up. The **run diagram** (a running plot of measurements, piece by piece, as the process continues) facilitates that assessment (see Example 4–2).

EXAMPLE 4–2   Run Diagram—Injection-molded Parts

Specifications: Outer diameter = 5.00 ± 0.05 cm.

Quality objective: Continually improve quality and productivity by reducing the fraction of parts that do not meet the specifications. Several distinct phases of the improvement process might be noted.

Phase 1: Operator measures every piece and plots outer diameter on the run diagram. Exhibit 4–18 shows diameters for 30 pieces. Pieces 7 and 23 are larger than the upper limit (5.05 cm), and pieces 17, 25, 26, 29, and 30 are smaller than the lower limit (4.95 cm). Also, there is a discernable drift downward over time. Action is needed.

Phase 2: Improvement team looks for causes. For example, the operator knows why the diameters are decreasing over time: machine heat buildup. Perhaps a faulty thermostat is replaced. The supervisor might suspect that raw material impurities are the cause for the diameters that were above the spec limits. The solution might involve placing a sheet of clear plastic over the containers of plastic pellets so passersby won't think the open box is a trash receptacle. Thus, efforts have been made to correct both the under- and overspec process output.

Phase 3: Operator constructs new run diagram by plotting 30 diameters measured after the process changes went into effect. Exhibit 4–19 shows that the second set of diameters falls within specs and appears to have no drift.

EXHIBIT 4–18   Run Diagram—Outer Diameters of 30 Pieces

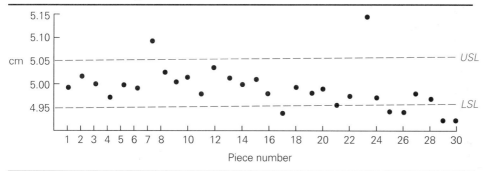

EXHIBIT 4–19   Run Diagram—Outer Diameters of 30 More Pieces

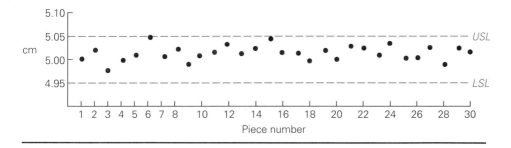

Conclusions: The run diagram is a simple tool, specification limits are easily understood, and using them for boundaries when plotting individual piece output is common sense. In the example, output has improved, so measurement frequency would decrease.

Process Control Charts

Process control charts (once referred to as quality control charts, reflecting a narrower view of application) plot the performance of a process output characteristic over time, typically using statistics from samples of output. Associates take the samples, derive upper and lower boundaries (called control limits) within which sample statistics are expected to fall, compute and plot those statistics, and then analyze the plots. Basically, control charts reveal whether process output variation is from common or special causes.

Many types of control charts exist. Exhibit 4–20 lists the more popular ones that can be traced to the work of Walter Shewhart in the 1920s and 1930s. Notice that the variables data charts are often used in pairs, one for the measure of location (e.g., average or median) and one for the measure of dispersion (e.g., range or standard deviation). Though Exhibit 4–20 suggests a variety of control chart applications, the procedure is similar for all types. In the following three examples, we examine control charts for both variables and attributes.

Exhibit 4–20   Types of Shewhart Control Charts

Control Charts for Variables Data

$\overline{X}$ and R charts: for sample averages and ranges.
$\overline{X}$ and s charts: for sample means and standard deviations.
$\widetilde{X}$ and R charts: for sample medians and ranges.
X charts: for individual measures; uses moving ranges.

Control Charts for Attributes Data

p charts: proportion of units nonconforming (sample size, n, may vary).
np charts: number of units nonconforming (sample size, n, must be constant).
c charts: number of nonconformities (sample size, n, must be constant).
u charts: number of nonconformities per unit (sample size, n, may vary).

EXAMPLE 4–3 $\overline{X}$ AND R CHARTS—INJECTION MOLDED PARTS

Let's return to our injection-molding process and assume that operators continue to measure outer diameters, but develop $\overline{X}$ and R process control charts—one logical next step after the run diagrams of Example 4–2. As with the run diagram, control chart creation has distinct phases.

Phase 1: Data collection and recording. Exhibit 4–21 shows diameters and ranges for 20 hourly samples of four parts each. Each sample mean, $\overline{X}$, shows process location, and the accompanying sample range (R) shows process dispersion or spread at the time the sample was taken. Alternatively, process variation may be shown using the standard deviation (the second item in Exhibit 4–20), but it takes more calculations. The range has long been preferred because it is simple and quick.

Phase 2: Calculate chart center lines and control limits. Sample averages and ranges are the first step; those values for the first sample are:

$$\overline{X}_1 = \frac{\Sigma x}{n} = \frac{5.06 + 5.00 + 5.03 + 5.01}{4} = 5.025$$

$$R_1 = 5.06 - 5.00 = 0.06$$

Ехнівіт 4–21   **Measurements for Designing $\overline{X}$ and R Charts**

Sample Number	Date	Measurements (cm)				Mean ($\overline{X}$)	Range (R)
		x_1	x_2	x_3	x_4		
1	10/10	5.01	5.00	5.03	5.06	5.025	0.06
2		4.99	5.03	5.03	5.05	5.025	0.06
3		5.03	5.04	4.99	4.94	5.000	0.10
4		5.05	5.03	5.00	5.01	5.022	0.05
5		4.97	5.04	4.96	5.00	4.992	0.08
6		4.97	5.00	4.99	5.02	4.995	0.05
7		5.06	5.00	5.02	4.96	5.010	0.10
8		5.03	4.98	5.01	4.95	4.992	0.08
9	10/11	5.05	5.03	5.05	4.98	5.028	0.07
10		4.99	5.03	5.01	4.96	4.998	0.07
11		4.98	5.05	5.05	4.94	5.005	0.11
12		4.95	5.04	4.99	4.99	4.992	0.09
13		5.00	5.05	5.01	4.97	5.008	0.08
14		4.96	5.03	5.05	5.00	5.010	0.09
15		5.08	5.01	5.02	4.96	5.018	0.12
16		5.02	4.98	5.04	4.95	4.998	0.09
17	10/12	5.02	4.99	4.99	5.04	5.010	0.05
18		4.99	5.00	5.05	5.05	5.022	0.06
19		5.03	5.02	5.01	4.96	5.005	0.07
20		5.02	5.04	5.04	5.04	5.040	0.02
Totals						100.195	1.50

The center lines for the $\overline{X}$ and R charts, respectively, are the grand average of the sample averages, $\overline{\overline{X}}$ (pronounced "X-double-bar"), and $\overline{R}$ (referred to as "R-bar"). In this case,

$$\overline{\overline{X}} = \frac{\Sigma \overline{X}}{k} = \frac{100.195}{20} = 5.010 \text{ cm} \tag{4–1}$$

$$\overline{R} = \frac{\Sigma R}{k} = \frac{1.50}{20} = 0.075 \text{ cm} \tag{4–2}$$

where k is the number of samples or subgroups (in this case, 20).

Next, calculate control limits. The *central limit theorem*, usually covered in statistics studies, applies. Since operators plot sample averages rather than individual piece measurements, they are actually dealing with a distribution of sample averages. The standard deviation of this distribution of sample averages, or simply standard error, depends on the size of the samples (n). The standard error is:

$$\sigma_{\bar{x}} = \frac{\sigma}{\sqrt{n}} \tag{4–3}$$

The central limit theorem also holds that (for our purposes) the distribution of sample averages will be approximately normal regardless of the population from which the samples were taken. Thus, a plot of all possible sample averages should approach the familiar bell shape of the normal curve. Further, approximately 99.72 percent of all sample averages should fall within three standard errors of the mean of the distribution of sample averages—that is *if* the process is within a state of statistical control.

Process control limits are typically—but not always—set at three standard errors above and below the center line and are commonly referred to as three-sigma limits. In practice, however, the standard error is not calculated; approximations are

EXHIBIT 4–22   **Process Control Chart Factors**

Sample (or Subgroup) Size (n)	Control Limit Factor for Averages ($\overline{X}$ Charts) (A_2)	UCL Factor for Ranges (R Charts) (D_4)	LCL Factor for Ranges (R Charts) (D_3)	Factor for Estimating Process Sigma ($\hat{\sigma} = \overline{R}/d_2$) ($d_2$)
2	1.880	3.267	0	1.128
3	1.023	2.575	0	1.693
4	0.729	2.282	0	2.059
5	0.577	2.115	0	2.326
6	0.483	2.004	0	2.534
7	0.419	1.924	0.076	2.704
8	0.373	1.864	0.136	2.847
9	0.337	1.816	0.184	2.970
10	0.308	1.777	0.223	3.078

used to obtain control limits. The most frequently used factors for $\overline{X}$ and R charts are shown in Exhibit 4–22. The table is derived from the basic mathematics of the normal distribution and the distribution of ranges.[9]

Control limits for the sample averages (the $\overline{X}$ chart) are:

$$\text{Upper control limit } (UCL_{\overline{X}}) = \overline{\overline{X}} + (A_2)(\overline{R}) \tag{4–4}$$

$$\text{Lower control limit } (LCL_{\overline{X}}) = \overline{\overline{X}} - (A_2)(\overline{R}) \tag{4–5}$$

As determined earlier, $\overline{\overline{X}} = 5.010$ and $\overline{R} = 0.075$. Thus, the control limits are:

$$UCL_{\overline{X}} = 5.010 + (0.729)(0.075) = 5.010 + 0.055 = 5.065$$

$$LCL_{\overline{X}} = 5.010 - (0.729)(0.075) = 5.010 - 0.055 = 4.955$$

For the R chart, $\overline{R}$ becomes the center line. The three-sigma limits are determined with the D_4 and D_3 factors from Exhibit 4–22, using sample size $n = 4$:

$$UCL_R = (D_4)(\overline{R}) = (2.282)(0.075) = 0.171 \tag{4–6}$$

$$LCL_R = (D_3)(\overline{R}) = (0)(0.075) = 0 \tag{4–7}$$

The control chart limits have nothing to do with specification (tolerance) limits, which should not be drawn on control charts. Remember: $\overline{X}$ and R control charts are for averages and ranges of a multipiece sample. Specification limits, on the other hand, apply to one-at-a-time (piece-by-piece) measures.

Phase 3: Draw the control charts. Most companies use preprinted forms or computerized templates to facilitate control chart drawing. Basically, the center lines and control limits are drawn, and then the data, sample averages and ranges in this case, are plotted. Exhibit 4–23 shows the $\overline{X}$ and R charts. Note that on either side of the center line, the charts are divided into three zones, C, B, and A, from the center line outward. Those zones represent one, two, and three standard deviations of the sampling data and are used as operators analyze the charts.

Phase 4: Analysis of control chart data. There are many tests that can and should be applied to control chart data. Basically, they are all designed to answer one fundamental question: Is the process in control—output stable over time and thus free from special variation? If a process is in control, plotted averages and ranges should

---

[9]The tables are based on an assumed normal distribution.

EXHIBIT 4–23 $\overline{X}$ and R Charts: Injection-Molding Process

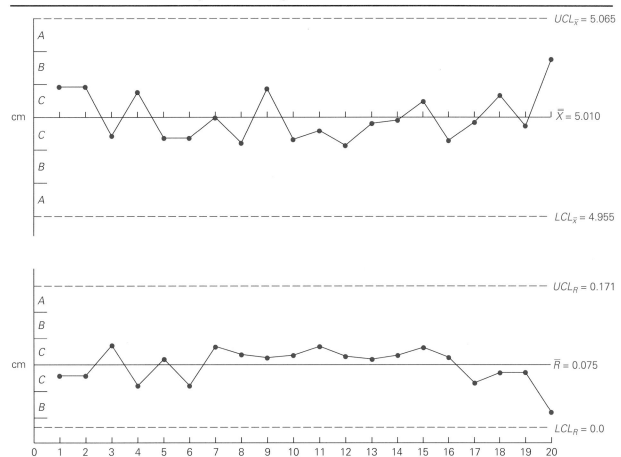

form small normal distributions within their (respective) sets of control limits. Since operators typically don't have enough data points to form those distributions, they rely on simple tests that may be used on limited data sets, such as our 20 samples. One popular set of tests is shown in Exhibit 4–24.

The first three tests are designed to reveal whether chart data conforms to expected normal distribution shape. The last four tests check to see if output is random, or free from any order that might show up if, for example, cycles or trends exist in the process. Let's see how our operators would apply the tests to their process control charts in Exhibit 4–23.

The first three tests pass; process output is close to center lines on both $\overline{X}$ and R charts. Furthermore, there are no runs up or down, so the fourth test passes as well. Test five fails, however, since 10 successive points are above the center line of the R chart. That usually signifies some shift in a process component, such as a different operator, new raw material lot, or a different measurement system (a new gauge, perhaps). Test six also fails on the $\overline{X}$ chart, since more than 15 successive points lie in Zone C; the operators would suspect mixing of process streams that are actually different. For example, the plastic injection molds might have multiple, and unintentionally nonidentical, cavities.

EXHIBIT 4–24   Tests for Process Control

A process is said to be out of statistical control if one or more of the following conditions occur on the process control chart:
1. One or more points falls outside Zone A; that is, outside the control limits.
2. Two of any three consecutive points fall outside Zone B.
3. Four of any consecutive five points fall outside Zone C.
4. Seven consecutive intervals either increase or decrease.
5. Eight or more consecutive points fall on the same side of the center line.
6. Fifteen consecutive points lie in Zone C.
7. Any obvious nonrandom patterns appear.

Phase 5: Check for causes of special variation. The control chart analysis revealed suspected sources of special variation. A process improvement team must investigate each one using various tools for improvement. Then, after appropriate process changes, they construct new control charts to confirm that the special causes are eliminated.

> Process control has nothing whatsoever to do with meeting specifications. A process may be in control and still produce totally unworthy output. Control means consistency only.

When process control is achieved, then what? The next step is investigation of process capability. We shall return to capability analysis for our injection-molding process after we examine two kinds of control charts for attributes data in Examples 4–4 and 4–5.

EXAMPLE 4–4   *p* CHART—BILLS OF LADING AT P*I*E NATIONWIDE[10]

The first use of process improvement tools at P*I*E Nationwide, fourth largest trucking company in the United States, was for billing errors. In eliminating special variation and bringing the billing process into statistical control, a P*I*E improvement team was able to eliminate all inspectors and cut the error rate from 10 percent to 0.8 percent in one year.

In the spirit of continual improvement, the team's next step was to use process control charting to track the proportion, *p*, of defective bills per day. That attribute, a defective bill, was defined as one having any type of error.

Phase 1: The first step with a *p* chart, as with any process control chart, is to make some decisions. The team decides on a sample size (*n*) of 50, to be taken every day for 20 days. Exhibit 4–25 summarizes the collected data.

Phase 2: Next, a team member calculates the chart center line ($\bar{p}$) and control limits ± 3σ from the center line. Since the **p chart** plots proportion defective, there are only two values for the attribute: good or bad (defective or nondefective). Thus, the binomial (two numbers) distribution applies. Sigma (σ) in the binomial distribution is:

> Attributes sample size is usually from 50 to a few hundred.

$$\sigma = \sqrt{\frac{\bar{p}(1 - \bar{p})}{n}}$$

where

$\bar{p}$ = Average (mean) fraction defective (or percent defective)
n = Number in each sample

Therefore, the control limits, at 3σ from the center line, $\bar{p}$, are:

[10]This is an actual case, with data slightly modified: Cort Dondero, ''SPC Hits the Road,'' *Quality Progress*, January 1991, pp. 43–44.

EXHIBIT 4–25   Attribute Inspection Data—Defective Bills

Day	Defective Bills	Proportion Defective	Day	Defective Bills	Proportion Defective
1	25	0.50	11	30	0.60
2	22	0.44	12	32	0.64
3	33	0.66	13	35	0.70
4	25	0.50	14	33	0.66
5	37	0.74	15	30	0.60
6	25	0.50	16	30	0.60
7	35	0.70	17	35	0.70
8	33	0.66	18	40	0.80
9	35	0.70	19	35	0.70
10	35	0.70	20	25	0.50
				Total 630	

$$UCL = \bar{p} + 3\sqrt{\frac{\bar{p}(1 - \bar{p})}{n}} \tag{4–8}$$

$$LCL = \bar{p} - 3\sqrt{\frac{\bar{p}(1 - \bar{p})}{n}} \tag{4–9}$$

The average fraction defective, $\bar{p}$, is total defectives divided by total items inspected, where total items inspected equals number of samples, k, times sample size, n:

$$\bar{p} = \frac{\text{Total defectives found}}{kn} \tag{4–10}$$

Since 630 defectives were found in 20 samples of 50 bills,

$$\bar{p} = \frac{630}{(20)(50)} = 0.63$$

The control limits are:

$$UCL = \bar{p} + 3\sqrt{\frac{\bar{p}(1 - \bar{p})}{50}}$$

$$= 0.63 + 3\sqrt{\frac{(0.63)(0.37)}{50}}$$

$$= 0.63 + 0.20 = 0.83$$

$$LCL = 0.63 - 0.20 = 0.43$$

Phase 3: The team member plots the points back on the chart. Exhibit 4–26 shows the resulting p chart. All points are within the control limits and all of the other tests of Exhibit 4–24 pass. If the process were out of control, bill processing associates would undertake a search for a special cause. For example, they might find an incomplete address for a major customer in computer memory. An address correction could reduce errors on days when that customer places several orders, or an associate may trace a pricing error back to a previous process, such as in sales.

Phase 4: Associates use the charts daily, watching them for an out-of-control condition that requires investigation and action. Meanwhile, the team employs other

EXHIBIT 4–26   *p* **Chart of Proportion of Defective Bills per Day**

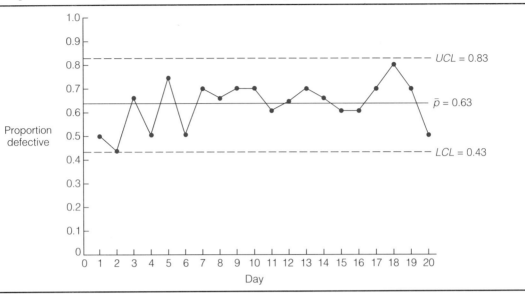

tools of process improvement in keeping up the attack on causes of defective bills and process variation. (With the aid of fishbone charting and Pareto analysis, the actual P*I*E team found "that 77% of the errors could be corrected by drivers during pickup and that only 23% were actual billing errors. The original error rate of 63% fell in less than a month to [below] 20% and was approaching 8%.")[11]

EXAMPLE 4–5   *c* CHART—HOTEL SUITE INSPECTION

A luxury hotel has five suites for visiting dignitaries and other VIPs—like operations management professors. As part of a TQM program, the housekeeping supervisor has implemented a program for daily inspection of those five suites immediately after housekeeping duties are performed. Housekeeping associates alternate inspection duties and record any deviation from established standards of excellence (a ruffled towel, wilting flowers, unstocked bar and refrigerator, etc.) as a defect. Daily the inspector records on a control chart the number of defects (*c*) found during the five-suite inspection.

Phase 1: As always, decisions about data collection are mostly defined by the circumstances. In this case, suites may be cleaned only at the guests' convenience, and the inspector must follow shortly thereafter. Defect totals apply to the entire five-suite inspection; Exhibit 4–27 shows those totals for a 26-day period.

Phase 2: Calculate center line and control limits. The center line ($\bar{c}$) is the sum of the defects found divided by the number of inspections (*k*, which should be at least 25). Here:

$$\bar{c} = \frac{\Sigma c}{k} = \frac{39}{26} = 1.50 \tag{4–11}$$

To get control limits, the supervisor needs to know the standard deviation. Since the basis for the **c chart** is the Poisson statistical distribution, rather than the binomial or normal, the formula for the standard deviation (σ) is very simple:

---

[11]Ibid.

EXHIBIT 4–27   Hotel Suite Inspection—Defects Discovered

Day	Defects	Day	Defects	Day	Defects
1	2	10	4	19	1
2	0	11	2	20	1
3	3	12	1	21	2
4	1	13	2	22	1
5	2	14	3	23	0
6	3	15	1	24	3
7	1	16	3	25	0
8	0	17	2	26	1
9	0	18	0		Total 39

$$\sigma = \sqrt{\bar{c}}$$

Thus the 3σ control limits are:

$$UCL = \bar{c} + 3\sqrt{\bar{c}} \qquad (4\text{–}12)$$

$$= 1.50 + 3(1.22)$$

$$= 5.16$$

$$LCL = \bar{c} - 3\sqrt{\bar{c}} \qquad (4\text{–}13)$$

$$= -2.16, \text{ or } 0^*$$

Next, the housekeeping personnel construct the process control chart (in much the same fashion as would be used with a p chart). They draw the center line and control limits and plot the 26 data points. Exhibit 4–28 shows the completed c chart. The process is within limits and does not violate any of the rules listed in Exhibit 4–24, so the group would conclude that the process is in control. The housekeeping supervisor and his staff, however, aren't satisfied with control; they want perfection.

Phase 3: Process improvement efforts continue. The group's ideas might include checklists to avoid forgetting, a closer supplier of freshly cut flowers (maybe just outside the hotel's front door), and prestocked bar and refrigerator shelves that are inserted each day and refilled at night.

Process Capability Analysis

The term **process capability** is a general statement of the ability of the process to meet specifications. Usually, process capability is expressed using one or more **process capability indexes;** perhaps the most popular is $\mathbf{C_{pk}}$. A process improvement team must know the specification for a quality characteristic and what the process output looks like before it can compute C_{pk}. The foundation for capability indexes, and perhaps a better understanding of their meaning, comes from a process capability graph.

Process Capability Graph.   To see how an improvement team could develop a process capability graph, let's return to the injection-molding process, used in Example 4–2 (run diagram) and Example 4–3 ($\bar{X}$ and R control charts). Assuming that injection-molding associates have attained process control, the only variation remaining in process output is

---

*There cannot be a negative control limit on attribute control charts.

Exhibit 4–28   *c* Chart for Hotel Suite Inspection

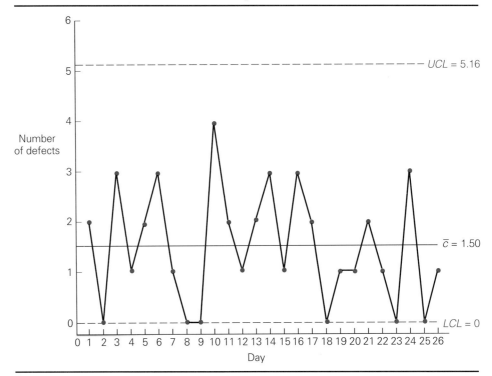

the natural or common variation. That variation, equal to six standard deviations (6σ) is referred to as the natural or inherent process capability. The team first determines inherent capability:

Since the standard deviation of process output is unknown, it is estimated as follows:

$$\hat{\sigma} = \bar{R}/d_2 \qquad (4\text{–}14)$$

where

$\hat{\sigma}$ = Estimate for σ

d_2 = Conversion factor found in quality control tables (see Exhibit 4–22); it is a function of sample size

From Exhibit 4–22, for a sample size (n) of 4, d_2 is 2.059; and from Example 4–3, $\bar{R}$ is 0.075 cm. Then:

$$\sigma = \frac{\bar{R}}{d_2} = \frac{0.075 \text{ cm}}{2.059} = 0.036 \text{ cm}$$

And the value for 6σ becomes:

$$6\sigma = 6 \,(0.036 \text{ cm}) = 0.216 \text{ cm}$$

This inherent capability, 0.216 cm, is a statement of variation only; it makes no claim as to location. Since process output location is already known, however (recall from Example 4–3 that the injection-molding process output is centered at 5.01 cm—the value

EXHIBIT 4-29   **Process Capability Graph: Injection Molding Process**

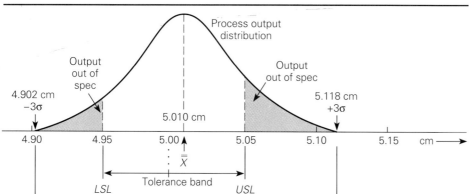

of $\overline{\overline{X}}$), the team can fully describe the expected process output distribution. It is centered at 5.01 cm and extends 3σ (0.108 cm) above (to 5.118 cm) and below (to 4.902 cm) that center.

To complete the process capability graph, the team adds the specification. In that outer diameter specification, 5.00 ± 0.05 cm, the tolerance band extends from the center (target) of 5.00 cm down to 4.95 cm and up to 5.05 cm. The allowable tolerance band is just 0.10 cm wide, much less than the inherent capability (0.216 cm) of the process. Exhibit 4-29 shows the process capability graph.

The shaded areas at each end represent molded parts that do not meet specifications. With the normal curve areas table (Appendix A), the team could compute the proportion of output that fails to meet specification. (We leave that for an end-of-chapter solved problem.)

C_{pk} Computation.   Improvement teams usually do not need to go to the extreme of constructing a figure such as Exhibit 4-29 in order to compare process output with specifications; they calculate C_{pk} instead. That index is a single number that conveys most of the information in Exhibit 4-29. The formula for C_{pk} is:

$$C_{pk} = \min\left(\frac{USL - \overline{\overline{X}}}{3\sigma}, \frac{\overline{\overline{X}} - LSL}{3\sigma}\right) \tag{4-15}$$

where

    USL = upper specification limit
    LSL = lower specification limit

If process output is not centered on the spec target, danger of out-of-spec output is greater at the nearer spec limit; hence, the focus on the minimum numerator value. In the present case, since $\overline{\overline{X}}$ (5.01) is closer to the upper limit than to the lower one, the minimum numerator is $(USL - \overline{\overline{X}})$, and the team calculates the value of C_{pk} as follows:

$$C_{pk} = \frac{5.05 - 5.01}{3(0.036)} = \frac{0.04}{0.108} = 0.37$$

$\mathscr{I}nto\ \mathscr{P}ractice$

Capability Index C_{pk}

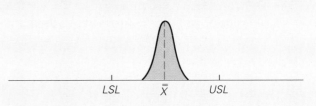

- If C_{pk} is negative, then $\overline{\overline{X}}$ is not within tolerance limits, indicating a very high defect rate; process improvement is urgently needed.

- If C_{pk} is positive but less than 1.0 — the case for the injection-molding process — the process is centered somewhere within the tolerance band but its width exceeds the tolerance band; again, serious work is needed, for some output is out of spec.

- If C_{pk} equals 1.0, the process just (barely) meets specs; it is centered somewhere within the tolerance band.

- If C_{pk} is greater than 1.0, all process output is within tolerances; the higher the value of C_{pk}, the better.

What does that value mean? Is it good or bad? The improvement team knows that — unfortunately for the customers or suppliers — it is a poor value for C_{pk}. It means that a large portion of the injection molding process output is not meeting specs, a discovery also evident in the process capability graph of Exhibit 4–29. In sum, C_{pk} reveals considerable process information, as the accompanying box shows.

C_{pk} shows not only whether process output is capable of meeting specs, it shows whether it does meet specs.

Some companies require their suppliers to show C_{pk} values of at least 1.33, a somewhat arbitrary indicator of acceptable performance. Teams increase C_{pk} in two ways. First, they improve process output location by getting the process average ($\overline{\overline{X}}$) closer to specs target. Second, they take actions to decrease variability (σ). Wouldn't capability also improve if they just extended the spec limits (widened the goal posts)? Yes, but that option is ridiculous. Continual improvement — better customer service — requires narrowing of spec limits, not extending them.

Why the persistent attack on process variability? Isn't it overkill, especially if C_{pk} satisfies customers? There are two reasons why improvement teams can't let up. First,

Into Practice

Variation Stackup

Isn't meeting specs enough? Not really. Output that meets specs may be unsatisfactory when the customer has to put it to use with other outputs. Variation stackup occurs when two or more outputs that must be used jointly each lie at the extremes of their spec limits. Consider this example:

- Door specification: 36.0 ± 0.25 inches.
  Frame specification: 36.5 ± 0.25 inches.

Even if all doors and frames are within their respective specs, one of the smaller doors placed within one of the larger frames results in gaps through which unwelcome weather passes. A larger door in a smaller frame? Well, there's lots of planing and sanding to do before the customer gets a good fit. Sorting and matching? That's just a time-consuming and expensive band-aid that doesn't solve the problem.

Variation stackup applies in services as well. Consider a municipal bus system:

- Commuters (riders): City specs—Get to bus stop up to five minutes before scheduled departure.

- Bus arrival time: City specs—Arrive at each stop no more than five minutes behind schedule.

If the commuter is five minutes early and the bus is five minutes late—which, "happens all too often," according to commuters—it's bad service. Just-in-time commuter plus early-departing bus? "Those @#&$%* buses!!!"

The best cure for these and other variation stackup problems is reduction of process variability. Make all doors close to 36.0 inches and all frames close to 36.5 inches. Put enough slack in the bus schedule so that busses are rarely late and set a rule that a bus may never leave a stop early. Northwest Airlines did exactly that in 1991 and went from being chronically late to having the best on-time performance of the major airlines operating in the United States.

The variation stackup problem is amplified in the mixing stages of continuous process production. Often several ingredients, not just two, are mixed together. Purities, specific gravities, and fineness of various liquid and solid ingredients may all be within specs, but on the high (or low) side. When mixed and processed, the result might be tacky rubber, cloudy glass, unstable chemicals, rough surfaces, crumbly pills, brittle plastic, or M&Ms that melt in your hands.

specifications limits are always somewhat arbitrary (even with maximum customer input). A customer might define *fresh fish* as fish caught that day, but would prefer fish caught within the hour, or even within a few minutes. Until the universe is perfect, quality is a matter of degree, though tolerance bands tend to make it yes-no (within specs, or not). No matter where one positions the spec limits, improvement can *always* be defined as getting more of the process outcomes closer to the target.

A second, and perhaps more practical, reason for continued improvement and narrower spec limits is a phenomenon called **variation stackup,** or tolerance stackup. The box provides details.

Precontrol Analysis

For companies that have many short production runs, gathering sufficient data for process control charts can be difficult. One option is **precontrol analysis,** a procedure that uses a set of simple rules to qualify a process as conforming to specifications or to guide process improvements until such qualification can be obtained.

Precontrol charts work directly with the tolerance band for a quality characteristic. Within the spec limits are lines setting off three zones on either side of the target; two outer red zones account for about 2 percent of the space, two yellow (middle) zones account for 23 percent each, and the innermost green zones take the final 50 percent (see

Exhibit 4–30   Precontrol Chart—Zones and Probabilities

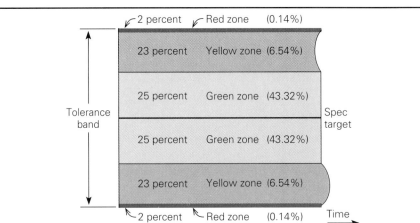

Exhibit 4–31   Precontrol Analysis—Rules for Implementation

1. Setup: Okay to run when five consecutive pieces are in green zone.
   a. If one in yellow zone, restart count (see No. 1).
   b. If two consecutive in yellow zone, adjust process and restart count.
   c. Return to setup (restart count) after any change in process components (any of the seven M's).
2. Running: Take two consecutive pieces (A and B) from process.
   a. If A is in green zone, continue to run.
   b. If A is in yellow zone, test B.
   c. If A and B are in yellow zone, stop and adjust process, return to step 1.
   d. If A or B are in red zone, stop and adjust process, return to step 1.
3. Continual improvement and process adjustments. Average six sample pairs between process adjustments. For example, if process adjustment occurs every eight hours, sample (two pieces) approximately every 80 minutes.

Source: Adapted from Dorian Shainin and Peter Shainin, "Precontrol versus $\overline{X}$&R Charting," *Quality Engineering* 1, no. 4 (1989), pp. 419–29.

Exhibit 4–30). If a process is centered at the spec target, and if its natural capability (6σ) is such that the process will fit within the spec limits, then the worst-case probabilities that pieces will fall into the respective zones are as shown in parentheses in Exhibit 4–30. If the process is narrower, the odds of a red zone occurrence are even lower.

Operators may apply precontrol rules during three phases of production: setup, running, and process adjustment for continuing improvement. After setup, an operator measures five consecutive pieces (on the quality characteristic of interest). After process qualification, the operator checks only two pieces at each test point. The rules are summarized in Exhibit 4–31.

In addition to reduced sampling and computational burden, precontrol is simple to implement. It uses spec limits rather than control limits, and spec limits are usually much easier to understand. Precontrol is not without its detractors, however. One criticism relates to precontrol's reduced level of inspection. Critics argue that precontrol doesn't reveal enough information about process behavior to guide process improvement. That same argument, however, might be leveled at control charts or any other tool used in isolation. Precontrol analysis, like all the rest, works best when it's integrated into a total effort, including a variety of coarse- and fine-grained analyses.

$\mathscr{C}$ontrast

Approach to Quality

Old Approach

- Worry about output volume first, and then worry about quality—when it becomes a problem.
- Produce large lots and rely on sampling inspection to accept or reject; sort to find good ones; scrap or rework bad ones.
- Declare some proportion defective (1–2 percent, perhaps) as acceptable quality level (AQL) and strive to meet that goal.

Superior Approach

- Everyone serves a customer and all customers want quality.
- Aim for fail-safe processes.
- Control processes for consistent output.
- Use capability analysis to guide continued efforts to improve processes.
- The only acceptable goal is zero defects.

Process Improvement in Perspective

Process improvement is a matter of attacking and reducing variation in output, that is, variation from the target itself and variation around the target. The approach applies to goods producers and service providers alike, for everyone has customers and all customers want quality. We might say that quality improvement efforts ought to grow in ever-widening circles because increasing use of all employees in empowered teams is the answer. Operators, engineers, lab technicians, sales representatives, and accountants—the list is as endless as the jobs people do—can and must take process improvement as a personal and team goal. The task cannot be delegated.

Summary

The responsibility for quality rests with the makers of products and providers of services. Team and individual actions that carry out that responsibility include process control, inspection and early warning, and continuing improvement. Time and quality are interrelated: better quality speeds up delivery and service to customers, and quick, delay-free response enables teams to attack causes for poor quality while the trail is still hot. Also, time taken for fail-safing, training, and other improvements enhances quality and removes delay-causing wastes. Small quality departments consisting of highly skilled professionals serve as facilitators and back-up to front-line associates in competitive organizations. Inspection's role is declining as emphasis shifts toward efficient, timely discovery of problem causes.

Modern quality management takes a process focus. Transformation processes are complex, consisting of materials, manpower, methods, machines, measurement, maintenance, and management. Process performance yields quality characteristics. Studying the distributions of those characteristics is at the heart of process improvement. Process output may exhibit common cause and special cause variation; when the latter is eliminated by removing assignable causes, the process is said to be in control or stable. Typically, those working closest to a process are better able to remove special cause variation, but management action (e.g., expenditures for new equipment) is often needed to reduce common cause variation. Process output may be viewed as variables data, where the degree of presence of a quality characteristic is measured, or as attributes data, where output is merely classified and counted.

Process improvement is guided by the scientific method. A growing collection of general, coarse-grained, and fine-grained tools are of proven help at each stage. General tools include team-building, group-interaction skills and specific process technology knowledge. Coarse-grained tools are the process flowchart, check sheets and histograms, Pareto analysis, fishbone charts, fail-safing, experimentation, and scattergrams. Fine-grained tools include run diagrams, process control charts, precontrol analysis, and process capability analysis. Many improvement efforts are accomplished with the general-level and coarse-grained tools alone, but more persistent problems may also require fine-grained tools.

In coarse-grained analysis and improvement, the focus is on the flow or relationships of materials, documents, or people. Data-sorting efforts to identify targets of opportunity also characterize this level of improvement. The process flowchart identifies each step in a process for analysis that detects the cause of error. Check sheets and histograms are simple, quick data collection and presentation tools. Pareto analysis arranges problems or possible causes in decreasing order and thus focuses attention on the most immediately promising targets of opportunity. Fishbone charts help teams break problems down into manageable segments of cause-effect linkages. Experiments support front-line efforts by testing the underlying relationships among variables. Fail-safing is a mind-set of prevention; it aids in both design and improvement efforts. The scatter diagram correlates behavior of one variable (such as a quality characteristic) with that of another (perhaps a deliberate team action on process components).

Fine-grained analysis affords a closer look at quality characteristic behavior. The run diagram is a plot of consecutive (or at least sequential) units of output. Comparison to spec limits is straightforward. Process control charts typically show plots of statistics taken from samples of process output and compared to computed control limits. $\bar{X}$ and R charts are the most widely used of the variables control charts. The $\bar{X}$ chart shows between-sample variation, while the R chart shows within-sample variation. Popular attributes control charts include the p chart (for proportion defective in samples) and the c chart (for number of defects in a sample, typically of one unit). Process capability analysis compares process output with specifications. The natural process width (6σ) is referred to as the inherent capability. Capability indexes such as C_{pk} combine in a single number most of the information of a process capability graph. Companies often set minimum values of C_{pk} for their suppliers to maintain. Precontrol analysis is viewed by some as a cheaper, faster alternative to control charts. One form compares a small number of process output units to specification limits in order to qualify the process as conforming to specs.

Process improvement at any level is a matter of attacking and reducing variation in output. It ought to occur in ever-widening teams of empowered employees dedicated to continuous improvement.

Key Words

Connector leads for electronic ignition components are produced to a specification of 8.000 ± 0.010 cm. The process has been studied, and the following values have been obtained:

$$\text{Process average} = \overline{\overline{X}} = 8.003 \text{ cm}$$

$$\text{Standard deviation (estimate)} = \hat{\sigma} = 0.002 \text{ cm}$$

Problem 1

Calculate:

a. The inherent process capability
b. The capability index C_{pk}

a. Inherent process capability $= 6 \times \hat{\sigma}$
$\qquad\qquad\qquad\qquad\qquad\quad = 6 \times 0.002 \text{ cm}$
$\qquad\qquad\qquad\qquad\qquad\quad = 0.012 \text{ cm}$

Solution 1

b. Since the process average (8.003 cm) is closer to the upper spec limit than to the lower, the appropriate form of Equation 4–15 (with values inserted) is:

$$C_{pk} = \frac{USL - \overline{\overline{X}}}{3\sigma} = \frac{8.010 - 8.003}{3(0.002)} = 1.167$$

The value of C_{pk} is greater than 1.0, so all process output meets spec. Some buyers in today's marketplace, however, would not be satisfied with so low a value. A process improvement team needs to take a look.

Samples of 180 units are drawn from production in order to construct a *p* chart. Develop the chart for the following 16 samples of percentages defective. Is the chart satisfactory for use on the production line? Explain.

Problem 2

Sample	Percent Defective	Sample	Percent Defective	Sample	Percent Defective	Sample	Percent Defective
1	2	5	1	9	6	13	4
2	5	6	0	10	2	14	3
3	5	7	2	11	7	15	2
4	3	8	2	12	1	16	3

First, calculate $\bar{p}$, *UCL* and *LCL,* using Equations 4–8 through 4–10.

Solution 2

$$\bar{p} = \frac{\text{Total percent defective}}{k}$$

$$= \frac{2 + 5 + 5 + 3 + 1 + 0 + 2 + 2 + 6 + 2 + 7 + 1 + 4 + 3 + 2 + 3}{16}$$

$$= \frac{48}{16} = 3 \text{ percent, or } 0.03$$

$$UCL = \bar{p} + 3\sqrt{\frac{\bar{p}(1 - \bar{p})}{n}} = 0.03 + 3\sqrt{\frac{0.03(0.97)}{180}} = 0.068$$

$$LCL = \bar{p} - 3\sqrt{\frac{\bar{p}(1 - \bar{p})}{n}} = 0.03 - 0.038 = -0.08, \text{ or } 0$$

Next, develop a chart and plot the 16 data points on it:

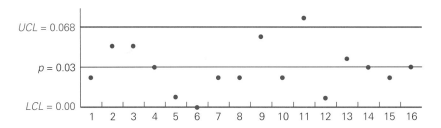

The chart is not satisfactory. Sample 11 is above the *UCL,* which indicates that the process is unstable, out of statistical control. Look for a special cause, eliminate it, and try again.

Problem 3

I. B. Poorly is director of Employee Wellness Programs for Alpine Escapes, a chain of winter sports resorts. He knows that Alpine's employee health care costs have risen 78 percent in the last three years. Absenteeism, low productivity, and poor attitudes (especially in the presence of customers) are other symptoms of poor health among employees. I. B. organized a largely volunteer process improvement team to turn things around. The team interviewed and tested a sample of 60 Alpine employees and recorded health problems on a checksheet. Join I. B.'s team and show how process improvement tools might be used to systematically tackle the health improvement task at Alpine.

Solution 3

First, analyze the following checksheet:

Health Problem	Occurrences	Total	Health Problem	Occurences	Total
Poor sleep habits	///// ////	9	Smoking	///// ///// ///// ///	18
High cholesterol	///// ///// ////	14	Overweight	///// ///// ///// ///// ///// ///// ///// /	36
High blood pressure	///// ///// ///// //	17	Alcohol abuse	///// ///	8
Poor circulation	////	4	Other problems	///// /	6

Clearly, some of the 60 members of the sample had more than one health problem, and perhaps there are interrelationships among the listed ills. A systematic approach, however, would call for early analysis of the most frequently occurring problem. Thus, the team ought to focus on weight by making it the spine of a fishbone chart. Such a chart, including some of the team's brainstorming (possible causes and effects), is sketched here:

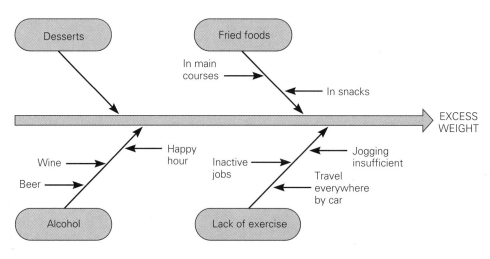

Each end point on the fishbone chart suggests action. The team might use process control charts to track percentage of employees who succumb to various poor health habits (snacks, no exercise, smoking, etc.). Effects of process interventions such as healthy cafeteria food, flexible work hours, exercise periods, and so forth, ought to show up on the charts.

Also, Pareto analysis could be used for the "jogging insufficient" end point. The accompanying Pareto chart provides concrete data on specific reasons for insufficient jogging. In this case, the dominant cause, "skipped entirely," might be used as the spine for another, finer fishbone analysis indicating reasons for skipping (e.g., bad weather or working late).

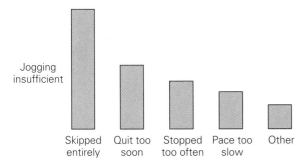

Problem 4

The fill process for nine-ounce bottles of Island Sunscreen Lotion is under scrutiny by a process improvement team. Sample averages and ranges from 20 samples of four bottles each are shown in the table below. Construct $\overline{X}$ and R charts and analyze the information given by the charts.

Sample Number	Average (Oz.)	Range (Oz.)	Sample Number	Average (Oz.)	Range (Oz.)
1	9.025	0.2	11	9.025	0.3
2	9.050	0.1	12	9.100	0.2
3	9.100	0.3	13	9.125	0.3
4	9.100	0.3	14	9.150	0.5
5	9.000	0.5	15	8.950	0.2
6	9.025	0.3	16	9.000	0.5
7	9.050	0.4	17	9.025	0.2
8	9.075	0.1	18	9.100	0.2
9	9.000	0.2	19	9.050	0.1
10	8.975	0.3	20	9.075	0.4

Solution 4

Following the procedure used in Example 4–3, calculate center lines and control limits for both $\overline{X}$ and R charts. First, the centerline for the averages chart:

$$\overline{\overline{X}} = \frac{\Sigma \overline{X}}{k} = \frac{181}{20} = 9.05 \text{ oz.}$$

For the ranges chart:

$$\overline{R} = \frac{\Sigma R}{k} = \frac{5.6}{20} = 0.28 \text{ oz.}$$

Next, (using factors from Exhibit 4–22) control limits for the averages chart:

$$UCL_{\overline{X}} = \overline{\overline{X}} + A_2\overline{R} = 9.05 + (0.729)(0.28) = 9.25 \text{ oz.}$$

$$LCL_{\overline{X}} = \overline{\overline{X}} - A_2\overline{R} = 9.05 - (0.729)(0.28) = 8.85 \text{ oz.}$$

Limits for the ranges chart:

$$UCL_R = D_4(\bar{R}) = 2.282(0.28) = 0.64 \text{ oz.}$$

$$LCL_R = D_3(\bar{R}) = 0(0.28) = 0$$

Place the center lines and control limits on the respective $\bar{X}$ and R charts and then plot the sample averages and ranges. The charts illustrate.

AVERAGES CHART

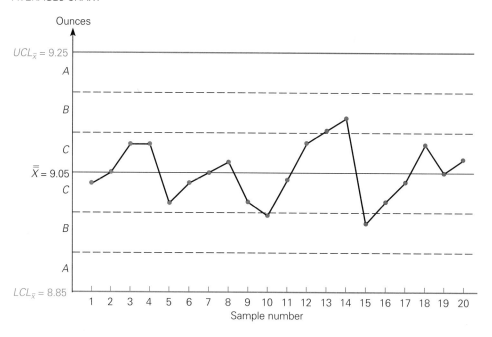

RANGES CHART

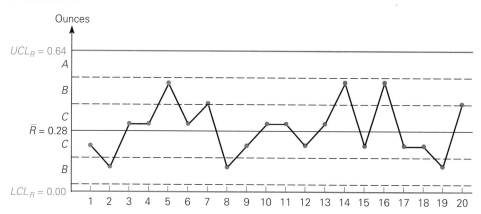

Comparison of chart patterns with tests for process control (Exhibit 4–24) reveals that all tests pass with the possible exception of test 7, obvious nonrandom patterns. On the $\bar{X}$ chart, cycling appears with a four-to-five sample period. In a close call like this, the team must examine the process environment to see what might be happening to cause such a cycle (perhaps the on-off cycling of large motors such as air-conditioners are affecting the lotion-filling machines). If a special cause for the apparent pattern is found, it must be eliminated.

The cycling might disappear on its own after a few more samples, and if stability continues, the team will begin capability analysis by comparing process output to specifications.

Quicksand Fidelity Life Insurance Company is getting serious about improving its service to customers. In addition to some image changes (a new name?), Quicksand has a customer service improvement team going after substantial process changes. Customer surveys revealed two major gripes: incorrect information in account records and excessive delay in records retrieval when customers phone in for service. The team recommended a new account information system; it is being installed and customer account records are being converted.

Problem 5

To track file accuracy, the improvement team randomly selected a converted account at two-day intervals during the installation, and verified the information in the record by contacting customers. The table below shows the number of errors in each sampled account. As a member of the team, your job is to use the data to construct a *c* chart and discuss its implications.

Sample Number	Errors	Sample Number	Errors	Sample Number	Errors	Sample Number	Errors
1	2	5	2	9	0	13	2
2	0	6	3	10	4	14	3
3	3	7	1	11	2	15	1
4	1	8	0	12	1	16	3

First, use Equations 4–11 through 4–13 to calculate the center line and control limits for the *c* chart. The center line is:

Solution 5

$$\bar{c} = \frac{\Sigma c}{k} = \frac{28}{16} = 1.75 \text{ errors}$$

Control limits are:

$$UCL = \bar{c} + 3\sqrt{\bar{c}} = 1.75 + 3\sqrt{1.75} = 5.72$$

$$LCL = \bar{c} - 3\sqrt{\bar{c}} = 1.75 - 3\sqrt{1.75} = -2.22, \text{ or } 0$$

Next, develop the chart and plot the sample data on it:

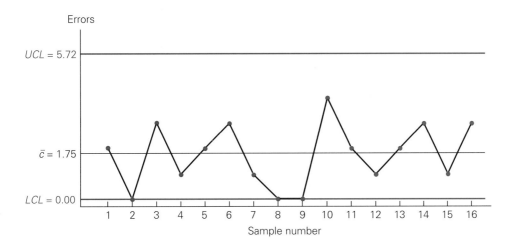

This problem is adapted from the authors' experiences with real-world information systems installations and conversions.

The chart shows a stable process that is in control. But it is important to reemphasize that *control* is not the aim. In this case, control merely shows that errors aren't getting worse. However, improvement is what the team wants. It looks as if the account conversion process is simply making what is already in the customer accounts compatible with the new information system.

Maybe the new system corrects the delay problem (screens of account information now appear faster when customers call in), but remember the other gripe. The *c* chart suggests that during the roughly one-month installation period, little was done to improve record accuracy. The team has work to do.

A final point: The analysis included only 16 samples (of one record each), 9 less than the recommended number of 25 for *c* charts. Does that make it invalid? Not at all. The idea is to listen to the process and make improvements as early as possible; there's no need for the team to wait longer at Quicksand.

Problem 6

Exhibit 4–29 is the process capability graph for the injection-molding process discussed in Example 4–3. The improvement team has asked you to compute the percentage of molding process output that fails to meet specifications and to comment on the implications.

Solution 6

Use the normal curve areas (see Table A–1 in Appendix A) to find the proportion of output that lies beyond each spec limit; that is, the areas that are shaded in Exhibit 4–29.
Recall from Example 4–3 that the process center is: $\overline{\overline{X}} = 5.01$ cm
Also, from Equation 4–14, σ is estimated as: $\sigma = 0.036$ cm
To use Table A–1, find the number of standard deviations (called *z* values) that each spec limit lies from $\overline{\overline{X}}$, the process average. The formula is:

$$z = \frac{\text{spec limit} - \overline{\overline{X}}}{\sigma}$$

Two *z* values are needed, one for each spec limit:

$$z_{LSL} = \frac{4.95 - 5.01}{0.036} = -1.67$$

$$z_{USL} = \frac{5.05 - 5.01}{0.036} = 1.11$$

From Table A–1, read directly the area between the distribution average and the *z* values. Then subtract each of those areas from 0.5, the area in half the distribution. The remainder is the area or proportion (or, for present purposes, percentage of output) that lies outside the respective spec limit. For the lower spec limit:

Table area = 0.4525, so $(0.5 - 0.4525) = 0.0475$, or 4.75 percent

For the upper spec limit:

Table area = 0.3665, so $(0.5 - 0.3665) = 0.1335$, or 13.35 percent

Add the two out-of-spec percentages, to get the total for the molding process:

$(4.75) + (13.35) = 18.1$ percent of output fails to meet specs

In your report to the improvement team, you might mention something about getting that errant output within specs—a free 18-percent boost in capacity! Tell the team about the key goal in all process improvement: Hit the target, the first time and every time!

For Further Reference

Books

Brassard, Michael. *The Memory Jogger Plus+* ™. Methuen, Mass.: GOAL/QPC, 1989.

Continuing Process Control and Process Capability Improvement. Dearborn, Mich.: Ford Motor Company, 1983.

DeVor, Richard E.; Tsong-how Chang; and John W. Sutherland. *Statistical Quality Design and Control.* New York: Macmillan, 1992 (TS156.D53).

Duncan, Acheson J. *Quality Control and Industrial Statistics,* 5th ed. Homewood, Ill.: Richard D. Irwin, Inc., 1986.

Juran, J. M., and Frank M. Gryna, eds. *Juran's Quality Control Handbook.* New York: McGraw-Hill, 1988.

Montgomery, Douglas C. *Introduction to Statistical Quality Control,* 2nd ed. New York: John Wiley & Sons, 1991 (TS156.M64).

Statistical Quality Control Handbook, 2nd ed. Indianapolis: AT&T Technologies, 1956.

Periodicals/Societies

Journal of Quality Technology, American Society for Quality Control (ASQC).

Quality, a Hitchcock publication.

Quality Engineering (ASQC).

Quality Progress (ASQC).

Technometrics (ASQC).

Review Questions

1. As TQM takes hold in a firm, how should emphasis shift among process control, inspection and early warning, and process improvement (the three actions for quality operations in Exhibit 4–1)?
2. Explain the time-quality connection.
3. What are the likely roles of quality departments in the future? What is the changing nature of inspection?
4. How does the process focus serve to reduce micromanagement?
5. What is a transformation process? How might process performance be described in terms of quality characteristics?
6. What is the difference between special cause variation and common cause variation? How do they relate to process control and process capability? How is each type of variation dealt with in improvement programs?
7. How do variables data differ from attributes data? Give examples of both.
8. What is the scientific method? What is its purpose in process improvement efforts?
9. What tools are commonly used in process improvement? Describe each.
10. How do flowcharts help identify value-adding transformations?
11. How is fail-safing used in improvement efforts?
12. How might check sheets and histograms complement one another in process improvement?
13. How might Pareto analysis and fishbone diagrams complement one another in process improvement?
14. How is a scatter diagram used in process control and improvement?
15. What are the roles of run diagrams and process control charts in improvement programs? What are the similarities and differences?
16. How do specifications and tolerances figure into process control? process capability?
17. In control charting for variables, why use two charts (e.g., $\overline{X}$ and R, or $\overline{X}$ and c)?
18. Compare and contrast $\overline{X}$, R, p, and c charts and their uses.
19. What are the tests for process control? How are they applied?

20. What does a process capability graph show? Is the same information given by the inherent capability? Explain.

21. What is C_{pk}? Discuss the meaning of different values for that index.

22. What is variation stackup? How does it affect good output? How might the effects of variation stackup be diminished?

23. What is precontrol analysis? How does it compare with run diagrams? control charts?

Problems and Exercises

1. Fix-M-Up, Inc., is a small chain of stores that clean and repair typewriters, photocopiers, and other office equipment. Define a process for the company along the lines of that discussed in the chapter for the manufacture of three-inch bolts. Prepare a list of quality characteristics you might wish to use if you were considering using Fix-M-Up as the maintenance contractor for your company's office equipment.

2. A food processing company has large tanks that are cleaned daily. Cleaning includes the use of packaged detergents, which dissolve in a solution inside the tanks. Detergent packages are purchased with a fill-weight specification of 12.00 ± 0.08 oz.

    A vendor representative claims that his company uses statistical process control and will promise an inherent process capability of 0.20 oz. for the fill-weight specification. The vendor's brochure says nothing else about the process except that the advertised weight of the detergent packages is 12 oz.

    a. Should the food processor buy detergent from this vendor? Why or why not?

    b. If the vendor had control chart evidence that its fill-weight process was in fact centered at 12.00 oz. and was in a state of statistical control, how would your answer to question *a* change? Does all output meet specs?

    c. Suppose the vendor is a reliable supplier of other products and can reasonably be expected to improve the detergent-packaging process. What advice would you offer to the food processor on seeking alternate suppliers? What advice would you offer the vendor regarding the relationship with the food processor?

3. Plug-N-Go, Ltd., makes valve covers to a diameter specification of 0.500 ± 0.020 cm. The normally distributed process is in control, centered at 0.505 cm, and has an inherent process capability of 0.024 cm. The process distribution is as follows:

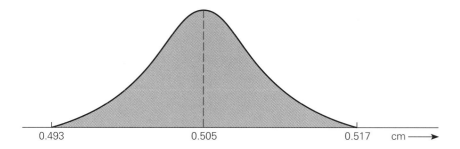

a. Calculate the process capability index C_{pk}.

b. Should Plug-N-Go be concerned about reducing the variation in the diameter process output? Why or why not?

4. Suppose the valve cover process in problem 3 is in control but centered at 0.510 cm. The inherent process capability and the diameter specification are as given in problem 3. The process would appear as:

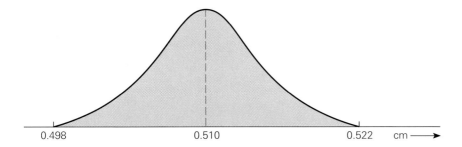

0.498   0.510   0.522   cm ⟶

    a. Calculate C_{pk}.

    b. Use Appendix A (areas under the normal curve) to determine what proportion, if any, of the valve covers would fall outside the specifications.

    c. What action, if any, should Plug-N-Go take regarding the valve cover process?

5. Wonderful Wisconsin Cheese Company packages 16 ounce chunks of longhorn cheese. Associates have designed $\overline{X}$ and R charts: $\overline{\overline{X}}$ is at 16.09 ounces, with $UCL_{\overline{X}}$ = 16.25 and $LCL_{\overline{X}}$ = 15.93; $\overline{R}$ is at 0.376 ounces, with UCL_R = 0.723 and LCL_R = 0.

    a. What sample size (n) would have been used? (It may be calculated.)

    b. Although the cheese packages are labeled as 16-ounce chunks, $\overline{\overline{X}}$ = 16.09. What is a reasonable explanation for the difference?

6. An improvement team for a medical supply manufacturer subjects hypodermic needles to a bend test, and the results, in grams, are plotted on $\overline{X}$ and R charts. A suitable number of samples have been inspected. The resulting $\overline{\overline{X}}$ is 26.1, and the resulting $\overline{R}$ is 5.0.

    a. For n = 8, calculate the control limits for the control charts.

    b. What should be done with the data calculated in question *a?*

    c. Assume that process control charts have been developed for the above data and that the operator has been using the charts regularly. For one sample of hypodermics, $\overline{X}$ = 26.08 and R = 0.03. Should there be an investigation for a special cause? Explain.

7. Spark-O-Plenty, Inc., periodically takes random samples, each with a sample size of six, from a production line that manufactures one-half-volt batteries. The sampled batteries are tested on a voltmeter. The production line has just been modified, and a new quality control plan must be designed. For that purpose, 10 random samples (of 6 each) have been taken over a suitable period of time; the test results are as follows:

Sample Number	Tested Voltages					
	V_1	V_2	V_3	V_4	V_5	V_6
1	0.498	0.492	0.510	0.505	0.504	0.487
2	0.482	0.491	0.502	0.481	0.496	0.492
3	0.501	0.512	0.503	0.499	0.498	0.511
4	0.498	0.486	0.502	0.503	0.510	0.501
5	0.500	0.507	0.509	0.498	0.512	0.518
6	0.476	0.492	0.496	0.521	0.505	0.490
7	0.511	0.522	0.513	0.518	0.520	0.516
8	0.488	0.512	0.501	0.498	0.492	0.498
9	0.482	0.490	0.510	0.500	0.495	0.482
10	0.505	0.496	0.498	0.490	0.485	0.499

    a. Compute and draw the appropriate process control chart(s) for the data.

    b. What should be done next? Discuss.

8. An associate measures current loss in a circuit and plots the means of sample measurements on an existing process control chart. Most of the means fall below the lower control limit—less current loss than before. What is the implication of this on such factors as pricing, marketing, purchasing, production, training, design, and control charts?

9. A process improvement team at Hang-M-High, a manufacturer of coat hangers, decided what constitutes a defective hanger. Samples of 200 hangers were inspected on each of the last 20 days. The numbers of defectives found are given below. Construct a *p* chart for the data. What should the team do next? Explain.

Day	Number Defective	Day	Number Defective	Day	Number Defective	Day	Number Defective
1	22	6	16	11	21	16	24
2	17	7	12	12	21	17	14
3	14	8	11	13	20	18	8
4	18	9	6	14	13	19	15
5	25	10	16	15	19	20	12

10. OK-Mart, a chain retailer, contracts with Electro Corporation to manufacture an OK brand of photo flashbulb. OK-Mart states that it wants an average quality of 99 percent good flashbulbs, that is, 99 percent that actually flash. Electro's marketing manager states that their goal should be for 99.9 percent to flash (better than OK-Mart's stated goal). After production begins at Electro, sampling on the production line over a representative time period shows 0.2 percent defective.

    a. Where should the center line be drawn on a process control chart? Why?

    b. What, if anything, needs to be done about the differences between goals and actual quality?

11. Exhibit 4–10 shows flowcharts of a travel authorization process, one before improvements and the other after. What principles of operations management were used to improve the process? State specifically how each principle you list was beneficial.

12. Rescue Services Training (RST) trains emergency rescue squads for state, county, and municipal police and fire departments. The training program development and improvement group at RST evaluates company training effectiveness, in part, by performance of trainee teams on the Simulated Emergency Rescue Exercise (SERE). During the SERE, trainee teams may err by omitting required steps as well as by committing acts that they shouldn't. The training group records total errors for each team. The table shows error data for the last 25 trainee teams:

SERE Team	Errors	SERE Team	Errors	SERE Team	Errors	SERE Team	Errors	SERE Team	Errors
1	4	6	1	11	3	16	3	21	3
2	3	7	4	12	7	17	6	22	2
3	11	8	3	13	4	18	4	23	4
4	2	9	2	14	1	19	4	24	1
5	6	10	4	15	8	20	12	25	3

    a. Plot the error data on a *c* chart.

    b. Analyze the chart and comment on process stability.

    c. Prepare a list of recommendations to the training program development and improvement group.

13. The training program development and improvement group at RST (see problem 12) suspects that the SERE error rate may depend on experience level, that is, trainee team members' years on-the-job in police or fire departments before coming to RST's program. How might that suspicion be investigated? Be specific in the tools and procedures that you recommend.

14. As a member of a process quality improvement team, you are evaluating vendor performance in meeting your specifications. A machined part from Ajax Components has a C_{pk} value of 2.0. Sketch a process capability graph for the component. Discuss.

15. Guarantee Seed Company applies process control charting to germination rates on its line of seeds. For one new type of seed, the inspection plan is to pull out samples of 100 seeds and test them to determine the germination rate. After production starts up, five samples of 100 are drawn, containing 1, 3, 3, 3, and 5 seeds that will not germinate. Calculate the center line and upper and lower control limits for a process control chart of germination rates. (Note: Usually 20 or more samples are taken to produce the charts, but in this problem use only 5 to simplify calculations.)

16. A pottery manufacturing firm constructs process control charts. Thirty pottery samples are taken, and the mean proportion of pottery samples that fail a strength test is 0.02, which becomes the center line on a *p* chart. Control limits are put in place, and the 30 defect rates are plotted on the chart. Two of the 30 fall above the upper control limit, but all 30 meet the requirements of the major customer, a department store. Explain the situation. What should be done?

17. Redraw the following chart. Fill in your chart to show the type of tool that could be suitable for each of the products on the left. Briefly explain each of your answers.

	Run Diagram	$\overline{X}$ and R Chart	p Chart	c Chart
Alcoholic content in beer batches				
Billiard balls—ability to withstand force in a destructive test				
Vibration of electric motor right after a process improvement				
New electronic component				
Number of fans that do not turn when plugged in				
Percentage of lenses having a scratch				
Number of scratches per table surface				

18. Orville's Ready-Pop Popcorn is packaged in jars. The jars are supposed to contain a certain quantity of popcorn, and the fill-machine operator inspects for quantity using statistical process control. Which of these three process control charting methods—X/R, p, and c charts—could or could not be used for process control of this product? Explain.

19. Explain why each of the three process control inspection techniques listed in problem 18 could be used in inspecting tabletops.

20. American Pen and Pencil (AmPen) has had most of the market for ball-point pens, but now it is under great pressure from a competitor whose product is clearly superior. AmPen operators have identified several quality problems, including viscosity of ink, which is affected by the temperature of the mixing solution; purity of powdered ink and amount of water; the ball-point assembly, which is affected by ball diameter, ball roundness, and trueness of the tube opening into which the ball goes; and strength of the clip, which is affected by the thickness of the metal and the correctness of the shape after stamping.
    a. Draw a fishbone chart for these ball-point pen factors. How should the chart be used?
    b. An inspection procedure at the ink-mixing stage reveals that 80 percent of bad samples are caused by impurities, 15 percent by wrong temperature, and 5 percent by wrong amount of water. Draw a Pareto chart. How should it be used?

21. A waiter is trying to determine the factors that increase tips. Some of his ideas are how long it takes to serve, how many words he speaks to a table of patrons, how long it takes the kitchen to fill the order, time between taking away dishes and bringing the check, and how far the table is from the kitchen.
    a. Arrange these few factors into a logical fishbone chart. Explain your chart.
    b. Which of the factors is likely to plot on a scatter diagram as an upside-down U? Explain.

22. Some mathematics instructors and students are developing a fishbone chart on how to improve the average math score on the Scholastic Aptitude Test (SAT). So far, the chart is as shown below; only the primary bone, "materials and machines," is filled out.
    a. Fill out the rest of the primary bones with reasonable cause and subcause arrows.
    b. Suggest three actions to be taken next.

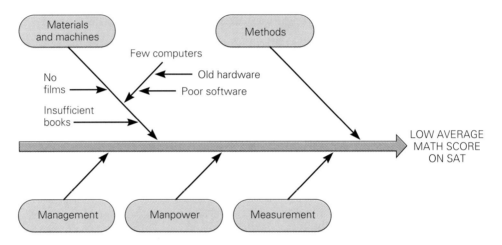

23. Following is a scatter diagram showing inches of deviation from the correct length of wooden blinds and humidity in the shop.
    a. What does the shape of the scattered points indicate?
    b. Sharpness of the saw blade is also known to affect the correctness of blind length. Make a drawing of how the scatter for those two factors (sharpness and deviation of length) would probably look.

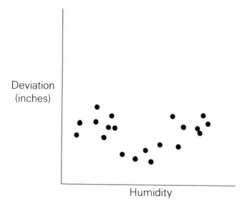

24. A listing of products/services follows. Select two from each column and do the following:
    a. For each of your four selections, decide on two attributes and/or variables that you think are most suitable for inspection. Explain your reasoning.
    b. Discuss whether a formal statistical sampling method or an informal inspection method is more sensible for each selection.

Column 1	Column 2
Telephone	Auto tire mounting
Ball-point pen	Bookbinding
Pocket calculator	Data entry
Dice	Proofreading
Space heater	Wallpaper hanging
Electric switch	Library reference services
Glue	Nursing care
Bottle of cola	Food catering
Watch	Cleanliness of dishes
Handgun	Bank teller service
Light bulb	Roadside rest stop

25. An office furniture manufacturer (which employees 1,000 people) is planning to adopt a total quality program. Following are some characteristics of its present production system:
    a. There is a quality assurance department of 50 people, including 30 inspectors.
    b. Rejected products discovered at the end of final assembly are sent by conveyor to a rework area staffed by 120 people.
    c. All purchased raw materials and parts are inspected on the receiving docks using acceptance sampling.
    d. All direct laborers are paid by how much they produce, which is measured daily.
    What changes would you suggest? Discuss.

26. Suggest a fail-safe device that could be used at a popcorn stand to prevent too many unpopped kernels from ending up in customers' bags.

27. Suggest a fail-safing approach for each of the following problems:
    a. Forgetting to set the alarm clock.
    b. Missing appointments.
    c. Running out of gas.
    d. Not having correct change for unattended tollway exit booths.
    e. Losing one sock, earring, or glove from a (matching) pair.

28. Give two examples of tolerance stackup for a goods producer.

29. Give two examples of variation stackup for a services provider.

CASE STUDY

AMERICAN CERAMIC AND GLASS PRODUCTS CORPORATION

The American Ceramic and Glass Products Corporation employed approximately 13,000 people, each of its three plants employing between 4,000 and 5,000 of this total. About three quarters of its sales volume came from standard glass containers produced on highly automatic equipment; the balance of the company's sales were of specialized ceramic and glass items made in batches on much less automated equipment. John Parr, production manager for American Ceramic and Glass Products, had just completed a trip that covered eight states, seven universities, and three major industrial centers. The purpose of his trip was to recruit personnel for American's three plants. He

Source: Adapted from Robert C. Meier, Richard A. Johnson, William T. Newell, and Albert N. Schrieber, *Cases in Production and Operations Management* (Englewood Cliffs, N.J.: Prentice-Hall, Inc. 1982), pp. 8–18. Copyright 1982 by Prentice-Hall, Inc. Reprinted by permission.

felt that his trip had been extremely successful. He had made contacts that would, he hoped, result in his firm's acquiring some useful and needed personnel.

Parr was anxious to hire a capable person to head up the inspection and quality control department of the largest of American's plants, located in Denver, Colorado. The position of chief of inspection and quality control had just been vacated by George Downs, who had taken an indefinite leave of absence due to a serious illness. There was little chance that Downs would be able to resume any work duties within a year and a substantial chance that he would never be capable of working on a full-time basis. During the 10 years that Downs was chief of inspection and quality control, he had completely modernized the firm's inspection facilities and had developed a training program in the use of the most modern inspection equipment and techniques. The physical facilities of Downs's inspection department were a major attraction for visitors to the plant.

Thomas Calligan

During his trip, Parr interviewed two men who he felt were qualified to fill Downs's position. Although each appeared more than qualified, Parr felt that a wrong choice could easily be made. Thomas Calligan, the first of the two men, was a graduate of a reputable trade school and had eight years of experience in the inspection department of a moderately large manufacturing firm (approximately 800 employees). He began working as a production inspector and was promoted to group leader within two years and chief inspector two years later. His work record as a production inspector, as a group leader, and as chief inspector was extremely good. His reason for wishing to leave the firm was "to seek better opportunities." He felt that in his present firm he could not expect further promotions in the near future. His firm was known for its stability, low employee turnover, and slow but assured advancement opportunities. His superior, the head of quality control, was recently promoted to this position and was doing a more than satisfactory job. Further, he was a young man, only 32 years old.

James King

James King, the second of the two men being considered by Parr, was a graduate of a major southwestern university and had about five years of experience. King was currently employed as head of inspection and quality control in a small manufacturing firm employing 300 people. His abilities exceeded the requirements of his job, and he had made arrangements with his employer to do a limited amount of consulting work for noncompeting firms. His major reason for wanting a different position was a continuing conflict of interests between himself and his employer. King did not wish to make consulting his sole source of income, but he felt that his current position was equally unsatisfactory. He believed that by working for a large firm he would be able to fully use his talents within that firm and thus resolve conflict between his professional interests and the interests of his employer.

King's work record appeared to be good. He had recently been granted a sizable pay increase. King, like Calligan, began his career as a bench inspector and was rapidly promoted to his current supervisory position. Unlike Calligan, King viewed his initial position of bench inspector primarily as a means of financing his education and not as the beginning of his lifetime career. King was 31 years old.

Role of Inspection and Quality Control

Major differences between the two men centered on their philosophies on the role of inspection and quality control in a manufacturing organization. Calligan's philosophy:

> Quality is an essential part of every product. . . . It is the product development engineer's function to specify what constitutes quality and the function of quality control to see that the manufacturing departments maintain these specifications. . . . Accurate and vigilant inspection is the key to controlled quality.

When asked how important process control was in the manufacture of quality products, he stated:

Process control is achieved primarily through the worker's attitude. If a firm pays high wages and provides good working conditions, they should be able to acquire highly capable workers. . . . A well-executed and efficient inspection program will, as it has done in my firm, impress the importance of quality on the employees and motivate high-quality production. In the few cases when quality lapses do occur, an efficient inspection program prevents defective products from leaving the plant. . . . Any valid quality control program must hold quality equal in importance to quantity. . . . Quality records must be maintained for each employee and be made known to both the employee and his or her immediate superiors. Superior quality should be a major consideration in recommending individuals for promotion or merit pay increases.

King's philosophy paralleled that of Calligan only to the extent that "quality was an essential part of every product." King made the following comments on his philosophy toward inspection and quality control:

If quality is properly controlled, inspection becomes a minor function. The more effective a quality control system becomes, the less inspection is required. . . . The key to quality control is process control, and inspection serves only as a check to assure that the process controls are being properly administered. . . . An effective inspection scheme should locate and pinpoint the cause of defects rather than place the blame on an often-innocent individual. A good rejection report will include the seeds from which a solution to future rejections can be developed. . . . One sign of an unsatisfactory quality control system is a large, impressive inspection program.

King was asked what steps he would take to develop such a program if he were to be offered and accept the job of chief of inspection and quality control in the Denver plant. He answered:

I would design and install a completely automatic inspection and process control system throughout the plant. By automatic I do not mean a mechanical or computer-directed system, but rather a completely standardized procedure for making all decisions concerning inspection and process control. The procedures would be based on a theoretically sound statistical foundation translated into layperson's terminology. The core of the program would be a detailed inspection and quality control manual.

When asked how long this might take, King continued,

I constructed a similar manual for my present employer in a period of less than 12 months and had the whole process operating smoothly within 18 months after beginning work on the task. Since your firm is somewhat larger, and accounting for my added experience, I would estimate it to take no longer than two years and hopefully significantly less time. . . . As previously stated, I would place major emphasis on process control and would minimize inspection by applying appropriate sampling procedures wherever possible. . . . Employee quality performance should be rated on the basis of process control charts rather than on the basis of final inspection reports. The employee should be trained and encouraged to use these charts as the chief tool toward achieving quality output.

King further stated that one of the reasons for his desire to find a new employer was that he had developed the quality control program in his present firm to the point where it was no longer offering him any challenge. He further stated that he felt this situation would recur at American Ceramic and Glass Products but that, because of the size of the firm, he could direct his attention to bigger and more interesting problems rather than be required to seek outside consulting work to satisfy his need for professional growth.

When asked what his real interests were, King stated, "Application of statistical concepts to the nonroutine activities of a manufacturing organization." He cited worker training, supplier performance, and trouble shooting as areas of interest. King submitted several reports that summarized projects that he had successfully completed in these or related areas.

This was the extent of information that Parr had on each of the two individuals he felt might best fill the position vacated by Downs.

Discussion Questions

1. What should be the role of the chief of inspection and quality control?

2. What was Calligan's philosophy toward quality control?

3. What was King's philosophy toward quality control?

4. Under what conditions would you expect Calligan and King, respectively, to be most effective?

5. Which of the two candidates, if either, should be selected for the position of chief of the inspection and quality control department? Explain your choice.

 **CASE STUDY**

QUADRUPLES RESTAURANT

Restaurants Limited, a Seattle-based restaurant group, has recently hired an aggressive person to manage Quadruples, which caters to business travelers. The new manager, a total quality management (TQM) enthusiast, is concerned over complaints about Quadruples' self-service breakfast buffet. In the interest of improving customer service, the manager develops a survey form, obtains responses from customers over a three-month period, and summarizes the results on a Pareto chart (see Exhibit 4S–1). The chart shows that customers' biggest gripe is having to wait too long to be seated.

Next, the manager collects base-line data on percentage of customers waiting over one minute; the results are plotted on a run diagram (see Exhibit 4S–2).

Officers at Restaurants Limited have observed these preliminary initiatives—in the interest of possibly applying TQM to other restaurant management issues. Several questions need to be answered, and a step-by-step project improvement methodology would need to be established.

Discussion Questions

1. Can these kinds of customer response data be obtained reliably, systematically, and cheaply enough for a restaurant? If so, how?

EXHIBIT 4S–1   Pareto Chart of Complaints

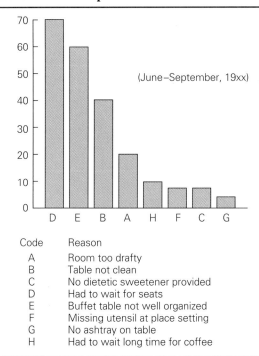

Code	Reason
A	Room too drafty
B	Table not clean
C	No dietetic sweetener provided
D	Had to wait for seats
E	Buffet table not well organized
F	Missing utensil at place setting
G	No ashtray on table
H	Had to wait long time for coffee

EXHIBIT 4S–2   Run Chart of Customers Waiting in Excess of One Minute to be Seated

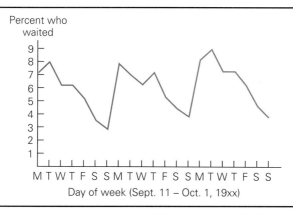

Percent who waited

Day of week (Sept. 11 – Oct. 1, 19xx)

2. Which of the Exhibit 4S–1 complaints are natural targets for continuous improvement in the restaurant (or any enlightened firm), thus, perhaps, not requiring solicitation of customer inputs to reveal the target for problem solving?

3. All of the complaints in Exhibit 4S–1 clearly are things customers would notice. If restaurant staff, instead of customers, were asked to express their complaints, suggest at least five complaints that would probably come forth. To what extent could the staff's mindset be altered so that they would worry about the same things as customers? How could this change occur?

Project Assignment

Devise a project for dealing with the complaint data from Exhibits 4S–1 and 4S–2. Consider the relative merits and uses (for this case) of each of the tools for process improvement listed in Exhibit 4–8 of Chapter 4 plus brainstorming, competitive analysis, benchmarking, and quality function deployment (QFD) (covered in Chapters 2 and 3).

TRANSLATING DEMAND INTO ORDERS

III

Customer demands enter the organization in assorted forms, some less specific than others. The organization's planners must sort out these demands and restate them as internal orders so that they can be executed without confusion or error. The six chapters of Part III detail the steps necessary for demand-sorting and order-planning procedures.

Chapter 5 examines overall demand management and specific demand forecasting techniques, and Chapter 6 addresses master planning to set overall capacity and output levels. Chapter 7 describes how orders should flow under careful control through the system, from order entry to delivery. Chapters 8 through 10 explain the many details that must be planned: selecting and buying from suppliers, planning the timing of each process, and grouping common orders into lots or avoiding grouping by improving process flexibility.

5 DEMAND MANAGEMENT AND FORECASTING

Chapter Outline

Transformation processes fill orders and those orders are expressions of demand. Demand is the lifeblood of any enterprise and it deserves good management. A customer-oriented approach to demand management and forecasting requires long-range vision as well as focus, and it includes:

- Planning for demand (developing readiness and flexibility).
- Recognizing all sources of demand.
- Processing demand.

Success in these and supporting activities is a shared demand management responsibility.

Responsibility for Demand Management

The importance of sharing demand management responsibility becomes clear when we consider the breadth of activities involved:

> **Demand management** is recognizing and managing all demands for products or services to ensure that the master planning team is aware of them. It includes forecasting, order entry and order promising—or direct selling—for external customers and for internal purposes.[1]

*P*RINCIPLE 3:

Achieve unified purpose through team involvement in planning.

A master planning committee or coordinating team, with ties to marketing, finance, and operations, needs to take charge of demand management activities. In the absence of a strong link among those functions, the likelihood of numerous errors and surprises is high.

While a coordinating team is basic, others also play key roles in demand management. Sales forces sell directly or book orders, order-entry clerks (or order-entry computer routines) further process orders, product managers (or computers) forecast demand for orders not yet received, warehouses confirm or deny material availability, and traffic checks delivery dates against shipping capabilities. On the internal side are people who determine capacity, financial, and other limits on what is to be produced and delivered.

There are short-, medium-, and long-term purposes of demand management. The short-term question concerns **item demand;** that is, the organization needs to know what demands exist in the near future for its mix of goods and services—the items it makes or provides.

Whether in short-, medium-, or long-term mode, demand management effort can be simplified if lead time, the time required to get things done, is shortened.

The medium term covers 6 to 18 months in manufacturing, but usually much less in the service sector. The purpose is to project aggregate demand so that productive capacity can be planned. In the medium term the plans particularly apply to labor, machine usage, and aggregate inventory, which we address further in Chapter 6.

Long-term demand management affects planning for buildings, utilities, and equipment, which we focus on in Chapter 17. Long-term demand management also affects the introduction of new products and services and the phasing out of older ones—already treated in Chapter 3.

Medium- and long-term demand management decisions are made infrequently. The short-term product mix (item demand) activities, in contrast, keep a good many employees busy all the time—handling orders or guessing about orders not yet formally booked. Processing current orders is our next topic. Later we consider guessing, more formally known as forecasting.

Order Processing

When things go well, operations is able to keep up with customer demand. To keep things going well, associates must play an active role in monitoring customer activities and processing orders. In most cases it is poor policy for a company to go for maximum customer traffic if that traffic just ends up in backlogs and waiting lines. Instead, the planning team needs to devise a responsive customer- and order-processing system. In retailing, some elements of this system occur all at once, at the point of sale. Elsewhere, order processing is a series of steps. In this section, we discuss the order-processing sequence, as well as orders in general.

---

[1]Adapted from a manufacturing-oriented definition in James F. Cox III, John H. Blackstone, Jr., and Michael S. Spencer, *APICS Dictionary,* 7th ed. (Falls Church, Va.: American Production and Inventory Control Society, 1992), p. 13

EXHIBIT 5–1   **The Order Processing Sequence**

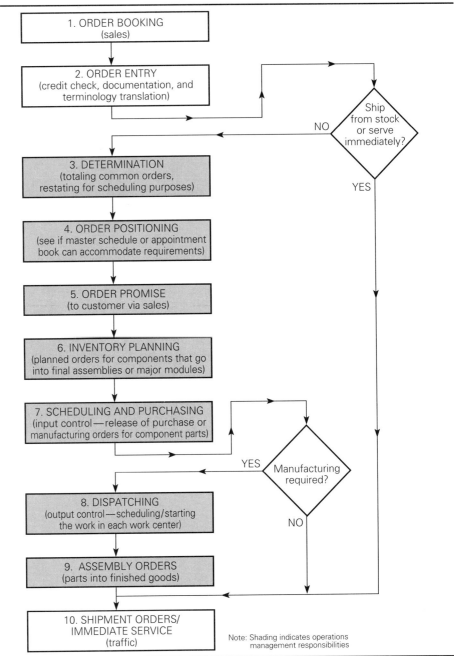

Note: Shading indicates operations management responsibilities

Orders   Even when considered only as a noun and only within an operations context, the word *order* has multiple meanings. For example, in manufacturing there might be individual sales orders, consolidation of sales orders into a few batch orders (for total requirements of each item), scheduled production orders for major modules, planned orders for component parts, shop or work orders, purchase orders for component parts and raw materials, final assembly orders, and shipment orders. Each type of order may have its own

---

Exhibit 5–1   *(concluded)*

Step 1. *Book orders.* A sales associate takes or books the order.

Step 2. *Enter order.* Really a subprocess in itself, **order entry** is the formal acceptance of the order into the order-processing system. Detailed order-entry activities include:

> Credit checks, especially for new customers.
>
> Documentation of pertinent customer data, such as requirements.
>
> Translation of requirements into specifications.
>
> Stock check; if order can be filled, the sequence goes directly to step 10.
>
> Assignment of an internal order number.

The next seven steps are primarily operations functions.

Step 3. *Determine total requirements.* The team totals multiple orders for the same output. In the manufacturing case, sales catalog terminology often needs to be translated into manufacturing part numbers, possibly including separate part numbers for (*a*) final assembly, (*b*) production of major modules like frames and engines, and (*c*) service parts, interplant transfers, or customer optional parts.

Step 4. *Position order.* A schedule positions the order in one or more schedules or appointment books, unless scheduling slots are unavailable.

Step 5. *Promise order.* If the schedule can meet a customer order, an order promise or reservation goes to the customer. Order promising completes order positioning of step 4.

Step 6. *Plan inventory.* Inventory planners divide accepted orders into requirements for component parts. If parts are not on hand, they generate manufacturing and purchase orders. Orders for common components may be consolidated; if they are, then at this point, customer identification for individual orders is lost.

Step 7. *Perform detailed scheduling and purchasing.* This step completes step 6. If the order is to be filled from purchased items only, buyers release purchase orders, and the sequence moves to step 10. If manufacturing is required, schedulers release in-house fabrication and component assembly orders so as not to overload shop capacity.

Step 8. *Perform dispatching.* Supervisors, production associates, or dispatchers control priorities as parts orders queue up for release to work centers.

Step 9. *Release assembly orders.* The customer order reemerges as the basis for orders for final assembly of end items (major components) and accessories into finished products.

Step 10. *Release shipment orders.* Associates prepare manufactured or purchased items for shipment, including geographically consolidated orders, or authorize immediate customer service.

---

numbering system and set of documentation. Thus, the question, ''Where's my order?'' is not always directly answerable.

In the service sector, too, the customer order sometimes breaks down into subtypes. Consider, for example, a medical clinic. You, the patient, are an order; when you go to X-ray, an X-ray order number is assigned; when you go to the lab, several lab orders are created; when you are finished, there will be a billing order with its own number for total services rendered.

With these meanings in mind, we now turn our attention to the order processing sequence.

The order processing steps are shown in Exhibit 5–1. While functions other than operations usually have responsibility for beginning and ending the sequence, the middle part (shaded area) rests with OM. Exhibit 5–1 makes order processing look complex, and indeed it can be if each of several staff departments does its own narrow set of order-processing tasks. Leading firms, however, rely on simpler visual, team-based approaches that combine, or even avoid, certain steps and significantly reduce documentation. Those firms focus on the objective: quick, on-time completion of quality goods and services at a reasonable cost, with flexibility to respond to new and changing customer needs.

*Order Processing
Sequence*

𝒫RINCIPLE 2:

Dedicate to continual, rapid improvement in quality, cost, lead time, flexibility, and service.

𝒥nto 𝒫ractice

Speedy Order Processing at Atlantic Envelope Company

Atlantic Envelope Company's seven plants had the same back-office problem: slow order entry. It was taking a week or so (nobody had actually measured it) from when salespeople booked a customer order (such as from a retail chain, an office supplies wholesaler, or perhaps a high-volume mail handler like Federal Express) to the start of envelope manufacturing.

Stage 1, 1990

Atlantic's effort to streamline order entry began at the company's home plant in Atlanta in the fall 1990. Earlier, office partitions had been removed so that four order-processing associates (order editor, order typist 1, order typist 2, and order checker) could operate more as a work cell. By itself, working in a common area as an order processing cell did not result in noticeable changes.

To establish a baseline for improvement, it was necessary to measure the processing time. It averaged five days, but was highly unstable. Moreover, all orders, except those designated for special routing, were treated alike. No rational priority system existed. One quick result: the mere act of measuring processing time resulted in its being cut to an average of three days, without conscious efforts on the part of the cell associates.

At that time the tasks of the four associates were as follows.

The order editor was responsible for pricing and commissions, order specs, packaging, paper cut-outs, production sequence, completion dates, dealing with incorrect or incomplete orders, and handling overprint and stock orders.

Order typists 1 and 2 were responsible for typing orders, assembling production jackets (containing production infor-

mation), typing corrections and change orders, filing, replenishing office supplies, and switchboard relief.

The order checker was responsible for proofreading orders, making outside purchases, processing change orders, overseeing B runs (large lots were split into A, B, etc., sublots), handling customer/sales service, and distributing proofs.

Stage 2, 1992

Then the team went to work. By fall 1992, they had cut average processing time from five days to about eight hours (and reduced their team from four to three associates). They made the following primary improvements.

- An order-entry associate screens incoming orders and puts them into color-coded folders: one color for standard manufacturing orders, a second for rush orders, a third for "jet" orders (overprinting on existing envelope stock using a jet printer), and a fourth for orders filled through purchasing from another Atlantic plant or an outside printer. Color-coding sets the stage for separate, focused treatment of each type of order.

- Jet orders, for example, are processed by a jet coordinator (a new position). She is able to get a sample to the art and composition department in about an hour (formerly it took one day). She determines which jet press to use, assigns the completion date, and returns the jet order to the order-entry cell for final processing (price, commissions, etc.) and forwarding to the jet press department. Jet orders are now processed in 5 days (15 days formerly).

If a customer can't be served immediately, as in on-demand service, the next best service is **order promising:** making a commitment to provide goods or services to a customer. That commitment must be in sufficient detail to provide sound information for making the sale, filling the order, and providing delivery. Also, the information must be current, which requires operations and sales to work together for speedy order processing. Aside from the few pure make-to-stock companies, where goods are produced to a forecast and placed in distribution warehouses, operations always has some order-promising function.

In client-oriented services, the order promise is known as an appointment. The order is not a legal promise; it just means that schedules have been checked and that, barring problems, the client should receive service at the appointed time. All parties realize that

- B runs and stock replenishment orders, both involving inventory actions, go directly to the inventory planner for more specialized handling.

- Order entry associates now hold regular order review meetings with raw materials and scheduling people; these meetings resolve order-processing problems faster and reduce errors.

- Order entry now sends incorrect and incomplete orders to sales service associates, who are better able to take corrective action with sales people and customers.

- Associates are participating in cross-training, which allows people to help at another order-processing desk and across department lines, as needed to handle surges in certain types of orders.

In the spirit of continuous improvement, further innovations are being considered. At the same time, Atlantic's large Nashville plant and five other smaller plants were involved in their own order-entry streamlining, mostly by adapting the Atlanta plant's system.

Order processing cycle times charted by order-entry associates at Atlantic Envelope Company's Atlanta facility. Shows average time to process 47 orders on Thursday, March 5, to be 7.9 hours. Large chart in the center shows average for the first four days in March. To the left are charts for prior months.

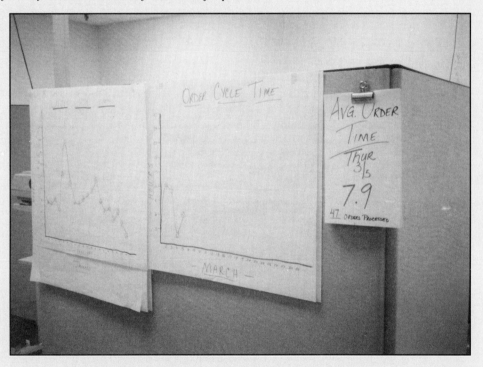

problems do occur and some services are going to be late. Just as obvious to all is that the firm with a good record of meeting appointments enhances its competitive position. The bottom line on the order-processing sequence? It is increasingly a target for improvement, as the box (Speedy Order Processing at Atlantic Envelope Company) illustrates.

Demand Forecasting

As a scratch golfer, you've been invited to play in the pro-am charity golf classic next week. Since your shabby golf shoes won't look good on the evening TV sports news, you head for the shoe-making department at the nearest sporting goods store. The cobbler takes your order, gets your size, and goes to work. Cleats, laces, and eyelets must be designed, tested, and then produced. Leather must be dried, tanned, softened, stained, cut, and matched, either in the cobbler's shop or by a subcontractor.

Though this scenario may sound ridiculous, old-time shoe making was very much as described. If things were still that way, you wouldn't get your shoes by next week, or want to pay the bill!

More likely, of course, you'll place your order by telling the sporting goods clerk, "I'll take those," get your shoes, and be back home within an hour or two. Many companies, like the modern golf shoe manufacturer, achieve success by producing for phantom customers—those who order goods that have already been made. Such make-to-stock companies produce to a demand forecast.

It could be said that a demand forecast differs from actual orders only in that actual orders are more certain. Forecasts are unlikely to be correct, but actual orders are uncertain, too, because they may be canceled or changed. Thus, the order-processing steps explained above take place whether production is triggered by orders or by a forecast. Our discussion of demand forecasting in the rest of this chapter will proceed from general what-and-why questions to specifics on forecast accuracy and forecasting techniques.

Components of Demand

The first what-and-why question is demand itself: what is it? Typically, the question is answered by reference to the components of demand and their behavior over time. The time-series approach may be useful in examining demand for individual items or for groups of items, such as product families or classes of resources.

In demand forecasting, time-series analysts look for different types of variations that occur in the series over time. Those variation types, or components of demand, are:

Time series:
A sequential set of observations of a variable, such as demand, taken at regular intervals; useful in both historical analyses and future projections.

1. **Trend,** or slope, defined as the positive or negative shift in series value over a certain time period.
2. **Seasonal variation (seasonality),** usually occurring within one year and recurring annually.
3. **Cyclical pattern,** also recurring, but usually spanning several years.
4. **Random events** of two types:
   a. Explained, such as effects of natural disasters or accidents.
   b. Unexplained, for which no *known* cause exists.[2]

The first three variations are shown in pure form in the three-year time series in Exhibit 5–2. Exhibit 5–2A has only trend, in this case positive. Exhibit 5–2B shows seasonality, with the seasonal high occurring at the first quarter of each year and the seasonal low at the third quarter. Exhibit 5–2C shows a series with a three-year cycle, peaking at about the middle of year 2. Exhibit 5–2D shows how a time series might appear with all three of the pure components along with some random events, shown as spikes.

Seasonal effects surround us (the flu season, the tourist season in a given locale, the harvest season) and all usher in demand peaks and valleys for goods and services. The magnitude may vary, but the pattern goes on and on.

Forecasting models exist for use with time series containing any or all of these components. Many demand forecasts are rather simple extensions of past series behavior into the future. For example, suppose the demand for tow-truck and jump-start services has peaked in the winter season in the 10 years for which records exist. This seasonal component would be expected to continue and would affect the tow-truck firm's projections in planning service to troubled motorists in the future.

Having defined and examined demand and its components, our next task is to do the same for forecasting. What is it? What are its purposes?

---

[2]UFDs (unidentified flying demands).

EXHIBIT 5-2   **Components of a Time Series**

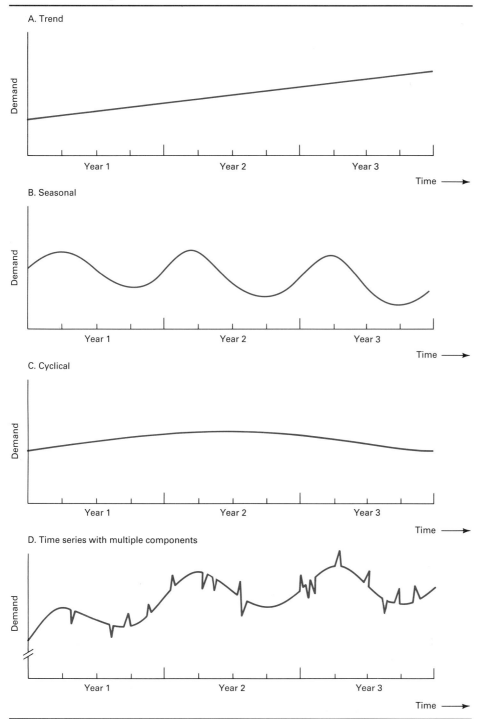

Purposes of
Demand Forecasting

Forecast and *forecasting* are popular terms. Weather forecasts, harvest forecasts, and even economic forecasts are beyond our scope, even though they can and do affect operations. Sales forecasts, however, are more within our focus. Whether expressed in dollars (or some other currency) or units, they reflect how much future demand for an organization's output is presumed to exist. In fact, we prefer the phrase **demand forecasting** because it applies to services offered by not-for-profit institutions as well as to sales-oriented profit-making enterprises.

The purposes of demand forecasting parallel the three purposes of demand management, but demand forecasting is more specific in that it helps plan both quantities and timing of:

1. Items/services provided or goods produced — in the short term.
2. Labor and inventories — in the medium term.
3. Facilities — in the long term.

1. Item forecasts are short-term and must express demand in natural item units. Examples are tons of steel and gallons of diesel fuel in the process industries, and clients, or client hours, light bulbs, paper tablets, trucks, and so forth, in discrete production businesses. Both the forecast and the schedule are expressed in those terms.

2. The medium term could cover just a few days for a firm that uses untrained labor and hires and lays off based on a few days' notice as demand rises and falls. Most firms adjust the labor force less often because of the cost of training labor. In that case, the medium-term forecast would extend several months or quarters into the future. Medium-term forecasts are often expressed in labor-hours' or machine-hours' worth of demand. Other units of measure, including dollars, are workable since they may be converted to labor, machine usage, and aggregate inventory.

3. Long-term forecasts for facilities (plant and equipment) may go 10 to 20 years into the future for plants that require extensive hearings, licenses, debate, and approvals. Nuclear power plants are one example. At the other extreme, the long-term forecast for a restaurant may need to extend only a few months out. Dollars are the preferred measure of long-term demand, but it is usually necessary to subdivide the total dollars into forecasts by type of product to indicate how the facility should be equipped: types of equipment, space, utilities, and so forth in each product area.

We have seen how the purposes of forecasting are affected by the time horizon. The complexity of forecasting, the next topic, depends on time horizon, plus another factor: type of industry or business.

Complexity of
Forecasting

Competition affects forecasting by defining the transformation process stages that must be forecast (see Exhibit 5–3). At the bottom of the chart are industries with competitive pressures to meet customer demand immediately on receipt of an order. Most services and deliveries from stock, such as your golf shoes, auto replacement parts, and cafeteria foods, require that everything except the delivery time be forecast and made ready in advance for phantom customers. That is, customers expect to have to wait only as long as it takes for shipment, delivery, or on-site purchase — and no longer: delivery is the allowable lead time.

Next up the ladder are industries in which customers expect to wait for assembly and delivery; everything else — capacity, raw materials, components, and so forth — must be forecast. These are make-parts-to-stock and assemble-to-order firms. Consider a Subway sandwich shop: customers wait and watch while their sandwich is assembled and delivered; components, however, have been forecast and prepared in advance. Other examples include machine tools, electronics, and custom assemblies.

Job-oriented firms form the next class. After placing orders, customers wait for manufacture or creation of components in addition to assembly and delivery. Organizations in

Exhibit 5-3   Demand Lead Times and Forecasts Required

PLAN CAPACITY	PROCURE RAW MATERIALS	CREATE OR MANUFACTURE COMPONENTS	ASSEMBLE PRODUCT OR SERVICE	DELIVER	CHARACTERISTICS OF INDUSTRY
Forecast required for planning capacity	← Allowable lead time →				Heavy capital goods: Ships Locomotives Missiles Heavy construction (Make-to-order industry)
Forecast required for planning capacity and raw materials		← Allowable lead time →			Job-oriented firms: Foundries Hospitals Restaurants (Make-to-order industry)
Forecast required for planning capacity raw materials, and components			← Allowable lead time →		Machine tools Electronics Custom assemblies Fast foods (Make-parts-to-stock/ assemble-to-order industry)
Forecast required for planning capacity, raw materials, components, and assemblies				← Allowable lead time →	Automotive replacement parts Consumer goods Cafeterias (Make-to stock/ ship-to-order industry) Services

SOURCE: Adapted from Figure 2–2 of G. W. Plossl and O. W. Wight, *Production and Inventory Control: Principles and Techniques* (Englewood Cliffs, N.J.: Prentice-Hall, Inc., 1967), p. 16. Copyright 1967 by Prentice-Hall, Inc. Reprinted by permission.

this class, such as foundries, hospitals, and landscape/nursery firms, forecast for capacity and raw materials; they make or provide to order, but from raw materials already on hand.

At the top of Exhibit 5–3 are industries with very long manufacturing lead times, such as ships, locomotives, and heavy construction. Customers know that these heavy-capital-goods firms are project oriented and make only to order. Thus, allowable lead time includes procurement of raw materials in addition to the other transformation stages already discussed. Companies in this class need only long- and medium-term forecasting for planning capacity; everything else happens after orders are received.

Two additional points about Exhibit 5–3: First, it suggests that up to four types of forecasts might be required for a firm. Implementation of just-in-time processing, with its tight stage-to-stage linkages, however, might cut this to as few as two forecasts: (1) a medium- to long-term forecast for facilities and labor, and (2) a shorter-term forecast of final product demand linking fabricated and purchased items.

Second, customers' judge competing firms' timeliness only on allowable lead time — the time from order placement until receipt of goods or services. The customer is blind to the preceding forecasting and demand management effort. Consider, for example, two competing companies in bicycle repair services. The one with the longer delivery time (allowable lead time in this business) is at a competitive disadvantage. Perhaps the opportunity for shortening lead time can be found in better forecasting and demand management activities. To reinforce a point made earlier: When lead times exceed those of competitors, it's time for smarter demand management.

*P*RINCIPLES 6 AND 11:

Organize chains of customers. Cut inventory all along the chain.

Delayed differentiation:
Keeping items in a
lower-cost state as long
as possible by delaying
transformation of raw
materials into
components, or standard
items into differentiated
items.

Standardization—
expressed as a design
guideline in Chapter 3
and as a goal for
effective purchasing in
Chapter 8—facilitates
delayed differentiation.

Wouldn't it be more competitive just to stock large inventories of finished goods and wait for the orders to roll in? Not really; there are risks of being stuck with costly inventories when forecasts have been too high just as there are risks of lost sales when forecasts have been too low. Demand management teams walk a thin line between those two risks, but sometimes they can help themselves by applying delayed differentiation.

Basically, the principle of delayed differentiation works like this: At each stage of operations and for each class of inventory, strive to keep items in a lower-cost or lower-value-added state as long as possible. For example, paint stores show a rainbow of available colors on small paper cards, but they certainly don't stock all those colors; rather, they make them up by mixing pigment (dye) in white paint after the customer has ordered a particular color. Grilled-to-order steak is another example: Keep the steak in its raw, lower-cost state until the customer specifies how it is to be done. Delayed differentiation works best when choice of type, style, or model is large but demand for each is low, as is true of nonstandard paint colors; or the value of the item changes a good deal from one state to the next, as with grilled steaks.

Demand Forecasting Sources

Your $1,000 certificate of deposit is maturing and you are thinking about a higher-yielding investment. A friend suggests stock, currently about $9 a share, in a company that has just diversified into the knee pad business (for skateboarders, volleyball players, tile layers, and spelunkers). Friendship is nice, but a little more checking is in order. You want to know about the company's past financial performance (time series of past stock prices, earnings, etc.), and operating performance (innovations, capacity, technology, management, etc.). In addition, you want more general information about what lies ahead. What are market projections? How is the general economy going to do? And what about demand for knee pads, as well as other goods and services provided by the prospective company?

Large multinational corporations are no different. They want to chart a course with inputs from a variety of sources. Consequently, demand forecasting is often three-pronged, perhaps coordinated by a corporate planning department. Exhibit 5–4 shows the three major groups of projections that help create a demand forecast.

- *Marketing projections.* Teams base marketing projections, typically measured in dollars, on sales projections, sales force estimates, test market results, and other kinds of consumer surveys.

EXHIBIT 5–4   Three Determinants of Demand Forecast

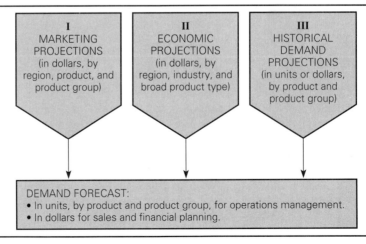

| I
MARKETING PROJECTIONS
(in dollars, by region, product, and product group) | II
ECONOMIC PROJECTIONS
(in dollars, by region, industry, and broad product type) | III
HISTORICAL DEMAND PROJECTIONS
(in units or dollars, by product and product group) |

DEMAND FORECAST:
- In units, by product and product group, for operations management.
- In dollars for sales and financial planning.

- *Economic projections.* Economists look at how the economy is likely to affect the organization's demand. Economic forecasting based on sets of computer-processed mathematical equations is known as econometrics.
- *Historical demand projections.* Computerized statistical packages also help teams project past demand patterns into the future.

While further exploration of marketing and economic projections is beyond our scope, we do recognize their roles in helping people get the big picture so that they can sharpen judgments about future demand and reduce variation between what customers want and what the firm provides. Historical demand projections, on the other hand, are of central importance in demand management, and various types are examined later in the chapter. At this time, however, we need to add a who to the discussion of what-and-why issues. That is, who should forecast?

$\mathscr{P}$RINCIPLE 10:

Improve accuracy; reduce variation.

The common view seems to be that forecasting should be done by those with responsibility for final products/services. That would limit forecasting to items earning revenue. Or, for non-revenue-producing organizations, forecasting would be restricted to major-mission items; for example, in social work, forecasting the number of eligible clients.

Forecasting in Support Organizations

That view of forecasting is too narrow. All managers should forecast. Put another way, all staff services and nonrevenue items should be forecast in addition to forecasting for revenue and major-mission items. Example 5–1 shows why forecasting is necessary in support departments.

EXAMPLE 5–1   APEX STEEL CABINET COMPANY

O. R. Guy is the new president of Apex. One of his first acts is to create the department of management science and assign corporate forecasting to it. Corporate forecasting applies to the firm's revenue-earning products: its line of steel cabinets.

Management science department analysts arrive at a forecast of a 10 percent increase in total steel cabinet sales for next year. Mr. Guy informs key department heads that they may consider 10 percent increases their targets for planning departmental budgets. Mr. Guy hears the following protests at the next department head meeting:

Engineering chief: O. R., I hate to protest any budget increase. But I'd rather wait until I need it. The engineering workload often goes down when cabinet sales go up. That's because marketing pressures us less for new product designs when sales are good. But then, in some years of good sales, we have a lot of new design and design modification work. This happens when several key products are in the decline phase of their life cycles. So you can see that our budget should not depend strictly on corporate sales.

Director of human resources: We are the same way, O. R. The personnel workload depends more on things like whether the labor contract is up for renewal. Sure, we need to do more interviewing and training when corporate sales go up. But we have bigger problems when they go down. Layoffs and reassignments are tougher. Also, when sales go down, we may get more grievances.

Marketing chief: Well, I hate to be the crybaby. But it's marketing that bears most of the load in meeting that 10 percent forecast sales increase. I was going to ask for a 20 percent budget increase—mainly for a stepped-up advertising campaign. I don't dispute the management science projection of a 10 percent sales increase. The market is there; we just need to spend more to tap it.

Based on those three comments, Mr. Guy rescinds his note about a 10 percent targeted budget increase. He then informs managers at all levels that they are expected to formally forecast their key workloads. That becomes the basis for their

---

EXHIBIT 5–5   Forecasting Plan—Human Resources Department, Apex Company

Workloads	*Forecast Basis*
1. Hiring/interviewing.	Number of job openings is based on data from other departments.
	Number of job applicants is based on trend projection and judgment.
2. Layoffs and reassignments.	Number of employees is based on data from other departments.
3. Grievances.	The number of stage 1, 2, and 3 grievances, estimated separately, is based on trend projection and judgment.
4. Training.	The number of classroom hours, and the number of on-the-job training hours; both are based on data from other departments.
5. Payroll actions.	Number of payroll actions is based on number of employees and judgment on impact of major changes.
6. Union contract negotiations.	Number of key issues is based on judgment.
7. Miscellaneous—all other workloads.	Not forecast in units; instead, resource needs are estimated directly based on trends and judgment.

---

plans and budgets. A management science department is assigned to advise those managers requesting help.

To explain what is meant by key workloads, Mr. Guy provides each manager with a simple forecasting plan developed by the director of human resources (see Exhibit 5–5).

The plan in Exhibit 5–5 provides for forecasting in units of demand as much as possible. The alternative is to skip this step and plan directly for staff, equipment, and other resources. That is the approach taken for item 7 in Exhibit 5–5, miscellaneous workloads. Some of the same methods (trend projection and judgment) may be used in that approach, but that is not demand forecasting. It is supply, or resource, planning.

Planning resources directly, rather than translating from a forecast of workload units, is the easy way. But a more precise approach is to forecast demand in units. The standard time to produce one unit may be determined—very precisely if the product is a key one. Then the unit forecast may be multiplied by the standard time to give staffing needs. Also, the unit forecast may be multiplied by material factors, space factors, and so on, to yield projected needs for other resources. The cost of all those resources then becomes the budget.

In the example, Mr. Guy is following a rational approach in requesting demand forecasts from all managers. It would be a mistake, however, to expect every manager to use extensive—and expensive—record keeping and historical data analysis. For lesser demands, a less formal approach should suffice.

Our discussion of types and sources of forecasting and influencing factors suggests that managers have discretion in deciding how much to forecast, how to forecast, what to use for reference data, and so forth. How is the exercise of this discretion evaluated? Quite simply, a forecast's accuracy serves as a simple but meaningful assessment of the people and procedures used to arrive at that forecast. Central to the concept of forecast accuracy is forecast error, considered next.

Standard time is the time a fully trained and experienced employee is expected to take to complete a task. Development of standard times is covered in Chapter 15.

Forecast Error

Forecast error has uses in item, product, product-or-capacity-group, and industry demand management. There are several popular ways of measuring forecast error. All, however, are after the fact; that is, a manager must wait one period (sometimes longer) to unearth the error in the forecast. In this section we discuss measures of forecast error, compare item forecast error to aggregate forecast error, and study error as we project forecasts further into the future.

In its basic form, **forecast error** is defined for a specific item in a given time period. Formally:

Measures of Forecast Error

$$E_t = D_t - F_t \qquad (5\text{–}1)$$

where

E_t = Error for period t
D_t = Actual demand that occurred in period t
F_t = Forecast for period t

Period t refers to any time period. Monthly, quarterly, and annual periods are popular in manufacturing, while service organizations might need to use weekly, daily, or even hourly time periods. Typically, the interest is in some representative measure of forecast errors over several periods rather than for a single time period. Exhibit 5–6 defines three such measures: mean absolute deviation, standard deviation, and mean absolute percent error.

EXHIBIT 5–6   Common Measures of Forecast Error

Mean Absolute Deviation
The **mean absolute deviation (MAD)** provides an accurate measure of the magnitude of forecast error. The MAD is the sum of the absolute values of the errors divided by the number of periods, that is:

$$MAD = \frac{\sum_{t=1}^{n} |E_t|}{n} \qquad (5\text{–}2)$$

MAD's use of absolute values removes evidence of positive or negative forecast model bias, but its realistic expression of mean or average error magnitude makes it one of the most popular error measures.

Standard Deviation
The **standard deviation (SD)** is obtained by taking the square root of the mean error squared, with $n-1$ in the denominator.

$$SD = \sqrt{\frac{\sum_{t=1}^{n} (E_t)^2}{n-1}} \qquad (5\text{–}3)$$

The standard deviation is useful in statistical analysis of forecast error data. If forecast errors are normally distributed, the standard deviation equals approximately 1.25(MAD). This relationship is explored later in the discussion of tracking signals.

Mean Absolute Percent Error
The **mean absolute percent error (MAPE)** relates forecast error directly to the target, actual period demand. It is calculated by dividing the absolute error for each period by the period demand, converting this ratio to a percentage, and computing the average of the percentage errors. We would show this as:

$$MAPE = \frac{\sum_{t=1}^{n} \left(\frac{|E_t|}{D_t}\right) \times 100\%}{n} \qquad (5\text{–}4)$$

Because absolute values are used, the MAPE will not reveal model bias. Its advantage is that it gives demand managers a common percentage basis for comparing forecasting models.

Example 5–2 shows the calculation of the three measures of forecast error for an eight-period time series (eight business days in a small, service-oriented start-up firm).

EXAMPLE 5–2   FORECAST ERROR—RESUMÉS-A-GLOW, LTD.

Kathy and Kyle have just opened their new business, a resumé preparation service, across from the university campus. As part of their business plan, needed to secure start-up financing, they forecast a level daily demand of 10 customers. After the first eight days of business, they evaluated the wisdom of the level forecast. The table below shows the day, actual demand (number of customers), and forecast in the first three columns. In column 1, −8 is the first business day, −7 is the next, and so on through the eighth business day.

(1) *Period* *(Day)* *(t)*	(2) *Demand* *(Customers)* (D_t)	(3) *Forecast* *(Customers)* (F_t)	(4) *Error* (E_t)	(5) *Absolute* *Error* $|E_t|$	(6) *Error* *Squared* $(E_t)^2$	(7) *Absolute Percent* *Error* $(|E_t|/D_t) \times 100\%$				
−8	10	10	0	0	0	(0/10)	×	100%	=	0%
−7	8	10	−2	2	4	(2/8)	×	100	=	25
−6	13	10	3	3	9	(3/13)	×	100	=	23
−5	5	10	−5	5	25	(5/5)	×	100	=	100
−4	9	10	−1	1	1	(1/9)	×	100	=	11
−3	8	10	−2	2	4	(2/8)	×	100	=	25
2	11	10	1	1	1	(1/11)	×	100	−	9
−1	12	10	2	2	4	(2/12)	×	100	=	17
		Sum:	−4	16	48					210%

Column 4 is calculated from Equation 5–1. Columns 5, 6, and 7, which are simple mathematical transformations from column 4, provide data for computation of the MAD, the SD, and the MAPE, as follows:

Mean absolute deviation (MAD, Equation 5–2):

$$MAD = \frac{16}{8} = 2.00$$

Standard deviation (SD, Equation 5–3):

$$SD = \sqrt{\frac{48}{7}} = \sqrt{6.86} = 2.62$$

Mean absolute percent error (MAPE, Equation 5–4):

$$MAPE = \frac{210}{8} = 26.25\%$$

Exhibit 5–7 is a plot of demand and forecasts for the eight-day period. With this small preliminary data set, it is of perhaps more interest than the error measures. What sort of pattern, if any, is emerging? Should Kathy and Kyle revise their forecast and make appropriate adjustments to their capacity? So many what-ifs, but then that's the nature of looking into the future. Perhaps our two entrepreneurs will watch closely for another week.

Forecast Error:
Item versus
Aggregate

We can appreciate the anxiety Kathy and Kyle face—the twin risks mentioned earlier. Sometimes, the risks of inaccurate forecasts, and the resulting overcommitment or undercommitment of resources, can be reduced with group forecasts.

Exhibit 5–7   Demand and Forecast Plot—Resumés-a-Glow, Ltd.

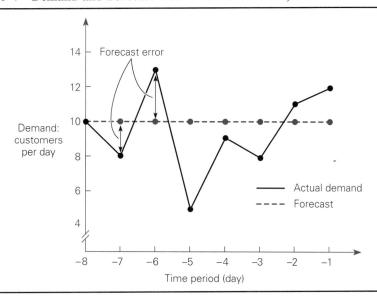

Exhibit 5–8   Item Forecast versus Group Forecast Accuracy

Item	(1) Third Quarter Actual	(2) Third Quarter Forecast	(3) Error $[(1) - (2)]$	(4) Absolute Percent Error $[|(3)|/(1)]$
Bracket	1,600	1,280	+320	20.0%
Doorknob	23,200	20,300	+2,900	12.5
Hinge	18,660	15,120	+3,540	19.0
Vise	22,210	32,010	−9,800	44.1
Tool case	7,960	7,880	+80	1.0
Grate	36,920	41,290	−4,370	11.8
Average item forecast error				18.1%
Group totals	110,550	117,880	−7,330	6.6%

An **aggregate demand forecast** is a forecast for an entire product or capacity group. It might be measured in output units (pieces, pounds, clients, etc.) or converted into capacity units (labor-hours, machine-hours, counseling time, etc.). If output or capacity groups are set wisely (discussed in Chapter 6), aggregate demand forecasts are helpful in planning work force and material levels.

The point here is that it is possible to rely on lower error rates of group forecasts. Exhibit 5–8 shows six items in a small group. The items could be members of a product family produced in a common work cell; this would imply that they share production resources. Exhibit 5–8 provides third-quarter actual demand, forecast, error, and absolute percent error for each item. The average error for the items as a group is 6.6 percent, while individual item errors range from 1.0 to 44.1 percent—a mean absolute percent error of 18.1 percent.

Caution is required in interpreting Exhibit 5–8. First, the figure may give the impression that a group forecast is merely the sum of item forecasts. However, that is not the best way to develop the forecast. It is better to examine trends, seasonality, and so forth,

EXHIBIT 5–9   Cumulative Forecast Error: Picture Frames

(1) Week Number	(2) Weekly Demand Forecast	(3) Cumulative Demand Forecast [(1) × (2)]	(4) Cumulative Actual Demand	(5) Cumulative Absolute Error [|(4) − (3)|]
2	500	1,000	1,162	162
5	500	2,500	2,716	216
10	500	5,000	5,488	488
15	500	7,500	8,110	610
20	500	10,000	11,250	1,250
26	500	12,500	14,010	1,510

for the group as a whole. The result is likely to be more accurate than the sum of item forecasts.

Forecast Error: Near versus Distant Future

Make an honest effort at answering these three questions: How many hours will you spend reading this week? How about the third week in April? The week of your 85th birthday? Obviously, forecasts are more accurate for near-future periods than for more distant ones. This somewhat intuitive point is illustrated in Exhibit 5–9 with data from a picture frame assembly shop.

Initially, the supervisor set a level forecast of 500 frames per week (column 2) for the next two quarters, far enough out for capacity-planning purposes. The cumulative forecast for selected weeks (2, 5, 10, 15, 20, and 26) appears in column 3; column 3 equals column 1 times column 2. Column 4 shows cumulative actual demand—for the same selected weekly periods. Cumulative absolute error (column 5) is actual (column 4) minus forecast (column 3). Error rises as the forecast takes in a longer time period.

The picture frame example raises several issues concerning length of forecast period and other more general points:

*P*RINCIPLE 2:

Cut lead times.

1. Long-term forecasting, even with the threat of increasing error, is often necessary in order to plan medium- and long-term capacity. Forecasts must project as far into the future as the firm's lead times.
2. Level or smooth demand is easier to serve. The demand pattern in the picture frame example is actually rather steady, about 540 frames per week, so a level forecast was the correct move on the supervisor's part. It was a good pattern guess, but a bit low on magnitude or amount.
3. As time passes, forecasts should be refined by interjecting newer data (e.g., recent demands) and rolling the forecast over. Had the frame-shop supervisor examined cumulative error after week 5, and perhaps switched to a weekly forecast of 600 frames at that point, the cumulative absolute error at the end of the 26-week period would have been slightly over 1,000, but in the other direction; that is, an over-forecast. Of course, making adjustments approximately every month could serve to reduce the cumulative error.
4. Forecast error analysis is hindsight. We can speak about what the frame shop supervisor should have done because we can see the entire two quarters—the historical demand time series. At the five-week point, however, the supervisor didn't have that knowledge; a guess had to be made.

If the frame shop supervisor asked you now what to forecast for the *next* two quarters, your response might be, "About 540 frames per week, that is, if the past demand pattern holds true for the future." You've just made a historical demand projection.

Historical Demand Projections

Recall from Exhibit 5–4 that historical demand projections are one of the three general sources for demand forecasts. Exhibit 5–10 shows eight forecasting techniques, grouped into three general categories, that all rely on historical demand data. The first two categories, multiperiod pattern and single-period projections, require time-series data. Associative projections, however, require that demand be tracked against some variable other than time.

All of the historical demand projection techniques rely on demand records. Larger firms that keep careful records are likely to have profuse data on past demand for goods and services. Minimal or no records at all might be the case, however, especially with start-ups, small firms, or smaller departments within organizations.

Where sufficient records don't exist, historical demand projections are still made but are totally judgmental. The manager uses experience to decide what future demand to expect. Inaccuracies possible in these rough forecasts could result in idle resources at some times and failure to meet demand at others—the twin risks. Record keeping is essential even for small firms. The high rate of failure among small businesses illustrates the danger of misjudging (really, mismanaging) demand.

Consideration of the historical forecasting models constitutes most of the remainder of this chapter. First are the three models used in multiperiod pattern projection.

Multiperiod Pattern Projection

Mean, trend, and seasonal variation, which are time-series patterns, identify forecasting models that project a past demand pattern several periods into the future. The forecast horizon may be limited to a few weeks, or it may extend years, depending on the firm.

EXHIBIT 5–10   Historical Demand Projection Forecasting Techniques

FORECASTING TECHNIQUE	UNIT OF MEASURE	FORECAST HORIZON		
		SHORT TERM	MEDIUM TERM	LONG TERM
Multiperiod pattern projection (mean, trend, seasonal)	Items or $	Yes	Yes	Yes
Single-period patternless projection (moving average, exponential smoothing, and simulation)		Yes	No	No
Associative projection (leading indicator and correlation)		Yes	Yes	Yes
		↑	↑	↑
		Product scheduling	Labor and inventory planning	Facilities planning
			FORECAST PURPOSES	

EXHIBIT 5-11   **Arithmetic Mean and Trend Projection—Data Services, Inc.**

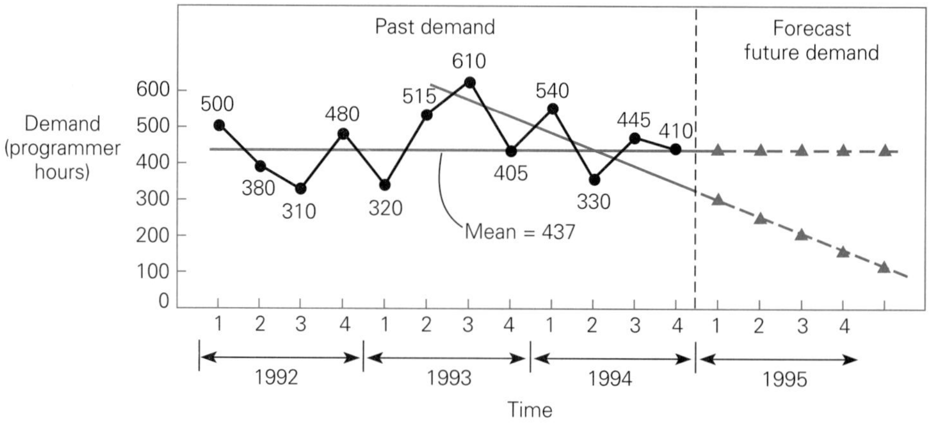

Mean and Trend

The simplest projection of a time series uses the arithmetic mean. When historical demand lacks trend and is not inherently seasonal, the simple mean may be suitable for forecasting. More often there is at least some upward or downward trend, which could even be projected as a curve. Exhibit 5–11 illustrates the mean and trend for Data Services, Inc., which offers commercial computer programming.

Three years of past quarterly demand in hours of programmer time are plotted. A first impression might be that there is no strong trend, and a bit of study shows no seasonal pattern either. If a certain quarter's demand is high one year, it looks as likely to be low the next. The up-and-down movement seems random. Also, one would not consider programming to be a service having some sort of seasonal demand pattern. What should the forecast be for upcoming quarters in 1995? Perhaps the mean (which works out to be 437) is the best way to minimize forecast error for such a nondescript demand; see the level dashed line.

However, another possible interpretation is to look at only the most recent data, say, the last seven quarters. The trend is downward; see the "eyeball" projection (done by eye with a straightedge) slanting downward in Exhibit 5–11. Data Services's analysts may consider the projection to be valid for one or two quarters into 1995. They do not accept it for the longer term, since it is trending toward out-of-business status! If they know the business is strong enough to carry on and prosper, the analysts would look for a more realistic way to project the future.

For a better forecast, better demand data might help. Let us assume that 20, not 12, quarters of past demand data are available. The demand history is displayed in Exhibit 5–12. Quite a different pattern emerges. The long-run trend is definitely upward. With a straightedge, the upward trend line is drawn and projected two years (eight quarters) into the future. The 1995 quarterly forecasts are now in the range of 500 programmer-hours instead of the 300 to 200 range resulting from the 7-quarter downward trend projection in Exhibit 5–11.

Another interpretation is that the 20-quarter demand data describe a slow curve. Exhibit 5–13 shows such a curve projected by the eyeball method through 1996. The 1995–96 forecast is now between the two previous straight-line forecasts. This projection is for a leveling off at about 450.

The curving projection looks valid. In other cases, of course, a straight-line projection may look valid. In any event, forecasting teams may use the graphic projection only

EXHIBIT 5–12   Twenty-Quarter Eyeball Trend—Data Services, Inc.

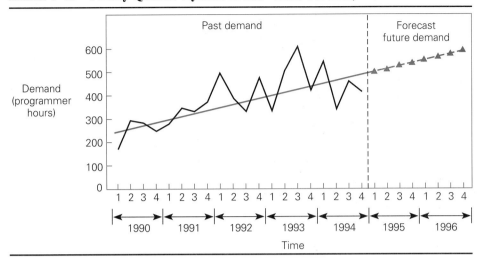

EXHIBIT 5–13   Twenty-Quarter Eyeball Curve—Data Services, Inc.

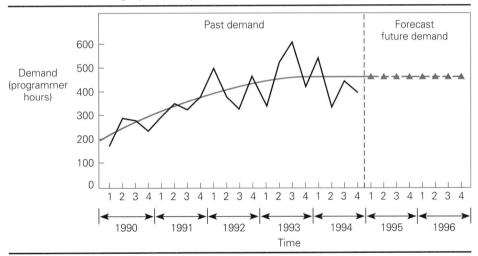

to sharpen their own judgment. For example, Data Services's people may have other information about their customers that leads them to a more optimistic forecast than the projected 450 programmer-hours. Even where such outside information seems to overrule historical projection, the projection is worth doing. It is quick and simple, when done by eye using a straightedge or curve template.

Another method of trend projection is less quick and less simple, but more precise: mathematical projection using regression analysis. The least-squares technique of regression analysis, discussed in the chapter supplement, results in an equation of a straight line that best fits the historical demand data. To get a trend projection, teams extend the line into the future. (The least-squares method may be modified to yield nonlinear projections as well.)

The accuracy of least squares is not its main value. Eyes and straightedge are generally accurate enough for something as speculative as forecasting. But drawing graphs for eyeball projections is time-consuming, prohibitively so if a large number of products must be forecast. Least squares takes time to set up, but after that it goes quickly, especially with a programmable calculator or computer. Computer-based forecasting routines have an extra benefit: they are usually able to print out mathematical formulas as approximations of the demand pattern, graphic projections, and tabular listings. Thus, least-squares regression is valued not for its forecasting accuracy but because it aids in routinizing some of the forecasting steps.

Seasonal

Often an item showing a trend also has a history of demand seasonality. In fact, perhaps most goods and services exhibit at least some seasonality. We'll see how teams use the **seasonal index** method of building seasonality into a demand forecast.

Seasonal Index: An Example.   The moving business is seasonal, so let's consider how a mover might make use of seasonal indexes. Exhibit 5–14 shows four years of demand data, in van loads, for Metro Movers, Inc. Since moving companies experience heavy demand surges during summer school vacations (June, July, and August), Metro groups its demand history into three-month seasons—that is, summer, fall, winter, and spring—rather than more commonly used fiscal quarters.

From the demand graph, summer demand is clearly the highest and fall demand is generally the lowest. Exhibit 5–15 shows calculations of seasonal indexes using the available 16 seasons of past demand data. (Note: Besides seasonality, there appears to be a slight upward trend over the 16 periods, but we'll ignore that trend for now.)

The third column in Exhibit 5–15 contains each season's mean seasonal demand, an intermediate figure needed to calculate final seasonal indexes. Each entry in column 3 is a four-season moving average centered on the appropriate season; it smoothes (averages) demands going back six months and forward six months. For example, the mean seasonal demand for fall 1991 (115 van loads, shown by the arrow) is the average of demand for the last half of spring 1991, all of summer 1991, all of fall 1991, all of winter 1991, and

Exhibit 5–14   Seasonal Demand History—Metro Movers

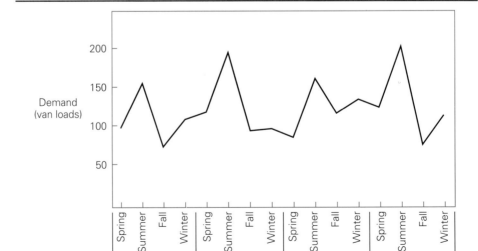

half of spring 1992. This calculation, and the one for the next (winter 1991) season, are shown at the bottom of Exhibit 5–15.

Column 4 in Exhibit 5–15 is actual demand divided by the mean seasonal average, or column 2 divided by column 3. Thus, the fall 1991 index is 70 divided by 115, or 0.61. In other words, the fall 1991 demand was only 61 percent of an average season's demand. The final step is to reduce the three indexes for each season into a single value (see Exhibit 5–16). Since no clear patterns emerge, a simple average will suffice. Thus, the seasonal indexes used to project demand for 1995 and beyond are as shown at the bottom of Exhibit 5–16.

Suppose Metro expects to move 480 vans of goods in 1995, based, perhaps, on projections of mean values of past years' demands. It would be foolish to simply divide

---

EXHIBIT 5–15   Seasonal Index Calculations—Metro Movers

(1)	*(2)*	*(3)*	*(4)*
	Actual	*Mean Seasonal*	*Seasonal*
	Demand	*Demand*	*Index*
Time	*(loads)*	*(loads)*	*[(2)/(3)]*
Spring 1991	90		
Summer 1991	160		
Fall 1991	70	115	0.61
Winter 1991	120	125	0.96
Spring 1992	130	132	0.98
Summer 1992	200	132	1.51
Fall 1992	90	124	0.73
Winter 1992	100	114	0.88
Spring 1993	80	115	0.70
Summer 1993	170	125	1.36
Fall 1993	130	136	0.95
Winter 1993	140	147	0.95
Spring 1994	130	146	0.89
Summer 1994	210	138	1.52
Fall 1994	80		
Winter 1994	120		

Example calculations; for fall 1991:

$$\frac{(90/2) + 160 + 70 + 120 + (130/2)}{4} = 115 \text{ loads} \qquad \text{Seasonal index} = \frac{70}{115} = 0.61$$

For winter 1991:

$$\frac{(160/2) + 70 + 120 + 130 + (200/2)}{4} = 125 \text{ loads} \qquad \text{Seasonal index} = \frac{200}{125} = 0.96$$

EXHIBIT 5–16   Summary and Projection of Seasonal Indexes—Metro Movers

		Spring	*Summer*	*Fall*	*Winter*	
	1991			0.61	0.96	
	1992	0.98	1.51	0.73	0.88	
Past	1993	0.70	1.36	0.95	0.95	
	1994	0.89	1.52			
Future	1995	0.85	1.46	0.76	0.93	←Mean of each column

480 by 4 and project 120 vans per season. Instead, the average-season value, 120 loads, is multiplied by the seasonal index for each season, yielding projected seasonal demands. The procedure is:

$$120 \times 0.85 = 102 \text{ vans forecast for spring 1995}$$
$$120 \times 1.46 = 175 \text{ vans forecast for summer 1995}$$
$$120 \times 0.76 = 91 \text{ vans forecast for fall 1995}$$
$$120 \times 0.93 = \underline{112} \text{ vans forecast for winter 1995}$$
$$\text{Yearly total} = 480$$

Seasonally Adjusted Trends.   Seasonal indexes may also be applied to projections when a trend component is present. Suppose forecasters at Metro Movers believed that the 1996 moving demand would reflect a 5 percent upward trend over the 1995 demand. On an annual basis, that increase would be calculated as:

$$480 \times 1.05 = 504 \text{ moves for 1996}$$

And the average-season demand for 1996 would be:

$$504 \div 4 = 126 \text{ moves}$$

Next, the seasonal indexes may be applied to the value of the average season. The procedure is:

$$126 \times 0.85 = 107 \text{ moves for spring 1996}$$
$$126 \times 1.46 = 184 \text{ moves for summer 1996}$$
$$126 \times 0.76 = 96 \text{ moves for fall 1996}$$
$$126 \times 0.93 = \underline{117} \text{ moves for winter 1996}$$
$$\text{Total} = 504 \text{ moves}$$

Steady growth, reflected by an upward trend, is great for business. Seasonal demand ups and downs, however, can give managers fits when they try to plan capacity to meet that demand.

Exhibit 5–17 shows the 1995 and 1996 forecasts. The figure shows what might be expected: trend effects, which are so important over the long run, tend to be overshadowed by seasonality when the short run, say, one year or less, is the focus. For forecasting and capacity management teams, the dominant message of Exhibit 5–17 is the seasonal pattern; the upward trend is secondary.

Cyclical Patterns—Natural and Induced.   Exhibit 5–2 illustrates seasonal demand patterns and cyclical demand patterns as different time-series components. The distinction, however, is merely the wavelength—the time it takes for the pattern to make a complete cycle. Thus, forecasting teams can treat seasonality, whether with a standard one-year wavelength or one that recurs, say, every 5, 10, or 15 months in much the same way. Other tricks of seasonal demand management depend somewhat on whether the cause of the pattern is natural or artificial.

Naturally occurring seasons are sometimes accompanied by extraordinary events that affect the magnitude of seasonal demand peaks. For example, a summer heat wave might raise temperatures from the seasonally normal high 80s to record 100-degree heat and create unusual demand for electricity. Accountants know that every spring is income tax season; newly revised tax laws, however, can further increase the peak demand for their services. In both cases, extra capacity is planned by further augmenting (normal) seasonal projections with percentage increases, based on past occurrences of the phenomenon. A

EXHIBIT 5–17   Seasonal Adjustment of Trend Projection—Metro Movers

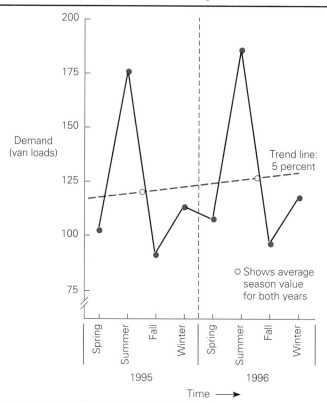

public accounting firm that saw a 17 percent increase in its tax-related business following the 1986 tax law change, for instance, plans on an additional 15-to-20 percent demand surge when new changes occur. Retailers have long known that holiday season sales create demand for more capacity (more clerks, longer store hours, etc.). They also know that extraordinary events, such as a mild winter, new toy or fashion craze, or negative report from a consumer advocacy group, further affect capacity needs in various departments or specialty shops.

Other seasonal patterns are artificial. For example, firms often fall into a pattern of inflating current sales totals—by various means—to meet some sort of goal. One version, well known in manufacturing circles, is called the end-of-month push (also end-of-week, end-of-quarter, and end-of-year push). People relax in the early part of the period and then go into a frenzy at the end to meet the target.

One company, Physio Control, a producer of a medical electronic product line, tried mightily to escape from its end-of-year demand-surge pattern. So far, it has been unable to do so because most of its customers, emergency and medical institutions, have money to spend at the end of the year and spend a lump of it on Physio's products.

Another version, *channel stuffing,* arises from pressures to meet sales quotas in selling to wholesalers and retailers. In a few cases, pressures to meet goals have driven people to desperate, sometimes illegal, acts (see the box entitled "Stuffing the Channel").

In such cases, where artificial demand patterns are a fact of life, seasonal analysis can and should account for them. That should not stop people from attacking the problem directly in an effort to eliminate the causes of spikey demand patterns.

To summarize the multiperiod pattern projections, keep in mind that their source is historical demand data described as time-series patterns. Finding the patterns can require

Into Practice

Stuffing the Channel

"Hitting the number became a company-wide obsession. Although many high-tech manufacturers accelerate shipments at the end of the quarter to boost sales—a practice known as *stuffing the channel*—MiniScribe went several steps beyond that. On one occasion, an analyst relates, it shipped more than twice as many disk drives to a computer manufacturer as had been ordered; a former MiniScribe sales manager says the excess shipment was worth about $9 million. . . .

"Other accounting maneuvers, starting as far back as 1986, involved shipments of disk drives from MiniScribe's factory in Singapore. Most shipments went by air freight, but a squeeze on air-cargo space toward the end of each quarter would force some shipments onto cargo ships—which required up to two weeks for transit. On several

occasions, says a former division manager, MiniScribe executives looking to raise sales changed purchase orders to show that a customer took title to a shipment in Singapore, when, in fact, title wouldn't change until the drives were delivered in the United States. . . .

"To avoid booking losses on returns . . . defective drives would be tossed onto a "dog pile" and booked as inventory, according to [a technician]. Eventually, the dog-pile drives would be shipped out again to new customers, continuing the cycle. Returns of defective merchandise ran as high as 15 percent in some divisions [according to the same technician]."

SOURCE: Andy Zipser, "How Pressure to Raise Sales Led MiniScribe to Falsify Numbers," *The Wall Street Journal,* Monday, September 11, 1989.

some computations, but projecting them into the future is direct and simple. If there is evidence suggesting that future conditions will differ markedly from past ones, the forecasting team should avoid the pattern projection techniques or use them with extreme caution.

We now turn to single-period patternless projection.

Single-Period Patternless Projection

The patternless projection techniques make no inferences about past demand data but merely react to the most recent demands. These techniques—the moving average, exponential smoothing, and simulation—typically produce a single value, which is the forecast for a single period into the future.

Rolling forecast:
Forecasts re-done or rolled over at intervals, for example, every week, month, quarter, or year.

In practice, forecasters extend the single-period projection several additional periods into the future. In the absence of trend and seasonality, extending the single value is appropriate and results in a rolling forecast. In each new period, the previous projection is dropped and the newly computed forecast becomes the new projection for periods in the new forecast horizon. It is like driving at night with headlights aimed 300 feet out, always reaching out another 300 feet as the car moves over the next stretch of pavement. These techniques are best suited to short-term forecasting for scheduling product mix. The forecast period typically is a week, a month, or a quarter.

Moving Average

The **moving average,** which became widely used in the 1950s and 1960s, is simply the mean or average of a given number of the most recent actual demands. Formulas and explanations for the moving average technique are presented in the following box.

The weighted moving average recognizes more important demands by assigning them higher weights. The advantages of weighting are somewhat offset, however, by the added burden of selecting weights: Just how much more important is last month's demand than

$$\mathscr{I}\text{nto } \mathscr{P}\text{ractice}$$

Moving Average: Formulas and Explanation

A general expression for the moving average forecasting model is:

$$F_t = \frac{\sum_{i=t-n}^{t-1} (D_i \times W_i)}{\sum_{i=t-n}^{t-1} W_i} \qquad (5\text{--}5)$$

where

F_t = Moving average forecast for period t

n = Time span, the number of demand periods included in the computed average

D_i = Actual demand for period i

W_i = Weight value given to data in period i

When different weights are used for the various data values, the computed forecast is referred to as the *weighted moving average*. Typically, higher weights are assigned to more recent periods. When the demand for each time period is weighted equally, usually with a weight of 1, we compute a *simple moving average* forecast. The sum of the weights (the denominator in Equation 5–5) will then equal the number of periods in the time span (n). The numerator is also simplified for simple moving averages, resulting in:

$$F_t = \frac{\sum_{i=t-n}^{t-1} (D_i)}{n} \qquad (5\text{--}6)$$

that from two months ago? From three months ago? Fortunately, exponential smoothing (discussed in the next section) provides an easier way to achieve about the same results as weighted moving averaging. Therefore, we shall limit our discussion of moving average forecasting to the simple moving average model.

Like other time-series methods, the moving average smooths the actual historical demand fluctuations, as illustrated in Exhibit 5–18. The data are for our moving company, Metro, except this time the demand history is in weekly instead of quarterly increments.

Demands for the last 16 weeks are shown on the left in Exhibit 5–18, where -1 means one week ago, -2 means two weeks ago, and so forth. On the right in Exhibit 5–18 is a calculation of three-week moving averages. A sample calculation for week -15 is shown below the figure. That result, 9.0, smooths the peaks in demand that actually occurred in the first three periods (6, 8, and 13).

In Exhibit 5–19, the three-week moving average for weeks -16, -15, and -14 is projected as the forecast for week -13. The result, 9.0, can be obtained from Equation 5–6.

The examples in the remainder of the chapter include much tabled data and calculation. We have, in most cases, rounded to the tenths place to facilitate presentation.

$$F_{-13} = \frac{\sum_{i=t-n}^{t-1} (D_i)}{n}$$

$$= \frac{\sum_{i=-13-3}^{-13-1} (D_i)}{n} = \frac{\sum_{i=-16}^{-14} (D_i)}{n}$$

$$= \frac{6 + 8 + 13}{3} = 9.0$$

Exhibit 5-18   Demand Data and Moving Average—Metro Movers

Week	Demand (van loads)	Three-Week Moving Average
−16	6	9.0
−15	8	10.7
−14	13	11.7
−13	11	12.7
−12	11	12.7
−11	16	11.7
−10	11	8.7
−9	8	10.0
−8	7	10.7
−7	15	12.0
−6	10	8.7
−5	11	8.3
−4	5	8.7
−3	9	11.0
−2	12	
−1	12	

Sample calculation for weeks −16, −15, and −14: $\dfrac{6 + 8 + 13}{3} = 9.0$

Exhibit 5-19   Three-Week Moving Average and MAD—Metro Movers

(1) Week	(2) Actual Demand	(3) Forecast Demand (Three-Week Moving Average)	(4) Forecast Error [(2) − (3)]	(5) Sum of Absolute Values of Forecast Errors
−16	6			
−15	8			
−14	13			
−13	11	9.0	2.0	2.0
−12	11	10.7	0.3	2.3
−11	16	11.7	4.3	6.6
−10	11	12.7	−1.7	8.3
−9	8	12.7	−4.7	13.0
−8	7	11.7	−4.7	17.7
−7	15	8.7	6.3	24.0
−6	10	10.0	0.0	24.0
−5	11	10.7	0.3	24.3
−4	5	12.0	−7.0	31.3
−3	9	8.7	0.3	31.6
−2	12	8.3	3.7	35.3
−1	12	8.7	3.3	38.6

$$\text{MAD} = \frac{38.6}{13} = 3.0 \text{ vans per week}$$

Since actual demand in week −13 was 11, the forecast error is $11 − 9 = 2$. That is a shortage or underestimate of two vans for that week. The moving average for weeks −15, −14, and −13 then becomes the forecast for week −12. The forecast error is $11 − 10.7 = 0.3$. The process continues, the average moving (or rolling over) each week, dropping off the oldest week and adding the newest; hence, a moving average.

EXHIBIT 5-20 Six-Week Moving Average and MAD—Metro Movers

(1)	(2)	(3)	(4)	(5)
		Forecast		*Sum of*
		Demand		*Absolute*
	Actual	*(Six-Week*		*Values of*
	Demand	*Moving Average)*	*Forecast Error*	*Forecast*
Week	*(loads)*	*(loads)*	*[(2) − (3)]*	*Errors*
− 16	6			
− 15	8			
− 14	13			
− 13	11			
− 12	11			
− 11	16			
− 10	11	10.8	0.2	0.2
− 9	8	11.7	− 3.7	3.9
− 8	7	11.7	− 4.7	8.6
− 7	15	10.7	4.3	12.9
− 6	10	11.3	− 1.3	14.2
− 5	11	11.2	− 0.2	14.4
− 4	5	10.3	− 5.3	19.7
− 3	9	9.3	− 0.3	20.0
− 2	12	9.5	2.5	22.5
− 1	12	10.3	1.7	24.2

$$\text{MAD} = \frac{24.2}{10} = 2.4 \text{ vans per week}$$

The three-period moving average forecast results in a forecast error (MAD) of 3.0 vans per week (see calculation at the bottom of Exhibit 5–19).[3]

Suppose forecasters decide to try a different time span, say, six weeks. The six-week moving average, forecast errors, and MAD calculations are shown in Exhibit 5–20. The mean error of 2.4 is better than the previous 3.0 value. They could try other moving average time spans and perhaps further reduce the error. In a larger firm with many products, searching for the best time span is a job for the computer.

Moving average time spans generally should be long where demand is rather stable (e.g., toilet tissue) and short for highly changeable demand (e.g., houseplants). Most users of moving average are producers or sellers of durable goods, which tend to have stable demand patterns in the short run. Therefore, longer time spans, say, 6 to 12 periods, are common.

The time span resulting in the lowest MAD is the best choice for actual use in forecasting future demand. But keep in mind that forecasters relied on past data. As long as they think that the future will be similar to the past, that is fine. If the future will be different, however, there is little point in expending much time analyzing past demand.

History-based forecasting methods such as moving average attempt to wash out some of the forecast error from historical demand data. The effect is a series of forecast values that are smoother—less variable—than the time series itself. These smoothing effects are illustrated in Exhibit 5–21 for the three-week and six-week data in the moving average example. The actual demand pattern, taken from Exhibit 5–18, exhibits some extreme high and low spikes. The three-week moving average data pattern, taken from Exhibit

---

[3]Use of the MAD in this and other examples is arbitrary. Another measure of forecast error would work just as well.

EXHIBIT 5–21   Smoothing Effects of the Moving Average

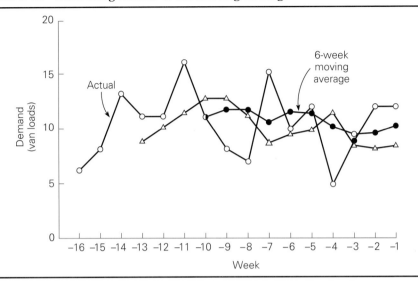

5–19, has spikes that are much less pronounced. The six-week moving average data pattern, taken from Exhibit 5–20, is smoothed to look like gently rolling hills. Taken to the extreme, the 12 weeks of actual data would be smoothed to a single flat prediction line, no peaks or valleys, which is the mean (discussed earlier). The correct amount of smoothing—the correct moving average time span—is the one resulting in the least amount of error (smallest MAD).

Exponential Smoothing

Many firms that adopted the moving average technique in the 1950s saw fit to change to **exponential smoothing** in the 1960s and 1970s. Today it is perhaps the most popular forecasting technique.

Simple exponential smoothing smoothes the historical demand time series. However, it assigns a different weight to each period's data and thus is really a weighted moving average. Weight values are obtained by selecting a single smoothing coefficient, α, such that $0 \le \alpha \le 1.0$. The exponential smoothing formula is:

$$F_{t + 1} = F_t + \alpha(D_t - F_t) \tag{5–7}$$

where

$$F_{t + 1} = \text{Forecast for period } t + 1$$
$$\alpha = \text{Smoothing constant}$$
$$D_t = \text{Actual demand for period } t$$
$$F_t = \text{Forecast for period } t$$

Equation 5–7 shows that each smoothed average has two elements: the most recent demand, D_t (new information) and the historical smoothed average F_t (old information). The term in parentheses, $D_t - F_t$, is the forecast error for period t. Thus, the exponential smoothing forecast for a period may be thought of as the forecast for the preceding period adjusted by some fraction (α) of the forecast error. That is:

Next forecast = Last forecast + α(Last demand − Last forecast)

For example, assume that the last forecast was for 100 units but only 90 were demanded. If α is set at 0.2, the exponential smoothing forecast is:

Exhibit 5–22   Exponentially Smoothed Demand Forecasts—Metro Movers

(1)	(2)	(3)	(4)	(5)	(6)	(7)	
Week	*Actual Demand*	*Forecast*	*Forecast Error [(2) − (3)]*	*Smoothing Adjustment [(0.2) × (Col. 4)]*	*Exponentially Smoothed Forecast [(3) + (5)]*	*Sum of Absolute Values of Forecast Errors*	
−5	11	10.6	0.4	0.1	10.7	}	Startup phase
−4	5	10.7	−5.7	−1.1	9.6	5.7	
−3	9	9.6	−0.6	−0.1	9.5	6.3	Forecasting
−2	12	9.5	2.5	0.5	10.0	8.8	phase
−1	12	10.0	2.0			10.8	

$$\text{MAD} = \frac{10.8}{4} = 2.7 \text{ vans per week}$$

$$\text{Next forecast} = 100 + 0.2(90 - 100)$$
$$= 100 + 0.2(-10)$$
$$= 100 - 2 = 98$$

This forecast of two fewer units than the forecast for last period makes sense because the last period was overestimated. Thus, exponential smoothing results in lower forecasts where teams have recently overestimated and in higher forecasts where they have underestimated. Exhibit 5–22 illustrates, again using Metro Movers as the example.

The data for Exhibit 5–22 come from Exhibit 5–18; α is set equal to 0.2. In exponential smoothing, there must be a start-up forecast; in this case, it is 10.6 for week −5. Following the suggestions of Brown,[4] the start-up value here is the simple mean of past demand data.

The underestimate for start-up week −5 was slight: only 0.4 units. Multiplying that 0.4 by the 0.2 smoothing constant yields an adjustment of 0.1, rounded off. Adding that 0.1 to the old forecast of 10.6 yields 10.7 as the forecast for the next week, week −4.

In week −4, the 10.7 forecast exceeds actual demand of 5; the error is −5.7. That times 0.2 gives an adjustment of −1.1. Thus, the next forecast, for week −3, is cut back by −1.1 to 9.6. And so on.

Exhibit 5–22 results may be compared with the three-week moving average results in Exhibit 5–19. Moving average absolute forecast errors for the last four weeks from Exhibit 5–19 sum to 14.3 (7.0 + 0.3 + 3.7 + 3.3). Exponential smoothing forecast errors in Exhibit 5–22 are better at 10.8 (week −5 is not counted). However, this is by no means a fair comparison, since the number of demand weeks is so small and exponential smoothing has not run long enough for the artificial start-up forecast to be washed out. Yet it indicates the tendency for exponential smoothing to be more accurate than moving average forecasts.

In testing for the proper value of α, the mean absolute deviation is again helpful. Using past demand data, forecasting teams could calculate the MAD for $\alpha = 0.1$, 0.2, . . . , 0.9, than adopt the α yielding the lowest MAD. It is common to use an α in

---

[4]Robert Goodell Brown, *Smoothing, Forecasting, and Prediction of Discrete Time Series* (Englewood Cliffs, N.J.: Prentice-Hall, 1963), p. 102 (TA168.B68).

the range of 0.1 to 0.3. The reason is the same as that mentioned earlier for using longer moving average time spans: most larger firms using exponential smoothing are makers or sellers of durable goods having rather stable short-run demand patterns. A small α, such as 0.2, fits this situation well. A small α means a small adjustment for forecast error, and this keeps each successive forecast close to its predecessor. A large α, say, 0.7, would result in new forecasts that followed even large up-and-down swings of actual demand. That would be suitable for the less-stable demand pattern of a luxury good or service.

It may appear that the next exponential smoothing forecast is always based solely on what happened last period, with no regard for all preceding demand periods. Not so. Metaphorically, if the forecast for next period, F_t, is the son, the father is F_{t-1}, the grandfather is F_{t-2}, the great-grandfather is F_{t-3}, and so forth. The current sibling, F_t, has inherited a portion, α, of the error attributable to the father, F_{t-1}, a smaller portion of the error attributable to the grandfather, and so forth.

Recall the manner in which weights are assigned in an exponential smoothing series. In a case where $\alpha = 0.2$, we would get the following results:

0.2 is the weight assigned to the F_{t-1} error.

$(0.2)(0.8)$ is the weight assigned to the F_{t-2} error.

$(0.2)(0.8)^2$ is the weight assigned to the F_{t-3} error.

$(0.2)(0.8)^3$ is the weight assigned to the F_{t-4} error.

In general, $(\alpha)(1 - \alpha)^{i-1}$ is the weight assigned to the F_{t-i} error.

The pattern of decreasing weights for $\alpha = 0.2$ is plotted in Exhibit 5–23. Also plotted are the calculated weights for $\alpha = 0.5$. The exponential smoothing weights extend back into the past indefinitely.

It is possible to construct a weighted moving average that closely approximates exponential smoothing. But why bother? Exponential smoothing is actually simpler and less expensive to perform than moving average; it requires but one small formula. Furthermore, exponential smoothing can be extended to handle forecasting chores for data

Exhibit 5–23   Weights for Moving Average and Exponential Smoothing

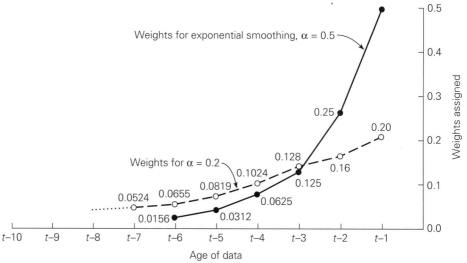

with trends and seasonality. Such models are beyond our scope, but may be found in forecasting texts.

Is forecasting model simplicity a true advantage? Research evidence suggests that it is. Simple models are not only easier to implement, but they frequently outperform more complicated ones. When two or three simple models are used together (e.g., with results averaged) performance improves even more.[5]

The main weakness of exponential smoothing and moving average is one of those pesky what-ifs. The underlying assumption of both models is that past demand data is the best indicator of the future. But what if it isn't? Sometimes the very fact that a good or service has been in very high demand causes demand to drop in the near future. Customers become sated and demand drops. As was observed earlier, wise managers use multiple forecasting sources.

Adaptive smoothing is usually used as an extension of exponential smoothing, and thus is often called adaptive exponential smoothing. Forecasters may adjust the value of the smoothing coefficient (α) if cumulative forecast error gets too large, thus adapting the forecasting model to changing conditions.

Adaptive Smoothing

Cumulative forecast error is called the running sum of forecast error (RSFE). To signal the need for a change in α, the magnitude of RSFE is divided by the MAD to compute what is known as a **tracking signal:**

$$\text{Tracking signal} = \frac{RSFE}{MAD} \tag{5–8}$$

Sustained increase in tracking signal magnitude reflects bias in the forecasting model, which the forecasting team would want to eliminate. Two bias conditions may arise; fortunately, both are corrected in the same manner:

1. *Tracking signal magnitude increases, positive direction:* The RSFE is getting larger in the positive direction due to underforecasting. The cure is to increase forecast values by increasing α, since the forecast errors are positive. A larger α then increases the forecast.

2. *Tracking signal magnitude increases, negative direction:* The RSFE is getting increasingly negative due to overforecasting. The cure is to decrease forecast values by increasing α, since forecast errors are negative. A larger α then decreases the forecast.

Recall from Exhibit 5–6 that when forecast errors are normally distributed, one standard deviation equals approximately 1.25 times the MAD. From the table of areas under the normal curve in Appendix A, we may obtain probabilities associated with various portions of a hypothetical tracking signal distribution assuming that no forecast model bias exists. The approximate probabilities are:

Area	Probability
0 ± 1 SD (or ± 1.25 MAD)	0.6826
0 ± 2 SD (or ± 2.50 MAD)	0.9545
0 ± 3 SD (or ± 3.75 MAD)	0.9972

[5]Nada R. Sanders, "The Dollar Considerations of Forecasting with Technique Combinations," *Production and Inventory Management Journal* 33, no 2 (1992), pp. 47–50.

Thus, the likelihood of the tracking signal's exceeding a value of ± 3.75 is very remote if the model is not biased. Continued tracking signal values with magnitudes less than 3.0, with some alternation in sign, usually denotes an unbiased forecasting model. A helpful rule of thumb is to consider changing the smoothing constant when the tracking signal exceeds 4 for high-value items or 6 for low-value items. For example, if the cumulative deviation is 650 and the MAD is 100, the signal is $650/100 = 6.5$, which is above the maximum. Forecast error is overly positive, that is, forecasts are too low. Larger α values should be tested on recent data to reduce the error.

Forecasting by Simulation

Trend and seasonal analysis, moving average, and exponential smoothing are standard forecasting tools, especially for durable-goods manufacturers. The techniques do not require a computer, but most firms have computerized them for efficiency reasons. The modern computer, however, provides the firm with computational power to run forecasting simulations involving several techniques. Forecasting simulation has the potential to surpass in accuracy any of the individual forecasting techniques.

In each simulated trial, the forecast values are subtracted from a set of actual demands from the recent past, giving simulated forecast error. The forecast method yielding the least error is selected by the computer, which uses it to make just the next period's forecast. For each successive forecast a new simulation is done, possibly based on a new technique. (In contrast, the search for a time span or a smoothing constant—for a moving average or exponential smoothing—is performed as an occasional review rather than every forecasting period.)

Perhaps the best known forecasting simulation routine is **focus forecasting,** which was devised for use by buyers for hardware stores.[6] In this system, each product is simulated every month for the next three months and seven forecast techniques are tested. Each is simple for buyers and other inventory people in the company to understand. For example, one of the seven forecasting techniques is a simple three-month sum (which is not quite the same as a three-month moving average). The simulation for that method uses historical demand data for only the past six months, which are grouped into two three-month demand periods.

Focus forecasting was developed by Bernard T. Smith, as inventory manager at American Hardware Supply, for use in buying 100,000 hardware products.

To illustrate the simulation, let us assume that demand for giant-size trash bags was 500 in the last three-month period and 400 in the period before that. In a three-month-sum forecasting method, the latest three-month sum is the forecast for the next period. Therefore, the computer simulation treats 400 as the forecast for the three-month period in which actual demand was 500. The simulated forecast error is $500 - 400 = 100$ trash bags. That forecast error is converted to a percent error so that it can be compared with six other computer-simulated methods for forecasting trash bags. The percent error is $1 - (400/500) = 0.20$, or 20 percent.

Six other simple, easy-to-understand methods (including simple trend and simple seasonal) are simulated to see what percent error results. If the three-month-sum method turns out to have a lower percent error than the other six simulated methods, the computer uses that method to make the next forecast. The forecast would be 500 for the next three months, and for each of those months the forecast is simply $500/3 = 167$ trash bags. The forecast rolls over (is recomputed) each month. The computer prints out the forecast for each of the 100,000 items, but buyers may overrule the printed forecast if they disbelieve it.

---

[6]Bernard T. Smith, *Focus Forecasting: Computer Techniques for Inventory Control* (Boston: CBI Publishing, 1978) (HD55.S48).

Associative Projection

In all of the preceding techniques, forecasters track demand over time. In associative projection, demand is tracked not against time but against some other known variable, perhaps student enrollment or inches of precipitation. The associative techniques are the leading indicator and correlation.

If changes in demand are preceded by changes in some other variable, the other variable is a **leading indicator.** The leading indicator is helpful if the patterns of change in the two variables are similar (i.e., they correlate) and if the lead time is long enough for action to be taken before the demand change occurs.

Leading Indicator

Few firms are able to discover a variable that changes with demand but leads it significantly. The reason probably is that demand for a given good or service usually depends on (is led by) a number of variables rather than one dominant variable. The search for such a variable can be costly and futile. Therefore, most of the work with leading indicators has centered on national economic forecasting instead of local demand forecasting. Nevertheless, the leading indicator should be part of the demand forecaster's tool kit, since it is a valued predictor in those cases where it can be isolated.

One story about leading indicators has been widely circulated. It is said that the Rothschild family reaped a fortune by getting advance news of Napoleon's defeat at Waterloo. Nathan, the Rothschild brother who lived in England, received the news via carrier pigeon. On that basis he bought depressed war effort securities and sold them at a huge profit after the news reached England.[7]

The leading indicator in this case was news of the war, and it led prices of securities. The Rothschilds' astuteness was not in realizing this, for it was common knowledge; rather, it was in their development of an information network with which to capitalize on that knowledge. A costly information system like that set up by the Rothschilds can provide highly accurate information rapidly. In contrast, personal judgment as a basis for action is cheap but tends to be less accurate and to be hindsight rather than foresight; that is, personal judgment often does not lead events.

In sum, leading indicators should have long lead times as well as accuracy. That requires good information systems. Example 5–3 illustrates.

EXAMPLE 5–3   STATE JOBS SERVICE AND LEADING INDICATORS

Mr. H. Hand, manager of the Metro City office of the State Jobs Service, sees the need for better demand forecasting. The problem has been that surges in clients tend to catch the office off guard. Advance warning of demand is needed in order to plan for staff, desks, phones, forms, and even space.

One element of demand is well known: many of the job seekers are there as a result of being laid off by Acme Industries, which is by far the largest employer in Metro City. Hand is able to obtain Acme records on layoffs over the past year. He plots the layoff data on a time chart, along with the Jobs Service office's data on job applicants, in Exhibit 5–24. The chart shows the number of job applicants ranging from a high of 145 (period 8) to a low of 45 (period 20). Layoffs at Acme range from a high of 60 (periods 6 and 7) to a low of zero (several periods).

---

[7]One historian disputes this story, asserting that the Rothschilds made more money during the war than at its end and that the news was forwarded by a courier in a Rothschilds ship, not a carrier pigeon. See Virginia Cowles, *The Rothschilds: A Family of Fortune* (New York: Alfred A. Knopf, 1973), pp. 47–50 (HG1552.R8C66).

Plotting the points seems well worth the effort because Hand notes a striking similarity in the shapes of the two plots. Further, the layoffs plot seems to lead the applicants plot. For example, the high of 145 applicants occurred two weeks after the high of 60 layoffs and the low of 45 applicants occurred two weeks after layoffs spiked downward to zero. Weeks 1, 3, 17, 21, and 22 are other places on the layoff plot in which a two-week lead appears; the lead is close to two weeks in weeks 11 through 15.

Does a two-week lead make sense, or could it be coincidence? Hand feels that it makes sense. He bases this on the impression that laid-off Acme people tend to live off their severance pay for a time—two weeks seems reasonable—before actively seeking other jobs. Hand therefore takes the final steps. First, he establishes an information system. This is simply an agreement that every two weeks Acme will release the number of its laid-off employees to the Jobs Service office. Second, he establishes a forecasting procedure based on that layoff information and the two-week lead pattern in Exhibit 5–24.

EXHIBIT 5–24   Layoffs at Acme and Job Applications at Jobs Service, with Time Scale

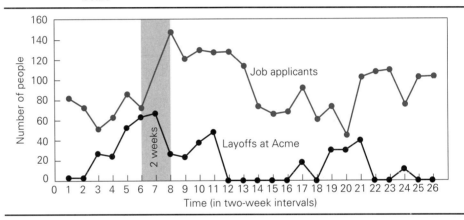

EXHIBIT 5–25   Correlation of Layoffs at Acme ($T-2$) with Demand at Jobs Service (T)

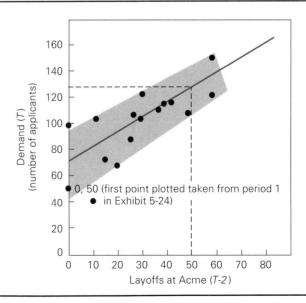

In establishing a forecasting procedure, Hand regraphs the data from Exhibit 5–24 into the form shown in Exhibit 5–25 (a scatter diagram); that is, layoffs at Acme for period $T - 2$ matched with applicants at the Jobs Service office for period T constitute points that are plotted as the two axes of the graph. For example, the first point plotted is (0,50), which is taken from Exhibit 5–24, where for period 1 layoffs are 0 and two weeks later applicants are 50. Every other point is plotted in the same way. The points tend to go upward left to right, clustering around the dashed line (an eyeball regression line).

The dashed line is used for forecasting. Suppose, for example, that Hand learns today that Acme is laying off 50 people this week. In Exhibit 5–25 a solid vertical line extending from 50 to the dashed line and leftward yields a forecast demand of about 125. Thus, the procedure tells Hand to plan for 125 applicants in two weeks.

Correlation

Correlation means degree of association.

How good is Mr. Hand's leading indicator? By one measure—the supporting information system—it is very good! The layoff data from Acme are cheap to obtain and highly accurate. But in terms of lead time, it is not so good. Two weeks' notice seems insufficient for the purpose of adjusting resources on hand. In terms of validity, the leading indicator seems good, but how may we measure good? One answer is: measure it by the correlation coefficient—our next topic.

The correlation coefficient, r, is a measure of degree of association. The value of r ranges from 1.0 for perfect positive correlation to 0.0 for no correlation at all to -1.0 for perfect negative correlation. In positive correlation, a rise in one attribute occurs along with a rise in the other; in negative correlation, a rise in one occurs along with a fall in the other. To calculate r, forecasters need a number of pairs of values. The chapter supplement provides a formula and sample calculations.

For the Jobs Service example, the correlation coefficient is quite good (about $+0.78$, calculations not given), which one can see by looking at Exhibit 5–25. The points tend to cluster along the broad, shaded band running upward at about a 30-degree angle. This is the pattern of a positive correlation. (Negative correlations go downward left to right.)

In the Jobs Service example, the amount of lead was determined visually. The two variables were plotted on the time scale in Exhibit 5–24, and brief inspection showed that the two curves were generally two weeks apart. Sometimes the amount of lead is hard to see, and where there are many potential leading indicators to check out, manual plotting and visual inspection become tedious. In such cases, computers may take over. It is simple for the computer to calculate r for a number of different lead periods. The one with the best r may then be selected.

Zero-lead-time correlation is usually covered in the introductory statistics course.

What about a lead period of zero? That would exist where a pair of events occur at the same time. Even if the correlation is perfect ($r = 1.0$), it appears that it is useless in forecasting. No lead time means no forewarning and, it might seem, no forecasting. This impression is incorrect. Correlation with no lead can be valuable if the indicator (independent variable) is more predictable than is demand.

As an example, phone company planners in a large city may know that new residential phone orders correlate nearly perfectly with new arrivals in the city—with no lead time. There is probably value in knowing this because in most large cities careful studies are done to project population increases. Fairly reliable projections of new residences may be available. The phone company need not spend a lot of money projecting residential telephone installations; instead, forecasters may use the city's data on new residences. For these reasons, most large firms are indeed interested in establishing good correlations, even without lead time.

Multiple regression/correlation is an extension of simple regression and correlation. In this method, multiple causal variables may be analyzed. The result is a formula with demand on the left side of the equal sign and each of the causal variables, properly weighted, on the right. For example, the phone company's forecasters may look for predictors other than new residences, such as level of savings in local thrift institutions and amount of phone advertising. A multiple regression equation might be put together with three causal variables: new residences (N), savings (S), and advertising (A). Then computer processing using past data would yield the parameters for each variable. As an example, the equation for forecasting next month's demand (D) for phone installations might be:

$$D = 0.36N + 2.81S + 0.89A$$

Since advertising effects may take awhile, the team perhaps should analyze advertising as a leading indicator. Maybe it could be shown that advertising leads demand by one month. The revised multiple regression equation might appear as:

$$D = 0.41N + 2.70S + 0.88A_{t-1}$$

Much more has been done with multiple regression/correlation in economic forecasting than in demand forecasting. The method, which is complex and requires a computer, is beyond the scope of this book. The approach often has proved futile at the level of the firm. Multiple regression has been used frequently, however, for large utilities or public agencies, whose demand is likely to be affected by a number of broad socioeconomic variables.

Summary

Though operations managers are key players, responsibility for demand management is shared. A master planning committee frequently coordinates demand management among marketing, finance, and operations associates.

Demand management has three purposes: short-term, which deals with item demand; medium-term, which projects aggregate demand for capacity groups; and long-term, which is needed for planning facilities and equipment. Long- and medium-term decisions are infrequent, but short-term demand management keeps people busy all the time processing orders.

Many kinds of orders exist; several occur within the demand management function. Consequently, customer satisfaction depends on a carefully constructed and well-maintained order processing system. The order processing sequence begins and ends outside the typical operations function. Most of the sequence, however—specifically, total requirements determination, order positioning, order promise, inventory planning, scheduling and purchasing, dispatching, and assembly—is the responsibility of operations.

Order promising is the act of making a delivery commitment to the customer and to the rest of the producing organization. In services, the appointment is the order promise.

Demand forecasting, or estimating future demand, is a major activity of demand management. Because planning usually must begin long before actual customer orders are received, forecasting is essential. The demand that is to be forecast consists of long-, medium-, and short-term components in addition to noise. Viewing demand as a time series suggests analysis of the time series components of trend, seasonality, cyclical patterns, and random events. Analyses of historical time series data often justify using simple projections of past patterns as forecasts of future demand performance. Demand is more certain in the immediate future, for which there usually exist customer orders specifying needed goods and services.

Forecasting results may be evaluated by studying forecast error. For a given time period, error is equal to demand minus forecast. Typically, however, a measurement of error over multiple time periods is more useful than that for single periods. Several measures of forecast error exist, including mean absolute deviation, standard deviation, and mean absolute percentage error.

Aggregate demand forecasts are used for planning product or capacity groups. Error percentage for group forecasts is usually lower than an average of comparable figures for individual items.

Forecast accuracy deteriorates as projections extend into the more distant future. Thus, as time passes, older forecasts should be refined in light of more recent developments. Also, planning and control systems dependent on forecasts should be segmented according to the importance of forecast accuracy.

Like demand management, demand forecasting has short-, medium-, and long-term components. Three primary sources of demand forecasts are marketing, economic, and historical demand projections. Accurate records greatly aid historical demand projection. Forecasting procedures are affected by industry and organizational variables such as required customer lead time, but all managers should forecast.

Demand forecasting often is based on a projection of a historical demand time series. Historical demand analysis addresses the simple mean, trend, and seasonality in time-series data.

Multiperiod pattern projection techniques are often used in a rolling-forecast mode. These techniques project the mean, trend, and seasonal components and are useful in short-, medium-, and long-term forecasting. The least-squares procedure for trend projection may be used when precision is desired or where many products or services must be forecast. Seasonal indexes are combined with trend to produce projections that are more sensitive to seasonal influences on demand. The multiperiod projection techniques are useful only when past demand patterns are expected to remain valid in the future. In the short run, forecast inaccuracies can stem from artificial conditions, such as stuffing distribution channels to make sales figures look good.

Single-period patternless projection tools include moving average, exponential smoothing, and simulation. Although they are most useful for short-term forecasts, they may be extended further into the future if certain conditions are met. A moving average is a mean of recent past demands, rolling over as time progresses. The number of periods used to compute the mean is the time span of the moving average forecast.

Exponential smoothing, perhaps the most popular of the single-period techniques, is really a form of weighted moving averaging. It is simple and inexpensive and has been shown to be accurate. The single or simple exponential smoothing forecast for a time period is the forecast for the last period plus some fraction (α) of the last period's forecast error. Adaptive smoothing uses a tracking signal—a ratio of the running sum of forecast error to the MAD—to permit adjustment of α should forecast error become too large.

The widespread availability of microcomputer-based forecasting software has resulted in computerization of much business forecasting. The computer is essential in forecasting by simulation, in which several forecasting models are studied simultaneously in the search for the best forecast.

In associative projection, demand is tracked against some variable other than time. Techniques include leading indicator and correlation. Attempts to isolate an association (correlation) between one known variable and demand are most productive if the predictor variable can be shown to lead demand. The greater the correlation and the longer the lead time, the better the leading indicator as a forecasting aid. Correlation without lead may itself be useful, however, if the correlated variable is more predictable than demand. Multiple regression/correlation permits use of more than one independent or predictor variable.

While all of the historical techniques are potentially useful, demand forecasting is inherently imprecise. No amount of mathematical analysis can change that. Recently, the preference seems to be for the simple models, such as those discussed in this chapter.

Key Words

Demand management 145	Time series 150
Item demand 145	Trend 150
Order promising 148	Seasonal variation (seasonality) 150
Order entry 148	Cyclical pattern 150

Solved Problems

Problem 1

Historical demand data and forecasts exist for the eight-period time interval shown below:

Period	-8	-7	-6	-5	-4	-3	-2	-1
Demand	100	110	104	98	106	102	100	98
Forecast	104	102	104	100	100	104	103	102

Arrange the information in a table similar to the one in Example 5–2. Compute the following measures of forecast error: MAD, SD, and MAPE. Plot the demand and forecasts as time series as in Exhibit 5–7.

Solution 1

The period, demand, and forecasts are shown in the first three columns of Exhibit 5–26. The rest of the table is constructed as in Example 5–2; it contains the computations necessary for determining the required error measures.

Exhibit 5–26   Forecast Error Measures: Sample Problem

Period (t)	Demand (D_t)	Forecast (F_t)	Error (E_t)	Absolute Error $|E_t|$	Error Squared $(E_t)^2$	Absolute Percent Error $(|E_t|/D_t) \times 100\%$
-8	100	104	-4	4	16	4.00%
-7	110	102	8	8	64	7.27
-6	104	104	0	0	0	0.00
-5	98	100	-2	2	4	2.04
-4	106	100	6	6	36	5.66
-3	102	104	-2	2	4	1.96
-2	100	103	-3	3	9	3.00
-1	98	102	-4	4	16	4.08
		Sum:	-1	29	149	28.01%

$$\text{MAD (from Equation 5–2)}: = \frac{29}{8} = 3.625$$

$$\text{SD (from Equation 5–3)}: = \sqrt{\frac{149}{7}} = \sqrt{21.286} = 4.614$$

$$\text{MAPE (from Equation 5–4)}: = \frac{28.01}{8} = 3.501$$

The actual historical demand and forecasts for the eight time periods are plotted in Exhibit 5–27.

Exhibit 5-27   **Demand and Forecast Plots: Sample Problem**

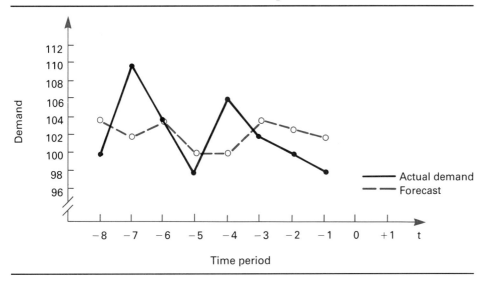

Time period

Consider again the historical demand and forecast data in solved problem 1. Determine the running sum of the forecast error (RSFE) at the end of each period, and calculate the tracking signal after period -1.

Problem 2

The following table contains the given data, forecasts, and error calculations in the first five columns. The sixth contains the RSFE values at the end of each period. The tracking signal at the end of period -1 is calculated below the table.

Solution 2

Period (t)	Demand (D_t)	Forecast (F_t)	Error (E_t)	Absolute Error ($|E_t|$)	RSFE
-8	100	104	-4	4	-4
-7	110	102	8	8	4
-6	104	104	0	0	4
-5	98	100	-2	2	2
-4	106	100	6	6	8
-3	102	104	-2	2	6
-2	100	103	-3	3	3
-1	98	102	-4	4	-1
				Sum $= 29$	

$$\text{MAD} = \frac{29}{8} = 3.625$$

$$\text{Tracking signal} = \frac{\text{RSFE}}{\text{MAD}} = \frac{-1}{3.625} = -0.276$$

Following are historical demand data for 12 periods:

Problem 3

Period	-12	-11	-10	-9	-8	-7	-6	-5	-4	-3	-2	-1
Demand	40	42	41	44	40	39	39	41	45	41	38	40

a. Calculate simple moving average forecasts and mean absolute deviation for the data, using a time span of 4.

b. Plot the demand data and the forecast on a time axis.

Solution 3

The time periods and historical demand data are shown in the first two columns of the following table. Moving average forecasts are in column 3 and error terms are in columns 4 and 5. Sample calculations and MAD values appear below the table.

(1)	(2)	(3)	(4)	(5)
		Simple Moving		Absolute
Period	Demand	Average Forecast	Error	Error
(t)	(D_t)	(F_t)	(E_t)	($|E_t|$)
−12	40			
−11	42			
−10	41			
−9	44			
−8	40	41.75	−1.75	1.75
−7	39	41.75	−2.75	2.75
−6	39	41.00	−2.00	2.00
−5	41	40.50	0.50	0.50
−4	45	39.75	5.25	5.25
−3	41	41.00	0.00	0.00
−2	38	41.50	−3.50	3.50
−1	40	41.25	−1.25	1.25
			Sum =	17.00

Sample calculations:
simple moving average (from Equation 5–6):

$$F_{-8} = \frac{\sum_{i=t-n}^{t-1}(D_i)}{n} = \frac{\sum_{i=-12}^{-9}(D_i)}{n}$$

$$= \frac{40 + 42 + 41 + 44}{4} = \frac{167}{4} = 41.75$$

$$MAD = \frac{17.0}{8} = 2.125$$

The plots of the 12 periods of historical demand data and the moving average forecast are shown in Exhibit 5–28. We see how the moving average technique smooths the peaks in the data.

Problem 4

The first five periods of demand data from the solved problem 3 are shown in the following table. Using a smoothing coefficient, $\alpha = 0.3$, compute simple exponentially smoothed forecasts for periods −4 through −1. Initialize the procedure with a forecast value for period −5 of 41.

Period	−5	−4	−3	−2	−1
Demand	40	42	41	44	40

Solution 4

The data, forecasts, and absolute errors for the five-period interval are given in the following table. Sample calculations and the MAD follow.

Exhibit 5–28   Historical Demand Data and Moving Average Forecasts

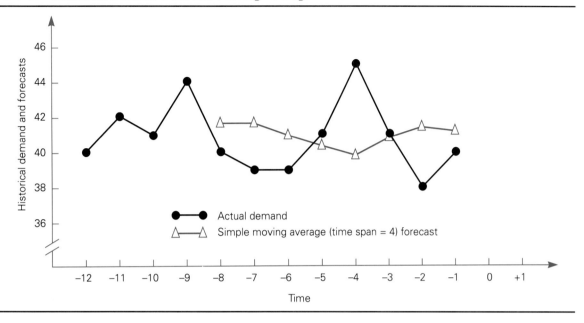

Solution 4 (continued)

Period (t)	Demand (D_t)	Exponentially Smoothed Forecast (α = 0.3) (F_t)	Error (E_t)	Absolute Error ($|E_t|$)
−5	40	41.000	−1.000	1.000
−4	42	40.700	1.300	1.300
−3	41	41.090	−0.090	0.090
−2	44	41.063	2.937	2.937
−1	40	41.944	−1.944	1.944
			Sum =	7.271

Sample calculations (from Equation 5–7):

$$F_{t+1} = F_t + \alpha(D_t - F_t)$$
$$F_{-4} = F_{-5} + \alpha(D_{-5} - F_{-5})$$
$$= 41 + 0.3\ (40 - 41)$$
$$F_{-4} = \underbrace{40.700}$$
$$F_{-3} = F_{-4} + 0.3\ (D_{-4} - F_{-4})$$
$$= 40.7 + 0.3\ (42 - 40.7)$$
$$F_{-3} = 41.090$$
$$\text{MAD} = \frac{7.271}{5} = 1.454$$

Problem 5

Historical monthly demand data for the past two years follow:

Period	−24	−23	−22	−21	−20	−19	−18	−17	−16	−15	−14	−13
Demand	10	12	14	12	10	8	6	8	10	12	14	12

Period	−12	−11	−10	−9	−8	−7	−6	−5	−4	−3	−2	−1
Demand	10	8	6	8	10	12	14	12	10	8	6	8

a. Compute a single exponentially smoothed forecast for the 24 months. Initialize the forecasting model by setting the forecast for period $t = -24$ to a value of 10. Use a smoothing coefficient of $\alpha = 0.2$. Repeat the forecast using $\alpha = 0.8$. Calculate the MAD for each forecast.

b. Plot the historical data and the forecasts on a time axis. Discuss the form of the demand data. Is the simple exponential model suitable for these data? What effects does the value of α have on the behavior of the forecasting model?

Solution 5

The time periods and historical demand data are shown in columns 1 and 2. Exponential smoothing forecasts are given for $\alpha = 0.2$ in column 3 and error and absolute error (or deviation) in columns 4 and 5. The forecasts computed with $\alpha = 0.8$ are in column 6, and error measures for this model are in columns 7 and 8. Mean absolute deviation (MAD) values for the two models are shown following the table.

Plots of the demand data and the two forecasts are shown in Exhibit 5–29. First, a note of caution: The data were created solely to illustrate some aspects of exponential smoothing. Do not infer that either exponential smoothing model is appropriate in this case. As can be seen, the data are perfectly seasonal and both forecasts lag the demand, illustrating why simple exponential smoothing generally is not a good model for obviously seasonal data. The model with $\alpha = 0.8$, putting 80 percent weight on new information and 20 percent weight on old data, is more reactive to peaks in the data. The model with $\alpha = 0.2$ reverses the weight emphasis and tends to smooth out peaks, being less sensitive to variations in demand data.

EXHIBIT 5–29   Historical Demand Data and Exponential Smoothing Forecasts

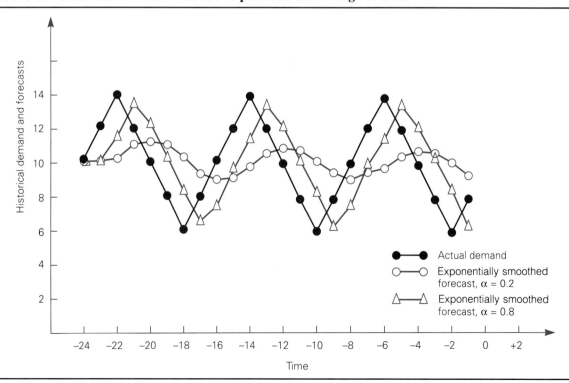

(1)	(2)	(3) Exponentially Smoothed Forecast ($\alpha = 0.2$) ($F_{t_{\alpha = 0.2}}$)	(4) Error ($E_{t_{\alpha = 0.2}}$)	(5) Absolute Error ($|E_{t_{\alpha = 0.2}}|$)	(6) Exponentially Smoothed Forecast ($\alpha = 0.8$) ($F_{t_{\alpha = 0.8}}$)	(7) Error ($E_{t_{\alpha = 0.8}}$)	(8) Absolute Error ($|E_{t_{\alpha = 0.8}}|$)
Period (t)	Demand (D_t)						
−24	10	10.000	0	0	10.000	0	0
−23	12	10.000	2.000	2.000	10.000	2.000	2.000
−22	14	10.400	3.600	3.600	11.600	2.400	2.400
−21	12	11.120	0.880	0.880	13.520	−1.520	1.520
−20	10	11.296	−1.296	1.296	12.304	−2.304	2.304
−19	8	11.037	−3.037	3.037	10.461	−2.461	2.461
−18	6	10.429	−4.429	4.429	8.492	−2.492	2.492
−17	8	9.544	−1.544	1.544	6.498	1.502	1.502
−16	10	9.235	0.765	0.765	7.700	2.300	2.300
−15	12	9.388	2.612	2.612	9.540	2.460	2.460
−14	14	9.910	4.090	4.090	11.508	2.492	2.492
−13	12	10.728	1.272	1.272	13.520	−1.502	1.502
−12	10	10.983	−0.983	0.983	12.300	−2.300	2.300
−11	8	10.786	−2.786	2.786	10.460	−2.460	2.460
−10	6	10.229	−4.229	4.229	8.492	−2.492	2.492
−9	8	9.383	−1.383	1.383	6.498	1.502	1.502
−8	10	9.106	0.894	0.894	7.700	2.300	2.300
−7	12	9.285	2.715	2.715	9.540	2.460	2.460
−6	14	9.828	4.172	4.172	11.508	2.492	2.492
−5	12	10.663	1.337	1.337	13.502	1.502	1.502
−4	10	10.930	−0.930	0.930	12.300	−2.300	2.300
−3	8	10.744	−2.744	2.744	10.460	−2.460	2.460
−2	6	10.195	−4.195	4.195	8.492	−2.492	2.492
−1	8	9.356	−1.356	1.356	6.498	1.502	1.502
			Sums =	53.249			49.695

$$MAD_{\alpha = 0.2} = \frac{\Sigma |E_t|}{24} = \frac{53.249}{24} = 2.219$$

$$MAD_{\alpha = 0.8} = \frac{\Sigma |E_t|}{24} = \frac{49.695}{24} = 2.071$$

For Further Reference

Books

Abraham, B., and J. Ledolter. *Statistical Methods for Forecasting.* New York: John Wiley & Sons, 1983 (QA279.2.A27).

Bails, Dale G., and Larry C. Peppers. *Business Fluctuations: Forecasting Techniques and Applications.* Englewood Cliffs, N.J.: Prentice-Hall, 1982 (HB3730.B25).

Box, G. E. P., and G. M. Jenkins. *Time Series Analysis, Forecasting, and Control.* Rev. ed. San Francisco: Holden-Day, 1976 (QA280.B67).

Chatfield, Christopher. *The Analysis of Time Series: An Introduction.* 4th ed. London: Chapman and Hall, 1989 (QA280.C4).

Makridakis, Spyros G., and Steven C. Wheelwright. *Forecasting Methods for Management.* 5th ed. New York: John Wiley & Sons, 1989 (HD30.27.W46).

Smith, Bernard T. *Focus Forecasting: Computer Techniques for Inventory Control.* Boston: CBI Publishing, 1978.

Willis, Raymond E. *A Guide to Forecasting for Planners and Managers.* Englewood Cliffs, N.J.: Prentice-Hall, 1987 (HD30.27.W55).

Periodicals

Interfaces.

Journal of Forecasting.

Journal of the Operations Research Society.

Management Science.

Review Questions

1. How does demand management differ for goods producers and service providers?
2. Why does the term *order* have different meanings to different people in a producing organization? Who is responsible for demand management?
3. In the order processing sequence, what are the effects of the provider's ability to ship or serve from stock? What happens when there isn't sufficient stock on hand to cover the order?
4. In an order promise, who promises what to whom? How firm is that promise? What constitutes order promise in a service organization?
5. How is the order processing sequence modified for human service processes?
6. What are the purposes of demand management? How do they compare with the purposes of demand forecasting?
7. What is a time series? What are its principal components?
8. What are the measures of forecast error? Identify advantages and disadvantages for each measure.
9. What is the relationship between lead time for providing a product and requirements for demand forecasts?
10. If a manager told you, ''I don't need to do demand forecasting,'' what arguments would you use to counter that statement?
11. Compare the accuracy of item and group forecasts. Explain.
12. Since forecast error is worse for distant future periods than for the near future, is it prudent to forecast only for the near term? Explain.
13. Marketing projections and economic projections are both done in dollars. How, then, do they differ?
14. What are the consequences for organizations that keep no demand records?
15. What does the term *historical demand pattern projection* mean?
16. When is a simple mean a suitable forecast? When would a trend forecast be preferable over the mean?
17. Is it permissible to make eyeball projections? Discuss. Under what conditions should the least-squares technique be used for trend projection?
18. Why is it sometimes difficult to decide whether to use the mean, straight-line trend, or curve trending as a forecast basis?
19. What is the purpose of calculating seasonal indexes? What is done with them?
20. How is one forecasting model compared with another in selecting a model for future use?

Problems and Exercises

1. Think back on your experiences with physician appointments, and select the appointment system that worked best. What demand management activities must be taking place among the staff who served you in order for the system to work well? Explain.
2. Following is a list of organization types. Exhibit 5–3 shows that forecasts may be required for planning (*a*) facilities and adjustable capacity, (*b*) raw materials, (*c*) components, and (*d*) assemblies. Refer to the concepts presented in the figure to match up the listed organizations with the four purposes. Briefly explain your matchups.

Furniture manufacturing	Roller-skating rink
Clothing manufacturing	Natural gas distributor
Air conditioning/heating contractor	Orthodontist

Highway construction   Church parish
Airframe manufacturing   Sound system manufacturing
Commercial printing   Small appliance manufacturing
Tractor manufacturing   Toy manufacturing

3. At Apex Steel Cabinet Company, the human resources director was the first manager to separately forecast key workloads (see Example 5–1). Mr. Guy, the president, wants key workload
forecasting extended to other departments. Your assignment is to prepare logical workload lists
and forecast bases, similar to Exhibit 5–5, for the following departments or sections: public
relations, advertising, and data processing.

4. Planners at county hospital are preparing a staffing plan and budget for next quarter. The
following listing is computer data on labor-hours in various departments for last quarter. The
trouble is, the average forecast error looks very high. Is the forecast error too high, or could next
quarter's computer forecast be useful as the basis for a quarterly staffing plan? Perform any
necessary calculations, and discuss.

Department	Last-Quarter Labor-Hour Actual	Last-Quarter Labor-Hour Forecast
Anesthesia	208	130
Cardiopulmonary	175	210
Emergency	589	650
Obstetrics	391	380
Pathology	68	90
Physical therapy	71	110
Radiology	277	200
Surgery	950	810

5. At Henry, Henry, and Henry, Public Accountants, the administrative vice president is responsible for forecasting demand for professional accounting services. The forecast for the preceding
six-month period (made six months prior to that) was 120 client-days of work per month. Actual
demand turned out to be 130, 100, 150, 150, 90, and 80. Calculate the MAD, SD, and MAPE
for the six-month time interval. From your calculations, what would you say about the pattern
of error? Is it about what you expect? Why or why not?

6. Metro Auto Sales forecasts new-car demand 12 months into the future. The forecast is updated
every month. Metro's supplier, a large U.S. auto maker, requires a 12-month forecast of total
number of cars of all types so that it may plan equipment, space, labor, and so on in its
manufacturing plants. It also requires a two-month forecast of numbers of each model. Internally
Metro finds the forecast useful for staffing (new-car salespeople) and for ensuring the correct
amount of lot space on lease. Metro and its new-car supplier clearly are practicing a number of
the concepts and principles of demand forecasting discussed in the chapter. Your assignment is
to discuss the principles and concepts that apply to this situation (as many as you can think of).

7. A study of forecast accuracy over a recent past time period for five products—A, B, C, D, and
E—reveals the following:

Product	Forecast Error	Percent Error
A	− 20	10%
B	− 10	5
C	+ 20	8
D	− 30	15
E	+ 40	12

Calculate the average percent error, first by item and second for the five items as a group. (Note: You will be able to make these calculations even without being given the raw data on forecast and actual demands.) Explain the resulting percent error for the group. Why are the item and group errors so different?

8. Following are the recent actual demands and forecasts for a *service part* (industry's term for a spare or replacement part).

Time (t)	−5	−4	−3	−2	−1
Actual demand	9	10	17	25	27
Forecast	10	12	15	19	25

   a. Calculate the MAD, SD, and MAPE.
   b. Plot the demand and forecasts on a graph similar to Exhibit 5−7. If you had to forecast the next two or three periods, what would your concerns be? Why?

9. Should the manager of a television or radio station forecast demand? Why or why not? What sort of demand are we talking about? (A brief interview with such a manager would be informative.)

10. In a certain time-sharing computer system, the quarterly number of "connects" or "logons" is one useful indicator of demand. Recent data are as follows:

	Quarter							
	−8	−7	−6	−5	−4	−3	−2	−1
Number of connects (in thousands)	8	9	11	10	11	13	16	12

What is your forecast for next quarter? Look for seasonality and trend. Explain.

11. Service part demands for lawn mower blades at Lawngirl Manufacturing Company, along with three-week and nine-week moving average data, are as follows:

	Week							
	−16	−15	−14	−13	−12	−11	−10	−9
Demand	800	460	630	880	510	910	420	740
Three-week moving average		630	657	673	767	613	690	650
Nine-week moving average					682	671	713	710

	Week							
	−8	−7	−6	−5	−4	−3	−2	−1
Demand	790	700	840	600	930	680	900	800
Three-week moving average	743	777	713	790	737	837	793	
Nine-week moving average	716	734	733	776				

   a. For weeks −12 through −5, plot the raw demand data, the three-week moving average data, and the nine-week moving average data on one graph. Comment on the smoothing effects of the different time spans (note that the raw data constitute a one-week moving average).

   b. Assuming a nonseasonal demand, what is the forecast for next week if a one-week moving average is used? If a three-week moving average is used? If a nine-week moving average is used?

   c. Consider your answers from question *b* and the nature of the product: lawn mower blades. Which moving average time span seems best?

12. Recent monthly caseload in a public defender's office was:

January	February	March	April	May	June
180	100	90	110	110	120
July	**August**	**September**	**October**	**November**	**December**
140	170	150	160	160	170

   a. Graph the demands as (1) a two-month moving average and (2) a six-month moving average. What do the graphs show about the smoothing effects of different moving average time spans?

   b. Calculate a five-month moving average centered on June. Then use that value to calculate a seasonal index for June.

   c. What factors would determine the usefulness of the seasonal index in question *b*?

13. Demand data and seven-month moving average data are as follows:

						Month						
	−12	−11	−10	−9	−8	−7	−6	−5	−4	−3	−2	−1
Actual demand	130	160	80	130	100	40	150	160	210	200	150	170
Seven-month moving average	133	121	107	113	117	124	141	144	154			

   a. Compute a seasonal index applicable to next month.

   b. If the trend projection, not adjusted for seasonality, is 168, what is the seasonally adjusted forecast for next month? Use the seasonal index from question *a* in your calculation.

   c. If the product is not seasonal but the seven-month moving average time span is optimal, what should be the forecast for next month?

14. Examine issues from the last two months of *Business Week*. In the "Business Week Index" section, find the production index and the leading index.

   a. How are they determined? Verify this with calculations of your own.

   b. Why would indexes such as these be smoothed? Discuss.

15. The stockroom manager at Citrus Life and Casualty Company forecasts use of office supplies by exponential smoothing using $\alpha = 0.3$. Three weeks ago, demand for letterhead envelopes and the forecast were both 12. Actual demands since then were 18 and 5 boxes, respectively. What is the forecast for next week?

16. The captain of the *Pescado Grande,* a sport-fishing boat that docks at Ensenada, Mexico, is trying to develop a plan for crew needs by day of the week. The basis is the number of paying customers per day. Following are data for the last three weeks:

	Monday	Tuesday	Wednesday	Thursday	Friday	Saturday	Sunday
Week −3	12	6	10	12	18	30	26
Week −2	9	4	5	8	22	32	34
Week −1	3	10	8	7	14	27	31

a. Calculate "seasonal" (daily) indexes for Sunday and Monday. Base the calculations on the appropriate seven-day average demand. What index should be used for planning the crew on Sunday and Monday of this week? Explain.

b. If the average number of paying customers per day next week is expected to be 16, how many should be forecast for Monday?

17. Huckleberry Farms, Inc., has three years of monthly demand data for its biggest seller, Huckleberry Jam. The planning director aims to use the following data for demand forecasting:

	Cases of Huckleberry Jam		
	Three Years Ago	*Two Years Ago*	*Last Year*
January	530	535	578
February	436	477	507
March	522	530	562
April	448	482	533
May	422	498	516
June	499	563	580
July	478	488	537
August	400	428	440
September	444	430	511
October	486	486	480
November	437	502	499
December	501	547	542

a. Calculate a six-month moving-average forecast. To which future time period is this forecast applicable?

b. Which of the following moving average time spans is best: three months, six months, or nine months? Prove your answer by calculating mean absolute deviations (MADs) using data for the last 12 months only. (If suitable computer facilities and software are available to you, use the full 36 months' data.)

c. If the most recent forecast—for December of last year—was 495, what is the next exponential smoothing forecast? Use $\alpha = 0.3$. To which future time period is this forecast applicable?

d. Which of the following alphas is best for exponential smoothing forecasting: 0.1, 0.3, or 0.5? Prove your answer by calculating MADs using monthly data for the last three months only. In each case, assume that 570 was the exponentially smoothed forecast for September of last year.

e. Although the given data are monthly, Huckleberry also needs a forecast for next quarter and next year. Manipulate the monthly data (i.e., create new tables of data) to make them useful for a quarterly and annual forecast. Now compute a quarterly and annual moving average forecast using a three-period (not three months, in this case!) time span. Then compute a quarterly and annual exponential smoothing forecast using $\alpha = 0.3$ and assuming that the last-period forecast was (1) 1,596 for quarterly and (2) 5,990 for annual.

f. Plot the data on a scatter diagram with time as the horizontal axis (use graph paper or carefully create a substitute on ordinary lined paper). Use the eyeball trend projection method to produce a forecast (not adjusted for seasonality) for Huckleberry Jam for the next 12 months. You may use either a straight or curving line—whichever fits better. Write down each of the 12 forecast values. (If suitable computer facilities and software are available to you, verify your plotted trend line by processing the data on a computer.)

g. Most consumer products show some degree of demand seasonality. What kind of seasonality pattern would you expect for Huckleberry Jam? Why? After responding to that question, examine the three-year history to see if the data tend to follow your reasoning.

You may find it helpful to plot the three sets of 12-month data on top of each other on a graph to see if there is a seasonality pattern. Now comment further on Huckleberry's demand patterns.

h. Select any 3 of the 12 months, and calculate seasonal indexes for those months for each year. Follow the method in Exhibit 5–15, modified so that the basis is a 12-month moving average. Now develop projected (next-year) seasonal indexes for each of the three months. (If suitable computer facilities and software are available to you, develop seasonal indexes for the full 12 months.)

i. Combine your results from (g) and (h), that is, your trend projection with your seasonal indexes. What are your seasonally adjusted trend forecasts for next year?

18. Seal-Fine Sash Company has three years' quarterly demand data for its standard bedroom window unit. The production control manager uses the following data for demand forecasting:

	Number of Window Units		
	Three Years Ago	*Two Years Ago*	*Last Year*
Winter	190	215	401
Spring	147	210	510
Summer	494	755	925
Fall	773	1,088	1,482

a. Calculate the three-quarter moving average forecast. To what future time period does this moving average apply?

b. Which of the following moving average time spans is better, three quarters or four quarters? Prove your answer by calculating mean absolute deviations (MADs) using all 12 quarters of data. (If suitable computer facilities and software are available, process the data by computer rather than manually.) Do the MAD values seem to show that moving average is a suitable method for quarterly forecasting of Seal-Fine's window units? Explain.

c. If the most recent forecast—for fall of last year—was 1,550, what is the next exponential smoothing forecast? Use $\alpha = 0.2$. To what future time period is the forecast applicable?

d. Which of the following alphas is best for exponential smoothing forecasting: 0.1, 0.3, or 0.5? Prove your answer by calculating MADs using quarterly data for the last three quarters only. In each case, assume that 540 was the exponentially smoothed forecast for winter of last year. Do the MAD values seem to show that exponential smoothing is a suitable method for quarterly forecasting of Seal-Fine's window units? Explain.

e. Plot the data on a scatter diagram with time as the horizontal axis (use graph paper or carefully create a substitute on ordinary lined paper). Use the eyeball trend projection method to produce a forecast (not adjusted for seasonality) for the window units for the next four quarters. Now combine the data to yield yearly forecasts for the next three years. You may use either a straight or curving line, whichever fits best. Write down each forecast value. (If suitable computer facilities and software are available, verify your plotted trend line by processing the data by computer.)

f. What kind of seasonal demand pattern would you expect for Seal-Fine's product line? Explain. After responding to that question, examine the three-year history to see if the data tend to follow your reasoning. You may find it helpful to plot the three sets of quarterly data on top of each other on a graph to see if there is a pattern of seasonality. Now comment further on Seal-Fine's demand patterns.

g. Select any two of the four quarters and calculate seasonal indexes for those quarters for each year. Follow the method in Exhibit 5–15. Now develop projected (next-year) seasonal indexes for each of the two quarters. (If suitable computer facilities and software are available, develop seasonal indexes for all four quarters.)

h. Combine your four-quarter trend projection from question *e* with your seasonal indexes from (*g*). What are your seasonally adjusted trend forecasts for next year?

19. Following are the last four months' demand data and exponential smoothing forecasts for the custom drapery department at a local department store. The data are in number of customer orders:

Month	Actual Demand	Forecast
−4	18	20
−3	6	18
−2	12	16
−1	9	15

a. Determine the mean absolute deviation of forecast error.
b. Calculate the tracking signal as of today. What does it suggest?

20. Q. R. Smith, owner-manager of Smith's Kitchens, Inc., sees some evidence that demand for kitchen cabinets is related to local tax mill rates, which are adjusted twice yearly. Following are recent data that Smith has collected:

	Half-Year Period									
	− 10	− 9	− 8	− 7	− 6	− 5	− 4	− 3	− 2	− 1
Cabinet demand	55	70	75	70	80	85	90	80	70	75
Mill rate	110	125	135	145	140	140	160	150	150	140

a. Develop a graph (scatter diagram) with cabinet demands (Y_t) on the vertical axis and mill rates three periods earlier (X_{t-3}) on the horizontal axis. Plot each combination of demand and mill rate three periods earlier (i.e., Y_t and X_{t-3}) on the graph. For example, the first point would be the demand, 70, for period −7 and the rate, 110, for period −10. Examine your graph. Is there enough association between demand and mill rates three periods (one-and-a-half years) earlier to be useful for forecasting? Explain.
b. Calculate the formula for the straight line of best fit for the data in question *a*. Using your formula along with the appropriate mill rate, what is the forecast cabinet demand for the next six-month period?
c. Calculate the coefficient of correlation. Is your impression from question *a* confirmed?

21. The chief of planning at North American Hotels, Inc., suspects that convention business may be associated with productivity indexes and tourist business with weather. The following graphs show two of his attempts to make these associations:

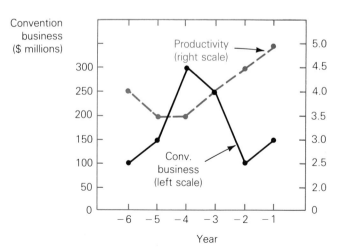

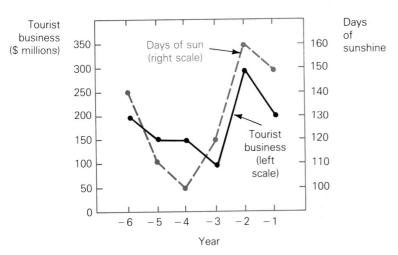

a. Based on your inspection of the productivity-convention business graph, what should the chief of planning conclude? Comment on the usefulness of the analysis for the hotel.

b. Based on your inspection of the sunshine-tourist business graph, what should the chief of planning conclude? Comment on the usefulness of the analysis for the hotel.

22. The safety division at Acme Manufacturing Company has written the following numbers of safety citations in the past seven months:

	Month						
	−7	−6	−5	−4	−3	−2	−1
Citations	71	63	60	58	61	40	42

a. Using the eyeball method, plot the data and project the number of citations that might be expected next month.

b. The chief safety inspector suspects that safety citations are related to number of new hires. She has collected the following data on new hires for the same seven months.

	Month						
	−7	−6	−5	−4	−3	−2	−1
New hires	40	31	27	33	10	25	25

Analyze the association between new hires and citations. Look for a leading indicator.

c. Calculate the formula for the straight line of best fit (line of regression) for the last seven months of citations. Use the formula to calculate the projected demand for the next two months.

d. Calculate the coefficient of correlation between new hires and citations. Make the same calculation but with new hires leading citations by one month. (Base the calculations on citations for months −6 to −1 and new hires for months −7 to −2.) Comment on the difference and on which type of associative forecast is more appropriate.

23. Anderson Theaters owns a chain of movie theaters. In one college town, there are several Anderson Theaters. Anderson wants to find out exactly what influence the college student population has on movie attendance. Student population figures have been obtained from local colleges. These, along with movie attendance figures for the past 12 months, are as shown (on the next page).

a. What is the correlation coefficient?

b. Is this correlation analysis useful for Anderson Theaters? Discuss fully?

							Month					
	1	*2*	*3*	*4*	*5*	*6*	*7*	*8*	*9*	*10*	*11*	*12*
Students*	8	18	18	18	15	9	11	6	17	19	19	13
Attendance*	14	15	16	12	10	8	9	7	11	13	14	17

*In thousands. The student figures are monthly averages.

24. Refer to the application box in the chapter, "Speedy Order Processing at Atlantic Envelope Company."
    a. To what extent has order processing become focused? What is it focused on?
    b. How can order processing times be further reduced while retaining a high degree of focus?

25. Large utilities typically forecast energy demands far into the future to ensure that adequate production facilities and distribution networks are available to meet customer needs. In 1992, Illinois Power Company prepared a 20-year forecast of the electrical power demand for its service territory; that forecast (not including reserve margin requirements) is shown in Exhibit 5–30.
    a. From the forecast, what would you conclude about the company's needs for financing, personnel, and facilities in the years to come? Why?
    b. Why are there three forecasts—high, medium, and low? Does the presentation of three sets of numbers detract from the credibility of the forecast? Discuss.
    c. Exhibit 5–30 is a demand forecast that does not include electrical power margin requirements. How might a company such as Illinois Power incorporate margin requirements into its forecasts? (You might want to interview a manager at a utility company.)

EXHIBIT 5–30   Forecasting in Utilities Services—Electrical Power Demand

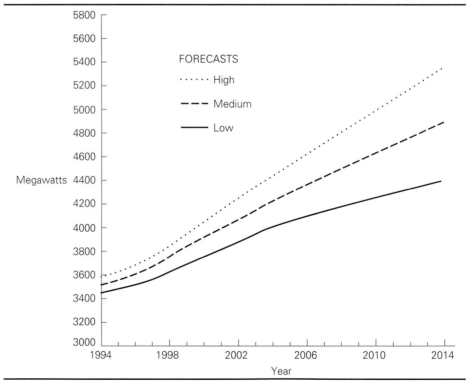

SOURCE: Data courtesy of Illinois Power Company. Used with permission.

LEAST SQUARES AND CORRELATION COEFFICIENTS

In this supplement we examine two related techniques. Both concern the straight line that most closely fits a set of plotted data points:

1. The least-squares technique, which yields an equation for the straight line of best fit (line of regression).
2. The correlation coefficient, which measures how well a given straight line or line of regression fits a set of plotted data points.

Least Squares

The general formula for a straight line is:

$$Y = a + bX$$

For any set of plotted data points, the least-squares method may be used to determine values for *a* and *b* in the formula that best fits the data points: *a* is the *Y* intercept, and *b* is the slope. Least-squares formulas for *a* and *b* follow, first in the general form and then in a simpler form for a special case.

General form:

$$a = \frac{\sum Y}{N} - b\left(\frac{\sum X}{N}\right)$$

$$b = \frac{N\sum XY - \sum X\sum Y}{N\sum X^2 - (\sum X)^2}$$

Special form (when $\sum X = 0$, i.e., an odd number of periods):

$$a = \frac{\sum Y}{N} \text{ and } b = \frac{\sum XY}{\sum X^2}$$

where

$$\sum Y = \text{Sum of } Y\text{-values for all plotted points}$$
$$N = \text{Total number of plotted points}$$
$$\sum XY = \text{Sum of product of } X \text{ value and } Y \text{ value for all plotted points}$$
$$\sum X^2 = \text{Sum of squares of } X \text{ values for all plotted points}$$
$$\sum X = \text{Sum of } X \text{ values for all plotted points}$$

The least-squares technique is shown in Example S5–1 using the special form of the equation.

Correlation Coefficients

The coefficient of correlation (*r*) ranges from ± 1.0 for perfect correlation to 0.0 for no correlation at all. An *r* of ± 1.0 applies to the case where all plotted points are on the straight line of best fit.
    A widely used formula for *r* is:

$$r = \frac{\sum XY - \sum X\sum Y/N}{\sqrt{[\sum X^2 - (\sum X)^2/N]\,[\sum Y^2 - (\sum Y)^2/N]}}$$

Example S5–2, an extension of Example 5–3, demonstrates the formula.

EXAMPLE S5–1   Least-Squares Trend Line—Data Services, Inc.

At Data Services, Inc., demand in the last seven quarters in programmer-hours was as follows: 510, 600, 400, 520, 340, 440, and 420. What is the trend line?

Solution:

The following table simplifies computation of a and b values. The fourth quarter, in which demand was 520, is treated as the base period; it is numbered as period 0. The three previous periods are numbered -1, -2, and -3; the three succeeding periods are numbered $+1$, $+2$, and $+3$. The low numbers simplify calculation and, since their sum is zero—that is, $\sum X = 0$—the simpler least-squares equations apply. The Y values are the seven demand figures.

Y	X	X^2	XY
510	-3	9	$-1,530$
600	-2	4	$-1,200$
400	-1	1	-400
520	0	0	$0 \leftarrow$ Base period
340	$+1$	1	$+340$
440	$+2$	4	$+880$
420	$+3$	9	$+1,260$
Sums = 3,230	0	28	-650

Since

$$a = \sum Y/N \text{ and } b = \sum XY/\sum X^2,$$

$$a = \frac{3,230}{7} = 461$$

$$b = \frac{-650}{28} = -23.2$$

The formula for the line of best fit is:

$$Y = 461 - 23.2X$$

The formula may be used to forecast, say, the next quarter. With the base or center-most period numbered 0, the next quarter is numbered $+4$. Then:

$$Y = 461 - 23.2 \, (+4)$$
$$= 368 \text{ programmer-hours}$$

Exhibit S5–1 summarizes the results of the least-squares computations and the forecast for next quarter; note the very close pattern of the demand data here with that in Exhibit 5–11. Dates are added to the figure to make it agree with the dates for Exhibit 5–11 in the chapter. Clearly the least-squares trend is very nearly the same as the eyeball trend in Exhibit 5–11, as we would expect it to be.

EXAMPLE S5–2   Correlation Coefficient—State Jobs Service

Layoffs at Acme two weeks earlier are plotted against job applicants at the Jobs Service office. Exhibit 5–25 shows the correlation visually. What is the calculated coefficient of correlation (r)?

EXHIBIT S5–1   Seven-Quarter Least-Squares Trend—Data Services, Inc.

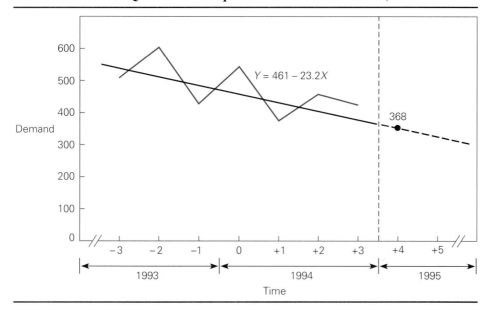

EXHIBIT S5–2   Working Figures for Computing *r*—State Jobs Service

Number of Applicants (Y)	Layoffs at Acme (T − 2) (X)	Y^2	X^2	XY
50	0	2,500	0	0
60	0	3,600	0	0
80	25	6,400	625	2,000
65	20	4,225	400	1,300
110	50	12,100	2,500	5,500
145	60	21,025	3,600	8,700
115	60	13,225	3,600	6,900
125	25	15,625	625	3,125
120	20	14,400	400	2,400
120	35	14,400	1,225	4,200
110	45	12,100	2,025	4,950
70	0	4,900	0	0
60	0	3,600	0	0
65	0	4,225	0	0
90	0	8,100	0	0
55	0	3,025	0	0
70	20	4,900	400	1,400
45	0	2,025	0	0
100	30	10,000	900	3,000
105	30	11,025	900	3,150
105	40	11,025	1,600	4,200
70	0	4,900	0	0
95	0	9,025	0	0
100	10	10,000	100	1,000
Sums = 2,130	470	206,350	18,900	51,825

Solution:

Exhibit S5–2 provides the necessary totals to solve for *r*. All *X* and *Y* values are taken from Example 5–3. Since there are 24 data items, $N = 24$. Calculation of *r* is as follows:

$$r = \frac{\sum XY - \sum X \sum Y / N}{\sqrt{[\sum X^2 - (\sum X)^2/N][\sum Y^2 - (\sum Y)^2/N]}}$$

$$= \frac{51,825 - (2,130)(470)/24}{\sqrt{18,900 - (470)^2/24)(206,350 - (2,130)^2/24)]}}$$

$$= 0.78$$

An *r* of 0.78 is rather high. Layoffs at Acme may be considered a good leading indicator.

MASTER PLANNING FOR CAPACITY AND OUTPUT

6

Chapter Outline

The following exchange is all too common:

   ''How's business?''

   ''Great! Demand's up 15 percent! Only problem is, they can't keep up in operations. I've noticed quite a few angry customers.''

That reply reflects one side of master planning: considerable demand, but inadequate **capacity** to serve it. Insufficient capacity to transform resources into desired outputs means delays in serving customers and probable loss of customers to the competition. The other side of master planning, excess capacity and output, raises costs and prices, which can also send customers to the competition.

Master Planning Basics

Grappling with capacity options is called **master planning,** and it occurs both broadly and narrowly (see Exhibit 6–1):

Aggregate demand:
Total demand, not broken down into different products; measured in broad units (e.g., customers, cartons, truckloads, or tons per day).

- At a broad level, the master planning team balances aggregate customer demand and the capacity to process demand. The result is a capacity plan.
- More narrowly, the master planning team steers the firm's capacity toward actual item demands as they occur, as well as toward specific process improvement activities. Results of narrow-level actions include an appointment book or master schedule of customers, services, or goods to be processed, plus time for training, improvement projects, housekeeping, and so forth.

Introductory Example

We can look more closely at the master planning effort to balance demand and capacity with the example of Anita's Studio, a small, service-oriented business. (The Anita's Studio example relates to two other chapter examples: Koji Film Co., a manufacturer whose product might be used by Anita's studio, and FastFotos, Inc., a service business that might process film for Anita's.)

EXHIBIT 6–1   Master Planning

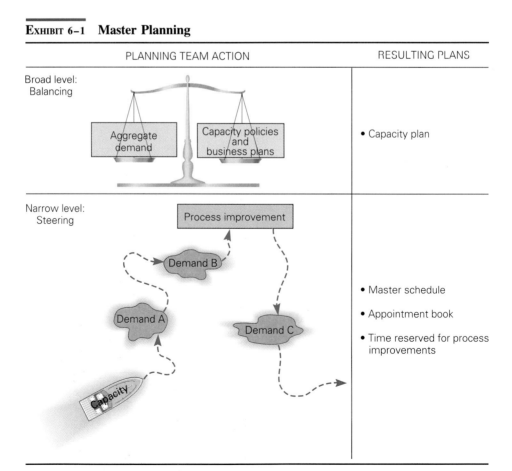

EXAMPLE 6–1   MASTER PLANNING—PHOTOGRAPHY SERVICES

Anita's Studio is a professional photography business. Anita specializes in individual and family portraits. She shoots in her own studio and does her own developing and printing. Demand may be expressed as the number of customers or, more precisely, the number of photos. But to Anita, demand has another, equally important meaning: demand for capacity. What capacity does she need to satisfy the demand for her services?

The first capacity item is Anita's time, which includes hours of studio time, developing time, packaging time, record-keeping time, management time, and so forth. Second is the demand for quantities of paper, developing chemicals, film, and other supplies. Next, she needs certain tools and equipment, such as cameras, lights, backdrops, enlargers, drying racks, and light meters. Finally, she needs the facility (studio) itself.

Anita must plan all these capacity elements if she is to succeed in serving her customers. Further, each item is limited. Anita's time is restricted to something less than 24 hours a day, the enlarger can handle only so many prints per hour, the studio accommodates only certain group sizes, backdrops, and so forth. If Anita knows that demand for her work is relatively stable, she may develop a relatively stable **capacity plan.**

But what if she wants to change her **business plan**, say, by expanding into event photography—weddings and other social or sporting events? For one thing, demand for photographs and capacity to process them will grow, which requires further capacity planning. Also, while some capacity items are common to both portrait and event photography, others must be separately planned. Event work will require new kinds of capacity. Although it places little demand on studio time, it creates the need for travel and on-site shooting time. Also, Anita may have to purchase faster lenses, battery packs, film winders, and other special equipment. Both event and portrait work, however, require capacity for developing and printing.

Another issue is the seasonality of event photography. Weddings, anniversaries, graduations, and proms pile up in May and June. Thus, more capacity will be needed in those months. Anita may consider buying more equipment, hiring assistants, and contracting out some developing and printing. On the other hand, she may choose simply to limit the amount of business she accepts, reasoning that any added springtime capacity will be unused during the rest of the year. She might wish to avoid the unpleasant task of dismissing assistants when there is not enough work. The point is that she has options in planning capacity.

Anita's business plan, including goals, strategies, and policies, will affect her thinking about the capacity plan options. What she wants to do influences what she plans to do.

In developing an appointment book (master schedule), Anita must consider demand for her services as well as her capacity to provide them. Total demand for all photography services (aggregate demand) will determine the load on her developing and printing capacity, as well as capacity to cover demand for billing and other clerical operations. The mix of portrait and event photography (major subgroups of aggregate demand) will determine the capacity requirements for studio shooting and travel/site-shooting times, respectively. Finally, planning for each capacity item, such as each type of film and each size of printing paper, will require forecasts of each type (item) of photography assignment, including number of shots, size and number of prints desired, and so forth. Actual customer bookings and ensuing print orders will most accurately help predict capacity needed, by type.

On the other side of the coin, the capacity plan Anita selects will determine how much and what type of demand she can satisfy. She might have to revise her appointment book, perhaps more than once, as she juggles demand and capacity, seeking a fit.

It is easy to see that inattention to demand for photography services might lead to investment in too much or too little capacity. Likewise, failure to consider capacity could lead to overbooking and promising more than can be delivered. Adverse effects may include delays, customer dissatisfaction, lost business, and overall careless and hurried business practices.

Several items emerge from the Anita's Studio example:

1. Capacity is needed in order to meet demand—without panic or shortcuts.
2. The business plan (including plans for expansion or contraction) influences capacity choices (equipment quantity, staff size, etc.).
3. Greater variety of products or services offered (portrait photography, event photography, etc.) complicates capacity planning.
4. Demand planning and capacity planning set limits on what the appointment book (master schedule) can accommodate.
5. In a given period, one or more revisions of the master schedule/appointment book might be required.

These points also apply to master planning in large firms, with the extra difficulty of developing consensus among the many manager-planners in large organizations.

Master Planning Teams

Except in very small businesses, like Anita's Studio, master planning is a two-team effort. A high-level team determines capacity for upcoming weeks, and a master scheduling team puts actual and forecast orders into time slots (see Exhibit 6–2).

These teams (with representatives from each key function) meet regularly, usually monthly for capacity planning and weekly for master scheduling. Lack of teamwork, an all too common problem, leads to capacity decisions and scheduling priorities based more on power and influence than on rationality.

For example, finance may push for greater capacity utilization to gain a higher return on existing fixed assets, while sales wants more capacity (never mind utilization) to meet peak demands. At the same time, senior management, fretting about high overhead costs, commissions a benchmarking study, which zeros in on the human resource department's budget. The study points to an abnormal amount of hiring/training to handle demand peaks, followed by layoffs and terminations when demand wanes—and the cycle repeats. Meanwhile, the vice president of operations bemoans layoffs of well-trained employees, who later are replaced by green new hires who aren't productive. These and other managers all have different views about capacity, utilization, and meeting demand. Decision making boils down to behind-the-scenes combat.

*𝒫*RINCIPLE 3:

Achieve unified purpose.

There are no magic formulas for resolving the conflict, which is irrational for the firm. However, divergent views on capacity stem from being out of touch. The best cure is regular teamwork, which forces each decision maker to confront the big picture.

Besides amount of capacity and output, master planning has a time component. As Exhibit 6–2 indicates, teams set capacity plans and master schedules to cover a medium-term planning horizon, from a few weeks to a few months out. As a capacity-planning example, Anita and her associates would want to plan labor and equipment needs at her studio a few weeks in advance of need. (By contrast, any associate could go out and buy film and paper, which is short-term planning, not our concern here.)

Like many service providers, Anita master-schedules her photographic assignments in an appointment book, which reserves a block of time. On-demand customers (who arrive occasionally, mainly to buy prints) are not an element of this medium-term master scheduling effort.

As noted in Chapters 3 and 5, readiness and flexibility reduce planning lead time. Thus, Anita can avoid the hazards of capacity planning in the distant future—where demand forecasting is poor—by being flexible and well prepared. She might obtain flexible equipment (e.g., a highly versatile camera and lenses), have on-call backup assistance, and make sure everything is well placed and orderly in the studio.

Anita must also do long-term planning for fixed assets, such as her studio and fixtures, often called facilities. (More on facilities planning in Chapter 17.)

Exhibit 6–2   Master Planning Teams

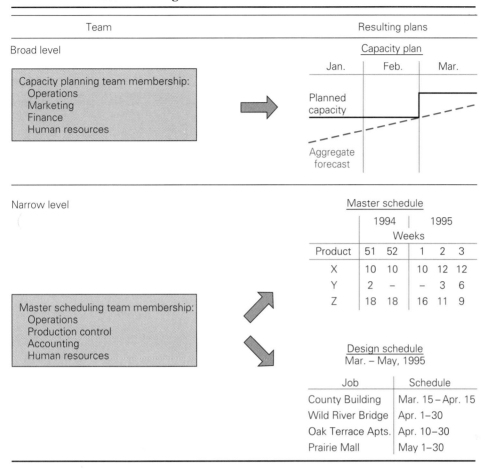

Balancing customer demand and capacity can be complicated and require detailed planning stages. In this chapter, however, we stick to the basics and save the detailed aspects for later chapters, where they fit well with other topics.

Exhibit 6–3 illustrates a basic master planning sequence. It shows one series of steps for prescheduled goods and services (e.g., dental appointments, contract home building, mail orders, or molding of plastic cases for camera assembly). A shorter sequence is shown for on-demand goods and services (e.g., freshly popped popcorn, electrical power outage repair, while-you-wait welding). For on-demand sales and services the capacity plan aims at providing the right amount of space, equipment, labor, and inventory (if any) to do business.

Prescheduling of demands, on the other hand, is in two steps. First, the planning team ensures that the master schedule or appointment book states what and when, but not in detail. Second, the team completes detailed planning and scheduling: step-by-step tasks and work flow (covered in Part IV).

At this point—their first brush with capacity planning—many students ask, Why not just forecast demand or book customer orders, then plan whatever capacity is required to meet that demand?

The answer: as stated in the opening paragraphs of the chapter, competition requires that plans for capacity and output levels must be sufficient but not excessive (incurring costly waste). Capacity strategies and policies (the filter between customer demand and the capacity and output plans in Exhibit 6–3) help ensure that both requirements are met.

*Basic Master
Planning Sequence*

Exhibit 6–3   Master Planning: Sequence Overview

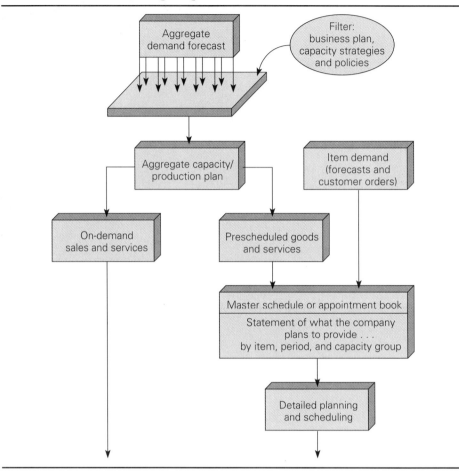

Capacity Strategies and Policies

When capacity is insufficient, customers have to wait or can't get what they want. But having too much capacity may result in costly idleness and invite bad work habits. What is too much? Some extra capacity is desirable because it lets associates upgrade skills, improve processes, and attend to deferred problems.

It is also needed to get the quality right and be on time, even in periods of peak demand (as indicated in Chapter 5, peak-and-valley demand patterns are common).

Thus, capacity planning is more than just matching numbers. Capacity is valuable and deserves good overall management, including allowing time for all the extras. To accomplish those aims, planning teams must deal with issues of capacity utilization.

Following are a few examples of master planning for a specified planning horizon and capacity utilization.

Capacity Utilization   While buildings and equipment are objects of long-term planning, the intensity of their use, or **utilization,** is an element of the medium-term capacity plan. Planning for utilization involves two questions: (1) What is full utilization? Some firms, or industries,

$\mathscr{C}$ontrast

Capacity Management

"By the Numbers" Capacity

Plan for full utilization of capacity—for hours of demand to equal available hours of labor and facilities or even to overutilize capacity (e.g., work overtime on a regular basis).

Well-Managed Capacity

Plan for enough capacity to ensure high quality, on-time performance every time, and reasonable time for improvement activities.

---

consider full utilization to be less than 24 hours a day, seven days a week. (2) What is planned utilization for the upcoming capacity planning period?

In photography studios, for example, full utilization might be eight hours a day, Monday through Friday, plus four hours Saturday morning: 44 hours a week. After the summer wedding season and before the school photo season, Anita may chose to close on Monday and Saturday. The capacity plan for her studio then is eight hours a day, Tuesday through Friday: 32 hours a week. Planned capacity utilization is 72.7 percent (32 divided by 44).

At some assembly plants full capacity is defined as 3 shifts per day, five days a week, or 15 shifts per week. If the planning team sets next quarter's capacity plan (based on the latest demand forecast) at 2 shifts of scheduled assembly per day, or 10 shifts per week, then planned capacity utilization would be 67 percent (10 divided by 15).

For paper and metal processors, because their equipment is so expensive, full capacity may mean 21 shifts per week (including scheduled maintenance time). If a paper plant's (see photos) demand is slack and its master planning committee runs only 18 shifts a week, planned capacity utilization is 86 percent (18 divided by 21).

Let's consider how to formulate a capacity plan. You'll recall (from Exhibit 6–3) that the capacity plan stems from the business plan, capacity strategies and policies, and the aggregate demand forecast.

A TV manufacturer's executive committee decides on a business plan calling for (1) shipment of 12,000 TVs next quarter (which equals the aggregate demand forecast) and (2) cutting finished goods inventory by 2,000 units, which yields (3) a net production plan of 10,000 TV sets for the quarter. Experience shows that production of 10,000 sets requires 5,000 labor-hours of TV assembly, 10,000 labor-hours of TV component subassembly, and so on. These figures are the labor component of the capacity plan for the quarter. They plan machine capacity similarly: 10,000 molded plastic cabinets for the TVs requires 2,500 machine cycles on a four-cavity injection-molding machine, forming 4 cabinets per cycle.

We see, then, that a capacity plan and a production plan are two sides of the same coin. For Anita's Studio, 10 portraits per day (production plan) might translate into five hours of studio time for Anita and two and one half hours of darkroom time for her or her assistant (capacity plan).

Studio capacity and darkroom capacity are treated as two separate elements of a capacity plan. Likewise, TV assembly capacity is logically different from plastic cabinet molding capacity. Different processes are required. As we learned in Chapter 5, each capacity element is a candidate for a separate aggregate forecast—but the fewer, the better, since aggregate forecasts are more accurate for larger capacity groupings.

Top left—Parent roll of tissue.
Top right—Team (amid rolls of tissue) examines partially converted segment.
Bottom—Product segment, plus packaged final product (conversion machines in background).

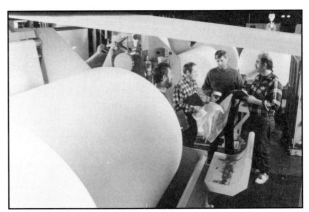

SOURCE: Courtesy of Pope & Talbot, Inc., Consumer Products Division.

Into Practice

Capacity Utilization at General Motors

"By the end of 1995, it's clear that GM will be a far smaller company. The projected North American work force— 71,000 white collar people and 250,000 hourly workers— will be about half the size of GM's total employment in 1985. . . . The 10 plants to be closed have the capacity to build about two million cars and trucks a year. Their elimination will slash the company's overall annual North American capacity to between five million and 5.5. million cars and trucks. That will allow the company to use 100% of its North American capacity by 1993, Mr. Stempel [GM's then CEO] said."

SOURCE: "GM Plans to Close 21 More Factories, Cut 74,000 Jobs, Slash Capital Spending," *The Wall Street Journal*, December 19, 1991.

Sometimes obstacles stand in the way of effective planning for capacity and resource utilization. Large numbers of restrictive job classifications, or products and services, cannot be reduced to a small number of capacity groupings. Thus, another reason for being organized into focused units with cross-trained employees is to make capacity planning simpler and more straightforward.

To sum up, an aggregate forecast for a capacity grouping (filtered by business plans and capacity policies) is input to a production plan and a capacity plan. The plans set limits on the master schedule or appointment book (omitted in master planning for on-demand sales and services). In the remainder of the chapter, we consider some of the key aspects of these activities.

*𝒫*RINCIPLES 6 AND 7:

Form focused chains of customers. Cross-train for multiple skills.

Capacity strategy often depends a good deal on the type of industry. As we've noted, capital-intensive process industries need high utilization of capacity. In labor-intensive businesses, especially services, capacity strategy centers on labor, a relatively flexible resource. At a tax preparation service, for example, the owner's strategy might be cost leadership, or keeping salary costs low. The owner might employ mostly part-time tax advisors, brought in only when required by current demand. This bare-bones labor-capacity strategy is known as **chase demand:** hire when demand is good, lay off when demand is poor.

An alternative labor strategy is known as **level capacity:** try to retain people through thick and thin. Level capacity is favored in labor-intensive operations when quality is a vital competitive factor. This is especially so if employees' skill qualifications are high or skills are scarce.

The level-capacity strategy sometimes governs materials and backlogs as well as labor. When demand dips for a firm that makes to stock (an inventoriable product), planners may allow inventory to grow in order to keep capacity (labor) level. In contrast, planners at a make-to-order firm may let order backlogs (instead of inventory) grow to keep capacity level.

Chase-Demand versus Level-Capacity Strategies

Backlog: Accumulation of unfinished work or unfilled orders.

Consider, for example, ABC, Inc., a Wall Street brokerage firm.[1] ABC handles transactions coming in from branch offices around the country. Securities and Exchange Commission regulations require all transactions to be settled within five days; that gives ABC managers time to smooth out the daily volume fluctuations so that transaction-handling capacity will not be strained one day and underused the next. But stock market volume can swing dramatically overnight. For example, a rumor about a peace agreement somewhere in the world might cause volume to soar. This could tax ABC's capacity to process stock transactions. How would ABC cope? Here are what two ABC managers might propose:

Manager A: Our capacity should be set at 12,000 transactions per day. This will allow us to meet demand most days. Last year we had a few hot periods when demand ran at 14,000–15,000 per day, and we probably will this year, too. We can handle those problems by overtime for a few days—until new clerks can be hired. Our labor turnover rate is high, so when transaction volume drops we can ease capacity down by not filling vacancies.

Manager B: I think we should keep capacity right at 17,000 transactions per day. That will be enough to handle the spurts in volume, which are very hard to predict.

---

[1] Adapted from W. Earl Sasser, R. Paul Olsen, and D. Daryl Wychoff, *Management of Service Operations* (Boston: Allyn & Bacon, 1978), pp. 303–05 (HD9981.5.S27).

$\mathcal{I}$nto $\mathcal{P}$ractice

Hewlett Packard's Flex Force: Level Capacity *Plus* Chase Demand

At Hewlett Packard's Lake Stevens Instruments division, demand spikes made capacity planning difficult. Their solution: flex force, a permanent pool of on-call temporary employees. At its inception, flex force was designed to meet these six requirements:

1. Provide 20 percent flexibility in the total capacity projections.
2. Assure short-term response (within 48 hours) to changes in capacity requirements.
3. Provide training necessary to maintain quality levels, regardless of changing workloads.
4. Be cost neutral. There should be no perceived cost advantage or disadvantage from using the flex force program.
5. Flex force employees should feel like HP employees and not be treated as second-class citizens. They

should be included in departmental meetings, enjoy equal access to the facility, and not be visibly identifiable as flex force employees.

6. Flex force employees should want part-time employment and not accept part-time employment as a means to attaining full-time employment.

Flex force has grown from an initial pilot-test group to 80 employees. The six requirements have generally been met, and "on-time delivery rates, frequently among the best in the company, have been largely attributed to the ability of the flex force to quickly respond to changing order rates on any product."*

*John Schneider, "Putting the Flex in a Flexible Work Force," *Target*, Special edition (1991), pp. 5–13.

Who is right? In this case both are—and here's the rest of the story. Each is managing a different end of the business of handling the stock transactions. Manager A is in charge of cashiering: processing certificates, cash, and checks. Clerks and messengers with uncomplicated tasks are the work force. Manager B, on the other hand, runs order processing. The work force has higher skills: data entry, data processing, programming, and information analysis. Equipment is expensive, and lead times to change information processing procedures are long.

Manager A is advocating chase demand, which seems rational for his department. Manager B prefers a level-capacity strategy, which is logical for her department. Since A's lower-skill people cannot handle the work in B's department, A and B should have different capacity plans based on separate aggregate demand forecasts. One plan for the whole transaction processing operation won't do.

Exhibit 6–4 outlines the two strategies. The conditions often dictate the strategy. Businesses that employ low-wage, low-skill people in possibly unpleasant working conditions use the chase strategy. With low skill levels, training costs are low per employee but could be high per year, since turnover tends to be high. Turnover also means high hire-fire costs and, along with low skills, contributes to high error rates. Forecasting and budgeting may be short-term since lead times for adding to or cutting the work force are short.

Level capacity has opposite features. To attract more skillful people, pay and working conditions must be better. Training costs per employee are high. The attractions of the job are meant to keep turnover and hire-fire costs low, and high labor skills hold down error rates. Forecasting and budgeting must be longer term, since hiring and training skilled people takes time.

EXHIBIT 6–4   **Comparison of Chase Demand and Level-Capacity Strategies**

	Chase Demand	Level Capacity
Labor skill level	Low	High
Wage rate	Low	High
Working conditions	Erratic	Pleasant
Training required per employee	Low	High
Labor turnover	High	Low
Hire-fire costs	High	Low
Error rate	High	Low
Type of budgeting and forecasting required	Short term	Long term

Is global competition making companies flip-flop on capacity strategies? Sometimes it seems so. Firms long admired for their level-capacity strategies have been shutting down or moving business units, laying off people, and cutting wages—which sounds like chase.

At the same time, however, some of the same companies are increasing training and process improvement. They had been paying high wages to employees who lacked the skills necessary to deliver world-class quality. By not spending enough on, or allowing time for, training and quality, the companies had not followed through with the full level strategy. Strategic correction, including a policy of underscheduling resources (explained next), is part of that follow-through.

Undercapacity Scheduling

A policy that allows time for training, getting the quality right, meeting just-in-time commitments even on busy days, and holding team improvement project meetings is sometimes called **undercapacity scheduling.** The policy usually applies just to the labor resource, but it presumes—and requires—that equipment will also be underscheduled. If equipment is too heavily scheduled, it won't be properly maintained, checked, set up, and improved; quality and JIT goals will not be met.

As a labor policy, undercapacity scheduling generally is determined numerically. A dental clinic, for example, might use a 15 percent undercapacity scheduling policy. If clinic capacity (measured in dentists' time, dental technician time, etc.) is 100 patients per day, the clinic will schedule 85 patients per day.

Is this practice wasteful of capacity? Not when TQM is active. When the schedule is met early (which is most of the time) the policy calls for data analysis, project work, preventive maintenance on equipment, training, and other activities aimed at reducing errors, rework, equipment trouble, and variation of all kinds. When fewer patients per day are planned for, there are valuable compensations: fewer unplanned stoppages, greater staff efficiency, lower operating costs, time to fit in emergency patients, time for unexpected patient problems, less rework, and happier customers. Happier customers lead to better customer retention, thus avoiding the costs of patient turnover or, worse, too few patients to keep the staff busy.

Example 6–2 illustrates some of the simple calculations that might be involved in applying undercapacity scheduling in high-volume manufacturing.

Special Capacity Policies

While underscheduling labor provides time, other specific capacity policies are needed to guide the attainment of specific strategies. Suppose, for example, that Anita's Studio follows a chase-demand strategy. Her customer-oriented policy is to promise finished prints no later than 72 hours after portrait photos are taken. To meet that commitment, her

EXAMPLE 6–2   Undercapacity Scheduling — Koji Film Co.

The star of the product line at Koji Co., a photographic film manufacturer, is 135 24-exposure, 100-speed color film. The yield per eight-hour shift has averaged 6,600 rolls, or 825 rolls per hour. Koji's master scheduling team has adopted a rate-based schedule of 6,000 rolls per shift—no more, no less—which is the current sales rate.

Is the schedule attainable? What is the underscheduling policy in percentage terms?

Solution:

The target of 6,000 should be attainable in one eight-hour shift most of the time. In a shift with average problems, the 6,000 rolls would be produced in about $7\frac{1}{4}$ hours (6,000/825 rolls per hour = 7.27 hours). On a bad day with two or three line stoppages, the 6,000 may still get produced—by working right up to the bell. On a very bad day, the 6,000 might be made by working some overtime.

The underscheduling policy is 6,000/6,600 = 90.9 percent.

Policy:
Guidance for carrying out strategy.

capacity policy is to make extensive use of subcontracting (to a friend's studio) for developing and printing. Other examples of specific policies are:

- A municipal power company has a strategy of providing high employee security in order to gain a stable work force (low employee turnover). Its enabling policies include (1) maintaining excess linespeople and installers in order to meet surges in demand and (2) subcontracting (to local electric contractors) extraordinary maintenance, especially repair of downed lines.
- A bowling lane proprietor's strategy is one of high utilization of bowling lanes. To act on that strategy, the proprietor offers lower prices for daytime bowling.
- At a food wholesaler, planners have adopted a competitive strategy of very fast service to retail grocers. Its supportive policies include shift work, weekend hours, overtime, cross-trained office associates who can help out in the warehouse or drive delivery vehicles, and large inventories.

Examples of these capacity policies, plus several other common ones, are listed as follows:

Hiring and layoffs.	Maintenance work as a filler.
Overtime and extra shifts.	Use of marginal facilities.
Part-time and temporary labor.	Renting space or tools.
Cross-training and transfers (of people or work) among departments.	Refusing, back-ordering, or postponing work.
Service pools (e.g., a typing pool).	Building inventories.
Quick changeover techniques to make capacity flexible.	Peak/off-peak price differences.

Setting capacity policies is, properly, a responsibility of top officers. These might include the general manager and the vice presidents (or department managers) of finance, operations, marketing, materials control, and production control.

Capacity policies may be expressed generally, such as "Avoid overtime and keep inventories low." Or they may be expressed numerically, with minimums, maximums, or ranges, and may be priority ordered. For example, a set of priority-ordered policies aimed at maintaining a level permanent work force might be:

$\mathcal{I}$nto $\mathcal{P}$ractice

Working Hard at Avoiding Layoffs

Kawasaki Motors Manufacturing in Lincoln, Nebraska, was faced with a double dilemma: just-in-time and quality improvements had raised productivity, resulting in a labor surplus. Then a recession hit, severely cutting motorcycle demand and killing off Kawasaki's entire line of snowmobiles. To correct the capacity-demand mismatch, the management team took the following actions, in chronological order:

1. Assigned excess direct labor to essential support tasks, including modifying, moving, and installing equipment.
2. Assigned excess labor to maintenance work, such as painting, caulking, and minor remodeling.
3. In fall 1981, Kawasaki lent 11 of its excess employees to the city of Lincoln, where they worked for

several months with Kawasaki paying wages and benefits.
4. The first layoffs (24 white-collar people) occurred in October.
5. In November, 16 blue-collar employees voluntarily took a six-month furlough with call-back rights.
6. In February 1982, 98 production employees were terminated.
7. In October 1982, the plant went to a four-day workweek to preserve jobs for the remaining work force.

The only policy governing those actions was that of seeking to avoid layoffs in the face of insufficient demand.

1. For insufficient demand:
   a. Keep employees busy by building inventory—maximum of 10 percent buildup above predicted demand.
   b. Lay off employees only after a 10 percent excess inventory is on hand.
2. For excess demand:
   a. Use temporary labor for the first 5 percent of excess demand.
   b. Use overtime for the next 5 percent.
   c. Reduce customer service (serve best customers fully, but for lesser customers, postpone or even refuse orders, offer partial shipments, etc.)

With such specific policies, master planning is straightforward; managers just follow the policies. Usually, however, a company will not hem itself in so explicitly. For example, the lifetime employment policy of some Japanese firms is really only a goal. The employee tends to have a lifetime (or career-time) commitment to a single company, but the company may or may not be able to retain the employee that long. Japan has a highly competitive economy, and each year many companies fail, laying off employees. Successful companies anywhere in the world, of course, often can claim with pride that they have never had layoffs.

While capacity strategies and policies apply to organizations, other master planning tools apply to units of output, goods, or services. One is the learning curve, explained in the supplement to this chapter. Another—and perhaps the most important—is aimed at natural capacity groupings, our next topic.

Group (Family) Capacity Planning

Group-based capacity planning, a commonsense partner of aggregate forecasting (discussed in Chapter 5), requires three implementation steps:

One of 16 U-shaped photofinishing cells at Ashton Photo, Salem, Oregon. Each cell has about nine members, focuses on one type of photo (e.g., sport teams or school photos), and processes the entire job from incoming film to outgoing finished work and invoice. (Ashton's customers are professional photographers.)

1. Group products into natural families and select units for aggregate capacity planning. Goods/services that employ units of capacity going through roughly the same processes form a family. It is a natural family only if capacity (skills and equipment) is flexible enough to process all the goods/services within the family.
2. Project aggregate customer demand for each capacity group. This forecast is in the units of measure chosen in step 1.
3. Develop a production plan (output units), and convert to capacity units if necessary. This step aims at having the right amount of aggregate resources on hand.

Capacity Planning for On-Demand and Make-to-Order Operations

The 1-2-3 capacity planning procedure applies to both on-demand (make-to-order) businesses and make-to-stock production. Our first example is for on-demand photographic services.

Does this method of capacity planning assume that future demand will be like past demand? No. While total demand may be fairly close, the week-to-week demand pattern is sure to be different. Thus, maximum backlogs can be much more or less than projected. Still, the simple method of Example 6–3 employs existing demand data. It can work quite well because overtime, job transfers, and other flexible responses are available in weeks when the plan goes wrong.

EXAMPLE 6–3   CAPACITY PLANNING—FASTFOTOS, INC.

FastFotos is a large photofinisher, handling both consumer and commercial film processing (including some contract work for Anita's Studios, especially in the school graduation season). It is an on-demand, make-to-order business.

EXHIBIT 6–5   Capacity/Backlog Options at FastFotos, Inc.

	Recent Demand	Option 1: 1,800 Orders per Week				Option 2: 2,100 Orders per Week			
Week	*Orders*	*Orders*	*Deviation*	*Backlog*	*Excess Capacity*	*Orders*	*Deviation*	*Backlog*	*Excess Capacity*
1	1,800	1,800	0		~~700~~	2,100	0		300
2	1,100	1,800	+700		7̶8̶0̶	2,100	+1,000		1,000
3	1,800	1,800	0			2,100	0		300
4	1,950	1,800	−150	−150		2,100	0		150
5	2,300	1,800	−500	−650		2,100	−200	−200	
6	2,800	1,800	−1,000	−1,650		2,100	−700	−900	
7	2,250	1,800	−450	−2,100		2,100	−150	−1,050	
8	1,200	1,800	+600	−1,500		2,100	+900	−150	
Total	15,200								

$$\text{Mean demand} = \frac{15,200}{8} = 1,900 \text{ orders per week}$$

The capacity-planning team (the personnel director and the operations manager) plans capacity a number of weeks in advance. Since there is plenty of equipment capacity, the plan includes labor only: the right skills, hiring, and training. Their day-to-day fine-tuning includes reasonable overtime and labor borrowing.

The capacity team uses the three-step method:

Step 1. They conclude that consumer and commercial photo processing make up separate capacity groups: consumer processing is routine; commercial customers usually require special processing. Routine processing and special processing take place in different areas of the building. The team agrees that number of orders is an appropriate capacity measure for both groups. The team plans capacity for its all-important commercial accounts first.

Step 2. The capacity team uses recent past demand (number of orders) as a simple, reasonable projection of demand for the next eight-week capacity planning period.

Step 3. Exhibit 6–5 is the team's capacity-planning work sheet for commercial business. It includes recent demand data (second column) and two capacity options, both tight on capacity (team members are very cost-conscious). Option 1 provides enough capacity to process 1,800 orders per week (100 less than the mean recent demand of 1,900 per week). Projected deviations range from +700 (excess capacity) to −1,000 orders per week. Since negative deviations signify backlogged orders, consecutive negative values carry over to the next week. The projected backlog grows to −2,100 orders in week 7, then falls to −1,500 in week 8. The capacity shortage in week 7 is over two weeks' backlog (2,100 orders /1,800 orders per week = 1.17 weeks), which won't do in FastFoto's competitive business. ⌐

Option 2 provides for 300 more orders per week than option 1. This results in projected excess capacity in the first four weeks, but insufficient capacity in the second four weeks; the backlog grows to a high of −1,500 orders in week 7. Since 1,050 orders is less than one week's backlog, the capacity planning team considers the plan workable (with the potential of marshalling additional labor hours during peak weeks).

Here *orders* is the unit of measure in a production plan and is also a suitable (surrogate) measure of capacity. (Cars per year serves a similar dual role in the auto industry—as noted earlier.)

Put another way, capacity planners generally should be able to reserve their flexible options for when the plan does not work out. If they build overtime, subcontracting, and so forth, into the capacity plan, there is no room for correction when actual demand patterns don't follow the plan.

In some businesses, such as transportation, restaurants, and lodging, an unmet order is lost; backlogs are not carryable. The method of Example 6–3 needs to be modified in those cases. The altered method treats demand as noncumulative so that negative deviations are lost sales, not backlogs.

Capacity Planning for Make-to-Stock Operations

In the make-to-stock case, capacity planning follows the three-step process and often adds a fourth step: refine the plan to provide for desired inventory levels. There may also be a fifth step: further test the feasibility of the plan by examining how it affects critical resources (e.g., a heavily used machine or a specially skilled associate). The first four steps are presented in Example 6–4.

EXAMPLE 6–4   CAPACITY (PRODUCTION) PLANNING—QUARK ELECTRONICS

Capacity planning at Quark Electronics was once reactive. If work was piling up in Shop A (long customer order backlogs), a planner in that shop would request more labor, extra shifts, or other reactive capacity changes. Planning capacity based on demand forecasts seemed hopeless because there were too many different products and forecasts were too inaccurate.

However, a capacity-planning team was formed, and they have learned to apply group-based forecasting and capacity planning in four steps.

Step 1: The team divided its production processes into three product families, groups 1, 2, and 3. Each group covers a large number of electronic items, including end products, subassemblies, and component parts.

The team studied product routings (flow paths) and found three dominant paths through the four shops (see Exhibit 6–6). A few products do not fit any of these

---

EXHIBIT 6–6   Common Routings—Quark Electronics

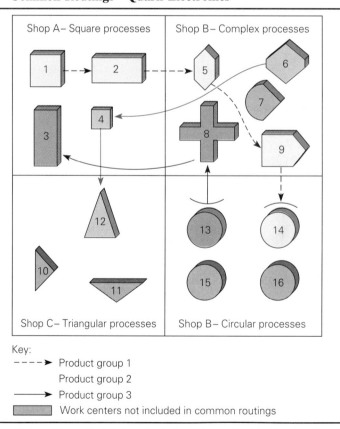

NOTE: Machines 13, 14, 15, and 16 are identical; thus 15 and 16 could be substituted for 13 and 14, if needed.

routings, but enough do to provide a solid basis for capacity (production) planning, with groups large enough for decent forecast accuracy.

Step 2: The capacity team obtains aggregate demand forecasts for each of the three product groupings; the forecast for group 1 is in pieces per week (see Exhibit 6–7).

Step 3: The team develops a capacity plan stated in pieces per week. The plan is based on careful evaluation to ensure that the plan is consistent with capacity policies and is realistic. The team's calculations (not shown) ensure that projected aggregate labor-hours in product group 1 are sufficient to meet projected demand each week, with time to spare for improvement work.

Step 4: Several years ago Quark's senior management decided to follow its competitors and focus, not on direct labor costs (which had fallen to less than 3 percent of production costs), but on intensive management of inventories (over 65 percent of costs). Thus, capacity planners are building inventory reductions into the capacity plans. The current four-week capacity plan shows a decline from 14,000 to 13,600 pieces (see last column in Exhibit 6–7). (But each year, just prior to Quark's busy season, the capacity planners allow a buildup of anticipation inventories. That is, they increase the production rate above the forecast sales rate in anticipation of a seasonal surge in demand.)

Quark's capacity-planning team must repeat all of these steps for product groups 2 and 3. But is that the end of it?

To be on the safe side, the planners want to know that their capacity plan does not overload certain critical resources. For example, Machine 5, a complex machine in Shop B, is nearly always the first to be overloaded, thereby becoming a bottleneck. Since the capacity plan is stated in pieces per week, which represents a nonspecific mixture of products, the team cannot precisely project the workload of Machine 5. Instead, they use historical average machine-hours per piece as the basis for the rough-cut stage of capacity planning. For Machine 5, the data show 0.0075 hours per piece. Thus, for Group 1 and week 1:

$$\text{Projected workload} = 10{,}100 \text{ pieces} \times 0.0075 \text{ hours per piece}$$
$$= 75.75 \text{ hours}$$

This is within Quark's upper limit of 80 planned hours of workload per week. (Company policy is to operate two 8-hour shifts a day, five days a week, or 80 hours.) The capacity team finds this too close for comfort. It leaves little margin for error, and forecasts are notoriously erroneous.

What to do? The marketing director (a member of the team) says, "No problem." Promotion costs are too high, and sales people have been booking orders from customers whose credit is shaky. Her actions to deal with these two problems will, she estimates, cut projected demand by 5 percent. Quick recalculations of all capacity figures yield a plan the whole team likes.

Marketing director's actions show capacity planning is more than translating demand into capacity numbers. If it were only number crunching, it could all be done by a computer—no need for a team.

Exhibit 6–7   Capacity Plan—Product Group 1

	Pieces through Product Group 1				
	Forecast		*Capacity (Production) Plan*		
Week	*Pieces per Week (000)*	*Cumulative*	*Pieces per Week (000)*	*Cumulative*	*Inventory*
0	—	—	—	—	14.0
1	10.0	10.0	10.1	10.1	14.1
2	10.0	20.0	10.1	20.2	14.2
3	10.4	30.4	10.1	30.3	13.9
4	10.4	40.8	10.1	40.4	13.6

Contrast

Capacity Planning

Reactive	Product-Group Based	Product-Group Based, Capacity Focused
Poor; hampered by functional organization and lack of product focus.	Good, but dispersed capacity for each product group hampers communication, cross-training, labor borrowing, and so on.	Very good; co-locating capacity and product groups simplifies planning, problem-solving, and adjusting to wrong forecasts.

Simplified Capacity Planning in the Focused Business

*P*RINCIPLE 6:

Form multiple focused chains of customers.

The method just reviewed represents good capacity planning for the firm that is organized by function. The modern movement to get focused (which requires breaking up functional departments, offices, and shops) yields a bonus: simplified capacity planning.

Exhibit 6–8 shows how Quark Electronics might get focused. The four shops (see Exhibit 6–6) are gone. The people, their equipment, and accessories have been moved into product-focused clusters, called cells or plants-in-a-plant. This way of grouping capacity makes it natural and easy for associates to become cross-trained, to switch jobs, and constantly to interact and solve problems with suppliers at the previous process and customers at the next one. When the demand forecast for their product family is wrong, the people in the focused unit may be able to quickly take corrective action on their own.

Master Scheduling

A capacity plan puts aggregate customer demands into time slots, but the master schedule puts actual orders into time slots, product by product. While all operations need a capacity plan, those providing on-demand services have no time to plan at the detailed level of a master schedule. That includes organizations catering to walk-in or call-in customers: retailers, fast-food restaurants, emergency rooms, police and fire departments, automobile registration facilities, buses, and so forth.

By contrast, reserved-seat businesses, professional services, and manufacturers draft a detailed master schedule. For services, the master schedule is the appointment book or reservation listing. It schedules a time slot for each client or order. At Anita's Studios, the appointment book schedules customers into Anita's available time slots. A bigger service business such as a medical clinic would have a separate appointment book for each physician, and might also have appointment books for scarce, high-cost facilities like X-ray.

Manufacturing is a bit more complicated. A master scheduling team (from operations, production control, sales, accounting, and human resources) weighs the master

EXHIBIT 6–8   **Cells—Quark Electronics**

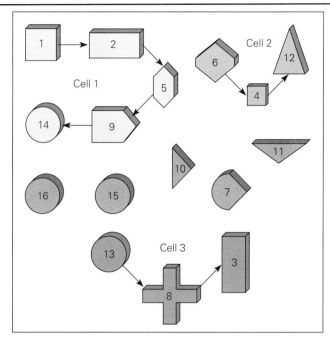

Note: Work centers not organized into cells are shaded. Centers 15 and 16 are mobile,
capable of quick replacement for center 13 or 14.

scheduling alternatives and sets priorities. Good customers, for example, get preferential slots in the master schedule; hence, the need for sales to be represented on the team. High-profit items ought to be preferred over marginal ones; hence, accounting needs a representative.

The master scheduling team may construct the master production schedule (MPS) around major capacity-consuming modules (end items) of the final product. Major modules (e.g., a personal computer's mother board, power supply, hard disk, etc.) are costly and warrant careful advance scheduling. (In contrast, putting the modules together into final products may be push-and-snap assembly, random testing, and a bit of packaging; it may take just a few hours and not cost much.) Since each module consumes different resources (capacity) with different timing, each gets its own segment of the master production schedule.

The complexity of master scheduling in factories will be explained with examples. But first we consider a very basic example, master scheduling classes in a college.

MPS	January	
	4-8	11-15
Mother boards:		
X-121	53	61
X-221	22	22
.		
.		
.		

Master scheduling is a key duty of department heads and administrators in educational institutions (see Example 6–5).

Basic Master Schedule: A Services Example

EXAMPLE 6–5   MASTER SCHEDULING IN DEPARTMENT OF MANAGEMENT—FUNK UNIVERSITY

Each department chairperson in the College of Business Administration at Funk University must prepare a master schedule consisting of one schedule for each course and covering the next few terms. The master schedule is prepared twice each term: one version is based on preregistrations; an updated version is based on general registration data.

The master scheduling steps are illustrated for the Department of Management (see Exhibit 6–9). The steps are the same for all other departments, but the aggregate forecast groups (block 2) would be different. The Department of Management's courses (30 to 40 offerings) cluster neatly into three capacity groups:

1. Quantitative/management information systems (MIS)/operations management (OM).
2. Behavioral/human resources.
3. General management/business policy.

Those groups are not intended to correspond to clusters of demand (though student demands may cluster that way). Rather, the purpose is to form natural units of capacity; that is, the courses in any given group should be similar enough to enable the group's faculty members to trade off teaching assignments. The groupings shown would not be perfect. Someone whose specialty is human resource management may, for example, have a secondary interest in general management instead of in behavior. Still, the groupings should be all right for the purpose: to arrive at a capacity plan (out of block 3) that matches up reasonably well with total course requirements (block 6), leading to a trial master schedule of course offerings (block 7).

The budget (education plan) and strategies and policies (block 1) are controls on the capacity plan. Policies generally exist regarding class sizes (faculty-student ratios), classroom space, teaching loads (per faculty member), use of teaching assistants, and utilization of faculty skills (the extent to which faculty teach in stronger or weaker areas of expertise).

Exhibit 6–9   Master Scheduling—Department of Management

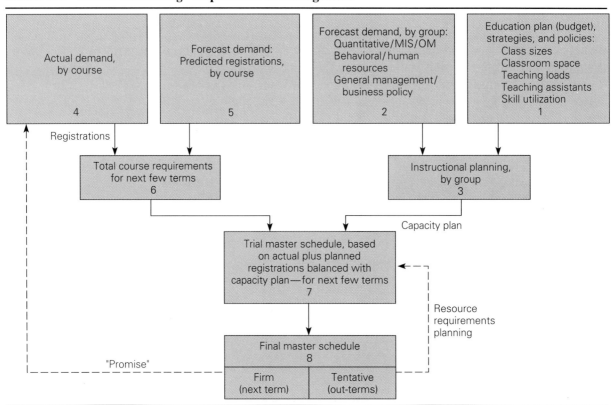

While blocks 1 through 3 deal with aggregate demand and capacity, blocks 4 through 6 deal with unit demand course by course. Actual demand, consisting of registrations by course, comprises block 4. Block 5 is forecast demand: predicted registrations, by course, based on historical patterns plus other knowledge.

Next, in block 6, the chairperson assembles course requirements for the next few terms into a list. Then she matches this shopping list against what is available in the capacity plan. The result is the trial master schedule of course offerings for the next few terms. The feedback arrow from block 8 to block 7 of Exhibit 6–9, resource requirements planning, indicates closed-loop control. It makes the master schedule an accurate reflection of capacity to meet demands by adjusting the master schedule until scarce resource overloads are eliminated.

A final master schedule emerges at block 8. It is firm for the upcoming term and tentative for future terms. At this point, Funk University's registrar sends out an order promise to students who have registered. The registrar either confirms or denies their registration for a given course. If denied, a substitute may be offered.

Exhibit 6–9 contains the basics of master planning. Exhibit 6–10, expanding the basics, yields a master planning model for the complex case of a manufacturer that fabricates and assembles in the job or batch mode.

Blocks 1 through 6 are the same for a manufacturer as for a service: A capacity planning team guided by business plans and capacity strategies (box 1) uses aggregate

Matching Capacity and Demand: A Complex Case

EXHIBIT 6–10   Capacity-Demand Matching Process

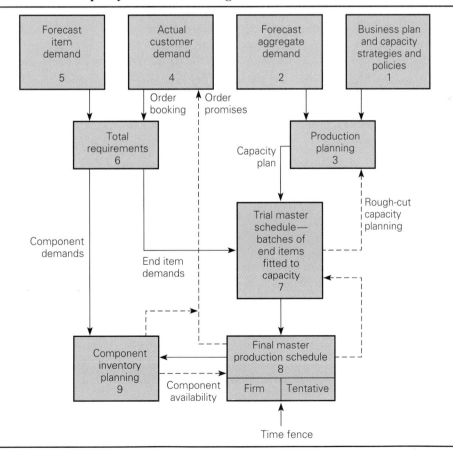

demand forecasts (box 2) to plan overall production activity (box 3), thereby yielding a capacity plan. The sales force goes to work booking orders (box 4), which combine with forecasts of future orders (box 5), adding up to total requirements (box 6).

Scheduling End Products and Components.   After block 6, there may be a split into two different types of schedules, one for end products and another for component parts. The one for end products is the master production schedule (MPS), block 7 (trial) and block 8 (final). The master scheduling team, in generating the MPS, tries to smooth out lumpy demand streams and may also collect demands for the same products into production lots.

Service parts:
In manufacturing lingo, spare parts and repair parts for after-sale service.

The schedule for component parts includes demands for parts needed to meet the master production schedule, and may also include independently demanded component parts, such as service parts (see arrows from blocks 6 and 8 to block 9 in Exhibit 6–10).

In previous editions of this text, things were more complicated. We described the practice, common in some industries, of breaking master production scheduling into two stages. One stage was for producing the major modules, which took weeks and was scheduled in the MPS based on forecasts. The second was for assembling the major modules into final products, which took days and was scheduled in the final assembly schedule at the last minute based on actual customer orders. However, some of today's producers—under a strategy of time-based competition—can produce the modules and assemble the final products in less than a week; they do it just in time to meet last-minute sales bookings. Indeed, some can make the component parts of the modules within the same week.

Cumulative lead time:
Total time from first activity (e.g., drawing materials from stock) to completion of the item.
Time fence:
Point in the future beyond the longest total lead time; separates firm scheduling zone from tentative zone.

Time Fence Policies (Avoiding Nervous Schedules).   JIT or no JIT, after suitable trials, the master scheduling team produces a final MPS. The firm portion typically covers the product's cumulative lead time, which ends at a time fence. A different master scheduling policy is needed for the two sides of the time fence. On one side (in the firm zone where work has already begun) schedule changes generate system nervousness—disruptions that ripple through many stages of planning and execution. On the other side of the time fence (in the tentative zone) schedule changes are just on paper. Thus, the firm portion of the schedule is changed only as a last resort, but the tentative portion may be changed frequently.

However, frequent schedule changes, even in the tentative zone, can upset schedules for suppliers. In some companies, therefore, the master planning team sets up a second time fence to cover maximum lead time for key supplier-partners. Capacity policy then calls for checking with those suppliers before making schedule changes in the zone between the first and second time fences.

Order Promise.   A primary concern of the customer is an order promise date, which comes from a salesperson. Salespeople must have reliable information from master scheduling so that they can make reliable promises. The importance of having a sales representative on the master scheduling committee has already been mentioned.

*𝒫*RINCIPLE 10:

Make it easy to avoid error or variation.

How else can companies improve delivery promises? They can install a complete information system that accurately calculates order completions. However, problems can persist under such a system. Alternatively, the firm can simplify and integrate ordering, planning, scheduling, purchasing, and production, and thereby eliminate causes of the usual delays such that all jobs are done quickly and predictably. Thus, salespeople can make promises based on firm order-promise policies (called rules of the game at Ahlström Pump, Mänttä, Finland, and Easley, South Carolina).

ontrast

Master Scheduling

Conventional Narrow Outlook	**Broad Competitive Outlook**
Master scheduling czar.	Master scheduling team.
Focus on internal lead times, time fence, lot sizes, and avoidance of schedule nervousness that would disrupt internal work in progress.	Focus on customers, and avoidance of schedule nervousness disruptive to customers, salespeople, and both internal and supplier work in progress.
Final assembly scheduled to actual customer orders and with short lead times.	Final assembly, major modules, and component processes scheduled as a unit in one stage, with short total lead times.
Major modules master-scheduled mostly to a forecast and long lead times.	
Component schedule tied to major module schedule, with long lead times.	

A special case of master planning in manufacturing is make-to-order production. An example is a producer of precision turntables for recording studios—no production without a firm order. The bane of the make-to-order producer is lack of planning lead time. Recording studios order turntables and want them right away. With no lead time, can a master production schedule extend far enough into the future to match demand with capacity reasonably well? The answer is yes. One approach is to use a flexible, customer-oriented procedure that involves what is called consuming the master schedule (or consuming the forecast).

Master Scheduling in Make-to-Order Plants

The method employs an MPS with three subdivisions: master schedule, actual demand, and available to promise (see Exhibit 6–11). The procedure begins with the master schedule, based on forecasting. As salespeople book orders, the master scheduler enters the quantities in the actual demand row. The term *available to promise* means the computed difference between master schedule and actual demand quantities.

We see in Exhibit 6–11 that in week 4, one unit of turntable A has been sold—to be completed or delivered in that week—and five are available to promise. In the same week, both master-scheduled units of turntable B have been sold, leaving none available to promise. The master schedule is said to be consumed by actual orders being booked by salespeople. The master schedule keeps sales informed about quantities available to promise so that the sales force will not overconsume the schedule.

The master scheduler revises the MPS periodically. For example, Exhibit 6–11 shows two of the four turntables as available to promise in week 1. If the firm never produces for inventory, the MPS would be revised at the last minute in order to produce just two, not four, units of turntable A.

The feedback loop from block 7 to block 3 in Exhibit 6–10 refers to **rough-cut capacity planning.** The aim is to assure the capacity-planning team that the production plan will not overload a scarce resource. Typically, a scarce resource is an expensive machine or a hard-to-get skill, such as a graphics designer or a programmer for a numerically controlled cutting machine.

Rough-Cut Capacity Planning

EXHIBIT 6–11   **Consuming the Master Production Schedule**

	Week				
	1	*2*	*3*	*4*	*5*
Turntable A:					
Master schedule	4	2	0	6	3
Actual demand	2	0	0	1	0
Available to promise	2	2	0	5	3
Turntable B:					
Master schedule	0	7	8	2	0
Actual demand	0	1	4	2	0
Available to promise	0	6	4	0	0

Another name for rough-cut capacity planning is *resource requirements planning* (*RRP*); in practice, some people treat one as a subset of the other.

Bill of labor: states amount (hours) of each skill needed to produce/provide one unit. (Similarly, bill of materials states amount of each material needed to produce one unit.)

In one sense, every organization does rough-cut capacity planning:

It might be as simple as saying, "I have a plan that calls for shipping $3 million worth of products this month, and I've always been able to ship $4 million per month. So we have the proven capacity to meet the plan." Alternatively, you might say, "Management wants us to ship $7 million a month during the summer season. We have no precedent for being able to do that—management's new plan appears to be unrealistic at this time."[2]

Running a rough-cut check requires data that show how much of the scarce resource is required per unit of product to be made or provided. Assume, for example, that a plastics manufacturer has a bill of labor stating that a newly designed plastic case for a computer keyboard requires, on average, 46 hours of mold-making labor. (The firm's senior mold-maker's skills are exceptional—nobody else has those skills.) To improve confidence that aggregate forecast demand will not overload the mold-maker, the capacity-planning team runs a rough-cut check on the amount of mold-making labor required.

Assume that the forecast is for eight new case designs in an upcoming quarter. Then:

$$8 \text{ cases} \times 46 \text{ hours per case} = 368 \text{ hours}$$

Since a standard quarter equals 520 hours (13 weeks $\times$ 40 hours per week), the production plan looks doable. Capacity for the scarce resource is adequate.

But providing only 368 hours of molding for the mold-maker in a 520 hour quarter seems inadequate to keep the expert busy.

Not so. In fact, being well below the 520 hour maximum is comforting at this stage of planning—no work has been scheduled and no orders have been received. When orders do arrive, they are unlikely to spread out evenly over the quarter. When orders pile up, the mold-maker will be quite busy. But when no orders require new mold design, the mold-maker will be occupied with repair and maintenance of existing molds and improvement projects. Vacations and possible illness may also intervene.

Load Profile

Load, as in load profile, is short for *workload.*

In addition to capacity planning, scarce resources are also an issue at the master scheduling stage (see dashed arrow from block 8 to block 7 in Exhibit 6–10). The master scheduling team may employ **load profiles** as a rather precise method. A load profile shows both how much of a given resource is required and when. However, like the

---

[2]John F. Proud, "Rough Cut Capacity Planning: The 'How To' of It," *APICS—The Performance Advantage,* February 1992, pp. 46–49.

EXHIBIT 6–12   Load Profile for a Mass Spectrometer, Model X

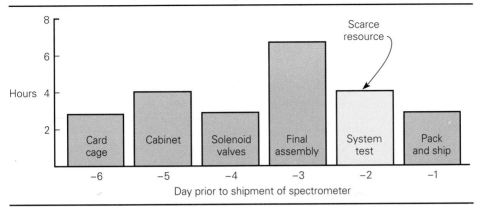

rough-cut method, the profile does not deduct inventories already on hand or on order. Therefore, requirements might be overstated.

For example, in assembly of mass spectrometers, a final-test machine might be the scarce, or bottleneck, resource. A load profile may show that a model X spectrometer requires four hours of system test time on the second day prior to shipment. Exhibit 6–12 is a complete load profile, showing time requirements for nonscarce as well as scarce resources (only the processes, not the resources themselves, are shown). Other spectrometer models would have different load profiles.

The profiles may exist as computer records or written data in a file cabinet. If the master production schedule calls for production of five model X spectrometers, two of model Y, and three of model Z, the master scheduler may pull out the profiles and multiply the processing times by 5, 2, and 3, respectively. The result is a composite workload profile showing whether the MPS will overload the scarce resource (the test machine). If so, the MPS quantities or timing may be changed.

Summary

The capacity (resource inputs) needed for meeting customer demand must be planned for, a procedure known as master planning. The merger of the capacity plan with demand yields a master schedule or appointment book, a statement of what the company plans to provide and when. Capacity planning and master scheduling are integral parts of all business ventures, including small, entrepreneurial ones such as a photography business.

Meeting customer demand and utilizing capacity (not too much utilization or too little) are the aims of capacity planning and master scheduling, which are best performed by cross-functional teams that meet regularly.

Capacity planning is balanced against aggregate demand far enough out to permit changes in work force, inventories, and other medium-range capacity elements. The capacity plan is based on aggregate forecasts for groupings of capacity or product families, and is easily translated into (or from) a production plan.

Capacity planning is governed by capacity strategies. A chase-demand strategy permits responsive customer service, but at a cost of fluctuating capacity. A level-capacity strategy has opposite characteristics. Policies translate the chosen capacity strategies into action and, along with strategies, are set by top management.

Often it is good practice to schedule under capacity by some percentage so that a fixed quantity of production is attainable in each run. When the quantity is produced early, employees engage in other useful activities, such as process improvement.

In companies with large order backlogs the capacity team may plan capacity in detail for months into the future. However, with or without backlogs, capacity planning may be improved by centering it around product families or capacity groups. By reorganizing resources into cells for each family or group, planning teams can avoid some of the hazards, inaccuracies, and complexities of capacity planning.

In a make-to-order business, options for capacity planning for a given capacity group may be tested on recent demand data, revealing effects on backlogs and order lead times. The capacity team may then select the plan that best fits company policies and customer needs.

In a make-to-stock business, capacity planning is also done by capacity groups. Based on demand forecasts, planners calculate the effect of a trial production rate on inventory levels and, in the complex case, on labor-hour and machine-hour requirements. They select the plan that yields the closest approximation to desired inventory levels while staying within available capacity.

Master planning for on-demand sales and services consists of capacity planning only. Pre-scheduled goods and services require an additional master scheduling step, which focuses on item demands for the next few periods. The capacity plan places upper limits on the master schedule or appointment book in an attempt to provide scheduled time slots for sales bookings plus item forecasts. An order promise conveys the firm's commitment to the customer.

In manufacturing, the master scheduling team creates the master production schedule, with separate sections for each major product. A subordinate schedule for component parts, plus parts sold outside, may also be developed.

Lack of planning lead time is the main problem in make-to-order plants, but an MPS based on forecasts can still work well. One approach—consuming the MPS—deducts actual customer orders as they arrive; MPS quantities not consumed are available to promise.

A rough-cut check shows capacity planners how the capacity plan affects scarce resources. Master schedulers also may use load profiles to do a more detailed check.

Learning-curve planning (see supplement) is helpful for large end products. As each unit is made, production time and costs tend to drop. The learning rate can be estimated and used in capacity planning and output scheduling and is a valued concept for management improvement.

Key Words

Capacity	201	Undercapacity scheduling	211
Master planning	202	Policy	212
Aggregate demand	202	Cumulative lead time	222
Capacity plan	203	Time fence	222
Business plan	203	Rough-cut capacity planning	223
Utilization (rate)	206	Bill of labor	224
Chase demand	209	Load profile	224
Level capacity	209	Learning curve	235
Backlog	209		

Solved Problems

Problem 1

Jack Sharp, a recent college graduate, seeks an entrepreneurial career. He started a consulting firm that helps small retail establishments and professional offices install microcomputer-based record keeping. Realizing that the only resources he has to sell are his expertise and workaholic tendencies, Jack plans on working about 280 hours per month. (Will all work and no play make Jack Sharp dull?) He has grouped his clients into three types: small retail outlets (such as shopping mall specialty stores), single-principal professional offices, and partnership professional offices. Jack estimates that time requirements for those clients will average 20, 40, and 50 hours, respectively.

Much telephone work and knocking on doors has resulted in a tentative client list for the next six months. Jack wants to match customer demand with available capacity (his time) and develop a trial schedule. The demand for each job type is as follows:

Client Type	Time Required (Hours)	Demand — Customers/Month (Month)					
		1	2	3	4	5	6
Retail store	20	4	—	6	3	4	2
Single professional	40	2	6	4	—	—	3
Multipartner professional	50	3	—	—	4	—	5

The following table shows Jack's capacity requirements by group (client type) for the six-month planning horizon as well as idle capacity or overload conditions:

Solution 1

Client Type	Demand — Resources/Month (Hours per Client × Number of Clients) (Months)						Cumulative (for Group)
	1	2	3	4	5	6	
Retail store	80	—	120	60	80	40	380
Single professional	80	240	160	—	—	120	600
Multipartner professional	150	—	—	200	—	250	600
Total capacity requirements (hours of time)	310	240	280	260	80	410	1,580
Capacity available	280	280	280	280	280	280	1,680
Extra capacity ("−" denotes overload)	−30	40	0	20	200	−130	100

For the total planning horizon, Jack has not overextended himself. He has 100 hours of excess capacity. He may have to work a few more hours during the first month, if demand estimates are accurate. His problem is months 5 and 6. He might try to entice some customers to use his services a month earlier than planned. But schedules very far out have a way of changing—often several times—prior to when the originally scheduled dates become current.

(Learning-curve problem; see supplement.) A company wants to bid on a contract to produce 50 glider aircraft. To prepare a reasonable bid, it must determine the demand for assembly labor-hours. The first glider requires an estimated 700 direct-assembly labor-hours, and the company uses an 85 percent learning rate in its planning.

Problem 2

a. For the first five gliders, determine the direct-labor-hours required for each unit. Also, find the cumulative average number of direct-labor-hours for the five units.

b. How many direct-labor-hours will be required for the 50th glider according to the learning-curve plan?

a. The learning-curve plan for the first five gliders is as follows:

Solution 2

Unit Number	Direct-Labor-Hours	Cumulative Total	Cumulative Average
1	700.00	700.00	700.00
2	595.00	1295.00	647.50
3	541.04	1836.04	612.01
4	505.75	2341.79	585.45
5	479.97	2821.76	564.35

b. For the 50th glider, we may use Formula 6–1 (logarithms to the base 10 are used, but the result is the same using natural logarithms):

$$
\begin{aligned}
Y &= aX^b \\
&= (700)(50)^{\left(\frac{\log 0.85}{\log 2.0}\right)} \\
&= (700)(50)^{\left(\frac{-.07058}{.30103}\right)} \\
&= (700)(50)^{-.2345} = 700(.3996) \\
&= 279.72 \text{ direct-labor-hours}
\end{aligned}
$$

(An interesting point: After 50 gliders are assembled, the average direct-labor-hour requirement is about 357 hours—about half the time planned for the first glider.)

For Further Reference

Books

Berry, William L.; Thomas E. Vollmann; and D. Clay Whybark. *Master Production Scheduling: Principles and Practice.* Falls Church, Va.: American Production and Inventory Control Society, 1979 (TS157.5.B46x).

Blackstone, John H., Jr. *Capacity Management.* Cincinnati: South-Western, 1989 (HD69.C3B63).

Plossl, G. W., and O. W. Wight. *Production and Inventory Control: Principles and Techniques.* Englewood Cliffs, N.J.: Prentice-Hall, 1967 (HD55.P5).

Vollmann, Thomas E.; William Lee Berry; and D. Clay Whybark. *Manufacturing Planning and Control Systems,* 3d ed. Homewood, Ill.: Dow Jones-Irwin, 1991 (TS176.V63).

Wight, Oliver W. *MRPII: Unlocking America's Productivity Potential.* Williston, Vt.: Oliver Wight Limited Publications, 1981 (TS161.W5x).

Periodicals/Societies

Decision Sciences (Decision Sciences Institute).

Journal of Operations Management (American Production and Inventory Control Society).

Production and Inventory Management (American Production and Inventory Control Society).

(All of these periodicals contain numerous articles on capacity management.)

Review Questions

1. What is capacity?
2. How much capacity is enough?
3. What are the broad and narrow aims of master planning?
4. Is capacity planning essential in small businesses? Explain.
5. What is the proper membership of the capacity planning team? Why?
6. Why does the master planning sequence for prescheduled demands include more steps than for on-demand sales and service?
7. How far in advance should capacity plans and master schedules be planned? Explain.
8. Give an example (other than those in the chapter) of planned capacity utilization.
9. Explain capacity plan versus production plan.
10. Is chase demand a capacity policy or a capacity strategy? Explain.
11. Why might one department in a company follow chase demand and another in the same company follow level capacity?
12. When is an undercapacity scheduling policy effective?
13. What is the advantage of making capacity policies explicit, specific, and (where possible) numeric?
14. Given the uncertainty of customer demand in on-demand and make-to-order businesses, how can capacity be planned intelligently in such businesses?

15. In a make-to-stock business, how could a capacity plan provide for rising inventory levels in anticipation of seasonal peak sales?

16. How can principle 6 affect capacity planning?

17. What is a time fence in master scheduling?

18. Why might a manufacturer have both a master production schedule and a component parts schedule?

19. Explain how a master schedule may be consumed.

20. How does rough-cut capacity planning improve the validity of the master schedule?

21. How is a load profile used in master scheduling?

22. What types of operating environments are best for using learning-curve planning? Why?

Problems and Exercises

1. Assume that you are president of a large company and have a strong aversion to laying off employees. Devise a multistep policy governing what your company would do if demand in certain product lines dropped, creating excess labor. Your last step should be employee terminations.

2. How has Hewlett Packard been able to down-size and still avoid laying off employees, given the competition and short life cycle of many products in the fast-changing computer and electronics industry? You may need to research the subject or interview H-P people to answer this question satisfactorily.

3. Investigate one company in three of the following industries to find out (*a*) what full capacity is in terms of hours or shifts per week, and why, and (*b*) what current capacity utilization is, and why:

Supermarket.	Overnight mail service.
Discount store.	Manufacturing plant.
Bank.	Certified public accounting firm.
Art gallery.	Charitable institution.

4. Investigate a retailer, a wholesaler, or a manufacturer to learn whether its current capacity plan includes both numeric labor and inventory levels. What are the plan's aims? Why? (If your company does not have a numeric capacity plan, find out why.)

5. City Sod is a small business that sells and lays sod (rolled strips of grass). The owner has devised a forecasting procedure based on demand history from previous years plus projection of demand in recent weeks. The forecast for the next six weeks, in labor-hours of sod laying, is:

860	880	900	920	930	940

   Currently City Sod has a staff of sod layers consisting of four crew chiefs and 15 laborers. A crew chief lays sod along with the laborers but also directs the crew. The owner has decided on the following staffing policies:
   a. A two-week backlog will be accumulated before adding staff.
   b. Plans are based on a 40-hour work week; overtime is used only to absorb weather or other delays and employee absence or resignations.
   c. The ideal crew size is one crew chief and four laborers.
      Devise a hiring plan for the six-week period covered by the forecast. In your answer, assume a current backlog of 1,200 labor-hours of sod-laying orders. Does City Sod follow more of a chase-demand or level-capacity strategy of production planning? Explain.

6. Bright Way Janitorial Service (see the case study at the end of the chapter) is considering a shift from a level-capacity to a chase-demand strategy of production/capacity planning. Bright Way managers know that chase demand would greatly simplify production/capacity planning. Explain why this is so. What new management problems would chase demand tend to create?

7. Coast Limited Railways has a car repair yard in Kansas City to repair its cars. In the six most recent months, Kansas City's car repair workload has been:

Month	1	2	3	4	5	6
Cars	83	72	71	90	49	56

    a. Coast Limited headquarters has directed Kansas City managers to plan for a capacity level that will exceed demand by no more than half a month's average demand during the six-month planning period. Prepare the capacity plan following the backlogging method of Example 6–3 in the chapter. Explain the positive and negative deviations.

    b. What important factors in question *a* could be analyzed in terms of dollars?

8. The purchasing director and two senior buyers at Windward Sportswear, an apparel manufacturer, jointly prepare the purchasing department's staffing (capacity) plan. They test alternative staffing plans using recent demand data. Demand is measured as the number of purchase orders (POs) per week, based on purchase requests from other Windward departments. Data for the past five weeks follow:

	Week				
	1	*2*	*3*	*4*	*5*
POs	128	98	155	150	83

    a. If the team elects to staff the department for 130 POs per week, will purchasing be able to serve its customers adequately? (Hint: Refer to the method of Example 6–3.) Explain.

    b. What capacity plan would you recommend? Why?

    c. If customers require very fast processing of purchase requests, what could the purchasing department do to efficiently accommodate the requirement?

9. Old English Tea Company blends and packages an average of 8,000 boxes of tea per shift. Eighteen people tend the production line, and the company follows a policy of undercapacity scheduling, scheduling labor at 90 percent of capacity. Demand is down, and the production rate must be reduced to meet the demand of 6,800 boxes per shift. How many people should be added or how many assigned to other work? Assume that labor and output rate are linearly related.

10. A computer software company has one production line that copies programs onto floppy disks and packages the disks. The line has been scheduled at full capacity and has been consuming 30 hours of direct labor per day. Demand recently has fallen from 1,400 to 1,200 packages per day; therefore, now is a good time to convert to undercapacity labor scheduling. (Problems in meeting schedules and resulting lost sales have brought about the policy change.) Determine the new labor-hour requirements for a policy of 10 percent undercapacity scheduling.

11. Dominion Envelope Co. produces a variety of paper and light-cardboard envelopes, often with customer-specified printing on them. Dominion formed an order-processing cell for its biggest customer, Bank of North America (BNA). The cell consists of one person each from sales, accounting, materials, and operations. Orders from other customers go from department to department, but BNA orders are processed in the cell, then sent to operations for production, packaging, and shipping.

  a. How would capacity planning differ for BNA orders versus other orders?

  b. How could capacity planning be improved for other customers?

12. Concrete Products, Inc., makes reinforced concrete structural members (trusses, etc.) for large buildings and bridges. Each order is a special design, so no finished-goods inventories are possible. Concrete members are made by using molds that are bolted onto huge shake tables. A vibrating action causes the wet concrete to pack, without air pockets, around reinforcing steel in the molds. Concrete Products uses a chase-demand strategy of hiring labor to assemble, fill, and disassemble the molds. If it takes a week to hire and train a laborer, how can Concrete Products make the chase demand strategy work well? What types of labor (capacity) policies would work? Recent work loads, in labor-hours, on the shake tables are as follows:

Week	1	2	3	4	5	6	7	8	9
Labor-Hours	212	200	170	204	241	194	168	215	225

13. At a fiberglass products company, the dominant product line is fiberglass bathtub and shower units, which sell to the high-quality segment of the market. The company's best employees work in tubs and showers, which are treated as a separate capacity group. Forecast demands for this capacity group are in labor-hours. For the next three months, demand is forecast at 300, 370, and 380 labor-hours. The present inventory is 620 labor-hours' worth of tub and shower units, in all sizes and colors. The plan is to reduce the inventory to 300 after three months because the slow season is approaching.

  a. Prepare a production plan for the next three months that minimizes labor fluctuation.

  b. How would the master production schedule differ from the production plan?

14. Gulf Tube and Pipe Company prepares monthly production/capacity plans for three capacity areas, one of which is the pipe-forming, -cutting, and -welding (FCW) processes. The forecast FCW demand for next month is as follows:

Week	Forecast Lineal Feet (000)
1	6,000
2	5,800
3	5,400
4	4,600

The present inventory is 16 million lineal feet.

  a. Devise a production plan following a chase-demand strategy that results in an ending inventory of 14 million lineal feet.

  b. Devise a production plan following a level-capacity strategy that results in an ending inventory of 14 million lineal feet.

  c. The following rule of thumb is used for purposes of capacity planning: two operators are required for every 1 million lineal feet produced. Develop two capacity plans (i.e., work force), one using data from question *a* and the other using data from question *b*.

  d. Cite data from questions *a* through *c* to explain the contrasting effects on inventories and labor of chase-demand and level-capacity strategies.

15. Devise a master scheduling diagram similar to Exhibit 6–9 but for draftspeople in an engineering firm. Explain your diagram.

16. Devise a master scheduling diagram similar to Exhibit 6–9, but for a maintenance department. Assume that maintenance includes janitorial crews, plumbers, and electricians, but does not include construction or remodeling personnel. Explain your diagram.

17. Capacity planning is never easy, and seems especially difficult in retail, where demand varies greatly throughout the day. Four retail situations are listed below. Pick any two and write a brief

analysis of how each deals with the unpredictability factor in planning capacity (labor). You may need to interview one or more people in a real firm.

Post office.   Fast-food restaurant.

Motel.   Bank.

18. At Gulf Tube and Pipe Company, the master scheduler has developed a trial master production schedule. Lately the growing demand for pipe products has strained capacity in the pipe-cutting work center. The work center consists of a single Dynacut cutoff machine with a single-shift daily capacity of 120,000 lineal feet. The master scheduler has been running a rough-cut capacity plan to ensure that the MPS quantities do not overload the Dynacut machine. Engineering has provided the master scheduler with a list of all end-item numbers that require cutoff; those items are starred in the following partial trial MPS:

End-Item Number	Week				
	1	*2*	*3*	*4*	*5*
0263	400	—	—	—	—
0845*	—	300	—	—	300
0997*	300	—	—	300	—
1063	—	200	800	—	—
.	.	.	.	.	.
.	.	.	.	.	.
.	.	.	.	.	.
Total for *-items (000 of lineal feet)	600	680	470	550	590

    a. Assume a five-day-per-week single-shift operation. According to rough-cut capacity planning, what should be done?

    b. Can you tell from the data given what Gulf's production/capacity planning strategy is (i.e., level capacity or chase demand)? Explain.

19. In general registration at your college, registering for classes probably requires you to pass through several work centers. Which work center is a bottleneck? Would the registrar's office find the rough-cut capacity planning idea useful in planning for that bottleneck work center? Explain. You will probably need to consider what the MPS would consist of in this case. (If you prefer, you can answer this question using drop-and-add or another administrative procedure instead of general registration.)

20. At Piney Woods Furniture Company, the scarce resource that most concerns the master scheduler is the wood-drying kiln. One product, a cabinet, uses three types of wood, which go through the kiln at different times in the manufacture of the cabinet. The accompanying bar graph shows the kiln load profile resulting from a minimum cabinet order (50 cabinets). The unit of measure is cubic-yard-hours, which accounts for size of the drying load and time in the kiln for one cabinet.

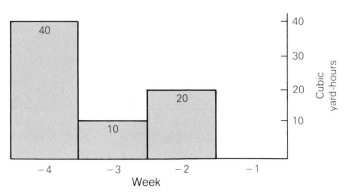

The current MPS includes an order for 1,000 cabinets in week 6 (six weeks from now). Projected kiln workload for all products other than the cabinet is as follows for the next six weeks:

	Week					
	1	*2*	*3*	*4*	*5*	*6*
Cubic yard-hours	5,000	5,200	5,300	5,800	5,700	6,000

a. Calculate the week-by-week kiln loads (workloads) for the cabinet order. (Assume that week −1 on the load profile means one week prior to the week in which an order is due on the MPS.)

b. If the kiln has a maximum weekly capacity of 6,000 cubic-yard-hours, will the MPS overload the kiln? Explain.

c. If the cabinet order is adjustable (the customer would accept a change in delivery date), what MPS changes would you recommend, if any?

(Problems 21 and 22: see learning-curve supplement.)

21. Iridion, Inc., has been awarded a contract to produce 200 rail-driven passenger cars for a large city. Based on Iridion's previous experience in guided-rocket manufacturing, an 80 percent learning curve is planned for the passenger-car contract. The first passenger car takes 1,400 direct-labor-hours to make.

a. If the city pays Iridion's accumulated direct-labor costs after the fourth unit, how many direct-labor-hours should the city expect to owe right after the fourth unit is produced?

b. The actual direct-labor usage for the first eight units produced is as follows:

1,400	1,206	1,172	1,145	1,101	1,083	1,033	1,005

Would you recommend that Iridion stay with its planning estimate of an 80 percent learning curve? Explain.

c. Answer question b for the following changes in actual direct-labor usage:

1,400	1,089	887	801	728	684	600	586

22. A manufacturer of ceramic products has been awarded a NASA contract to produce ceramic-based heat shields for space vehicles. The contract calls for a total of 20 heat-shield units. If the estimated learning-curve rate is 94 percent and the first unit takes 60 hours to produce, how long will it take to produce the fifth, tenth, and final units?

CASE STUDY

BRIGHT WAY JANITORIAL SERVICE

Bright Way Janitorial Service has established three categories of capacity:

1. Wet processes (mopping, buffing, etc.).
2. Dry processes (vacuuming/dusting).
3. Glass cleaning.

Those categories were set because they define separate kinds of employee/equipment processes. Each category can be forecast based on historical data. Bright Way uses the forecasts, along with its labor, service, and pricing policies, to arrive at a production/capacity plan for a three-week period by week.

The forecast and production/capacity plan are updated (rolled over) every two weeks. The short forecast interval is suitable because hiring and training require less than two weeks. Updating the production/capacity plan need not be done every week because there is a staff of irregular employees on call. They serve as a cushion against inaccurate forecasting.

Bright Way has a strategy of seeking more affluent customers, paying a slightly higher wage, and gaining a somewhat more stable work force than its competitors. In support of that strategy it has developed the following capacity policies:

Labor:
  Priority 1: 18–22 percent full-time labor, no overtime.
  Priority 2: 65–75 percent part-time labor.
  Priority 3: 8–12 percent irregular labor.
  Priority 4: 20 percent of full-time and part-time staff cross-trained for possible temporary transfer to secondary work category.
  Priority 5: subcontract (make advance agreements) for excess short-term demands, where possible.

Service (responsiveness):
  Priority 1: maintain all schedules for regular customers.
  Priority 2: next-week response to new customers (up to limits of staffing) for routine cleaning (work categories 1 and 2).
  Priority 3: integrate special cleaning demands into the schedule as soon as possible without disrupting regular schedules.
  Pricing: no pricing incentives. This policy subject to change if competition warrants.

Bright Way's production/capacity plan for the next three weeks is as shown in Exhibit CS–1. The plan shows forecast labor-hours of demand for each work category and for each week. The forecast labor-hours are assigned to full-time, part-time, and irregular labor. For the entire three-week period, there is no planned need for subcontracting. The totals at the bottom include percentages. These fit the percentage goals Bright Way set in its capacity policies.

For example, in week 1, the total forecast demand for category 1 (wet processes) is 1,240 labor-hours of business. Janitorial staff assignments for that demand are 240 labor-hours of full-time labor, 860 of part-time labor, and 140 of irregular labor. Since 240 + 860 + 140 = 1,240, the plan meets forecast demand with no need for subcontracting.

Forecast demand for all three work categories in week 1 totals 3,620 labor-hours. To meet that demand without subcontracting, the plan calls for 760 full-time labor-hours, 2,540 part-time, and 320 irregular. In percentages, full-time labor is 21 percent, within the priority 1 goal of 18–22 percent; part-time labor is 70 percent, within the priority 2 goal of 65–75 percent; and irregular labor is 9 percent, within the priority 3 goal of 8–12 percent.

All priorities are met in week 1. The production plan is to fully meet the demand forecast. The capacity plan that enables demand to be met is the staffing plan at the bottom of Exhibit CS–1.

In weeks 2 and 3, hiring is called for because forecast demand is on the increase. Since hiring normally is possible in less than two weeks, this plan provides the necessary lead time.

Case Discussion Questions

1. Compared with its competitors, is Bright Way's strategy chase demand or level capacity? Develop a table such as Exhibit 6–4, with Bright Way's strategy in one column and the more typical janitorial service in the other. Discuss each row in your table.

2. If Bright Way changed to the capacity strategy of its competitors, would capacity planning, and overall management, be simpler or more difficult? Explain.

3. What demand forecasting techniques would you recommend for Bright Way? Why?

EXHIBIT CS–1   Three-Week Group Forecast and Production/Capacity Plan—Bright Way Janitorial Service

		Labor-Hours, by Week					
		1		**2**		**3**	
Work Category	Labor Type	Forecast	Assigned	Forecast	Assigned	Forecast	Assigned
1: Wet		1,240		1,160		1,100	
	Full-time		240		240		240
	Part-time		860		860		860
	Irregular		140		60		
	Subcontracted						
2: Dry		1,900		2,000		2,260	
	Full-time		400		400		480
	Part-time		1,320		1,320		1,400
	Irregular		180		280		380
	Subcontracted						
3: Glass		480		520		480	
	Full-time		120		120		120
	Part-time		360		400		360
	Irregular						
	Subcontracted						
	Totals	3,620		3,680		3,840	
	Full-time		760 (21%)		760 (21%)		840 (22%)
	Part-time		2,540 (70%)		2,580 (70%)		2,620 (68%)
	Irregular		320 (9%)		340 (9%)		380 (10%)
	Subcontracted						
	Change in hours			+60		+160	
	Staffing plan			Hire two part-time; assign to glass. Add 20 hours irregular.		Hire two full-time and two part-time; assign to dry. Add 40 hours irregular.	

SUPPLEMENT

LEARNING-CURVE PLANNING

As people learn, the time required for them to do a given task decreases. In industry this is known as the **learning-curve** phenomenon, which applies to the direct work force plus those who provide technical and other support services. More broadly, the learning curve is related to the well-known economy-of-scale concept: greater volumes yield lower unit costs.

Where the learning-curve effect is significant, planners of production rates and capacity should build on it. With learning effects, production rates may rise over time with no change in capacity level, or capacity levels may be cut over time without reducing production rates.

The learning-curve phenomenon was observed in airframe manufacturing as far back as 1925.[1] Later, aircraft manufacturers found a dominant learning pattern—the 80 percent learning curve. The second plane required 80 percent as much direct labor as the first; the fourth 80 percent as much as the second; the tenth 80 percent as much as the fifth, and so forth. The rate of learning to assemble aircraft was 20 percent between doubled quantities.

---

[1]The commander of Wright-Patterson Air Force Base was reported to have observed it in 1925. See Winfred B. Hirshmann, "Profits from the Learning Curve," *Harvard Business Review*, January–February 1964, p. 125–139.

EXHIBIT S6–1   80 Percent Learning Curve

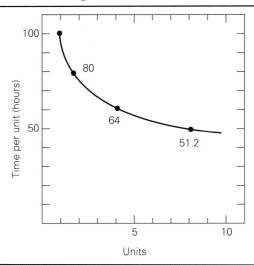

Exhibit S6–1 illustrates an 80 percent learning curve. Mathematically, a learning curve follows the general formula:

$$Y = aX^b \qquad (6\text{–}1)$$

where

Y = Labor-hours per unit
X = Unit number
a = Labor-hours for first unit
$b = \dfrac{\text{Logarithm of learning-curve rate}}{\text{Logarithm of 2}}$

Learning Curve Calculations

When using the learning curve for capacity planning, production-hour requirements are calculated over time, as Example S6–1 shows.

EXAMPLE S6–1   LEARNING-CURVE PLANNING—BELLWEATHER ELECTRIC, INC.

Bellweather has a contract for 60 portable electric generators. The first unit requires 100 production hours. Therefore, Bellweather planners develop an aggregate capacity plan using learning-curve calculations. They use a 90 percent learning curve, based on previous experience with generator contracts.

Using Formula 6–1, the labor requirement for the second generator is:

$$
\begin{aligned}
Y &= aX^b \\
Y &= (100)(2)^{\left(\frac{\log 0.9}{\log 2.0}\right)} \\
  &= (100)(2)^{-0.152} \\
  &= (100)(0.9) \\
  &= 90 \text{ hours}
\end{aligned}
$$

The result of 90 for the second unit is expected because there is 10 percent learning between doubled quantities for a 90 percent learning curve.

For the fourth unit:

$$Y = aX^b = 100(4)^{-0.152} = (100)(0.81) = 81$$

This result may be obtained more simply:

$$(100)(0.9)^2 = (100)(0.9)(0.9) = (100)(0.81) = 81$$

For the eighth unit:

$$Y = aX^b = 100(8)^{-0.152} = (100)(0.729) = 72.9$$

This result is also obtained by:

$$(100)(0.9)^3 = (100)(0.9)(0.9)(0.9) = (100)(0.729) = 72.9$$

This way of avoiding logarithms works for any unit that is a power of 2 (the 16th, 32nd, 64th, and so on, units). But for the 3rd, 5th, 6th, 7th, 9th, and so forth, units, a logarithmic calculation is necessary.

Exhibit S6–2 displays some of the results of the learning-curve calculations. With those figures, Bellweather may assign labor based on the decreasing per-unit production-hour requirements. For example, the 60th generator requires 53.7 production-hours, only about half that required for the first unit. Completion of finished generators can be master-scheduled to increase at the 90 percent learning-curve rate.

Exhibit S6–2   Production-Hour Requirements for Generator Manufacturing— Bellweather Electric, Inc.

Generator Number	Production-Hours Required	Cumulative Labor-Hours Required
1	100	100.0
2	90	190.0
3	84.6	274.6
10	70.5	799.4
20	63.4	1,460.8
30	59.6	2,072.7
40	57.1	2,654.3
50	55.2	3,214.2
60	53.7	3,757.4

Team Learning and Continuing Improvement

Learning-curve planning is most closely associated with production of large-scale items: airplanes, earthmovers, and so on. At first, no one is familiar with the work, and the production system needs to be debugged. As units are produced, improvements are natural. Thus, the learning curve may apply to any repetitive manufacturing if the work climate is favorable for continuing improvement. Of course, in many companies, it is not, for various reasons. Labor may denounce a productivity-enhancing idea, considering it a speedup, or employees may resist changes in less vocal ways. (In an entertaining book about his working life, Robert Schrank explains how employees tend to set their own informal output norms or "bogeys" and enforce them through peer pressure.[2] In either case, the system is prevented from learning).

But blaming the work force for improvement failures, though easy, begs the question, especially considering the many companies that do have a climate conducive to improvement. The

PRINCIPLE 2:

Dedicate to continual, rapid improvement in quality, cost, lead time, flexibility, and service.

---

[2]*Ten Thousand Working Days* (Cambridge, Mass.: MIT Press, 1978) (HD8073.S34A37).

quality management initiatives in many companies succeed in making continuing improvement part of every associate's job. Resulting rates of learning-driven productivity improvement can be impressive.

The fact that most companies enjoy some tendency to improve suggests that the learning curve could be widely used for labor-capacity planning, costing, budgeting, pricing, and so forth. But the learning curve fails as a planning aid unless improvements are measurable over each planning increment, such as each month or quarter. Moreover, some poorly performing companies get measurable improvements mainly at model changeover time, when advanced equipment is bought and when plant expansion is undertaken. In between, the climate for improvement may be so poor that none takes place. How operations can be managed to achieve steady improvement is a central issue in this text and is treated in most chapters.

FLOW-CONTROL SYSTEM OVERVIEW

Were you out of coffee this morning? Was the milk spoiled? Car battery dead? Situations like these interrupt the flow of work (or play). These are failures of the **flow-control system**, and they can include inventory problems, faulty equipment, and various people and system shortcomings.

Getting a flow-control system on target—and keeping it there—is a challenge. This chapter begins the discussion of how to do it. We treat the topic in greater detail in the two chapters on inventory management (Chapters 9 and 10) and in Chapters 11 through 14 (Part IV) on managing the different types of operations. We begin by looking at variability, the root cause of many possible problems.

A flow-control system in wholesaling is mostly an inventory system; in manufacturing, a production and inventory system; in human services, a customer processing system.

239

System Variability

A business flow-control system is like your own personal flow-control system, except that many more things can vary and break down in the business's system. In any organization, multiple process elements can vary at the same time, and the combined variations can result in extreme mistakes, delays, failures, and total shutdowns. Two common examples for purchased materials are variations in delivery time and in quality (see Exhibit 7–1).

*𝒫*RINCIPLE 10:

Eliminate process variation.

In the exhibit, the T stands for the performance target: what should happen every time. The variabilities are not pluses (goods) and minuses (bads) that cancel out over the long run: one uncooked cake and one burned cake do not add up to great baking. All variabilities are bad, and combining them only makes matters worse: bad-quality material is not forgiven if delivery is too early.

Consider the following:

- Material records showing more or less material than is actually on hand.
- A machine running too fast or too slow, too hot or too cold, and so on.
- Equipment (e.g., computer, punch press, transparency projector) breaking down randomly.
- An associate overcompensating or undercompensating.
- A team member present or absent (early or late, sometimes doing the job right and sometimes wrong, etc.)
- Yield (percentage of output that is good) varying randomly.

Variability, variation, uncertainty, and *undependability,* are used more or less synonymously, as are *invariability, certainty,* and *dependability.*

The list could go on, and every variability element adds to customer annoyance.

Additive process variability annoys, both because it yields bad results and because it equals uncertainty. If a bus is late by 10 minutes dependably, we might be able to live with it. But if it's 10 minutes late on average—sometimes much later, on time, or early—we may give up on bus riding.

Keeping buses on time requires controlling just a few sources of variability. But flow control in a complex organization involves many interacting sources of variability, such as multiple internal processes using many different external materials and other resources. Reducing interacting variability requires a three-pronged attack:

1. System designers avoid complexity so that there are fewer sources of variability.
2. Every associate and team finds ways to control process variation.

EXHIBIT 7–1   Variability: Deviation from Target

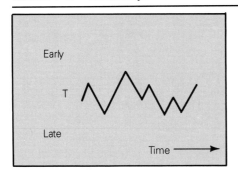

Late or early delivery of material

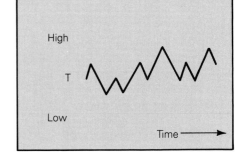

Material out of specification (bad quality) on the high side or low side

3. A cross-functional team develops the flow-control system so that the team can detect and plan around or adjust to sources of variability, thus producing a satisfactory result.

Developing the flow-control system is this chapter's focus, and it requires a basic understanding of inventories, carrying costs, demand dependency, system delays, combined effects of timing and quantity, and measurements of success. The remainder of the chapter addresses these topics.

Flow Control: Avoiding Slacks and Gluts

A tailor, a tax advisor, or a ticket-taker each seeks a steady flow of customers to and through the processes. This means avoiding both slack resources and "inventories" of customers waiting impatiently for services. To be successful, these businesses must keep their cloth, tax forms, and ticket revenues flowing.

In manufacturing, wholesaling, and retailing, inventories of materials must be kept flowing, while avoiding slacks that anger customers and gluts that raise the costs of carrying the inventories. Inventories are a major cost, typically over 50 percent of expenditures in manufacturing, 70 percent in retailing, and 90 percent in wholesaling. In these businesses, controlling inventories is a key to success. Highly efficient Wal-Mart spends less on inventory mistakes (too much or too little inventory), which enables it to spend more (85 percent) of its expenditures on the revenue-earning inventories themselves.

As the Wal-Mart example illustrates, control does not mean elimination. Inventories (materials, documents, or customers) must flow. But like life-giving rivers, they should neither dry up nor flood too often.

The world's best retailers team up with freight carriers and manufacturers at several levels in the supply chain in order to keep goods flowing through those levels.

Whether linked to retailers or not, each manufacturing plant must keep the work flowing. Buyers and schedulers play a central part. They plan for materials to arrive just in time for processing or, for seasonal manufacturing, they plan for building stock to meet the seasonal peak.

In any business, planning and timing do not work out if equipment is down. Thus, equipment maintenance is part of flow control. Also, long get-ready and changeover times often necessitate scheduling in large lots (batches), but each large-lot process is a lump in what otherwise could be a relatively smooth work flow. Therefore, efforts to cut change times and batch sizes are also important.

*C*ontrast

Having the Right Inventory

No One Responsible	Everyone Responsible
Inventory managers *care for* inventory; processing and transporting is in batches.	Everyone at every process keeps the work flowing.
Shortages of supply are blamed on purchasing, suppliers, operations, maintenance, and so on.	Stops and starts, large process and transit batches, unnecessary storages, equipment stoppages, and so on, are avoided.
Wrong items in inventory are blamed on marketing and the demand forecast.	Everyone connects with and responds quickly and flexibly to customers and suppliers.

Quality is especially important. If quality is erratic, work may arrive on schedule but go directly to scrap, to rework, or to the complaint department.

The point should be clear—poor flow control has diverse causes, including disconnection between supply chain levels, long get-ready times, batching, erratic processes, and poor quality.

*𝒫*RINCIPLE 10:

Eliminate error and variation.

These causes are commonly addressed defensively or reactively. A common defense is flooding the distribution warehouses and internal processes with extra, just-in-case inventories. Common reactions are rerouting, rescheduling, or rearranging priorities of stalled orders. However, what's needed is to solve the problems in the first place.

Failure to solve problems causes flow control, as a separate function and cost center, to become highly complex. Indeed, the costs of managing the delays and changes may rival the direct costs of the operations being controlled.[1]

Managing the Delays (The Carrying Costs)

To reiterate, the work must flow. That advice becomes doubly important when cost is considered, for cost is like dust—it tends to settle on anything that is sitting around. Rapid processing allows little time for costs to accumulate. Unfortunately, in almost any business the work is mostly in a state of delay or idleness. For example, for every minute that a piece of metal is under a cutting tool, it is likely to spend 5, 10, or even 100 minutes in front of the machine waiting. When material is idle, it incurs a cost above and beyond its unit price. That cost is called an **inventory carrying cost.**

Office work involves delays and carrying costs too. Little time is spent working on office documents compared with the time documents are in an in-basket, and jobs on personal computers are usually sitting in a file rather than being completed. In human services work, the carrying cost includes the cost of clients standing in line.

Costs of Idleness

What do those delays cost? For a client the cost is hard to judge because most of it is poor-service cost, that is, the cost of the client's involuntary idleness. Likewise, for documents and files the cost of idleness is mostly the cost of slow service to the customer; costs of storing and carrying the documents and files are minor.

What about materials in a hospital, restaurant, or factory? First are the physical costs of holding inventory and the financial costs of having working capital tied up in idle inventory. But those are the obvious carrying costs, which inventory management writings have always recognized. Inventory costs are now under closer scrutiny because of an awareness of so-called hidden inventory. Obvious, semiobvious, and hidden inventory carrying costs are listed in Exhibit 7–2.

Obvious Costs

In order to be a true inventory carrying cost, a cost must rise with the growth, and fall with the reduction, of inventory. **Capital cost,** first on the list, clearly qualifies. Company financial managers frequently attempt to secure bank loans or lines of credit to pay for more inventory. Banks often use the inventory as collateral for loans.

Only in abnormal situations can a company avoid capital costs. For example, Harley-Davidson people like to crow about the time when they got paid for production before they had to pay for the raw materials. On the books, the effect appears as negative inventory. (The product was not motorcycles but a subassembly they had contracted to make for

---

[1]Jeffrey G. Miller and Thomas E. Vollmann, "The Hidden Factory," *Harvard Business Review,* September–October 1985, pp. 142–50.

EXHIBIT 7-2   Carrying-Cost Elements

Obvious carrying costs:
    Capital cost—interest or opportunity costs of working capital tied up in stock
    Holding cost—stockroom costs of:
        Space
        Storage implements (e.g., shelving and stock-picking vehicles)
        Insurance on space, equipment, and inventories
        Inventory taxes
        Stockkeepers' wages
        Damage and shrinkage while in storage
Semiobvious carrying costs:
    Obsolescence
    Inventory planning and management
    Stock record keeping
    Physical inventory taking
Hidden carrying costs:
    Cost of stock on production floor:
        Space
        Storage implements (e.g., racks, pallets, containers)
        Handling implements (e.g., conveyors, cranes, forklift trucks)
    Inventory transactions and data processing support
    Management and technical support for equipment used in storage, handling, and inventory data processing
    Scrap and rework
    Lot inspections
    Lost sales, lost customers because of slow processing

---

another company.) The negative inventory situation arose because of Harley's successful just-in-time efforts: work sped through the plant—raw materials to finished goods—in a day or two versus the weeks that it would have taken in Harley's pre-JIT days.

Next on the list is **holding cost,** which is mainly the cost of running stockrooms. While the accounting system may consider space and storage implements as fixed costs, they exist only to hold stock; therefore, many companies see them as true carrying costs. The other more or less obvious holding costs are insurance, taxes, material department wages, damage, and shrinkage costs.

Semiobvious carrying costs include inventory obsolescence and costs of inventory man-   *Semiobvious Costs*
agement and clerical activities (see Exhibit 7–2). People involved in inventory planning, stock record keeping, and physical inventory counting do not actually handle stock, and their offices often are far from stockrooms. Perhaps for these reasons, some companies include those costs as general or operating overhead. Clearly, however, they are inventory carrying costs.

Obsolescence cost is nearly zero when materials arrive just in time for use, but it can be high if companies buy in large batches and then find that the need for the items has dried up. High-fashion and high-tech electronics companies should be acutely aware of obsolescence as a cost of carrying inventory. Old-line manufacturers, however, might write off obsolete stock only once every 10 years; if so, they may fail to include obsolescence routinely in their calculated carrying-cost rate.

Carrying costs that commingle with other costs tend to be hidden. A prime example is   *Hidden Costs*
stock released from a stockroom to operations (factory, sales floor, kitchen, etc.), where it sits idle between operations, tying up cash and occupying costly floor space. In manufacturing, idle in-process inventories commonly occupy half or more of factory floor

space. Idle stock often sits on racks, conveyors, automatic storage systems, and other costly equipment, and it adds up to a major hidden carrying cost component.

Most companies once invalidly charged those costs as production costs. Today, accountants and operations managers and associates are increasingly asking, Does it add value? Does the activity produce something saleable or directly serve a paying customer? If not, treat it as an inventory carrying cost. Illustration: a conveyor literally carries inventory and adds no value to the product.

Another so-called **nonvalue-adding (NVA)** activity is processing inventory transactions, including the cost of associates' time for entering inventory usage and scrap data into terminals plus the cost of the terminals, usually treated incorrectly as operating costs. Much greater are the associated central processing costs (hardware, software, and computer operations) and the costs of corrections and report processing. In inventory-intensive firms, inventory management is the dominant computer application; its costs have been conveniently bundled into the information system department's total costs, but they are actually hidden inventory carrying costs. Costs of management and technical support for storage, handling, and data-processing equipment are also carrying costs, but they are rarely treated as such.

Scrap and rework costs also fall with decreases in inventories, including decreases in lot sizes. This is true in processing perishables (such as cutting off rot from food items), in wholesaling and retailing (e.g., an entire lot of garments missing a buttonhole), in information processing, and in manufacturing.

As an information processing example, suppose telephone sales associates send sales orders forward once a day in batches averaging 800 orders. Order entry clerks in the next department might find numerous defects, such as missing quantity, incomplete address, or lack of a promise date. Sometimes, especially for a new promotion, an entire lot of 800 orders will contain the same error. More commonly, errors will occur at some average percentage. Either way, order entry clerks end up sending the faulty forms back to the sales office for rework, probably the next day (see Exhibit 7–3A). Meanwhile, time has passed and sales people are busy with other orders. They are no longer clear about the details of yesterday's orders and the likely root causes of yesterday's order-processing errors.

If salespeople processed and forwarded orders in lots of 20 instead of 800 (Exhibit 7–3B), maximum damage would be 20, which could be sent back while the trail of causes is still warm.

Best of all would be for a sales associate to hand the order directly to an order entry clerk (Exhibit 7–3C). They become a team, intolerant of errors on order forms. Large defective lots are no longer possible. When an error occurs, it is usually discovered right away while the cause is still obvious. The team finds ways to permanently eliminate the cause of the errors, steadily driving down the rate of defective order forms.

Inspection costs merit similar scrutiny. Inspectors facing large lots have the big job of sorting out the bad ones. However, some companies avoid large lots by adopting just-in-time techniques. They avoid large *bad* lots by implementing strict process controls to prevent defects rather than merely detecting defects. The tie-in between inspection costs and lot-size quantities is becoming clear, and the conclusion is that even inspectors may be treated as a carrying cost. (We leave it to the reader to speculate on machine repair-people, parts expediters, and others who respond to work stoppages and stockouts, which are negative inventories, incurring inventory shortage costs. Are those too a type of carrying cost?)

Last and most important are the costs of lost sales and lost customer allegiance when the flow-control system is plagued by stalled orders. Thus, the negative impact of idle inventories on customer responsiveness is also a carrying cost. But by keeping lot sizes,

---

𝒫RINCIPLE 11:

Cut inventory.

Independent inspectors conducting sampling inspections may reject a whole lot based on a bad sample and send the lot back for rectification.

𝒫RINCIPLE 13:

Decrease cycle interval and lot size.

EXHIBIT 7–3   **Effect of Lot Size on Rework/Scrap**

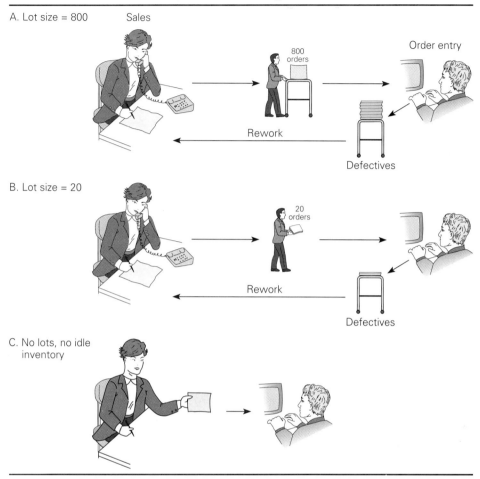

A. Lot size = 800   Sales

800 orders

Order entry

Rework

Defectives

B. Lot size = 20

20 orders

Rework

Defectives

C. No lots, no idle inventory

---

queues, and transport distances short, the firm can ensure that the work flows through the system cleanly and quickly—perhaps surprising, delighting, and retaining the customer.

Often inventories are such a dominant company cost that virtually every investment proposal has an inventory effect. Therefore, it is important to use a realistic carrying cost when doing a financial analysis for a proposal. *Uses of Carrying Cost*

Traditionally, carrying cost has been stated as an annual rate based on the item's value. Older books on inventory management suggested a rate of 25 percent as a good average. Many North American manufacturers still use 25 percent (or 24 percent — 2 percent per month). But that rate is based on the obvious carrying costs (Exhibit 7–2) and possibly some of the semiobvious costs.

If all carrying costs are included, as they should be, what is the proper rate? No studies have answered that question definitively. However, the rate is surely at least 50 percent. Indeed, several manufacturers have upped their rates to 50 percent or higher. When researchers have unearthed all carrying costs, more companies may use higher rates, perhaps as high as 100 percent. To see what 100 percent means, imagine a $50 chair sitting in a stockroom for a year. The owner would be paying another $50 for the chair in the form of the costs of carrying it.

Thinking about moving a machine and its operator across the building to team up with a machine and operator at the next process? How much inventory savings are there, and what carrying-cost rate is being used? Suppose that the cost of moving is $2,000 and that $3,000 of inventory would be eliminated. At a 25 percent rate, the savings are $750 per year ($0.25 \times \$3,000$); without doing a discounted cash flow analysis, payback on the investment will take $2\frac{2}{3}$ years ($\$2,000 \div \$750$ per year), maybe not very attractive. At 100 percent, carrying-cost savings are $3,000 per year and the investment pays for itself in less than a year:

$$\text{Note: Simple payback period} = \frac{\text{Investment cost}}{\text{Annual savings}} \qquad (7\text{--}1)$$

The best-known financial analysis that uses carrying-cost rates is in calculating an economic order quantity (see Chapter 10). Another issue that bears on flow-control systems is whether demand for an item is dependent or independent of other items.

Dependent and Independent Demand

A taco that you buy and eat is an **independent-demand** item; it does not go into a **parent item.** The taco's ingredients, however, are **dependent-demand** items, which is the demand category for a **component item** that goes into a parent item. In delivery of services, client demands are independent, but supplies consumed and capacity engaged in service delivery may be dependent.

Sometimes an item appears to be dependent but its parent is unknown. An example is a new tire for sale in a service station. What kind of car or truck will it go on? The item must be treated as independent. However, that same tire, if destined for a car in an auto assembly plant, is a dependently demanded component.

The classification reasoning is as follows: The production or delivery schedule for a dependent item matches the demand for the parent; production of the component and parent can be tightly synchronized with little fuss or idle inventory. The schedule for the component is completely accurate relative to the schedule for the parent item or items.

Scheduling the independent-demand item is less simple. The service station keeps common tires on hand, which generates a carrying cost. But which common tires and how many of each should be on hand? The station manager can only guess (forecast), and that introduces inaccuracy. To ensure an adequate level of customer service, the manager keeps **buffer stock** on hand in order to provide protection in the face of forecast inaccuracy.

Buffer stock:
Stock inserted at any stage of production or delivery to ensure continued supply when demand increases or production stalls; also called safety stock.

Retail and wholesale inventories generally are independent-demand items, as are service parts (spare or replacement parts) in factories, since the parents into which they go are unknown to the provider.

A few decades ago, flow-control systems were too primitive and data processing too costly to permit companies to sort out parent-component dependencies. Most parts were ordered based on guesses about how quickly they would be used up, and buffer stock provided protection. Modern systems, especially **quick response program (QRP), just-in-time (JIT),** and **material requirements planning (MRP),** simplify the planning of dependent items. These systems handle independent-demand items, too, but with less precision and higher costs since independent demands must be forecast. JIT and MRP, briefly mentioned in this chapter, are fully treated in Chapter 9. QRP, a powerful multi-stage application of JIT, is our next topic.

Into Practice

QRP at Wal-Mart

"A manufacturer like Gitano can access Wal-Mart's point-of-sale terminals to track sales of its jeans. This way, Gitano knows when to crank up production to resupply a Wal-Mart store before the store runs out of merchandise. Wal-Mart's electronic data interchange system enables it to electronically place orders with a manufacturer.

"But Wal-Mart goes further. It works with its suppliers and with its suppliers' suppliers. For example, with a company like Gitano it will work with the fabricmaker and even the fiber producer. According to David Glass, Wal-Mart's president and CEO, "We just tie everyone into the loop. You won't call the apparel manufacturer and have them say, 'Gosh, we'd make that for you, but we don't have any fabric.' "

Source: "Cutting Out the Middleman," *Forbes*, January 6, 1992, p. 169.

QRP at Luxottica Group SpA of Italy

"Luxottica [the world's largest eyeware manufacturer] reorganized its U.S. sales staff and started sharing with customers the advantages of computer power. It is equipping [independent] retailers with software that checks Luxottica's stock and orders goods for overnight delivery. In the past, delivery took days or weeks."

Source: Bill Saporito, "Cutting Out the Middleman," *Fortune*, April 6, 1992, p. 96.

QRP at VF Corporation

"VF Corporation [maker of Wrangler, Lee, Jantzen, and Vanity Fair apparel] has devised and implemented a Market Response System (MRS), designed to reduce cycle time and inventory, lower costs, and offer retailers and consumers the products they want, when they want them. MRS is executed through a series of simultaneous rather than sequential marketing, production, and supply activities, linked by information technology."

According to Lawrence Pugh, CEO, "If we eliminate organizational barriers and encourage such a free flow of information, we can get a specific product replaced on the retail shelf in less than seven days—in an environment where 60 to 90 days has been considered good practice. . . . [By implementing MRS] we can make it so that the consumer can count on having the right product, size, and color in the store every day."

Source: Advertising supplement, *Fortune*, September 21, 1992.

QRP links different companies in several stages of production, supply, and freight hauling to final points of sale. The ultimate aim is tight synchronization: pick the cotton that's spun into thread that's woven into cloth that's dyed and finished into fabric that's cut and sewed into a shirt that's delivered to the store just before you walk in to buy it—all of this, and transportation, too, in synch. Synchronization at each stage affects scheduling, purchasing, storage, logistics, capacity, and cash flow planning. The accompanying box gives examples of QRP.

Quick response program's unofficial kickoff was in June 1986 in Chicago. Roger Milliken, chairman of textile manufacturer Milliken & Co., was instrumental in getting together a few dozen retailers and textile and apparel suppliers to discuss foreign competition. The main issue was how North American fiber-textile-apparel industries could compete with low-wage companies off shore. Participants at this and following meetings:

Quick Response Program for Intersector Flow Control

*P*RINCIPLE 13:

Operate at the customer's rate of use.

Bennetton's and The Limited's home-grown versions of QRP existed before 1986. But the Milliken-led group brought QRP into general use.

SURVIVAL OF THE QUICKEST.

This photo is reprinted with the expressed written consent of Automatic Identification Manufacturers, Inc. (AIM USA). For more information, contact AIM USA 412/963-8588.

wanted to use technology to exploit the proximity of U.S. companies to the American market, and the goal was to set standards so everyone from raw materials to the retail store could speak the same electronic language and share data.

The reasoning was that if U.S. companies could respond faster to market shifts, they could overcome the advantage of low wages paid by Third World competitors.[2]

QRP has rapidly expanded. An international conference, Quick Response 91 (now an annual event), drew participants from companies that make hand tools, furniture, greeting cards, hardware, floor sweepers, household cleaners, batteries, cosmetics, toys, consumer electronics, office equipment, motor oil, and others, as well as textiles and apparel.

Technology is part of the QRP equation: universal product codes, scanning equipment at the retailer, data communications hardware, and electronic data interchange (EDI) software. However, according to Joe Berger, corporate director of EDI at Springs Industries, "Technology is 10 percent of the issue." The other 90 percent, he says, involves tight "relationships with trading partners, reduction of inventories, and recrafting production processes."[3]

QRP and JIT: Linking External and Internal Flow Control

QRP is the offspring of just-in-time and it embodies JIT's core concept of final customers "pulling the strings" to cause production and delivery, back through the chain of supply. For QRP to work, firms at each echelon in the supply chain must improve their internal processes—in office support, distribution, and freight areas, as well as in front-line

---

[2]Jon Van, "Retail and Apparel Trades Tailor New Technology, Systems," *Chicago Tribune,* Monday, March 16, 1992.

[3]Ibid.

$\mathscr{I}$nto $\mathscr{P}$ractice

Quick Response by Fax: How Auto Dealers, an Automaker, a Seatmaker, a Fabricmaker, a Yarn Dyer, and a Yarnmaker Adopted Quick Response

"The automaker regularly got information from dealers about what car models were selling, what colors were popular, and so on. The automaker could pass that information on to its seatmaker to help anticipate what styles and colors of seats would be needed in the near future. The seatmaker dealt with a fabricmaker who in turn dealt with a yarn dyer who got material from a yarnmaker.

"Like most other customers and suppliers in traditional competitive industries, they kept most business affairs secret from each other, fearful that shared information might cause a competitive disadvantage and lost profit. [A consultant] found [that] the time it took for the yarnmaker's product to find its way into a car seat installed by the automaker averaged about 71 days."

It took seven months "to persuade everyone in the chain that it would be mutually advantageous to share information. . . . Once everyone agreed, the information was regularly distributed by fax. They could have installed computer linkups and shared information electronically, but that would have taken another two years to implement and wouldn't be any more efficient," the consultant maintained.

Results: "On average, everyone in the chain was able to cut inventory by 75 percent, and the time from yarnmaker to installed car seat dropped to 28 days."

Source: Jon Van, "Firms Tool Up With Information," *Chicago Tribune,* Tuesday, November 5, 1991.

operations (see Exhibit 7–4). These firms can use a broad array of proven JIT techniques for responding to customers' demands, plus TQM techniques for getting it right.

Perhaps the main QRP contribution is that the program attracts retailers, who in turn often press manufacturers to step up their own JIT activities. At a Quick Response 91 press briefing, Thomas Rittenhouse, who chaired the conference and is controller at Strawbridge & Clothier (13 department stores and 22 discount stores in three states), advised laggard manufacturers to enact JIT in their own operations so that they will be able to meet their retail customers' JIT requirements.

By involving retailers, QRP uses sales scanning data that big retailers had collected for years but never used to good advantage. Before QRP's introduction, firm-to-firm JIT arrangements were widespread, but mostly limited to manufacturing: processed-material or component suppliers linked (by kanban, fax, EDI, etc.) to fabrication or assembly plants. QRP establishes a common basis for sector-to-sector flow control, linking goods and service sectors seamlessly.

JIT was born in Japan and is now practiced worldwide, but QRP is a uniquely North American contribution to good management. America's large open market and relatively efficient distribution system offered a favorable environment for QRP's development. The necessary alliances may be difficult to attain in Europe with its many national borders and in Japan with its many layers of middlemen between manufacturers and retailers.

While QRP is the hot, new innovation in flow control, its alter ego, JIT, is for many companies a still-new and untried flow-control system. Even material requirements planning (within-company computer-based flow control) is relatively new (circa the 1970s).

JIT and MRP for Internal Flow Control

Since we treat JIT and MRP fully in Chapter 9, only a brief illustration is needed here. MRP calculates demand for components based on demand for parent items (items the components go into). JIT relies on simple signals (called kanban signals) of actual parent-item usage to trigger production or delivery of the component.

EXHIBIT 7–4   **Smart New Way to Get Goods to Consumers**

Top row: Consumers lose when manufacturers periodically stuff excess goods into distributors' warehouses (sometimes called trade loading). Here a typical grocery item takes 84 days to go from factory to store shelf.

The manufacturer stockpiles ingredients and packaging supplies to meet peak production levels.

Plants prepare huge runs. Scheduling is chaotic, with more overtime and temporary workers.

Freight companies charge premium rates for the manufacturer's periodic blow-out shipments.

No more panic purchases are necessary. The company cuts down on inventories, freeing up cash.

Factories run on normal shifts. The company cuts down on overtime pay and supplemental workers.

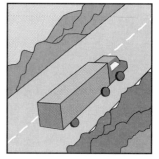

The manufacturer eliminates peak-and-valley distribution. That helps it save 5% in shipping costs.

SOURCE: Patricia Sellers, "The Dumbest Marketing Ploy," *Fortune*, October 5, 1992, pp. 88–94. Used with permission. Jim McManus, Illustrator.

For example, the MRP approach to ordering eggs for a home would be to calculate on, say, Saturday that you will run out of eggs on Thursday. So, you schedule a buy of one dozen eggs on Wednesday. In contrast, a JIT system might employ three reusable egg containers (each holding a dozen) along with a rule that says when a container is empty (kanban signal), you *may* go for a refill, but when all three are empty, you *must* go refill without delay.

One issue that keeps people busy embellishing basic MRP, JIT, and other flow-control approaches is how to keep work from getting stuck in a bottleneck.

Bottleneck Management

If you're standing in line waiting to buy a ticket and the ticketing machine or computer breaks down, you get annoyed. You are idled at a **bottleneck,** which is any process (office, work cell, machine, manager, etc.) that impedes the flow of work. Generally, we

---

EXHIBIT 7–4   continued

Bottom row: Speeded-up cycle is more efficient, improves company's cash flow, and gives consumers a fresher product at a better price.

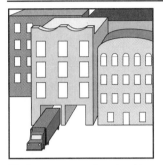

Distributors overstock as they binge on short-term discounts. Cartons sit for weeks inside warehouses.

At distribution centers, the goods get overhandled. Damaged items go back to the manufacturer.

Twelve weeks after the items leave the production line, they may not be fresh for the consumer.

Wholesalers' inventories get cut in half. That means storage and handling costs decline 17%.

Retailers receive undamaged products. Their perception of the manufacturer's quality improves.

The consumer gets the goods 25 days earlier, and—even better news—at a 6% lower price.

---

say that demand exceeds capacity at a bottleneck. Repair of the ticketing computer removes the bottleneck in this situation.

When you finally buy your ticket and surrender it to a ticket taker, you may head for the restroom only to find a long queue there. In this case, the bottleneck stems from failing to plan enough restroom capacity.

Bottlenecks are serious and costly and they drive off customers. The cause of a bottleneck must be fixed, but that takes time; meanwhile, the flow-control system must go to work to minimize damages. We shall briefly consider four topics pertaining to flow control in the face of bottlenecks: finite and infinite capacity assumptions, capacity cushions, capacity enhancement, and the theory of constraints.

Typically, computer-driven flow-control systems, such as material requirements planning (MRP), have operated in the **infinite-capacity planning** mode: the system's scheduling routine sets order start and finish dates assuming that equipment, labor, and other resources are available infinitely to produce the required parent-item components.

Capacity: Finite or Infinite?

However, capacity is finite. In the case of a bottleneck, it is insufficient, and the schedule is said to be overstated. That need not be serious because:

1. Various kinds of flexibility (not easily captured in a computer routine) have always existed; they are used to their fullest in firms with a commitment to serving the customer and improving continuously, including improving things associated with bottlenecks (such as long changeover times or breakdown-prone equipment).

2. Priorities can be rearranged as the work proceeds from process to process. As we shall see in Chapters 9 and 13, advanced MRP systems can issue a new priority report every day. The report for in-progress jobs rearranges priorities, so the highest priorities go to the jobs farthest behind.

Composition of Demand.   Where departmental barriers have been removed, permitting the formation of a multifunctional master scheduling team, another approach to defeating bottlenecks is available. The team looks closely at the composition of orders flowing toward a bottleneck resource and separates good orders from not-so-good ones.

Exhibit 7–5A shows an apparent bottleneck situation. Demand has grown so that it consistently exceeds capacity. The master scheduling team breaks down current demand into three categories: orders for high-profit items, for low-profit items, and for loss items (see Exhibit 7–5B). The team immediately gives preference to high-profit items by removing loss and lower-profit items from the current demand stream (delaying, canceling, or subcontracting those orders). Longer-term actions might include removing items from the product line; changing pricing, advertising, and promotion; and impressing salespeople with the need to discourage sales of loss items.

Besides segmenting demand by profitability, the master scheduling team may also segment by type of customer: vital customers, average customers, and difficult customers. Good customers are well served but the business of annoying ones is refused. Thus, the

> Cost systems often don't yield true item cost; the master scheduling team may need to do its own activity-based costing audit to get good cost data for finding true profit.

Exhibit 7–5   Analysis of Demand at an Apparent Bottleneck

A. Apparent Bottleneck (Capacity Constraint)

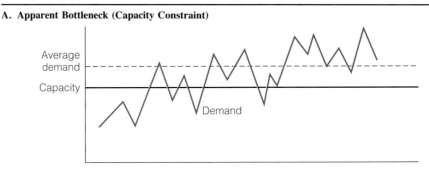

B. Composition of Orders

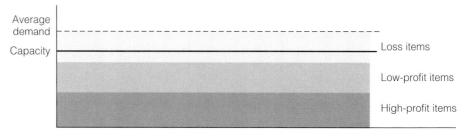

team rejects the view that "a sale is a sale." It segments demand on overloaded resources and takes commonsense actions to relieve the overloads.

Dissecting demand by profitability or customer importance is good business anywhere. Why wouldn't every company do it? we might ask. One reason is that companies have lacked team structures for joint planning across departmental lines. Another is that companies often expect too much from their computer systems. Prudence calls for retaining and enhancing offline organizational and planning mechanisms for influencing scheduling decisions.

Finite-Capacity Planning.   Computer-based flow-control systems that operate under **finite-capacity planning** assumptions are also available. The methodology is as follows. The computer plans the workload for a certain work center or machine. If the workload exceeds capacity, creating a bottleneck, the computer moves some of the workload to the following period's schedule for that work center. The enormous complexities in such systems prevented widespread use of finite-capacity planning until recently. In the mid-1980s, a high-priced finite-based computer software package called optimized production technology (OPT) became available, and a number of finite-capacity planning systems are now on the market (some OPT software is still in use, mainly in Europe).

While computer-based flow-control systems offer ways for companies to plan around capacity obstacles, some companies are able to avoid the problem by planning for sufficient capacity in the first place. Not investing in enough capacity became common in North America and may have contributed to the productivity crisis that became apparent in the 1980s. Even some highly admired North American companies commonly suffered numerous permanent bottlenecks. This was caused largely by misguided strategies: managers milked cash out of existing facilities and failed to invest to expand capacity or to improve the reliability and flexibility of existing capacity.

Capacity Cushion

Failures to invest in needed capacity improvements sometimes reflects a myopic fixation on internal financial numbers.

*C*ontrast

Capacity Planning

Finite-Capacity Planning

Complex scheduling system: If a computer-calculated schedule overloads a bottleneck resource, move some jobs to later (or earlier) time slots.

Only a dream of flow-control system developers in the 1970s, some finite-capacity systems are now up and running.

Infinite-Capacity Planning

Traditional, now in third generation:

First generation: Human expediters use wits to overcome bottlenecks.

Second generation: Computer issues daily priority report, allowing delayed jobs to catch up.

Third generation: Low tolerance for bottlenecks or complex central planning. Emphasis on flexible, cross-trained people, under-capacity scheduling, continuous bottleneck elimination, and identifying/restricting less-desirable orders that create bottlenecks.

No approach works well in conditions of chronic capacity constraints. The most successful firms have understood that. Merck Company (pharmaceuticals) and Milliken & Company (textiles and chemicals), for example, as well as most supermarkets, hotels, hospitals, and transportation companies, plan for a healthy cushion of capacity. This enables them to respond to demand surges, rather than falling into periodic bottlenecks. The Mercks and Millikens of the world are setting an example for other companies, and perhaps prudently shifting to a policy of maintaining a reasonable capacity cushion will become a trend. Companies are also taking cues from JIT writings, which call for undercapacity scheduling so that firms can meet demand surges and serve customers dependably even with lean inventories.

Capacity Enhancement

Superior companies are also finding ways to make existing capacity more dependable and versatile. Exhibit 7–6 lists six approaches that teams of associates can take to reduce the firm's vulnerability to bottlenecks or constraints. The first two items (reducing service and capacity consumption for low-profit items and increasing flexibility to gain capacity) need not be discussed further. But the other four items need some explanation.

Well-trained standby labor (number three) protects against bottlenecks as long as there is enough available, not theoretical, physical capacity (equipment and space) for the standby labor to use. Having standby equipment capacity ties in with the ninth principle of operations management, calling for multiple smaller units of capacity. The rationale is simple. If one small unit breaks down, others of the same type keep humming, but if a single, large-capacity unit goes down, production comes to a halt.

Principle 9:

Multiple units of capacity.

Number four aims at getting more output from existing capacity through improvement projects. Improvement teams especially focus on eliminating stoppages and preventing losses from bad quality.

In the lore of JIT, the main purpose of cutting buffer stocks (number five) is to stimulate problem solving. The procedure is to cut inventories between a pair of processes until the user process sometimes runs out of work (a stockout). Creating a bottleneck, though not a severe or permanent one, makes people in the process feel the actual pain of a shortage in order to create the incentive to expose and fix the underlying cause of variability. That is, you create a small, temporary bottleneck in order to prevent a large, chronic one. This is an aggressive, enforced-problem-solving approach that has sometimes been associated with JIT; it is not for the fainthearted.

Number six is a way of avoiding a trade-off dilemma. Prudent managers have followed the apparently commonsense practice of inserting buffer stocks wherever there is a capacity constraint. The trouble is that buffer stock adds lead time, which has multiple negative effects.

Let's turn this technique around: Where there is a serious but infrequent capacity constraint, move the protective buffer stock offline. For example, an Ontario, Canada,

---

Exhibit 7–6   Toward Capacity Enhancement

---

1. Less service (and therefore less demand on capacity) for less-profitable items or less-valued customers.
2. Cross-training and faster equipment changeovers to gain capacity, flexibility, and speed.
3. Maintaining capable standby capacity, including trained on-call labor.
4. High involvement in improvement projects that cut capacity losses due to down equipment, lack of materials or information, rework, scrap, and low process yields.
5. Deliberately cutting stock to create temporary bottlenecks, thereby stimulating the need to solve basic problems.
6. Moving emergency buffer stock offline, thus cutting throughput time while retaining protection against random bottleneck conditions.

manufacturer keeps one day's supply of six sizes of steel blanks in a low-cost, offline location; historically the blanking equipment breaks down a few times a year. When it does, someone fetches the buffer stock, and operations carry on, avoiding late deliveries, while the equipment is fixed. If the buffer stock was in line, it would add one extra day of lead time all year long, even though it is needed only a few times a year. Furthermore, if in line, it would take up premium space and require constant handling and the usual administrative expenses of work-in-process inventory.

Offline buffer stock avoids these costs. In addition, offline stock can be purified, or subjected to 100 percent quality checking to ensure that, if needed, it will be good stock. If buffer stock is in line, constantly being used and resupplied (first-in, first-out), there is the chance of getting poor quality buffer stock just when it's needed.

Another approach to bottleneck management is Eliyahu Goldratt's **theory of constraints** (an extension of OPT).[4] Emphasis is on scheduling and forwarding work so as to maximize throughput: the rate of work flow and, therefore, cash flow. Managers may be especially attracted to an emphasis on throughput when their capacity is busy 24 hours a day, seven days a week, and still demand cannot be met. In a more normal situation managers should place first emphasis on decreasing throughput time, which we emphasize throughout this text as a basic, customer-oriented, long-term objective. While also important, increasing throughput is more of an internal, shorter-term financial objective.

Theory of Constraints

Constraint:
Inability to keep up with demand because of a capacity bottleneck or a demand surge.

One feature of the theory of constraints is to treat a process batch and a transfer batch separately: if the process batch is large, break it down into smaller transfer batches. The next process, then, gets started on the job sooner, with a smaller amount, instead of waiting until the whole process batch arrives. Another feature is to increase the process batch size (on a bottleneck machine) to cut down on time lost stopping for machine changeovers to another product.

To these concepts (which were OPT elements) the theory of constraints adds policies on buffer stock, formalized rules for inserting buffer stocks either before or after certain bottlenecks. Examples include stocking already machined parts just after (past) a breakdown-prone machine, and placing finished stock as a buffer before an erratic-demand item.

There are two reasons for today's special emphasis on buffer stock policies:

1. In conventional manufacturing and distribution, lot sizes were very large. It was common to buy or produce weeks' or months' worth of most items at a time; that meant weeks or months before supplies dwindled to the point where stockout became a concern. In effect, the huge cycle stocks (lot-size stocks) did double duty, providing buffer stock protection as well.

   The convenience of using cycle stock as buffer stock disappears as lot sizes and cycle intervals shrink, as they do under QRP or JIT. For example, if a dairy makes apple-lemon flavored ice cream every day instead of once a month, dairy managers had better think carefully about how much buffer stock to keep on hand. The amount of buffer stock (raw materials, including apple and lemon flavorings, and semifinished product, such as apple-lemon mix) should be based on recent data on fluctuations of demand, yield, on-time deliveries, machine problems, and so forth. While all those variabilities were present when apple-lemon ice cream was

---

[4]An elaboration of the theory of constraints, called synchronous manufacturing, is described in M. Michael Umble and M. L. Srikanth, *Synchronous Manufacturing* (Cincinnati: South-Western Publishing Co., 1990) (TS155.U48).

Improving the Flow

Theory of Constraints	**Capacity Enhancement**
Maximize throughput (e.g., cash per day generated by moving work quickly through the plant).	Minimize throughput time by solving a wide assortment of work-flow and quality problems.
Potential weakness: Old-line managers may use the theory as an excuse to continue watching short-term productivity reports and profit statements.	Has long-term customer-oriented emphasis.

made only monthly, the possibility of stockout occurred so seldom that the buffer stock decisions were relatively unimportant, not worth much thought.

2. In pursuing just-in-time, some managers become sidetracked and begin to believe that the goal is to eliminate inventory. Most JIT authorities, however, stress that inventory reduction is a lesser benefit (by-product) and that the primary goals are quick, high-quality service to the customer. That often requires prudently placed buffer stock.

We've seen that flow control may involve two kinds of inventory: that arising from lot size and that serving a protective buffering purpose. Are these two kinds of stock related? A caterer's egg-buying behavior provides an answer.

Relating Inventory Timing to Quantity

Kevin and Karin systematically ensure that their catering business doesn't run out of key ingredients. For example, they always write *eggs* on their buy list when the stock in the refrigerator gets down to 10 eggs. At that point, they buy seven dozen eggs.

These two decisions—timing and order quantity—may seem independent but they are not, and here's why.

Kevin and Karin have two aims: (1) don't tie up too much money and refrigerator space on eggs (seven dozen plus 10 eggs is enough), and (2) hold down the chance of running out (10 eggs as the trigger for restocking is the right amount of protection).

Reorder point:
Quantity of on-hand inventory that serves as a trigger for placement of an order for more.

If Kevin and Karin maintained 10 eggs as their **reorder point** but changed their order quantity from seven dozen to one dozen, they would risk running out too often. That is, their egg supply would drop to the danger zone for running out (10-eggs) seven times more often than before. Their catering business won't stand for that much risk, so they would either need to go to a larger order-quantity or raise their reorder point, say, from 10 eggs to two dozen. Either step reduces the long-term frequency (risk) of running out.

Measuring Flow-Control System Performance

What is a gung-ho, high-performance flow-control (or production-control) group striving to achieve? Exhibit 7–7 summarizes traditional and newer answers to that question.

EXHIBIT 7–7   Measurements of Flow-Control Performance

	Traditional	*New*
Pipeline control	None	Order-to-receipt time (supplier performance)
		Advance-shipping-notice-to-receipt time (freight carrier performance)
		Receipt-to-selling floor time (retailer performance)
Operation control	On-time order completion	Lead time (throughput time, response time)
		Response ratio
Inventory control	Stock-record accuracy	Invariable quantity of items/containers in fixed locations between each pair of processes
	Inventory turns, company	Joint inventory turns, company plus suppliers

Traditional (and still common) examples of flow-control measures include 95 percent on-time performance against internal schedules, 99 percent inventory accuracy, and five inventory turns per year.

Companies still care about each of these factors, but emphasis is shifting from internal due dates, stock records, and inventories to speedy response through the supply chain and customer chain.

Pipeline Efficiency

Quick response programs look beyond the department or company walls. QRP-connected firms in the supply pipeline all work from the same scanning data: real customer demand. The supporting information system usually allows suppliers to send advance shipping notices to freight carriers via electronic data interchange (EDI) or fax transmission.

New pipeline-oriented measurements need to be devised to reflect flow control among suppliers, freight carriers, and retailers. Examples for suppliers include time from ordering to receipt of material by the customer; for carriers, time from receipt of the advance shipping notice to customer receipt of the goods; and for the retailer, time from receipt of the goods to their availability on the sales floor.

Short Lead Time

A prominent internal performance measurement (complement to external pipeline measures) is lead time, including time to process all information related to production or service. Aside from measuring quickness of response, lead time serves as an overall indicator of flow control. Long lead times (e.g., many weeks) are evidence that the work flow is out of control.

Ironically, better flow control means a smaller flow-control staff. That is, as lead times fall and the work flow becomes more tightly controlled, the firm needs fewer expediters, schedulers, dispatchers, and clerical staff.

For example, JIT implementation teams at Physio Control (an Eli Lilly company manufacturing defibrillators) were able to create 11 JIT cells (or *team-built* lines, as they are called at Physio). The focused cells used daily rate scheduling, revised monthly, thus eliminating thousands of work orders. Work-in-process (WIP) inventories plunged, emptied WIP stock rooms were torn out, and remaining small stocks became the property of each team-built line. Physio's 10-member production control department had no scheduling or inventory management to do and was abolished, and the 10 people were retrained for other duties, such as supplier certification and supplier development.

Response Ratio

Lead time is a fine measurement of overall flow through several processes, but what about measurements within each of those processes? The **response ratio** fills the need.

The three response ratios are lead time to work content, process speed to use rate, and pieces to workstations or operators. The ideal ratio for each is 1 to 1, but in practice it is typically 5, 10, 100, or 1,000 to 1. What does a ratio of, say, 100 to 1 mean? Examples for each ratio serve to illustrate:

- In a drop-and-add line (at registration for college classes), there is an average of 99 minutes of delay for a 1-minute transaction to have a form signed. The 99 minutes of delay plus the 1 minute for signature is a ratio of 100 minutes of total lead time to 1 minute of work content (when value is added).

- A wire-cutting machine currently is cutting 1,000 pieces of electrical power cord per hour for a certain model of lamp. Lamp assembly, the next process, installs that model of cut cord at only 10 per hour. The ratio or process speed to use rate, thus, is 1,000 to 10, or 100 to 1.

- A clerk in a purchasing department typically has a stack of 99 invoices in an in-basket and just 1 invoice being worked on. This constitutes a pieces-to-operator ratio of 100 to 1.

In each case, high ratios mean long queues of idle materials, documents, or customers. Team members may calculate the ratio, post it in the workplace, and then work to lower it. But they cannot do so without making improvements: cut changeover times, limit the queues (use kanban), have a system for borrowing labor when lines get too long, eliminate disruptive rework by doing it right the first time, keep all facilities clean and well organized, run equipment at the use rate instead of at maximum speed, and so forth.

Following an improvement, the new ratio can be posted on the graph for all to see. The process continues, one improvement at a time, with 1 to 1 as the ultimate (though sometimes unattainable) goal. It is often a good idea to post before-and-after photos or schematic drawings showing waiting-line reductions as the ratios drop.[5] Use of the ratios is also intended to instill the habit of improvement at the operator level (*kaizen* in Japanese) so that improvement becomes primarily a line, not staff, responsibility.

Some firms use response ratios for an entire sequence of operations (total lead time to theoretical minimum time). This overall ratio can be useful for senior managers, but it is not very meaningful for front-liners, who should be concentrating on their own process responsiveness.

Inventory Control

For material-intensive businesses, inventory control is an important aid to flow control of the work itself. In fact, it was clear from the outset of material requirements planning systems use that MRP success requires high stock record accuracy (perfect accuracy is 100 percent agreement between counts of stock in the stockrooms and on-hand stock record balances in the inventory master file).

Successful implementation of just-in-time doesn't require high stock record accuracy so much as it yields record accuracy. One reason is that, to the extent that JIT cuts inventories, there are fewer chances for inventory record inaccuracy. More important in advanced JIT, inventories are held in a set number of special fixed-quantity containers (see Exhibit 7–7). Thus, associates can count their own stock quickly and accurately.

Conventional large-batch production lacks that discipline. Items are likely to exhibit considerable stock variability, from zero (a back-order condition) to thousands of pieces on shelves or in nonstandard containers scattered throughout the facility. Since chances for

---

[5]Examples of use of photos and schematic drawings, as well as more on the response-ratio technique, may be found in Richard J. Schonberger, *World Class Manufacturing Casebook: Implementing JIT and TQC* (New York: Free Press, 1987).

error are high (sometimes baskets of parts are simply lost or misplaced), stock counting is a major undertaking and may be done only once a year.

To summarize, emerging external and internal flow-control focus is on fast processing—on time against real customer needs—and stable inventories.

One more flow-control measure shown in Exhibit 7–7 is **inventory turnover.** For manufacturers, wholesalers, and retailers, inventory turnover remains a good overall measure accounting for many of the wastes tied up in inventory. Corporate management or improvement teams can use it to assess site performance, and site managers/teams can use inventory turnover, or turnover improvement, to measure their own performance.

Inventory Turnover

Beyond that, improvement teams should measure joint inventory turnover (see Exhibit 7–7), which includes the total of within-company inventory and supplier inventory. This measurement prevents companies from dumping inventories on suppliers to make internal inventory performance look good.

An implementation team at one of IBM's first continuous flow manufacturing (JIT) facilities, in Raleigh, North Carolina, chose joint inventory as a performance measure.

Annual inventory turnover is cost of goods sold divided by the value of average inventory:

$$T = \frac{CGS}{I} \qquad (7\text{--}2)$$

where

T = Turnover
CGS = Cost of goods sold (annual)
I = Average inventory value

To illustrate, assume that a modem costs $30 to produce, is selling at a rate of 1,000 per year, and average inventory is worth $6,000. What is the inventory turnover?

$$\text{Cost of goods sold (CGS)} = \text{Unit cost} \times \text{Annual sales}$$
$$= \$30 \times 1,000 = \$30,000$$

$$T = \frac{CGS}{I} = \frac{\$30,000}{\$6,000} = 5 \text{ turns per year}$$

The firm is selling its inventory, or turning it over, five times per year. Compared with an average of between three and four turns for North American industry, that's not bad. (The industry average is much higher in high-volume, continuous production and lower in one-of-a-kind production.) However, some North American plants that used to turn their inventories 3 or 4 times have, through implementing JIT, improved that to 10, 20, 30—even 100—turns.

A poor turnover (below three) could arise from flow times stretching out over many weeks or months. It could also result when demand response is fast but achieved with high inventories. Thus, turnover is a good measure of flow-control system performance.

It may be useful to calculate turnover by category: raw materials, work-in-process, finished goods, and total inventory. Extending the example of the modem manufacturer, assume that $1,500 of the $6,000 average inventory is finished goods, $1,500 is raw materials, and $3,000 is WIP. Assume further that the cost of labor and overhead to convert raw materials to finished goods is $12,000, which is used in calculating WIP turnover as follows:

$$T_{WIP} = \frac{\text{Manufacturing costs}}{WIP} \qquad (7\text{--}3)$$

$$= \frac{\$12,000}{\$3,000} = 4 \text{ WIP turns per year}$$

To calculate raw material (RM) and finished goods inventory (FGI) turnover, we may assume the price of purchased materials plus purchasing overhead to be $14,000 and the overhead cost to carry finished goods to be $4,000. Then,

$$T_{RM} = \frac{\text{Purchasing costs}}{RM} \qquad (7\text{--}4)$$

$$= \frac{\$14,000}{\$1,500} = 9.3 \text{ RM turns per year}$$

$$T_{FGI} = \frac{\text{Finished goods overhead costs}}{FGI} \qquad (7\text{--}5)$$

$$= \frac{\$4,000}{\$1,500} = 2.7 \text{ FGI turns per year}$$

Some firms also compute an RIP turnover, which includes both raw materials and WIP. One company that uses the RIP measure is TRW's Mission Products Division in Texas. The division, one of the more successful JIT converts, improved its RIP turnover from 3 to about 35 per year.

Summary

The flow-control system in any business experiences variabilities: arrivals too early or too late; performance too high or too low, too fast or too slow; or machine breakdowns and yields varying randomly over time. The variabilities are undesirable and detract from serving the customer. When added to poor performance in meeting other customer wants, variability makes things worse. Flow-control systems try to plan around the variabilities; better flow control tries to eliminate them.

Managers/caretakers can only partially control the inventory element (documents and customers as well as materials) of the flow-control system. Inventory slacks and gluts are caused by process variabilities and thus must be dealt with by marketers, engineers, plant maintenance and quality specialists, and others who have the skills to dampen process variability. Their failures call the flow-control system into action, but the system costs themselves are high.

With inventory comes inventory carrying costs: capital invested; stockrooms; obsolescence; inventory administration; space, storage, handling gear for front-line inventories, and support for them; data processing; scrap and rework; lot inspections; and lost business resulting from slow, inconsistent response. The last four items are hidden inventory costs, commonly commingled with other cost categories.

Annual carrying cost is commonly set at 25 percent of the inventory's cost. With hidden costs included, the rate goes as high as 50 percent or even 100 percent. The rate is important since in many businesses inventory is a dominant cost affected by almost any proposed major change.

Modern flow-control systems take advantage of the dependency of component parts on the parent item. The dependency can be reduced to computer calculation using material requirements planning (MRP) software, or to the simplicity of a visual just-in-time (JIT) signal from parent to component.

While MRP and JIT have operated mostly on dependencies within a firm (plus some first-echelon suppliers), quick response programs (QRP) reach well back into the supply chain. QRP requires extensive intercompany teamwork to install a system that feeds retail sales scanning data back through layers of suppliers, who may use it to synchronize schedules to recent actual sales.

One of the challenges to a flow-control system is coping with capacity bottlenecks and constraints. The MRP method is initially to presume infinite capacity and then adjust to bottlenecks by rescheduling affected jobs and by reprioritizing jobs already in process. A newer set of coping approaches is a theory of constraints, which aims at maximizing throughput rate and cash flow. It includes adjusting the sizes of transfer batches and production quantities, and prudently placing buffer stocks after an undependable process or before a spikey demand. Today's emphasis on buffer stocks stems from loss of buffering as JIT drives down lot-size (cycle-stock) inventories; too much inventory reduction causes too much exposure to risks and variabilities.

The multifunctional master scheduling team can often avoid bottleneck problems by examining the composition of the demand stream. Typically it contains some unprofitable orders or those from difficult customers; by canceling or delaying those orders, the team relieves the bottleneck.

While flow-control systems help in dealing with capacity constraints, they do not deal with the root cause of many capacity problems: failure to invest in sufficient capacity. Spending enough on capacity avoids the chaos resulting when demand exceeds capacity. Fixed bottlenecks and the severity of temporary or floating bottlenecks are thus reduced.

Other ways of averting bottleneck problems include provision of capable, on-call backup labor, and improvement team projects that cut changeover times, keep equipment working, and so on, thereby continually freeing up wasted capacity. The JIT technique of putting buffer stock off line allows lead times to be compressed at the same time that risks of stoppages are reduced. Finally, the aggressive JIT approach of drawing down buffer stocks to the pinch point, thus making every process a temporary bottleneck, can drive the pace of improvements, many of which relieve capacity constraints.

Lot-size and buffer inventories are related; smaller lots mean more instances of low stock levels. Flow-control designs should allow for this and avoid increasing risks as stocks are drawn down.

Flow-control system performance had been measured by on-time work order completions and stock record accuracy. With JIT driving lead times down and inventories down and into exact positions in known quantities, the old perfection criteria are becoming givens. The new measures center around pipeline efficiency for QRP-involved firms; short lead times and low response ratios covering every process; stable, invariable inventories between processes; and overall high inventory turnover jointly with suppliers.

Inventory turnover is the number of times average inventory is sold annually. Some JIT and QRP facilities are driving up annual turnover from industry average values of 3 or 4 to 10 or 20 times that high.

Key Words

Flow-control system   239
Inventory carrying cost   242
Capital cost   242
Holding cost   243
Nonvalue-adding (NVA)   244
Independent demand   246
Parent item   246
Dependent demand   246
Component item   246
Buffer stock   246
Quick response program (QRP)   246

Just-in-time (JIT)   246
Material requirements planning (MRP)   246
Bottleneck   250
Infinite-capacity planning   251
Finite-capacity planning   253
Offline buffer stock   255
Theory of constraints   255
Reorder point   256
Response ratio   257
Inventory turnover   259

Solved Problems

Problem 1

A print shop often has numerous jobs stacked up before the huge paper slicing machine. Even by running the slicer overtime and with extra shifts, some days the slicer cannot keep up with the workload. What is a JIT solution to the problem? What solutions would be consistent with the theory of constraints concept?

Solution 1

The JIT approach, based on continuous improvement, would be to seek permanent solutions to the capacity limitations. An improvement team might recommend acquiring one or two small, simple paper-cutting machines that could provide backup and ease the bottleneck. Other techniques favored under JIT are quick setup to reduce the machine time lost in changing from one paper size to another, high levels of preventive maintenance on the machine to keep it from breaking down in the middle of a busy day, high levels of quality control so that the machine's limited capacity will not be eaten up by rework, and moving materials from process to process in small quantities.

Usable theory of constraints concepts include (1) consolidating similar orders (e.g., same paper sizes) into a large production batch, thus minimizing setup frequency, and (2) moving small transfer batches forward from the slicer to the next processes rather than waiting for completion of an entire production run (same as one of the JIT solutions). Both concepts help get more work per day through the bottleneck machine during busy times.

Problem 2

At Computer Services, Inc., small software jobs start at the chief analyst's desk, where each job is assigned to one of the 10 systems analysts. On average, a job sits in the chief's in-basket for 7¾ hours before the chief starts processing it. Average processing time is 15 minutes. In systems analysis, there typically are 60 active jobs.

Use the appropriate response ratios to analyze the delay situation at the chief's desk and in systems analysis.

Solution 2

Chief: Lead time to work content is the proper ratio:

$$\text{Total lead time} = 7\ \tfrac{3}{4}\ \text{hours delay} + \tfrac{1}{4}\ \text{hours work content}$$
$$= 8\ \text{hours}$$

Then:

$$\text{Ratio (lead time to work content)} = 8\ \text{to}\ \tfrac{1}{4},\ \text{or 32 to 1}$$

Analysts: Pieces to operators is the proper ratio:

$$\text{Number of pieces} = 60\ \text{jobs}$$
$$\text{Number of operators} = 10\ \text{analysts}$$

Then:

$$\text{Ratio (pieces to operators)} = 60\ \text{to 10, or 6 to 1}$$

Problem 3

One division of J. W., Inc., produces detergent. Its current RIP inventory turnover is 9. Another division, producing a line of electronic timing devices for home and industrial use, has a RIP turnover of 4. Both divisions have about the same annual costs of purchased materials plus cost to convert them to finished goods: $2 million.

a. What is the average total of raw materials and WIP for each division?
b. Should the turnovers be used for comparing the two divisions or for some other purpose?

Solution 3

a. The turnover formula must be inverted from

$$T_{RIP} = \frac{\text{Purchasing and manufacturing costs}}{RIP}$$

to

$$RIP = \frac{\text{Purchasing and manufacturing costs}}{T_{RIP}}$$

Then:

For detergent: $RIP = \$2,000,000/9 = \$222,222$
For timers: $RIP = \$2,000,000/4 = \$500,000$

b. It is unreasonable to compare turnovers. Detergent is made in a continuous process, which should not give rise to nearly as much idle inventory as do timers. It is reasonable to regularly assess the trends in RIP turnover separately for each product. Higher RIP turnover is an overall sign of improvement in division performance.

For Further Reference

Books

Goldratt, Eliyahu M., and Jeff Cox. *The Goal: Excellence in Manufacturing*. Croton-on-Hudson, N.Y.: North River Press, 1984.

Hall, Robert W. *Attaining Manufacturing Excellence*. Homewood, Ill.: Dow Jones-Irwin, 1987.

Plossl, G. W., and O. W. Wight. *Production and Inventory Control*. Englewood Cliffs, N.J.: Prentice-Hall, 1967 (HD55.P5).

Schonberger, Richard J. *Building a Chain of Customers: Linking Business Functions to Create the World Class Company*. New York: The Free Press, 1990 (HD58.9.S36).

Vollmann, Thomas E., William L. Berry, and D. Clay Whybark. *Manufacturing Planning and Control Systems*. 3rd. ed. Homewood, Ill.: Richard D. Irwin, 1992 (TS176.V63).

Periodicals/Societies

Journal of Operations Management (American Production and Inventory Control Society).

Production and Inventory Management (American Production and Inventory Control Society).

Target (Association for Manufacturing Excellence).

Review Questions

1. Describe three types of process variabilities. What are their effects on work flow? On customer service?

2. Can material managers control inventory excesses and shortages? Explain.

3. What are capital costs and holding costs?

4. Why have some costs of carrying inventory been semiobvious or even hidden?

5. What is the meaning of a 35 percent carrying cost? Is it realistic today? Discuss.

6. Give an example of a dependency chain four levels deep (component into parent, which goes into its parent, etc., through four levels).

7. Why are buffer stocks more necessary for independent-demand items than for dependent-demand items?

8. How are quick response systems (QRS) different from JIT? Similar?

9. How does MRP treat the relationship between parent and component items?

10. Can a flow-control system be effective under an infinite-capacity assumption? Explain.

11. When and why should a master scheduling team analyze the composition of demand?

12. What does the theory of constraints do about bottlenecks?

13. What is a good way of coping with fixed bottlenecks?

14. How is JIT supposed to handle bottlenecks?

15. How does lot size affect risk of stockout?

16. When should buffer stock be off line and why?

17. Why is 100 percent on-time completion of work orders inadequate as an indicator of perfection in operation control?

18. What is the usefulness of calculating inventory turnover?

Problems and Exercises

1. Process variabilities induce firms to carry protective excess inventories; the greater the excess, the greater the inventory carrying costs. Process variabilities also can result in inventory shortages. The greater the shortage, the greater which cost? Explain.

2. Iota Company produces bicycle reflectors. Currently Iota buys the main raw material, bags of plastic pellets, in large quantities about three times a year. Its policy is to order another lot when

stock on hand falls to five days' worth (the reorder point). Now Iota is considering a just-in-time purchasing approach: small quantities ordered frequently, perhaps as often as every two weeks.

There is a risk that the supplier will deliver late. Will JIT purchasing increase or decrease the risk? Should the reorder point be changed? Explain.

3. A plant specializing in precision machining is considering buying a numerical control (NC) machine with an installed cost of $200,000. The NC machine can perform multiple metal-cutting operations by successively rotating a mounted metal work piece and selecting cutting tools from a magazine. Thus, it would incorporate operations now done at scattered machine centers and would eliminate idle materials between machine and stockroom. Average inventory reduction from using the NC machine is estimated at $60,000. Also, the single machine will cost less to set up and operate than the present multiple machines, an additional savings of $50,000 per year.

   a. If 20 percent is used as the inventory carrying cost, how quickly can the investment pay for itself (what is the payback period)?

   b. Suggest four more important kinds of savings that are likely but less obvious than savings from materials and direct labor. Recalculate the payback period using a larger, more realistic carrying cost (your best estimate).

4. When Hewlett-Packard's Boise division converted to JIT, it eliminated all work orders. One result was 100,000 fewer computer transactions per month.

   a. In what sense may those eliminated transactions be considered as nonvalue-adding? An element of inventory carrying cost?

   b. This story is detailed in Rick Hunt, Linda Garrett, and C. Mike Merz, "Direct Labor Cost Not Always Relevant at H-P," *Management Accounting,* Feb. 1985, pp. 58–62. Find this article and explain how the transactions were eliminated.

5. Jack is an assembler at Penrod Pen Company. His job is to pack a gold-plated pen and pencil, plus guarantee card, into a gift box. He puts the completed box on a chute, which feeds a machine that applies an outer wrap. (The chute holds a maximum of five boxes.) As an employee, Jack exhibits normal human failings, especially these:

   Occasionally he drops a pen, pencil, or card and while he searches for it on the floor, the outer-wrap machine runs out of boxes to wrap and stops. Several times the machine has lost 50 to 100 cycles while Jack was searching.

   Every few hours the assembly line is changed to produce a different model of pen and pencil set, which requires a different guarantee card. But Jack sometimes forgets to change to the correct card. (Inspectors discover the error through random sampling.) As many as 1,000 boxes may have to be torn open and reworked, and when that happens an order for an important customer is usually late.

   The supervisor has a solution to Jack's variable performance: extra inventory.

   a. Explain exactly how extra inventory can serve as a solution.

   b. Jack has ideas for certain types of fixtures and automatic checkers that, he feels sure, would immediately catch either of his chronic errors. The devices, installed at his end of the feeder chute, would eliminate the need for the extra inventory that his supervisor has proposed. The supervisor weighs the cost of the devices against the savings on inventory carrying costs using Penrod's usual carrying cost rate of 25 percent. Jack feels the rate is too low. Is Jack right? Be specific in your answer.

6. The director of purchasing and materials management at Ivy Memorial Hospital wants her hospital to be the first in the area to implement a quick-response program with its suppliers of medical devices. How should she proceed?

7. Rate the following four types of businesses, one to four, as to the applicability of quick-response systems in the business. Explain your ratings.

Welfare agency.   Producer of pigments.

Fast-food restaurant.   Trucking company.

8. Review the QRP examples in the chapter, of Wal-Mart, Luxottica, and VF Corp., all of which employ EDI. Also review the example "Quick Response by Fax."

   a. Are there any significant differences between the first three examples and the last one, other than choice of communications media? Explain.

   b. Having adopted fax communications, should the fabric-to-auto chain upgrade to EDI? Why or why not?

   c. As other chains of customers, perhaps in other businesses, consider a quick-response alliance, would you recommend EDI or fax? Why?

9. Over-Nite Mail Corporation experienced two serious problems as business grew in the past 18 months: (1) Over 10 percent of its service orders take three days or more for successful delivery; (2) record accuracy (showing where orders are in its delivery system) is poor; random sampling shows that 30 percent of the records are inaccurate (e.g., a log book shows that a piece of mail is in the delivery truck while it is really still in the sorting room). A recent investment in a computerized order-tracking system has improved record accuracy to 99.5 percent. Should that give the company a significant competitive edge over competing overnight delivery companies? Explain. In your explanation, describe how the company should measure the effectiveness of its order control system.

10. A plant that produces industrial thermostats has successfully implemented MRP. One result is that mean production lead time (from raw material to finished goods) has improved modestly, from 9.3 to 8.7 weeks. Two large improvements are (1) stock record accuracy has risen from 68 to 99.2 percent, and (2) on-time completion of work orders is up from 60 to 97 percent. Plant management and the consulting company that assisted in the conversion to MRP are delighted; they claim that inventory control and production control are approaching perfection. They expect the results to stem some of their business losses to domestic and foreign competitors. Are their expectations realistic? Are the inventory and production control really so good? Discuss.

11. Currently the major bottlenecks at a plant that makes electrical fixtures are the paint line and the 600-ton press that stamps out sheet metal parts. Hundreds of different kinds of parts must pass through those processes, and many jobs get stalled in queues before one or both.

    a. What kinds of solutions would be recommended if theory-of-constraints concepts were employed?

    b. What are likely to be the main kinds of solutions to these bottleneck problems under JIT?

12. The equipment used in a campus testing service includes order-entry terminals, optical scanning equipment, computers, and printers. At certain times, one or more of the machines has days' worth of jobs queued up. What do you recommend? Why?

13. Elmo's Burger Shoppe sells $50,000 worth of plain burgers per month. The profit margin is 10 percent. Total inventory on hand averages $12,000. What is the inventory turnover? Should Elmo separately calculate turnovers for purchased materials, WIP, and finished goods?

14. ABC Specialties, Inc., produces a wide variety of office and home products, one of which is a small mail scale. Annual cost of goods sold for the scale is $100,000, which includes $60,000 to purchase raw materials and $35,000 to convert them to finished goods. The average value of recently purchased plastic and metal parts and materials, plus fasteners, is $10,000; the value of partially completed production is $5,000; and the value of completed finished goods is $15,000. Compute separate and total inventory turnovers. Is ABC managing scale production well? Explain.

15. Exhibit 7–1 shows variability in relation to target performance. The point was made in the chapter that positive and negative variations do not cancel one another out. How do these ideas compare with Taguchi's social loss concept (discussed in Chapter 2)?

 **CASE STUDY**

RIO BRAVO IV

The Packard Electric division of General Motors is the leading producer of power and signal distribution products in the United States and wanted the same reputation internationally. The company believed it was as capable as any producer anywhere, but that view was not shared in some foreign markets. There was one way to gain worldwide respect: take on an important international project and show everyone just how competent we were.

Little did I realize that I'd be in the middle of this project or that it would start as it did, when my boss drove me to an industrial section of Juarez, Mexico, and mysteriously stopped on a small street.

"You always wanted to do something in manufacturing," he began. "Here's your chance. Jim, it's all yours."

With knowing irony he motioned dramatically toward my new domain—a dilapidated warehouse building, previously used to store furniture, with weeds growing through the surrounding pavement. It was hardly what I envisioned when I imagined myself as manager of a manufacturing plant.

From this dirty, cobwebbed structure, our team would be expected to produce wiring harnesses for the most demanding company Packard had ever supplied: New United Motor Manufacturing Incorporated (NUMMI), a joint venture of General Motors and Toyota in Fremont, California. And initial units for the pilot vehicle were to be shipped in just four months.

Thus, I became manager of Plant IV of Rio Bravo Electricos, S.A. de C.V., a subsidiary of Packard Electric.

Packard decided to perform the manufacturing in northern Mexico, where other Packard facilities were in operation. The former furniture warehouse was leased and converted to an assembly plant, equipment was quickly installed in a layout similar to that of other Packard plants, and a management team was gathered.

It was an unlikely team. My background was primarily in quality control and sales; I had never supervised a manufacturing operation. Our manager of industrial engineering was a long-term tool-and-die guy who had no industrial engineering experience. The materials manager was an ex-U.S. Army captain whose involvement with automotive wiring had been nine months of scheduling production for a battery line in Ohio. We had three other Packard transferees. Only one of these five men spoke any Spanish. Completing the team were three Mexicans. One had worked two years at a wiring plant. The second had been in the clothing business with his father, and the third had been a mining engineer at an aluminum operation.

From our hastily equipped facility, this team had to supervise the prompt production of products that met NUMMI's lofty expectations. We thought we were a very high quality producer, but we didn't realize that NUMMI was demanding something we had never had to accomplish: Not only did the parts have to be of the highest quality, but they had to be delivered

- In precise quantities.
- At the specified hour of the day.
- To the correct location.
- At an acceptable price.

Case Topics:

Quality.	Eliminating nonvalue-adding wastes.
Housekeeping.	Disciplined stock location practices.
Continuous improvement (kaizen).	Supplier partnership.
Queue limitation (kanban).	Visual management.
Quick die change.	Globalization and culture.

SOURCE: Adapted from James P. Walker, "A Disciplined Approach to Continuous Improvement," Packard Electric Corp., 1988.

It might be difficult, but how tough could it be? After all, we were good at making harnesses. What could be expected that we couldn't handle?

We quickly found out.

The Awakening

Despite Packard's long and successful history of producing wiring harnesses and electrical components, it did not take long for us to see that NUMMI's expectations were on a different plane from any we had previously encountered. Satisfying them was sometimes humiliating, often painful, and nearly always an ordeal.

When Packard was instructed to send 200 samples for a prototype vehicle, the Packard general manager decreed that the samples be flawless, regardless of the effort required. He wanted to impress NUMMI with Packard quality.

A special group was formed to assemble the samples. The division's best people were used. Every component was carefully checked. The samples, all in perfect order, were sent to NUMMI managers then located at Toyota in Japan.

We eagerly awaited the anticipated flattery. Instead, the Toyota people expressed grave disappointment. They disliked the tape used to wrap the assemblies! Our tape had small notches along one edge, cut intentionally to facilitate tearing. To the NUMMI people, the notches were unattractive, and the appearance of the wiring harnesses, not just their performance, was important.

We could not believe such nit-picking. We were certain they were creating objections in order to make us look bad. Nevertheless, we had to do something.

> Question 1. Are there any justifiable reasons for this response by NUMMI/Toyota people? Or was it just nit-picking?

So we entered into a joint technical agreement with Sumitomo Wiring, a company with a reputation for outstanding quality and a major supplier to the Japanese auto industry, including Toyota. Sumitomo sent a team of six engineers and a translator to Rio Bravo IV where they spent six months with us, living and working, teaching, and criticizing. Mostly teaching by criticizing. These advisors not only showed us how to read the NUMMI blueprints but also helped us institute the philosophies, techniques, and discipline necessary to produce harnesses acceptable to NUMMI.

The agonizing details of this six-month period of criticizing and learning are set down in the original, longer version of this report. I'll make that longer story short by skipping to our first shipment to NUMMI. It was rejected. The reason: There was too much variation in the colors of the cables.

Despite the negative evaluation and the initial rejection and the lack of appreciation for our efforts, Packard hung in there, and so did most of our work force, though not without doubts and frustration. The pressure on everyone was disheartening.

One afternoon, two of my top Mexican managers said they wanted to quit. They complained that, no matter how hard they worked, I was never satisfied. After some conversation, the managers agreed to sleep on their decisions and talk about it the next day.

That day, by chance, Packard Electric staff members, including general manager Elmer Reese, visited the plant. In front of his staff and many of our beleaguered workers, our general manager optimistically announced, "Things look bad now, but I predict this plant will be a success." Buoyed by this show of faith from Mr. Reese himself, the Mexican managers decided to stay on, hoping eventually to share in the rewards.

During the same visit, Elmer said to me: "This is the cleanest plant I've ever seen at Packard Electric or General Motors. You can't serve a gourmet dinner from a dirty kitchen; I know this team will be successful."

Putting the Theories to Work

The many lessons we learned, with the guidance of the Sumitomo advisers, had to be put into effect in ways that fit the local culture. Still, we have instituted these techniques: customer is king, build it right the first time and every time, no repeat problems, eliminate waste, planned maintenance, minimal inventories, supplier involvement, kanban, visual controls, people power, and so on.

Kaizen.   Kaizen (continuous improvement) sheets are posted on boards around the plant. When a problem is identified, it is listed on the sheet. A sketch or Polaroid snapshot is placed on the board to illustrate the problem. There are columns for writing in the cause of the problem, the irreversible corrective action that will eliminate the cause, the person or persons responsible for the corrective action, the date when the action is completed, and a sketch or photo of the correction. Posting the problems not only establishes our desire to remove them but gives all members an opportunity to be involved in solutions.

We have also hastened problem solving by a very simple technique: reducing the size of our reject holders. A large rack encourages procrastination in taking corrective steps and makes it easier to discard the rejected item and think about it later. By cutting the size of our racks in half, the decision-making process was hurried. Since then, we have eliminated the reject racks altogether. Now, whenever there is a reject, the associate must immediately decide what action should be taken.

> Question 2. This practice (restricting the reject holders) is an application of what concept from this chapter?

Die Changes.   The delay caused by die changes has also been reduced. We have cut the time required of our cutting machine operator by 80 percent. All possible adjustments are made in a trial press before the die leaves the crib for the cutter. This minimizes the loss of the operator's production time and is an example of external adjustments, which, where possible, should be made offline before interrupting production.

Lead Time Reduction.   We use a simple diagramming method to look at ways to streamline our procedures (see Exhibit S7–1).

Blocks representing each step in a procedure are drawn proportionally to the amount of time that step consumes. The blocks are laid out along a time line, with value-added steps on the left side of the line and nonvalue-added steps on the right. Our goals are to reduce the size of the boxes (i.e., the time required for each step) and eliminate steps on the nonvalue-added side of the line.

> Question 3. In what Rio Bravo IV operations would this diagramming method be effective? Discuss.

Inventory Control.   Inventory is like a drug; it makes you feel good, but it can be very expensive and even deadly (in a tough competitive environment). We order and maintain inventories of

Exhibit S7–1   Lead Time Reduction Diagram

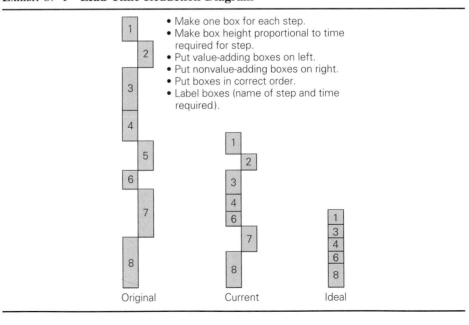

supplies that are as small as practicable. And we produce only what is needed for that day's shipments; when operators complete their scheduled work before the end of the shift, they spend the remaining time cleaning their work stations or checking their equipment or working on a plant problem or training.

To ensure that inventories are kept small, we build racks to accommodate only the size and number of boxes that we determine are necessary. This applies to our drinking water as well as our production materials.

One morning, while on a plant tour, I spotted two bottles of drinking water on the plant floor next to a completely filled bottle rack. I asked the water service man why they were there. He replied that two extra bottles were needed because of demand. I explained our everything-in-its-place philosophy and agreed to have another rack built to meet his needs.

A couple of days later I noticed that both racks were filled and two bottles were again on the plant floor. I waited for the water service man to arrive and, once he could see me, I broke one of the bottles with a hammer. The problem was eliminated.

Kanban.   We control inventory through the use of kanban. With kanban, material is pulled from the supplier to the customer. The cards make it easy to see how many pieces have been ordered, how many have been built, and how many remain to be built. The kanban card is the pull signal.

Kanban works; we have reduced inventories and related floor space by 80 percent (and we are not finished yet), discovered process and quality problems in their early stages, and cut the time necessary to make engineering changes. However, kanban works best only in combination with other measures. For optimum results, production schedules received from the customer must be level or with plus or minus 10 percent variation.

Three of our local suppliers (providers of pallets, boxes, and cable) have recognized the benefits of kanban and have adopted their own systems. Every day, at a specified time and loading dock, we receive from them exactly those materials we need for that day, and only that day.

Suppliers.   By involving a supplier or just by asking, How about doing this for us? it is surprising how often problems are eliminated. Occasionally, however, it is necessary to find another supplier.

For example, some of the shipping boxes we used were too easily crushed. The weak boxes were affecting the quality of our products—broken connectors were one of the biggest problems reported to us by NUMMI. Besides, boxes are not supposed to get damaged in normal handling.

We looked into the problem and found that (1) the boxes were too spacious for the amount of material being shipped within, (2) the box walls were probably too thin, and (3) internal liners would add support and protection, but also add cost. We discussed the needed changes with our box supplier. They were unable to make satisfactory modifications.

A supplier was found who designed and fabricated a stronger box, with internal dividers, that met our needs. In addition, the new box cost less than the box we had been using (see Exhibit S7–2).

Question 4. What benefits in addition to protection do the box dividers offer? Discuss.

Visual Management and Discipline.   As a visual control above critical equipment, we've installed a system of lights. When the machine is running, the green light is illuminated. The yellow light means the machine is momentarily idle, and red indicates assistance is needed.

Also above cutting machines are placards that show the date of the equipment's last maintenance work and when the next maintenance is scheduled. It is planned maintenance as opposed to crisis maintenance. In addition, daily adjustments are made by operators who consider the machines their own.

Another simple visual control appears on the doors of our terminal die cabinets. On the metal doors, blocks are lined off that relate in size and position to the compartments inside. Each block is labeled with the compartment's part number and has small spaces corresponding to the dies within. When dies are in the compartment, magnets are put in the spaces. A green magnet indicates that a die is in use in a press, and a red magnet shows that a die is being serviced or replacement parts are on order.

With visual controls such as these, anyone passing can tell at a glance where things stand. There is no need to check computer screens, printouts, or reports.

EXHIBIT S7–2   **Shipping Containers**

We have a rule: when a light goes out in the plant, it is to be replaced within ten minutes. (Fixtures are not supposed to hold burned-out lights and, more importantly, poor lighting obscures the operator's view of the work.) It is not left to a maintenance person to spot it; anyone can do it.

There is a place for litter, as there is for barrels of cable, terminal dies, and bottled water. Orderliness takes effort to establish but, once instituted, makes many tasks more efficiently done.

"Everything in its place" applies to the office area as well as to the production area. In our conference room is a small holder with slots for five felt tip markers. We placed bars of color on each slot to show what particular color of marker goes in that specific slot. All slots are to be filled with the properly colored marker. I've threatened going even a step further and having a kanban card for each marker.

You may have thought that such details are ridiculous, but I hope by now you understand their significance. I have a quick way of judging how well things are going at Rio Bravo IV: if the markers are in their holder properly and if there are no burned out lights in the plant and if the terminal reels are stacked correctly, I can be fairly sure that everything is proceeding as it should and the harnesses are marching into their shipping containers.

The Beginning

The trials of Rio Bravo IV have been difficult, but the lessons learned have helped to establish Packard Electric as a worldwide leader in the manufacture of signal and power distribution systems. That was our objective when the NUMMI contract was bid, and it remains our objective today.

It would be comfortable to think that the goal has been reached and now we can relax. But the principle of continuous improvement does not allow for complacency. There is always opportunity for improving quality or productivity or costs; there is always a better way.

Though we have made giant strides in our first three-and-one-half years, the ongoing attention to continuous improvement will show that the steps taken so far are just the beginning.

Question 5. What does this case suggest about management of the global company? What does it suggest about the influence of culture?

8 PURCHASING: QUEST FOR HIGH-QUALITY SUPPLIERS

In 1992, nearly $1,000 of the cost of every car that General Motors produced went to buy health care services for employees.

Raw materials and purchased components typically account for 60–70 percent of the final cost of manufactured goods. If we include costs of *services* purchased to enhance or support manufacturing operations, the purchased (bought) component of product cost is even higher. Unlike the previous focus on price of purchased items, managers now believe that the best way to improve value received for purchasing expenditures (thus lowering total costs) is to have better suppliers. In one study, top manufacturing executives ranked improving supplier quality as the number two strategic objective for the 1990s, surpassed only by the objective of improving one's own quality.[1]

---

[1]Jeffrey G. Miller, Arnoud DeMeyer, and Jinichiro Nakane, *Benchmarking Global Manufacturing* (Homewood, Ill.: Business One Irwin, 1992), p. 83 (HD 9720.5.M55).

Like manufacturers, service organization managers are realizing the strategic importance of their purchasing activities. Government agencies, schools, hospitals, and private-sector service firms are seeking high-quality suppliers. Yesterday's isolated buyer, intently searching in catalogs and by phone for a better price, has been replaced by teams of associates from throughout the organization working toward quality-oriented partnerships with a few preferred suppliers.

In this chapter, we first explore the specifics of a growing movement toward team-based supplier-customer partnerships. We then turn to a few of the better known purchasing procedures that apply to the team/partnership approach.

Purchasing: A Changing Role

Purchasing played a small role in the first modern upheaval that occurred in materials management. The material requirements planning (MRP) wave of the late 1970s and early 1980s improved the planning for purchased items, but traditional purchasing organization and practices survived. However, the second phase, featuring just-in-time and total quality, proved too much for traditional purchasing. Today it is one of the radically changing disciplines within organizations. In this section, we look at traditional purchasing and examine new challenges facing associates who buy goods and services.

Traditional purchasing departments are organized by commodity group. Each buyer is responsible for one or a few commodities, such as sportswear, shoes, steel, electronics, paper and supplies, and contracted services. A typical week may bring hundreds of requisitions and purchase orders to be processed and forwarded to dozens of suppliers. Large quantities of data from the receiving department must be reconciled or used to evaluate vendors. Also, associates are constantly trying to find new suppliers, then soliciting and processing bids. All the while, they are handling complaints from unhappy internal and external customers with unmet materials needs.

Traditional Purchasing

A requisition, prepared in another department, is a request for purchasing to place an order for a specific item.

Poor quality, wrong quantity, wrong item, and, especially, late deliveries keep requisitioners anxious and buyers busy. Changing delivery dates or quantities, arranging alternative transportation, and attending to the large flow of paperwork keeps buyers from getting to know suppliers.

Management may choose not to know what happens in the supplier's system, in effect, to treat it as a black box (see Exhibit 8–1). Order information (orders, requisitions, inquiries, change requests, etc.) goes into the box, and status information (acknowledgements, responses, etc.) and, eventually, goods and services themselves come out of the box. But what's inside remains a mystery.

Of course, in a few companies purchasing professionals have attempted to probe the black box (e.g., by phone or on-site visit to the supplier) to learn about suppliers. However, the result too often is like the following exchange:

EXHIBIT 8–1   Black Box View of the Supplier's System

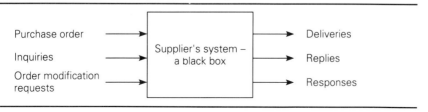

Buyer: ''What is the status of my order?''

Supplier's representative: ''According to my current information, it is on time.''

Buyer: ''What do you mean by current information?''

Supplier's representative: ''Well, I haven't received a delay notice.''

Buyer: ''Do you receive regular delay reports?''

Supplier's representative: ''Yes.''

Buyer: ''How often?''

Supplier's representative: ''Monthly.''

Buyer (mentally noting that month-old delay reports are badly out of date): ''Could you please check to see where the order is in your shops?''

Supplier's representative: ''No, I've tried that before. Manufacturing tells me there are just too many orders on the floor to go searching for a particular one.''

Buyer: ''OK. Then could you just check with your master scheduler to see where my order is on your MPS?''

Supplier's representative: ''MPS?''

Clearly, the supplier's representative is not in the habit of checking with production control or operations. The aggressive buyer will have scored a coup if the supplier's rep is induced to go to production control for order status information and succeeds in getting it.

Purchasing's New Challenge

It becomes easier for buyers to probe the black boxes of their suppliers when the purchasing department gets focused. This requires the breakup of central purchasing departments so that some buyers can join product- or customer-focused teams.

A focused unit may have broad responsibilities, perhaps encompassing the entire process (see Exhibit 8–2). Purchasing's responsibilities in that process may include

EXHIBIT 8–2   The Purchasing Challenge

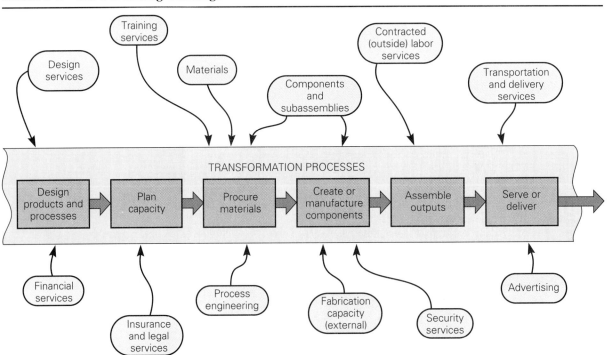

𝒞ontrast

The Purchasing Associate

Traditional	**Modern**
• Commodity-oriented.	• Captain of a purchasing team of colleagues and suppliers.
• Burdened with paperwork.	• Quality-oriented and challenged by task variety.
• Out of touch with suppliers.	

---

buying materials and also various services, such as design services, advertising, and training. The team structure improves the effectiveness of buying such services: engineers on the team can help procure outside design services, marketing people can assist in selecting advertising agencies, human resource associates can participate in contracting with outside training organizations, and so on.

Increasingly, businesses and government agencies are outsourcing these and other kinds of services instead of performing them internally. Buying services, which are less tangible than goods, introduces special contract compliance issues, to be explored later in the chapter. The demand for quality stands firm, however, whether you buy goods or services.

In sum, the challenge for the modern buyer is to become a team-oriented buyer/planner/manager. Dedicated professionals are needed to carry out these duties, of course. Demand for purchasing professionals is increasing and should continue to rise throughout the 1990s.

From the catalog-and-telephone-limited buyer to an integrated purchasing team is a big step, but it's not enough. The next step is to tap the suppliers' expertise, that is, to get them on the team as partners.

Focused organizational unit—or **focused factory**: facilities dedicated to doing one or a few things well instead of all things for all customers.

Affiliation with the National Association of Purchasing Management (NAPM) provides a window to career opportunities in purchasing and related fields.

Toward Partnerships with Suppliers

Getting to know suppliers became a strong movement in the 1980s and early 1990s. The old approach was ineffective. Buying companies distrusted suppliers and changed suppliers often; in response, suppliers did not do their best for customers, which made their replacement by other suppliers likely.

The trend away from detached, even adversarial, relationships is strongest among big industrial companies and major retailers, such as McDonald's and Wal-Mart. Some are calling the new approach partners in profit, and a few companies are adopting new job and department titles, such as Frito Lay's vice president of supplier development.

Exhibit 8–3 contrasts the old and new approaches. The second column describes adversarial relationships. Few companies have been totally adversarial with suppliers, but most have been that way to some degree. By contrast certain leading-edge companies have embraced nearly all of the partnership items, and many others have adopted them in part. The extremes of adversary and partnership are anchors for discussion of the 12 dimensions in Exhibit 8–3.

EXHIBIT 8–3   **Supplier Relationships**

	Adversary	*Partnership*
1. Tenure	Brief	Long-term, stable
2. Type of agreement	Sporadic purchase orders	Exclusive or semiexclusive contracts, usually at least one year
3. Number of sources	Several sources per item for protection against risk and for price competition	One or a few good suppliers for each item or commodity group
4. Volume of business	Limits on amount of business with any one supplier	High; sometimes supplier dedicates small plant to single customer
5. Prices/costs	High on average; low buy-in bids (below costs) can lead to unstable suppliers	Low; scale economies from volume contracts; suppliers can invest in improvements
6. Quality	Uncertain; reliance on receiving inspections	Quality at source; supplier uses statistical process control and total quality management
7. Design	Customer developed	Make use of suppliers' design expertise
8. Delivery frequency/order size	Infrequent, large lots	Frequent (sometimes more than one per day), small lots just-in-time
9. Order conveyance	Mail	Long-term: contracts. Short-term: kanban, phone, fax, or electronic data interchange
10. Documentation	Packing lists, invoices, count/inspection forms	Sometimes no count, inspection, or list—just monthly bill
11. Delivery location	Receiving dock and stockroom	Direct to point of use
12. Openness	Very little; black box	On-site audits of supplier, concurrent engineering/design, visits by front-line associates

Tenure

Under the adversarial approach, suppliers are changed often. A new supplier's catalog price list might catch a buyer's eye and trigger a switch from the old to the new supplier. For larger volume (or big-ticket) items, bids are requested from several suppliers at least yearly; the lowest bidder (often not the present supplier) usually gets the contract.

In the partnership approach, the idea is to not change suppliers. Stay with one so that the learning curve has a chance to work for the benefit of both parties. Suppliers who get to know a customer's real requirements are valuable participants on product and process improvement teams, quality function deployment programs, and other continuous-improvement efforts.

Type of Agreement

In the adversarial approach, sporadic purchase orders for single shipments are the norm, and orders for a single item may rotate among 5 or 10 suppliers. Some blanket orders cover multiple shipments over a longer time period, but a blanket order may also go to several suppliers for a single item.

Special, one-time buys will probably always require a purchase order. For regularly used items, however, the trend is toward contracts. Five-year contracts have become widespread in the North American auto industry; one-year contracts are more common in the volatile electronics industry. For example, the Lincoln, Illinois, plant of Eaton Corporation's Power Distribution Division treats selected vendors as internal departments and uses yearly master pricing agreements.

Some contracts, like blanket orders, may not commit to a quantity. Others go beyond blanket orders to specify the quantity in fairly precise terms for the next few months and as a forecast for the rest of the year. Also, the contract may grant the supplier an exclusive arrangement, although exact quantities are not stipulated.

Number of Sources

Having several sources for each purchased item was the common practice, especially among adversarially oriented buyers. And government regulations still require it for certain classes of goods and services to encourage price competition and a sense of fairness in public expenditures. In most cases, however, fear of supplier failure accounted for the many-supplier rule.

There is price competition with multiple sourcing, but it is short-term. Over time, multiple sourcing raises each supplier's costs and thus costs to the customer.[2] But sole- or preferred-supplier sourcing gives the supplier confidence that demand will continue, thus encouraging supplier investment in process and product improvements that offer economies of scale. Indeed, some believe that widespread multiple sourcing in North America and Europe in recent decades ruined part of the supplier base, which drove buying companies off shore, primarily to the Far East, in search of quality goods from reliable suppliers.

Multiple sourcing is also costly to buying organizations: expenses associated with vendor selection, evaluation, and certification; data processing; communications; and administrative and clerical activities are obvious examples. A less tangible cost of having many suppliers is the loss of the opportunity to get to know and take advantage of suppliers' capabilities.

Competitive organizations strive to reduce these wastes, and a total quality or JIT program is often the impetus. A survey of North American companies revealed the average number of suppliers to be 1,096 prior to JIT. The number dropped to 759 after one year of JIT, to 656 after two years, and to 357 after five years. On average, the companies had cut their number of suppliers by over 67 percent in five years.[3] Other companies' programs aim at reducing the number of suppliers as a goal in itself. For example, a 3M factory in New Ulm, Minnesota, trimmed its active vendor list from 2,800 to 600 in the first year, and to 300 in the second year.[4] Furthermore, the trend has spread from manufacturing to fast-food companies, hotels, retailers, and wholesalers. Wallace Company, a distributor of oil-drilling repair parts and a winner of the Malcolm Baldrige Quality Award, cut its number of valve suppliers from 2,500 to 325.[5] Reductions of suppliers usually are competitive rather than arbitrary, and buying companies are usually up-front about their intentions to cut suppliers.

Despite the obvious cost benefits of vendor-base reductions, some companies fear that the sole supplier might fail. Sole-sourcing is not always the answer; often firms maintain two suppliers for each commodity group but just one for each part within a group. For example, they buy business forms 1, 3, 5, 7 and so on, from supplier A, and forms 2, 4, 6, 8 and so on from supplier B. If disaster strikes one supplier, the other is able to help, without the expense of developing new supply channels. Added protection of buyer-supplier contingency plans (what to do in case of fire, flood, strikes, etc.) further reduces buyer's exposure.

*𝒫*RINCIPLE 5:

Cut the number of suppliers.

Volume of Business

Many large companies have had a policy of not accounting for more than, say, 25 percent of any supplier's total sales. Some supplier companies have had a similar policy; for example, not allowing more than 15 percent of total sales to be with any single customer. The reason is the potentially severe impact on a supplier if the customer decides to change suppliers or cancel the business.

Under the partnership approach, a supplier may elect to build a small satellite plant next to a big customer and do up to 100 percent of its business with that customer—to

*𝒫*RINCIPLE 1:

Get to know the customer.

---

[2]James P. Womack, Daniel T. Jones, and Daniel Roos, *The Machine that Changed the World* (New York: Rawson Associates, 1990), chap. 6.

[3]Larry C. Giunipero, "AME Survey Report: A Survey of JIT Purchasing in American Industry," *Target,* Winter 1988, pp. 25–28.

[4]Roy L. Harmon, *Reinventing the Factory II* (New York: The Free Press, 1992), p. 126.

[5]Michael Barrier, "Overcoming Adversity," *Nation's Business,* June 1991, pp. 25–29.

Into Practice

Staying Lean with Low Risk

"Our inventory levels are at a fraction of where they were in the mid-1980s, but we feel there's no higher risk of shortages developing now than then," said Allen Hagstrand, in charge of purchasing for the Stamford, Connecticut, unit of Schweppes PLC, the London food and beverage producer.

Closer cooperation with a smaller but better informed assortment of suppliers has helped, according to Mr. Hagstrand. "Today we get close to 80 percent of our glass containers from a single company, whereas seven years ago no one supplier provided more than 30 percent," he said. "We used to play one off against the other and keep them guessing, while now we all work very closely together, providing sales forecasts and other data we once kept to ourselves."

SOURCE: Alfred L. Malabre, Jr., "Firm's Inventories Are Remarkably Lean," *The Wall Street Journal*, November 3, 1992.

---

become a dedicated supplier plant but remain independent. Customers sometimes encourage this. Under that concept, a supplier company may grow by building many satellite plants, each serving just one or a small number of nearby customers. Each supplier plant then becomes a close partner with its customer plant, but total risk is spread among many supplier-customer pairs.

Prices/Costs

In the adversarial approach, price is the dominant basis for selecting a supplier. The idea is to find several suppliers capable of providing the desired item and then select the one with the lowest catalog or bid price. Bidding rather than catalog price is the basis when the item requires special engineering or design work or the volume is high enough to warrant a special price.

Buyers attempt to play suppliers off one another on price. Sometimes a supplier will buy in with a discount or a bid price that is below costs, but it then must overcharge on other contracts in order to stay in business. Also, when big customers with clout are able to force suppliers into making recklessly low bids, the suppliers become unstable and financially unable to invest in improvements. That instability, along with frequent changing of suppliers, introduces high change costs for both parties. Thus, while the adversarial approach focuses on getting good prices, it often gets the opposite.

By contrast, the partnership approach, offering stable high-volume contracts with opportunities for economies of scale, is attractive to suppliers and persuades them to try to improve and do their best for customers.

Quality

When suppliers are distrusted, customers must protect themselves. The insurance may be a sizable staff of inspectors at the receiving dock or in a holding area. Sometimes it takes days to clear incoming inspection, while users watch their own schedules slip. For purchased services, the distrusted supplier's work must be checked, reports and claims must be filed and reconciled, and sometimes the service must be re-done.

Instead of spending so much time discovering postreceipt errors, firms need to follow the partnership idea and send customer teams to visit, develop, certify, and then nurture suppliers. Numerous original equipment manufacturers (OEMs) furnish training and technical assistance to suppliers to prevent mistakes (fail-safing) or to help the supplier discover and correct them (process control). Sometimes supplier nurturing extends throughout an industry. For example, after decades of using unique SPC rules (thus

*P*RINCIPLE 10:

Make it easy to provide goods and services without error.

forcing suppliers into the expense of multiple manuals, nomenclature, and reporting formats) General Motors, Ford, and Chrysler jointly developed the *Fundamental Statistical Process Control Reference Manual*.[6] That common set of procedures for inspection and reporting significantly reduces industry suppliers' costs of meeting carmakers' quality requirements.

If the customer buys out of a catalog or off the shelf, the supplier clearly has control of the design specifications. However, the customer often wants a specially designed product or service. In the adversarial approach, the customer typically does the design work, passes the specs on to the supplier, and expects them to be followed. But that approach has come under attack from wise customers. Programs such as early supplier involvement, design-build teams, and quality function deployment tap suppliers' expertise and can reduce development time significantly.

Design

Shipping costs depend partly on whether the volume is great enough to fill a truck (or barge or sea container). Since volume for a certain item traditionally has been split among several suppliers, each supplier must ship less often in order to get full-load freight rates. Thus, it has been normal for customers to have to receive large lots infrequently; many weeks' supply per shipment is common.

Delivery Frequency/Order Size

Under the partnership approach, in which a smaller number of suppliers each has a greater volume of business, shipping more often—weekly, daily, or even more frequently—becomes economical. If the bulk is insufficient to fill a semitrailer, then a smaller truck or van may make the deliveries.

For remote suppliers, frequent, small-lot deliveries are made economical by what the auto industry calls milk runs. A single truck stops at several suppliers, collecting a small amount from each; when the truck is full, it delivers to one or more customers. Milk runs range from one a week to several loops per day.

Distance need not be a serious problem. One Chrysler milk run, extending from El Paso, Texas, to the Detroit area, takes 56 hours. Small-lot deliveries are even occurring across oceans; for example, a ship departing from a Far Eastern port may carry in a single sea container just a day's worth of several dozen different bulky auto parts; each day another similarly loaded ship departs, and each spends five weeks on the sea, but one arrives at a North American port to offload every day.

*P*RINCIPLE 13:

Operate at the customer's rate of use; decrease cycle interval and order size.

Conventionally, the truck or ship would carry one or more months' supply of a given item per delivery, and would visit a given supplier just once every month or two for a pickup. That is a costly amount of inventory for the supplier to build up for each shipment and a costly amount to dump on the customer. While it may seem that loading and paperwork costs are much greater when pickups and deliveries are daily instead of monthly, that need not be the case. When partnered companies, including the freight hauler, get a regular milk run going, they usually are able to greatly simplify the data processing, including invoicing just once a month instead of per delivery and per part number.

Exhibit 8–4 illustrates the order conveyance and documentation aspects of purchasing. We deal with order conveyance here and discuss documentation in the next section. In traditional, large-lot, infrequent delivery systems, a mailed purchase order from the customer or an order booked by a salesperson starts the ball rolling in the supplier's plant (see the top portion of Exhibit 8–4A).

Order Conveyance

---

[6]Chester Placek, "GM, Ford, and Chrysler Get Together to Develop Uniform SPC Procedures for Suppliers," *Quality,* December 1991, p. 13.

EXHIBIT 8–4   Purchasing—Order Conveyance and Documentation

A. Traditional approach

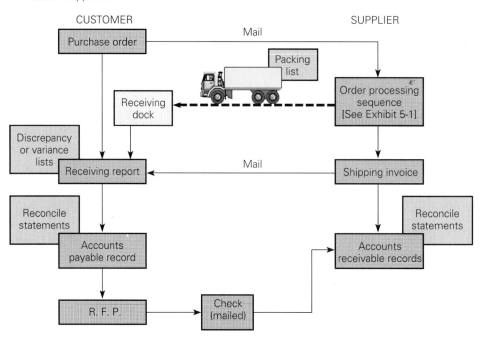

B. Partnership approach

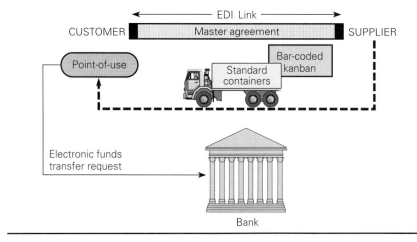

Under partnership with frequent deliveries, mail is too slow. New, faster methods of transmitting order information include phone, facsimile copier, and **electronic data interchange** (EDI), (see Exhibit 8–4B). EDI is a standardized computer-to-computer messaging system open to any company and usable for billing and perhaps funds transfers as well as for ordering.

According to the National Association of Purchasing Management, EDI improves purchasing productivity by reducing paperwork, improving information management, and bettering supplier relationships.

Still another communications method is basic kanban. A kanban (identification card) is attached to the container, which is returnable; its return to the supplier is the authorization to forward one more container-full to the customer. Basic kanban is also usable in conjunction with electronic messaging. Standardized returnable containers provide physical discipline and control, while an electronic message or faxed kanban card provides early warning, before the empty container itself is delivered back to the supplier.

Critical documentation associated with traditional purchasing occurs after the supplier receives the purchase order, completes required transformations, and ships goods to the customer (see Exhibit 8–4A). When the shipment arrives, receiving inspectors verify its correctness: right item, right quantity, and right quality. The supplier's packing list is checked against the receiving dock's copy of the purchase order, and discrepancies are noted on forms that go to purchasing and accounts payable. After reconciliation, accounts payable issues a request-for-payment (RFP) to the controller's office where a check is cut and mailed.

> *Documentation*

    The partnership approach tries to eliminate or simplify paperwork. In an ideal system based on a master agreement (see Exhibit 8–4B) there is no purchase order, packing list, or receiving report. A bar-coded kanban card identifies standard containers as to contents, quantity, and so forth. Inspection isn't needed; supplier and item are certified. When an associate scans the kanban bar code upon receipt of the order, accounts payable receives payment authorization.

> *𝒫*RINCIPLE 16:
>
> Cut transactions and reporting.

    Some plants even skip the notification to accounts payable. Operators scan bar codes on kanbans that accompany received goods, thus recording the receipt in appropriate inventory accounts and stock records. Periodically, monthly perhaps, the customer's computer generates RFPs, which may be checked by point-of-use operating managers prior to payment. As partnerships mature, even that checking should disappear, and electronic funds transfer requests will arise from the periodic inventory account record processing. Perhaps semiannual or even annual reconciliation will be required. Sound too trusting? That's what the partnership idea is designed to promote.

Deliveries have historically gone to a single receiving dock (see the top portion of Exhibit 8–5; the dark, heavy arrows depict flow of purchased items). The traditional relationship between the customer and Supplier A is costly, time-consuming and wasteful. Materials may be handled four times: onto the dock for a quick check of contents and quantity, into quality hold in the receiving stockroom for counting and inspection, then to a free-to-use area of the stockroom, and finally to the point of use.

> *Delivery Location*

    In the partnership approach (sec quality-certified Supplier B in Exhibit 8–5), materials skip some of those nonvalue-adding steps. In industry parlance, they go dock-to-line (or dock-to-use), right to their destination in the plant, lab, kitchen, sales floor, or office. Some companies are remodeling their buildings to provide receiving docks and doors at multiple locations around the building so that trucks can deliver close to use points.

    In some cases, the driver is authorized to carry or push a trolley of parts through the dock to an interior user location. This is the case for paper and packaging materials delivered from Smurfit Company, a JIT supplier to Microsoft-Ireland, a Dublin-based plant producing software products for the European market (see Exhibit 8–6). The trolleys shown are specially designed, the paper quantities are counted out in 20s (Microsoft's lot quantity), and the driver pushes each to its proper location on a kanban square.

> More on kanban squares in Chapter 9.

The adversarial approach is one of arm's-length relationships. The buyer, in the office or at trade shows, sifts through many suppliers' offerings and finally selects a few; from then on, communication is by mail and fax (except in times of materials scarcity, when the suppliers put their customers "on allocation"— 1,000 Nintendo game sets to this store chain, 1,200 to that one, and so forth).

> *Relationship Openness*

EXHIBIT 8–5   Delivery Location: Dock versus Point-of-Use

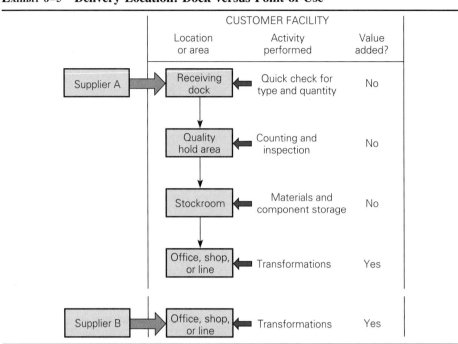

The partnership approach requires the buying company occasionally to send teams to the supplier's plant. That includes sending operations employees who use the purchased items. The visitors get to know people at the supplier's facility and acquire an understanding of the supplier's culture, skills, processes, nagging problems, and potential sources of misunderstanding, and invite the supplier's people to reciprocate the visit.

Some buying companies, in what is called supply-chain management, actively seek to extend the partnership to the supplier's suppliers and beyond. Sometimes the catalyst for such linkages is a supplier's trying to forge partnerships with customers and their customers. Such companies as Baxter Healthcare, Milliken & Co., and Levi Strauss & Co. have engaged in this form of customer development or customer-chain management.

Buying companies also should do formal audits of the supplier's quality and processes. Failure to visit and perform audits invites misunderstanding, bad feelings, and a return to adversarial relationships. It is perhaps like gardening: till the soil, or weeds will grow.

Throughout this section we have focused on relationships between buyer and seller; to a large extent, these relationships determine how purchasing is accomplished. We will obtain additional insight by addressing our next topic, purchasing policies and practices.

Purchasing Policies and Practices

Purchasing activities are guided by commonsense policies relating to value and kind of item bought. In this section, we consider those policies, looking first at the use of ABC analysis and its influence on common buying procedures. Related topics include measurement and compliance issues, the value analysis method, and the positive benefits of standardization.

EXHIBIT 8–6   **Delivery of Paper Items to Point of Use at Microsoft-Ireland**

It makes sense to manage costly materials tightly and cheap materials loosely. That logic is the basis of **ABC analysis,** an old and still important tool of materials management.[7]

ABC Analysis

ABC analysis begins by classifying all stocked items by annual dollar volume (or annual demand times cost per unit). Class A items, those needing close control, are the high-dollar-volume group. They may include 80 percent of total inventory cost but only 1 percent of total items bought. Class B is a medium-dollar-volume group, perhaps 15

---

[7]ABC analysis is another example of Pareto's observation concerning maldistribution. Here, most of the value lies in but a few of the inventory items.

$\mathscr{I}$nto $\mathscr{P}$ractice

Supplier in Residence

The purchasing department at Bose Corporation, producer of high-end speakers and sound systems, is a pioneer in an extension of the supplier-partnership concept. Their approach, registered under the trademark JIT II, features suppliers in residence at the Bose headquarters facility in Framingham, Massachusetts, as well as at Bose factories. Conceived in 1987, the Bose program has grown to include nine suppliers, of metal, plastics, packaging, printing, stationery, export/import, and transportation goods and services. The supplier representatives are "stationed at the Bose facility at the [supplier's] expense, on a full-time basis, [given] access to customer data, people, and processes, and granted the right to place purchase orders with their own organizations on behalf of Bose. . . . Simply put, JIT II eliminates buyer and salesman, and the [supplier] and customer work closely together."

SOURCE: Adapted from "JIT II: An Inside Story," *APICS—The Performance Advantage*, October 1992, pp. 20–22.

percent of cost and 30 percent of items. Class C is the rest, say, 5 percent of cost and 69 percent of items. Some firms continue with D and perhaps E categories.

Computer processing makes ABC analysis easy to do. Item cost is available in the inventory master file. Any measure of annual usage may be used, such as actual usage last year, actual usage last month times 12, or a forecast. The computer multiplies item cost by annual usage, giving annual dollar volume. The ABC formula is fed into the computer, and the output is a complete list of items in descending dollar-volume order. The listing is grouped into three parts: A items first, B items second, and C items third.

ABC analysis may be used as follows (the details will vary from firm to firm):

At a TQM team's suggestion, Microsoft USA provides each group assistant (serving a group of software engineers) with a credit card for buying low-value items, thus bypassing the purchasing department for nearly 40 percent of the firm's purchases.

1. *Purchasing.* Have each purchase order for a class A item signed by the president or chief financial officer, for a class B item by a department head, and for class C item by any buyer.

2. *Physical inventory counting.* Count A items weekly or daily, B items monthly, and C items annually.

3. *Forecasting.* Forecast A items by several methods on the computer with resolution by a forecasting committee, B items by simple trend projection, and C items by buyer's best guess.

4. *Safety stock.* No safety stock for A items, one week's supply for B items, and one month's supply for C items.

ABC dipped a bit in popularity in the 1970s. Experts were saying that falling computing costs made it economical for a material requirements planning system to give B and C items as much attention as A items; one ordering system could be used for all items. The emergence of just-in-time brought us back to more conventional ABC thinking.

Class A items are often the best prospects for full JIT treatment because they have the volume to most easily justify frequent small-lot deliveries, perhaps daily. It is no small achievement to switch an item to daily deliveries; typical delivery intervals/lot sizes in the non-JIT mode are monthly or greater. JIT policies for B and C items are more modest: perhaps weekly deliveries for class B items and quarterly for class Cs.

Actually, many companies have found ways to do much better than that for some Bs and Cs. For example, a sizable number of manufacturing plants now buy all their hundreds of hardware items (screws, bolts, grommets, etc.) from a single supplier.

Commonly, that supplier visits the customer at least once a week, goes right out to the factory floor to fill the bins and trays, and just invoices the customer monthly. While each hardware item is class C in annual value, the whole commodity group adds up to class A value, which makes it economical for the supplier to provide that kind of customer service.

A different twist on the same general idea is coming into use in several industries, especially automotive, but also major appliances and large electronic systems: buying completed modules instead of the individual parts. Past practice in automotive assembly, for example, was to buy and receive hundreds of class B parts for instrument panels, doors, and so forth for installation, one by one, on the assembly line. It was a receiving and material-handling nightmare.

The current trend is to have a subcontractor, a specialist in instrument panels or doors, for example, deliver completed modules to the assembly plant. While the individual parts are class B, the modules are class A in value, which makes daily deliveries (sometimes several times a day) economical.

ABC applies as well to inventory-intensive wholesaling and retailing as it does to manufacturing (see Example 8–1).

EXAMPLE 8–1   ABC Analysis—Wholesaler

At Universal Motor Supply Company, the buyer has arranged 10 inventory items in order of annual dollar volume. Exhibit 8–7 shows the ordered list, with dollar volume expressed in percentages. The buyer examines the list to arrive at an ABC classification of the items.

Exhibit 8–8 shows the 10 items as the buyer grouped them into classes A, B, and C. The groupings seem natural: the three B items account for over seven (9.8 ÷ 1.3) times as much annual dollar volume as the five C items; the two A items account for about nine times as much as the three B items. It is clear that A items should receive major attention. Have them delivered often in small quantities, store them in flow racks at or near the receiving/shipping docks, and carefully monitor and control them. Class Bs should receive moderate attention, and class Cs little attention; for example, handle them manually and store them in conventional racks in a remote part of the warehouse.

Exhibit 8–7   Inventory Items in Annual-Dollar-Volume Order—Universal Motor Supply Company

Stock Number	Annual Demand	Unit Cost	Annual Dollar Volume	Percent
407	40,000	$ 35.50	$1,420,000	59.53%
210	1,000	700.00	700,000	29.35
021	2,000	55.00	110,000	4.61
388	20,000	4.00	80,000	3.35
413	4,400	10.00	44,000	1.84
195	500	36.00	18,000	0.76
330	40	214.00	8,560	0.36
114	100	43.00	4,300	0.18
274	280	1.00	280	0.01
359	600	0.25	150	0.00
		Totals	$2,385,290	~100.0%

Besides ABC analysis, there are other common purchasing practices and terms that managers should know. They have to do with arranging the supplier-seller agreement and the terms of that agreement, and they group fairly well into the A, B, and C categories.

Purchasing and Contracting Procedures

EXHIBIT 8–8   ABC Classification—Universal Motor Supply Company

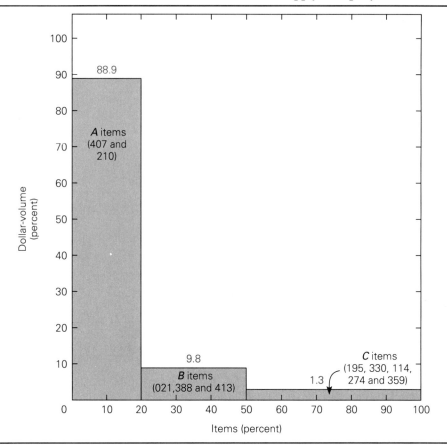

Class A Items.   A class A item may be an expensive, seldom-ordered item or a low-cost item that is ordered often or in large quantities. Common purchasing measures are:

Soliciting competitive bids on specifications. The buyer mails an invitation to bid or a request for quotation to prospective suppliers. The item to be bought is specified in detail; the description may consist of technical specifications (physical or chemical properties), performance specifications (mean time until failure, rated output, etc.), and procedural specifications (e.g., consultant will conduct an employee attitude survey). Specifications may be necessary because the item is nonstandard or because the buying firm wishes to exclude low-quality suppliers. Also, specifications can provide a sound basis for determining compliance with the buyer's requirements. Engineers often play a key role in developing specs, and blueprints may be attached. Attorneys may ensure that contractual obligations are legally correct.

Governments, especially the federal government, intermittently buy based on publicly available specs. Regulations require that for many types of purchases the invitation to bid be published in a widely circulated government document.

Certification. As Chapter 2 noted, quality-conscious companies conduct formal studies to quality-certify suppliers and items bought from them. Older approaches, which rank suppliers rather than certify them, are based on external price data, delivery timeliness, defect rates, and a few other factors. Quality-certification sometimes is broadly defined to include such factors as quality of design, training, and lead-time or delivery performance (see chapter supplement).

Negotiation. Where sources of supply are stable, there may be no need to solicit formal bids. Instead, purchasing teams may just periodically negotiate with the regular source for better price or delivery terms. Typically, negotiation applies to nonstandard class A goods and services.

Buying down and **speculation.** Buying down means trying to buy an item with a history of cyclic price swings when its price is down. It is a form of speculative buying. In pure speculation, purchases are made for price reasons rather than for meeting an actual need for the goods.

Hedging. Hedging applies especially to commodities, such as wheat, corn, silver, and lumber. Organized futures markets exist for some commodities. A buyer can pay cash to buy a commodity now and at the same time sell a like amount of a future delivery of the commodity. Price changes will mean that losses on one order are offset by gains on the other.

Class B Items. Class B goods and moderate-cost services usually warrant less purchasing effort. That applies to many kinds of standard off-the-shelf goods, such as maintenance, repair, and operating (MRO) supplies, as well as standard services, such as those of a plumber or auto body shop. For nonstandard items in the class B cost range, specifications might be necessary, but the expense of soliciting bids is harder to justify than for class A items. Order procedures for the class B category include the following:

Approved supplier lists. Companies like to buy from proven suppliers. Buying teams rely on the approved supplier list, especially for class B items, though it also is used for class A and class C buying. The approved supplier list may be based on an old-style performance rating or on a full certification study.

Catalog buying. Perhaps the most common purchasing procedure for off-the-shelf (MRO) goods is buying out of current catalogs, sometimes with the help of salespeople. Most buyers have shelves full of suppliers' catalogs for this purpose.

Blanket orders. Where there is an ongoing but varying need for an item with class B annual volume, the purchasing team may draw up a blanket-order contract with a supplier. The blanket order covers a given time period, and deliveries are arranged by sending a simple release notice to the supplier. Price and other matters are covered in the contract.

Systems contract. A systems contract is similar to a blanket order, but it is longer term and more stringently defined. The purchasing department negotiates the systems contract; purchasing then typically monitors, but does not participate in, ordering. The contract may name certain responsible employees who may order, by mail, phone, or other means, directly from the supplier.

Class C Items. Class C or low-cost items are worthy of little attention by purchasing specialists. Buying such items from a supplier on an approved supplier list provides a measure of control. For many items even that is too much control and red tape, and to avoid these, using departments are provided with petty cash funds with which to buy directly and in cash. Until recently, petty cash buying has been restricted to office employees. Now a few progressive North American manufacturers provide each factory employee or improvement team with a petty cash fund for purchasing small tools or other devices that can improve performance.

Exhibit 8–9   Tangibility of Purchased Goods

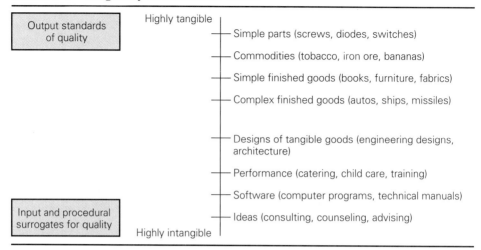

Performance and Compliance: The Tangibility Factor

When teams buy intangibles (things that cannot be seen, touched, tasted, etc.), they must employ different purchasing practices than when buying tangibles. The distinction arises largely because the quality characteristics of tangibles can be measured (variables) or classified and counted (attributes). An intangible item, however, is sometimes difficult to identify, much less specify. Consequently, it may be hard to hold the provider accountable for the buyer's performance/compliance wishes.

Intangibility is relative (see Exhibit 8–9). At the highly tangible end of the scale, quality is generally determined by objective, measurable output standards. At the highly intangible end of the scale are few, if any, measurable output quality characteristics on which teams may judge compliance with requirements; thus, emphasis shifts to input or procedural factors as surrogate indicators of quality. Specific attention to these two extremes, as well as the intermediate levels of tangibility is warranted:

- Highly tangible items include simple parts like screws, diodes, and switches. Teams may judge quality with straightforward process capability analysis (discussed in Chapter 4).

- Commodities (corn, iron ore, bananas, etc.) are tangible but some of their properties are costly to measure. Therefore, associates often augment measurement with slightly more subjective eyeball judgments to grade quality, thus moving from variables into attributes.

- Simple finished goods are less tangible than commodities. Books, furniture, and fabrics, for example, have several measurable physical properties, but visual inspection for scratches, flaws, and so on, may be more important. Again, buyers mix attributes assessment and variables assessment.

- Complex finished goods (autos, ships, mobile homes) have thousands of measurable physical properties of *form* (e.g., dimensions) and *function* (such as turning radius and speed). Nevertheless, partly subjective judgments of effectiveness (how well a destroyer protects the fleet, or a mobile home keeps the elements out) are also important. For complex goods aimed at consumer markets, even more subjective judgments come into play, about style, comfort, and even status.

- Designs for tangible goods, such as those rendered by architects and engineers, are harder to judge until the end result (the tangible good itself) becomes reality. If a bridge caves in or a door handle keeps breaking off, teams can (in hindsight) judge the design to be bad. The engineer might even be liable for damages. Perhaps the best *up-front* help for buyers of these items is design expertise on the buying team.

- Contracting for performance is growing explosively; catering, child care, and employee training are examples. Enterprising college students capitalize on the trend by starting part-time businesses to provide janitorial, yard care, computer dating, and a variety of other services. The end products or outputs are good food, well-adjusted children, requalified employees, clean floors, weed-free lawns, and well-matched dating couples. It is difficult to write standards for those outputs into a contract. Consequently, there has been growing use of measures of compliance such as mean number of customer complaints and opinion polling involving customers, experts, or impartial panels using some form of Likert scale (a rating scale from 1 to 5, 1 to 7, etc.).
- Software (computer programs, technical or training manuals, operating instruction booklets, etc.) is slightly more intangible. Buyers of these items must distinguish between the quality of the item specified, a television set, for example, and the quality of the software (operating instructions manual) being purchased. A benchmark-class health care package may not impress employees because the benefits description booklet is poor. Buyers may set contract limits such as number of pages or lines of code, but these hardly measure quality, and the supplier is likely to receive full pay (even for a shoddy job) just by meeting those limits.
- Highly intangible items, at the bottom of Exhibit 8–9, have no physically measurable properties. Therefore, purchase contracts may be based on input and procedural factors. In a contract with a consultant, input factors may include specifying level of education and years of experience of the consultants sent out on the job; procedural factors may include number of people to be interviewed and number of pages on the final consultant's report. Those do not comprise the quality of the consultant's services, but they are often treated as surrogates for output quality.

From the foregoing discussion, we can conclude that the most serious measurement and compliance assessment problems occur when teams buy performance, software, and ideas, items at the intangible end of the scale. Buying from certified suppliers, or at least from those with good reputations, helps. But performance service providers tend to come and go rather than stay and build clientele and reputation. Software firms and consulting firms are somewhat more stable. Ironically, poor software or consulting is not notably destructive to firms' reputations. The reason is that dissatisfied customers tend not to admit their displeasure (1) because of the risk of defamation suits (bad quality is difficult to prove) and (2) because dissatisfaction would be an admission of having wasted time and money on poor software or consulting services.

On occasion, however, service providers' failure to perform is publicly recognized, especially when those providers charge stiff fees for their failure. An example is the attempted leveraged buyout of UAL Corp. (United Air Lines' parent) that fell through on October 13, 1989. Already reeling from plummeted stock values, UAL shareholders nevertheless received a bill for $58.7 million for professional services rendered by the lawyers and bankers hired to complete the deal. Irked by this high price for failure, shareholders and other observers criticized the banks and law firms involved and questioned the wisdom of the UAL Corp. board for its purchase of the services.[8] Even large corporations can have problems in buying service performance.

Public and corporate officials are increasingly relying on consultants to help them with sticky decisions. But the inability to write tough contracts leaves the officials at

---

[8]"In Failed Bid for UAL, Lawyers and Bankers Didn't Fail to Get Fees," *The Wall Street Journal,* November 30, 1989, p. A1.

the consultants' mercy. Fortunately, most consultants are professionally dedicated and motivated to maintain self-respect. Still, contracting for intangibles is a major challenge for buyers, one that permeates all organizational transformations. Clearly, trust, openness, and a few good suppliers are key to meeting the purchasing challenge.

Value Analysis

Purchasing means spending money. But purchasing professionals also may become involved in projects that offer long-term substantial savings (making money) for their company. Value analysis projects are of this type.

In large organizations, file cabinets in purchasing and design may be filled with specs developed years ago. New technology outdates some of the old specifications. Each time such items are reordered, the obsolescence becomes more apparent and purchasing takes the heat for not "buying modern." It is no surprise that VA was developed and promoted by purchasing people. As engineers got more involved, the concepts were extended to include new designs as well as old specs.

Value analysis (VA): Team analysis of existing product design specifications with the aim of improving value; developed in the purchasing department of General Electric in 1947.

In some companies and in the federal government, engineers conduct the analysis, calling it **value engineering (VE).** While value analysis could be applied to services, it is mostly restricted to goods, especially where material costs and usage rates are high.

The VA step-by-step procedure has been adopted worldwide. The steps are a variation of the scientific method:

1. *Select product*. Select a product that is ripe for improvement.
2. *Gather information*. The team coordinator collects drawings, costs, scrap rates, forecasts, operations sheets, and so forth, before the team first meets. Team members provide whatever information they have.
3. *Define function*. The team meets and defines each function of the product. A function is defined in two words: a verb and a noun (e.g., "A barrel *contains fluid*."). Only essential functions are included. Next, the team estimates the present cost of each function. That reveals which functions are costing far too much. (Note: Defining functions in this way is unique and sets VA apart from other cost reduction techniques.)
4. *Generate alternatives*. Team members suggest ideas for new and different ways to accomplish the functions (known as brainstorming). Ideas are recorded and later culled to a list of manageable size.
5. *Evaluate alternatives*. The team evaluates alternatives based on feasibility, cost and other factors, which cuts the list to one (or a few) good ideas.
6. *Present proposals*. Refine the final alternatives and present them to a management committee as change proposals.
7. *Implement plan*. Translate the approved change proposal into an engineering change order (ECO) and put it into effect.

In Example 8–2, the description of a real VA study helps show how the procedure works.[9]

Impressed by the results of VA and VE in private industry, the Department of Defense issued VE regulations applicable to all DOD contracts costing more than $100,000. In 1964, the American Ordnance Association conducted a survey that randomly sampled 124 successful VE changes in the DOD.[10] The survey report showed not only impressive cost

---

[9]Based on Arthur E. Mudge, *Value Engineering: A Systematic Approach* (New York: McGraw-Hill, 1971), pp. 263–64 (TS168.M83).

[10]*Reduce Costs and Improve Equipment through Value Engineering,* Directorate of Value Engineering, Office of the Assistant Secretary of Defense for Installations and Logistics, Washington, D.C., January 1967 (TS168.U5).

EXAMPLE 8–2   VA Procedure for Improving a Bearing Housing-Support

After selecting a dust-collector valve for value analysis, a VA team, in the information phase, found that the valve assembly was composed of five parts: bearing, left- and right-hand bearing housing support, and left- and right-hand seal. The team reviewed the assembly and the five parts and their costs, finally deciding to focus further analysis on the bearing housing supports (see Exhibit 8–10A).

The pair of housing supports, cast from gray iron, had a direct material and labor cost of $36. The team noted that the function of the supports was to *locate* the *bearings*, which, in turn, had the function *support* and *locate* the *main shaft.*

The study centered on those two functions. The team searched a number of bearing manufacturers' catalogs. All the catalogs included a sealed, self-mounting bearing as a standard item. When the team's solution to the functions to reduce friction and provide seal was combined with its solution to the functions to provide support and provide location, the team knew that it had a workable solution.

The team realized that the self-mounting bearing could be mounted on either side of a common piece of steel plate, as shown in Exhibit 8–10B. This design cut the total housing subassembly cost by 33 percent, to under $25 per pair. Since only minor engineering changes were required and no tooling was needed, the annual net savings of about $3,100 began in the first year.

Exhibit 8–10   Bearing Housing-Support Undergoing Value Engineering

A. Before value-analysis   B. Value-analysis proposed design

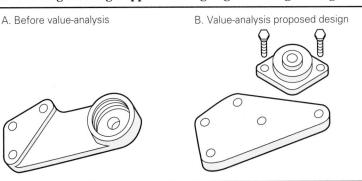

Source: Arthur E. Mudge, *Value Engineering: A Systematic Approach* (New York: McGraw-Hill, 1971), p. 263 (TS168.M83). Used with permission.

savings but also, in many cases, collateral gains in the areas of reliability, maintainability, producibility, human factors, parts availability, production lead time, quality, weight, logistics, performance, and packaging. The DOD then implemented a formula for sharing VE savings (usually 20 percent) with contractors; that gave the contractors' VE teams added incentive to squeeze savings out of the design specifications.

An informal method of value analysis has recently come into use. In a JIT plant a problem might arise that threatens to stop production. That summons a buyer or engineer to the shop floor; a foreman and perhaps an operator will join in the problem analysis. Blueprints may be marked up and taken immediately to the inside or outside maker of the parts that are causing the problem.

Conducting value analysis in that way—on the fly—requires that blueprints and design specs not be too limiting. Design engineers traditionally have tried to specify every dimension, type of material, finish, and so on, which greatly limits options for producing the item. The nonrestrictive specs concept aims at giving the maker latitude over nonessential design attributes so that easy, cheap ways of making the part may be searched for and easily changed when someone sees a better way.

Principle 3:

Achieve team involvement in implementation of change.

The purist might say that making design decisions on the floor should not be called value analysis because the formal steps (defining functions, generating alternatives, etc.) are bypassed. While that is true, the less formal approach has the advantage of giving more attention to how product design affects producibility, a key element in overall product cost. Also, producibility is a vital concern in just-in-time production in which a production problem can starve later production stages of parts and bring operations to a halt.

Standardization

Industrial **standardization** means settling on a few rather than many sizes, shapes, colors, and so forth, for a given part. Value analysis sometimes leads to standardization. But some companies have a permanent standardization committee, often headed by an engineer or buyer.

Lee and Dobler state that "standardization is the prerequisite to mass production." They credit Eli Whitney's development of standardization (initially of musket parts) as having led ultimately to the emergence of the United States as the world's dominant mass producer in the 20th century.[11] The idea is to make not standardized end products but a wide variety of end products from a small number of standardized parts and materials. The cost savings can be substantial. (Standardization is a key to delayed differentiation, discussed in Chapter 5.) Fewer items means less purchasing, receiving, inspection, storage, and billing. Internally, fewer different kinds of production equipment and tooling are required, and production of some parts may be relatively continuous and just-in-time, which is efficient, instead of stop-and-go with intermittent delays.

*𝒫*RINCIPLE 5:

Cut the number of components in a product or service.

The American National Standards Institute (ANSI) is a federation of over 100 organizations that develops industrial standards. After research and debate, ANSI may approve a recommended standard for adoption nationwide. Perhaps the most vexing standardization issue in America is metrics, since the United States is the only nonmetric country among major industrial countries. However, most American companies with good export markets have gone metric on their own.

Make or Buy

The strategic question of whether to make or buy is often a complex issue. Its basic cost elements, however, reduce to a simple type of break-even analysis (see Exhibit 8–11).

As Exhibit 8–11 shows, if the item is bought, there is no fixed cost. Instead, the total cost (TC) is simply the unit price (P) times demand (D):

$$TC_{buy} = P \times D \qquad (8\text{--}1)$$

If the item is made, there is a fixed cost (FC) of setting up for production. The other element of total cost is the variable cost of production, which equals the assumed constant unit variable cost (V) times demand (D). Then:

$$TC_{make} = (V \times D) + FC \qquad (8\text{--}2)$$

We see in Exhibit 8–11 that the break-even demand (B) occurs where the total costs are equal. For demand less than B, the total cost to buy is lower; thus, buy is preferred. For demand greater than B, offsetting the fixed cost by the lower unit cost results in a lower cost to make; so make is preferred. The analysis should be based on annual demand and cost if the item is a stocked one that is bought year after year. The demand and cost of a single order should be used for a nonstocked item that may or may not be reordered in future years.

[11]Lamar Lee, Jr., and Donald W. Dobler, *Purchasing and Materials Management: Text and Cases,* 3rd ed. (New York: McGraw-Hill, 1977), pp. 54–55 (HD52.5.L4).

EXHIBIT 8-11   **Make-or-Buy Break-Even Analysis**

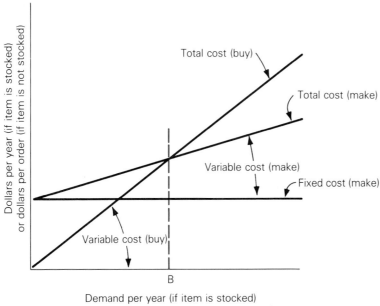

Since the total costs are equal at the break-even point, a break-even formula is easily developed. Using B (for break-even demand) instead of D, we have:

$$TC_{buy} = TC_{make}$$

$$P \times B = (V \times B) + FC$$

$$(P \times B) - (V \times B) = FC$$

$$B(P - V) = FC$$

$$B = \frac{FC}{P - V} \qquad (8-3)$$

For example, assume you can buy candles at the store for $1 each. Or you can pay $50 for candle-making apparatus and make your own candles for a unit variable cost (wax, wicks, etc.) of $0.75. What volume is necessary in order to recover your fixed cost, that is, break even?

Solution:

$$B = \frac{50}{1 - 0.75} = \frac{50}{0.25} = 200 \text{ candles}$$

Classical make-or-buy seems simple enough, but what about its overall usefulness? Make-or-buy analysis, like any technique, requires certain assumptions. First, we must assume that make (or buy) is a realistic option. This goes beyond the cost of the candle-making apparatus and into the technical knowledge and other competencies required to be a producer. Do we have such resources? Having to acquire them, perhaps by hiring candle makers or training some existing personnel, will increase fixed costs and thus raise the volume required for break-even.

Second, we must assume that the variable costs associated with making are less than the variable (unit) cost of buying, or we could never reach break-even. What if new technology, simplified production techniques, or other change led to a drop in the buy price? We would have to match the change or see erosion in the economic advantage of making. That is, we would have just acquired another business (candle making) to keep up in. Even if we spent the capital on equipment required for making, could we keep up with candle-making technology? Do we even want to?

Concern over these assumptions seems trivial for the candle-making example. But what if a shopping mall is considering a $10 million capital expenditure for building its own power-generating facilities instead of buying power from the local utility? Now the issues (hiring and retaining competent technical staff, availability and prices of fuel, etc.) are important indeed; major costs and risks are involved.

The classical make-or-buy approach is fine for small-value items, where entry barriers are low. If in moving from buy to make or from make to buy we don't have to pay much, learn much, change much, or worry much, then a basic make-or-buy analysis is appropriate. Changing our minds later if new tactics are required will entail no substantial economic hardship.

For sourcing decisions that fall outside the simple category, classical make-or-buy must yield to more detailed analysis. One key issue is backward integration, treated next.

Backward Integration versus "Stick to Your Knitting"

Backward integration: Setting up to make goods or provide services formerly bought, or buying a supplier company and making it part of the business.

When materials are scarce or supplier performance is inconsistent, panic sets in. Anxiety makes some companies opt for **backward integration.**

One result is that purchasing may no longer have to scramble to get delivery commitments or to handle problem suppliers. Backward integration is a major financial commitment, and it consumes a lot of managerial energy. However, when the material shortage evaporates or suppliers upgrade their performance, the company that absorbed another of its suppliers may wish it hadn't.

The authors of "Managing Our Way to Economic Decline," an acclaimed 1980 article, commented on backward integration. Companies with stable, commodity-like products, such as metals and petroleum, often can gain economies and profit improvements through backward integration. The strategy may backfire, however, for companies in technologically active industries. Backward integration "may provide a quick, short-term boost to ROI figures in the next annual report, but it may also paralyze the long-term ability of a company to keep on top of technological change."[12]

Concentrating on doing a few things well and acquiring the rest from outside is popularly known as "sticking to your knitting."[13] This approach, which runs counter to backward integration, has been widely applied to services in recent years. Companies hire caterers to run employee cafeterias and vending machines, janitorial services to clean the premises, contract truckers to haul goods, and consultants to provide advice.

The stick-to-your-knitting viewpoint has its adherents in manufacturing as well, especially in electronics. For example, the strategic plan for the Apple Macintosh plant in Fremont, California, is to focus on assembly. In other words, most of the cost is for purchased materials. Apple controls critical factors, including design and marketing, and lets outside experts in microprocessors, sheet metal, CRTs, and so forth, produce the

---

[12]Robert H. Hayes and William J. Abernathy, "Managing Our Way to Economic Decline," *Harvard Business Review,* July–August 1980, pp. 67–77.

[13]That old saw became a buzzword in management circles when a best-selling book gave it a whole chapter. See Thomas J. Peters and Robert H. Waterman, Jr., *In Search of Excellence: Lessons from America's Best-Run Companies* (New York: Harper & Row, 1982), chap. 10, "Stick to the Knitting."

$\mathscr{C}$ontrast

Competitive Sources

Out-Sourcing	In-Sourcing
1980s: Not cost competitive? Search the globe for lowest cost and then move.	1990s and beyond: Not cost competitive? Slash nonvalue-adding wastes and stay (or return) home. Not quality competitive? Adopt TQM.

parts. Most other successful producers of computers and allied products have adopted a somewhat similar strategy.

Shifting processing outside or off shore, however, can be done too hastily. At Compaq Computer, cost concerns sent engineers around the globe searching for suppliers who could provide parts for less than Compaq's own costs. They settled on a Taiwanese producer that could deliver circuit boards for 30 percent less. At a briefing of plant associates, "one 'crusty old' employee stood up and [argued] that Compaq workers should be allowed to bid on the job." The point hit home. Team engineers found a way to simplify board manufacturing, enabling in-house personnel to make a new computer model on one line, saving a lot of down time.[14]

In a variation on this idea, a number of companies have been bringing operations back to the United States or Canada to cut costs or improve quality — the same reasons for leaving some years earlier. An article on the subject notes further reasons for coming home:[15]

- Automation and "new product designs that shrink the number of parts and simplify assembly."
- Quick response. "What many companies compete on today is service — the ability to produce with lead times of a day or two."
- Fast product development. It is better for the "design and manufacturing folks to be physically close so that they can talk elbow to elbow, modifying continuously."

Any advantages of stick-to-your-knitting or out-sourcing depend on having reliable suppliers. The ideal is for the buyer company to exert control over a few vital factors of the supply channels, leaving the supplier free to innovate and keep up with technologies in its area of manufacturing expertise. Reliable suppliers don't just happen; they must be nurtured.

Related to standardization, make or buy, and backward integration is purchasing in already-put-together modules. This has special advantages for companies whose products are made from many hundreds or thousands of parts. Processing large numbers of parts in a single location tends to overload the system, causing quality problems, cascading shortages and work stoppages, and physical congestion.   *Modular Buying*

---

[14]Michael Allen, "Bottom Fishing: Developing New Line of Low-Priced PCs Shakes Up Compaq," *The Wall Street Journal,* June 15, 1992.

[15]Edmund Faltermayer, "U.S. Companies Come Back Home," *Fortune,* December 30, 1991, pp. 106–112.

How to tell if a plant has too many parts: Have a look. If most of what you see are vehicles, overhead conveyors, and storage systems, the plant is sinking in a sea of parts.

If the firm is adversarial with suppliers, it tries to cope with these difficulties itself. But partnership companies look to their suppliers for a solution, such as having a supplier acquire and preassemble a collection of loose parts into a module, to be delivered with certified quality just in time for use. Though it takes years to implement, this solution has become attractive to manufacturers of such complex products as automobiles, aircraft, large appliances, and mass spectrometers. (A car has over 13,000 parts, and the newest Boeing airplane, the 777, has 132,000 engineered parts and over 3 million fasteners.)

Sometimes the initiative comes from supplier companies. The automotive group at Eagle-Picher Company has proposed to its automotive customers that it supply multipurpose rubber floor mats. The mats would include the underlayment, plus electrical wiring for tail lights and accessories. That gets wiring inside the car, for more reliable quality, instead of strung beneath the car exposed to the elements. Eagle-Picher wants to become a stronger, more valuable supplier with more parts, while helping its customers to become stronger with fewer parts.

Summary

Raw materials and purchased components typically make up about two thirds of the final cost of manufactured goods. The addition of purchased support services pushes the what-gets-bought component even higher. Evidence suggests that top manufacturing executives place high strategic importance on improving supplier quality.

Traditionally, purchasing has operated by commodity groups, with each purchasing agent responsible for one or a few commodities. Relationships between buyer and supplier have often been adversarial and standoffish. The supplier came to be viewed as a black box, whose internal workings could only be surmised. Some buyers attempted to probe the black boxes through plant visits and other modes of inquiry, but the majority accepted the adversarial relationship as the norm.

Disappointment with supplier performance, such as late deliveries, poor quality, and incorrect quantities, kept purchasing professionals busy searching for and switching to new suppliers. Suppliers had little commitment to do their best, sensing lack of support from customers. Each new prospective supplier created necessary but time-consuming supplier evaluation procedures, and new startup costs and problems.

In the 1980s, a movement to replace the buyer-supplier adversarial relationship gained momentum. Supplier development programs came into existence as buyers began to view suppliers as partners-in-profit. Today characteristics of the partnership relationship include longer contracts, more exclusivity in agreements, fewer (but better) suppliers, high volume between buyer and supplier, lower prices, quality at the (supplier) source, supplier-centered design, frequent delivery of small lots, less burdensome order conveyance, delivery to point of consumption (rather than to a receiving inspection), and mutual openness. Visits between buyer and supplier help maintain the open relationship.

Purchasing procedures depend on what is being bought. The ABC method of classifying materials uses annual dollar volume to assign items to one of three classes. High-valued (class A) items are purchased and controlled with more care than medium-valued (class B) items, which in turn are managed more closely than low-valued (class C) goods.

Purchasing intangibles, such as ideas and services, presents special problems for buyers because the quality of intangibles is difficult to measure. Often the buyer is at the mercy of the seller, and the seller's professionalism and self-respect are the only guarantees for quality.

Value analysis is a procedure that purchasers developed to meet materials needs (functions) with lower-cost materials and designs. Value engineering (VE) emerged as engineers began to influence value analysis efforts. VE has received federal government support in the form of higher profits for contractors able to lower costs through VE studies of government specifications.

Industrial standardization may result from value analysis programs or it may be spearheaded by a permanent standardization committee. Long heralded as the prerequisite to mass production, standardization is also the key to delayed differentiation. Organizations such as the American National Standards Institute (ANSI) play an active role in standardization efforts. In the United States, debate continues on the standardization issue of metrics.

Classical make-or-buy analysis is an acceptable policy for relatively low-impact materials. Its simplifying assumptions suggest that it not be used for more complex decisions. One historically popular sourcing strategy was backward integration; it calls for making rather than buying materials even if suppliers must be acquired. A recently popular view is to beware of backward integration and "stick to your knitting"; in other words, buy more of the goods and services you need and concentrate on doing a few things well.

Shifting to foreign suppliers, however, has become a volatile issue. Economic pressures to keep jobs at home, as well as better quality and delivery performance from reenergized domestic producers, have created a movement to bring some operations back to the United States and Canada.

Companies whose products are made of hundreds or thousands of components may help reduce part counts through modular buying. Suppliers may take the initiative by creating multipurpose items that combine functions previously accomplished by separate parts.

Key Words

Focused factory   275

Electronic data interchange (EDI)   280

ABC analysis   283

Soliciting competitive bids on
    specifications   286

Certification (of supplier)   286

Negotiation   287

Buying down   287

Speculation (in buying)   287

Hedging   287

Approved supplier   287

Catalog buying   287

Blanket order   287

Systems contract   287

Value analysis (VA)   290

Value engineering (VE)   290

Standardization   292

Backward integration   294

Solved Problem

Consider the following list of parts, their unit costs, and annual requirements:

Part Number	Unit Cost	Annual Demand	
M2	$ 20.00	120	2400
A5	2.00	155,000	310,000
A7	8,000.00	13	104,000
L8	950.00	6	5700
L4	0.30	7,000	2,100
A6	10.00	9,400	94000
M9	6,000.00	70	420,000
Q2	400.00	240	96,000
Z1	0.50	200	100

1,034,300

Compute the annual value and percentage of total value for each part. Arrange the nine parts into ABC categories. Plot the cumulative percentages in order from the greatest- to least-valued part.

First, we compute the annual value for each part, obtain the total annual value of materials, and derive the required percentages:

Solution

Part Number	Annual Value	Percentage of Total	Cumulative Percentage
M9	$420,000	40.61%	40.61%
A5	310,000	29.97	70.58
A7	104,000	10.06	80.64
Q2	96,000	9.28	89.92
A6	94,000	9.09	99.01
L8	5,700	0.55	99.56
M2	2,400	0.23	99.79
L4	2,100	0.20	99.99
Z1	100	0.01	100.00
	Sum = $1,034,300		

Thus, we see that two parts, M9 and A5, account for over 70 percent of the total annual materials value and are likely candidates for treatment as A parts. We might select the next three parts, A7, Q2, and A6, as our class Bs. The remaining items, L8, M2, L4, and Z1, would be the C items. The plot is shown in Exhibit 8–12.

EXHIBIT 8–12   Cumulative Percentage of Total Annual Inventory Value

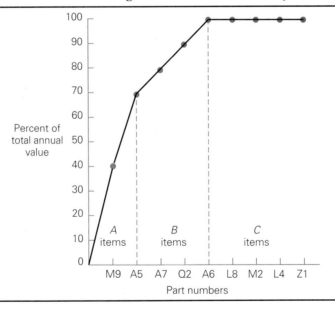

For Further Reference

Books

Ansari, A., and B. Modarress. *Just in Time Purchasing*. New York: The Free Press, 1990 (TS156.A56).

Colton, Raymond R., and Walter F. Rohrs. *Industrial Purchasing and Effective Materials Management*. Reston, Va.: Reston Publishing, 1985.

Dobler, Donald W. *Purchasing and Materials Management: Text and Cases*. 5th ed. New York: McGraw-Hill, 1990 (HD39.5.D62).

Fearon, H. E.; K. H. Killen; and D. W. Dobler. *The Purchasing Handbook*. New York: McGraw-Hill, 1992.

Leenders, M. R.; H. E. Fearon; and W. B. England. *Purchasing and Materials Management.* 9th ed. Homewood, Ill.: Richard D. Irwin, 1989.

Zenz, Gary J. *Purchasing and the Management of Materials.* 6th ed. New York: John Wiley & Sons, 1987 (HD39.5.W47).

Periodicals/Societies

Journal of Purchasing and Materials Management (National Association of Purchasing Management).

Production and Inventory Management (American Production and Inventory Control Society).

Purchasing.

Review Questions

1. Contrast the black-box and the probing-buyer approaches to purchasing.
2. How has team-based purchasing affected the role of the purchasing professional?
3. In general, how are buyer-supplier relationships changing?
4. Explain why the partnership approach favors fewer suppliers.
5. What nontraditional roles does the supplier assume under the partnership approach?
6. What does the term *backward integration* mean? How does it compare with get-focused and stick-to-your-knitting concepts?
7. What is out-sourcing? Discuss its advantages and disadvantages.
8. How does the partnership approach affect freight and information handling?
9. What is ABC analysis? What are its uses?
10. What are MRO items? How should associates purchase them?
11. Identify ways that buying intangibles differs from buying tangibles.
12. Compare value analysis and standardization.
13. How do supplier certification and approval programs fit into modern purchasing?
14. Why should operating groups share in the responsibility for purchasing goods and services that they consume?
15. Under what conditions would classical make-or-buy analysis be appropriate?
16. How can an assembly plant choking in too many parts obtain help from its suppliers?

Problems and Exercises

1. The chapter discussion on partnership versus adversarial buyer-supplier relationships examines 12 dimensions on which the relationship might be rated. A number of organizational types are listed below. For each type, identify the relationship's most crucial dimensions. Explain your reasoning.
   a. Aerospace company that is highly project oriented.
   b. Chemical company.
   c. Foundry.
   d. Major accounting firm.
   e. U.S. Navy shipyard.
   f. Private shipyard faced with severe cost problems.
   g. Machine tool manufacturer.
   h. Retail hardware store.
   i. Integrated circuit manufacturer.
   j. Hairstyling salon.

2. You would like to negotiate a long-term (two-year), exclusive contract to sell your automobile repair services to a city government. The city's purchasing agent believes that such a contract would not be in the city's best interests because "free competition wouldn't get a chance to work." Prepare a rebuttal, giving specific ways in which the city might benefit from a contract with you.

3. How do the terms *licensed* and *certified* affect the quality of services rendered by an individual holding either title? Discuss the merits of these measures.

4. John Revere, operations director at CalComp, Inc., a producer of graphics peripheral products, "was given an ultimatum: Shape up the factory or it would be shipped to Singapore" (Bruce C. P. Rayner, "Made in America: CalComp Plots a World-Class Future," *Electronic Business,* August 1, 1988, pp. 28–32). Among Revere's actions to preserve U.S. operations was his challenge to the team designing the new 1023 model pen plotter: Design it with no more than 20 fasteners (screws, bolts, etc.) bought from no more than 20 suppliers located no farther than 20 miles from the CalComp facility in Anaheim, California.

    How would achievement of these three objectives help keep production in Anaheim? Cite concepts from the chapter in your answer.

5. David N. Burt reports ("Managing Suppliers Up to Speed," *Harvard Business Review,* July–August 1989, pp. 127–35) that Xerox's copier division was in a cost squeeze and losing market share in the 1970s. Corrective actions included reducing its supplier base from 5,000 to 400 companies. Further, "it trained suppliers in statistical quality control (SQC), just-in-time (JIT) manufacturing, and total quality commitment (TQC). Under a program of continuous improvement, it included suppliers in the design of new products, often substituting performance specifications for blueprints in the expectation that suppliers should design final parts themselves."

    Which of the 12 characteristics of supplier partnership given in the chapter was Xerox following in these actions? Explain.

6. A home remodeling contractor presently subcontracts concrete work, mainly pouring concrete patios. The patios cost an average of $400 each. If the remodeling company were to do the patios itself, there would be an initial outlay of $8,000 for a concrete mixer, wheelbarrows, and so forth, but the cost per patio for labor, materials, and extras would drop to $200.

    a. What is the break-even volume?
    b. Draw and fully label the break-even graph.

7. Othello Corporation has a company uniform that employees may wear if they choose. Othello spends $60 for each new uniform. If Othello made its own uniforms, the variable cost (labor, materials, etc.) would be only $50 each, but it would have to lease a sewing machine for $200 per year.

    a. What number of uniforms per year would be required to break even on the $200 lease cost for the machine?
    b. If 15 new uniforms per year is the projected need, is it better to make or buy uniforms? Explain.
    c. Draw and fully label the break-even graph.

8. A large corporation is considering establishing its own travel department, which would earn commissions on airline tickets. The current cost of airline tickets averages $122 per trip. With an internal travel department earning commissions, it is estimated that the ticket cost would drop to $105 per trip. The salaries and expenses of the travel department would come to $40,000 per year.

    What number of tickets per year would the corporation need to process in order to break even on writing its own tickets instead of buying tickets from an outside agency? If the corporation projects 2,000 trips per year, should it buy or make? Why?

9. Following are eight items in a firm's inventory. Devise an ABC classification scheme for the items. Show which class each item fits into.

Item	Unit Cost	Annual Demand
A	$ 1.35	6,200
B	53.00	900
C	5.20	50
D	92.00	120
E	800.00	2
F	0.25	5,000
G	9,000.00	5
H	15.00	18,000

10. Several examples of uses of ABC inventory classification were discussed in the chapter. Suggest four more uses and discuss their value.

11. Arrange the following six item numbers into logical A, B, and C classes (put at least one item into each class):

Item Number	Quantity Demanded Last Year	Unit Price
24	2	$ 800
8	10	15,000
37	1,000	0.05
92	3	12
14	80	50
35	20	1.25

12. Arrange the following five item numbers into logical A, B, and C classes (put at least one item into each class):

Item Number	Quantity Demanded Last Year	Unit Cost
109	6	$1,000
083	400	0.25
062	10	10
122	1	280
030	10,000	3

13. Danielle Weatherby is director of purchasing at Spark-o-Mation. Her company, a producer of sophisticated control and security systems, has had a successful supplier certification program in place for six years; Danielle herself laid much of the groundwork for the program. She attended several good seminars, benchmarked other supplier certification programs, and ensured that her own associates, as well as prospective suppliers, were well trained and informed as the program evolved.

Spark-o-Mation's supplier base has been reduced to approximately 20 percent of its size since Danielle came on board, and the current suppliers are treated as partners. They've earned it; JIT delivery to the point-of-use is in place, receiving inspection at Spark-o-Mation is a thing of the past, EDI has reduced the paperwork, and suppliers have active roles in Spark-o-Mation's design efforts. Danielle feels that further reduction in the supplier base would be detrimental to Spark-o-Mation's performance.

She reads a memo she just received:

Memo to all Department Heads:

As you know, earnings have been flat for three quarters, and last quarter's orders were disappointing. Several large customers cite problems with the quality and timely delivery of our product, and some are threatening to go elsewhere for their control systems. I want you all to conduct a thorough (internal) audit of your departmental operations with an eye for change. Let's get together next Tuesday at 8:00 a.m.

> Thanks,
> Mark Smith
> VP, Operations

Danielle has several thoughts:

- Clearly, Mark needs help from all of us; I must be a team player on this one.
- We've already done so much in purchasing. Can we be expected to improve on an already great system?
- I know we're getting good materials; the quality problems must be occurring elsewhere. How can I say that without pointing the finger?
- We get great delivery, but we can't give it? I wonder why?

How should Danielle respond?

14. Adam Pendleton is director of purchasing for THIS Company. THIS (The Healthcare Industry Supply) provides a broad line of MRO items to hospitals and clinics in several western, Rocky Mountain, and plains states and in the western provinces of Canada. One of the best performing of those items is uniforms. THIS offers surgical gowns and laboratory coats in many styles and colors as well as uniforms for nurses, technicians, orderlies, cafeteria employees, and so forth. THIS buys almost all of its uniforms directly from an apparel manufacturer with two plants located in two southeastern states. In both cases, the plant is the town's major employer.

   THIS accounts for approximately 35 percent of the apparel manufacturer's sales. Over the years, THIS has lived with slow but steady price increases. Delivery from the supplier has been adequate, but there is room for improvement. Quality is average at best; often shipments have to be returned for some correction of sizing, color, special insignia, or other mistake.

   Already today, Adam has had to make two calls to the supplier to straighten out details in orders. The uniform supplier stays in his mind as he reads a memo he just received:

Adam,

As you know, everyone is screaming about health care costs; our customers are getting hammered to keep their costs down, and the buck is being passed back to us. We've simply got to do two things: First, get our own costs down so we can be more price competitive; second, build up a better quality image. Maybe I've got those two reversed, but you get the idea. I've been wondering about getting rid of some of our poorer suppliers; I think there are better and cheaper sources out there. Any ideas? We can't sit on this, I'd like to get with you early Tuesday morning if possible.

> Thanks,
> Nell Jones
> Executive VP

As Adam mulls over Jones's note, several thoughts come to mind:

- Clearly, Nell needs help and is counting on me to play a key role in this matter.
- The supplier certification program that I tried to implement three years ago—with little support from upper management—would have made things easier now.
- If changing suppliers is the answer, the uniform supplier ought to be among the first to go.

How should Adam respond?

15. The purchasing department at OK Industries uses different buying techniques for various items bought. What are two appropriate buying techniques for each of the following items?

    a. Bearings and seals for the factory machinery.

    b. Gear assemblies bought as direct materials in quantities of 8,000 per year.

    c. A special bottle of drafting ink for the company's one draftsperson.

    d. Nails used in the maintenance department.

16. Several types of organizations are listed below, each with different kinds of purchases to make:

Fashions (apparel)	Car rental company
Liquor wholesaler	Glass manufacturer
City government	Plastics manufacturer
Major home appliance manufacturer	Computer manufacturer
Electric power company	Food wholesaler
Furniture manufacturer	Shipbuilder
Construction contractor	Aerospace company

    a. Discuss some key purchasing techniques that would be useful for four of the organization types.

    b. Which types of organizations on the list are most likely to be heavily involved in buying intangibles? Explain.

    c. Which types of organizations on the list are more likely to use an approved supplier list? Bid solicitation based on specifications? Blanket orders? Explain.

    d. Which types of organizations on the list are most likely to use value analysis? Explain.

17. Some years ago, the public school system in Gary, Indiana, contracted with a company to run the Gary schools. The contract featured incentive payments for raising scores on standardized math and verbal tests. What weaknesses do you suppose were present in this contract? Discuss.

18. Value analysis often begins by selecting VA projects from old specifications found in the design engineering files. How is value analysis modified in companies using the just-in-time production system? Why?

19. Following is a list of products to be analyzed by value analysis:

Classroom desk	Bookends
Mousetrap	Electric fan
Backpack-style book toter	Bike handlebars
Fireplace grate	Bike lock
Coaster on which to set drinks	Lamp part shown in the accompanying sketch

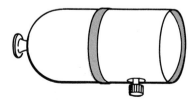

    a. Select any four of the above and define their function or functions in two words as discussed in the chapter.

    b. Why is function definition an early and precisely done step in value analysis/value engineering? Explain what this step accomplishes, using some of your examples from question *a*.

20. Jane A. Doe has just moved to another city and taken a job with a company that manufactures lawn sprinklers, which was exactly the kind of company she had worked for in her prior city

of residence. She finds that her new company has three or four times as many different part numbers going into essentially the same models of sprinkler. Is this good or bad? Discuss.

21. The last paragraph in this chapter mentions Eagle-Picher's proposal to deliver modular floor mats to its automotive customers. The proposal is aimed at strengthening both Eagle-Picher and those customers. Explain the various ways that each would be strengthened.

SUPPLEMENT

PURCHASING AT FORD MOTOR COMPANY: THE TOTAL QUALITY EXCELLENCE (TQE) PROGRAM

Ford Motor Company, like many other large companies, has an active program of supplier selection and evaluation. Ford people refer to their supply base management program by the name of the award that top-level suppliers receive: Total Quality Excellence (TQE). The roots of TQE lie in Ford's quality-oriented Q1 supplier certification program.

The Q1 Supplier Certification Program

Ford started the Q1 program in 1981 to improve the quality of materials from outside suppliers. In the mid 1980s, Q1 was extended to internal (captive) suppliers and later to Ford's assembly plants. In 1989, Ford made Q1 certification a prerequisite for all suppliers. Under Q1, suppliers are required to have certain quality-related programs in place (e.g., incoming quality, SPC, and process capability) and to assist Ford with advanced quality planning and manufacturing feasibility studies. Though crediting the Q1 program for the firm's success during the 1980s, Ford planners realized the limitations of a program that focused solely on quality, and in 1987 the TQE program was launched. Exhibit S8–1 shows evolution of both Q1 and TQE.

EXHIBIT S8–1   Ford's Supplier Certification Program Evolution

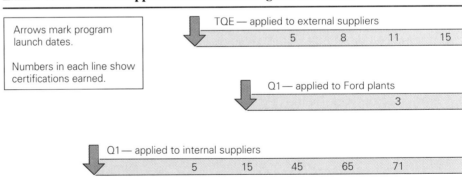

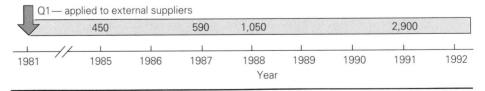

SOURCE: Adapted from James Welch, Laddie Cook, and Joseph Blackburn, "The Bridge to Competitiveness: Building Supplier-Customer Linkages," *Target*, November–December, 1992, pp. 17–29.

TQE Overview

Ford purchasing personnel provide potential suppliers with the *TQE Orientation Guide*. It outlines the TQE application, or petition, procedure and describes the program. For example:

- TQE criteria stem from the Supply Base Management process, which evaluates product quality, engineering, delivery, and commercial performance.
- The program requires a commitment to ensure excellence and continuous improvement in all aspects of business.
- TQE mandates involvement by executives, management, and employees in creating a culture that emphasizes leadership, information analysis, strategic quality planning, human resource utilization, quality assurance of products and services, quality results, and customer satisfaction.
- The highest recognition full-service suppliers can achieve is TQE certification. It represents a superior level of excellence and continuous improvement in everything suppliers do to meet Ford's customers' needs and expectations.

Although Ford considers TQE an extension of its Q1 quality award, company personnel emphasize that quality alone—even backed by Q1 certification—is inadequate. Suppliers must demonstrate continuous improvement in product quality, engineering, delivery, and commercial performance. Exhibit S8–2 shows ratings expected in those four evaluation areas by each of the three levels of recognized suppliers, defined as:

- *Preferred long-term:* Suppliers committed to meeting Ford's overall quality, engineering, commercial, and delivery requirements.
- *Potential long-term:* Suppliers judged to have the potential to achieve preferred status within a reasonable period of time.
- *Short-term:* Suppliers that seem unable to become preferred/potential, suppliers scheduled for elimination, or suppliers of commodities being phased out because of technology shifts.

The Continuing Improvement Mandate

The arrow at the right side of Exhibit S8–2 reflects the heart of TQE: Suppliers are expected to maintain active programs of continuing improvement in all aspects of business. In fact, Ford

EXHIBIT S8–2   Ford's TQE Supply Base Management Process

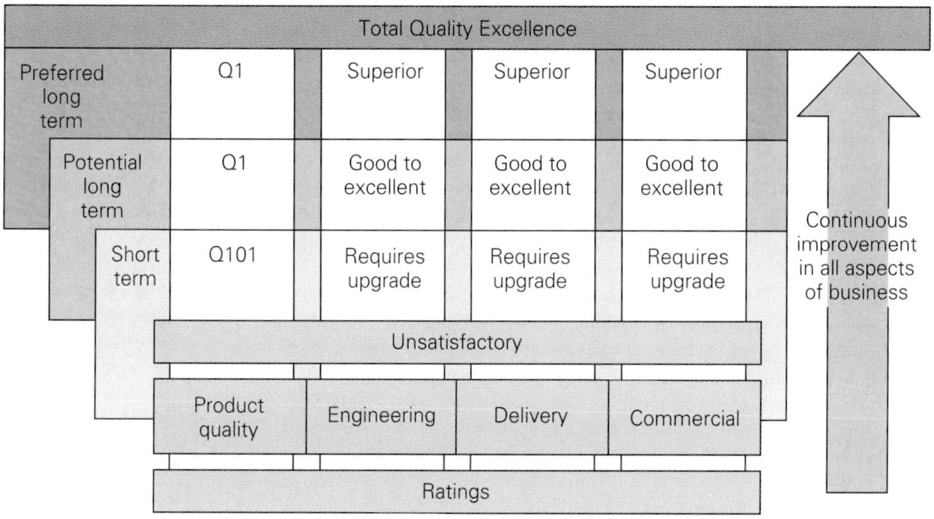

SOURCE: Courtesy Ford Motor Company. Used with permission.

maintains that the evidence of continuous improvement is what distinguishes TQE recipients from other excellent suppliers.

Getting to Know Suppliers

The *TQE Orientation Guide* and the *TQE Assessment Manual* identify numerous dimensions along which continuous improvement is expected. For instance, in human resources utilization, a dimension that transcends all four areas of evaluation, suppliers must:

- Utilize cross-functional teams and employee involvement concepts, and continuous improvement management tools such as team-oriented problem solving and the Plan-Do-Check-Act approach.
- Provide employees with opportunities for education and training related to quality and other disciplines throughout their careers.
- Demonstrate commitment to employee health and safety issues, including developing and implementing ergonomically designed man/machine interfaces and work environments.

In commercial performance, Ford wants to know about a supplier's worldwide cost competitiveness (commitment to productivity, engineering change costs, innovative designs, etc.) level of support (management depth, financial resources, and manufacturing technology and flexibility), and responsiveness to various business issues. In general, throughout the TQE petition process, prospective suppliers will find Ford's purchasing teams aggressively probing for partnership potential.

How rigorous is the TQE certification process? After more than five years, only 15 suppliers had made the grade.

SOURCES: *Total Quality Excellence Award Program Orientation Guide* (Plymouth, Mich.: Ford Quality Related Publications, 1990); *Total Quality Excellence Assessment Manual* (Plymouth, Mich.: Ford Quality Related Publications, 1990); James Welch, Laddie Cook, and Joseph Blackburn, "The Bridge to Competitiveness: Building Supplier-Customer Linkages," *Target,* November–December, 1992, pp. 17–29.

The authors thank Ms. Susan E. Kobet, Manager of Supplier Relations and Quality, Ford Motor Company, for her cooperation and assistance in the preparation of this supplement.

TIME-BASED COMPETITION: JIT, MRP, AND RELATED TOPICS

Chapter Outline

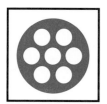

Anita's Studio is being refurbished. New lighting fixtures, carpeting, drapes, display cases, storage cabinets, and furniture have already arrived. The studio is crammed. The painters are here but not the plasterer, who needs to fix wall cracks and holes before painting. Anita's assistants are moving heavy items out into the hall. Anita is phoning the plasterer. She's frantic.

Anita's problem is clear: bad timing. Furnishings have arrived too early, the plasterer too late. The furnishings will be handled several times before finding their final resting places, which is wasteful and costly.

Timing, like quality, is a basic issue. It is of central importance to the customer (Anita in the above example). Therefore, timing is an important issue in nearly every chapter, discussed in connection with topics such as competitive strategy, design-to-market, forecasting, capacity planning, flow control, purchasing, scheduling, maintenance, and facilities location and movement. But timing gets a chapter of its own because it has its own concepts, language, practices, and systems. In considering these matters, we begin with broad, new concepts and practices: JIT, queue limitation, kanban, and the pull system. Later we discuss older concepts associated with inventory timing: material requirements planning, reorder point, and safety stock.

Just-in-Time

Just in time (JIT) has been discussed as a broad set of operating concepts, but here we focus on its *time* component. While the business press associates JIT more with inventory reduction than time compression, the main competitive advantages relate to time: responding to the customer dependably and quickly, without waste or delay, and beating the competition in satisfying customer requirements.

JIT's beneficial effects in reducing *average* throughput times are well known. Less well understood is its important role as a reducer of *variation* in throughput times. Throughput time consistency is often as important for customer satisfaction and retention as product or service performance consistency. In fact, predictable throughput time has become a competitive weapon in human services such as retailing, banking, and fast food, where the unit being served is free to take its business elsewhere.

To deliver dependably short throughput time, JIT must include ways of keeping the provider attuned to the customer's usage. That role is filled by queue limitation, better known as kanban.

Kanban, from the Japanese, means card or visible record. An ancient Japanese meaning of kanban is shop sign. This book's cover photo is an example for a paint shop, and Exhibit 9–1 is a kimono shop example. The colorful, artistic shop sign conveys simple, accurate information about a shop's product or service to the passing shopper. Less artistically but just as simply and exactly, a kanban card tells what and how much to forward to the customer. No transactions are necessary, since the kanban recirculates.

*𝒫*RINCIPLE 16:

Cut transactions.

Queue Limitation (Kanban)

Queue limiter:
A device that limits the queue (waiting line)—and queue time—of items waiting for service.

Kanban is a **queue limiter,** that is, it tightly links a provider's service with a user's need. Thus, it limits the queue of work in front of the provider (the quantity/amount of items waiting and the time each item waits). Queue limitation replaces lax flow control with discipline, which results in customer satisfaction and competitive advantage. Exhibit 9–2 lists various queue limitation methods (not intended as an exhaustive list), which are discussed below.

Classical Card Kanban.   In this system, kanbans recirculate; any container with parts in it must have a kanban attached. Printed on the kanbans are item name, stock number, quantity, user, provider, and card number.[1] Exhibit 9–3 illustrates this version of kanban for an item, Part A, that might be a desk drawer going to desk assembly (user) from a desk drawer manufacturing cell (maker). In this example, with three carts of desk drawers (kanban = 3), the cards are numbered 1 of 3, 2 of 3, and 3 of 3. When an assembler takes the first desk drawer from the cart, the card is pulled, to be collected by (or sent to) the desk drawer production associates. At the drawer production cell (maker), no card, no production.

---

[1]For details on kanban variations and rules of use, see Yasuhiro Monden, *Toyota Production System* (Norcross, Ga.: Industrial Engineering and Management Press, 1983).

EXHIBIT 9–1   **Japanese Shop Sign (Kanban) for Kimono Shop**

SOURCE: Dana Levy, Lea Sneider, and Frank B. Gibney, *Kanban: The Art of The Japanese Shop Sign* (San Francisco: Chronicle Books, 1983), p. 75.

EXHIBIT 9–2   **Queue Limiter (Kanban) Variations**

- Classical card kanban: Recirculating containers with detachable cards.
- Labeled containers: Recirculating containers and carts, permanent kanban identifying labels attached.
- Unlabeled containers or kanban squares: Contents of flow path obvious, so no identifying label (card) necessary.
- Timer or warning light or bell: Queue time limitation, instead of quantity limitation.
- Queue limit policy: Prominently displayed, hard-to-ignore queue limit.
- Colored golf balls, poker chips, abacus beads, discs, flags, and so on: Queue depletion below queue limit signaled by a colored indicator.
- Electronic or oral signal: Notification of queue depletion below queue limit via electronic communication or oral message.
- Automatic queue limiter: In automated system, notification of queue depletion, below queue limit, via automatic device.

Labeled Containers.   Here the card is permanently affixed to recirculating kanban containers, carts, dollies, trolleys—a limited number per item. At Harley-Davidson's engine and transmission plant in Milwaukee, nearly all component parts are controlled this way. Kanban for a certain gear, going from a machining cell to transmission assembly, might be set at four recirculating parts boxes (kanban = 4), each holding exactly 20 gears, and each having a plate riveted to it on which the usual kanban information is

Exhibit 9–3   Card (Kanban) System

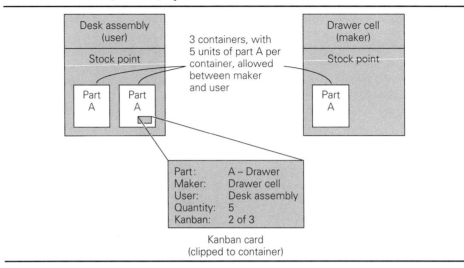

Kanban card
(clipped to container)

written. No box, no production (of that part) at the cell. (Harley had tried detachable kanbans, inserted into a box slot. But the cards got lost, torn, and grease-stained too often.)

Unlabeled Containers or Spaces (Kanban Squares).   Some firms use unlabeled recirculating kanban containers (carts, dollies, trolleys, etc.) or kanban squares, (spaces on the floor or a table). An identifying label is unneeded under each of the following conditions:

- The container holds only one (homogeneous) item, such as a certain size gas tank. Exhibit 9–4 illustrates two special containers for defibrillators, made by Physio Control Company. The three-level container—queue limit (kanban) = 3 — was devised for one of Physio's products in its first assembly-and-test cell. Associates assembling a similar product in Physio's second cell, seeking an improvement, adopted a one-unit version of the container (queue limit = 1) .
- Various (nonhomogeneous) items are flowing through the same process sequence, such as different customer orders through order processing, or successive 10-person groups of tourists on a fixed-sequence guided tour.
- The empty square signals the need for production. For example, unlabeled kanban squares are common in electronic assembly plants. Typically, one square is taped off on each table on an assembly line (kanban = 1). Each assembler looks to the square at the next table for the customer's signal—an empty kanban square—that more work is needed. For big units, the kanban square is on the floor, and some kind of lifting/moving apparatus is usually needed for transport to the next process.

Timer or Warning Light or Bell.   Each Seafirst Bank has a clock and a sign, where customers queue up for a teller, that says the bank will pay $5 to anyone who waits more than five minutes for a teller (queue limit = 5 minutes). Since customer arrivals are extremely uneven, Seafirst uses part-time and flexible labor to keep queues below the limit. Some tellers work only the noon rush, some only on Mondays, Fridays, paydays for the area's biggest employer, and so forth.

EXHIBIT 9–4   Kanban Containers at Physio Control Company

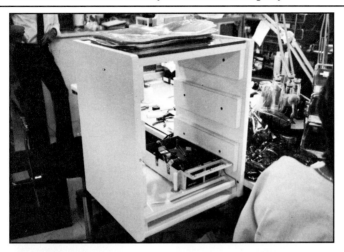

Queue Limit Policy.   Ernst Home and Garden stores put up signs above cashier stations proclaiming the Three-Person Promise (queue limit = 3; see Exhibit 9–5). The sign explains that if a fourth person enters a line, an Ernst clerk comes immediately to open another cashier station.

Colored Golf Balls, Poker Chips, and Abacus Beads.   At a Kawasaki engine plant, when a certain part in subassembly is down to its queue limit, the assembler rolls a colored golf ball down a pipe to a machine center, which tells the operator what part to run next. Associates at an Imprimis disk drive plant in Minneapolis came up with red and blue poker chips and abacus beads, one row for each product, where red means don't make it (we still have some), blue means make it (we are down to the queue limit).

Electronic or Oral Signal.   Usage, or notification that queue limit has been reached, is conveyed electronically (using fax or bar-code scanning and electronic data interchange) or orally (by intercom, phone, or even a shout). As noted in Chapter 7, these kinds of

EXHIBIT 9–5   "Three-Person Promise" at Ernst Home and Garden

notifications are employed in quick-response programs, involving retailers, wholesalers, and manufacturers.

Automatic Queue Limiter.   When automated conveyor systems link processes, limit switches governing each feeder machine can keep the queues short before each user machine. Exhibit 9–6 is a schematic illustration of this method, with a contrasting verbal example. The limit switch, positioned in the conveyor or feed mechanism of Machine Y, limits the queue. When piece 2 slides into a position where it blocks the switch (queue limit = 2), a signal halts Machine X. When Machine Y pulls the next unit forward for processing, the switch is tripped and Machine X gets a signal to make and forward another piece.

Queue Limitation and Dependability

In each of the previous examples, queue limitation serves two basic customer needs: short lead time and invariability. It shortens the lead time by bringing average waiting delays below the queue (kanban) limit, and it prevents extreme wait-time variations.

Exhibit 9–7 shows eight customer experiences with a certain business, perhaps a bank. In part A, with no queue limits, the customer's total time commitment (wait time plus service time) is highly variable, ranging from a low of 3 minutes (fourth instance) to a high of 28 minutes (eighth instance). The average is 16 minutes. In part B, with a queue limit of 5 minutes, the variation is slight, ranging from 3 to 7 minutes, and the average is 5.25 minutes.

A high ratio of queue time to production or service, as in Exhibit 9–7A, is the norm in manufacturing and office work as well as in human services. Therefore, queue limitation is where the service leverage is.

Exhibit 9–6   Automated and Verbal Queue Limitation (Kanban) Examples

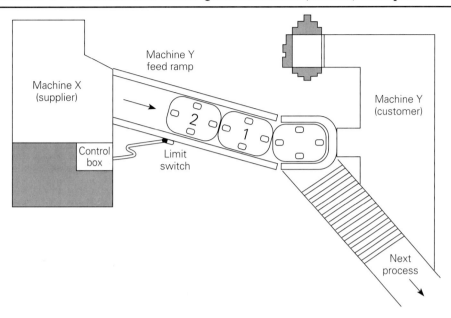

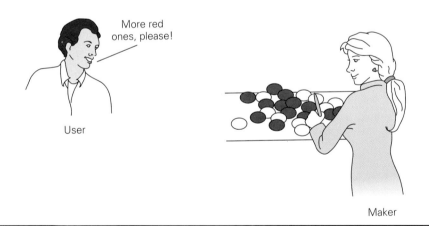

In some companies, success with queue limitation in the direction of Exhibit 9–7B has led to the following results:

- The guesswork is removed. Rob Henderson, plant manager of Corning's ceramic filters business in Corning, New York, says: "We used to negotiate on the request date. We don't do that anymore." With a known, dependably fast throughput time, the Corning salesperson and customer needn't negotiate, which partly explains why this Corning plant was chosen "one of America's best plants" by *Industry Week*.[2]

---

[2]"America's Best Plants," *Industry Week,* October 20, 1990.

EXHIBIT 9-7   Effects of Queue Limit on Total Customer Time

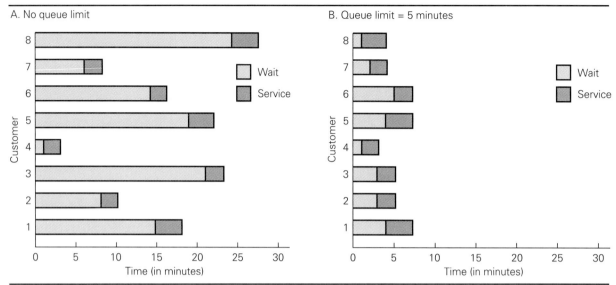

$\mathcal{P}$RINCIPLE 10:

Eliminate variation.

- Reliable order promise dates are easy to set. At Ahlstrom Pump (Finland and U.S. facilities), the multifunctional product strategy team has worked out a rules-of-the-game lead-time policy, based on its dependably quick time to produce any pump, large or small. Nearly all parts, made or bought, are kanban controlled.
- On-time performance improves. In extensively employing kanban, Baldor Electric, a specialty (high-mix) electric motor manufacturer, has cut its throughput time from an unstable average of four weeks to a fixed five days. As a result, in March 1991, associates at Baldor's Westville, Oklahoma, plant celebrated a full year of on-time deliveries.

Continuous Improvement (Kanban Removal)

A special attraction of kanban, as described in early writings on it, is the kanban removal feature, a simple way of incrementally reducing the queue (See Example 9–1).

EXAMPLE 9–1   KANBAN/EDI SERVICE AGREEMENT—MEDIVICE, INC. AND MUNY HOSPITAL

Last year, Muny Hospital contracted with Medivice, Inc., to provide medical devices under a kanban/electronic data interchange (EDI) contract. The initial, trial agreement included 30 high-use items, for example bar-coded cartons of H1 disposable hypodermic needles.

For that item Muny Hospital's stores manager and a Medivice salesperson agreed to an initial kanban quantity of eight cartons. Whenever Muny's demands for H1 needles requires a stores clerk to break open another carton, the clerk uses a wand to scan the carton's bar code. That sends an EDI message to Medivice, authorizing shipment of one carton next time the truck goes to the hospital. If the hospital has used, say, three cartons since the previous delivery, Medivice learns about it through EDI and ships three cartons instead of one.

But was eight the right kanban quantity? Experience quickly provided the answer. In the midst of a serious flu epidemic, Muny Hospital quickly went through all eight cartons of H1s and experienced a stockout. The medical staff was in a panic until Medivice made a special midnight needle delivery. That seemed like an

Exhibit 9–8 Kanban Status and Stockout Check Sheet—Hospital

Items on Kanban	Last Year					This Year					
		J	F	M	A	M	J	J	A	S	...
Hypodermic needle, H1											
Kanbans	10——→8	8	8	7	6	6	6	6			
Stockouts	5				//						

Comments: April problem (damaged needle packages—two stockouts) quickly resolved by supplier; no need to increase kanban quantity.

.
.
.

IV bags, I1											
Kanbans	14——→10	10	10	10	9	8	8	7			
Stockouts	0										

Comments: No stockouts last year or this year to date.

.
.
.

Nurserver carts											
Kanbans	30——→25	25	25	25	22	22	22	22			
Stockouts											

Comments: June late delivery (8:30 A.M. instead of 5:30) due to large turnover of drivers (e.g., graduation of student drivers). Freight co. has set up backup driver system, so no change in kanbans.

Note: Data shown for only 3 of 30 kanban items.

isolated exception, but several more stockouts occurred in the next two months, caused by various system failures (miscount of cartons, a late truck, a stockout at Medivice's warehouse, and a defective lot of H1 disposable needles). As a result, the stores manager and the salesperson increased the kanban quantity of H1 needles to 10 cartons.

On I1 intravenous solution (IV) bags, the opposite happened. The initial kanban quantity, 14 containers, proved to be more than enough. Despite a few startup problems in getting I1 IV bags on kanban, they were always available at the hospital. The service rate on this item was 100 percent, which spelled too much inventory to the stores manager and called for kanban removal. The manager and the salesperson reduced the kanban quantity to 10 containers of IV bags. (More kanbans were subsequently removed, primarily because hospital improvement teams, including representatives from the freight carrier and the supplier, implemented overall improvements in the kanban system.)

Stores associates wanted a simple, easily noticed record of stockout incidence for H1 needles, I1 bags, and the 28 other kanban-controlled items. They developed a large wall-chart check-sheet with preprinted categories of problem causes. A stores clerk makes a check mark beside the probable cause whenever a stockout occurs. Improvement teams later investigate the most frequently checked causes.

Stores associates treat reduction of kanban quantities as one measure of success; response ratios, in pieces rather than boxes, are another useful measure. Associates make check marks for stockouts, and they track kanban reductions on the same wall-chart, shown in part in Exhibit 9–8. Out of Muny's several thousand stockkeeping units (SKUs), only 30 are currently under kanban, so it's feasible to chart them all.

Exhibit 9–8 includes two individual SKUs (H1 hypodermic needles and I1-IV bags) and the Nurserver cart, a shelved cart filled with common supplies (tape, swabs, tongue depressors, etc.). Medivice takes Nurserver carts away each day for restocking and return.

Exhibit 9–8 shows a pattern of few stockouts (high fill rates), which is to be expected since kanban is a disciplined, highly reliable system. The exhibit shows that

Service rate or **fill rate:** Percentage of demands (items) filled out of existing stock (or immediate production).

𝒫RINCIPLE 11:

Cut wait time and inventory.

Stockkeeping unit (SKU): An item at a particular geographic location; a stocked item requiring separate management. SKU is used in retailing, manufacturing, and elsewhere.

the kanban quantity for H1 needles fell from 10 to 8 last year, with further reductions this year. The stockout problem that occurred twice in April this year was quickly resolved, but Muny's cautious associates agreed to keep kanban at six cartons for awhile. Good service experience has led to intermittent kanban removal for both I1 IVs (14 to 10 to 7 kanbans) and Nurserver carts (30 to 25 to 22 kanbans; a single late Nurserver delivery problem causing the June stockout was successfully resolved).

Push versus Pull Systems

Just-in-time and kanban are often associated with the **pull system.** In the following sections, we'll explore the difference between pull and push, why push is so commonplace, subtle pull-push distinctions, and when kanban is used in the push mode.

Vending Machine—Pure Pull System.   Imagine a coffee machine that keeps filling cups and setting them on a conveyor, regardless of the presence of coffee drinkers. That would be a **push system.** Driven by the maker (or provider), a push system pushes out product without queue limits or linkage to usage (user demand) and usage interruptions.

Of course, coffee machines are not push systems; they respond on demand, with a queue limit of zero. In other words, they respond to a pull signal, money dropped in the slot by the customer. Unless demand is present, the machine is inactive.

Dominance of Push Systems.   The push system has dominated nearly every type of operations. Factories typically contain conveyors, storage racks, pallets on the floor loaded with stock, and more being pushed out with no queue limits. In services, long lines of customers form, and providers have no response that would shorten the queues.

Although apparently wasteful and insensitive to customer wants, the push mode has dominated for three main reasons:

1. *Inflexibility.* A surge in customers or order arrivals will cause the queue to lengthen unless the provider can quickly muster more resources. Sufficient physical capacity, plus cross-trained labor and a backup labor supply (as at Seafirst Bank), are some ways of providing necessary flexibility.

2. *Geographical distances.* In manufacturing and distribution, provider and users are often geographically distant, which tempts the maker/supplier to keep producing product and pushing it forward.

3. *Erroneous costing.* Costs of producing an item in advance and carrying it are often grossly underestimated (see discussion of carrying costs in Chapter 7).

ontrast

Materials Management

Conventional Stocking Systems	Kanban
Failure-prone: Rely on fallible stock records, separated from actual stocks; stocks often poorly segregated, counted, containered, and susceptible to damage and unauthorized usage	Few failures: Stock location and count well defined, easily verified; stocks well packaged or ''containered''; simple, visual, disciplined.

Operator hitting line-stop button at Ford assembly plant, Louisville, Kentucky.

SOURCE: *Manufacturing Engineering Magazine,* Society of Manufacturing Engineers. Photo courtesy of Mid-West Conveyor
Co., Kansas City, Kansas

Push-Pull Distinctions.   Fast-food restaurants often keep a small inventory of already cooked and wrapped sandwiches in a kanban-like slide, one for each product. When a slide is full, the cook stops preparing that item; when a server withdraws one or more, that is the pull signal authorizing the cook to make one or more.

For heavier stock, such a slide is called a flow rack and is often equipped with rollers.

In this system, slides are short, so the link between customers and cooking is short too. If the slide was long (holding dozens of sandwiches) the close linkage between customers and cooking would be lost. Quality deterioration (e.g., cold burgers) signals that the cooks are operating in the push mode, keeping the slides overflowing rather than serving customers fast with high quality.

Sometimes the push system is built in. Conveyor-driven production lines (for bottling, canning, tableting, assembly, etc.) are examples. This kind of processing is relentless and associates describe it as "push, push, push." Increasingly, however, companies in these businesses are installing stop and slow-down switches accessible to any operator. Numerous automotive and appliance assembly lines have been so equipped, and the main reason is to give associates ownership of quality: the means, the authority, and the duty to stop the line to get the quality right (and eliminate the rework lines). Associates are likely to carry out their duty if (*a*) the schedule includes time for stoppages (undercapacity scheduling, discussed in Chapter 6), and (*b*) expert help is nearby (many companies have moved key technical-support people and engineers to the front lines so that they can respond just-in-time). When these changes are made, associates are less inclined to use the word *push* to describe their work environment. It begins to *feel* like a pull system to associates—and so it is. Thus, the pull system is, in some sense, a state of mind.

Kanban in the Push Mode?   Earlier we noted Ahlstrom Pump's "rules of the game" and Baldor Electric's success in driving throughput times down from four weeks to five days. Both companies produce a wide variety of models, some in one-piece lots (non-homogeneous production); both have achieved dependably short throughput times (a matter of days) through extensive use of kanban; and both launch orders at the first process (e.g., blanking or rough-machining of a cast metal part) rather than pulling orders through from the last process. Is this the push system? It is not.

Though orders are pushed (launched) at first process (to identify which model of motor or pump to produce), all remaining processes are governed by queue limits, which disallow pushing. At Baldor, a coil-winding-machine operator may not produce unless an empty kanban container has come back from stator assembly (coil assembled, with other components, into a stator). A few specially designed containers (holding a fixed kanban quantity of various coils) enforce the queue-limit rule, but they are not labeled with a particular coil's stock number. Usage at stator assembly empties a container, the pull signal to coil winding.

We've seen the advantages of good user-provider contact, enforced by queue limitation. But what if the provider is plagued by inflexible capacity, buried in other work, or far removed in time from the next process? Can there be reasonable coordination between provider and user? In manufacturing, yes, there can be, by using a timing system called material requirements planning, our next topic.

Material Requirements Planning

Material requirements planning (MRP), perfected in North America in the 1970s, harnessed computer power to carry out complex manufacturing planning. Its first applications were in assisting order planners to determine parts needed to meet a known master schedule for end items.

At its inception, MRP combined two old procedures, **bill of materials (BOM) explosion** and **netting,** with a new one, **backscheduling.** New in that the computerization made it feasible, backscheduling means subtracting required lead time from the due date to find when a required item should be started into production or ordered from a supplier.

MRP has been extended into distribution (distribution requirements planning) and updated to include the planning of resources other than materials (manufacturing resource planning, or MRPII). Basic MRP, discussed next, applies as well to MRPII.

Basic MRP

MRP is said to be a push system, but that is an oversimplification. Though MRP usually plans a push schedule a week at a time, it may include a production activity control subroutine to adjust the work flow somewhat every day (more on that topic in Chapter 12). Also, MRP can be set to plan everything daily instead of weekly.

A process can switch from push to pull as the situation changes. Drink machines, labeled as natural pull systems earlier in this chapter, come to mind. A cola machine in the student lounge might better serve its clientele (and make more sales per day) with the following modification. Three minutes before change of classes, the machine converts itself from pull to push; it fills cups with cola and ice and pushes them onto a short conveyor inside the machine. Customers put in their money and get their cola right away; when customers don't come (rarely), the cups are dumped. In either case, the machine changes back to pull after the conveyor is emptied.

Though a fanciful example, it helps clarify push and pull and the value of each, or both in tandem. Example 9–2, also for a food product, illustrates basic MRP graphically. Since MRP is easier to grasp graphically than in words, some MRP computer systems even show MRP results in graphical form. Two new terms are introduced: **planned order**

EXAMPLE 9–2   MRP for a Caterer

Imagine you are a caterer and have a master schedule of parties to cater every night for the next two weeks. Your inventory policy is zero inventories (except for incidentals like seasonings). To plan for zero inventories, you consult menus for every food dish to be provided for each catering order in the next two weeks. Menu quantities times number of servings equals gross requirements. Let us say (without showing calculations) that gross requirements for salami are as shown in part A of Exhibit 9–9. Salami is required in the quantities shown on days 3, 6, 11, and 13.

You normally order salami from a deli two days ahead of time (purchase lead time for salami is two days). Therefore, you plan to release salami orders as shown in part B of Exhibit 9–9. Each planned order release is two days in advance of the gross requirement shown in part A.

The schedule of planned order releases is correctly timed and in the exact quantities needed. It is a material requirements plan for one of the components that go into the foods to be catered. It is a plan for zero inventory, and is achieved if the deli delivers the salami orders in the planned two days. If deliveries come a day early, inventory builds. Also, if an order of salami arrives on time but a customer cancels the catering order, residual (leftover) inventory builds. Such supply and demand uncertainties create some inventory when MRP is used, but MRP cuts inventory considerably from what it is when the producer (caterer) *plans* to keep components in stock.

Exhibit 9–9   Planned Order Release Determination—Salami

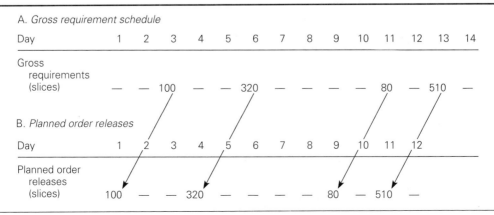

release, which is found by backscheduling from the date of need, and *residual inventory,* which is inventory left over when an order is canceled or reduced in quantity.

MRP Computer Processing

Clearly MRP is a simple idea. The MRP calculations for salami (Exhibit 9–9) are easy because from salami slices to a master schedule of catered food dishes is only a single level of dependency. Now consider the partial product structure in Exhibit 9–10. (A product structure visually depicts a bill of materials and sometimes is used as a synonym for *bill of materials*). It is a dependent-demand chain having five levels below the end item, an automobile. The end item typically is designated the zero level in a computer file storing a bill of materials. The figure shows raw metal (5) cut into a gear (4), fitted onto a shaft (3), placed in a gear box (2), installed in an engine (1), and assembled into an auto (0).

The timing and quantities of parts to be ordered at each level depend on needs for parts by the parent item directly above. Planned-order-release calculations must cascade, that is, proceed from the first level to the second, to the third, and so on. Cascading calculations are a good reason for planners to use computers, especially for products having thousands of parts.

But cascading or level-by-level netting is not the only complication. The same raw metal that is cut into a gear might also go into other parent items that ultimately become the vehicle. Moreover, the raw metal (and, perhaps, the gear, shaft, gear box, and engine) may go into other parent items that become other types of vehicles. Finally, dependent demands (i.e., demands that descend from parent items) for parts at any level must be combined with independent demands. Independent demands arise, for example, from

EXHIBIT 9–10   Partial Product Structure Showing Dependency Chain

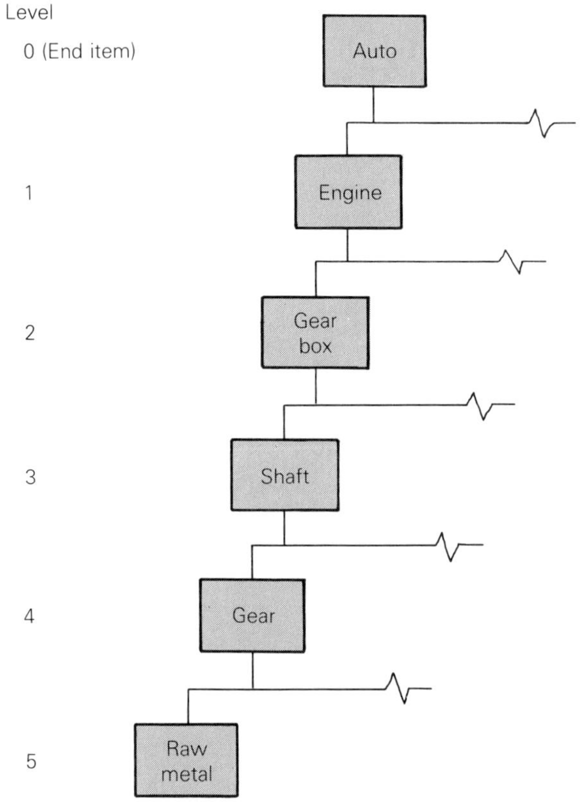

orders for spare parts (service parts). Computers are needed to total and properly time-phase all those requirements.

Exhibit 9–11 shows the necessary inputs and outputs of an MRP computer run. The inputs are a master production schedule, an item master file, a bill-of-materials file, and an open-order file. The outputs include a planned-order-release listing, rescheduling notices, and management reports.

Master Production Schedule.   The master production schedule (MPS) is the action input. The end-item schedule (of the MPS) drives MRP. In most MRP-using firms, the master scheduling team plans in weekly time buckets (periods) extending a year into the future and updated monthly. As the month passes, the master production schedule gets increasingly out of date; that is, toward the end of the month some of the scheduled quantities are out of line with sales orders being booked. Often, the master scheduling team leaves the MPS as it is and deals with inaccuracies via weekly MRP runs, by component parts schedule changes, and by activity control measures on the shop floor.

Item Master File.   The **item master file** holds reference and control data, including on-hand stock balances and planning factors for every component item. The on-hand balance is simply the quantity that is supposed to be in stock.

The on-hand balance is used by MRP to compute planned orders. First, the system computes gross requirements for a given part. Then it calculates projected stock balances to see if there is a net requirement, which would indicate a need for a planned order; that calculation is called netting. A net requirement is the same as a negative projected stock balance, where:

$$\text{Projected stock balance} = \text{Previous stock balance} - \text{Gross requirements} \qquad (9\text{–}1)$$
$$+ \text{ Planned and scheduled receipts}$$

Exhibit 9–11   MRP Computer Run

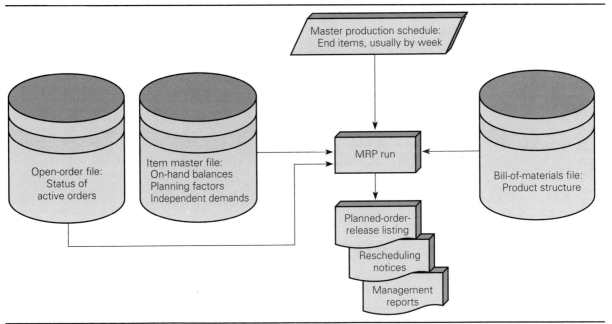

Example 9–3 extends Example 9–2 to allow for an on-hand stock balance. Also, let's change salami into salamite, a hypothetical chemical compound. In keeping with the usual industry practice of scheduling in weeks, gross requirements for salamite are stated as a 14-week rather than 14-day schedule.

EXAMPLE 9–3   MRP FOR A CHEMICAL PRODUCT

Let us say that 220 units of salamite is the on-hand balance at time zero (the start of week 1). Gross requirements are as shown in Exhibit 9–9 (for salami), but with days changed to weeks. For week 3:

$$\text{Projected stock balance} = \text{Previous balance} - \text{Gross requirements} + \text{Receipts}$$
$$= 220 - 100 + 0 = 120$$

The positive projected stock balance (120) shows that there is no need for an order. The projected balance stays at 120 in weeks 4 and 5. In week 6:

$$\text{Projected balance} = 120 - 320 + 0 = -200$$

Now the projected stock balance is a negative 200, which is a net requirement. In MRP, a net requirement is covered by a planned order. The planned order quantity is 200, and the planned order release, obtained by back scheduling, is two weeks earlier, since the planned lead time (*LT*) is two weeks.

Exhibit 9–12 shows MRP results as a four-row display. This type of display might be available for viewing on a video terminal or as printed output. (The scheduled-receipts row, which is empty in this example, is explained later.)

The net requirement of 200 in week 6 is covered by a planned order release of 200 in week 4. A negative stock balance is thus averted; therefore, the −200 is crossed out and replaced by a zero balance. Recomputation of the stock balance in week 6 to account for the planned receipt of 200 is as follows:

$$\text{Projected stock balance} = \text{Previous balance} - \text{Gross requirements} + \text{Receipts} = 120 - 320 + 200 = 0$$

The projected balance goes negative twice more, in weeks 11 and 13. Planned orders cover the net requirements; thus, the negative quantities are crossed out and replaced by zeros.

EXHIBIT 9–12   MRP Computations—Salamite

LT (lead time) = 2 Week		1	2	3	4	5	6	7	8	9	10	11	12	13	14
Gross requirements				100			320					80		510	
Scheduled receipts															
Projected stock balance	220	220	220	120	120	120	0 ~~−200~~	0	0	0	0	0 ~~−80~~	0	0 ~~−510~~	0
Planned order releases					200					80	510				

↑ *LT* = 2   ↑ *LT* = 2 ↑ *LT* = 2

Planning factors stored in the item master file include lead time, lot size, safety stock, and so forth. Those factors need less updating than stock balances. In Example 9–3, the lead time (LT) of two weeks would have been extracted from the item master file.

So far we have assumed that the planned-order-release quantity is the same as the net requirement. That policy is known as lot-for-lot (i.e., production lot size exactly equals lot quantity required). Sometimes the item master file specifies a preset order quantity or lot size, Q (for quantity). Example 9–4, adapted from Example 9–3, provides for a fixed Q.

Fixed order quantities compromise the MRP goal of low (or zero) inventories. Order-quantity policies are the topic of the next chapter.

Bill-of-Materials File.   A bill of materials (BOM) is not the kind of bill that demands payment; rather, it is industry's term for a list (often a structured list) of component parts that go into a product. The BOM names the parts detailed on the engineer's blueprints. Like the item master file, the computerized BOM file serves as a reference file for MRP processing.

The BOM file keeps track of which component parts, and how many of each, go into a unit of the parent item. In each MRP run, the computer (1) calculates planned order timing and quantity for the parent item, (2) consults the BOM file to see what goes into the parent, and (3) translates the parent's planned order requirement into gross requirements for each component. For example, if there are three of a certain component per parent, the gross requirement for that component will be equal to triple the planned order quantity for the parent. (The grand total of gross requirements for the component would also include requirements derived from other parents and from independent demands.) Example 9–5 continues the salamite example to demonstrate the role of the BOM file.

EXAMPLE 9–4 MRP for a Chemical Product—Fixed Order Quantity

Assume that salamite is produced in a vat that holds 500 units. Even though 500 is unlikely to be the net requirement, it seems economical to make the salamite in full 500-unit batches. The excess is carried as a stock balance.

Exhibit 9–13 shows the MRP computations for the case of a fixed order quantity, Q, equal to 500 units. A net requirement of 200 arises when the computed stock balance goes negative by 200 in week 6. The computer covers the net requirement with a planned order two weeks earlier (since $LT = 2$). The order is for $Q = 500$, the fixed order quantity, which brings projected stock balance in week 6 to $+300$. The balance drops to 220 in week 11 and to -290, indicating a net requirement, in week 13. To prevent the negative balance in week 13, the computer plans an order for 500. The planned order release is in week 11, which eliminates the negative balance in week 13 and leaves 210 units to spare.

EXHIBIT 9–13   MRP with Fixed Order Quantity—Salamite

$LT = 2$ $Q = 500$ Week	1	2	3	4	5	6	7	8	9	10	11	12	13	14
Gross requirements			100			320					80		510	
Scheduled receipts														
On hand 220	220	220	120	120	120	300 ~~200~~ 300	300	300	300	300	220	220	210 ~~290~~	210
Planned order releases				500							500			

EXAMPLE 9–5   MRP FOR A CHEMICAL PRODUCT WITH TWO LEVELS

Planned order releases for salamite have been calculated. The computer consults the BOM file to find what goes into salamite. The first ingredient is a chemical compound known as sal. There are two grams of sal per unit of salamite. Therefore, the planned order quantities for salamite are doubled to equal gross requirements for sal. This simple translation of salamite orders into sal needs is shown in Exhibit 9–14. (The salamite data are from Exhibit 9–13.)

Projected stock balances and planned order releases may now be calculated for sal as shown in the figure. Then the computer does the same for the next ingredient or component of salamite.

EXHIBIT 9–14   BOM Reference Data and Scheduled Receipts in MRP

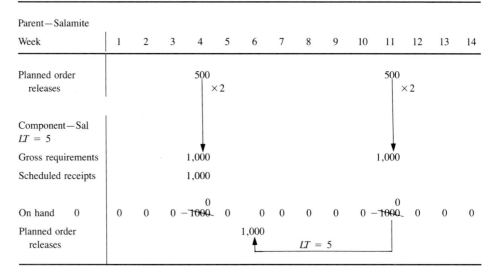

Parent—Salamite

Week	1	2	3	4	5	6	7	8	9	10	11	12	13	14
Planned order releases				500 $\times 2$							500 $\times 2$			

Component—Sal
$LT = 5$

Gross requirements				1,000							1,000			
Scheduled receipts				1,000										
On hand 0	0	0	0	0 ~~1000~~	0	0	0	0	0	0	0 ~~1000~~	0	0	0
Planned order releases						1,000			$LT = 5$					

Developing the master production schedule and forecasting MPS requirements are cumbersome for planners if large numbers of products are in the BOM file. Therefore, the BOMs provided by the engineering department (called engineering bills) may require consolidation. The usual approach is to judiciously combine some engineering bills into modular bills and phantom bills (or superbills). The full approach, called restructuring the bills of materials, is often a valued step in MRP implementation; the method is somewhat complicated, however, and is reserved for advanced studies.[3]

Computer Runs.   MRP computer runs are usually weekly; a total regeneration of material requirements is performed, generally over the weekend. A few companies use regenerative MRP processing every two or three days or even daily. An alternative to regeneration is net-change MRP. Net-change computer software is designed to update only items affected by a change in quantity or timing for a related item. Since not all part numbers need be regenerated, net change saves on computer time.

---

[3]See Joseph Orlicky, *Material Requirements Planning* (New York: McGraw-Hill, 1975), chap. 10, "Product Definition" (TS155.8.O74).

Another MRP factor is scheduled receipts. Returning to Exhibit 9–14, we see a scheduled receipt of 1,000, which is the gross-requirement quantity in week 4. A scheduled receipt represents an **open order** instead of a planned order. In this case, an order for 1,000 has already been released, for make or buy, and is scheduled to be delivered in week 4. Since the lead time is five weeks, the order would have been released, opened, and scheduled two weeks ago. (Remember, we're at time zero, the beginning of week 1.)

Scheduled Receipts and the Open-Order File

Let's examine the events that change a planned order into a scheduled receipt. The following table is a partial MRP for sal as it might have appeared on Monday morning two weeks ago.

Lead time = 5	1	2	3	4	5	6
Gross requirements						1,000
Scheduled receipts						
On hand 0	0	0	0	0	0	0 −1,000
Planned order releases	1,000					

Any time a planned order release appears in the first time-bucket, action to schedule the order is called for. Therefore, sometime on Monday the scheduler writes a shop order to make 1,000 grams of sal. The effect of scheduling the order is to remove it from the planned-order-release row and convert it to a scheduled receipt, as follows:

Lead time = 5	1	2	3	4	5	6
Gross requirements						1,000
Scheduled receipts						→1,000
On hand 0	0	0	0	0	0	0
Planned order releases	( )					

On the next MRP run, the scheduled receipt for 1,000 grams will be included. The order is shown as a scheduled receipt each week until the shop delivers the 1,000 grams. (But the scheduler could cancel the order or change its quantity or timing. Also, the shop may successfully produce more or less than the planned quantity of 1,000 grams.)

Referring back to the system flowchart in Exhibit 9–11, we see that computer processing for MRP makes use of an open-order file, which holds data on open orders (scheduled receipts). Each time a scheduler releases a shop order or a buyer releases a purchase order, the order is recorded in the open-order file. (Alternatively, item master file records may contain fields indicating if there is an open order for a given item.) When orders are received (or canceled), they are closed and removed from the file.

One step in an MRP computer run, usually after calculation of planning order releases, is to evaluate open orders, which can occur after calculating planned order releases. Then the computer checks to see whether quantities and timing for each order in the open-order file are still correct. The check may show that a certain open order is still needed, but perhaps a week later or in a different quantity; or perhaps the order is no longer needed at all. The system issues **rescheduling notices,** which highlight the difference between present requirements and open orders. If the open order is overstated, the shop scheduler or buyer will sometimes ignore a rescheduling notice and allow the order to be completed early or in a quantity in excess of current need, because rescheduling for every new requirement would be too disruptive for the suppliers or shops doing the work. (Order changes and rescheduling notices are normal; the disruption resulting from reacting to every rescheduling notice is often called system nervousness.)

Multiple Parents and Scrap Allowances

So far, we've examined simplified MRP examples. MRP is at its best, however, for complex product structures that can benefit from the computer's sorting powers. Exhibit 9–15 is a partial bill of materials for a bicycle. There is enough room to show only a sample of the bicycle's 300-odd component parts. The complete BOM breaks down into as many levels as are necessary to get to the purchased part. Take the breakdown of the front and rear wheels. Each wheel has a tire, an axle assembly, a rim assembly, 28 spokes, and 28 nipples; each spoke is fabricated (cut, bent, and threaded) from 11 inches of raw wire stock. The nipple is a second-level purchased item and the wire is a third-level purchased item. Spoke nipples and wire stock appear at two locations in the BOM; they also would occur in the BOMs for other bicycle sizes. The computer is efficient for totaling the quantities needed for parts occurring in multiple locations, which is a step in exploding the BOM. (Before computers and MRP were available, BOM explosion was done by legions of clerks using index cards and adding machines.)

Example 9–6 uses some of the bicycle components to show how MRP treats multiple parents and scrap calculations. In the example, netting with scrap allowance included is done as follows:

$$\text{Net requirement} = \frac{\text{Shortage amount}}{1 - \text{Scrap rate}} \qquad (9\text{--}2)$$

Independent Demands for Component Parts

Independent demands for component parts may be entered into the item master file. The subset of MRP for handling independent demands is often called **time-phased order point (TPOP).** TPOP requires that the independent demands be forecast since they cannot be computed; there are no parent demands from which to compute.

EXHIBIT 9–15   Partial Bill of Materials for a Bicycle

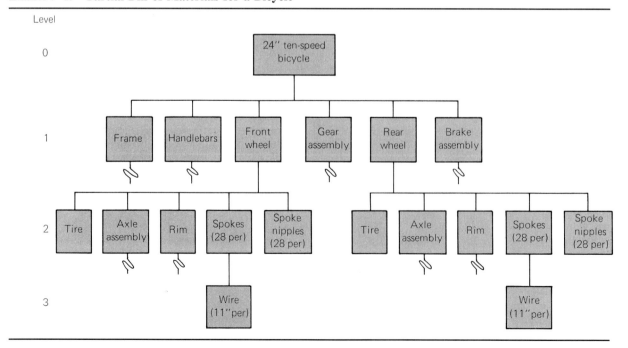

EXAMPLE 9-6 MRP Processing—Bicycle Spoke Nipples

Exhibit 9–16 shows generation of gross requirements for spoke nipples and their translation into planned order releases. Planned order releases for front and rear wheels are given for three sizes of bicycle: 20-inch, 24-inch, and 26-inch. Requirements for wheels would have been derived from master production schedules (level 0) for all bike models. Planned order releases for spoke nipples emerge after higher levels of MRP processing have been completed.

In the figure, orders for more than one parent are consolidated to become gross requirement for a next-lower-level part. The requirement for nipples in week 5 is based on 84 + 60 + 24 + 24 = 192 wheels. At 28 nipples per wheel, the gross requirement is 192 × 28 = 5,376. For week 6, the basis is 36 + 36 + 72 + 84 = 228 wheels: the gross requirement is 228 × 28, which equals 6,384. (Front-wheel and rear-wheel planned orders may be unequal, because there may be extra demand for one or the other as service parts, to make up for scrap losses, etc.

The 2,500 nipples on hand at week 0 are projected to stay on hand (in stock) through four weeks. In week 5, 5,376 are needed but only 2,500 are available; there is a projected shortage of 2,876. The possibility of a shortage triggers the following: the MRP program subtracts the purchase lead time (LT), three weeks, from week 5, giving a planned order date of week 2. The lot size is lot-for-lot. Thus, the planned purchase order is for 2,935 units, a quantity that, allowing for 2 percent scrap, would cover the projected shortage of 2,876 units. Similarly, the projected shortage of 6,384 in week 6 is covered by a planned order back-scheduled to week 3. The order quantity (6,515) again allows for 2 percent scrap.

Note the treatment of the scrap factor. The planned-order-release amount includes the 2 percent so that the extra amount will be placed on order. Planned receipts do not include it, since 2 percent is expected to be scrapped.

EXHIBIT 9-16 **MRP Generation of Planned Order Releases—Spoke Nipple Example**

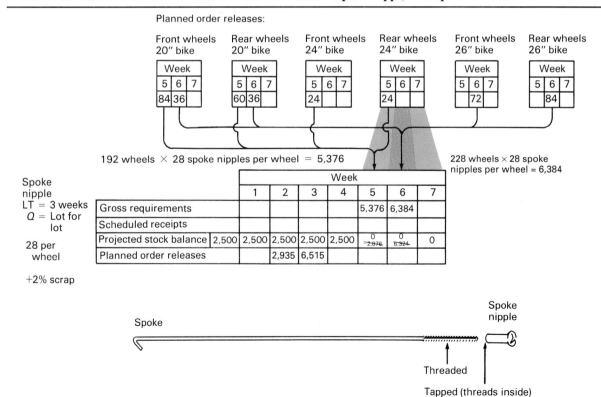

The main difference between MRP and TPOP is this: dependent demands are calculated based on parent-item needs (MRP), while independent demands are forecast (TPOP). TPOP actually loses its identity when the independent demand is merged with demands derived from MRP; MRP takes over from there. Example 9–7 illustrates the method.

We have seen how TPOP handles independent demands from outside the company. But what about independent demands from inside, for example, from company-operated distribution centers? We consider an approach to such demands next.

Distribution Requirements Planning

Traditionally, finished goods inventories in distribution centers have been planned independently of manufacturing. The distribution centers use reorder points, which randomly trigger orders from the manufacturing plants. It makes more sense to fit distribution

---

EXAMPLE 9–7   INDEPENDENT DEMANDS—BICYCLE SPOKES

For a bicycle manufacturer, most of the gross demands for spokes are dependent demands derived from planned orders for wheels. Some independent demands for spokes come from parts wholesalers and other bicycle manufacturers that do not make their own spokes.

The independent sources do not make their demands known very far in advance. Thus, independent spoke demand is forecast. The most recent forecast for 11-inch spokes is for 800 units. That quantity is used as the forecast for the next 52 weeks. Exhibit 9–17 shows the 800-per-week projection at the upper left. The upper right shows a dependent demand for 672 spokes in week 5; that demand is derived from MRP processing at the level of the parent item, 24-inch bike wheels.

The two sources of demand merge into gross requirements for spokes. The independent-demand quantities, 800 per period, are extended directly; the single dependent demand of 672 is computed from the planned order of 24 wheels times 28 spokes per wheel. From this point, MRP logic takes over; the figure shows a net requirement in week 6 covered by a planned order release with a fixed quantity of 4,800 a week earlier.

EXHIBIT 9–17   TPOP—Spoke Example

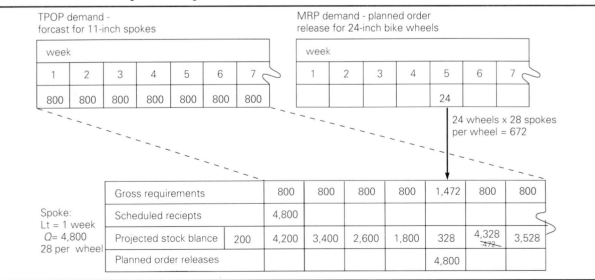

requirements into master production schedules, a procedure known as **distribution requirements planning (DRP).**

DRP works in various ways, but one sound approach is to centralize the planning of distribution requirements. Some of the key steps are:

1. A team at central planning sends historically based demand forecasts (usually weekly, for perhaps a year into the future) to each distribution center.

2. Each distribution center manager adjusts the forecasts based on local factors. Any known large orders or expected demand surges resulting from product promotions are added to the forecast.

3. Forecasts are returned to central planning and totaled. The master scheduling team uses the totals as a basis for developing the master production schedule. Some of the requirements will probably be for lower level components needed in the distribution centers as service parts. In that case, the totals will bypass the MPS and be added directly to gross requirements for the component when the next MRP run is made.

Under DRP, requirements are based on actual forecast needs, not just shelf replenishment. Thus, inventories may be cut even as customer service improves. The manufacturing side of the business operates better as well, because the MPS may be developed based on long-term projections rather than on sudden demands from distribution centers that have found that shelf stock is low.

Closed-Loop MRP

Early MRP systems were one-way streets. They fed plans to production associates but received no feedback from production as to how well schedules were being met. The advent of **closed-loop MRP** brought file control, rescheduling actions, and production activity control on board. We will see how these three innovations make the street run both ways, after we examine obstacles to staying on schedule.

Obstacles.   MRP generates valid schedules in that they are logical extensions of parent demand. But once planned orders are launched, some of the planning factors begin to stray off course.

Lead-time estimates often turn out wrong. This happens when machines break down, delivery trucks are delayed, goods are damaged, the power fails, and so on. If one such incident delays the arrival of 1 part number out of, say, 100 that go into an end item, the schedules for all of the remaining 99 will be thrown off.

A second planning factor that can go wrong is quantities. MRP plans for 1,000 of the component part, but 200 may be ruined or fail quality inspection. The order may be on time but short. The other 99 part numbers going into the end item will be affected by the shortage.

A third factor is customer requirements. The master production schedule, which drives MRP, is partly actual customer orders and partly forecast orders. The forecasts may be off by some amount, and customers may change actual orders. Customers may ask for more or for earlier or later delivery. This changes the MPS, throwing off all component orders.

Finally, the staff may be continually tinkering with product designs and issuing change notices, thus changing the component parts that go into end items.

File Control.   How may valid schedules be maintained in the face of all these changes? First, reference file information must be updated regularly. Notification of design changes goes into the BOM file; changes in scrap rate, lead time, order quantity, and other

Experience shows that the item master file and BOM file need to be at least 95 percent accurate before MRP is activated, or people will lack confidence in MRP outputs. But 99+ percent (or zero defects) is the only reasonable goal, which some companies do achieve.

planning factors go into the item master file; and order completion data go into the open-order file. Finally, regular counts of stockroom inventory ensure that inventory records in the item master file are accurate.

If the information in the files is inaccurate, factory associates and people in scheduling and purchasing will lose confidence in the system. The MRP system may continue to churn out advice, but an informal system will take over. The MRP systems that have failed to meet expectations usually did so because of shoddy record keeping.

Rescheduling Actions.   The MRP system's rescheduling notices are sometimes ignored (thereby avoiding system nervousness), but at other times require action. A scheduler or buyer might find the old schedule impossible to meet and decide to reschedule part or all of an order, to move its due date to a later week. The next computer run would recalculate due dates for all parts affected by the change.

Production Activity Control.   After deciding to reschedule, schedulers send new due dates and quantities to the factory and supplier companies. With jobs based on the old schedules already in progress, change is disruptive. For example, some supplier orders may already be in transit on a truck, some factory orders may have passed through several work centers already and are currently set up and running in another work center. Plants and suppliers will have to halt jobs, backtrack, and change priorities. But how can they even find a given job in order to change its priority?

One way is to tap the pulse of the workplace: know where the work is, what the delays are, and how much is being ruined or scrapped. The usual method is this: as associates in each work center complete a job and send the work onward, they send a message to the computer telling how many units were sent forward and the date. That information is enough to allow the MRP system to provide each work center with daily notices or priority changes. The completion data fed to the computer and the daily priority reports are part of a loop-closing MRP subroutine known as **production activity control** (more on that topic in Chapter 12).

Manufacturing Resource Planning (MRPII)

Closed-loop MRP closes small loops within operations. The operations department also fits into a grand loop that includes capacity planning, marketing, financial planning, and overall business planning. **Manufacturing resource planning (MRPII)** is an extension of basic MRP that closes parts of the grand loop.

MRPII uses the master production schedule to schedule capacity, shipments, tool changes, some design work, and cash flow. It requires several additions to the reference files. One is a bill of labor, which states labor needs, by skill category, to produce a unit of product. The MRPII system can use the bill of labor to project labor shortages. That gives the human resources department advance notice useful in assigning, hiring, and training.

MRPII can also project needs for support staff, including design engineering support in firms in which a customer order normally entails design work on the front end. Some sort of bill of support labor is necessary in order for MRPII to provide that kind of projection.

While basic MRP is well defined (standard files and subroutines), the meaning and composition of MRPII is fuzzier (many possible subroutines) and not easily illustrated with a few tables.

With still more reference data, MRPII can keep track of tool wear and recommend when to replace or resharpen tooling. It can also keep track of machine loads and projected machine capacity shortages, which may call for using alternate machines or arranging to subcontract work to an outside producer.

For financial planning, MRPII treats cash flow almost like materials. The master production schedule is exploded into component parts requirements as usual. Then the system converts planned order releases into cash outflows using unit cost data. Normal delays for bill paying are fed into the computer, and the output is a prediction of future cash outflows. The outflows include payments to suppliers and shippers for bought items and payment of wages, power consumption, and so forth, for made items. Budgeting is simple under MRPII. Cash outflows by expense category and organizational unit may be projected out one year or more. The projection may be refined into budgets.

Projected cash outflows also are valuable for predicting excessive needs for cash, such as in periods of heavy purchasing. Knowing this in advance, the finance department has time to shop for favorable loans and lines of credit and to consider other options for raising short-term cash. The master production schedule (or shipping schedule) is also converted to cash inflows for projected goods sold. Past rates of payment on accounts receivable are used to project the timing of cash inflows for goods sold. Different price structures may be simulated to see the projected effects on profitability.

As to overall impact, Wight states that "MRPII results in management finally having the numbers to run the business." And when "everybody uses the same set of numbers," MRPII serves as "a company game plan."[4]

In the narrow sense, the chief benefit of MRP/MRPII is its ability to generate valid schedules and keep them that way. Valid schedules have broader benefits for the entire company. They include the following, roughly in order of importance:

Benefits of MRP and MRPII[5]

1. *Improves on-time completions.* Industry calls this improving customer service, and on-time completion is one good way to measure it. MRP/MRPII companies typically achieve 95 percent or more on-time completions, because completion of a parent item is less apt to be delayed for lack of a component part.

2. *Cuts inventories.* With MRP/MRPII, inventories can be reduced at the same time customer service is improved. Stocks are cut because parts are not ordered if not needed to meet requirements for parent items. Typical gains are 20 to 35 percent.

3. *Provides data (future orders) for planning work center capacity requirements.* This benefit is attainable if basic MRP is enhanced by a capacity requirements planning (CRP) routine (discussed in Chapter 12).

4. *Improves direct-labor productivity.* There is less lost time and overtime because of shortages and less need to waste time halting one job to set up for a shortage-list job. Reduction in lost time tends to be from 5 to 10 percent in fabrication and from 25 to 40 percent in assembly. Overtime cuts are greater, on the order of 50 to 90 percent.

5. *Improves productivity of support staff.* MRP/MRPII cuts expediting ("firefighting"), which allows more time for planning. Purchasing can spend time saving money and selecting good suppliers. Materials management can maintain valid records and better plan inventory needs. Production control can keep priorities up-to-date. Foremen can better plan capacity and assign jobs. In some cases, fewer support staff are needed.

6. *Facilitates closing the loop with total business planning.* That includes planning capacity and cash flow, which is the purpose and chief benefit of MRPII.

JIT also yields benefits 1–5, but much more so. Some firms lay JIT on top of MRP; others implement JIT by turning off some MRP subroutines.

---

[4]Oliver W. Wight, *MRPII: Unlocking America's Productivity Potential* (Williston, Vt.: Oliver Wight Limited Publications, 1981), p. 58 (TS161.W5x).

[5]Data on MRP/MRPII gains are drawn from two sources: Wight, *MRPII,* chap. 4, and Roger G. Schroeder, John C. Anderson, Sharon E. Tupy, and Edna M. White, "A Study of MRP Benefits and Costs" (Working Paper, Graduate School of Business Administration, University of Minnesota, May 1980).

ontrast

MRP Coverage

Wide MRP Coverage	**Reduced MRP Coverage**
A goal of Class A MRP requiring:	A goal of disciplined simplicity requiring:
High record accuracy.	High record accuracy.
All MRP subroutines in use.	Reduction of subroutines, except for data files.
All part numbers on MRP.	Migration of parts off MRP and onto JIT, regular-use parts first.

Benefits of MRP/MRPII are offset somewhat by its complexity. Considerable time, training, preparation, and discipline make MRP or MRPII yield the promised benefits. The next technique, reorder point, does not offer those benefits, but it is simple.

Reorder Point

Inventory timing with **reorder point (ROP)** is probably as old as humanity (maybe older; some animals, such as squirrels, also replenish low stocks). The ROP provides for replenishing stocks when they reach some low level. Let's look at some ROP variations.

Perpetual System

The classic use of the reorder point occurs in a **perpetual inventory system.** Perpetually—every time an issue is made—the stock on hand is checked to see whether it is down to the ROP. If it is, someone places an order. In the informal case, stock clerks perpetually examine the physical stock level itself. More formally, records clerks examine the balance on a stock record.

Reorder points are part of our personal lives. We may reorder (go out to get) postage stamps when we have only three left, or we may buy a new half gallon of milk when there is about two inches left in the old container. Sometimes we get reminders from the manufacturer: the desk calendar or box of personal checks containing a reorder notice.

Two-Bin System

A version of the perpetual reorder point called the two-bin system is often used in small stockrooms. Two adjacent storage bins hold a single item, and users are told to withdraw from bin 1 first. The rule is this. When the first bin empties, place an order. The second bin contains the ROP, a quantity that covers the lead time for filling the order and allows for some additional buffer or safety stock.

There are many variations. A colored sheet of paper may be inserted in a stack of forms on a shelf to show when the ROP (the second bin) has been reached. Indirect material, such as washers, screws, and nails, is often placed in trays on assemblers' workbenches; a painted line partway down inside the tray can designate the ROP. Transistors, diodes, and so on, are often stored in corrugated boxes on shelves; a small box in the larger box may be used to contain the ROP (the second bin). Exhibit 9–18 shows two component parts (left side and right side of a bin) controlled by a two-bin system at Upright-Ireland. At Upright, the two-bin system is an element of JIT, which covers

Exhibit 9–18   Two-Bin (Kanban) System at Upright-Ireland

virtually all of Upright's parts, bought or made. When an associate breaks into the second bin, that is the kanban signal to order another package.

The two-bin system works best when one person is in charge of the stockroom or is in charge of a daily check to see which items are down to the ROP. Otherwise, people can get too busy to note the need for an order; associates can blame each other if the second bin is emptied but no one has reordered.

In firms with partial computer control of inventories, order cards with bar codes can be placed near bin 2. Then, when bin 2 is entered, it is easy to initiate the reorder: Just scan the bar code, which holds identifying data. Associates are less likely to forget to order when ordering is so simple.

Planners and buyers may set the reorder point (the quantity in bin 2) by judgment and experience or by an ROP formula. Judgment would tend to follow the concepts embodied in the basic ROP formula:

ROP Calculation

$$ROP = DLT + SS = (D)(LT) + SS \qquad (9\text{--}3)$$

where

ROP = Reorder point
DLT = Demand during lead time
SS = Safety stock (or buffer stock)
D = Average demand per time period
LT = Average lead time

ROP calculation is simple, but it does require reliable numbers if it is to be trusted. The planner or buyer often uses recent averages for demand rate and replenishment lead time. Safety stock could be set judgmentally or by using a formula; more on how to do that after we consider two ROP examples.

EXAMPLE 9–8   ROP CALCULATION—FUEL OIL EXAMPLE

Assume that a building heated by fuel oil consumes an average of 600 gallons per year and the average lead time is two weeks. Thus:

$$D = 600 \text{ gallons per year}$$
$$LT = 2 \text{ weeks/52 weeks per year} = 0.04 \text{ year}$$
$$DLT = (D)(LT) = (600)(0.04) = 24 \text{ gallons}$$

Then, if desired safety stock is 40 gallons:

$$ROP = DLT + SS = 24 + 40$$
$$= 64 \text{ gallons}$$

Replenishment Cycle

In Example 9–8, an average demand rate of about 24 gallons was calculated based on an average replenishment lead time of two weeks. Average values tend to smooth things out, masking the existence of stock outages and inventory peaks. A more realistic picture of ROP replenishment cycles is explained in Example 9–9.

EXAMPLE 9–9   REPLENISHMENT CYCLES FOR DISCRETE DEMAND—RADIATOR CAP EXAMPLE

Radiator caps are issued in discrete units; that is, you cannot issue half a radiator cap. (In contrast, a continuous item, like fuel oil, can be issued in fractions of a gallon). Exhibit 9–19 shows two replenishment cycles for radiator caps. The graph shows a stairstep depletion pattern. It also shows early and late order arrivals, including a case in which backordering occurs.

In the first cycle, radiator caps are being issued at a slow pace (i.e., slower than past average demand). In the fourth time period there is a spurt, and at the end of the period stock on hand drops below the ROP. An order is placed. During lead time, stock issues start out slowly, then speed up in periods 6 and 7. All radiator caps are gone by the beginning of period 7, and orders still come in.

The shaded zone below the zero line indicates orders unfilled because of the stockout condition, caused by the combination of slow delivery (greater-than-average lead time) and a late spurt in demand.

Backorder:
Order accepted when stock is out.

The second cycle begins when the order arrives in period 7. The order quantity (lot size) brings the stock level up from zero to Q units, and the backorders are immediately filled, dropping the stock level somewhat. The stock depletion rate is about average through period 10. In period 11, demand for radiator caps surges. The surge continues into period 12, and it reduces stock to below the ROP. An order is placed.

This time, delivery is faster than average (see actual LT as compared with average LT), and there is little demand during the lead-time period. The result is little use of the DLT quantity and no use of the SS amount. Stock is high when the order quantity (Q) arrives. The order arrival pushes up the stock level to near the maximum possible, which is the ROP plus Q.

Periodic System

The ROP method of replenishment requires perpetual checking of the balance on hand. Why not just check the balance at fixed time intervals? The periodic system does just that. The regularity in order intervals makes the periodic system popular with retailers, who

EXHIBIT 9-19   ROP Replenishment Cycles—Radiator Cap Example

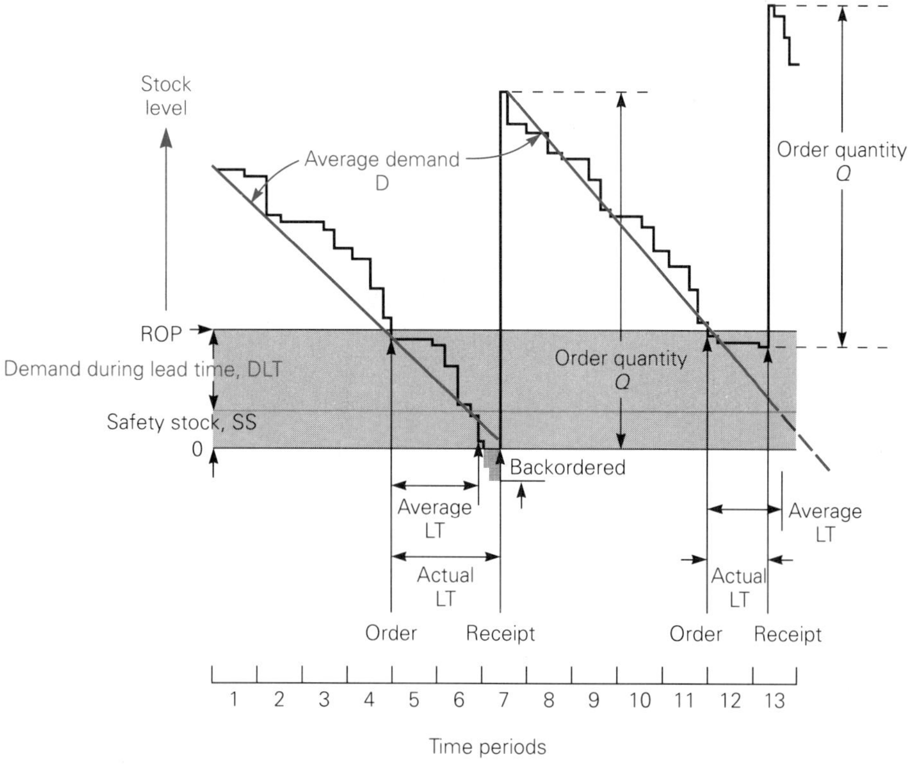

often set up a schedule of checking stock levels in slack periods each day, once a week, or perhaps monthly. Grocers, restaurants, gas stations, clothing stores, and auto parts stores are some of the many kinds of businesses that favor a periodic system.

Often the periodic system of timing orders is combined with maximum-minimum quantity criteria. For example, a grocery store might periodically reorder laundry soaps, with two days as the order interval. The maximum shelf space, and therefore maximum inventory, for one item—say, Whiter-White Detergent—might be four cases and the desired minimum, one case. The periodic system works like this:

1. Check stock of Whiter-White on Monday, Wednesday, Friday, and so on.
2. If shelf stock is below one case, reorder enough to bring the stock as close to four cases as possible without exceeding that amount.
3. If stock is above one case, don't reorder.

Note that the minimum is really a reorder-point quantity used in conjunction with the reorder-point interval; the maximum governs what the lot size must be in order to bring up stock to the maximum level.

Buffer Stock (Safety Stock)

Regardless of the system used for inventory timing, keeping customers well served is difficult. Consumption and output rates vary, and stoppages, accidents, and natural disasters sometimes disrupt operations. These difficulties lead managers to rely on protection in the form of buffer stocks, also called safety stocks.

Factory people tend to call it buffer stock: a buffer between one machine and the next. To retailers and wholesalers, where reorder points are most common, it's safety stock.

Even well-run just-in-time operations and quick-response programs must rely somewhat on buffer stocks. Buffer stock, a special class of inventory, is like the spare tire in
your auto or your homeowner's insurance policy: you hope you don't need it, but you
don't dare operate without it. Buffer stock is expensive, however, and needs careful
management.

In Chapter 7, we introduced the concept of offline buffer stock, which provides
protection but does not consume throughput time. Sometimes it is appropriate to calculate
the quantity of buffer stock; the calculation procedure and comments about its limitations
round out our discussion of careful buffer-stock management.

Statistical Safety Stock

In retailing and wholesaling, safety (buffer) stock must be far greater than in dependent-
demand situations. Customers must be served, but their demands for a given item tend to
be highly variable. Fortunately, demand variability and customer service can be expressed
in numbers. Manipulate the two numbers (the desired customer service level and the
demand variation level) in a certain way, and the result is a calculated statistical safety
stock.

The first step is to decide on the desired customer **service level.** Among the many
possible definitions of service levels the following is popular: Service level is the percentage of orders filled from stock on hand. That, plus its converse, the **stockout rate**,
must equal 100 percent. For example, a planned service level of 0.98 means that customer
orders would be filled 98 percent of the time, with a stockout the remaining 2 percent of
the time.

Safety stock is calculated from service level by the following formula (assuming
independent demands, normally distributed):

$$SS = z \sqrt{LT \, (SD)^2} \tag{9–4}$$

where

    SS = Safety stock
    z = Value from normal distribution table (see Appendix A), based on service level
    LT = Lead time
    SD = Standard deviation of demand

(Note: LT and SD must be stated in the same time units; for example, if SD is calculated
based on variability over one-month time periods, LT must be expressed in months.)
Example 9–10 illustrates use of the formula.

Limitations and Broader Buffer-Stock Issues

Unfortunately, the statistical safety stock method omits factors that affect safety stock.
One is the effect of lot size. In Chapter 7, we learned that large lot sizes act as buffer
stock; if the lot size is very large, a calculated statistical safety stock will be insignificant
(compared with the buffering effects of the large lots) and not worth calculating. Small lot
sizes have the opposite effect: it is better to keep larger safety stocks on hand than the
calculated statistical quantity.

In retailing and wholesaling, lot sizes normally are moderate, which means that the
statistical model is valid enough. Exceptions are hard-to-get items or items from undependable suppliers. In those cases, the main concern may be with variable supply, but the
statistical model accounts only for variable demand.

The same types of limitations restrict use of the statistical model in setting buffer
stocks for semifinished factory materials and other dependent-demand items. The big

EXAMPLE 9–10   SAFETY STOCK—LOAVES OF BREAD

Assume that mean demand for bread at your house is 100 slices per week and that demand varies by a standard deviation of 40 slices per week. The desired service level is 97.72 percent. It takes just one day to replenish the bread supply. How much safety stock should you carry? What is the reorder point?

Solution:

All data must be in the same time units. Thus, replenishment lead time of 1 day is converted to ⅐ weeks.

The service level, 0.9772, represents a probability: 0.50 (the left half of the area under the normal curve) plus 0.4772. We look for 0.4772 in Appendix A and find it where $z = 2.00$. Insert the data into the formulas, and solve as follows:

$$SS = z\sqrt{LT(SD)^2}$$
$$= 2.00\sqrt{1/7(40)^2} = 30.2 \text{ slices}$$

and, from Equation 9–3:

$$ROP = (D)(LT) + SS$$
$$= (100)(1/7) + 30.2 = 44.5 \text{ slices}$$

---

problems are the variabilities in supply (the maker), which the statistical model does not address.

Other miscellaneous factors that affect buffer stock are:

Cost. For very costly items, keep very little (even zero) buffer stock on hand. For low-cost items (washers, paper clips), keep perhaps as much as a year's worth.

Space. If the item is very bulky, keep the buffer stock small, and vice versa.

Consequences of a stockout. Sometimes a wide variety of options, such as substitute items, are available in the event of a stockout; in such cases, keep the buffer stock small.

Obsolescence. In high-tech industries, large buffer stocks mean large obsolescence costs; thus, keep buffer stocks small.

With so many factors not present in the model, how can the model be effectively used? To answer this question, let's consider a company that takes particular pride in its high service level. The centerpiece of Frito-Lay's corporate culture is its ability to provide its customers with a 99.5 percent service level.[6] Current-demand data (captured by bar-code scanning or collected by Frito-Lay's 10,000 store representatives) go into company computers, which calculate demand, standard deviation of demand, safety stock, and reorder point for each product. Armed with computer listings of calculated ROPs for each product, product managers can decide whether to change any of them in light of other safety-stock factors such as cost and space.

---

[6]Thomas J. Peters and Robert H. Waterman, *In Search of Excellence* (New York: Harper & Row, 1982), pp. 164–65 (HD70.U5P424).

Summary

Just-in-time processing not only cuts throughput time on average, but also reduces variation around the average. A key to achieving dependably quick response is the use of queue limitation devices. These include classical card kanban, labeled containers (where the item is uniform), unlabeled containers or kanban squares (which can be used for nonuniform items), timers (for queue-time limits), queue limit policies (less disciplined than physical limiters), colored indicators, electronic or oral signals, and automatic (e.g., electric) stop devices.

While queue limiters do not deal with service times, they place upper limits on waiting times, which in most cases are far larger consumers of throughput time. Thus, queue limitation can eliminate variation to the point where customers can be given certain delivery (or appointment) dates or times, with no need to speculate or negotiate.

A server employing queue limitation would normally begin with enough units, say, 10 kanban containers, to protect against delivery problems or surges in demand. As delivery problems are solved or customer demands are smoothed out, the server then reduces units (kanban removal), which cuts throughput time.

Vending machines operate as pull systems in which the customer's coin drop is the pull signal that actuates the serving mechanism. More common are push systems in which customers push forward on the server, or the producer pushes the parts on to the next process; the main concern is keeping busy, not fast service. Competitiveness is increased by inducing firms to shorten the queues, which makes the processes feel more like customer-pull systems.

While JIT/queue limitation has the feel of a pull system, material requirements planning (MRP) is usually considered a push system; it generates planned orders rather than responding quickly to customer pull signals.

In MRP, a master production schedule for many periods into the future is exploded into gross requirements for all component parts in the bill of materials. The current stock balance for each part is found in the item master file, and projected stock balances are calculated for each future period. Where a negative projected balance is found, the computer backschedules (offsets for lead time) in order to plan an order in a quantity large enough to prevent the negative balance. Scrap allowances and independent demands for service parts can be included in MRP processing.

Basic MRP just launches orders, but closed-loop MRP provides for production progress data to be fed back to the computer, which then issues any needed rescheduling notices. By prudently acting on the notices, schedulers and buyers can keep make rates and use rates better coordinated with less risk of large residual inventories, more like the pull concept.

An extension of MRP called time-phased order point (TPOP) allows for blending independent demands (e.g., for service parts) with calculated demands based on parent-item requirements. Another extension, distribution requirements planning, ties demands for distribution inventories to planning for manufacturing inventories.

The unique feature of MRP is not the explosion of bills of materials for items in the master schedule; that was done years before MRP was developed (the method produced a list of shortage items that the reorder point system failed to provide enough of). What is unique is that MRP plans far enough into the future to allow lead-time offsetting for ordering parts. People will trust MRP outputs only if the item master file and bill of materials, the key inputs, are accurate.

MRP is effective in that it plans material needs based on demand projections, not just to refill a stockroom shelf. MRPII extends MRP into the planning of almost any manufacturing resource, including cash flow, and provides a basis for ties to overall business planning.

The oldest inventory-timing approach is replenishment by reorder point (ROP) methods. In the perpetual system, stock is replenished when it drops to a reorder quantity, the ROP. The ROP equals enough stock to cover average demand over an average lead time, plus some safety stock to protect against nonaverage surges in demand or lengthy lead times. In a periodic replenishment system, reorders are at fixed intervals rather than when stock gets low.

Statistical safety stock calculation employs standard deviation of demand, desired customer service level (service from stock), and lead time. The formula works where demand uncertainty is the dominant variable, as in retailing and wholesaling. Other businesses involve variabilities in supply, which makes the statistical method less useful.

Key Words

Solved Problems

Problem 1

At Computer Services, Inc., small software jobs start at the chief analyst's desk, where each job is assigned to one of the 10 systems analysts. On average, a job sits in the chief's in-basket for 7¾ hours before the chief starts processing it. Average processing time is 15 minutes. In systems analysis, there typically are 60 active jobs. Is queue limitation (kanban) usable at either work center? Explain.

Solution 1

Queue limitation could be used in several ways. For the chief, the rule could be to have zero jobs in the in-basket (queue limit = 0) at the end of the day and stay late, if necessary, to meet the rule. Another possibility is to set the queue limit = 5; if the in-basket ever has more than five jobs, call for help from the most senior analyst.

For the analysts, a general queue limitation policy is one possibility. For example, set an overall response ratio at 2 to 1, with no more than 20 jobs assigned to the 10 analysts. Stay late, borrow programmers for use as analysts, or subcontract work to avoid exceeding the ratio. A rule such as queue limit = 2 at each analyst's desk will yield the same overall ratio. It is hard to say whether the overall ratio or queue limit = 2 at each analyst's desk would work better.

The result of using queue limitation is to speed work through in much less total lead time (but the same work content time per job). In the office, queue limitation forces people to start one job and finish it instead of starting many jobs, switching among them and stretching all of them out.

Problem 2

The same extruded plastic case is used for three different colors of highlighter felt-tipped pen, A, B, and C. Demand for each color for the next five weeks is as follows (numbers are in thousands):

	Week				
	1	*2*	*3*	*4*	*5*
A	10			10	
B	18		18		18
C	8	8	8	8	8

a. What is a plausible reason for demands for A and B to occur in alternate periods whereas demands for C occur in every period?

b. Calculate gross requirements for the plastic case. Then, given an on-hand balance of 70,000 at time 0, a lead time of 2 weeks, and an order quantity of 20,000, calculate planned order releases.

Solution 2

a. Demand for colors A and B appears to come from planned orders for a higher level parent item, perhaps a package containing both colors of highlighter pen. Color C's demand could be independent, perhaps direct orders from a wholesaler or retailer.

b.

		Week				
	0	*1*	*2*	*3*	*4*	*5*
Gross requirements		36	8	26	18	26
Scheduled receipts						
Projected stock balance	70	34	26	0	2 ~~−18~~	16 ~~−24~~
Planned order releases			20	40		

Explanation: The projected -18 in week 4 requires a planned order of 20 backscheduled by 2 weeks to week 2. The projected -24 in week 5 requires a double lot size—40 instead of 20—backscheduled to week 3.

Problem 3

A wholesaler's computer records show the following for one of its inventory items:

Mean monthly demand = 8,000
Standard deviation of demand = 1,000 per month
Replenishment lead time = 1 month

If the desired service level is 95 percent, what is the statistical safety stock? What is the reorder point?

Solution 3

The service level, 0.95, represents a probability: 0.50 (the left half of the zone under the normal curve) plus 0.45. We find 0.45 in Appendix A where, by interpolation, $z = 1.645$. Then:

$$SS = z\sqrt{LT(SD)^2}$$
$$= 1.645\sqrt{1(1,000)^2}$$
$$= 1,645$$

Next, compute mean demand for the lead time period:

$$DLT = 8,000 \text{ per month} \times 1 \text{ month} = 8,000$$

Then:

$$ROP = DLT + SS$$
$$= 8,000 + 1,645$$
$$= 9,645$$

For Further Reference

Books

Hall, Robert. *Zero Inventories*. Homewood, Ill.: Dow Jones–Irwin, 1983.

Japan Management Association, ed. *Kanban: Just-in-Time at Toyota.* Trans. David J. Lu. Stamford, Conn.: Productivity, Inc., 1986 (originally published in Japanese in 1985) (TS157.T6913).

Monden, Yasuhiro. *Toyota Production System: Practical Approach to Production Management.* Norcross, Ga.: Institute of Industrial Engineers, 1983.

Orlicky, Joseph. *Material Requirements Planning.* New York: McGraw-Hill, 1975 (TS155.8.O74).

Periodicals/Societies

Schniederjans, Mark J. *Topics in Just-in-Time Management.* Needham Heights, Mass.: Allyn & Bacon, 1993 (TS155.S3243).

Schonberger, Richard J. *Japanese Manufacturing Techniques: Nine Hidden Lessons in Simplicity.* New York: Free Press, 1982 (HD70.J3S36).

Wight, Oliver W. *MRPII: Unlocking America's Productivity Potential.* Williston, Vt.: Oliver Wight Limited Publications, 1981 (TS161.W5x).

Journal of Operations Management (American Production and Inventory Control Society).

Journal of Purchasing and Materials Management (National Association of Purchasing Management).

Production and Inventory Management (American Production and Inventory Control Society).

Target (Association for Manufacturing Excellence).

Review Questions

1. What is the role of the maker or provider under push systems and under pull systems?
2. Why is it desirable for the queue limit to be small? Why must it usually be larger than zero?
3. What types of queue limitation signals might be used to trigger materials movement?
4. Under what circumstances would kanban removal be appropriate?
5. How might queue limitation be applied to patrons awaiting service?
6. How can queue limitation be made to work when the demand rate is highly variable?
7. What are the marketing and competitive advantages of queue limitation?
8. How does MRP differ from MRPII?
9. What is the role of the item master file in MRP?
10. How does an open order differ from a planned order?
11. How does DRP improve on the usual way in which distribution centers are managed?
12. What is the hazard in using the computer and MRP to reschedule whenever any manufacturing variables change?
13. What is closed-loop MRP?
14. Why is the ROP system considered a perpetual system?
15. Given a safety stock, what else is needed to arrive at a reorder point? Explain.
16. Contrast visual and records-based ROP.
17. To what extent can safety stock determinations be computerized? Does it depend on type of industry? Explain.
18. Is the periodic system simpler or more complex than the perpetual system? Explain.

Problems and Exercises

1. Sentrol, Inc., maker of premier sensor products for the security industry, employs nearly every kind of queue limiter in its plant operations, which has cut its average production throughput time to four hours. A remaining problem is cutting the time to refill assembly teams' kanban containers with purchased components from the stockroom in the next room. Most containers are about the size of a one-quart ice cream carton and hold lightweight resisters, wire sets, screws, and so on. It takes about 50 minutes for a stockroom associate pushing a trolley of full kanban containers to make a complete circuit around the assembly floor; the circuit includes collecting empty kanban containers.

   On a trial basis, a stockroom associate on roller skates (with crash helmet and knee pads) has been making the circuit, carrying two or three cartons at a time. Does this idea sound feasible? What would its advantages be? How would they be measured? Are there disadvantages?

2. Sentrol, Inc., maker of premier sensor products for the security industry (motion detectors, door and window entry detectors, etc.), receives hundreds of orders and other inquiries from resellers and final users by phone each day. Sentrol's customer strategy team has rejected the use of an automatic answering system. The team believes that good service requires real people answering the phones within four rings every time. The trouble is, the calls arrive unevenly, sometimes 5 per hour and sometimes 50 per hour. Is the customer strategy team's preferred policy practical? If so, how can it be made to work?

3. An accounts payable office consists of three people. Their work flow includes passing piles of invoices among them in the process of authorizing payment. Recently the average number of invoices on the three desks was 150 and the typical time an invoice spent in the office was three days. Select a response ratio, and explain how it might be used to improve the operation. What results might be expected?

4. A manufacturer of X-ray machines presently has partially completed machines scattered around the assembly areas, with only a few actually being worked on by the department's five assemblers. The units accumulate in assembly because parts and subassemblies from other departments arrive whenever the departments happen to complete them.
   a. Is the current system push or pull? Explain.
   b. Suggest an improved system.

5. Four ways to limit queues are (1) kanban squares, (2) special-purpose containers, (3) general-purpose containers with kanban (cards) attached, and (4) a powered assembly conveyor with no container or card necessary. Which of the four should be used in each of the following situations? Explain your answers.
   a. A book printer; books are printed and bound in a route through four different departments.
   b. Final assembly of 13-inch TV sets.
   c. Production of vitreous china products (sinks of all sizes, toilets, tubs, etc.); involves molding, glazing, firing in kilns, and so forth.
   d. Repetitive production of several different large, highly polished precision metal parts.
   e. Internal mail delivery in a large office building.

6. The following matrix shows partial MRP data for one component part. Scheduled receipts are missing, as is the planned-order-release row. Lead time is three weeks. A fixed order quantity (rather than lot-for-lot) is used.

	Week					
	0	*1*	*2*	*3*	*4*	*5*
Gross requirements		80	80	90	90	90
Scheduled receipts						
Projected stock balance	190	270	190	100	10	80

What fixed order quantity is used? When is a scheduled receipt due in? In what period is there a planned order release?

7. A partial master production schedule and material requirements plans for a bicycle manufacturer are shown in the accompanying figure.
   a. Complete the calculations of gross requirements, projected stock balances, and planned order releases for handlebars and cut tubes.
   b. Recalculate the planned order release for cut tubing given a scrap allowance of 3 percent.

0-level

Master schedule — 26-inch bicycles

	Weeks							
	1	2	3	4	5	6	7	8
	40	0	50	0	0	60	0	60

First-level MRP

Handlebars — 1 per bicycle

LT = 4, Q = 100

Gross requirements		40	0	50	0	0	60	0	60
Scheduled receipts				100					
Projected stock balance	80								
Planned order release									

From first-level MRP — 24-inch bike
From first-level MRP — 27-inch bike

Second-level MRP

Cut tubes

¼ tube per handlebar

LT = 5, Q = 200

Gross requirements		50						120	
Scheduled receipts									
Projected stock balance	190								
Planned order release									

8. Six companies produce and sell irrigation equipment in the same region of the country. Company A has a reorder point system. Company B uses MRP, but only to launch orders. Company C has full closed-loop MRP. Company D uses MRP plus distribution requirements planning. Company E has an MRPII system (including DRP). Company F produces orders as they are booked, with each assembly triggering pull signals back through all processes and small kanban quantities of all parts kept on the plant floor. Discuss each company's likely competitive strengths and weaknesses.

9. Acme Wood Products Corporation makes wooden picture frames. The 10-by-12-inch size is made with three finishes: oak stained, walnut stained, and mahogany stained. The parts needed for final assembly and finishing for each frame are two 10-inch and two 12-inch wood pieces and four corner brackets. Inventory planning is by MRP. Lot sizes are 10,000 for wood parts and 5,000 for brackets.

   a. Construct the BOM structure. You need not limit yourself to the given data.

   b. What should go into the item master file? Be as specific as possible given the above data, but you need not limit yourself to these data.

   c. Assume that for every oak-stained frame, two walnut-stained and three mahogany-stained frames are made. Also assume that gross requirements for 10-inch wood pieces in the next five weeks are 0, 600, 0, 240, and 300. Compute all parent-item gross requirements based on these gross requirements for the wood pieces (work backward).

   d. Based on the gross requirements information from (c), compute the planned-order-release schedule for 10-inch wood pieces only. Assume a current on-hand balance of zero and a lead time of one week.

10. The following sketch shows the two main parts of a transparent-tape dispenser: molded plastic housing and roll of tape. A master production schedule for the dispenser is shown below the sketch.

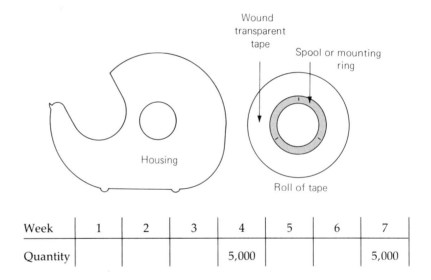

Week	1	2	3	4	5	6	7
Quantity				5,000			5,000

   a. Draw a structured bill of materials for the tape dispenser. Include the main parts and one level of parts below that.

   b. Assume that lead times are one week for the roll of tape and two weeks for the spool (mounting ring). Beginning on-hand balances are 0 for the roll of tape and 3,000 for the spool. Draw the MPS, with MRPs for the roll of tape and the spool below it. (Do not include housing and wound transparent tape.) Compute gross requirements, scheduled receipts (if any), on-hand balances, and planned order releases for the roll of tape and the spool. Use lot-for-lot order quantities (not fixed order quantities). Show your results in the usual MRP display format.

   c. Explain your entries or lack of entries in the scheduled-receipts row for both the roll of tape and the spool.

     d. Assume that the rolls of tape are sold separately as well as being a component of the tape dispenser. Make up a forecast of independent (external) demand for rolls of tape for each of the seven time buckets. Merge your forecast of independent demand with the dependent demand from the parent item. Also, assume an on-hand balance of 2,000 for the roll of tape and a scheduled receipt of 4,000 in week 2 for the spool. Recompute the MRPs as in (*b*.) What could explain the quantity 4,000 as a scheduled receipt in week 2?

11. Assume you are employed by a company that makes a type of simple chair (you decide on the chair's design). MRP is to be the method of inventory planning for the chair.
     a. Draw a bill-of-materials structure for the chair. Briefly explain or sketch the type of chair.
     b. Develop an 8- to 10-week MPS for the chair.
     c. Develop MRPs for three or four of the chair's components, with the following restrictions:
          (1) Include level 1 and level 2 components (e.g., a chair arm might be level 1 and the raw material for making it level 2).
          (2) Make your own assumptions about lead times, order quantities, and beginning inventories.
     Your answer should be realistic; no two students should have the same answer.

12. Repeat problem 11 using a ball-point pen as your product.

13. Select a product composed of fabricated parts (not one referred to in the text explanation of MRP or in preceding MRP problems). In one page, develop an MPS for the product, plus a level 1 MRP for a major module and a level 2 MRP for a part that goes into the level 1 module.
     a. Develop an 8- to 10-week planning period.
     b. Draw the MPS at the top of your page, with time buckets for the two levels of parts MRPs lined up below it. The material requirements plans for the parts should include four rows: one for gross requirements, one for scheduled receipts, one for projected stock balance, and one for planned order releases. Make up the following data: realistic quantities for the MPS; beginning on-hand balances, lead times, and order quantities for each part (make one order quantity fixed and the other lot-for-lot); and one or more scheduled receipts based on a previous, already released order (be careful about the timing and quantity of scheduled receipts).
     c. For level 1 and level 2 parts, calculate the timing and quantities of gross requirements, scheduled receipts, on-hand balance, and planned order releases. Display results on your charts, and:
          (1) Include a safety stock for one of the parts.
          (2) Include a scrap allowance for one of the parts.
          (3) Include demands from an external source (rather than from parent planned order releases) for one of the parts.

14. Following are bills of materials for two sizes of kitchen knife. Two parts are common to both knives: rivets and 8-foot wood bars. Also, a 6-inch cut wood block is common to two different parents (handle, left, and handle, right) for the medium-size knife. Presently there are no parts of any kind on hand or on order. Order quantities are lot-for-lot rather than fixed. The master schedule for the next seven weeks is as follows:

	Week						
	1	*2*	*3*	*4*	*5*	*6*	*7*
Small knife	0	0	0	0	1,200	0	960
Medium-size knife	0	0	0	800	0	1,200	400

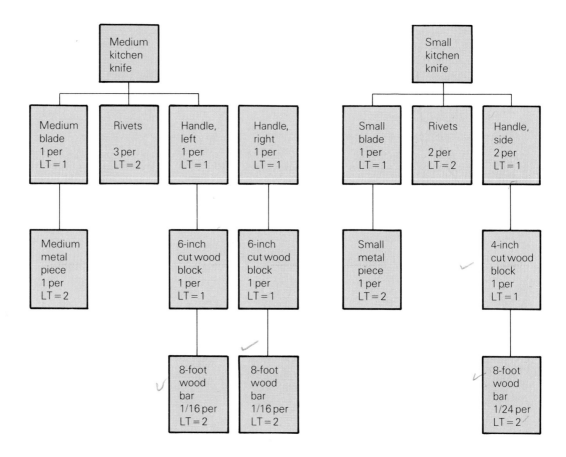

   a. What is the first planned order release for rivets? Calculate quantity and week.

   b. What is the total number of 4-inch cut wood blocks that should be ordered to cover MPS demand in weeks 1 through 5?

   c. How many 8-foot wood bars should be ordered in week 3?

15. The following table shows partial MRP data for one component part. Lead time is two weeks.

		Week				
	0	*1*	*2*	*3*	*4*	*5*
Gross requirements		80	0	80	90	90
Scheduled receipts				70		
Projected stock balance	90					

   a. If the order quantity is lot-for-lot (just enough to meet requirements), when should there be a planned order release?

   b. If a scrap allowance of 10 percent is included in planned order releases, what should the planned-order-release quantity be?

16. Following is a list of inventory items that might be found in various locations in a hospital. For each item, pick what you feel are the two factors that should most influence safety stock for the item. Also, state whether the item should have a high, medium, or low safety stock as measured in weeks' supply. Explain.

Toothpicks.	Pillows
Disposable hypodermic syringes.	Rare blood.
X-ray film.	Aspirin.
Coffee cups (pottery).	Soap solution for mopping floors.
Daily newspapers (for sale).	Prosthetic devices (artificial limbs).

17. A beer distributor reorders when a stock item drops to a reorder point. Reorder points include statistical safety stocks with the service level set at 95 percent. For PBR beer, the forecast usage for the next two weeks is 500 cases and the standard deviation of demand has been 137 cases (for a two-week period). Purchase lead time is one week (a five-day work week).
    a. What is the safety stock? How many working days' supply is it?
    b. What is the ROP?
    c. How many times larger would the safety stock have to be to provide 99 percent service to PBR customers? How many working days' supply does the 99 percent level provide?
    d. Statistical safety stock protects against demand variability. What other two factors do you think are especially important influences on size of safety stock for PBR beer? Explain.

18. Brown Instrument Company replenishes replacement (service) parts based on statistical reorder point. One part is a 40-mm thumbscrew. Relevant data for the thumbscrew are:

$$\text{Planned stockout frequency} = \text{Once per year}$$
$$\text{Planned lead time} = 1 \text{ week}$$
$$\text{Forecast for next week} = 30$$
$$\text{Batch size} = 300$$
$$\text{Standard deviation of demand} = 25 \text{ (per week)}$$

    a. What is the reorder point? (Hint: Convert planned stockout frequency to service level.)
    b. What would be the effect on ROP if lead time were four weeks instead of one? (Just discuss the effect; don't try to calculate it.)

19. An auto muffler shop reorders all common mufflers, and the like, every Tuesday morning. (Rarely needed mufflers are not stocked.) Two of the biggest-selling models are muffler A and muffler B. Each is ordered if stock is below 3, and enough are ordered to bring the supply up to 10; under this reordering system, the average inventory of each is about 8. It takes two days to replenish.

    A reorder-point policy with a service level of 90 percent is being considered as a replacement for the present policy. To see whether ROP would reduce costly inventories, the following data are provided:

	Muffler A	Muffler B
Item cost	$7	$39
Daily usage (average)	2	2
Standard deviation of daily usage	1.5	1.5

    a. What kind of reorder policy is the present one? Are there names for it?
    b. What safety stocks and ROPs would there be for mufflers A and B under a perpetual system?
    c. Should the muffler shop go to a perpetual system? Stay with the present system? Devise a hybrid system? Discuss, including pros and cons.

20. One storeroom item has an average demand of 1,200 per year. Demand variability, as measured by standard deviation, is 25 (based on monthly calculations).
    a. If the desired service level is 90 percent and the lead time is 2.5 months, what is the statistical safety stock?
    b. The item is bulky, costs over $1,000 per unit, and is bought from a variety of suppliers. What effects should these factors have on the safety stock? Explain.

21. Star City Tool and Die has been using a certain 2-inch square metal insert at an average rate of 200 per five-day week with a standard deviation of 125. Star City makes the inserts itself on its punch press. Only one day is needed to make more of them.
    a. The insert is so critical that management wants the item to be available (in stock) 99.9 percent of the time. What is the statistical safety stock? What is the statistical reorder point?
    b. The insert has been required for only the past six weeks and is inexpensive to make. Should these factors affect safety stock and reorder point? Explain.

22. Fuel oil is one source of heat in a northern university. Average fuel demand in winter is 6,000 gallons per month. The reorder point is 6,400 gallons, the average lead time is two weeks, and the order quantity is 8,000 gallons.
    a. How many orders are there in an average five-month winter season?
    b. What is the demand during lead time? What is the safety stock?
    c. Draw a graph showing three replenishment cycles for the fuel oil. Construct the graph so that:
       (1) In the first cycle, delivery takes more than two weeks (with normal demand during lead time).
       (2) In the second cycle, delivery takes less than two weeks (with normal demand during lead time).
       (3) In the third cycle, lead time is average but demand during the lead-time period is low. Note: Since fuel-oil usage for heating is continuous rather than discrete, your line showing actual usage should waver downward rather than follow a downward stairstep pattern.

23. One of the products manufactured by a maker of hand tools is pliers. There are four parts, shown in the accompanying illustration. The status of each part at a given point is shown below the sketch; reference data are also given.

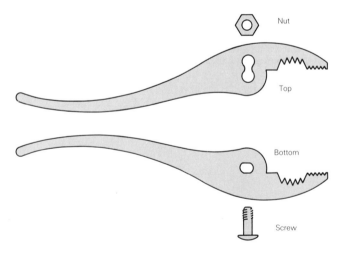

Item	Inventory Status	ROP	Q	LT
Nut	8,000 on hand, none on order	4,000	10,000	10 days
Top	2,200 on hand, none on order	2,000	5,000	10 days
Bottom	3,800 on hand, none on order	2,000	5,000	10 days
Screw	1,700 on hand, 10,000 ordered two days ago	4,000	10,000	5 days
Pliers	2,700 on hand, none on order	3,000	3,000	5 days

For the given data, the following partial table lists required ordering actions and resulting inventory status. Complete the table (determine the correct ordering actions and inventory statuses for the blank cells).

Item	Ordering Actions	Inventory Status
Pliers	Shop order for 3,000 to replenish low (below ROP) stocks.	2,700 in stock
Nut	Release 3,000 from warehouse for pliers shop order.	3,000 on order
Top		
Bottom		
Screw		

CASE STUDY

HYGAIN-TELEX

The HyGain-Telex plant in Lincoln, Nebraska, manufactures antennas. It currently has a U.S. Army contract for Model X32 antennas. The contract requires a production rate of 200 Model X32s per day. The contract quantity may be changed quarterly.

Chris Piper, the foreman, is collecting data for a JIT project. Piper has selected the X32 antenna base (not the whip part of the antenna, which is fairly simple) for the JIT project. Exhibit S9–1 is a photograph of the base.

Manufacture of the X32

The X32 base, a cylinder 6 inches in diameter and 10 inches high, goes through several stages of manufacture. Piper's data collection involved the following basic production processes and standard times:

Mold the Lexan plastic base: Some holes are molded into the base by use of core plugs; 2.50 minutes.

Drill and tap (eight operations): Seven drill or tap operations, taking from 0.12 to 1.02 minutes; install helicoils, 1.82 minutes. (The eight operations include drilling a dozen more holes; half of the drilled and molded-in holes are tapped, and half are installed with helicoils, which are self-threaded inserts, a rather old technology.)

Assemble (epoxy) a "birdcage" (ferrite core, coaxial cable, etc.) inside the Lexan base: 1.78 minutes. (Note: The birdcage is produced as a subassembly, going through 12 operations.)

Case topics:

Lead-time-to-work-content ratio.   Statistical process control.
Pieces-to-workstations ratio.   Total preventive maintenance.
Distinction between preventive   Simplifying the schedule.
  maintenance and setup.   Partnership with customer.
Frequency of delivery.   Cellular manufacturing.
Kanban.

SOURCE: Adapted from the *World Class Manufacturing Casebook: Implementing JIT and TQC*. Copyright © 1987 by Richard J. Schonberger. Reproduced by permission of The Free Press, a Division of Macmillan, Inc. The characters and some of the data in this case study are fictitious, but much of the process data are based on a real product at HyGain-Telex.

EXHIBIT S9–1   **Base for X32 Antenna**

Foam the assembly: 2.61 minutes.

Paint: 1.82 minutes.

Flow Data

Piper thought that the place to start was between drill-and-tap and assembly. Drill-and-tap ran one shift, and assembly usually ran two shifts. Piper asked L. G. Smith, the industrial engineer, to find out the flow distance between processes, especially those two processes. Smith scaled off the distances on the factory blueprints and came up with a total flow distance of 1,296 feet, which breaks down as follows: from mold to drill-and-tap, 192 feet; from drill-and-tap to tank assembly, 144 feet; from assembly to paint, 480 feet; and from paint to final prep, 480 feet.

Piper wanted to be sure. "Are those prints current?" he asked. Smith assured him that they were. Just to make sure, Piper got a tape measure and checked some of the distances; they were indeed correct.

For flow-time data, Piper went to Raul Nieves, the scheduler. Nieves pointed out that the flow time from molding to final prep had been "as short as about five days for a few lots, but we are quoting six weeks to marketing." Piper asked Nieves to come up with some sort of average. Nieves did so by putting pieces of colored tape on a few molded bases from several lots over the space of three weeks. The average flow time, found by noting how long it took for the taped units to get to final prep, was seven weeks. One week of that was the flow time from the start of drill-and-tap to assembly (see Exhibit S9–2 for summary data).

Question 1. What is the ratio of actual production lead time (or flow time) to work content time from the start of drill-and-tap to final prep? (Note: You will not need to be concerned with the issue of one or two shifts.)

Nieves also provided Piper with scheduling and unit-load data. Scheduling released work packets in lot quantities of 2,000. Drilled and tapped bases were forwarded to assembly by forklift

Exhibit S9–2   HyGain-Telex—Flowchart

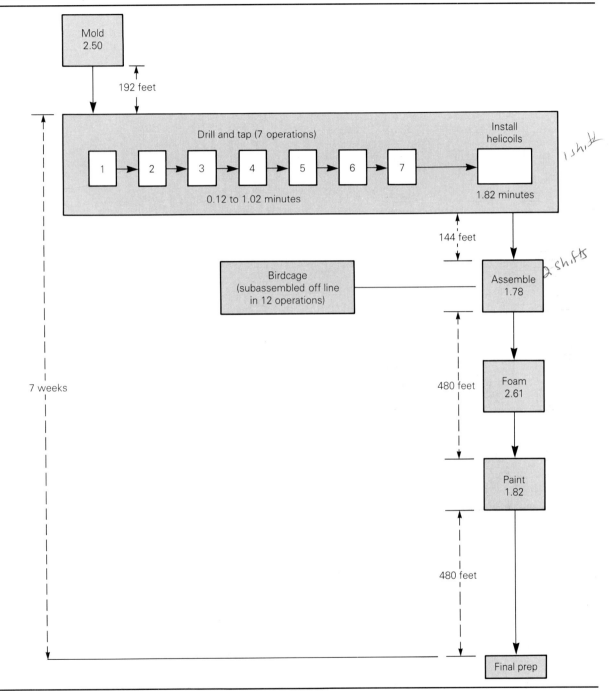

truck, in wire-bound pallets holding about 400 bases. In other words, about five forklift trips were required to move one packet-release quantity to assembly.

Problems

At this point Piper called a meeting. Smith and Nieves were there, along with Karen Jones, manager of quality assurance; Bob Crane, an inspector; Doug Atkins, a drill press operator; and Ellie Olson, an assembler. Piper announced that the purpose of the meeting was to "brainstorm what can and maybe can't be done to reduce WIP and flow time" between drill-and-tap and assembly. Piper explained that the purpose was to improve and not look for blame. In that spirit, "please speak frankly."

Piper's first question was directed to Atkins: "Doug, there's no setup time on the drill press that you use for the X32 — it's a dedicated tool, right?" Atkins said that it was.

"How about up time on the drill press? Is it reliable?" asked Piper. Atkins replied that the drill press itself was fine but that the tapping head with spindles in the taps was a problem sometimes: "They break, or the bushings loosen," which results in off-center taps or a marred surface around the outside. "Then I have to call maintenance to make adjustments or replace the head."

"About how many hours per month are you down waiting for them to make those adjustments or replacements, Doug?" Atkins estimated about five hours.

Ellie Olson was next. "Ellie, do you have any problems with the bases? Quality problems or running out of bases?" Ellie said that sometimes she did have to wait for the fork truck to bring another wire-bound; she estimated six hours of wait time per month.

The quality problems were the biggest headache, Olson felt, and she looked at Bob Crane, the inspector, for corroboration. Crane agreed that the defect rates were high, especially cracks and fractures around the helicoil inserts. Some, "maybe 5 percent," they thought, were minor defects that Crane or Olson let pass. Crane had figures on how many were defective but repairable and defective-scrapped: 2 percent repaired, 4 percent scrapped.

Karen Jones, quality manager, pointed out that their customer, the Army, had been rejecting an average of 7 percent in recent months. "I believe that the majority of the problems can be traced back to drill-and-tap," she stated.

Piper then asked if anyone knew how many bases were in work-in-process.

Nieves said he had just made a rough count; there were six wirebounds full at drill-and-tap and eight and a half full at assembly.

Question 2. If 15 direct-labor employees are involved in the production of the Lexan base, what is the ratio of pieces in process to people who could work on them?

JIT Opportunities

At this point, the group began brainstorming on JIT opportunities. Here are some of the options they discussed:

1. Setup reduction (adjust and replace spindles/bushings) on the drill presses. To this suggestion, everyone nodded their heads, but no one commented pro or con.
2. Cut transit quantities. Nieves (scheduler) protested: "The fork truck drivers would be making more trips." (conveyor belt or)
3. Adopt kanban. Nieves liked the idea.
4. Use process control charts in drill-and-tap. Everyone thought it was about time to do some of this.
5. Adopt total preventive maintenance. This was Piper's (the foreman's) idea. The others showed little reaction; they seemed not to know what that meant.
6. Put in conveyors. Smith (the industrial engineer) offered that one; nobody challenged the idea.
7. Slash the buffer stock. Nieves suggested this, pointing out that inventory counting was a headache anyway. Olson was indignant: "I run out of bases too often as it is."

8. Get rid of the packet-release quantities. Smith suggested this but admitted that he did not know what kind of scheduling might replace the packet-release system.

9. Bring the design engineers in to come up with a better design of the base. Everyone smiled and nodded vigorously.

10. Expand the size of the task force (which they were calling themselves by that time), including a customer (Army) representative. This was Jones's suggestion, which was met by a couple of favorable nods.

11. Move a drill press into the assembly department. This was Smith's idea. Crane (inspector) said that "if we do that I won't have to inspect the bases—and I'm not complaining; it's a boring job."

The meeting broke up with plenty of ideas but no decisions.

Question 3. What should be done? Should all the ideas be implemented? None of them? A different set? What order? To what extent? What time period? What guidance and direction? Discuss each of the eleven options that came out in the brainstorming session.

10 LOT SIZING AND QUICK-CHANGE FLEXIBILITY

JIT processing of dishes at a restaurant would go like this: Clear a plate after patron finishes, take it away to wash and dry, and carry it back for placement on another table. Do the same, in turn, for each plate, fork, cup, and so on. Just-in-time it may be, and lean-and-mean (minimal investment in dishes), but efficient it is not.

Good management requires handling dishes in lots, whether busing and cleaning them or setting tables. Serve customers as quickly as possible (pure just-in-time) but save up dishes for processing in non-JIT lots of some size. But what is the correct size?

In this chapter, we consider various **lot sizing** models for part of the answer. Another part lies in the second principle of operations management: continual improvement. One avenue is refined determination of the lot size itself. A related avenue is quick changeover flexibility, which makes smaller lots economical. Since quick-change flexibility is a basic goal of operations management (regardless of the lot-size issue), we consider it first.

PRINCIPLES 2 AND 12:

Continual improvement in lead time and flexibility. Cut changeover and start-up times.

Quick-Change Flexibility

How long does it take an Indy 500 pit crew to change four tires, fill the tank, clean the windshield, and squirt Gatorade into the driver's mouth? Fifteen seconds? Less? Regardless of how long, the workings of an efficient pit crew capture many concepts of quick-change teamwork and readiness. Those concepts can be expressed as guidelines for action.

Although some businesses are famous for their quick changeover expertise (e.g., stage crews and airline caterers), others, including most members of the manufacturing sector, have only recently given it attention. But elevated competition in many businesses demands quicker, error-free service and enhancing the firm's ability to continually reduce changeover and get-ready times. The training materials that address these concerns are based on a few guidelines (see Exhibit 10–1), which we discuss next.

Changeover Avoidance.   Guideline one is the special case of a single service, product model, or type of customer that gets its own dedicated process. If, say, three quarters of McDonald's customers wanted a Big Mac and a medium Coke, the restaurant would set up a dedicated Mac-and-a-Coke line, with no flexibility or changeovers to worry about. All companies would love to have products that popular. The simplicity, low cost, and uniformly high quality of this mode of processing yields high profits and large numbers of loyal customers.

Be-Ready Improvements.   The next three guidelines provide natural, low-cost improvement projects for teams of associates.

Guideline two is doing all possible setup steps while the process is engaged on its previous product model, type of customer, or service. That minimizes the time the process is stopped and unproductive. Alternatively stated: Convert internal setup time (while the process is stopped) to external steps (done offline, while the process is running a prior job). At a laundromat, for example, have your next load sorted and the detergent and other additives measured out before the machine stops.

Exhibit 10–2A shows detailed analysis of setup steps on a packing machine at Microsoft, Dublin, Ireland. The analysis includes separate columns for steps to be done while the machine is stopped versus those to be done beforehand. Packaging machine changeovers are frequent because this plant duplicates and packages diskettes just in time for many Microsoft products in many different languages for the European market.

Guideline three (an extension of two) provides the discipline of "A place for everything, and everything in its place." Have you had to wait to sign something while a clerk looks for a 49 cent pen? Or has one but it won't write? By contrast, an Indy pit crew is ready with gasoline hoses, tire-changing devices, and tires correctly positioned and in tip-top shape. Surgical teams in operating rooms adopt the same kinds of readiness habits and discipline.

Guidelines

A milestone achievement for a quick-changeover team is one-touch setup, meaning virtually no setup time; next best is single-digit setup (less than 10 minutes).

Experience shows that the be-ready improvements can often cut changeover times by 50 percent or more.

Setup or **changeover:** Timed from end of previous productive output to the start of the next, including all checks for quality and adjustments to get it right.

EXHIBIT 10–1   Quick Changeover, Set-up, and Readiness Guidelines

Changeover avoidance:
1. A dedicated, single-purpose process.

Be-ready improvements—developed by teams of associates:
2. External (offline) steps performed while process is active.
3. Setup implements close, clean, in top condition, and ready.
4. For costly equipment, trained crew and clockwork precision.

Modifications—technical assistance on improvement team:
5. Eliminate/immobilize unneeded devices and adjusters.
6. Add positioners and locators.
7. Simplify/standardize equipment, fixtures, fasteners, and accessories.
8. Employ externally loadable magazines and work-element holders.

EXHIBIT 10–2   Changeover Analysis and Shadow Board at Microsoft-Ireland

A. Setup steps.

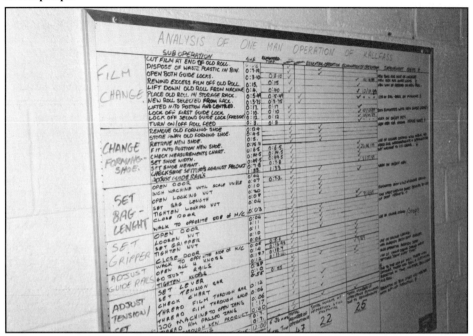

B. Shadow board.

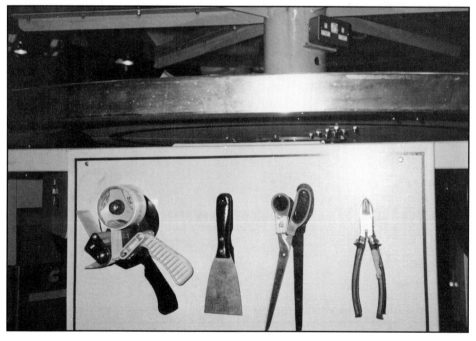

In factories, readiness may include hanging precleaned and sharpened hand tools on "shadow boards" at the work place: no fumbling through a drawer or tool box, or walking to a tool room. Exhibit 10–2B shows a shadow board holding four simple tools used by teams assembling instruction manuals at Microsoft's plant in Dublin, Ireland.

Where equipment is expensive—a race car, a surgical room, or a massive press line that stamps out automobile body parts—a sizable, well-trained changeover crew is justified. Guideline four is deftly applied, for example, in well-managed conference centers: dozens of people assemble the minute a conference ends, and quickly and acting in parallel, they dismantle the speaker's platform, remove water pitchers and other table-top items, fold and stack tables and chairs, clean the area, and set up for an evening banquet or wedding party.

> In some firms, operators rig pegboards on which to hang tools. A shadow board, with silhouettes of tools painted on, provides better visibility.

Too often the opposite occurs in factories of well-known companies, such as a $5 million packaging line for a headache remedy halted for four hours while one or two maintenance technicians make hundreds of adjustments, one-by-one (serially), for the next package size or type of tablet. The JIT movement has caused many manufacturers to change their human resource practices so that such expensive equipment can be set up more efficiently, more like an auto-race pit crew or a conference center setup crew. In some manufacturing companies, for example, labor and management have agreed to have teams of operators, trained by maintenance technicians, do their own changovers.

> *P*RINCIPLE 7:
>
> Develop human resources through cross-training.

Modifications. Guidelines five through eight generally require that the improvement team call on an expert for technical assistance. Since the modifications may be costly, these guidelines would usually take affect after the be-ready guidelines (two through four).

Guideline five calls for eliminating or immobilizing devices and adjusters that come with the equipment, or that were once part of the process but are no longer needed. For example, an overhead projector has a focus knob, but if the projector stays in the same classroom anchored to a table facing the same screen year after year, the focus adjustment unit is an invitation for unnecessary, nonvalue-adding tampering and variable image quality. In one company, a conference room user had wound strapping tape around the adjustment knob at the right focus setting so that other users could skip the adjustment step.

> Experience shows that following be-ready and modification guidelines can often cut total changeover time by 80 or 90 percent.

Why not just order the projector with a fixed focal length to suit the room layout? Because it would be a costly special order, and the manufacturer would have to charge a higher price. Equipment designers usually include many adjustment features, which broadens appeal, increases demand, produces economies of scale, and lowers the price. After the sale, however, teams of users should work on removing or immobilizing unneeded adjustment devices.

Guideline six is the opposite of five: adding special features not provided by the equipment manufacturer. For example, to make recycling easier, a team might come up with a plan to equip all the firm's pop machines with a bin that receives, crushes, and holds empty cans.

In manufacturing, setup teams frequently devise locator pins, stops, air-cushion glides, and guide paths that make it easier to change a mold or a die. Exhibit 10–3 shows huge "sleds" on rails, used for quickly and accurately moving multi-ton dies in and out of stamping presses.

Guideline seven calls for simplified, standardized designs. Too many brands of computers, typewriters, and drill presses (each a bargain price) expand exponentially the array of supporting tools, loaders, carriers, adjustment devices, and sets of instructions needed for setup and changeover. Standardization also applies to accessories; for example, if all

---

Exhibit 10–3   Quick Die Change Equipment, GM Stamping Plant

Die-handling sleds on rails are among the quick-die-change innovations on this six-press tandem stamping line, for auto body parts, at this General Motors stamping plant in Pittsburgh. This plant was the winner in a nationwide competition, called the Die Change Challenge, clocking a single-digit die change at 9 minutes 41 seconds (compared with an average 23 hours at the same plant a few years earlier). The resulting plant flexibility was a key factor in a corporate decision to remove the Pittsburgh facility from GM's plant closure list.

SOURCE: "Industry News," *Manufacturing Engineering,* July 1992, p. 24.

Exhibit 10–4   Washer, Bolt Hole, and Threads Simplified for Quick Installation

---

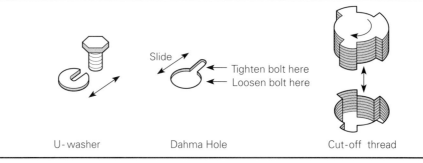

U-washer   Dahma Hole   Cut-off thread

SOURCE: Adapted from Kiyoshi Suzaki, *The New Manufacturing Challenge: Techniques for Continuous Improvement* (New York: Free Press, 1987), p. 38.

fastening bolts on a machine are the same size, only one size of wrench is needed in machine changeover.

The other part of this guideline is simplification, which should take place before standardization. Exhibit 10–4 shows three examples of how an accessory might be altered so that its use in a changeover takes much less time:

- A U-shaped washer can be slid against a bolt; no need to remove a nut first.
- Pear-shaped bolt holes allow the head of the bolt to slip through the large hole, then slide into the narrow slot for tightening.
- A bolt with cutaway threads may be inserted all the way down into a hole with similarly cutaway threads; then, just a quarter turn of a wrench fastens the bolt tightly.

Quick-change teams worldwide have been trained to make use of these kinds of simplified devices.[1]

Guideline eight specifies having extra holders for the work elements, such as component parts, tools, or paper feedstock. Think of a fondue party where each person loads a backup fondue fork while having another already loaded fork in the hot oil.

The eight guidelines assist project teams organized specifically to improve readiness and cut changeover times. In practice, by cutting setup time, the project team usually also improves process consistency, quality, safety, maintenance, ease of operation, housekeeping, and other factors for the target process. Similarly, a team organized to reduce process variation will often also cut setup time. In other words, many of the goals of continuous improvement and competitiveness overlap and are largely inseparable.

Quick Changeover Projects

This inseparability can be bothersome to veteran managers and technicians, who are used to seeing the work subdivided into many specialties and allocated to specialty departments. However, as we have reiterated throughout this text, superior companies have discovered the power of continual improvement led by teams of front-line employees, who call on experts only as needed and usually after several rounds of low-cost improvements have already been implemented.

$\mathscr{P}$RINCIPLE 15:

Improvement led by front-line teams.

$\mathscr{C}$ontrast

Setup/Changeover/Readiness Projects

No Viewpoint	**Specialist Viewpoint**	**Broadened Viewpoint**
Setups not viewed strategically.	Improve only at bottlenecks.	Improve at all processes.
Process set up by outside experts.	Improvement talent & funds scarce, so focus on bottlenecks.	Improvement talent includes every associate; most improvements are low cost.
Once setup procedure is established and (sometimes) timed, it is fixed (no improvement).	Work speeding through setup at a non-bottleneck will just stall later at a bottleneck.	Can't divorce from other process improvements going on.
		Each cut in setup time frees some labor and reduces startup problems.
		This year's slack process is next year's—or next week's—bottleneck.

---

[1]A basic reference for manufacturing processes is Shigeo Shingo, *A Revolution in Manufacturing: The SMED [Single-Minute Exchange of Die] System* (Cambridge, Mass.: Productivity Press, 1985).

In organizations yet to reach this stage of all-employee involvement, responsibility for improvement projects may be housed in the specialty departments. Or front-line improvement teams are dominated by supervisors, managers, or outside experts. In such cases problem-solving talent is viewed as a scarce resource that should be directed toward highest priority projects, such as setup/changeover improvement at bottleneck processes. Some advisors maintain, as well, that quick setup on a nonbottleneck process will speed the work through that process only to be idled at a bottleneck. While that can be true in the short run, it is not a good reason for making quick setup a low priority for improvement-minded teams in non-bottleneck work centers.

Add a second, low-cost machine at a bottleneck process (or use subcontracting) to eliminate the bottleneck.

Also, situations change. Today's nonbottleneck process is likely to become a bottleneck before long. Bottlenecks change with changes in markets, suppliers, products, and processes, and that rate of change accelerates when continuous improvement is taking place throughout the organization.

In inventory-intensive operations, the focus on quick setup is closely related to the goals of cutting lot sizes and throughput times, which we address in the remainder of the chapter.

Lot Sizing: Fundamentals

Common sense is plentiful at Poge, Poge, Perry, and Wacker. In the mail room, Arvin follows the commonsense practice of accumulating two hours' worth of incoming mail and faxes (interdepartmental as well as external) before delivering them to the departments. In accounts receivable, Cheryl generally spends mornings on problem accounts, then completes her work on new invoices and forwards them to another desk in the afternoon. Every other desk in every other office follows similarly sensible practices: accumulating a reasonable pile of similar items to work on before attacking the pile, and accumulating a reasonable load before forwarding it to its next stop.

The Poge employees are missing the consequences of their so-called reasonableness. Important letters and faxes arriving in the early afternoon may not reach the addressee until late in the day or the next morning, and then they may end up in a high in-basket pile. Moreover, invoices for completed work must pass from desk to desk and department to department before being mailed to clients who owe the firm money. New business also gets the same slow treatment, which undoubtedly sends some clients to the competition.

Process lot:
Lot undergoing a value-adding transformation.

Transfer lot:
Lot being transferred (moved) to the next value-adding transformation.

These inefficient business practices are common in firms such as law offices, banks, insurance companies, government agencies, hospitals, and manufacturing companies. The necessary remedy is to cut the process lot sizes and transfer lot sizes.

In discussing this topic, we consider a basic approach and a lot-sizing model, including lot-sizing economics and model variants. Then we return to the theme of continual improvement (reduce lot size toward the ideal of one), along with the new economics. We begin with the basic lot-for-lot approach.

Lot-for-Lot Processing

Lot-for-lot works well in the parent-component dependency chains of MRP—and can also be the lot-sizing policy in a JIT situation.

Lot-for-lot calls for the parent lot size to be the lot size for components. Lot-for-lot may be passed down through several stages of supply: "The customer bought four premium tires, so we pulled four from stores, and they ordered four from our distributor, who ordered four from the manufacturer." With no batching into larger lots, orders are frequent, which might cause order-processing costs to be high, but inventories are low, and supplier activities closely match real demand. We see the synchronizing and smoothing effects of lot-for-lot, as compared with batching, for two sizes of canned food items, apple juice and apple sauce, and two layers of components going into those end products.

Into Practice

When Large Lots Are *Required*

Firms such as drug and medical-device manufacturers are required by government regulations to conduct lot-acceptance sampling inspections. This involves testing a statistical sample drawn at random from a large lot. According to statistical sampling tables, as lot size increases, the percent sampled from the lot gets smaller; therefore, larger lots save on inspection costs. Thus, inspection department managers are motivated to delay sampling until a large lot accumulates.

However, this practice can be frustrating to other managers striving for the just-in-time ideal of making and forwarding items in small lots at the customer's use rate. Gradually, regulations and policies are being rewritten in favor of online process control, which is more effective in controlling quality than acceptance sampling, and more JIT-friendly.

Exhibit 10–5A shows a smooth demand pattern for the four products at the canning level. The smooth pattern is carried downward to apple processing and to apple picking. An obvious benefit is the uniform workload for apple pickers, apple processing associates and equipment, and apple canning line operators and equipment; capacity planning is simple, and capacity may be kept uniformly busy, with little or no overtime or idleness.

The buying of cans, labels, boxes, sugar, and other ingredients and supplies is also uniform. Scheduling and purchasing may be greatly simplified, perhaps to the point where schedules are simply a daily rate, with no need for separate orders and order follow-up for each lot. Queue limitation and kanban might be easily introduced. When even demand is passed back to outside suppliers, they can pass it back through some of their own operations, thus cutting their costs, which can mean price reductions to our apple company.

In Exhibit 10–5B we see a much different pattern. The canning is done in batches, which are fixed in quantity and in excess of daily demand. Maybe somebody has decreed, "Let's can on Monday, Wednesday, and Thursday, and try to save Tuesday and Friday for maintenance on the canning lines." But what may be good policy for canning certainly is not good for apple processing, which now has lumpy demands (150, 0, 0, 100, and 0 for cut and trim; 350, 0, 150, 200, 0 for core and peel).

Not to be outdone, processing also decides on fixed-batch lot sizes (200 and 400, respectively) that are larger than, and unsynchronized with, parent demands. Those lot sizes become an even lumpier demand pattern for the apple pickers (600 on Monday, none on Tuesday, 400 on Wednesday, 200 on Thursday, and none on Friday). If the pickers can find steadier work, they will surely leave.

This example makes a strong case for keeping lot sizes from growing, and for trying to maintain the synchronization inherent in the lot-for-lot approach. We'll keep the synchronization factor in mind as we consider the economic order quantity.

The **economic order quantity (EOQ)** is one of the oldest tools of management. EOQ concerns the inventory costs of a single item. Unlike lot-for-lot, which uses actual parent item demand, EOQ calculations use forecast demand, often based on past average demand. (Since reorder point, presented in Chapter 9, is also calculated based on past average demand, EOQ and ROP are sometimes treated as a knife-and-fork-like pair.)

Economic Order Quantity

F. W. Harris developed a basic EOQ formula in 1915.

EXHIBIT 10–5   Lot-for-Lot versus Batched Ordering

A. Lot-for-lot ordering

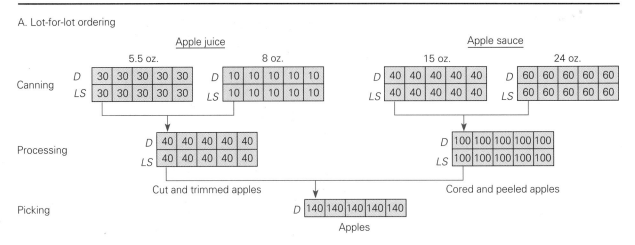

B. Batched orders

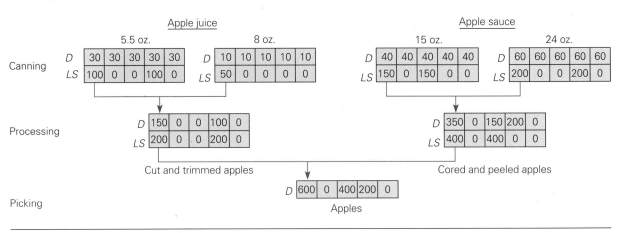

D = Demand   * All numbers in bushels or, for processing and canning, bushel-yields.
LS = Lot size

Like most models, the basic EOQ makes a few simplifying assumptions. While the real world never quite matches the assumptions, the matchup is sometimes close enough for the EOQ to be helpful. The assumptions are:

1. Demand is known and constant, without seasonality.

2. Order processing (or setup) costs are known and constant (do not vary with quantity ordered).

3. Cost per unit is constant (no quantity discounts).

4. The entire lot is delivered at one time, instantaneously. This is typical of purchased goods, but not of items produced by the user.

5. The carrying cost rate is known and constant. Total carrying costs are a linear function and depend on carrying cost rate and quantity ordered.

6. On average, one half of inventory is in stock.

Costs of Inventory.   The period inventory costs that EOQ seeks to minimize are of three types: order processing cost, carrying cost, and item cost.

   1. *Order processing cost.* In a given time period (say, a year) an item may be reordered once, twice, three times, or more, even daily in some JIT cases. If it is ordered once, the lot size is large enough to cover the whole year's demand; if ordered twice, a half-year's demand is the lot size; and so on.

   The costs of processing an order include the clerical costs of preparing the purchase order or work order. If it is a purchase order, costs of order expediting and processing the invoice are included; if it is a work order, the main cost may be process setup cost. Let S (for setup) be the average cost of processing an order, Q (for quantity) be the lot size, and D be the forecast annual demand for a given item. Then, for the item:

$$\frac{D}{Q} = \text{Number of orders per year}$$

$$S\left(\frac{D}{Q}\right) = \text{Annual cost of processing orders}$$

   Forecast demand (D) could cover a period other than a year. For example, if D represents monthly demand, $S(D/Q)$ equals the monthly cost of processing orders.

   2. *Carrying cost.* Carrying cost (discussed at length in Chapter 7) is the cost to finance inventory and hold it in idleness. Thus, carrying cost increases as number of idle units increases. If an item is reordered infrequently in large lots, its carrying costs will be large; if ordered often in small lots, its carrying costs will be small.

   Total carrying costs per period divided by value of all inventory items yields what is known as the annual inventory-carrying-cost rate (I). Cost analysts may set one rate for all items carried in a given firm. To compute annual carrying cost for a single item, we need the unit cost (C) for the item. Then:

$$IC = \text{Cost to carry one unit for one year}$$

   Let's take a look at some lot-sizing concepts that apply in the typical situation. (Less typical cases are treated later.) For any given lot size (Q), annual carrying cost equals annual cost to carry one unit times average number of idle units, ($Q/2$). Symbolically, for a given item we have:

$$IC\left(\frac{Q}{2}\right) = \text{Annual carrying cost}$$

   Why is the average inventory equal to $Q/2$? Exhibit 10–6 illustrates the repetition of EOQ order cycles during the year. Inventory increases from 0 to Q (the EOQ) on receipt of each order. Demands during the order cycle reduce inventory from Q to 0. The average amount of inventory, then, is simply the average of the maximum amount (Q), and the minimum amount (0), or $Q/2$. (The mathematically inclined might prefer to make the point with a geometrical proof that triangles I and II in Exhibit 10–6 are identical.)

   3. *Item cost.* The annual cost to make an item, or the total price paid for it, is treated as a constant in the basic EOQ model. We pay the same per item regardless of whether it is obtained in small or large lots. The annual item cost, then, is annual demand (D) times unit cost (C).

   4. *Total cost.* We may compute a total annual cost by summing the order processing costs, carrying costs, and item costs:

$$\text{Total cost} = TC = \left(\frac{D}{Q}\right)(S) + (IC)\left(\frac{Q}{2}\right) + DC \qquad (10\text{--}1)$$

EXHIBIT 10–6   EOQ Order Cycles over Time

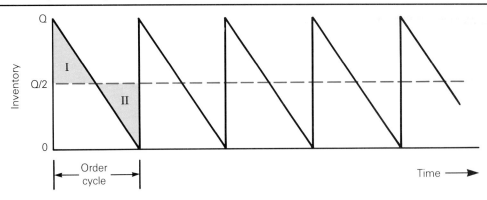

EXHIBIT 10–7   Graph of Annual Inventory Cost and Lot Sizes

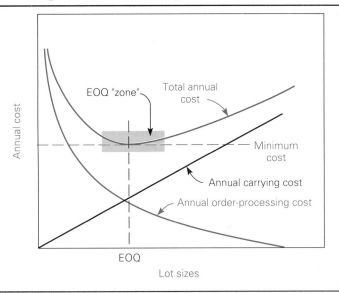

EOQ Calculations.   By using calculus (see chapter supplement), we can reduce Equation 10–1 to the classic EOQ formula:

$$Q = \sqrt{\frac{2DS}{IC}} \tag{10–2}$$

Exhibit 10–7 shows the EOQ as the minimum cost point on a total annual cost curve, as well as the point where annual carrying cost equals annual order-processing cost. (Annual cost of the item itself is not included in the graph since that cost does not vary with lot size.)

Note that the minimum cost is shown in a shaded zone. In that zone, which is fairly large horizontally, total annual cost does not deviate much from the minimum. Thus, in a practical sense EOQ may be thought of as a zone or range of lot sizes, not just the exact EOQ quantity.

Development of input data and use (and misuse) of the basic EOQ model are demonstrated for a small bookstore in Example 10–1.

EXAMPLE 10–1   ECONOMIC ORDER QUANTITY—BOOKSTORE

B. K. White, manager of Suburban Books, is thinking of purchasing best-selling titles in economic order quantities. White has assembled the following data:

Inventory on hand (books):	
Estimated average last year	8,000
Estimated average cost per book	$10
Average inventory value	$80,000
Annual holding cost:	
Rental: Building and fixtures	$7,000
Estimated shrinkage losses	700
Insurance	300
Total	$8,000
Annual capital cost:	
Capital invested (tied up in books)	$80,000
Interest rate	15%
Total	$12,000
Annual carrying cost (Annual holding cost + Annual capital cost):	
$8,000 + $12,000	$20,000
Carrying cost rate, I (Annual carrying cost ÷ Inventory value):	
$20,000/$80,000	0.25
Purchase order processing cost, S:	
Estimate for preparation and invoice handling	$4 per order

Now White has the cost data needed to calculate EOQs. He selects his biggest seller as the first book to be ordered by EOQ—*Gone with the Wind,* which is enjoying a burst of renewed popularity in the store. The paperback recently sold at a rate of 80 copies per month and wholesales for $5 per copy. Thus, for the EOQ equation:

$$C = \$5 \text{ per unit}$$
$$D = 80 \text{ units/month} \times 12 \text{ months/year}$$
$$= 960 \text{ units/year}$$

Then:

$$EOQ = \sqrt{\frac{2DS}{IC}} = \sqrt{\frac{2(960)(4)}{0.25(5)}} = 78 \text{ copies/order}$$

The EOQ, 78 copies, is about one month's supply (78 copies/order ÷ 80 copies/month = 0.98 months/order); it is also $390 worth ($5/copy × 78 copies/order = $390 per order).

White's assistant, M. B. Ainsworth, cannot resist pointing out to her boss a fallacy in this EOQ of 78 copies. She puts it this way: "Mr. White, I'm not so sure that *Gone with the Wind* is the right book to order by EOQ. The EOQ is based on last month's demand of 80. But demand might be 120 next month and 150 the month after. Also, the average carrying cost rate, I, was based mostly on larger hardcover books, which cost more to store. Maybe we should use EOQ only on our stable sellers in hardcover. How about Webster's *New Collegiate Dictionary?*"

Users may employ variations on the basic EOQ to offset some of the model's limiting assumptions. We consider two variations: EOQ with quantity discounts and the economic manufacturing quantity.

EOQ with Quantity Discounts

Sometimes the cost for purchased items varies stepwise via quantity discounts, or price breaks. Annual item cost then becomes a relevant cost along with annual carrying and order processing costs.

In the quantity-discount situation, the analyst may calculate an EOQ for each price, but the true economic order quantity is the amount that minimizes total annual cost, including item cost. A method for finding the true EOQ is:[2]

1. Calculate EOQs for each price. Reject any EOQ that is not within the allowable quantity range for the price used.
2. For feasible EOQs, calculate total annual cost.
3. Calculate total annual cost at each higher price break.
4. Pick the quantity having the lowest total annual cost. This is the true economic order quantity.

Example 10–2 employs the method by continuing the bookstore example.

EXAMPLE 10–2   EOQ with Quantity Discount—Bookstore

B. K. White, manager of Suburban Books, has applied basic EOQ to *Gone with the Wind*. But he didn't allow for quantity discounts. Popular Publications, Inc., offers the following price breaks for *GWTW:*

Quantity Range	Price per Copy
1–48	$5.00
49–96	4.70
97 and up	4.40

Other data, from Example 10–1, are:

$$I = 0.25$$
$$S = \$4 \text{ per order}$$
$$D = 960 \text{ units/year } (12 \times 80)$$

White's first step in finding the true economic order quantity is to calculate EOQs for each price:

$$EOQ_5 = \sqrt{\frac{2DS}{IC}} = \sqrt{\frac{2(960)(4)}{0.25(5)}} = 78$$

He rejects this EOQ since it is not within the quantity range (1 to 48) that applies at the $5.00 price.

$$EOQ_{4.70} = \sqrt{\frac{2(960)(4)}{0.25(4.70)}} = 81$$

This EOQ is within the allowable range, 49 to 96, for the $4.70 price, and therefore is feasible.

$$EOQ_{4.40} = \sqrt{\frac{2(960)(4)}{0.25(4.40)}} = 84$$

---

[2]This is not intended to be the most efficient algorithm; we leave that to the computer programmers.

He rejects this EOQ, which is outside the allowable quantity range (97 and up) for the $4.40 price.

Next, White computes total annual costs for the feasible EOQ, 81, and at the next higher price break, 97:

$$\text{Total annual cost} = \text{Annual order processing cost} +$$
$$\text{Annual carrying cost} + \text{Annual purchase price}$$
$$= \frac{D}{Q}(S) + IC\left(\frac{Q}{2}\right) + DC$$

$$\text{Total annual cost}_{81} = \frac{960}{81}(4) + 0.25(4.70)\left(\frac{81}{2}\right) + 960(4.70)$$
$$= 47.41 + 47.59 + 4,512 = \$4,607.00$$

$$\text{Total annual cost}_{97} = \frac{960}{97}(4) + 0.25(4.40)\left(\frac{97}{2}\right) + 960(4.40)$$
$$= 39.59 + 53.35 + 4,224 = \$4,316.94$$

The true economic order quantity is 97, since its total annual cost, $4,316.94, is less than the total of $4,607.00 for a quantity of 81.

The cost-volume pattern for *Gone with the Wind* has been clarified. Exhibit 10–8 is White's sketch of the cost-volume pattern. It shows that annual order-processing cost drops smoothly and is not affected by the quantity discounts. The annual carrying-cost line has two small bumps, one at each price break. The annual item cost plunges at each price break, and those effects are dominant in the makeup of total annual cost. The feasible EOQ of 81 at a unit price of $4.70 is not economical compared to the true economic order quantity of 97 at the $4.40 price break.

Basic EOQ is suitable for purchased items—an economic purchase quantity—in which the whole lot is usually delivered at one time. When an item is made instead of bought, the quantity ordered is available in trickles as it comes off the production line. This complicates figuring average inventory, on which annual carrying cost is based, and results in a modified EOQ formula. The modification may be called an **economic manufacturing quantity (EMQ)** formula.

Economic Manufacturing Quantity

EMQ formula also applies to the rare case in which a purchased lot is delivered in trickles, instead of all at once.

The EMQ formula calls for one new term, the production rate (P). P is measured in the same units as D (demand rate), typically in units per year. P must be greater than D in order for the demand to be covered. $P - D$ is the rate of inventory buildup; that is, producing at rate P and using at rate D. The difference equals the rate of increase in stock. (Some prefer to use weekly or monthly build-and-use rates, which work just as well in the EMQ model.)

In developing the model, let us consider a time unit T. If a lot is made in time T:

$$Inv_{max} = Q_{max} = \text{Rate} \times \text{Time} = (P - D)(T)$$

Since Q_{max} is maximum planned inventory and $Q_{max}/2$ is average inventory:

$$\text{Average inventory} = \frac{Q_{max}}{2} = \frac{(P - D)(T)}{2}$$

The extra term T may be eliminated by substitution. The time needed to produce a lot, Q, is:

$$T = \frac{\text{Quantity}}{\text{Rate}} = \frac{Q}{P}$$

By substitution:

$$\text{Average inventory} = \left(\frac{P - D}{2}\right)\left(\frac{Q}{P}\right) \text{ or } \left(\frac{P - D}{P}\right)\left(\frac{Q}{2}\right)$$

EXHIBIT 10–8   **Annual Cost Graph of Lot Sizes with Quantity Discounts**

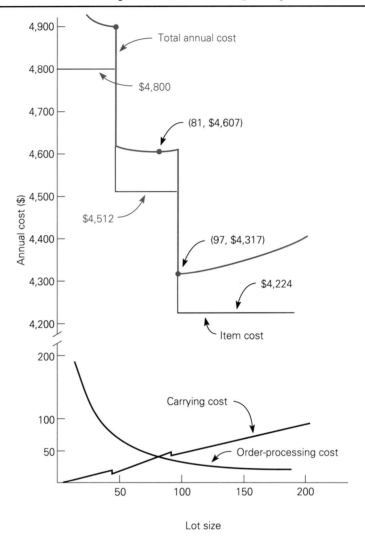

We can express the carrying costs as:

$$CC = (IC)\left(\frac{P - D}{P}\right)\left(\frac{Q}{2}\right)$$

Substituting into Equation 10–2, with the $(P - D)/P$ ratio included at the appropriate point:

$$\frac{DS}{Q^2} = \left(\frac{IC}{2}\right)\left(\frac{P - D}{P}\right)$$

$$Q^2 = \left(\frac{2DS}{IC}\right)\left(\frac{P}{P - D}\right)$$

$$Q = \sqrt{\frac{2DS}{IC}\left(\frac{P}{P - D}\right)}$$

EXHIBIT 10–9   **Basic EOQ and EMQ Replenishment Patterns**

A. Basic EOQ pattern of instantaneous replenishment

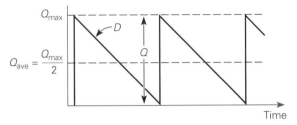

B. EMQ pattern of noninstantaneous replenishment

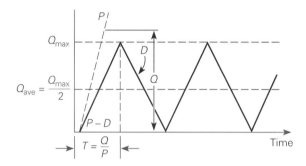

Alternatively:

$$\text{EMQ} = \sqrt{\frac{2DS}{(IC)(1 - D/P)}} \qquad (10\text{–}3)$$

Differences between basic EOQ and EMQ may be shown graphically. Exhibit 10–9A shows the general pattern of usage and replenishment for basic EOQ. It looks like a ripsaw blade. The vertical line represents the increase in stock that occurs when the whole EOQ is received at one time (instantaneous replenishment). The downward-sloping line is the average demand rate (D). Maximum quantity ($Q_{max.}$) is equal to Q, and average quantity ($Q_{ave.}$) is equal to $Q_{max.}/2$.

Exhibit 10–9B shows the general inventory pattern for EMQ. It looks like a cross-cut saw blade. The upward-sloping solid line represents the rate of inventory buildup ($P - D$); the production rate (P) is shown as a dashed line for reference purposes. The downward-sloping line is the average demand rate (D). Maximum inventory ($Q_{max.}$) is not equal to Q; the stock level never reaches Q because some of Q is being used up (delivered) as it is being produced. $Q_{max.}$ is, instead, equal to $(P - D)(T)$ or $(P - D)(Q/P)$, as was shown earlier, and $Q_{ave.}$ equals half of $Q_{max.}$.

Note that for otherwise equal conditions, EMQ is larger than basic EOQ. Inspection of the EMQ formula shows this to be mathematically obvious, because the factor $1 - D/P$ in the denominator makes the denominator smaller and the EMQ larger. The logical reason is that with EMQ there is less stock to carry since part of Q is used as it is produced; with less to carry, it is economical to produce a bit more per lot.

Preference for Simple Models

There are more elaborate lot-sizing algorithms than those just discussed. The problem with some of the models that look good on paper however, is that they require cost calculations for future periods, which means reaching into the future for a demand forecast. But we saw in Chapter 5 that forecasting accuracy drops the further into the future one projects.

Ready access to computers allows any of the lot-sizing models to be run dynamically; that is, lot sizes can be recomputed every time demand projections change. The effect, however, is unstable planned lot sizes. Ever-changing forecasting signals cause the entire inventory planning and control system to become nervous. Costs of replanning, rescheduling, and other shuffling of resources outweigh any apparent lot-sizing savings.

Thus, many feel that one lot-sizing method is as good as another. Historically, the simpler models, such as lot-for-lot and basic EOQ, have been preferred in business. The preference for simpler models continues today and probably will in the future, judging by the findings of a recent survey.[3] Researchers surveyed firms that provide MRP software to over 25,000 worldwide manufacturing locations. They found that lot-for-lot is the most commonly used lot-sizing technique, fixed-order-quantity is second, fixed-period-quantity is third, and EOQ fourth. The users' rationale for choosing the simple models includes (1) simplicity, (2) employee acceptance, (3) recognition that real-world conditions prevent any savings promised by more complicated optimization models, and (4) realization that lot-sizing is not nearly so important as taking steps to drive lot sizes down.

Lot-Sizing under Attack

Today, with just-in-time and total-quality-management zealots looking for waste under every rock, some rethinking about lot-sizing models is taking place. Instead of asking, What is the economic lot? the new question is, What must be changed to move toward piece-for-piece, or lotless, operations? As we consider that question, we must bear in mind that much of the business world still is not very JIT/TQM-minded, and therefore some of the fundamentals of lot-sizing continue to have a useful role.

We begin our discussion of the pursuit of lotless operations by contrasting a conventional lot-sizing issue and its modern counterpart; then we consider some of the benefits and methods of lot-size reduction. We conclude with graphs that illustrate changes in lot-sizing concepts.

Benefits of Smaller Lots

For many years, experts advised manufacturers, wholesalers, and retailers to employ economic order quantity models in lot sizing. That advice was widely heeded, especially by professional managers. EOQ models may have become (and still may be) the most used of all management science models.

However, many who once favored use of EOQ models now support the principle of driving lot sizes down continuously.[4] Benefits of smaller lots cut across departments and reach out to customers (and thus would not be apparent to an isolated inventory manager or model builder). They include:

1. Smaller lots get used up sooner; hence, defectives are caught earlier. This reduces scrap and rework and allows sources of problems to be quickly caught and corrected while the evidence of possible causes is still fresh.

---

[3]Jorge Haddock and Donald E. Hubricki, "Which Lot-Sizing Techniques Are Used in Material Requirements Planning?" *Production and Inventory Management,* Third Quarter 1989, pp. 53–56.

[4]Gene Woolsey, well known in the management science community for his colorful "reality check" writings, wrote an editorial attacking the EOQ model's unrealistic assumptions: "A Requiem for the EOQ: An Editorial," *Production and Inventory Management,* Third Quarter 1988, pp. 68–72.

*C*ontrast

Capturing Lot-Sizing Savings

Old Wisdom

Space

Storage space not easily converted, so smaller EOQ lots will capture capital-cost savings but not holding-cost savings.

Money

Business plan may limit investment in inventory, so if EOQ calls for larger lots, financial policy may not allow them.

Staff

People who process orders and set up processes may not be easily retrained/reassigned, so larger EOQ lots may fail to capture staff-reduction savings.

New Wisdom

Within a few months, space will be reemployed; until then, cordon it off and cease charging it as inventory-carrying cost.

Follow **Principle 13,** ever smaller lot sizes, which puts pressure on simplifying and cutting costs of processing orders (e.g., via kanban and setup time reduction).

Follow **Principle 7,** cross-training all associates; also, if ordering is reduced, or "order-less" processing employed, buyers/order processors have more time for process improvement; setup people have more time to attack setup times and help train operators to set up their own jobs.

2. With small lots, floor space to hold inventory can be cut and workstations can be positioned very close together. Then employees can see and talk to one another, learn one another's job (which improves staffing flexibility), and function as a team.

3. Small lots allow tasks to be closely linked in time. A problem at one workstation (or supplier firm) has a ripple effect; subsequent operations (or customer sites) are starved of inventory. Provider and user must treat the problem as a joint problem, and a team attack on such problems becomes natural and common.

4. Activity control is simplified, and costs of support staff, handling and storage devices, control systems, and so forth, are reduced.

5. Most important, customers are served more quickly and flexibly, which increases revenue and avoids the expenses of attracting new customers when present customers exit.

The benefits become more pronounced as lot size decreases. The limit? An ideal lot size of one. Two key steps in making small lots feasible are reduction of setup costs (discussed earlier) and order-processing costs (via kanban, rate-based scheduling, and supplier-customer partnerships).

This discussion of benefits of small lots supersedes a topic formerly common in OM studies: difficulties in capturing the benefits of economic order quantities. The old and new way of looking at lot-sizing benefits are contrasted in the contrast box.

$\mathscr{I}$nto $\mathscr{P}$ractice

Smaller Trains at Conrail

In a strategic shift, Conrail is putting fast freight movement, a requirement of its just-in-time customers, ahead of productivity. The key change is keeping trains shorter. "Although longer trains saved on crew and locomotive costs, they resulted in freight sitting in yards and missing connections."

SOURCE: Daniel Machalaba, "Highballing Along: New Conrail Resembles a Growth Company," *The Wall Street Journal*, November 20, 1992.

Transfer Lot Reduction

While process lot sizing has received plenty of attention, transfer lot sizing has not. But much of the rationale presented for process lot-size reduction (Principle 13 of operations management) also applies to transfer lots.

In Exhibit 10–5A, lot-for-lot is the policy for process lots. The transfer lots, however, can be larger or smaller than the process lots. For example, the process lot of 140 bushels per day in picking might be transferred to processing in sub-lot quantities of 20 bushels every two hours, assuming two 7-hour shifts.

Large tour groups are often handled in much the same way. If a group of 100 college freshmen are to tour the library, the tour leader will break them up into, say, five groups of 20, and stagger the start times as several tour guides lead the groups through the building.

Smaller transfer lots might also be good policy for the mail room clerk in the earlier chapter example. If the clerk made deliveries every 15 minutes instead of every two hours, the transfer lot size and the nonvalue-adding delivery delay would be reduced eightfold, greatly improving customer responsiveness.

Would delivery of mail every 15 minutes make sense? Would transfer of apples from the orchard to processing every two hours be reasonable? It depends partly on the distance, and partly on the mode of transport. A 15-minute delivery interval would make sense if all the offices were together on one floor of an office building. If the offices are geographically disbursed, maybe it's time to bring them together. It might make sense to form office cells with complete teams in the same room, thus avoiding the mail room for all internal transfers.

For apples, a golf cart or other small vehicle might be efficient for delivering 20 bushels every two hours from orchard to plant. If competition requires cutting the transfer lots even more, how about a processing unit on the back of a truck, which follows the pickers through the orchards?

$\mathscr{P}$RINCIPLE 6:

Organize focused cells.

To summarize:

1. The economic justification for cutting transfer lots is innovation-based reduction of handling costs, which is similar to reducing the cost of changeovers in the case of process lots.
2. Typical innovations involve simplifying the method of transfer (usually toward a less costly mode) and cutting transfer distances by moving people or processing units closer together.

Exhibit 10–10   Modifying the EOQ Concept

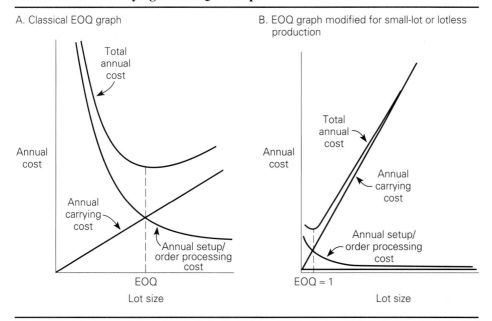

A. Classical EOQ graph

B. EOQ graph modified for small-lot or lotless production

Exhibit 10–7 illustrates the components of the economic order quantity. With small-lot or lotless production, the graph changes a good deal. Exhibit 10–10A is the classical EOQ graph. Part B is the modified graph showing wholesale changes. First, in part B the setup/order-processing cost curve has lost its steepness. The cost of ordering frequently in small lots is not much more than ordering infrequently in large lots. Why? Because for made items, setup times have been engineered downward, first to single-digit setup and finally toward one-touch setup. For bought items, kanban has simplified ordering, and stable contracts with a few (perhaps nearby) suppliers have cut the costs of negotiations with suppliers.

The New Economics of Lot Sizing

The second major change is in carrying cost per year. The cost to carry one unit for one year is modest in part A; the rate is represented (arbitrarily) by a 30-degree angle. In part B, the angle is 60 degrees, reflecting added external costs of carrying large inventories, namely, customer- and quality-related costs (items 1 through 5 in the previous section) and lumpy workload costs (discussed early in this chapter).

In sum, Exhibit 10–10 shows that lot sizes should be smaller than the classical EOQ because classical EOQ neglects process benefits of smaller lots (and therefore understates the carrying-cost rate). A new EOQ model incorporating the process benefits could be developed. But it is unclear which benefits (or negative costs) would be entered into the equation for such externals as better teamwork and quicker customer response. Perhaps because such a question has no easy answer, practical people have simply set forth a goal of piece-for-piece or lotless operations and striven for it by making small improvements month after month and year after year.

Summary

While just-in-time processing may be efficient as well as competitive, sometimes it's necessary to process and transfer work in larger lots. By following the guidelines for quick changeover and setup, it becomes feasible to continually cut process lots, toward the ideal of one unit.

The first guideline is changeover avoidance, via a process dedicated to one type of work. There are three be-ready guidelines useful to front-line improvement teams: convert internal changeover steps (while the process is stopped) to external, offline steps; keep setup implements close, clean, and in top condition; and, for costly equipment, employ a crew who do the changeover steps in parallel. There are four modification guidelines, usually calling for technical assistance: remove unneeded process adjustment devices, add needed positioners and locators to simplify and standardize equipment and accessories, and use externally loadable work holders and feeders.

Following the guidelines can often cut changeover times by 80 to 90 percent. Changeover-time reduction usually carries with it improvements in process control and consistency, operability, and several other factors. Regardless of the main goal of an improvement team, other improvements are likely. Consequently, the old practice of parceling out improvement work in pieces to specialty departments is giving ground to broad-spectrum project teams. These teams may be formed of front-line associates, who call on specialists as necessary. Also, the view that setup time projects should target only the bottleneck processes is erroneous since associates should be at work on all kinds of process improvements in every process, and since bottlenecks aren't fixed.

The lot size, or quantity ordered, must be decided each time an order is planned. Several orders may be grouped together (batched) to save on setup and order-processing costs, but that increases inventory carrying costs (holding costs plus capital costs). Also, large orders or batches tend to result in unbalanced or lumpy workloads in processing. Thus, lot-for-lot ordering has some advantages.

Acting on a need for an inventory item generates an order-processing cost, mostly the cost of equipment setup for manufactured items and the cost of processing purchase orders for purchased goods. In addition to the cost of ordering inventory, there is the cost of having or carrying it. Carrying costs include foregone interest on capital tied up in inventory plus physical holding or storage costs.

At the economic order quantity (EOQ), annual order-processing costs equal annual carrying costs, and the sum of the two is minimized. Since the sum varies little on either side of the minimum-cost point, the EOQ may be treated as a fairly wide zone. EOQ computation requires four inputs: annual demand, order-processing cost rate, carrying cost rate, and unit cost of the item being ordered. Variations in the basic EOQ model include allowance for quantity discounts and inclusion of a production-rate minus usage-rate adjustment.

Dynamic lot sizing may be used when real-world conditions change, but it tends to result in nervous operations. Although simpler lot-sizing models are preferred, there is a growing challenge to the basic assumptions of lot sizing. In particular, the just-in-time ideal is piece-for-piece, or lotless, production.

Operations with smaller lots are beneficial throughout the production process. Benefits include catching errors and correcting causes sooner, reducing inventory space to put front-line employees closer together, linking operations more closely so that employees face problems jointly, simplifying the inventory management system, smoothing workloads, and becoming more flexible and quicker to respond to customer demand.

The new economics of lot sizing favors efforts to reduce lot sizes. The goal is lotless operations, and continuing improvement is the path.

Key Words

Solved Problems

A manufacturer of industrial solvents has been buying for its own use about 18,000 bottles of solution X4X annually for several years. The cost is $10 per bottle, and $100 is the approximate cost of placing an order for X4X. The firm uses a carrying cost rate of 30 percent. Calculate the EOQ, the annual ordering cost, and the annual carrying cost for this item.

What would you expect to occur if lot sizes were made larger than the EOQ? Smaller? (Hint: Base your answer to these questions on Exhibit 10–7.)

The EOQ may be found using Equation 10–2:

$$EOQ = \sqrt{\frac{2DS}{IC}} = \sqrt{\frac{2(18,000)(\$100)}{(0.3)(\$10)}}$$
$$= \sqrt{1,200,000}$$
$$= 1,095.45 \text{ bottles}$$

Equation 10–1 contains the annual ordering and carrying cost terms. The annual ordering costs are:

$$\text{Annual } OC = \left(\frac{D}{Q}\right)(S) = \left(\frac{18,000}{1,095.45}\right)(\$100) = \$1,643.16$$

The annual carrying costs are:

$$\text{Annual } CC = \left(\frac{Q}{2}\right)(IC) = \left(\frac{1,095.45}{2}\right)(0.3)(\$10) = \$1,643.18$$

Thus, we see that at the EOQ, the annual ordering cost and the annual carrying cost are equal, the very slight difference due to rounding. Exhibit 10–7 shows the equality of the two costs graphically.

At any lot size other than the EOQ, the total annual cost will increase, as shown by the total cost curve in Exhibit 10–7. If the lot size were increased, we would expect carrying cost to increase and ordering cost to decrease. A lot size of less than the EOQ will result in a reduced carrying cost but a higher ordering cost.

Suppose the firm in problem 1 decides to begin making X4X instead of buying it. An initial estimate of production rate is 150 bottles per day during a production run. The daily usage, assuming 250 workdays per year, averages 72 bottles. The firm elects to continue valuing the X4X at $10 per bottle and, because it is an experienced solvent manufacturer, believes that it can set up to run a lot for approximately $100, the same as it has been costing to place a purchase order.

a. Calculate the EMQ, the annual ordering cost, and the annual carrying cost.
b. The plant manager thinks the calculated EMQ is much too high. She wants to produce small lots on more of a just-in-time basis. To justify this move, the manager directs that the EMQ be recalculated using a carrying cost rate of 80 percent. What is the recalculated EMQ?
c. Suppose that after recalculation using the 80 percent rate, the plant manager still thinks the lot size is too large. How can a smaller one be justified?

a. We use Equation 10–3 to find the EMQ:

$$EMQ = \sqrt{\frac{2DS}{IC(1 - D/P)}}$$
$$= \sqrt{\frac{2(18,000)(\$100)}{(0.3)(\$10)(1 - 72/150)}}$$
$$= 1,519.11 \text{ bottles}$$

Annual ordering cost is:

$$\text{Annual } OC = \left(\frac{D}{Q}\right)(S)$$
$$= \left(\frac{18,000}{1,519.11}\right)(\$100)$$
$$= \$1,184.90$$

Annual carrying cost is:

$$\text{Annual } CC = (IC)\left(\frac{P-D}{P}\right)\left(\frac{Q}{2}\right)$$
$$= (0.3)(\$10)\left(\frac{78}{150}\right)\left(\frac{1,519.11}{2}\right)$$
$$= \$1,184.91$$

The annual ordering cost again equals the annual carrying cost, and their total is less than the comparable total for problem 2. Also note that a larger lot size (about 1,519 units rather than 1,095) is suggested since the firm never has the entire production lot in inventory. As X4X is produced, some of it is consumed.

b. Again using Equation 10–3:

$$EMQ = \sqrt{\frac{2DS}{IC(1 - D/P)}}$$
$$= \sqrt{\frac{2(18,000)(100)}{(0.8)(10)(1 - 72/150)}}$$
$$= 930.26 \text{ bottles}$$

c. The setup time must be reduced. Currently, setup cost is estimated at $100, which could represent about five hours at $20 per hour for setup wages and benefits. In setting up to make solvent, pipes and mixing vessels must be cleaned out. Perhaps the firm could use precleaned pipe lengths and a throwaway liner for the mixing vessel. Quick coupling/uncoupling of pipes may be another promising avenue for improvement.

Problem 3

T-Square, Ltd., an engineering firm, uses packages of plastic tape of different patterns, widths, and shading to create layouts and other design drawings. About 2,000 packages are consumed each year. The supplier, an office supply company, offers quantity discounts as follows:

Quantity/Order	Unit Price
1–99	$10.00
100–499	9.50
500 and up	9.00

T-Square uses a 35 percent carrying-cost rate and spends about $30 placing a tape order. Use the EOQ with quantity discount procedure, as explained in Example 10–2, to determine the appropriate tape lot size.

Solution 3

First, calculate the EOQ for each of the three price values, rejecting those that do not fall within the allowable quantity range:

$$EOQ_{10.00} = \sqrt{\frac{2(2,000)(\$30)}{(0.35)(\$10.00)}} = 185.16 \text{ (reject—too large)}$$

$$EOQ_{9.50} = \sqrt{\frac{2(2,000)(\$30)}{(0.35)(\$9.50)}} = 189.97 \text{ (feasible)}$$

$$EOQ_{9.00} = \sqrt{\frac{2(2,000)(\$30)}{(0.35)(\$9.00)}} = 195.18 \text{ (reject—too small)}$$

Next, calculate the total annual cost associated with the only feasible EOQ, (approximately) 190 packages, using Equation 10–1:

$$TC = \left(\frac{D}{Q}\right)(S) + (IC)\left(\frac{Q}{2}\right) + DC$$

$$= \left(\frac{2,000}{190}\right)(\$30) + (0.35)(\$9.50)\left(\frac{190}{2}\right) + (2,000)(\$9.50)$$

$$= \$315.79 + \$315.88 + \$19,000.00 = \$19,631.67$$

Now calculate the total cost if the lot size were made equal to the next quantity break point, 500 units in this case:

$$TC = \left(\frac{D}{Q}\right)(S) + (IC)\left(\frac{Q}{2}\right) + DC$$

$$= \left(\frac{2,000}{500}\right)(\$30) + (0.35)(\$9)\left(\frac{500}{2}\right) + (2,000)(\$9)$$

$$= \$120.00 + \$787.50 + \$18,000.00 = \$18,907.50$$

Since the total annual cost of ordering at the best quantity discount amount, 500 units, is less than that associated with the EOQ, the more economical lot size for T-square is 500 packages.

For Further Reference

Books

Shingo, Shigeo. *A Revolution in Manufacturing: The SMED [Single-Minute Exchange of Die] System.* Cambridge, Mass.: Productivity Press, 1985.

Suzaki, Kiyoshi. *The New Manufacturing Challenge: Techniques for Continuous Improvement.* New York: The Free Press, 1987 (HD9720.5.S98).

Periodicals/Societies

Decision Sciences (Decision Sciences Institute).

Journal of Purchasing and Materials Management (National Association of Purchasing Management).

Production and Inventory Management (American Production and Inventory Control Society).

Review Questions

1. Why does lot-for-lot tend to ease the problem of lumpy workloads?
2. Why are lumpy workloads a problem?
3. How can process changeovers be avoided entirely?
4. Who should lead the effort to convert internal setup time to external? Why?
5. How does Principle 7, involving cross-training, relate to quick changeovers?
6. When should experts be called in to assist in a quick-setup project? What would the experts' role be?
7. Why is setup/changeover time reduction important for lot sizing?
8. Explain how order-processing/setup costs and carrying costs relate to lot size.
9. In what sense is the EOQ a zone?
10. Why is construction of the ultimate EOQ model, with all costs included, an impractical goal?
11. What does the EMQ model assume that differs from the basic EOQ model?
12. What benefits are associated with smaller lot sizes?
13. How may order-processing costs be cut in order to make it economical to buy in small amounts?
14. How does reducing lot size improve quality? Work force communication? Problem solving?

15. If EOQs (or a lot-size reduction campaign) result in small lots and less inventory, will there be savings from emptying out storage space? Explain.

16. If process lots are unyieldingly large, is it practical to turn to transfer lots for improvement in responsiveness? Explain.

Problems and Exercises

1. Clerks at your local post office must be prepared to sell stamps, weigh and post several types of letters and parcels, insure mail, and perform dozens of other operations. Find out about and discuss two of the quick-changeover guidelines that seem to be followed by post office clerks to enable them to quickly switch from one operation to another.

2. What is done in well-managed restaurants to enable staff to quickly and easily switch from breakfast to lunch to dinner operations? Which of the eight guidelines for quick changeover apply?

3. From your own experience as a client or customer, give an example of especially good server readiness and especially poor server readiness.

4. Exhibit 10–3 shows die-handling sleds on rails along a stamping line, which presses a steel sheet between upper and lower dies into auto body parts (the steel goes into the first press for partial shaping, then into the next for more shaping, etc., for progressive shaping into the final part). Changeover time from, say, a fender to a door panel—an extreme changeover—is 30 minutes. The plant has several identically equipped stamping lines and racks containing dies for hundreds of different auto body parts that go to auto body repair shops (not to GM assembly plants).
   a. From the photo and this explanation, which of the eight quick-changeover guidelines have been followed? Explain.
   b. What would be necessary to reduce this type of changeover to single-digit minutes (which is the next goal at this GM plant) or less? (Hint: Carefully consider the eight quick-changeover guidelines.)

5. Exhibit 10–2B is a photo of four tools hanging on a shadow board just below the edge of a round table used for assembling instruction manuals for Microsoft software products. The location of these tools below the table edge might be an obstacle to reducing changeover time still further. Suggest an improvement that would cut changeovers further; cite the quick-changeover guidelines that apply to your improvement.

6. Would the comparison between lot-for-lot and batch (Exhibit 10–5) make sense if clients were being processed instead of apples? If so, develop a brief example and explain. If not, explain why not.

7. The master scheduling team at a plant producing steel chain is considering a lot-for-lot policy, instead of batching into larger lots. The following is their partially completed analysis for three levels of chain making (final chain making, fed by fabrication of cut steel pieces, fed by purchased steel rods).

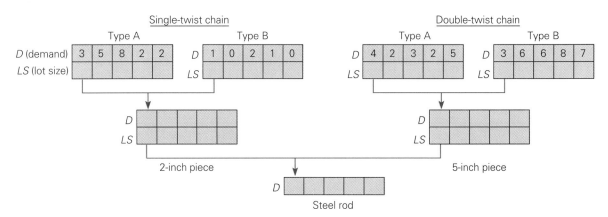

      a. What is the economic manufacturing quantity for three-inch pipe? For four-inch pipe?

      b. Assume that each of the three types of pipes is stored in a rack that is made to fit the pipe diameter; that is, a storage rack for one size of pipe may not hold another size (this changes the method of calculating EMQ). Explain why this might change the calculated EMQ's for the pipes. (Hint: What EOQ assumptions would be violated?)

17. A small company adopts buying by EOQs for all items in its stockroom. The EOQs show that many items formerly had been ordered in quantities far larger than their EOQs. The company has one buyer and one enclosed stockroom with one storekeeper.

      a. What savings can the company expect to derive from its EOQ ordering? What potential savings may prove to be difficult to capture?

      b. If the company adopts a full just-in-time effort, including flexible resource policies, how would that affect the answers to the questions posed in part *a?*

18. For the first time, Ordinaire, Inc., has calculated economic order quantities for items carried in stock. The calculations show that, for years, the supplies stockroom has been ordering quantities that are too large and the direct material stockroom has been ordering quantities that are too small. The comptroller is convinced that adopting the EOQs will save over $100,000 per year in reduced inventory cost. Critique the comptroller's viewpoint. (Hint: What expected savings, if any, may fail to be captured?)

19. Among other things, Marksman Industries makes 10 different models of gun-cleaning rods. Presently, the 10 models are manufactured one at a time, each for about one week's worth of production (average). The schedule is supposed to provide enough of a given model during the week-long production run to satisfy about 10 weeks of consumer demand (it will not be made again for 10 weeks). The problem is that by the end of the 10-week cycle for a model, expected consumer demand may have changed. By the time of the next production run, Marksman may have run out of a given model or accumulated a large excess. How can Marksman be more responsive to actual consumer demand? Explain.

20. Federal Time Corporation makes and sells clocks. Plastic lenses for clock faces are molded in Federal's own facilities. One popular table model has an annual demand of 40,000 clocks; its lens costs $0.60 to make. Setup to mold the lens, consisting of inserting and clamping the correct mold in the injection molding equipment, costs $80 per production run. (Setup time is about four hours.)

      a. Federal has been using EOQ to determine number of lenses per production run. It uses an inventory carrying cost rate of 0.25 and the formula $EOQ = \sqrt{2DS/IC}$. What is the *EOQ* for this lens?

      b. The plant manager has become convinced that there are benefits in running lenses in much smaller lots than EOQs. The four-hour setup time must be reduced in order to make small lots economical. What kinds of improvements does Federal need in order to achieve single-digit setup? To achieve one-touch setup?

21. Argo Electronics has a subsidiary plant in Wisconsin that produces electronic games and various other products. The plant produces its own circuit boards, which are used at a steady rate on the assembly line. Demand for one type of board is 7,000 per year, and the production rate is 40,000 per year. The standard cost is $6 per circuit board. It costs $200 to set up a production run for that kind of board.

      a. If 0.30 is used as the carrying-cost rate, what is the economic manufacturing quantity for circuit boards?

      b. An improvement team believes the carrying cost rate should be increased to 0.70. Recalculate the EMQ. Comment on why the team should favor a higher carrying-cost rate.

22. A well-known phenomenon in the semiconductor industry (making microprocessors and memory chips) is that fast processing of a production lot has a higher process yield than slow processing. (*Process yield* means number of good chips from a wafer, i.e., chips that pass electronic tests of quality.) The reason is that the wafers are susceptible to handling, dust, and other kinds of damage that are reduced if the production run is completed and the chips sealed over quickly.

One semiconductor manufacturer has several models of memory chip to run, one at a time. A production run of a given model normally takes five weeks, but a few small, special runs have been completed in as little as two weeks, with high process yields. How can a manufacturer gain these advantages all the time instead of only in special cases?

23. A producer of precision instruments has initiated a just-in-time effort. One of its early achievements was reducing setup time on a milling machine for making a key component part. The old setup cost was $200; now it is $8. As a result, the new economic lot size is only 16 units, whereas the old one had been much higher.

   a. If the company is serious about obtaining full just-in-time benefits, what lot size should be run? Explain.

   b. What was the old EOQ? (Hint: Use the new EOQ along with the ratio of new to old setup cost. No other data are needed.)

SUPPLEMENT

DERIVATION OF THE BASIC EOQ FORMULA

From Equation 10–1, we know that:

$$\text{Total cost} = TC = \left(\frac{D}{Q}\right)(S) + (IC)\left(\frac{Q}{2}\right) + DC$$

where

Q = Economic order quantity
D = Forecast annual demand
S = Setup or order-processing cost
I = Annual inventory carrying cost rate
C = Unit cost of the item

The economic order quantity is the quantity that minimizes total annual costs, that is, where the slope of the total cost curve is zero. Thus, by taking the derivative of the total cost function with respect to Q and setting it equal to the slope (zero), we obtain an expression for the EOQ:

$$\frac{d(TC)}{d(Q)} = \frac{d\left[\left(\frac{D}{Q}\right)(S) + (IC)\left(\frac{Q}{2}\right) + (D)(C)\right]}{d(Q)} = 0$$

$$= -\frac{DS}{Q^2} + \frac{IC}{2} = 0$$

Rearranging the terms, we obtain:

$$\frac{DS}{Q^2} = \frac{IC}{2}$$

or

$$Q^2 = \frac{2DS}{IC}$$

By taking the square roots of both sides:

$$Q = \sqrt{\frac{2DS}{IC}}$$

TRANSLATING PLANNING ORDERS INTO OUTCOMES

IV

Planned orders generate activity that results in customer service and product outcomes. The kind of activity depends on such factors as the volume and variety of orders. The subject of Chapter 11 is how different volume and variety combinations lead to three different systems of managing operating activities. We discuss each of these systems in the remaining chapters in Part IV: continuous and repetitive operations in Chapter 12, job and batch operations in Chapter 13, and projects in Chapter 14.

11 VOLUME AND VARIETY ISSUES

Chapter Outline

Operations and Operating
Environments
   Basic Operations Types
   Operations Environments

Toward Streamlined Operations
   Streamlining—Examples
   Streamlined Operations—A
   Continuum

Facilities Layout
   Layout Types
   U-Shaped Layout
   Layout Features

Case Study: Streamlined Patient
Transfers: Hours to Minutes

In Part IV, we spotlight the translation of orders into the activities that result in the goods and services we consume. A trip to a shopping mall offers many examples of the outcomes of diverse operations and operating environments. For example:

- Low on cash? The 24-hour automatic teller at the branch bank in the mall's parking lot, an example of *continuous service* operations, can solve that problem.

- A dedication plaque in a courtyard or atrium of the mall reveals its opening date, construction costs, and other information—reminders that the planning and building of a mall is a massive one-of-a-kind *project* that consists of many smaller operations.

- Inside the mall is a shop offering interior decorating services. Each decorating job, though smaller in scale, shares with the mall the uniqueness of a one-of-a-kind effort typical of *job operations*.

- We may stop for a soft drink, the product of a *continuous production* process at the manufacturer's plant. An accompanying cookie is the result of *batch* production in a bakery.

- *Assembly lines* or *cells* have provided the televisions and computers available in the electronics store and the shoes and clothing in the department store.

Of course, we could add to our list many other examples of goods and services as evidence of underlying operations. A key to learning how to manage diverse operating

EXHIBIT 11–1   **Types of Operations—Size and Volume Classification**

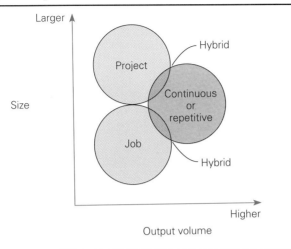

environments is understanding volume and variety issues, the focus of this chapter. We will consider classification of operations and operating environments, operations streamlining, and an overview of layout concerns.

Operations and Operating Environments

Those who provide society with shopping malls, cookies, or decorating services share basic strategic aims—broadly, improving service to customers—that have been covered in earlier chapters. Clearly, however, very different types of operations and operating environments are required to create these diverse outcomes.

Exhibit 11–1 illustrates the basic types of operations. As the axes indicate, operation size and output volume are factors that govern classification.

 Projects are unique, large-scale endeavors. A single project typically takes the project team months or years to complete and, if large enough, may be divided into subprojects. Project output volume is considered to be one, even if other similar projects are planned. For example, a series of spacecraft-tracking stations built around the world might call for nearly identical facilities, antennas, communications, power support, and so forth. But each site is different; climate, terrain, national policies and building codes, and other variables will make each station construction unique.

 A **job** is a small-scale, small-output-volume effort; painting a room or performing surgery are examples. Like the project, a job may be one-of-a-kind, although jobs frequently provide a small volume of like units. For example, a job might call for installing two soccer goal nets or staining eight matching dining chairs.

 When output volume must be higher, as with most consumer goods, **continuous operations** or **repetitive operations** are needed. Continuous and repetitive operations are together in one circle in Exhibit 11–1 because both have little variety, an issue we explore in the next section. But there are important distinctions between the two. Output from repetitive operations occurs in discrete units (e.g., production of circuit breakers or

Basic Operations Types

The basic types of operations are projects, jobs, and continuous (or repetitive) operations; hybrids are also common.

EXHIBIT 11-2   Operations Environments—Characteristics and Examples

Output variety	Highest	Highest	High	Low	Lowest
Equipment flexibility	Highest	Very high	High	Low	Lowest
Output volume	Lowest (one item)	Very low	Low	High	Highest
1. Project.	Construction Computer network installation R&D effort				
2. Job.		Tool-and-die shop Repair services Portfolio review			
3. Batch.			Heavy equipment Printing services Cement mixing		
4. Repetitive.				Auto assembly License processing School registration	
5. Continuous.					Steel plant Brewery 24-hour laundry

computer disks, or processing of insurance claim forms); by contrast, continuous output flows, or even pours, and is not identifiable as a discrete unit (e.g., petroleum products from a refinery or electrical power from a utility).

The two overlapping areas in Exhibit 11–1 indicate hybrid operations. The upper one represents the special case when a large project consists of multiple nearly identical units, most likely produced at the same location. An example would be an order for 25 destroyer escorts by the navy. The lower overlap region represents larger-quantity job orders. For example, a welding service business might receive an order to perform 500 identical welds.

In manufacturing, large-quantity-job operations occur so frequently that they have their own name: **batch operations.** Companies that thrive on filling multipiece job orders are sometimes referred to as batch producers or batch processors.

Having defined the basic types of operations, we will now address the environments in which those operations occur.

Operations Environments

Exhibit 11–2 identifies the five common operations environments, along with examples of each environment's goods and services output or the types of facilities used. The exhibit also describes how output variety, equipment flexibility, and output volume vary among the operations environments. Let's look more closely at each environment.

Exhibit 11–2 introduces the more detailed treatment of managing operations environments found in Chapters 12 (continuous and repetitive operations), 13 (job and batch operations), and 14 (projects).

1. *Project.* Projects provide a wide variety of outputs; construction, installation of a computer network, and research and development (R&D) efforts are examples. Furthermore, operations and the people assigned to them change as the project progresses. With large numbers of diverse operations in process at any one time, planning and control of operations sequence and timing are critical. Typically, equipment found in project environments is quite flexible, useful in a variety of ways in multiple projects.

2. *Job.* Intermittent job operations are found in machine shops, restaurants, and throughout the mostly job-oriented service sector. In the goods-manufacturing

sector, job-shop operators make small volumes of special parts for use in assembly operations. Others repair equipment or make tooling. Volume tends to be low.

Output in most job shops is highly variable, so equipment must be flexible. Since each customer wants something special or slightly different, operations management tends to be chaotic; much of the work is nonstandard and unfamiliar. Waiting lines and priority-ordering schemes are common. The management challenge is to reduce complexity of operations while still providing the sense of unique service that customers expect.

3. *Batch*. In common usage, batch may be anything from a pan of cookies in your kitchen to a massive vessel of chocolate, raw rubber, or molten metal in a factory. Our usage is more restrictive. We consider small-scale baking at home to be a job; production in massive vessels is part of continuous processing. Batch processing falls somewhere in between. Further, it is intermittent (like job processing), but output consists of standard, familiar items. Equipment is flexible and output volume is low or moderate. In a commercial bakery, for example, bakers may produce several types of bread and cookies, perhaps a batch of each type daily. Though batch-processing environments share some of the difficulties found in job operations, familiarity with the output mix precludes many of the surprises faced by job-shop personnel.

4. *Repetitive*. In repetitive operations, variety is low, equipment is designed for a narrow range of applications, and output volume is high. Repetitive production of discrete items is planned, scheduled, counted, and controlled by the unit or piece; in manufacturing, the assembly industries provide many examples. Repetitive services also exist, however; examples include forms processing, registrations, and tanning salons.

5. *Continuous*. Continuous processors are often referred to as the **process industry** (short for *continuous-flow process*). Production of fluids, grains, flakes, and pellets, as well as the mining of ores, coal, and so forth, fit into the process industry. Makers of small, discrete items (e.g., nails, toothpicks, and pens) are also sometimes considered part of the process industry. Such products are planned, scheduled, counted, and controlled by volume, rather than by unit or piece. Output volume is very high, but variety is low. Equipment is specialized, and the process industry is capital intensive.

Both continuous- and repetitive-production environments require elaborate advance planning but are relatively easy to control. Simple, rather inflexible rules and rigid standards govern operations. The benefits of continuous or repetitive operations are many, as we shall see in the next section, so companies naturally strive to operate in a more repetitive or continuous manner, that is, to become more streamlined.

Toward Streamlined Operations

City driving is harder on a car than highway driving. Mileage is lower, wear and tear is greater, and service is needed more frequently. In addition, the driver's time is wasted in stop-and-go traffic and in the time required for extra auto maintenance. In much the same way, stop-and-go operations can cause extra waste, inefficiency, high cost, and so on, in companies.

The benefits of steady-flow operations are considerable, including high efficiency, consistent high quality, shorter throughput times, less setup, lower inventory, lower labor

Streamlined operations: Steady or smooth flow operations, fewer, or less disruptive, starts and stops.

costs, simpler planning and scheduling, and fewer surprises. Thus, transforming irregular or intermittent operations into more streamlined operations is a goal that managers in all environments ought to pursue. To better understand how streamlining can work, even in job-shop and batch processing environments, we turn to some historical examples.

Streamlining—
Examples

Place the goods and services that we consume on a variety axis. At the high-variety end, we have **custom items** (or customized items); they are highly differentiated, even unique. At the other end are **commodities,** very common or undifferentiated goods and services.

At one time, all products were made in the job-shop mode as custom goods. For example, if you needed to have a tooth filled during the 1849 California gold rush, the dentist might melt down freshly panned gold from the South Fork River and fill your tooth by the light of a lamp burning the oil of a muskrat trapped near the same river. Of course, fuel and gold are commodities today, produced more or less continuously, but they were custom products made in the job mode in 1849.

As demand for any good expands, the low-volume job environment must give way to repetitive or continuous production if that demand is to be met. Around 1438, for example, the Arsenal of Venice turned out 10 fully armed warships per day. Carpenters fashioned and tarred hulls, and floated them in canals through a maze of assembly-line stations. Sails, oars, weapons, and supplies were added by artisans skilled in each respective trade.

Four and one-half centuries later, John D. Rockefeller's oil wells steadily pumped product into Rockefeller pipelines and rail tanker cars, which forwarded the product to Rockefeller tank farms and retail stations. Also, Andrew Carnegie's steel manufacturing empire included railroads and lake steamers that moved ore to the great furnaces and then to the finishing mills of Pittsburgh.

Today, one of the purest examples of streamlined processing may be found in the Western coal fields, where the output of lignite mines goes into trucks that drive a mile or so to giant electric power plants and dump their loads onto conveyors. The conveyors move the coal into furnaces that drive the generators that convert steam to electric power. The power is pumped through wires for immediate consumption by millions of users. Coal, the raw material, is a commodity, as is electric power, the end product.

The products in these examples—gold, muskrat oil, coal, electricity, even the Venetian ships—could be produced as commodities as long as customers demanded little variety. (Some of history's most skillful entrepreneurs were able to cultivate mass demand and keep it continuously or repetitively supplied with relatively undifferentiated goods or services.) But what happens when customers require variety?

Perhaps the most quoted accolade to the efficiencies of streamlined operations comes from a pioneer of the automobile industry. Ford Motor Company once transformed commodities such as iron ore into a commodity-like end product, the Model T automobile: "Our production cycle is about 81 hours from the mine to the finished machine in the freight car, or three days and 9 hours."[1] Ford's repetitive-flow mode of manufacture began

Ford's other quotation: "They can have any color they want, so long as it's black."

to unravel when customers started demanding variety: big cars and small ones, luxury models and sporty models with rumble seats. Changing customer tastes affected producers. The auto industry, from assembly plants to parts makers to steel mills, moved well away from commodity-like product uniformity and turned to intermittent production—one model at a time, with long cycle intervals.

Must a firm choose between satisfying customers' needs for variety and enjoying the benefits of streamlined operations? Exhibit 11–2 indicates that only low-variety

---

[1] Henry Ford, *Today and Tomorrow* (Garden City, N.Y.: Doubleday, 1926), p. 115.

environments (repetitive or continuous) are likely to reap those benefits. While that has been the common wisdom, today's more positive view is that firms with less continuous operations can share the wealth. An example from the aerospace industry, discussed in the box, illustrates.

In addition to these cases, we've already discussed a wide variety of concepts and techniques for becoming more streamlined: better process design (Chapter 3), smoother order processing (Chapter 5), improved flow-control and quick-response techniques (Chapters 7 and 10), reduced documentation and materials handling (Chapter 8), and queue limitation (Chapter 9). The chapters ahead include other equally effective techniques. The big picture? Perhaps a continuum of increasingly streamlined operations.

The case study of the hospital at the end of this chapter is another example of streamlining operations.

The range of product/service variety, from custom to commodity items, is represented by the horizontal axis of Exhibit 11–3.[2] The vertical axis reflects *process* (or operations) environment; its range covers the five environments shown in Exhibit 11–2. A sampling of industries lies along the diagonal—from electrical power, a continuously generated commodity, at the bottom-right, to intermittent, custom jobs or services at the top-left.

Placement of industries on the diagonal is not set in concrete. It is natural to want to move downward along the diagonal, and perhaps to the right, thereby taking advantage of the benefits of streamlined operations. For a prime example, let us return to the automotive industry.

Streamlined Operations—A Continuum

Exhibit 11–3   Product/Service versus Process Matrix

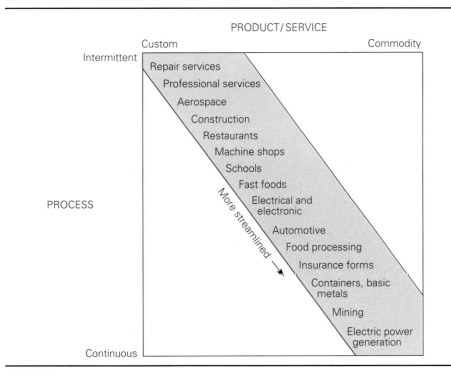

[2]The original idea for the matrix comes from Robert H. Hayes and Steven C. Wheelwright, "Link Manufacturing Process and Product Life Cycles," *Harvard Business Review,* January–February 1979, pp. 133–40. This version of the matrix is adapted from Sam C. Taylor, Samuel M. Seward, and Steven F. Bolander, "Why the Process Industries Are Different," *Production and Inventory Management,* Fourth Quarter 1981, pp. 9–24.

Streamlining in the Aircraft Industry

"Because of the low production volume of commercial aircraft, assembly hasn't changed much over the years," said Charles Carter, vice president of technology of the Association for Manufacturing Technology in McLean, Virginia. That fact didn't stop Giddings & Lewis, a machine-tool builder headquartered in Fond du Lac, Wisconsin, from teaming up with Boeing Company to build the biggest automated assembly machine ever.

Known as the Automated Spar Assembly Tool 2, or ASAT, the machine builds wing spars for Boeing's 777. Each spar—four are needed for an aircraft—is 106 feet long and requires 6,800 fasteners. Prior to the ASAT, spar assembly was accomplished manually in a project layout fashion. ASAT is capable of building four spars simultaneously.

The crux of its operation is the fastening process, in which a spar's large metal plate is connected to the stiffeners and flanges that hold it together. While driving along on adjacent tracks, eight massive tool carriages, each weighing nine tons, periodically measure the spar plate's thickness, drill holes, select appropriate fasteners by length and diameter, and then install the fasteners.

Thus, the tool rather than the workpiece does the "flowing" along the length of the spar. As for the low volumes of aircraft assembly, consider the numbers: 27,200 repetitive fastening sequences on each plane for the wings alone!

SOURCE: Adapted from Chuck Murray, " 'Coloring Outside Lines' in a Big Way," *Chicago Tribune*, Section 3, p. 1, November 4, 1992.

The Automated Spar Assembly Tool (ASAT 2) at Boeing's Everett, WA, facility is used to assemble, drill, and install fasteners for wing spars on the Boeing 777. Courtesy of Boeing Commercial Airplane Group, Boeing Aircraft Company. Used with permission.

ontrast

Variety, Volume, and Flow

High Variety Characteristics

Conventional:	**Contemporary:**
Disruptive processing.	Smoothing out the disruptions.
Long setups/changeovers.	Reducing setup/changeover times.
Skills/equipment grouped by specialty.	Skills/equipment grouped by product/customer family.
Long transport distances.	Transport distances shortened by cellular organization.
Complex flow control.	Flow controls simplified via visual queue limitation devices.
Overtime and undertime for narrowly skilled employees.	Cross-trained associates moving to where the work is.

High Volume Characteristics

Streamlined flow, a special case (opposite of high variety processing).	Ideal is always to strive to behave like streamlined, high-volume processors.

With the exception of Ford's Model T era, the automotive industry's dominant processing mode had been production in lots. Over three decades after the Model T was introduced, Toyota of Japan began developing a system of synchronized production, which means synchronizing the stages of manufacturing much like Henry Ford had done. But there was a difference. Toyota's method, unlike Ford's, allowed mixed-model assembly and therefore was able to accommodate customers' demands for variety. In Toyota's case the variety is high, because its customers' tastes vary worldwide. (Its Japanese customers can order a particularly large variety of configurations.) Thus, Toyota has moved downward toward streamlined operations without much rightward movement toward commodity products.

Part of the streamlining equation—whether at Ford in the 1920s, Toyota 50 years later, or any firm today—is the way that facilities are positioned within the work environment, that is, facilities layout.

Facilities Layout

The operations management masterminds at the Arsenal of Venice in the 15th century understood the importance of layout.

Layout:
The physical organization or geography found at a facility; basic types include process (or functional), product, cellular, and fixed-position.

> And as one enters the gate there is a great street on either hand with the sea in the middle, and on one side are windows opening out of the houses of the arsenal, and the same on the other side, and out came a galley towed by a boat, and from the windows they handed out to them, from one the cordage, from another the bread, from another the arms, and from another the balistas and mortars, and so from all sides everything which was required, and when the galley had reached the end of the street all the men required were on board, together with the complement of oars, and she was equipped from end to end. In this manner there came out ten

galleys full armed, between the hours of three and nine. I know not how to describe what I saw there, whether in the manner of its construction or in the management of the workpeople, and I do not think there is anything finer in the world.[3]

That description identifies the Arsenal of Venice as having a product layout. In this section, we examine basic layouts and their features.

Layout Types

There are four basic types of facilities layout:

1. **Process layout.** Also known as the **functional layout,** the process layout is characterized by grouping like facilities or functions together: human resource people in the HR department, sheet-metal equipment and people grouped in the sheet-metal shop, and so forth. The process layout tends to emerge as small organizations grow, and functional groups appear (e.g., bookkeeping and accounting, sales and advertising, packing and shipping and so on). Such a layout may facilitate use of common tools, maintenance of like items, utility hookups, and waste control. Also, putting people with like functions together creates a climate for mutual support and learning. Job-shop environments, for either goods or services, have tended toward process layouts. However, the process layout has a substantial disadvantage; it puts distance between provider and customer. For example, the customer who receives output from the human resource department or the sheet-metal shop is not close by.

2. **Product layout.** In the product layout, facilities are arranged along the flow of goods or services. The customer (next process) is adjacent to, or very near, the provider. Cafeterias or assembly lines are examples. In manufacturing, product layouts can require substantial investment and may be ill-advised if output volumes are projected to be low. The major disadvantage to product layouts, however, is with how they are managed. If associates along a flow line are allowed to do only one small job day in and day out, they can hardly be expected to grasp the overall operation. Their worth is diminished, boredom sets in, and morale drops. With cross-training and flexible product-flow cells, however, those problems can be eliminated.

3. **Cellular layout.** In the cellular layout, the idea is to arrange work stations and machines into cells that process families of goods or services that follow similar flow paths. Cells perform better with the addition of a number of subconcepts: items deliberately designed to have as many common features as possible, high-use tools and data located within the cell, cross-trained cell operators, and the cellular layout itself. A cellular layout is similar to a product layout, although most people think of product layouts (production lines) as handling only one or just a few products instead of a family. Cellular layout became one of the more important operations management concepts in the 1980s.

   Cells are often created when customer-oriented companies break apart process layouts. Drill presses may be transferred from a press room to a cell making a family of parts. A stamping machine may be moved so it can make and feed a single part to a using station on a production line. The photo in Exhibit 11−4 shows just that; a stamping machine that makes junction box brackets is positioned at the point-of-use, where the brackets are used on the line, in a General Electric dishwasher plant.

*P*RINCIPLES 6 AND 9:

Organize resources by item families. Assign equipment to focused cells.

---

[3]This description is from Pero Tafur, *Travels and Adventures* (London: G. Routledge & Sons, Ltd., 1926) p. 1435, cited in R. Burlingame, *Backgrounds of Power* (New York: Charles Scribner's Sons, 1949).

EXHIBIT 11–4   Point-of-Use Manufacturing

Junction box brackets stamped at the point where they are used.

The same concepts apply in processing documents or human clients, or whenever people are moved into cells to be near the customers they serve. Human resource specialists, accountants, and engineers (along with their desks, file cabinets, computers, etc.) may join cells that either make a family of parts or perform a family of services. For the Bank of Boston, such a service family is its securities-processing business, as the box explains.

The Bank of Boston case illustrates conversion to focused (cellular), delay-free (JIT) processing—a contemporary term for which is **re-engineering**.

4. **Fixed-position layout.** In the fixed-position layout, it is the product whose position is fixed, and resources (people, machines, materials, and so on) must come to it. Construction is a good example. Another is the manufacture of items too large to be easily moved, such as aircraft and locomotives. Still others are patients in hospital beds, or an actor being dressed, made up, and coached before the performance.

Mixed layouts—two or more layout types in a single facility—are common, if not the norm. An example is a restaurant that sets up a buffet brunch line on Sundays. The patron has the choice of going through the buffet line or sitting down and ordering from the menu. A patron entering the restaurant may be thought of as raw materials; a patron leaving is finished goods. The operations are to transform a hungry patron into a fed one. The two types of patrons are processed through two types of facilities layout. The buffet customer goes through a product or cellular layout (hard to narrow it down to one or the other). It is a flow line. The menu customer receives service in a fixed layout: Menu, waiter, food, drinks, and check come to the fixed position.

Exhibit 11–5 is a sketch of such a restaurant, identifying the product layout and fixed layout. It also shows that the restaurant includes a process layout in the kitchen. There

Into Practice

Moving Facilities for Moving Money

"Garbage—or something like it—was what the Bank of Boston found when it looked at its securities-processing business . . . , which handles stock transfers, dividends and interest payments, pension plan administration, and related tasks—about 25 million transactions a year. It had six separate operations, each with its own mainframe, scattered over 11 locations. Work for one customer could shuffle through several systems—one for dividends, another for stock sales, a third for bond interest—costing time, labor, and money at each point.

"[Working with a consulting firm,] the bank put everyone in securities processing at one location with two computer systems and set up the work around its core process, moving money. Computer cables run across the ceiling like track lighting, allowing the bank to change the layout overnight. The idea was to mimic a just-in-time, flexible factory. Says senior vice president John Towers: 'We created a utility that could service all the product lines.' Productivity soared: After 2½ years, with 17% fewer employees, the division does 80% more securities-processing business."

Source: Adapted from Thomas A. Stewart, "U.S. Productivity: First but Fading," *Fortune*, October, 1992, pp. 54–56.

foods, not patrons, are the products being transformed. The process areas include grill, salad area, range, dessert area, ovens, freezer, and pantry. Arrows show the jumbled flow patterns.

Compared with a single-layout facility, a mixed-layout facility is more difficult to plan, more costly to equip, and more troublesome to maintain. But it may be easier to keep busy because it serves a wider variety of customers or products.

U-Shaped Layout

The main feature of both production lines and workcells is the close proximity of workstations, speeding up flow, and reducing in-process inventory. Another feature is layout of stations into a U shape. At least six advantages for cells or lines result from **U-shaped layout.**

1. *Staff flexibility and balance.* The U shape allows one associate to tend several workcenters, adjacent or across the U, since walking distance is short. Also, more options for balancing work among personnel exist; as demand increases, labor may be added until every station in the cell is tended by an associate.

   Exhibit 11–6 shows a typical U-shaped layout. As many as eight employees, or as few as one, might attend the machines, depending on demand. Also note that kanban squares link each station with its customer station.

Principle 1:

Team up with the customer—the next process.

2. *Teamwork.* Getting all staff into a cluster enhances teamwork and joint problem solving. Slowdowns or stoppages quickly ripple through the cell, and cell members form a natural team that must collectively solve the problems and get the process going again. Natural teams can hardly form, much less work effectively, if employees are strung out along long lines or dispersed and separated by walls of inventory.

3. *Rework.* When a mistake occurs, a common policy is to send the customer to the complaint department or the product to a separate rework line. But a tenet of total quality management is quality at the source, which calls for correcting mistakes

EXHIBIT 11–5   Mixed Layout in a Restaurant

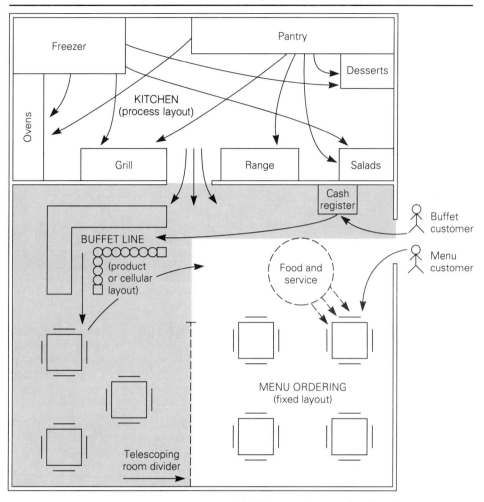

(solid arrows show product flows)

right where they occurred. In the U-shaped layout, the distance to return a mistake is short, making it easier to follow the TQM tenet.

4. *Passage.* A long, straight line interferes with travel of people and vehicles. We object when supermarket aisles are too long, and people protest when a freeway cuts through a neighborhood. A long, straight production line is a similar imposition.

5. *Work and tool distribution.* Since all stations in a U are immediately accessible from the center, it is easier to distribute materials, parts, instruction sheets, and so on. A single person may be able to handle distribution tasks while also tending a starting or ending station in the U. In unmanned cells, a robot at the center may distribute work and tools and also perform assembly operations.

6. *Linking with other U-shaped layouts.* The U shape provides many more arrangement options for linking feeder and user cells. Simple kanban squares control

EXHIBIT 11–6   U-Shaped Layout—Manufacturing Cell

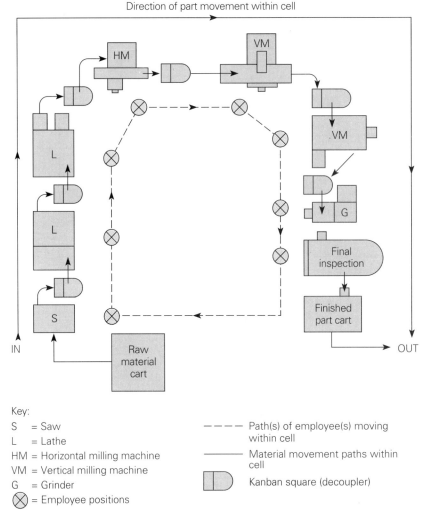

Key:
S   = Saw
L   = Lathe
HM = Horizontal milling machine
VM = Vertical milling machine
G   = Grinder
⊗ = Employee positions

– – – – Path(s) of employee(s) moving within cell

———— Material movement paths within cell

Kanban square (decoupler)

SOURCE: Adapted from J. T. Black, *The Design of the Factory with a Future* (New York: McGraw-Hill, 1991), p. 67. Used with permission.

flow. Exhibit 11–7 shows a linked-cell system consisting of final assembly, subassembly, and fabrication cells—all U-shaped. Each fabrication cell might resemble the one shown in Exhibit 11–6 and would provide a different parts family to the subassembly and assembly cells at the appropriate point of use. In a well-balanced system, fabrication cells would have the same degree of demand-mix and volume flexibility as the subassembly and assembly cells.

There are cases where these advantages of the U shape do not fully apply. For example, with a high degree of automation and few parts or tools to be handled, the teamwork benefits are absent. Also, a line processing wide sheets of steel, aluminum, glass, and so on, perhaps should run straight because transfer between machines is simpler if there are no changes in direction.

EXHIBIT 11–7   Linked-Cell Manufacturing System

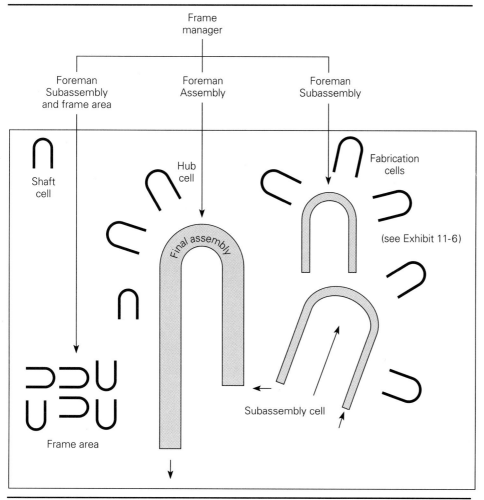

SOURCE: Adapted from J. T. Black, *The Design of the Factory with a Future* (New York: McGraw-Hill, 1991), p. 66. Used with permission.

Some of the distinguishing features of the primary layout types are shown in Exhibit 11–8. It lists eight resource factors and the ways in which each is commonly treated for each layout type.

Layout Features

The first factor, facilities arrangement, states the main differences among the layout types. They have already been discussed.

Type of operations is the second factor. Process layout is dominant in job and batch operations; product layout is typical in repetitive and continuous operations. The JIT mandate is to identify all items that have the potential for more or less repetitive operations and to organize product layouts for those items. Cellular layout is suitable for small lots of first one part in a family and then another. Fixed layout is common in construction and industrial projects and for production of large-scale products (e.g., missiles and dynamos). Fixed layout is also found where special human services are provided. For example, the resources come to the client or customer in surgery, grooming, feeding, and home TV repair.

EXHIBIT 11-8   Resources and Layouts—Common Characteristics

	Types of Layout		
Resource Factors	*Process Oriented*	*Product or Cellular*	*Fixed Position*
1. Facilities arrangement	Facilities grouped by specialty	Facilities placed along product-flow lines	Facilities arranged for ease of movement to fixed product
2. Type of operations	Job and batch	Continuous and repetitive	Construction and industrial projects; large-scale products, special human services
3. Cost of layout/re-layout	Moderate to low	Moderate to high	Moderate to low
4. Facility utilization	Usually low	High	Moderate
5. Type of operating facilities	General purpose	Special purpose	Mostly general purpose
6. Handling equipment	Variable path	Fixed path	Variable path
7. Handling distance	Long	Short	Moderate
8. Employee skill level	Skilled	Unskilled	Unskilled to skilled

Cost of layout/re-layout is third. In process layout, machines, desks, and the like generally are not tightly linked; thus, process layout usually is not costly. For a product or cellular layout, the cost is high if pieces of equipment are closely interlinked as in automated lines; the cost may be moderate if production is more labor intensive; that is, one person hands work to the next. Fixed layout of a construction site requires temporary parking and storage space for operating resources, which usually are not costly. Fixed layout for goods production and for special human services may take more than just parking space; it may require a well-equipped bay for assembling a missile or aligning wheels, or a well-equipped operating room. The layout cost can be low if the facilities are mainly general-purpose hand tools, but can be higher (moderate) if special lighting, holding fixtures, work pits, and so forth, are involved.

Fourth is facility utilization. In process layouts, facilities tend toward low utilization. That is not desirable, but it is typical because the job mix changes all the time and different jobs use different facilities. High facility utilization—little idleness—is a goal of product layout. Line balancing helps achieve it. Fixed layouts tend to have moderate facility utilization because the product mix is not very diverse.

The fifth factor is type of operating facilities. Process layouts usually hold standard, general-purpose equipment, tools, handling aids, and so forth. Special-purpose facilities are worth investing in if the volume is high, as it normally is with product or cellular layouts. In fixed layouts, special products call for some special-purpose facilities, such as an overhead crane or a mounting fixture, but most of the facilities will be general purpose since production volume is not high.

Sixth is handling equipment. In process layouts, variable-path equipment (hand-carry or on wheels) provides needed handling flexibility. Fixed-path handling equipment (conveyors, elevators, chutes, etc.) helps cut handling time in product layouts. Variable-path handling equipment is used in fixed layouts because a variety of resources come to the site from different places.

Seventh is handling distance. Long distances occur in process layouts. In product and cellular layouts, the opposite is true. In fact, a purpose is to tightly cluster the facilities in order to cut distance and handling time. Fixed layouts are in between. The product stays put, but the resources do not flow to the product by fixed routes; resources move to the product from various locations over moderate handling distances.

The eighth factor is employee skill level. In process layouts, employees tend to be skilled. Clerks, machinists, plumbers, computer operators, nurses, and accountants fit the category. If the skill is based on higher education or apprenticeship, the pay tends to be high; if based on vocational training, the pay tends to be moderate or low. Employees along product layouts are often hired without a particular skill. Such employees may become adept, but they are classed as unskilled because they are easily replaced from an unskilled labor market. In fixed layouts, skilled craftspeople, such as carpenters and welders, often work alongside unskilled laborers, such as shovelers or riveters.

While many more operating-resource factors could be discussed, these eight are enough to show the basic nature of each layout type. Exhibit 11–8 is not intended as an if-then analysis device; that is, we would not conclude that if people are skilled, facility utilization is low, and so on, then a process layout should be developed. There are better ways to plan the right kind of layout. We consider some of them in Chapter 17.

Summary

As associates transform orders into outcomes, the arrangement of their workplaces and the tools they use depends to a great extent on customers' volume and variety demands. Of specific interest in this chapter are types of operations and operating environments, streamlining efforts, and facility layout.

There are three basic types of operations: projects, jobs, and continuous or repetitive. Those basic types may be found in five common environments: (1) Projects are large-scale efforts that provide a wide variety of output with flexible equipment, but volume is very low, typically only one unit. (2) For smaller-scale output, employees use flexible equipment to perform intermittent job operations, providing low-volume, high-variety goods and services. The terms *nonstandard* and *unfamiliar* describe much job work. (3) Batch processing is also intermittent, but output is standard and familiar. Low volume and flexible equipment are characteristic. (4) Repetitive operations occur when demand calls for high volume, but output variety is low. Equipment is specialized. (5) Continuous processing requires highly specialized equipment to provide a continual flow of largely undifferentiated output.

The efficient creation of quality goods and services and other benefits of continuous and repetitive operations is a worthy aim; to obtain those advantages, associates try to streamline operations. Throughout history, entrepreneurs who knew how to streamline flows often amassed sizable fortunes. Today, better process design, improved flow-control and quick-response tools, reduced documentation, queue limitation, and employee cross-training are helping with streamlining programs. Also, today's streamlining is accomplished with a concurrent goal of retaining variety.

Layout is the physical organization or geography found at a facility; basic types include process (or functional), product, cellular, and fixed-position. The process layout is accomplished by grouping like functions, tools, or facilities together; it tends to evolve as organizations grow. In product layout, facilities are arranged along the flow path of goods or services. Provider-customer pairs tend to be closer together. To create a cellular layout, employees arrange work stations and machines into cells that process families of goods or services that follow similar flow paths. More complete cells include supporting-service associates, such as accountants, engineers, and human resource specialists. The fixed-position layout is used when the output—a product or a person receiving service, for example—is stationary, and people, materials, and equipment must come to it. Mixed layouts, where two or more of the basic types occur within a single facility, are common, if not the norm.

U-shaped layouts are increasingly appropriate for product lines and work cells. Advantages of the U shape include greater staffing flexibility and teamwork, rework performed at the point of error, easier passage through the facility, smoother work and tool distribution, and simplified linkages between feeder and user cells.

Resource factors receive varying treatment under the different layout types. Arrangement, cost of layout and re-layout, utilization, type of facilities, handling equipment and distance, and general employee skill level are among the more noteworthy.

Key Words

Project   385
Job   385
Continuous operations   385
Repetitive operations   385
Batch operations   386
Process industry   387
Streamlined operations   387
Custom items   388
Commodities   388

Layout   391
Process layout   392
Functional layout   392
Product layout   392
Cellular layout   392
Fixed-position layout   393
Re-engineering   393
U-shaped layout   394

For Further Reference

Books

Black, J. T. *The Design of the Factory with a Future*. New York: McGraw-Hill, 1991.

Harmon, Roy L. *Reinventing the Factory II*. New York: The Free Press, 1992 (HD56.H37).

Schonberger, Richard J. *Building a Chain of Customers*. New York: The Free Press, 1990 (HD58.9.S36).

Steudel, Harold J., and Paul Desruelle. *Manufacturing in the Nineties*. New York: Van Nostrand Reinhold, 1992 (HD9725.D68).

Periodicals/Societies

APICS: The Performance Advantage (American Production and Inventory Control Society).

Industrial Engineering (Institute of Industrial Engineering).

Industry Week.

Production and Operations Management (Production and Operations Management Society).

Review Questions

1. Explain the main differences among the three basic types of operations.
2. Five common operations environments were discussed; explain how each of the following would vary among those environments:
   a. Output variety.
   b. Equipment flexibility.
   c. Output volume.
3. What are streamlined operations? Which industries tend to be among the more streamlined? Among the less streamlined?
4. In transforming operations to make them more streamlined, must there be movement from a custom to a commodity orientation? Discuss.

5. What is layout? Distinguish among the four major layout types.

6. What are the primary advantages and disadvantages of process or functional layout?

7. Suppose plant associates convert part of their facility from process to cellular layout. What might be the advantages of such a move?

8. What kinds of goods and services are produced in fixed-position layouts? Why?

9. What is a mixed layout? Cite advantages and disadvantages of mixed layouts.

10. Why is the U-shaped layout well suited for cells or flow lines?

11. Discuss the ways in which U-shaped layouts help associates follow the tenets of TQM?

Problems and Exercises

1. For each of the following types of organization, try to determine the main kind of operation: repetitive or continuous, batch, job, or project. Discuss each.

Medical clinic	Cafeteria	Commercial fishing
Crane manufacturing	Book printing	Grocery checkout
Auditing	Petroleum refining	Farming
Architecture	Purchasing	Mowing grass on campus
Shoe repair	Bottling	Law practice
Radio manufacturing	Construction	Welding shop

2. Why does operations management tend to be more highly developed in repetitive than in job or project operations?

3. As organizations grow, their productive character may change, for example, from batch or job (custom) to repetitive or from project to repetitive. Describe how this might happen for a type of organization of your choice. Also describe the accompanying changes in the management of operations; that is, why would different kinds of planning and control models be called for?

4. Fifteen examples (three from each of the five common operations environments) are shown in Exhibit 11–2. Select one example, interview someone who works in your selected job environment, and prepare a report addressing the following:
   a. Describe the nature of the industry, the company or agency's mission, the volume and variety of output, and other items of general interest.
   b. From your interview results and your own observations and research, describe the various uses of any major tools or equipment used by the person you interviewed.
   c. Describe the layout of two primary areas (office, plant, cafeteria, laboratory, and so forth) in the facility in which your interviewee works.

5. Arrange the following industries on a product/service versus process matrix similar to Exhibit 11–3: motels, shoe manufacturing, processing welfare recipients, shipbuilding, furniture manufacturing, employee skills testing, toxic waste site cleanup, natural gas mining and distribution. Discuss.

6. Some golfers occasionally need a sand wedge. Would such an item be a custom product or a commodity item? Discuss.

7. What is the basic layout of the college or university in which you are enrolled? What are the advantages of such a layout? The disadvantages?

8. The music and theater departments at State University will jointly present *The Sound of Music* at four locations around the state during the upcoming season. Two shows, a matinee and an evening performance, will occur at each site.
   a. What form of layout will this eight-performance effort require? (Hint: Don't rush to limit your options.) Explain fully.
   b. Discuss the effects of volume and variety. How would your response change if a different performance were to be given at each site?

       c. Fred and Freida, the production managers of the show, have asked you for ways in which they might streamline the entire effort. What would you suggest?

9. Greg Bailey and Greta Benson are executive partners at Bailey & Benson, Ltd., a CPA firm that specializes in personal taxes, estate planning, and other related accounting services for a small but growing number of wealthy clients. Both Greg and Greta feel that Bailey & Benson's reputation for high-quality custom services is largely responsible for their success.

    To help serve their growing client list, they have recently hired Haley Johnson and Harold Jones as junior associates. Haley feels strongly that a streamlining effort would help Bailey & Benson increase its efficiency and serve an even greater number of clients. She has a strong ally in Harold; he believes that greater use of high-quality software with state-of-the-art computer-generated standard forms is in the clients' best interests.

    Greg and Greta have reservations. Can they streamline, as Haley puts it, and continue to provide custom service to discriminating clients? Discuss.

10. What is the usual operations environment under which corneal transplant surgery is performed? Suppose such a procedure were scheduled for a large number of people at the same time. They would move along through a form of assembly line, with each of several surgeons doing a small piece of the operation. Is this streamlining? Is surgery a custom service or is it a commodity? Discuss.

 **CASE STUDY**

STREAMLINED PATIENT TRANSFERS: HOURS TO MINUTES

The process of admitting patients to Northwest Hospital's Transitional Care Unit (TCU) was cumbersome. It took 6 to 12 hours just to get the necessary approvals when a physician referred a patient to the TCU. Then the patient's chart had to be reviewed, which was delayed until the next day. Thus, it took at least 24 hours and often 48 hours for the patient finally to be moved to the TCU.

"Five people evaluated each patient" because, explained Gayle Ward, assistant director of nursing, "there were two different philosophies" for admission. One centered on control of patients and payments, the other on smooth management of evolving patient care. Because of the cumbersome admissions procedure, some physicians had become reluctant to refer patients; the TCU's beds were underutilized, and the unit had become a financial problem for the hospital.

Thus, the TCU admission process was ripe for improvement when TCU's total quality management training program began in July of 1992. In conjunction with training in the quality sciences by an outside consultant, a project team was formed composed of Becky Larson from care management; Matt Quaterman, admissions coordinator; Rebecca Pelroy, from TCU billing; Pat Ford, utilization review coordinator; and the acute care case managers, Jo Croot and Gayle Ward. The team developed a process flow diagram for the admissions process and then "streamlined it by eliminating complexity and rework. The staff didn't think [the new process] would work."

Jo said, "Give me one week. . . . That first day I had about 40 calls and messages with questions about the process. I kept saying, 'Stick to the diagram.' We started turning referrals around from six hours to less than one hour and filling beds as soon as they became empty."

Within two weeks, the new process of relying on the judgment of the case managers rather than on the several review stages was working. It reduced the admissions workload by eight hours a day for Jo and her staff. Delays for hand-carrying of paperwork were also eliminated. "We do almost everything by phone [and let the] paperwork catch up." Admissions that once took as long as two days were cut to 20 minutes. "Physicians are happier with the service, beds fill quicker, there are more admissions from outside the hospital, and the evening shift is also admitting patients."

The streamlined procedure has exposed underlying stumbling blocks, according to Jo Croot. After implementation, however, Jo had continued to feel frustrated by the number of referrals that were refused admission. "I tracked down the reasons why and made a bar chart." Her chart, tracking 51 such refusals, showed the following:

- One patient was admitted instead to the rehabilitation unit.
- One was sent instead to an outside gero-psychiatric unit.
- Two had no insurance.
- Two had died.
- Twenty-five had been discharged directly to their homes.
- Twenty had been placed in some other nursing home, hospital, or other facility.

The study confirmed that ''these 51 referrals were appropriately screened and placed elsewhere by our case managers.'' Thus, by her bar chart, Jo had developed the evidence that the new admissions process was not only quick but also producing correct (high-quality) referral decisions.

Discussion Questions

Question 1. Two competing philosophies were at work under the old TCU admissions process; the ''smooth management of evolving patient care'' one seemed to win out under the new approach. Does the makeup of the project team suggest that outcome? Is it reasonable to expect that proponents of both philosophies will come to appreciate the new procedure? Discuss.

Question 2. Are the human reactions to the new process (staff doubt that it will ever work, the 40 calls that Jo got the first day and so forth) normal? Why? In this case, positive changes were apparent almost immediately. But what might have happened if those changes were much slower in developing? Was Jo wise to suggest rapid results when she said, ''Give me one week?'' Why?

Question 3. Jo's chart is offered as evidence that the streamlined TCU admissions procedure produces quality admissions decisions. Do you agree? Why or why not?

SOURCE: Adapted from Jodi B. Torpey, *Northwest Hospital Quality Case Studies* (Seattle: Quality Health Systems of America, 1992), pp. 48–54. Used with permission.

12   MANAGING CONTINUOUS AND REPETITIVE OPERATIONS

Chapter Outline

For many of us, the word *production* conjures up images of rapidly moving products streaming down long assembly lines, or of liquids flowing continuously through a maze of pipes until forced through nozzles into bottles, cans, or other containers. Perhaps plant tours or films have provided glimpses of the manufacture of item brands that we consume: food and beverages, cleansers, shoes, hardware, tools, and electronics. The list seems as endless as the flow lines themselves.

As we learned in Chapter 11, the process industry consists of companies that produce fluids, grains, ores, and other commodities in continuous fashion; its close partner provides widely used consumer products in highly repetitive production. In this chapter, we look more deeply at the management of these types of operations.

Process Industries

Many process industry companies actually have both continuous and highly repetitive operations. Typically, the front end is continuous—raw materials start as flows—but the

EXHIBIT 12–1   **Streamlined Flow Process**

Continuous-flow operations are in evidence at British Arkady Company's Briscoe Lane, Great Britain, plant in the production of frozen dough paste—a composite ingredient for the baking industry. Courtesy of British Arkady Company. Used with permission.

end products emerge as units. In candy factories, for example, sugar, chocolate, water, and other ingredients flow in, and cartons of candy bars or boxed candy come out. Potatoes, salt, vegetable oil, and so forth, flow into a potato chip plant, and cartons of sacked chips emerge. Sugar, water, flavoring, and active ingredients flow into a drug-producing plant, and out come boxes of bottled cough medicine. Exhibit 12–1 illustrates typical production of food items. Continuous flow of dough through the mixing stage gives way to individual pieces for subsequent freezing and packaging in highly repetitive fashion.

The streamlined flow is the distinguishing feature regardless of whether the output is continuous or repetitive. Efforts to achieve streamlined flow can be intensive, as is shown by the achievements of another food-processing company, the Pepperidge Farms division of Campbell Soup.[1] Pepperidge's problem was the same as most food processors': too many different products, package sizes, and types competing for very few production lines. The schedule for a certain product allowed intervals of days and even weeks between production runs; large lots, or poor service, resulted.

Faster changeovers from production of one product to another would allow more frequent production of all items. Pepperidge scoured the world to find equipment that could be quickly changed over. Now the new equipment in one plant permits production of nearly 10 times the number of products per day as the old. With more frequent production—closer to continuous—the company has come closer to synchronizing baking with store sales. Bake-to-store lead times for cookies and breads have been roughly halved; this is a sizable competitive advantage, since the product on the shelf is fresher.

*P*RINCIPLES 9 AND 12:

Use simple, flexible equipment. Cut changeover times.

---

[1]"A Smart Cookie at Pepperidge," *Fortune,* December 22, 1986, pp. 67–74.

EXHIBIT 12–2   **Success Factors for Process Industries**

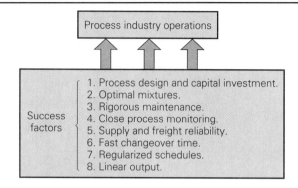

Employees at Pepperidge Farms took steps to make the company more responsive to customers' wants. Let's pursue that theme and examine process industry success factors more closely.

Key Success Factors

> The Cypress Plant was built with quality, just-in-time, and total employee involvement in mind; the plant was designed internally, and those who designed it run it. All associates are cross-trained on every task, and a weekly job rotation includes every facet of the plant. Obvious benefits include flexibility and enhanced problem solving. Rapid response to customer requirements has been attained through an 80 percent reduction in changeover times, receipt of materials in the exact (containerized) quantity needed and at the point-of-use, process stream-lining, buffer inventory reductions, and quick-response shipping. Brainstorming, partnerships with suppliers, benchmarking, and elimination of non-value-adding steps are other activities contributing to success.[2]

These comments have a familiar ring. They reflect prescriptions for success that appear throughout this text that are applicable to any organization. In this case, they refer to success in the chemical industry; they describe Milliken Chemical's Cypress plant in Blacksburg, South Carolina. In general, success in the chemicals business is obtained just as it is elsewhere: give customers quality, flexibility, responsive just-in-time service with short lead times, and eliminate wastes to drive down costs.

By delving into process industry specifics, however, we can identify targets of opportunity for managers and employees. Exhibit 12–2 identifies some key factors that provide direct support for successful process industry operations.

1. *Process design and capital investment.* Most stages from mixing through packaging tend to be quite automated (capital intensive). Some advantages can be gained by having more modern equipment than one's competitors, but it is often more important to keep the equipment in good condition so that the process yield is high and dependable.

2. *Optimal mixtures.* One of the more important uses of linear programming, a mathematical technique, is in determining optimal (best) mixtures of ingredients or other resources in some process industries. For example, product planners in

---

[2]This description of Milliken's Cypress plant was supplied by Mr. Sam P. Gambrell, director of Milliken Industrial Engineering Services, in a personal correspondence, December 1990.

companies that produce dog food, chicken feed, and so on, use linear programming to select the lowest-cost mix of ingredients that will meet nutrition and other standards. Since volumes are usually large, savings of a few cents per pound can be significant.

3. *Rigorous maintenance.* An equipment breakdown idles a whole process, for example, the whole mixing or the whole bottling process in the case of a food or drug company. When the product is perishable, there is further reason for wanting to avoid breakdowns. Perishability is also a reason for being unable to use buffer stocks between process stages as protection against breakdowns. In other words, perishability forces more of a just-in-time (stockless) mode of production.

4. *Close monitoring of the process.* In the process industries, federal law or industrywide standards often govern product quality, purity, and sanitation. Process monitoring must be rigorous to ensure that standards are met and products are safe and salable.

5. *Reliability of supply and freight.* This includes careful selection of a plant site close to markets and supplies of raw materials. Regardless of where the plant is located, the freight haulers bringing in raw material must be reliable, because raw materials are the lifeblood of process industries. Stockpiling as protection for shaky supply or freight is possible. But most of the process industry produces in such large volumes that even a few days' supply of ingredients can take up too much storage space. "Disaster stock" may be stored offline to keep it from interfering with the continuity and speed of flow.

6. *Fast changeover time.* Nearly all process-industry plants are able to change production lines to run different blends and container sizes. Sometimes it takes several days for a line changeover, which may include completely cleaning out all equipment. Fast changeovers make it easier to fit more jobs, large and small, into the schedule in a given time period.

7. *Regularized schedules.* Dominant products (say, the 10 most popular of 200 fabrics woven in a textile plant) deserve special treatment. An effective solution is to fit these products into regularly scheduled processing time slots, based on average demand rates. This approach provides predictable output for planners in sales and throughout the chain of customers and predictable materials usage for the supply chain. Nondominant products do not have enough volume to make this approach feasible, and so those products (the other 190 fabrics) would be scheduled irregularly, as demands dictate.

Regularized schedule: A schedule in which key items are made, or key services provided, at regular intervals.

8. *Linear output.* Regular processing slots are an improvement, but since yield per run may vary, a linear output plan provides extra insurance of getting predictable output for sales and predictable resource requirements for providers. Some call the linear output concept making to a number.

Linear output: Processing mode under which output quantity is the same each specified time period (e.g., hour, shift, or day).

Historically, competitive process industry companies have emphasized items 1 through 5 in Exhibit 12–2. In recent years, operations managers and employees have begun to address item 6 as well. Unfortunately, little attention has been given to items 7 and 8. Increased pressure from customers and from competitors, however, mandates continuous improvement for greater responsiveness in all eight success factors. The accompanying list suggests examples.

Increased Responsiveness

1. *Process design and capital investment.* Use concurrent design for outputs and processes, employ interfunctional teams for process design efforts, and keep an eye towards fail-safe devices.

2. *Optimal mixtures.* Take steps to secure superior process ingredients, including research and development, supplier certification, and early supplier involvement in process and materials improvement.

3. *Rigorous maintenance.* Employ total preventive maintenance programs, aimed at eliminating expensive downtime caused by equipment malfunctions, and practice cleanliness and regular calibration of measurement equipment.

4. *Close process monitoring.* Rely on automated monitoring and inspection, use statistical process control, and aim for early discovery of malfunctions, fast detection and removal of defects, and rapid correction of causes.

5. *Supply and freight reliability.* Use JIT purchasing, with delivery (to point-of-use) closely matching production schedules, and establish partnerships with a few good suppliers.

6. *Fast changeover time.* Incorporate fast setup and changeover techniques like single-minute-exchange-of-die (SMED) and offline setups, coupled with employee cross-training for mastery of multiple jobs.

7. *Regularized schedules.* Use regular slot schedules for dominant items, and cells for regular production of family-group components.

8. *Linear output.* Ensure linear output through consistently attainable output targets, obtained in turn by meeting (short) period demand with undercapacity scheduling and occasional overtime if needed.

Also, on a broader scale, process industry responsiveness means looking ahead. Reliance on typically large facilities filled with expensive equipment—resources with long purchase and installation lead times—forces process industry managers to plan well into the future; often substantial risks must be taken. Managers at Archer Daniels Midland (ADM), for example, spent years building a greater presence in Europe long before the iron curtain fell, opening the potential of Eastern European markets. In 1986, ADM purchased its Europoort facility in Rotterdam, the Netherlands (see Exhibit 12–3). Since that time, the plant has undergone continuous expansion and upgrading, and is now the largest and most modern grain processing facility in the world. Indeed, ADM seems well poised to play a large role in meeting Europe's agricultural products needs. Among oil companies, steel producers, and other process industry stalwarts that rely on high-volume production, success often depends on recognizing where mass markets might emerge and taking steps to build production facilities nearby.

What changes might we expect to see in future process industry operations? For one thing, regularized schedules and linear output, two largely ignored success factors, should receive increased attention. Let's examine them more closely.

Regularized Schedules and Linear Output

Despite the razzle-dazzle of new high-technology equipment, improvement in continuous processing and high-volume repetitive operations often hinges on better scheduling and on greater accuracy in providing the scheduled amount (hitting the target) consistently. Proven techniques for accomplishing these and other aims include processing with regularized schedules and linear output. To fully appreciate their usefulness, the negative consequences of irregular schedules and output need to be understood.

Consequences of Irregular Processing

The bar chart in Exhibit 12–4 represents what a typical process industry production schedule for item X might look like. Item X is one model or size in a family of products.

EXHIBIT 12-3   ADM's Europoort: World's Largest Soybean Processing Facility

Archer Daniels Midland Company's Europoort, in Rotterdam, the Netherlands, is the world's largest soybean processing facility. A destination for global soybean suppliers, the plant produces a variety of soy-based products and distributes them by sea, river, rail, and land. Courtesy of Archer Daniels Midland. Used with permission.

EXHIBIT 12-4   Schedule, in Work Shifts, for Item X

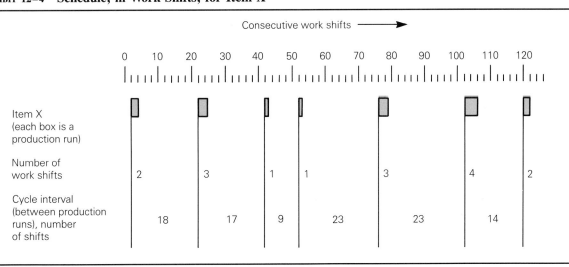

$\mathcal{I}$nto $\mathcal{P}$ractice

From High to Low in Brewing

In recent years, at a South African brewery, senior management keenly watched the weekly production total (amount of beer packaged). When the total hit a new record, management threw a "barbey" and beer party for all employees. So employees would occasionally summon a special effort to achieve that. But, "in the week following the record, everyone was so tired that they approached new lows. Management was stimulating their own instability."

SOURCE: Tongue-in-cheek report from Dr. Norman Faull, partner in the Faull and van der Riet consulting firm, specializing in consulting for brewing, paper-making, and other process industry businesses. Their approach is built around the "success factors for process industries" in Exhibit 12–2.

It might be standard-size 60-watt light bulbs, eight-ounce cans of tomato sauce, type-AAA batteries, rolls of 135 24-exposure, 100-speed color film, twin-bed-size white percale sheets, 3.5-inch Brand Z floppy disks, half-gallon cartons of cherry nut ice cream, six-packs of canned root beer, bottles of 50 decongestant tablets, 100-foot spools of 12-gauge, red-coated copper electrical wire, or four-by-eight-foot sheets of 3/8″ plywood.

Note the tendency to schedule not in pieces or volume, but in work shifts. Now, notice the variabilities. The number of shifts (length) of each production run varies: 2, 3, 1, 1, 3, 4, and 2. The interval between production runs also varies: 18 shifts, then 17, 9, 23, 23, and 14. Between production runs, other models of the same basic product occupy the schedule: other types or sizes of light bulbs, canned tomato products, batteries, and so on. Normal sales variations, special marketing promotions, and the end-of-the-month push to meet a sales quota cause demand variability, to which the production schedule must react.

Output is another source of variability not shown in Exhibit 12–4. In the process and high-volume assembly industries, the schedule is reasonably definite as to number of shifts but often rough as to units. For example, consider the first bar in Exhibit 12–4, a production run of two shifts. If Item X is standard 60-watt light bulbs and an average of 10,000 can be produced in a shift, the bar is interpreted as follows: The production run is two shifts, which might yield 20,000 bulbs. But the yield varies. If all goes well 20,400 may be produced, but on a poor day, only 18,500. Once in a while there will be a serious equipment or raw material failure, and output may be only 8,000. Production of only 8,000 risks a stockout and lost sales; thus, 60-watt bulbs will need to be fitted into the schedule again quite soon. The whole schedule gets adjusted now and then for such reasons.

Overtime or extra shifts are a possibility if the plant is not running at or near full capacity. However, traditional standard accounting systems often press manufacturing managers to run costly equipment near to full capacity even if inventory builds as a result. Change capacity—close a plant or shut down a production line—if sales fall, but let the records show high use of capacity without large cost variances.

To sum up, irregular production intervals, run times, and output release clouds of uncertainty. Since sales is uncertain about how much product to expect from operations, it tries to keep protective, and costly, buffer stocks in the distribution system. The greater costs are at the supplier side: What supplies of all the ingredients should be kept on hand?

Exhibit 12–5   Three Products with Regularized Schedules

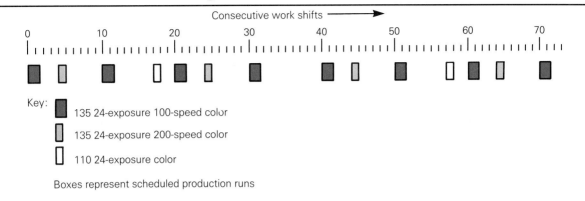

Key:
■ 135 24-exposure 100-speed color

▯ 135 24-exposure 200-speed color

▯ 110 24-exposure color

Boxes represent scheduled production runs

When and how much should each supplier deliver? How can suppliers ever achieve regular production schedules and thereby hold down their wasteful buffer stocks and costs? Irregularities pass backward through all prior stages of supply and production.

Something must be done. There is a crying need for regularity and stability.

Regular-Slot Processing

Giving the stars in the product line regular slots in the schedule is one fairly easy way to gain some regularity and stability. The stars are the models or sizes that sell in some quantity every day and earn a high proportion of total revenue. If they sell every day, the ideal is to make some every day, from 8 to 9 A.M., perhaps. The slots should be equal in hours of run time, should be changed when the demand rate changes, and should be spaced at regular intervals.

*P*RINCIPLE 2:

Reduce variability.

The superstar (the number one revenue earner) gets first claim at regular slots in the schedule, followed by some of the starlets. The regularized portion of the schedule may appear as in Exhibit 12–5. The example is for three sizes of photographic film (it could also be three or more flavors of ice cream, sizes of plywood, etc). Perhaps the manufacturer has a total of 80 film products. Schedulers fit the other 77 into the schedule in the old, irregular fashion.

While the benefits—more predictable needs for ingredients and more predictable deliveries to sales—apply to only 3 out of 80 products, that may represent a sizable percentage of costs and sales dollars, perhaps 15 or 20 percent. That 15 or 20 percent deserves the very best management, not average management.

Two points about regular-slot processing deserve further emphasis. First, shorter setup or changeover times facilitate regular-slot processing. If it takes four hours to change a line over, it might make little sense to schedule a one-hour production run each day, even for a star product. In that case, the star might be given a regular, but less frequent slot, say, once every six shifts.

Second, notice in Exhibit 12–5 that the 135 100-speed film (the superstar) is produced for 1½ shifts out of every 10 and it is produced on a regular interval of every 10 shifts. The 135 200-speed film is produced for 1 shift out of every 20, and the 110 film 1 shift out of every 40. Those production run lengths and cycle intervals are not set capriciously; together with information about production rates per shift, that schedule should reflect recent average demand for the various film products.

Regular slots improve predictability, but yield per run still can be quite variable. In many cases, regularizing of schedule slots should be combined with a policy of linear output.

Linear Output

Linearity index:
Measure of consistency
in hitting output target
quantity, expressed as a
percentage.

That means setting an attainable output target, running production until it is achieved, and not allowing overproduction.

No matter how attainable the target quantity is supposed to be, it cannot be met every time. A good way to monitor degree of success is with a linearity index (which apparently was devised by Hewlett-Packard Company). The index equals 100 percent minus the mean percent deviation, where mean percent deviation is the sum of absolute percentage deviations from schedule quantity divided by number of production runs. Mathematically, it is:

$$L = 100\% - \frac{\sum |D|}{N} \qquad (12–1)$$

where

L = Linearity index
D = Deviation from schedule quantity as a percentage of schedule quantity per run
N = Number of production runs

Typically, associates calculate the index monthly, and number of production runs (N) equals number of working days in the month. Calculation of the index is more simply illustrated, assuming only one production run per week, in Example 12–1.

EXAMPLE 12–1   Calculation of Linearity Index

Given:

500 units of a certain model of a product are to be run one shift a week on Mondays. Actual production last month was 500, 490, 510, and 500. Compute the linearity index for the month.

Solution:

The deviations from schedule, in units, are 0, −10, +10, and 0. To convert to percent, associates divide each by the schedule quantity per run, 500. That yields 0, −2, +2, and 0 percent, respectively. By Equation 12–1 (ignoring minus signs, since the absolute sum of deviations is used),

$$L = 100\% - \frac{\sum |D|}{N}$$

$$= 100\% - \frac{0\% + 2\% + 2\% + 0\%}{4}$$

$$= 100\% - \frac{4\%}{4} = 100\% - 1\%$$

$$= 99 \text{ percent}$$

The linearity index mathematically reflects that any deviation, over or under schedule, is undesirable; both over- and underproduction cause problems for suppliers and uncertainty for users. In Example 12–1, the shortfall of 10 units in week 2 was made up by deliberate overproduction of 10 in week 3 to get back on target. (The index does not reward getting back on target. However, an alternate form of the index, calculated based on a cumulative schedule, does encourage getting back on schedule; the cumulative basis might be useful in some cases.) Note too that the index will always be 100 percent if the schedule is met every time.

At some Hewlett-Packard plants, linearity is calculated for every product and every production line every shift every day. The daily results are used to compute a monthly linearity index, which is posted on a graph for all to see.

*C*ontrast

Processing Mode

Irregular Processing	**Regular-Slot, Linear Processing**
Variabilities: high variability in output quantity, length of production run, and time between runs.	*Variabilities:* constant-run length at regular intervals, with linear output, provides known quantity.
Capacity planning/usage: tendency is to run at or near full capacity, little margin available to meet demand upswings or cope with processing problems.	*Capacity planning/usage:* undercapacity scheduling provides capacity margins to meet demand upswings and time to fix problems.
Inventory: costly buffer stocks out of synch with market demand, supply and delivery uncertainty.	*Inventory:* knowledge that supply is regular reduces reliance on buffer stocks.
Customer service: sales personnel unsure as to production quantity and timing.	*Customer service:* predictable processing and delivery schedules.

The linearity index is usable in continuous processes, but it seems to have been first used in repetitive operations, our next topic.

Improving Repetitive Operations

Once the product's state changes from continuous flow to discrete units, we call it repetitive rather than continuous. Of course, a good share of the world's products are discrete from start to finish. In producing discrete units, a worthy goal is to increase repetitiveness and get away from lots.

As with continuous-processing, facilities layout is critical in repetitive operations. Typically, product or cellular layouts are favored, for they afford the opportunities for the streamlining that high-volume repetitive operations demand. Managers and employees could begin improving repetitive operations by addressing the factors deemed crucial for the process industry in general, for all the factors listed in Exhibit 12–2 and discussed earlier in the chapter are applicable to repetitive processing.

Actions specifically targeted at repetitive operations also result in improved responsiveness (see Exhibit 12–6). We consider them next.

After a product or cellular layout has been developed, task assignments must be divided among work stations along the line or in the cell, a procedure called line balancing. It is important to emphasize from the outset that line *re*balancing is a useful tool for continuous improvement as conditions change. Even simple line-balancing problems can become quite detailed, however, and we reserve most of the procedural specifics for an example appearing later in the chapter. Here, we focus on a more general overview of the tool.

Some products can be made either in a fixed layout or in a product/cellular layout; line balancing applies only to the latter case. Furthermore, some work is done entirely at a single workstation; an invoice may be prepared, checked, and paid by a single clerk, or a computer printer may be completely assembled by one operator. These are **autonomous**

Line Balancing and Rebalancing

Line balancing:
Dividing work among stations along a production line or within a work cell.

EXHIBIT 12–6   Repetitive Operations Improvement Factors

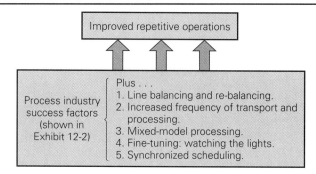

operations, and no line balancing is needed. However, if items being worked on are passed from station to station, that is, in **progressive operations,** line balancing comes into play.

Several other concepts fundamental to the line-balancing task are explained, with a brief example, in the accompanying box.

In the example in the box, if associates get the needed production rate of slightly more than 17 per hour with just 35 minutes of throughput time instead of 105 minutes, they are far more efficient: less inventory, less floor space, less time until discovery of errors, faster response to change (design and demand changes), closer dependency and better

Line efficiency is often measured by computation of balance delay, described in the line-balancing example later in the chapter.

𝒥nto 𝒫ractice

Line Balancing: Basic Concepts

The designer charged with initial or rough line balancing is often an industrial engineer or another associate familiar with time standards, methods-study information, and process flow. Suppose demand is such that the line or cell is to provide a unit of work every 3.5 minutes. The designer wants to assign each workstation precisely 3.5 minutes of work so that the work load is balanced and so that each pass to the next station occurs just as the downstream station (the customer) has completed its tasks and has demand for the next piece.

That 3.5 minutes is the **cycle time.** Perhaps time standards show that the total **work content time** to make one unit is 35 minutes. Then, with each station working 3.5 minutes, 10 workstations are needed.

For a piece having 35 minutes of work content, the **throughput time** or production lead time is unlikely to be

35 minutes. Handling among stations and various delays may add time. Also, there may be small buffer stocks between some processes. For example, most high-volume conveyor-driven, or paced, production lines making TVs, cameras, videocassette players, keyboards, and so forth, have several units between stations. If there are two idle units between stations for every one being worked on, the throughput time is 3 times 35 minutes, or 105 minutes; that is, a unit gets 3.5 minutes of work at station 1, then waits for 7 minutes, then gets 3.5 minutes more work at station 2, then 7 minutes' wait time, and so on, through 10 stations. Raw material enters every 3.5 minutes and completed units emerge every 3.5 minutes, but each unit spends 105 minutes in the system. The **production rate** is 17.14 units per hour.

atmosphere for teamwork, and close connection between each provider and customer. As a production line ages, a goal should be to cut throughput time, as well as cycle time, in order to decrease waste and improve efficiency.

In sum, process designs should be flexible. Rebalancing or other activities for improving the workload balance should go on continuously.

There are numerous examples of businesses that achieve roughly repetitive operations in final assembly but are far from it in earlier processes. The term *roughly repetitive* allows for variety within limits. In a Mr. Steak restaurant, the cook who grills steaks has a repetitive job, but the steaks vary in size and quality of meat. Routine purchase orders (POs) in a purchasing department are similar. Each PO is slightly different but is basically a repetitive operation. In the first case, the preceding process is in lots, not repetitive—purchased lots of steaks. In the second, both the preceding and next operations are in lots—batches of incoming requisitions (requests to buy) received by internal mail and batches of outgoing mailed purchase orders.

Is there room for improvement? Often there is. If a Mr. Steak restaurant currently receives steaks every three days, improvement would be receiving in smaller (more repetitive) daily amounts. Obvious advantages are less cold storage, better control of aging, and less forecast error. In the case of POs, a modern improvement is electronic communication. Send orders to suppliers electronically via facsimile, one at a time, immediately as needs are known. That gets the supplier working on the order sooner.

Steaks and POs have what are called shallow bills of materials. (For grilled steaks there are just two BOM levels: raw and grilled.) Many products with deep BOMs are, like steaks and invoices, roughly repetitive in the last process, final assembly, but not in earlier processes (lower levels on the BOM). Examples are cars, trucks, tractors, and small aircraft. In final assembly, each successive unit may have its own set of options, but the assemblers perform almost the same operations over and over.

For such products, a way to improve operations is to extend the repetitiveness backward into subassembly, fabrication, and purchasing. The easy way is to cut transit quantities: smaller loads moved more frequently, ideally with the discipline of kanban. Next, cut lot size and cycle interval (interval between production runs); this often requires reducing setup or changeover times. (When the transit quantity is one unit, that is as repetitive as is possible for a certain production run or lot.) These topics were addressed in Chapters 7 through 10 and need no further discussion here.

The production schedule interval for the film in Exhibit 12–5 was shown in work shifts, each perhaps eight hours long. Schedules can be repetitive in much longer or shorter cycle intervals. When a variety of products must be produced and the cycle interval is very short (a day, a few hours) teams might employ mixed-model processing.

Consider the irregular, long cycle-interval schedule for products L, M, and N shown in Exhibit 12–7A. The boxes represent production runs; they vary in duration, as do the intervals between them. For example, in February and March, nearly two months pass between production runs of product N. Suppose that L, M, and N are standard products that enjoy regular, perhaps daily, sales; thus, they show good potential for repetitive regularized production.

Exhibit 12–7B shows a regularized repetitive schedule with a fairly short cycle interval (one day) between repetitions. Let's examine how a scheduler might determine the mixed-model processing cycle. The objectives are to match production to demand with a regularized schedule that gives star products priority status.

Increasing Frequency of Transport and Processing

Mixed-Model Processing

Mixed-model processing: Short cycle-interval production of a variety of types, sizes, or models of a product family on the same line or within a single cell.

EXHIBIT 12–7   **Irregular, Repetitive, and Mixed-Model Schedules**

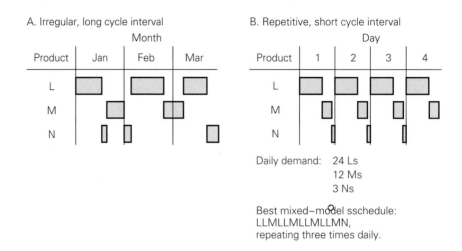

A. Irregular, long cycle interval

B. Repetitive, short cycle interval

Daily demand: 24 Ls
12 Ms
3 Ns

Best mixed–model sschedule:
LLMLLMLLMLLMN,
repeating three times daily.

Assume that daily sales average 24 Ls, 12 Ms, and 3 Ns, for a total of 39 units. First, reduce those requirements to the minimum ratio; dividing each demand amount by 3 yields 8, 4, and 1. Second, sum the minimum ratios, obtaining the number 13. That becomes the number of units in the repeating processing cycle. That is, every cycle will contain 13 units; 8 will be Ls, 4 will be Ms, and 1 will be N. To meet daily demand, the cycle will repeat 3 times each day. Third, find the mix of the 13 units that is most repetitive, minimizing the interval between production of each type of product.

This last step might require trial and error, but one or two simple passes will usually suffice. Consider two possible solutions that meet the daily demand requirement:

> There are two levels of repetition in mixed-model processing: (1) cycle repetition during the processing period (day or shift) and (2) repetition within the cycle itself.

1. LLLLLLLLMMMMN—Repeat three times per day. Assessment: Not repetitive within cycle; must wait up to 6 units for next L, up to 10 units for next M.
2. LLMLLMLLMLLMN—Repeat three times per day. Assessment: Repetitive within cycle, four repeating triplets followed by singleton; maximum wait to next L is 3 units, and maximum wait to next M is 4 units. (This is the best schedule for this product mix.)

One advantage of going to the lowest-ratio, most-repetitive mix is that it allows providers of component parts to consider low-capacity processes and cheap equipment. Assume that the products L, M, and N in Exhibit 12–7 are (respectively) 24-, 20-, and 18-inch bicycle wheels, which are made from cut metal strips. If the whole day's requirement of each size is cut in one batch, what cutting equipment is appropriate? A good choice might be a costly, semiautomatic cutting machine that takes an hour to adjust for length changes (setup) but then cuts pieces fast.

On the other hand, if production of each size wheel is spaced out in the lowest-ratio model mix, the need for cut metal strips is also spaced out. Instead of the costly, high-speed cutter, why not use a simple band saw? It is much slower, but it takes virtually no time for a length change, and the low-ratio mixed-model schedule requires many length changes per day. In our example, the band saw would cut two 24-inch strips, one 20-inch strip, two 24s, one 20, two 24s, one 20, two 24s, one 20, and, finally, one 18-inch strip. That 13-unit sequence repeats two additional times throughout the day, exactly matching demand at the next processes, which are rim forming and wheel assembly.

What if the high-speed cutter is already owned and the producer, as part of a continual improvement effort, is changing the schedule from a daily batch to lowest-ratio mix? An attractive option is to treat 24-inch wheels as the star. Set up the high-speed cutter permanently for that length and cut two at a time intermittently throughout the day. This has the advantages of speed, no more one-hour length changes, and perfect stockless synchronization with the next process. Buy a band saw, if one is not already owned, to cut the 20- and 18-inch lengths.

The benefit of being able to use cheaper, simpler equipment as a result of low-ratio mixed-model scheduling may seem small, or rarely applicable. Not so! Toyota Motors, which has followed this scheduling and frugal equipment policy (capital expenditure avoidance), perhaps more extensively and longer than any other manufacturer, finds itself with massive retained earnings.

Thus far, our discussion of mixed-model processing has been limited to issues and benefits associated with scheduling. Line-balancing algorithms have also been developed for mixed-model assembly lines. For example, in a mixed-model doll clothing line, male dolls, female dolls, large dolls, small dolls, and so forth, may be clothed in a mixed sequence.

Mixed-model line-balancing involves (1) determining the sequence of products (model numbers) moving down the line and (2) balancing the line. Some line-balancing methods allow for restrictions and special conditions: subassembly lines that feed main lines, distance and direction requirements, safety needs, special groupings of elements, zoning restrictions, maximum and minimum conveyor speeds, and so forth.

Example 12–2 illustrates some factors involved in mixed-model line balancing.

*𝒫*RINCIPLE 9:

Look for simple, flexible, low-cost equipment.

EXAMPLE 12–2   MIXED MODELS—BORING HOLES IN PUMP HOUSINGS

A machine center bores holes in pump housings. It used to take twice as long to set up and run a lot of large pump housings as it did small housings. After a vigorous improvement effort, the setup times are now nearly zero for either size of housing. With negligible setup times, it seems reasonable to run mixed models down a mini-production line composed of machines that bore the holes.

The schedule calls for 22 large (L) and 88 small (S) pump housings per day. Run times are 12 minutes per large unit and 2 minutes per small unit. What cycle of mixed models will produce the scheduled quantity with balanced production?

Solution:

Model sequence:	L	S	S	S	S	L	S	S	S	S	...
Operation time:	12	2	2	2	2	12	2	2	2	2	...
			20					20			

This cycle takes 20 minutes and repeats 22 times per day. The production requires 20 × 22 = 440 minutes out of a 480-minute workday, which leaves 40 extra minutes for problem solving, equipment care, and so forth.

Fine-Tuning:
Watching the Lights

Line-balancing seems precise and accurate but it isn't. A good typist can type twice as many words per minute as an average one. Similarly, a good welder, solderer, or painter can work twice as fast as an average one. In a line balance based on standard pace, the fast people will not have enough to do and the slow ones will have trouble keeping up. Fine-tuning is needed. The supervisor or operating team will see who the slow ones are and can fine-tune by reassigning some work elements from slower to faster people. A novel method called watching the lights serves to make fine-tuning a bit easier.

It is fairly common for trouble lights to be mounted above production lines to alert troubleshooters and supervisors when there is a slowdown or line stoppage. Typically, a red light signals shutdown and a yellow signals trouble. Yellow lights may also aid in fine-tuning the line balancing. Here is how it works:

1. A new production schedule is issued, rough line balancing takes place, and work begins.
2. Anyone who has trouble keeping up will turn on the yellow light frequently. Those who have no trouble keeping up will not turn on their yellow lights. The message to the supervisor and team is clear. Take a few small duties away from those with too much to do and reassign them to those whose lights have not been coming on. When everyone's yellow lights are coming on at about the same frequency, the line is balanced, and no one is pushed into making errors out of haste.
3. With the line balanced, yellow lights no longer suggest line imbalance; they indicate trouble. For the remaining days or weeks of the schedule, the problem signaled by a yellow light is recorded so that there are good data for problem solving.

When industry veterans first hear about this approach, they tend to be dubious or full of questions: "But some people will have much more to do than others. Is that fair? Won't the faster operators complain? Or won't they deliberately go slow and push the yellow button in order to avoid getting more tasks to do?"

The first question is not so hard. It is true that the fast people will end up with more tasks to do, but surely that is more fair, not less. The system should not mask the abilities of the fast employees, nor should it unduly pressure the slower ones. There will be complaints from some of the faster people. The complaints may be resolved in two ways:

1. Give the faster employees bonuses, incentive pay, merit wage increases, pay for knowledge, or special training or other rewards.
2. Evolve a performance appraisal approach that rewards for problem solving, quality control, and work improvement. These activities focus on innovativeness, leadership, and communication skills. Make sure that enough labor is available to make it possible to meet the schedule every day and on most days still allow time for problem solving, quality control, work improvement, and maintenance.

Synchronized
Scheduling

As we have seen throughout this chapter, streamlined operations require changes in scheduling. The ultimate is to let a final assembly schedule serve as the schedule for all major assemblies, which in turn would serve as the schedules for fabricated parts, and so on, back to purchased parts and beyond. That ideal may be called synchronized scheduling. It involves meshing the timing of delivery or production of an item with the use rate of the next item at the next higher process level. Synchronizing delivery with usage is good; synchronizing operations and delivery with usage is even better: Make one, deliver one, use one.

As an example of synchronization, consider what happens to a written sales order sent in to a home office for action. Typically, the action is hard to find amid all the order-processing delays. The order may spend two days in central sales, two in accounting for a credit check, three in order filling and packing, and finally one more in shipping. And we should probably add a day for passage through the company mail room between each action activity. The total throughput time in this out-of-synch, snail-paced operation is about 11 days.

One way to synchronize these operations would be requiring each office to process this hour whatever came in last hour, mail service included. That cuts throughput time from 11 days to 7 hours!

As an example of synchronization in a factory, imagine a plant that makes blue jeans. If the schedule for the next two hours calls for the sewing machines (final assembly) to sew stovepipe-cut 28-inch-waist and 30-inch-length jeans, the schedule for the next two hours in the cutting room should call for cutting fabric for the same size and style. Cut one pattern, send it forward, and immediately sew it. If zippers, thread, labels, and rivets are also on the same schedule, the schedule is highly synchronized. While there may still be some idle inventories, for example, because of delivery problems, potential stoppages or defects, and differences in process speeds, none result from mismatched schedules.

Of course, one way to get synchronization is to relocate far-flung processes into a cell, for example, an order-processing cell in which orders are passed from desk to desk in one room, or a blue jeans cell complete with cutting, sewing, and packaging.

> **Synchronized scheduling (or *synchronized processing*):** Scheduling or processing such that the timing of delivery or production of an item coincides with the timing or usage rate of the parent item.

Line-Balancing Example

Any of several line-balancing methods may be used in the rough, or initial, balancing stage. They include trial and error, as well as heuristics, algorithms, and mathematical models. Computer programs are available for many of the algorithms and models; study of those tools is reserved for more specifically focused texts. Here, we look at a manual heuristic line-balancing procedure, which begins, like other line-balancing methods, with a precedence diagram.

> A heuristic is a search procedure that may give an optimal solution to a problem but offers no guarantee of doing so. If it can be proven that an exact solution exists, the method becomes an algorithm.

The **precedence diagram** charts the work elements and their required sequence. To get the work elements, the entire process is divided into tasks and subtasks. This division of labor is carried down to where a task is assignable to a single station.

One popular type of precedence diagram shows the earliest stage of production where each work element may be done. Element durations, numbers, and sometimes descriptions go on the diagram; arrows show which elements must come before which others.

Example 12–3 demonstrates the precedence diagram. The assembly task is clothing a male doll. In real doll making, all of the work elements for such assembly would probably be done by a single assembler, because the element times are very short. But for the sake of illustration, we shall assume progressive, rather than autonomous, assembly. Precedence diagramming can allow for a variety of special restrictions, but this example is kept simple.

Precedence Diagram

Once the precedence diagram has been completed, actual line balancing may begin. A perfectly balanced line has zero balance delay, which means no wait time at any workstation. **Balance delay,** *d,* is:

$$d = \frac{nc - \sum t}{nc} \tag{12–2}$$

Line-Balancing Analysis

EXAMPLE 12–3   PRECEDENCE DIAGRAM FOR LINE BALANCING—DOLL ASSEMBLY[3]

A toy company is coming out with a new male doll. The doll is to be clothed on an assembly line, with different items of clothing put on at different stations. The company wants a balanced assembly line.

Methods engineers have broken up the whole job into 13 separate items of clothing, each of which is a work element, with element times as follows:

Element	Element Time t (in 0.01 Minutes)
1. Put on undershorts.	10
2. Put on undershirt.	11
3. Put on left sock.	9
4. Put on right sock.	9
5. Put on slacks.	22
6. Put on shirt.	42
7. Put on left shoe.	26
8. Put on right shoe.	26
9. Put on belt.	30
10. Insert pocket items (wallet, keys, and handkerchief).	20
11. Put on tie.	63
12. Put on coat.	32
13. Put on hat.	6
Total work content time, $\sum t$	306

Solution:

Using the elemental data, associates develop the precedence diagram shown in Exhibit 12–8. Work elements are in the circles and element times are beside the circles. The four elements under stage I have no predecessors and can be started anytime. No elements may begin until their predecessors have been completed.

In a column, work elements are independent of one another. Three elements (left sock, right sock, and hat) have lateral flexibility; that is, they may be moved one column to the right without disturbing precedence restrictions. With these kinds of flexibility, a large number of combinations of workstation layout sequences can satisfy precedence restrictions.

where

n = Number of workstations
c = Cycle time
$\sum t$ = Total work content time for one unit

A manual heuristic line-balancing method is shown in Example 12–4, again using the doll assembly.

EXAMPLE 12–4   MANUAL HEURISTIC LINE BALANCING—DOLL ASSEMBLY

Total work content ($\sum t$) for the doll assembly is 306 hundredths of a minute (see data given in Example 12–3). A first step in line-balancing analysis is breaking $\sum t$ into its prime numbers. There are five prime numbers:

$$306 = 1 \times 2 \times 3 \times 3 \times 17$$

---

[3]Adapted from Theodore O. Prenting and Nicholas T. Thomopoulos, *Humanism and Technology in Assembly Line Systems* (Rochelle Park, N.J.: Spartan Books, 1974), pp. 131–32 (TS178.4P73).

Exhibit 12–8   Precedence Diagram—Clothing a Doll

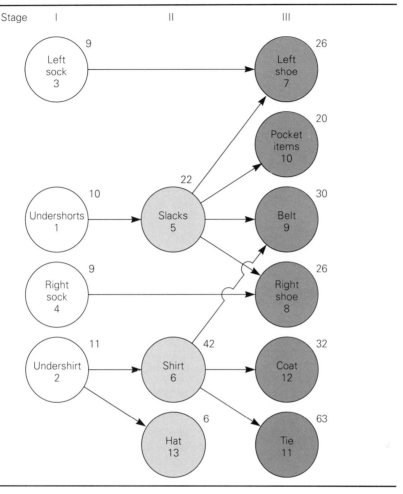

Source: Theodore O. Prenting and Nicholas T. Thomopoulos, *Humanism and Technology in Assembly Line Systems* (Rochelle Park, N.J.: Spartan Books, 1974), p. 132 (TS178.4.P73). Used with permission.

For a balanced line, the cycle time must equal the product of some combination of these prime numbers. However, a cycle time shorter than the longest single work element time is not feasible (unless a way can be found to divide the element into two distinct elements). The combinations yield 12 possible cycle times:

$$c_1 = 2 \times 3 \times 3 \times 17 = 306 \qquad\qquad c_7 = 17$$
$$c_2 = 3 \times 3 \times 17 = 153 \qquad\qquad c_8 = 3 \times 3 = 9$$
$$c_3 = 2 \times 3 \times 17 = 102 \qquad\qquad c_9 = 3 \times 2 = 6$$
$$c_4 = 3 \times 17 = 51 \qquad\qquad c_{10} = 3$$
$$c_5 = 2 \times 17 = 34 \qquad\qquad c_{11} = 2$$
$$c_6 = 2 \times 3 \times 3 = 18 \qquad\qquad c_{12} = 1$$

Now we want to see how many workstations (n) we would end up with in a balanced line. To find out, we simply divide cycle times into the total work content, 306:

$$n_1 = \frac{\sum t}{c_1} = \frac{306}{306} = 1 \text{ station} \qquad n_3 = \frac{\sum t}{c_3} = \frac{306}{102} = 3 \text{ stations}$$

$$n_2 = \frac{\sum t}{c_2} = \frac{306}{153} = 2 \text{ stations} \qquad n_4 = \frac{\sum t}{c_4} = \frac{306}{51} = 6 \text{ stations}$$

Exhibit 12–9   Tabular Form of Precedence Relationships in Assembling Clothes

(A) Column Number in Precedence Diagram	(B) Element Number	(C) Remarks	(D) Element Time, (t)	(E) Sum of Element Times	(F) Cumulative Sum of Times
I	3	→ II	9		
	1		10		
	4	→ II	9		
	2		11	39	39
II	5		22		
	6		42		
	13	→ III	6	70	109
III	7		26		
	10		20		
	9		30		
	8		26		
	12		32		
	11		63	197	306

Note: Six or more stations would be poorly balanced, since the minimum cycle time is 0.63 minutes, which is the time it takes to install the tie on the doll, element 11. Thus, there are just three feasible perfectly balanced options: n_1 through n_3.

The choice of number of stations may be dictated by the production schedule. Assume the schedule calls for 400 dolls per day and there is one shift of 400 working minutes. The required cycle time, then, is 400/400 = 1.00 minutes per doll. Option n_3, which has a cycle time of 1.02 minutes and calls for 3 stations, is almost perfect.

To develop a plan for a well-balanced line with three stations, we begin by rearranging the precedence diagram, Exhibit 12–8, into a table, Exhibit 12–9. Columns A, B, and D in the table are taken directly from the precedence diagram. Column C shows elements that could just as well be performed in a later stage. Column E sums the element times for each stage, and column F cumulatively sums the times for the three stages.

Now, we inspect for ways to achieve a well-balanced line, which must have three stations, each with work content close to 102. We can see from Exhibit 12–9 that the cumulative sum of stages I and II is close at 109. A way to reduce it closer to 102 presents itself: Move element 13, with a time of 6, from stage II to stage III. This reduces the time for stages I through II to 103, which is very close to the 102 that would give perfect balance.

Moving element 13 to stage III increases the stage III sum from 197 to 203. Now we want to split stage III into two stations, with cycle times close to 102, the ideal. To find a set of work element times whose sum is close to 102 or 101, it is efficient to begin by adding the larger numbers. Adding elements 11 and 12 — 63 and 32 — gives 95; adding 6, the time for element 13, gives us 101. The remaining four elements — 7, 10, 8, and 9 — total 102.

Exhibit 12–10 gives us the nearly perfect solution, with station times of 103, 102, and 101. This means that one doll may be clothed every 103 hundredths of a minute, not counting transit time between stations. Station 1's capacity is fully used

EXHIBIT 12-10   **Improved Line-Balancing Solution for Assembling Clothes**

(A) Column Number in Precedence Diagram	(B) Element Number	(C) Remarks	(D) Element Time, (t)	(E) Sum of Element Times	(F) Cumulative Sum of Times	
I	3		9			↑
	1		10			
	4		9			Station
	2		11			1
II	5		22			
	6		42	103	103	↓
III	7		26			↑
	10		20			Station
	9		30			2
	8		26	102	205	↓
	13	From Stage II	6			↑
	12		32			Station
	11		63	101	306	3
						↓

each cycle; station 2 wastes 0.01 minutes per cycle; and station 3 wastes 0.02 minutes per cycle. The waste or underuse of capacity for the whole assembly line is the balance delay, which, by Equation 12-2 is:

$$d = \frac{nc - \Sigma t}{nc} = \frac{(3 \times 103) - 306}{3 \times 103}$$

$$= \frac{309 - 306}{309} = \frac{3}{309} \approx 1\%$$

Note that fewer than three stations is unfeasible, since the precedence diagram, Exhibit 12-8, shows several sequences that include all three stages (for example, 1 to 5 to 7). It is feasible to have four or five stations, but it seems unlikely that either would cut the balance delay below 1 percent, because the resulting cycle times would not be products of primes. Therefore, we select n_3, and the analysis ceases.

The heuristic method yields good, but not necessarily optimal, results, and development of optimizing algorithms and models continues. Though a variety of line-balancing computer software is available to ease the computational burden, manual heuristic and trial-and-error line balancing efforts are widespread.

Line Balancing in Perspective

For one thing, line balancing is not easily reduced to simple models or algorithms; there are simply too many choices, given the flexibility and variability of humans. Employees can run one machine or several, push a broom or wield a paintbrush between machine cycles, handle machine setup and inspection duties or leave those chores for special crews, speed up or loaf, stay at their work or wander off, fix broken equipment and suggest improvements or leave it up to the specialists, and file documents or sit around waiting for file clerks to do it.

Get to know the
customer. Operate at
the customer's rate of
use.

How can balance be designed into a process with those uncertainties? The answer is: One can design only a roughly balanced line. Supervisors and the work group itself need to fine-tune it and redo it often as customer demand rates change.

Scope of Application

The techniques of transforming irregular operations into repetitive, synchronized operations apply not only to high-volume production; they may also apply to building, say, one ship every two weeks or one passenger aircraft every three days. If each ship or plane is a special order for a different customer, that is only a partial obstacle to repetitive operations. In manufacture of ships and planes, thousands of parts are the same from unit to unit and are therefore unaffected by special orders. Those thousands of standard parts may be made to highly repetitive schedules—repeating only every two weeks or every three days—with some levels synchronized with the level directly above. The massive problem of scheduling all those parts thus can be partly simplified, and some flows of parts can be put on kanban.

One of the most pressing needs in operations management is extending the benefits of continuous and highly repetitive processing (the stuff of this chapter) into job and batch operations. We take up that challenge in the next chapter.

Summary

Many process industry companies have both continuous and highly repetitive operations. As they make goods that pour or flow, they are plagued by large lots and long cycle intervals in much the same way job-oriented firms are.

Although the general factors that spell success in process industries are the same as for other firms, there are some specific opportunity targets for managers and employees in process industry companies. Traditionally, the process industry's concerns have been modern, well-maintained equipment for achieving process control and high-volume, low-cost flows; optimal mixtures of ingredients for minimizing raw material cost; and reliable supply and freight. Today, worldwide competition presses for fast equipment changeover, regularized schedules, mixed-model processing, and linear output.

In the process and high-volume assembly industries, production intervals typically are irregular. Quantities produced are also irregular, because the tendency is to schedule a definite number of shifts per production run but get a variable yield per shift. One way to avert the high costs of irregularities is to give the star (high-revenue) product regular slots in the schedule and let lesser products fill the gaps.

In linear processing, employees strive to produce the same output quantity within a specified time period (e.g., hour, shift, or day). They measure performance with a linearity index, where 100 percent linearity means meeting exact target quantity every time.

Balancing workstation capacity is a primary concern in production-line layout. Line balancing usually begins as associates divide a job into work elements or tasks and show the task sequence on a precedence diagram. A manual heuristic method makes use of precedence diagram data to yield a nearly balanced line, specifying cycle time and number of workstations. A perfectly balanced line has zero balance delay, or full utilization at each workstation while the line is running.

Line balancing is more difficult in mixed-model situations. Sequencing becomes critical, and a work cycle may call for mixed sequences of several short-cycle-time models along with one long-cycle-time model. The work cycle repeats. Fine-tuning is required with any line balance. By watching the lights, supervisors and operators may adjust workloads away from those who turn on their yellow trouble lights most often.

Sometimes products start out in continuous flow and later, perhaps in packaging, end up in discrete units produced either irregularly or repetitively. One technique for increasing repetitiveness is more frequent moves and production lots in smaller quantities. Another is to synchronize production schedules from one processing level to the next. When people synchronize two levels, they eliminate costly inventory and pave the way for the simplest of scheduling techniques for the lower level: kanban.

A very short cycle repetitive schedule could use mixed-model processing. The shorter the cycle, the better, because short cycles slow the production pace for each model in the mix. Simpler, cheaper, slower equipment may be considered.

Repetitive techniques can apply to both low-volume products, such as airplanes, and high-volume ones, such as telephone sets. Extending benefits of streamlined processing into job and batch operations is a critical need.

Key Words

Regularized schedule	407	Work content time	414
Linear output	407	Throughput time	414
Linearity index	412	Production rate	414
Line balancing	413	Mixed-model processing	415
Autonomous operations	413	Synchronized scheduling	419
Progressive operations	414	Precedence diagram	419
Cycle time	414	Balance delay	419

Solved Problems

Problem 1

An assembly line currently staffed with 10 assemblers produces an average of 190 units per day. The current sales rate for the product is 200 units per day. If the company follows a policy of scheduling at 85 percent of capacity, what should it do? (Options include setting a new production rate or changing capacity.)

Solution 1

The production rate must be 200 units per day, exactly the number being sold. Then 200 is set equal to 85 percent of capacity, and capacity is solved for algebraically:

$$0.85X = 200$$

Then:

$$X = 235.3 \text{ units per day}$$

Since 10 assemblers can produce 190 on the average, we need to know how many assemblers are needed to produce 235.3. Therefore:

$$\frac{10}{190} = \frac{X}{235.3}$$

$$190X = 2,353$$

$$X = 12.38, \text{ or } 13 \text{ assemblers}$$

Thus, the company must assign three more assemblers to the production line.

Problem 2

The accompanying table shows 22 working days of production against a regularized schedule for a somewhat new product. The schedule rate, seven per day, was set on the 15th of the prior month. It gets changed in midmonth only when actual orders are greatly deviating from plan, as happened on August 22 to 26. Calculate the linearity index.

Date	Working Day	Pack Schedule	Actual Pack	Comments
8-1	1	7	3	No card cages
2	2	7	3	
5	3	7	10	
6	4	7	11	
7	5	7	4	Door latch problems
8	6	7	9	Two people short
9	7	7	9	
12	8	7	1	No drives
13	9	7	5	Rework required
14	10	7	4	Rework required
15	11	7	5	Rework required
16	12	7	6	Rework required
19	13	7	10	
20	14	7	7	
21	15	7	10	
22	16	0	0	No orders
23	17	0	0	No orders
26	18	0	0	No orders
27	19	7	5	
28	20	7	2	
29	21	7	3	
30	22	7	1	

Solution 2

Step 1: Insert working columns for calculation of absolute deviation (ignore minus signs) and percent deviation:

Working Day	Pack Schedule	Actual Pack	Absolute Deviation	Percent Deviation
1	7	3	4	4/7 = 57%
2	7	3	4	4/7 = 57
3	7	10	3	3/7 = 43
4	7	11	4	4/7 = 57
5	7	4	3	3/7 = 43
6	7	9	2	2/7 = 29
7	7	9	2	2/7 = 29
8	7	1	6	6/7 = 86
9	7	5	2	2/7 = 29
10	7	4	3	3/7 = 43
11	7	5	2	2/7 = 29
12	7	6	1	1/7 = 14
13	7	10	3	3/7 = 43
14	7	7	0	0/7 = 0
15	7	10	3	3/7 = 43
		—Omit zero schedule days—		
19	7	5	2	2/7 = 29
20	7	2	5	5/7 = 71
21	7	3	4	4/7 = 57
22	7	1	6	6/7 = 86
Total = 19 working days				Total = 845%

Step 2: Calculate the linearity index (L):

$$L = 100\% - \frac{845\%}{19} = 100\% - 44.5\% = 55.5\%$$

Consider the following elemental precedence diagram (element times are in units of 0.01 minutes):   *Problem 3*

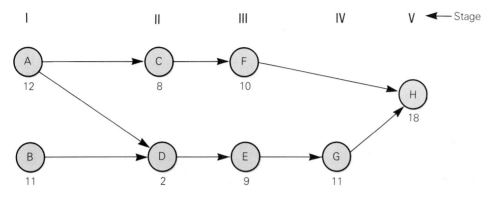

a. What would be the cycle time for a line with one workstation (autonomous production)?

b. What would be the maximum daily capacity of such a line assuming 420 minutes of work time per day?

c. What is the shortest possible cycle time?

d. Assuming we used this shortest cycle time, what would daily line capacity be?

e. Plan a balanced line for the assembly operation using a cycle time of 0.29 minutes. Compute the balance delay for your solution. What will be the approximate capacity of the line assuming a 420-minute workday?

f. Try to reduce the balance delay in your solution to question e by adjusting element assignments. What effect would you hope to obtain regarding cycle time? Compute the balance delay and the approximate daily capacity assuming a 420-minute workday.

g. The solution in question f cuts balance delay. In what ways, if any, does that benefit the customer?

a. With one workstation, the sum of the element times would be a reasonable estimate for the   *Solution 3*
cycle time. In this case, the sum is 0.81 minutes.

b. With 420 minutes of available work time per day, the maximum capacity possible with a cycle time of 0.81 minutes would be: $420/0.81 = 519$ units

c. The shortest possible cycle time equals the time of the longest element, or 0.18 minutes. We would not necessarily want to use this as the cycle time, but it is possible to do so.

d. If we were using 0.18 minutes as the cycle time, again assuming a 420-minute workday, the maximum capacity would be: $420/0.18 = 2,333$ units

e. Cycle time $= 0.29$ minutes

Precedence relationship table:

(A)	(B)	(C)	(D)	(E)	(F)
				Sum of	Cumulative Sum
Element Stage	Element Letter	Remarks	Element Time	Element Times	of Element Times
I	A		12		
	B		11	23	23
II	C	→ III	8		
	D		2	10	33
III	E		9		
	F	→ IV	10	19	52
IV	G		11	11	63
V	H		18	18	81

By assigning the elements in stage I to the first workstation, stages II and III to the second, and stages IV and V to the third, we arrive at the following balance:

Station	Element	Element Time	Cumulative Station Work Time	Station Idle Time
1	A	12	12	
	B	11	23	6
2	C	8	8	
	D	2	10	
	E	9	19	
	F	10	29	0
3	G	11	11	
	H	18	29	0
				Total idle time 6

Balance delay $\dfrac{(3 \times 29) - 81}{87} = 0.069$, or 6.9%

Capacity = 420/0.29 = 1,448 units per day

f. Station 1 in the solution for question *e* has 0.06 minutes of idle time, so we might begin by moving element D to station 1, raising the work time from 0.23 to 0.25 minutes. Next, we could assign elements C, E, and G to station 2, resulting in a work time of 0.28 minutes. The remaining elements, F and H, would be assigned to station 3; it too will have a total work time of 0.28 minutes.

Since 0.28 minutes is the largest amount of work time in a station (for stations 2 and 3, in this case), we could have a cycle time of 0.28 minutes. The slight reduction, from 0.29 minutes in question *e,* might be desirable. As we see below, we will have a lower balance delay and will be capable of slightly greater capacity. The balance appears as follows:

Station	Element	Element Time	Cumulative Station Work Time	Station Idle Time*
1	A	12	12	
	B	11	23	
	D	2	25	3
2	C	8	8	
	E	9	17	
	G	11	28	0
3	F	10	10	
	H	18	28	0
				Total idle time 3

Balance delay $\dfrac{(3 \times 28) - 81}{84} = 0.036$, or 3.6%

Capacity = 420/0.28 = 1,500 units per day

*Based on a cycle time of 0.28 minutes.

g. The solution in question *f* raises daily line capacity slightly from the 1,448 units found in question *e* to 1,500 units. Rebalancing to achieve 1,500 per day and producing at that rate are worthwhile only if sales are 1,500 per day; if sales are less, the excess production will just go into storage, which will add an unnecessary cost and ultimately force a price rise. The point is that the production line should be run at the customers' buying rate and balanced accordingly. Sales rates usually change every few weeks, requiring that the supervisor work on rebalancing and reassigning people every few weeks.

For Further Reference

Books

Schonberger, Richard J. *World-Class Manufacturing: The Lessons of Simplicity Applied.* New York: The Free Press, 1986 (HD31.S3385).

Shingo, Shigeo. *Non-Stock Production: The Shingo System for Continuous Improvement.* Cambridge, Mass.: Productivity Press, 1988 (TS155.S45613).

Stephanou, S. E., and F. Spiegl. *The Manufacturing Challenge: From Concept to Production.* New York: Van Nostrand Reinhold, 1992 (TS155.S775).

Periodicals/Societies

Assembly Engineering.

Chemical Processing.

Industry Week.

Review Questions

1. Differentiate between continuous and repetitive operations. Give examples of industries where we might find both types in the same facility.
2. What are key success factors in the process industry? How might continuous improvement be obtained for each factor?
3. What is regularized processing?
4. What is the advantage in changing from a schedule of making each star product once a day to a minimum-cycle, mixed-model schedule?
5. What kinds of technological obstacles stand in the way of synchronized operations? Give an example other than those in the chapter.
6. In the process industries, what have been the success factors for operations in the past? What are more recent success factors?
7. In continuous operations, production usually is scheduled in shifts rather than units. Does this change under the concept of regularized scheduling?
8. How can a schedule of 5,000 different parts or models be regularized?
9. Explain the linearity index.
10. What, if anything, can be done if the goal is to synchronize schedules for multiple process levels but some processes have very long setup times?
11. How is synchronized production related to mixed-model production?
12. Can the concepts of regularized, synchronized schedules be applied to low-volume production? Explain.
13. Define (*a*) cycle time, (*b*) work content time, (*c*) throughput time, (*d*) production rate, and (*e*) balance delay.
14. What is meant by a mixed-model line? Are there any special problems associated with balancing a mixed-model line? Explain.
15. What does the phrase *watching the lights* refer to? How can it lead to increased productivity?

Problems and Exercises

1. List characteristics of process industries. Give four examples of process industry goods. Are there service providers that are in the process industry? Discuss.

2. In the following industries, which stages of processing are best considered as continuous flow and which as repetitive? Discuss.
   a. Soft drink manufacturer.
   b. Aspirin tablet producer.
   c. Breakfast cereal producer.
   d. Nursing care for hospitalized patient.
   e. Banking (account maintenance).

3. Modesto Farms operates a high-volume cannery for tomato products: canned whole tomatoes, tomato sauce, tomato paste, and the like. Discuss three vital success factors in the area of manufacturing for this company. Be as specific as you can, even though you have to speculate on the nature of this type of company.

4. Detergent is manufactured in a continuous process through a network of pipes, vessels, and pressure chambers. First, petroleum is distilled into paraffin, which is oxidized and then catalytically hydrogenated under pressure to form fat alcohols. Sulphuric acid is added, and water cools the mixture to yield fat alcohol esters. Bleaching agents and alkalies are injected, and an emerging paste of fat alcohol sulphate is processed through a "spray tower" into finished detergent. Discuss two vital manufacturing success factors for a detergent manufacturer; be as specific as you can.

5. Edsom, Inc., a maker of keyboards for computer products, has a department in which instruction manuals are assembled into three-ring binders and another in which the pages are printed. There are four stages of production for the complete binders:
   a. The print shop slices large sheets of paper to size. It prefers to run as many jobs as possible on a recently acquired heavy-duty slicer, which runs faster than two older model slicers still in the shop. All the slicers require some setup time for any job.
   b. The printshop prints pages for manuals. Because of long setup times, print jobs for manuals compete with other print jobs for slots in the schedule.
   c. A high-speed collator collates the pages. The collator, a dedicated machine in the assembly department, is only used for manuals.
   d. Human assemblers open binders, insert sets of pages, and close binders.
      Elsewhere in the plant, the keyboard assembly line runs to a daily rate and achieves nearly perfect linearity.
   Can the four stages of manual production be synchronized to the assembly rate for the keyboards? Should they be synchronized? Discuss fully, giving an example with sample numbers.

6. Building A delivers several kinds of bulky component parts to building B four miles away. The components are made in three production stages in building A. Setup times on some of the equipment and parts assembly lines have been driven down nearly to zero. Building B houses final assembly and packing, each with negligible setup time from model to model of the family of end products.
      Can five production stages in two buildings, plus deliveries between, be completely synchronized to the sales rate? Is a fully mixed-model synchronized schedule feasible?

7. Line 1 at the East Texas plant of Feast Frozen Foods has been troublesome. Its average production has been 5,000 12-ounce packages of frozen vegetables per shift, which is equal to average sales. But the variation around that average has been unacceptable. For the 10 shifts last week (a typical week) output was 4,728, 4,980, 5,009, 4,822, 5,860, 5,121, 5,618, 4,899, 4,620, and 4,900.
      About 35 percent of line 1's output consists of Feast's top-selling product, frozen young peas. A production run of peas usually is one shift, but sometimes a half-shift run is scheduled; peas are packaged three or four times per week. The other 65 percent of production is split among 17 other products. Recently, the line 1 crew has been working overtime on about half its shifts. Changing the speeds of the tray-filling and packaging equipment is no problem.
   a. Calculate the linearity for last week.
   b. Recommend a plan for increasing predictability of output on line 1.

8. Faiko Time Company produces grandfather clocks. Customers (mostly retailers) can select from over 100 styles of fine wood and glass outer enclosures, which are made in Faiko's wood and glass shops. In contrast, only three types of clock mechanisms can be ordered; these are assembled in another Faiko shop.

The past two weeks' production orders have been as follows, in numbers of clocks ordered each day: 8, 9, 5, 7, 7, 9, 7, 4, 6, 10. Can Faiko adopt a workable production plan with a regularized production schedule and linear output? Explain why, why not, or to what extent.

9. A bicycle manufacturer has implemented a schedule of assembling every bike model every day (instead of long production runs for individual models). Can it use the same repetitive daily schedule in making handlebars, frames, and wheel assemblies? If so, can the repetitive schedule extend downward to tires, wheels, and spokes? Can it go further downward to wire extruders that make reels of spoke wire and to the steel plant that makes the commodity steel that is drawn into wire? Discuss the possibilities, obstacles, and benefits.

10. As a first step in a line-balancing analysis, the following precedence diagram has been developed.

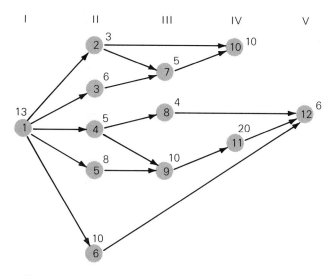

a. Calculate Σt. Now calculate all the possible cycle times and numbers of stations that could be used in a perfectly balanced assembly line.

b. Which of the options developed in question *a* are not worth pursuing further? Why?

c. Balance the line as best you can, and calculate the resulting balance delay.

11. The following precedence diagram has been developed for circuit breaker assembly:

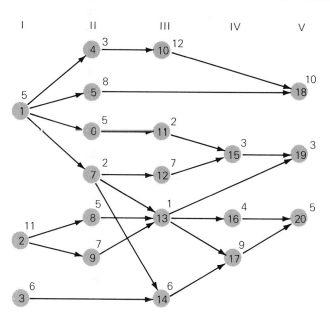

    a. Calculate all the possible cycle times and numbers of stations that could be used in a perfectly balanced assembly line.

    b. Balance the line as best you can for six stations. Explain. Calculate the resulting balance delay.

12. The processing of worker's compensation claim forms in a state office is being organized as a production line. Work elements have been divided as far as possible and have been organized into the following precedence diagram:

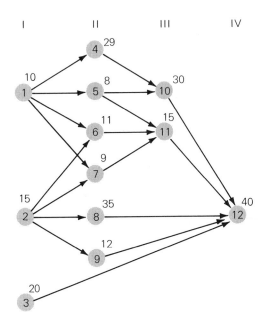

    a. Calculate all combinations of cycle time and number of stations that would result in zero balance delay.

    b. Which combinations (from question *a*) are not reasonable for further analysis? Explain.

    c. Balance the line for five stations and again for six stations. Which is better? Why?

13. Crow's Eye Foods, Inc., has patent rights to a special type of segmented dish for perfect warming of foods in a microwave oven. The dish permits Crow's to launch a new line of frozen breakfasts. Crow's kitchens are planning for the first breakfast: two strips of bacon, one egg, and two slices of buttered toast.

    a. Develop a precedence diagram for use in balancing the production line for this breakfast. Make your own (reasonable) assumptions about work elements and element times. Explain your diagram.

    b. Determine all sets of cycle time and number of stations that would result in a balanced line.

    c. Balance your line.

14. Zeus, Inc., makes three models of personal computers: large, medium, and small. One purchased part is an internal cooling fan: a large fan for the large computer, medium fan for the medium, and small fan for the small. Zeus produces and buys components purely just-in-time. The end-product schedule calls for producing one large, two medium, and four small computers every 10 minutes during the day, and the schedule is frozen for four weeks into the future. Suppliers deliver component parts (such as fans) once a day.

    a. What are the advantages of the daily mixed-model delivery schedule for the fan supplier? (One supplier provides all three sizes.)

    b. During one 5-day period, Zeus has trouble meeting its daily schedule, falling short by 30 units the first day, 5 units on the second, 2 on the third, 25 on the fourth, and 8 on the fifth. What difficulties does this create for the just-in-time supplier?

    c. Zeus's schedule works out to 48 large, 96 medium, and 192 small computers per eight-hour day. What is wrong with the schedule (a possible contributor to the schedule problems described in part *b*)?

15. A production line assembles two models of hair dryer: standard (S) and deluxe (D). Each S requires 4 minutes of assembly time and each D 12 minutes. Marketing sells twice as many Ss as Ds. Develop a mixed-model sequence for the two dryers. Make it as well balanced as possible. What is the cycle time, and how many times can it repeat in a 480-minute day?

16. Parts A and B must be heat treated. The heat-treat time for part A is 5 minutes; for part B, it is 10 minutes. The schedule calls for 36 As and 12 Bs per day. Develop a balanced mixed-model sequence for the two parts. How many hours will it take to produce the scheduled amount?

17. Demand for a certain product averages 250 units per day. The product is made and sold in three styles; recently the split among them has been: style 1, 60 percent; style 2, 30 percent; and style 3, 10 percent. Devise a mixed-model schedule with minimum cycle interval for this product line.

18. Find the lowest-ratio mixed-model schedule for four models of typewriter table, where daily market requirements are 6 model Ds, 18 model Es, 12 model Fs, and 24 model Gs.

19. When production volume is high and product variety low, dedicated production facilities may be used to run a streamlined make-to-a-number operation. What can be done to streamline production of medium-volume products?

20. In a bank, customers arrive irregularly. Are there any processes in a bank that can escape from that basic customer-driven irregularity and get onto a repetitive schedule? Discuss, including any possible benefits.

21. In a department store, customers arrive irregularly. Are there any processes in a store that are important to customer service but that can be put onto a regularized schedule? If so, what are the benefits?

CASE STUDY

GETTING READY FOR MIXED-MODEL PRODUCTION AT KAWASAKI MOTORS USA

Mixed Models in Motorcycle Assembly

In September 1981, a Japanese management team replaced the American plant manager at the Kawasaki motorcycle plant in Lincoln, Nebraska. One goal of the new managers was to convert the main motorcycle assembly line to mixed-model production. The line had been running production lots of at least 200 of each model between line changeovers.

    The conversion was expected to take about three months. It required two kinds of exacting preparation:

    1. Identification: All parts, tools, cartons, racks, and so forth, had to be clearly labeled so that an assembler would be able instantaneously to identify and select the right one. With a different motorcycle model next on the conveyor, delay in identifying it and all of the parts and tools to go with it would be intolerable. A color-coding system was devised so that, for

Case topics:

Preautomation.

Mixed-model assembly sequence.

Benefits of mixed-model assembly when sales are falling.

Benefits of setup time reduction on presses.

example, all items related to a KZ650 motorcycle would be labeled with a gummed red dot. Even the position of the colored dot on the carton, part, or tool had to be precisely designed.

2. *Placement*. Engineers, material controllers, foremen, and assemblers all pitched in to devise exact locations for all parts and tools at workstations along the assembly line. The assembler, on seeing what the next model of motorcycle is, should be able to reach for the correct parts and tools blindfolded. Better racks, containers, and holding fixtures were designed to feed parts and hold tools in the right positions.

The preparations (which today we would refer to as preautomation) were successful. On January 1, 1983, the main assembly line fully converted to mixed-model production. ·

At that time, the production volume was at about 200 motorcycles per day. That 200 might consist of the following models: 100 KZ440s, 60 KZ650s, and 40 KZ1000s.

Discussion Questions

Question 1. For that mixture, what is the lowest-ratio mixed-model assembly sequence?

Question 2. Would there be any benefits of mixed-model assembly in a period when motorcycle sales were falling and excess bike inventories were building up in the distribution system (as in 1982)?

Mixed Models in Motorcycle Parts Fabrication

Perhaps the main subassembly made in the Lincoln plant is motorcycle frames. The frame parts are formed from steel tube stock, and the parts are welded together into frames.

At one time frame parts were punched out on punch presses in lots of thousands at a time. The large lots were economical because it typically took half a day or so to move a heavy die into place on a large-size punch press and to get all of the die adjustments and machine controls just right. Part of the setup time was running off trial pieces, inspecting their dimensions, changing settings, running and inspecting a few more, and so forth.

Exhibit S12–1   Carousel Conveyor on Punch Press

In 1980–1981, the presses were modified for quick die changes and adjustments. Common roller conveyor sections were welded to form a carousel around the punch press; all dies were shimmed up so they had standard "shut heights"; and insertion and fastening were simplified. A dozen or more dies could be lined up around the carousel conveyor in the morning, and each die could be quickly and precisely rolled into place during the day in shifting from one frame part model to another (see Exhibit S12–1). The changes cut average setup time to under 10 minutes (including zero inspection time). Instead of running thousands of a model between setups, it became economical to run in lots of 200, 100, or perhaps 50; while that is not the one-piece-at-a-time mixed-model ideal, it comes close.

But Kawasaki wanted to achieve the ideal: one-touch setup and one-piece-at-a-time production. That was accomplished for high-use frame parts in the summer of 1982. To achieve one-touch setup, large general purpose punch presses were replaced with small special-purpose screw presses. Each screw press has a die permanently built in so that there is no die change time and therefore no setup time—a dedicated machine. The small screw presses apply pressure slowly rather than punch suddenly, but their slowness is more than offset by the zero setup time. With dies exactly positioned, defective parts are much less likely. The screw presses were relocated to the welding shop, where a welder can set up several screw presses to make several different frame parts; as each part is completed, the welder may immediately weld it onto the growing frame. There are no lot-size inventories. Much of the punch press shop has been abolished, since welders now make each part as they go.

Question 3. What kinds of resource costs did Kawasaki reduce through their way of first achieving single-digit setup and then one-touch setup?

13 MANAGING JOB AND BATCH OPERATIONS

Chapter Outline

Jumbled Jobs

Scheduling
    Lead-Time Elements
    Work in Process
    Lead-Time Accuracy
    Backward and Forward Scheduling
    Resource Scheduling
    Gantt Charts

Work Center Loading
    Capacity Requirements Planning
    Load Shifting

Capacity Control

Expediting
Lot Splitting
Overlapping

Activity Control
    Input Control
    Priority Control (Dispatching)

Simplification: Reduction of Variables
    Paperless and Visual Systems
    Other Antidotes
    Forklift Trucks and Roller Skates
    Reforming the Job Shop: An Example

Much of life's work breaks down into **jobs,** each having a defined end point and tangible results: a broken fence board repaired, six copies made, a process flowcharted, 20 tennis rackets strung, or a client visited. The job mode of operations covers nearly all human services, most office work, and industrial job shops.

A job might yield one or a dozen units, or even a few thousand, in which case we may call it a **lot,** or job lot. A **batch** is a certain type of job, usually a standard lot size or container quantity. In the process mode, a batch involves mixing ingredients to create an output measured by volume or weight: a yard of concrete, a ton of sand, or a gallon of sulfuric acid. We treat jobs, batches, and lots together because they require similar management. For convenience, we use the term *job* when referring to any of these operations involving smaller, irregular quantities.

Jumbled Jobs

If the schedule consists of a long succession of jobs that are identical, or nearly so, they aren't actually jobs; it's continuous or repetitive operations, which involve a small number of variables to manage. The comparatively simple management concepts of Chapter 12 apply.

The trouble with job operations is the typically large number of variables: irregular and randomly changing colors, sizes, and styles; numbers of units, process steps, and routings through the processes; and specifications, components, and customer expectations. Managing the jumble of jobs requires a combination of the following skills:

1. *Job planning, scheduling, and control.* This approach, grounded in information systems, has been highly developed, especially in North America.

2. *Simplification, sorting, and elimination of non-value-adding steps.* This approach, on the other hand, entails less information system support because it reduces the number of variables to be managed. It requires a high degree of cross-functional team effort and barrier breaking.

In order to properly discuss system simplification and variables reduction, we must first examine the full job operations system and its variables. Exhibit 13–1 shows the job processing sequence in manufacturing, processing documents, or serving clients. First, the master scheduling committee (or person) positions the work in a master schedule or appointment book, sometimes with other similar work. Inventory planning, as necessary, comes next (even in pure services, some inventory actions are generally needed so that the job will not be halted for lack of a certain item, say, a special tax form).

If all required inventories are on hand or due in, scheduling at a detailed job-by-job level may take place; for a multi-operation job, this may involve a scheduler's putting start and completion dates on each operation. In the dispatching step, jobs in progress get positioned one more time; dispatching is what we call prioritizing jobs in queue at a given work center. Finally, during or after the transformation, comes reporting and corrective control.

Well-known use of dispatching: Phone for a taxi, and a dispatcher assigns you to a cab, or a cab to you.

From Exhibit 13–1, we see that scheduling can take place at multiple levels, from master scheduling to dispatching. Can it go still lower? It can. Orders for component parts or services are often processed in several steps, called **operations.**

EXHIBIT 13–1   Job Planning, Scheduling, and Control

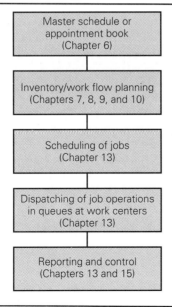

Master schedule or appointment book (Chapter 6)

Inventory/work flow planning (Chapters 7, 8, 9, and 10)

Scheduling of jobs (Chapter 13)

Dispatching of job operations in queues at work centers (Chapter 13)

Reporting and control (Chapters 13 and 15)

An operation is one step in a job, and each operation requires a new setup, change-over, or get-ready. Since setups introduce a variety of problems (startup mishaps, variation, delays, and non-value adding costs), reducing setups and standardizing operations are often high-priority projects for improvement teams.

A job (or batch or lot or job lot), on the other hand, is the whole work activity needed to fill a service order or a production order. The order itself (documentation about the job) may be called a service order, job order, work order, or shop order.

There are several reasons why each operation might be separately planned, scheduled, and controlled. One is that special setup people, different from the regular staff, are sometimes brought in to set up for each new operation (e.g., bus people setting up for each meal change at a restaurant or tool setters in a factory). Another is that each new operation may require that new materials, instructions, specifications, and tools be brought in. Finally, before each operation, work queues can build up and require some kind of queue management, including priority assignment. Example 13–1 further distinguishes between operations and jobs.

_{*P*}RINCIPLES 5 AND 12:

Cut number of operations. Cut setup times.

EXAMPLE 13–1   DISTINCTION BETWEEN OPERATIONS AND JOBS—BOOKCASE SHELF

As is customary in manufacturing, operations are numbered by tens, that is, 10, 20, 30, instead of 1, 2, 3.

Upon appearing on the master schedule, an order for production of bookcases is exploded. In bookcase manufacturing, the bookcase appears on the master schedule and is exploded into component parts. One part is a shelf. Making a quantity of the shelf involves planning and controlling one job and several operations. Exhibit 13–2 shows a job consisting of 10 bookcase shelves. The shelf part number is 777, and the shop order is shown as a five-operation job. We see in the figure five operations and the inventory conditions between them. Operation 10: Withdraw boards from the stockroom. Operation 20: Saw boards. Operation 30: Plane sawed boards. Operation 40: Sand planed boards. Operation 50: Apply finish to sanded boards. The result is 10 finished shelves, which are component parts that go into the next-higher-level item on the bill of materials for the bookshelf order.

Each operation, even stockroom activities, requires setup time. After each operation, work-in-process (WIP) inventories form and sit idle for a time. The setups and heaps of WIP require attention. A dispatcher assists the wood shop foreman in scheduling and controlling the operations: saw, plane, sand, and finish. But the due date for the whole bookshelf job was set earlier by a scheduler in the production control department.

The bookcase example exposes a few of the common complications in planning a job: multiple routings, setups, moves, queues, inventories, scrap, and value-adding operations. Another complication is scheduling the job, our next topic.

Scheduling

In common usage the word *schedule* usually means a completion time or date and perhaps also a start time. Master schedules state the quantity and the completion day, week, or month, but usually not start times. Detailed scheduling, job by job, at the component level does include start times. Detailed scheduling, simply called scheduling in business and industry, is our concern here (master scheduling was discussed in Chapter 6).

Scheduling a service or job order requires answers to three questions:

1. When can the job be completed? (Based on standard times.)
2. When should the job be completed? (Based on date of customer or parent-item need.)
3. When will the job be completed? (Based on realities in operating work centers.)

Exhibit 13–2   Job and Operations for 10 Bookcase Shelves

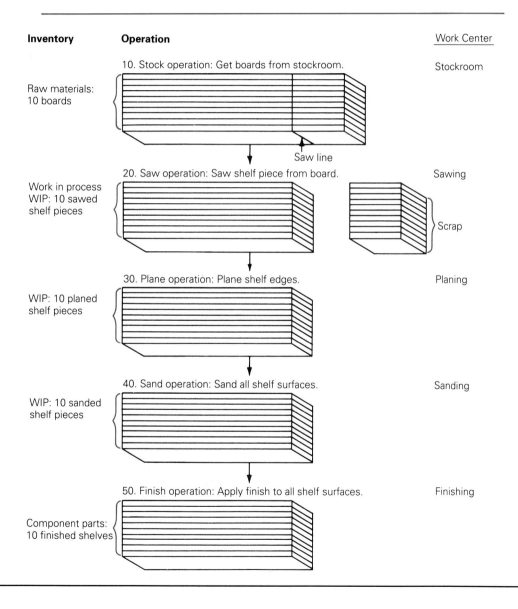

It simplifies things if all three questions have the same answer. For example, suppose a patient is undergoing a complete physical examination. An early step is withdrawing specimens of various body fluids. The physician may want the results of laboratory analysis of a certain specimen to be ready at the end of the exam, say, 30 minutes later; that answers question 2 (when should it be completed?). Perhaps the standard time, adjusted for efficiency and utilization, is also 30 minutes; that answers question 1 (when can it be done?). Suppose the lab has no higher-priority jobs that would interfere with this lab test; then the job can be expected to be completed in 30 minutes, which answers question 3 (when will it be done?). Since all three questions have the same answer, it is clear that the lab test should be scheduled to start upon withdrawal of the body fluids and be completed 30 minutes later.

Actually, it is not very likely that a lab can complete its testing as soon as the physician desires the results. A lab is a job shop, and in job shops queues of job orders form and jostle for priority. In repetitive operations, in contrast, jobs generally do not compete for the same resources, because job uniformity allows work to flow smoothly from station to station, sometimes without queues of WIP inventory.

Lead-Time Elements

In job operations, lead time to produce or deliver something or provide a service usually contains much more delay time than actual work; that is, the part, client, or document spends far more time idle than being processed. In manufacturing, according to Orlicky,[1] the elements of production lead time for a given part are as follows, in descending order of significance:

1. Queue time.
2. Run time (service time).
3. Setup time.
4. Wait time (wait for instructions, transportation, tools, etc.).
5. Inspection time.
6. Move time.
7. Other.

Orlicky and others maintain that queue time (the first element) in metal fabrication shops normally accounts for about 90 percent of total lead time. It's often the same for customers buying tickets or paying tolls. Other delays (items 3 through 7 in the above list) take up part of the remaining 10 percent, which leaves run time (value-adding operations) with a very small percentage of total lead time.

Run time may be precisely measured using standard time techniques (see Chapter 15). Total lead time, however, is hard to pin down. Accurate estimates of lead times, and therefore accurate schedules, are likely only when work centers are uncongested; only then can the typical job sail through without long and variable queue times at each work center. One of the scheduler's jobs is to keep things uncongested, that is, without too much work in process.

Work in Process

The WIP problem is attacked directly with just-in-time techniques. But the evils of WIP were receiving attention in Western industry well before JIT found its way across the Pacific. For 20 years or more, production control books and dinner speakers at professional meetings for production control people preached the following benefits of keeping WIP low:

---

[1] Joseph Orlicky, *Material Requirements Planning* (New York: McGraw-Hill, 1975), p. 83 (TS155.8.O74).

1. *Service*. Low WIP means less queue time and quicker response to customers; also, with less queue time there is less uncertainty in the schedule and customers may be given better status information.
2. *Forecasts*. We know that forecasts are more accurate for shorter periods into the future, that is, for the shorter lead times that result from smaller amounts of WIP.
3. *Production control work force*. Less WIP means less congestion and less need for operations control by expediters and dispatchers.
4. *Floor-space and inventory costs*. These are lower when fewer jobs are in process.

In services we could add another benefit: Customers are happy when they don't have to wait in long lines (note: the customers are the WIP). They get angry and may take their business elsewhere if lines get too long. Manufacturers have it easier, since inanimate parts waiting for machine time are unable to express anger.

Despite the advantages of low WIP, it can also make managers nervous, fearful that some work centers will run out of work. Each job in the work stream usually will require different operation times at each work center it visits. This causes work to pile up and overload some work centers and, potentially, underload others. As the job mix changes, and it often changes quickly, the pattern of over- and underloading changes. The scheduler is under pressure to overload on the average in order to hold down the number of underloaded work centers. Supervisors get nervous about cost variances when workloads get low.

$\mathscr{P}$RINCIPLE 11:

Cut wait time and inventory.

The scheduler seems caught in a bind: Scheduling enough work to keep centers busy means that queue times will grow and make schedules less realistic. Queue time for an average job is hard to predict, because the average varies with the changing job mix. Queue time for a particular job is even harder to predict, because the job may queue up at several work centers as it completes its routing. Therefore, the scheduler sometimes follows a rule of adding a fixed number of days for queue time and other delays.

Lead-Time Accuracy

A dynamic scheduling approach is another possibility, usable when the system is highly computerized. Here queue time includes an extra-time allowance for current or projected congestion. A simple measure of congestion is the number of open job orders, which the computer can find in the open-order file. (The open-order file is discussed in Chapter 9 in connection with material requirements planning.) An alternative measure of congestion is the number of operations in all open orders. To find number of operations, the computer searches the open-order file and then the routing file, which tells the route taken by an order.

With so much uncertainty and use of fudge factors in estimating lead times, is it possible to do a reasonable job of planning and controlling work flows? The answer is yes. In closed-loop material requirements planning, work flows are monitored and schedulers and dispatchers are kept informed. If they find that lead-time estimates, and therefore schedules, are wrong, they can make adjustments.

One way to adjust is to simply change the due date for a job. Advice on the need to change due dates may take the form of rescheduling notices from the weekly MRP run. While planned order releases from an MRP run trigger inventory planning (ordering) actions, rescheduling notices trigger scheduling actions. Together those two MRP outputs provide full support for planning and controlling the movement of component parts. A second type of adjustment may be made each day (between weekly MRP runs). A daily dispatch list from the computer tells the dispatcher of the need to change the priorities of work in process in order to meet due dates. (We discuss dispatch lists later.)

Inaccurate lead times have a more severe effect on capacity control. **Capacity requirements planning (CRP)** is a computer-based extension of MRP in which future work center loads are computed. Accuracy of computed loads may be improved by including some kind of queue-time allowance in lead-time estimates. Allowances based on shop congestion (the dynamic scheduling idea mentioned above) may help. Planning around capacity bottlenecks (the theory-of-constraints idea) is another approach. More accurate load projections permit work center capacity to be planned so that there is less need for last-minute capacity control measures.

Backward and Forward Scheduling

For services offered on demand, the usual customer need date is "as soon as possible" (ASAP is the well-known abbreviation). The customer order is scheduled forward from the current date or from the date on which resources are expected to be available.

For services provided by appointment, **backward scheduling** may be used. An example is deliveries of checks and deposit slips from a small bank to a larger bank's computer service center. The service center may require delivery by 9 P.M. each day. If so, schedules for each delivery stop are backward scheduled; that is, the scheduler successively subtracts operation lead times (times at and between stops) from 9 P.M. The resulting schedule might appear as shown in the accompanying diagram.

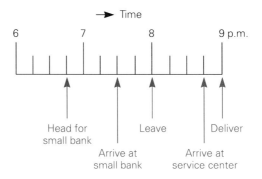

Backward and **forward scheduling** may be used in tandem. A scheduler might be asked to estimate the earliest date on which a job can be completed, which calls for forward scheduling. The date of need could be beyond the calculated earliest completion date; backward scheduling might then be used to determine the scheduled start date.

Goods producers also use both forward and backward scheduling. Generally, manufacturing inventories that are replenished by reorder point (ROP) are forward scheduled. But MRP yields planned order releases that are backward scheduled from the date of the net requirement. Actually, in most MRP systems the planned-order-release date is not the scheduled start day. The computer backward schedules to determine the start *week*, which the scheduler uses to calculate the start *day*. Example 13–2 illustrates.

EXAMPLE 13–2   SCHEDULING A SHOP ORDER—QUIDCO, INC.

The weekly MRP run at QUIDCO, Inc., shows a planned order in the current time bucket for part number 1005CX. The part is due on Monday of time bucket (week) 3, which is shop calendar date 105 (see Exhibit 13–3A).

The inventory planner validates the need for the order and the order quantity and timing. He decides that it should be a make rather than a buy order and therefore requests a shop order.

The scheduler finds the part number in the routing file, and the routing and time standards for each operation on a video display terminal. She prepares a shop

EXHIBIT 13–3 Generating Shop Order from Current Planned Order Listing

A. MRP Listing of Planned Orders Due for Scheduling

Week of 90
Orders Planned for Release This Week
QUIDCO Inc.

Part Number	Due Date
0052X	110
0077AX	115
⋮	⋮
1005CX	105
⋮	⋮

B. Shop Order, Backward Scheduled

Shop Order Number 9925
Part Number 1005CX   Quantity: 50   Release Date: 92

Operation	Description	Work Center	Setup	Cycle Time	Standard Hours	Finish Date
20	Bend rod	16	4.2	0.05	6.7	99
30	Finish rod	85	0.4	0.18	9.4	102
40	Inspect rod	52				105
					Due Date:	105

order using the data from the routing file (see Exhibit 13–3B). She uses backward scheduling, along with QUIDCO's rules for computing operation lead times:[2]

1. Allow eight standard hours per day; round upward to whole days.

2. Allow one day between operations for move/queue time and other delays.

3. Allow two days to inspect.

4. Release shop order to the stockroom five days before the job is to be started into production.

5. All dates are treated as end of the eight-hour day.

She begins backward scheduling with the due date, 105, in the lower right corner. That is the finish date for the last operation, inspect. She subtracts two days for inspect and one day between operations, which makes 102 the due date for the finish operation. Finish takes 9.4 standard hours [$0.4 + (0.18 \times 50$ pieces)], which rounds upward to two days. Subtracting that plus one day between operations equals 99 as the due date for the bend operation. Finally, she subtracts one day (6.7 hours rounded upward) for bend, five days for stockroom actions, and one day between operations, which makes day 92 the release date. The scheduler therefore holds shop order 9925 in her *hold-for-release* file on Monday and Tuesday (days 90 and 91) and releases it on Wednesday (day 92).

A shop calender of consecutively numbered work days, omitting weekends and holidays, is common among manufacturing firms, because it makes computation easy.

A week goes by. The inventory planner notifies the scheduler that part number 1005CX has a new need date: the week of 110 instead of 105. (The latest MRP run informed the inventory planner of the later date.) The scheduler recomputes operation due dates as follows:

New job due date = Inspect due date	=	Day	110
Less inspect time	=		2 days
		Day	108

---

[2] Adapted from Oliver W. Wight, *Production and Inventory Management in the Computer Age* (Boston: CBI Publishing, 1974), pp. 81–82 (TS155.W533). Note that operation lead times are detailed, whereas job-order lead times, discussed earlier for computing planned order releases, are gross.

Less move/queue time	=		1	day
Finish due date	=	Day	107	
Less finish time	=		2	days
		Day	105	
Less move/queue time	=		1	day
Bend due date	=	Day	104	

The scheduler enters the three new operation due dates into the computer. The computer uses the new dates in printing out a daily dispatch list. Copies of the list go to the three work center supervisors to tell them about the changes in operation due dates.

In this system, the scheduler need not issue new paperwork giving revised due dates, because the computer issues daily dispatch lists giving *operation* due dates based on latest *job* schedules. She does need to assemble a planning package that may include job tickets, inspection tickets, and forms on which to record such things as material usage, scrap, and labor changes.

In a manual system, there may not be a daily dispatch list. In that case, the scheduler will need to put due dates on job tickets or other planning-package paperwork. A problem with the manual system is keeping everybody informed of new due dates when schedules change. It can be a paperwork mess.

In the QUIDCO example, a human scheduler performs the backward scheduling. This could be done at a terminal, with the computer handling the calculation chores following the lead-time rules.

Some companies have their MRP systems plan in days rather than weeks. Schedulers then may plan in hours instead of days. That cuts work-in-process inventory further and shortens lead times, which can make the firm stronger financially and competitively. Shop-floor recorders can provide the scheduler with faster feedback on how jobs are doing so that schedule changes can be more responsive.

Resource Scheduling

We have been talking about scheduling jobs and job operations: the ends. At the same time, schedulers must make sure that the right operating resources (means) are there at the right time for the scheduled jobs. The schedules for ends and means must match.

In an earlier era, the tendency was to schedule jobs and operations with little regard for whether resources would be on hand. This was the case for two main reasons:

1. Labor resources were largely unskilled, and labor laws were weak. Companies therefore could adjust labor up or down, on short notice, as job schedules required.

2. Material resources, purchased and made, were planned by reorder point, because there was too little data processing power to schedule those resources based on future net requirements, today's MRP process. The same was true of reusable resources such as tools, gauges, fixtures, dies, machines, and space.

Over time businesses developed ever larger numbers of labor classifications, and moving labor around as job mixes changed became difficult. Scheduling became more complicated. Availability of the right labor skills and other resources had to be considered in scheduling jobs.

MRP systems were developed to provide notices of needs for certain component parts, and the MRP systems were embedded in a broader system that checked on resource availability. Aggregate and rough-cut capacity planning, which can roughly check for resource availability (see Chapter 6), come before the MRP run. Capacity requirements planning, typically after an MRP run, checks critical resources more precisely. MRPII extends the MRP concept to aid in scheduling labor skills, gauges, tools, dies, machines, and cash flow, all based on explosion of the master production schedule.

Resources sometimes may be scheduled in advance of need by making reservations. A reservation more clearly defines the resources to be used than does an appointment; in fact, in human services a reservation often amounts to presale of a resource, like an airplane seat or hotel room.

While schedules can be stated in words and numbers, they also may be displayed visually on a calendar or, better yet, on a Gantt chart, our next topic.

Henry Gantt's name is attached to a family of widely used scheduling charts. A few *Gantt Charts* examples appear in Exhibit 13–4. In the basic **Gantt chart** form, much like Exhibit 13–4A, vertical divisions represent time, and horizontal rows, the jobs or resources to be scheduled. Lines, bars, brackets, shading, and other devices mark the start, duration, and end of a scheduled entity. The purpose of the charts, as with any visual aid, is to clarify, improve comprehension, and serve as a focus for discussion.

The charts in Exhibit 13–4 are for scheduling three different resource types: equipment, space, and line employees. Each also identifies the jobs to be performed by the

---

EXHIBIT 13–4   Common Forms of Gantt Charts

A. Schedule for machine

Scheduled summer jobs	M	T	W	T	F	S	S	M	T	W	T	F	S	S	M	T	W	T
Payroll			▨							▨							▨	
Accounts receivable				▨							▨							▨
MRP					▨							▨						

B. Schedule for classrooms

Classroom schedule	(Monday) Hour							
	6	7	8	9	10	11	12	1
BA 101		ECON 205		MGM 331	ACCT 101 / ECON 400	FIN 394		MGM

C. Schedule for labor

	Dentist's appointments
Mon. 8:00	Mrs. Harrison
8:30	↓
9:00	J. Peters
9:30	Steve Smith
10:00	
10:30	↓
11:00	↓

resources. Note too that each is a services example. While Gantt's original chart was for the control of repetitive manufacturing, today simpler forms of Gantt charts are more widely used in services, where routings are short and queues have few chances to form.[3]

In goods production, Gantt charts may be usable if:

1. *There are not many work centers.* With many work centers, a carefully developed Gantt display of schedules tends to be a piece of gross fiction, because queuing effects (discussed earlier) make lead times unpredictable. Keeping the chart up-to-date under such conditions would be time-consuming and pointless.

2. *Job times are long—days or weeks rather than hours.* One example is a construction project. Drywallers, painters, cement crews, roofers, and so on, may each spend several days or weeks at a work site. With such a long job time, a schedule on a Gantt chart will hold still and not become instantly out of date as it would with very short jobs.

3. *Job routings are short.* In parts manufacturing, routings can be long. A single job may pass through 5, 10, or even 15 work centers, with unpredictable queue time at each stop. With so much unpredictability, the Gantt schedule is not believable and thus not worth displaying.

Maintenance is a service (though it is goods that are maintained) Thus, it's not surprising that maintenance, like other services, may benefit from Gantt scheduling.

Sometimes a Gantt chart is used for both scheduling and schedule control. This is especially the case in maintenance work. Examples are renovation, major maintenance, and extensive overhaul work; nonmaintenance examples in which Gantt control charts might be used include computer systems analysis and programming projects, as well as computer program maintenance.

Exhibit 13–5 shows a Gantt control chart for renovation work. The Gantt chart in Exhibit 13–5A is an initial schedule for three crews. An arrow at the top of each chart identifies the current day.

Exhibit 13–5B shows progress made after one day. The shading indicates amount of work done, which probably is estimated by the crew chief, in percent of completion. Two thirds of the first paint job was scheduled for Monday, but the paint crew got the whole job done that day. While the paint crew is one half-day ahead of schedule, drywall is one quarter-day behind. Carpentry did Monday's scheduled work on Monday and is on schedule.

Exhibit 13–5C for Tuesday shows painting falling behind, drywall on schedule, and carpentry ahead.

Commercially available schedule boards use velcro or magnetic strips, pegs, plastic inserts, and the like to block out schedules and to show progress. Such boards are common in construction offices, project managers' headquarters, and maintenance departments.

Work Center Loading

Scheduler: "In a nutshell, what is your advice on how we should load your work centers?"

Supervisor: "Keep 'em busy. But not too busy."

The above exchange describes one concern of schedulers: loading the work centers. Whereas a multifunctional team plans overall capacity in light of predicted aggregate

---

[3] The original purpose was to display variances from planned production rates in repetitive production.

EXHIBIT 13–5   **Gantt Control Chart—Renovation Work**

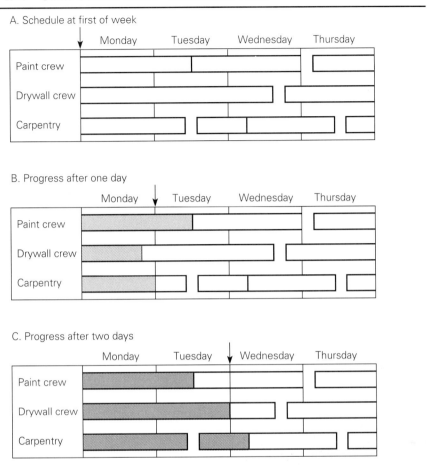

A. Schedule at first of week

B. Progress after one day

C. Progress after two days

work load (Chapter 6), the scheduler (a role sometimes retained by supervisors) has the task of fitting jobs into the schedule so as not to overload or underload work centers day to day and week to week. In some companies, especially those that have implemented material requirement planning, the scheduler may perform loading with the aid of an MRP supplement, capacity requirements planning.

Loading:
Assigning workload to a work center.

Capacity requirements planning (CRP) is a computer-based method of revealing work center loads. A CRP run requires three inputs. One is planned order releases for compo nent parts. Planned order releases are calculated by the computer in an MRP run (see Chapter 9). The second is open orders for component parts. These are orders released by scheduling (or purchasing) in an earlier period and still in process. The third input is routing data that tell which work centers each component-parts order goes through and how long it takes. Both the open-order file and the routing file must be computerized in order to run CRP. (Because of the cost of creating and maintaining valid computer files of routing and operation timing data, most MRP-using firms have not implemented CRP.)

Schedulers would want to apply CRP where it can do the most good: to work centers that have trouble achieving planned output, thus becoming bottlenecks. CRP projections

Capacity Requirements Planning

in those work centers can warn of insufficient capacity far enough in advance for schedulers to do something about it. (There is little sense in asking the computer to run CRP projections for all work centers and for 52 weeks into the future, because the real problems are in the near future and likely only in certain work centers.) Common corrections include training new operators, shifting labor to new jobs, layoffs, subcontracts, and so on. With CRP's potential to alert managers so as to keep work center capacities reasonably close to planned loads, the usual chaotic atmosphere in the job-shop may give way to reasonable order and tranquility. Differences between traditional and CRP load projections are examined next.

Load Shifting   **Infinite-capacity loading** (presented in Chapter 7) means scheduling job orders without regard for resulting work center loads. Exhibit 13–6 shows two versions of a visual loading report. Exhibit 13–6A shows the usual falling-off load projected for a work center in a firm relying only on open orders for parts that are low in the warehouse. The week 0 load is a backlog of parts orders already in the work center; the remaining loads are for parts orders due in this work center after passing through upstream (prior) work centers. The backlog and the week 1 load are shown to be (together) more than double the work center's weekly capacity. That is not a great problem, however, since only a few of the orders are needed for current production, and they may appear on a shortage list. Expediters will see that they are run first. Other orders are for stock replenishment (filling warehouse supplies) and may be safely delayed.

Exhibit 13–6B shows the up-and-down loading pattern common for work centers in firms that use the computer for inventory planning and CRP-based loading. A line divides open orders, those the scheduler has already released to the shops, from planned orders calculated by the computer to meet future needs. Overloads are shown in weeks 1, 2, and 7. Daily dispatching of more urgent jobs in those weeks can deal with most of the overload problem.

When overloads are severe, the work center scheduler needs help. The master scheduler, who schedules end products but not components, may need to move end-item (end-product) orders on the master production schedule. Moving many end items to an earlier or later period also moves the dates of need for component parts that go into the end items. It may not be easy to trace a component part back to its end items. (That kind of tracing, called pegging, sometimes can be performed on the computer by calling up a pegging subroutine of MRP.) Once the linkage has been established, the master scheduler may move an end-item lot and thereby move all the other links in the chain down to the level of the overloaded work center, thus relieving the overloading.

Capacity Control

While capacity planning and load shifting deal with blocks of jobs and capacity, **capacity control** operates at the level of single jobs and single work centers. The capacity control problem is to make on-the-spot capacity adjustments in order to get a certain job through. Special capacity adjustments may stem from the press to get one or more hot jobs through the system. One way, considered here, is for expediters to push the work through. Another way, discussed in the final section of the chapter, is to select from a range of tools that simplify the processing or the handling so that special push activities are unnecessary—in other words, solve the root causes.

Expediting   When a job is late or a key customer is getting impatient, our usual reaction is to **expedite:** do whatever is necessary to push the job through, and never mind the chaos and

EXHIBIT 13–6   **Visual Load Report**

A. Manually calculated loads

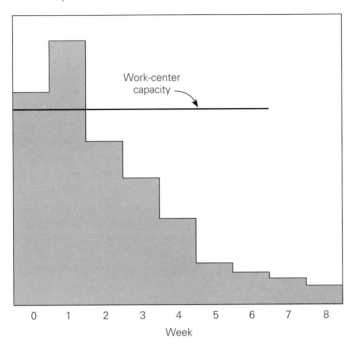

B. Computer-calculated (CRP) loads

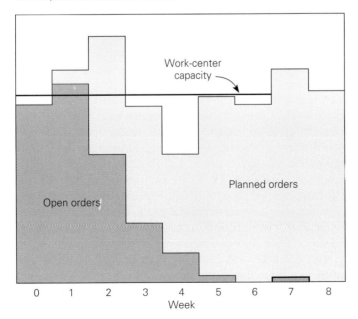

interruptions that might ensue. In almost any line of work, unexpected hot jobs and processing obstacles make expediting necessary at least once in a while.

In the complex case of dozens, or hundreds, of jobs in process at any given time, the job mixture will generally include many nonurgent jobs along with a few hot ones. The scheduler's tendency (and the firm's policy) is to overload the schedule for each work center, let the less urgent jobs or customers wait, and push the hot jobs through via some form of expediting. In formal systems, sometimes people called *expediters* may physically move jobs along, mustering whatever resources are necessary and pushing aside any less-important work.

It's easy to see how this system works in the case of an emergency patient at a clinic or hospital. Medical staffers simply make a judgment as to criticality and process more-critical patients before others who had earlier positions in the queues. In other cases, the expediting may take the form of *lot splitting* or *overlapping*.

Lot Splitting

Lot splitting:
A nonurgent job split by a hot job.

Say that a grinding machine is in the middle of an 18-hour job to produce a lot of 9,000 pieces. An expediter drives up in a forklift truck with a pallet load of castings: Hot job! They need to be ground right away. Stop the machine and run the hot job! That splits the lot of 9,000 that was on the machine and necessitates another machine setup once the hot job is finished.

Variants of lot splitting are found in services as well. The regular scheduled job might be interrupted in payroll to permit processing of a special paycheck; in accounts payable, for meeting tight discount terms on a very large purchase; in sales, for processing a big sales order; or in guided tours, for guiding a group of VIPs.

Lot splitting has always been considered, at best, a necessary evil; expediting itself has been viewed the same way. Thinking on this matter is changing. The JIT emphasis on quick setup reduces the costs of splitting lots. In fact, when large numbers of machines have been retrofitted for quick setup, lot splitting is no longer expediting; it is just normal practice. The 18-hour lot of 9,000 pieces on the grinding machine perhaps becomes half-hour runs of 250 pieces. Since we are talking about job operations with unsteady demands, those 250-piece runs would be scheduled irregularly as needs arise in the processes that use the ground castings.

Overlapping

Overlapping:
A hot job forwarded in multiple, smaller transfer lots.

A close relative of lot splitting is overlapping. Perhaps the hot job is the 9,000-piece lot (a process lot) set up and running on the grinding machine. Common practice is to wait 18 hours for all 9,000 to be ground and then move the entire lot to the next process. But this is a hot job! Can't wait 18 hours! The expediter needs some or all of those 9,000 pieces to be moved forward fast.

The expediter has an easy solution. Move small sublots (transfer lots) forward to next processes and get them started right away. For example, each time 200 pieces have been ground, hand carry or push them on a wheeled cart to the next work center. The expediter might repeat the action between the next several work centers. The result is a lot that is in overlapped production at two or more work centers at the same time. It resembles assembly-line production, except that the work centers typically are not lined up in close proximity.

These examples of expediting apply when it is too late to adjust the plan. But various activity control actions, considered next, may be taken while still in the planning stage.

Activity Control

The workplace is out of control if it is choked with partly completed jobs. That is true for a restaurant, clinic, or bank as well as for a goods producer. In Chapter 6, we studied production/capacity planning and master scheduling, which help to keep an overall balance between workload and capacity, and in the preceding section we considered work center loading concepts. There are two steps to be taken in the quest for balanced loads in work centers. They involve input control of work releases to either gateway or bottleneck work centers (scheduling) and priority control of operations in each work center (dispatching). When all else fails, someone may have to expedite an urgent job (expediting was discussed earlier).

These topics comprise activity control. Manufacturers may prefer calling it either production activity control or shop floor control.

Input Control

The first half of the scheduler's job is to set due dates for each operation and a release date for the whole job. The second half is to release orders in trickles so as not to overload the work centers. This is often referred to as **input control.** Two techniques of input control are load leveling and firm planned order.

Load Leveling.   The scheduler typically maintains some form of hold-for-release file. The file contains jobs with a mix of priorities. It may also include orders that were due for release on a previous day but were withheld because something (e.g., instructions or materials) is missing, or in order to avoid overloading certain work centers. The scheduler is attempting input **load leveling;** as the term suggests, the purpose is to release a level load, which is a mix of orders that neither overloads nor underloads a work center. Load leveling works well only for gateway work centers, those at the input end of the operation sequence. The foundry (producing castings) is a common gateway in metal fabrication, a component sequencing machine (used in printed circuit board assembly) may be a gateway in electronics, and order entry or customer arrival is a gateway in many service businesses.

A scheduler could, with computer help, work up a schedule to level not only gateway but also downstream work centers. But it won't work. Variable queue times at later work centers get in the way, so that later operations are unlikely to follow the schedule closely enough for the loads to remain level.

Firm Planned Order.   The **firm planned order** is an MRP tool that may be used to overrule the automatic rescheduling feature of MRP. That can be helpful in load leveling. A firm planned order may be scheduled earlier than the actual need to get the order into a gateway work center in a slack (underloaded) week (See Exhibit 13–7). To invoke the firm planned order, the scheduler instructs the computer to flag a particular planned order and move it to a given time bucket. In the figure, planned order 688 is moved from week 3, its calculated date of need, to week 2, which helps level the load imbalance in weeks 2 and 3. The next MRP run will not reschedule the flagged job back to its need date. It will issue a reschedule message, which may be ignored.

The firm planned order may also be used to move a job to a later week. There is no point in going far into the future, however, since conditions will change the future before it arrives.

Priority Control (Dispatching)

Controlling capacity (by input/output control) is only one aspect of work center management. Priorities of the jobs and lots flowing through the work centers also must be controlled because jobs are unlikely to arrive at a work center in an orderly manner. Some jobs arrive earlier than planned and some later, and often there are jobs in queue awaiting their turn. Jobs already behind schedule should be given a higher priority in order to go through first. Priority rules (dispatching rules) need to be established, and a dispatcher may be on hand to release the jobs according to the rules. Priority control concepts, the daily priority report, and centralized versus decentralized dispatching are discussed next.

EXHIBIT 13–7   Firm Planned Order for Load Leveling in Gateway Work Center

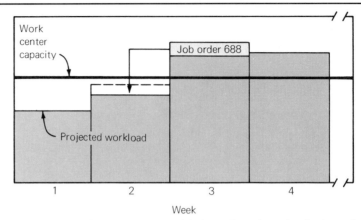

Action taken: Job order 688 is scheduled as a firm planned order in week
2 instead of week 3, its MRP-generated date of need.

Priority.   At retail, the priority system is simply first come, first served. Customers are considered homogeneous; that is, one is not more important than another. First come, first served runs itself. The retailer need not pay a dispatcher to pick and choose among customers.

Are wholesalers and factories blessed with such simplicity? Yes, but only if orders can be processed quickly enough, with no queuing or other delays at each work center. If wholesale or factory orders can be filled in, say, a day or less, the company probably will elect just to process orders as they come in; an exception might be an urgent order, which can receive high-priority treatment, such as hand carrying.

Some jobs-shops (wholesalers, offices, labs, and so forth, as well as factories) are striving for delay-free processing, but are still far from it. If it takes many days or weeks to process an order, the orders may need to be sorted by priority. Factors to consider in setting priorities for jobs include:

1. Customer importance.
2. Order urgency.
3. Order profitability.
4. Impact on capacity utilization.

For example, customer orders for items in the U.S. Department of Defense supply system are scheduled to be filled based on a priority composed of two factors. One is urgency. The other, called the force activity designator, is the customer's importance. A combat unit deployed in a combat zone is treated as a most important customer. If the unit orders bullets, the order will probably receive a high-urgency factor. The combination of customer importance and urgency yields an overall priority number calculated by computer, probably priority 1 in this case. The supply system has procedures for very fast delivery (say, 24 hours) for priority 1 requisitions; orders with very low priority call for delivery to take a certain number of weeks or months. Note that priority decisions are simplified here because profitability is not a factor; neither is capacity utilization (though it affects the supply system's delivery performance).

EXHIBIT 13–8   Some Work Center Dispatching Rules

Timing-Based Rules	Other Rules
First come, first served and kanban	Profitability rules
Shortest operation processing time	Cost rules
Longest operation processing time	Preferred customer rules
Earliest operation due date	Work center capacity rules
Earliest operation start date	
Least operation slack	
Critical ratio	
Hot list	

Scheduling component parts for end items involves simpler priority decisions than does scheduling the end items themselves. At the component level, orders for the same part are often batched. In batching orders, customer identification is lost, making it hard to schedule parts orders based on end-item profits or customer importance. Therefore, dispatching priorities (for dependent-demand parts) are usually based on order urgency and impact on capacity, not on profitability or customer importance.

Various priority rules have been proposed to aid in dispatching. Some are given in Exhibit 13–8 and discussed next.[4]

First Come, First Served and Kanban.   First come, first served was discussed earlier as the dominant priority rule in retailing. This simple priority rule is often used in industry as well. The first job arriving at a machine or desk is the first job done. First come, first served is also a common priority rule in kanban. Empty containers with kanban identifiers go back to a provider; the provider fills the containers in order of their arrival.

Shortest Operation Processing Time.   Operation processing time means setup time plus run time. In the QUIDCO example (Exhibit 13–3), the operation processing time for "bend rod" (operation 20) at work center 16 was shown as 6.7 standard hours, of which 4.2 hours was setup time.

The shortest operation processing time priority rule is noteworthy because in computer simulations it has been shown to be superior to several others. The simulations show more on-time completions when the rule is used. Even so, few firms have adopted the rule. Instead, more advanced manufacturers, especially MRP users, usually base priority decisions on some measure of relative lateness. The next four rules are based on due date and thus measure relative lateness. Each has its adherents among MRP authorities, and all yield about the same good results.

Earliest Operation Due (or Start) Date.   The earliest operation due date (or start date) priority rule simply considers the operation dates for jobs in queue at a work center. First priority goes to the job with the earliest operation due (or start) date.

In MRP firms, job due dates may be updated with each MRP run, typically weekly. The computer may then back schedule from the job due date to recompute operation due (or start) dates. Thus, the operation dates that were assigned before the job was released may change while the job is in the factory, and priorities will then change too.

---

[4] These are local priority rules, applied to operations performed at work centers. Global rules, applied to the job as a whole rather than to an operation, may be used for initially scheduling the job. Also, there is a less-precise work center priority system based on the timing of the whole job rather than the operation.

Least Slack.   Earliest due (or start) date has a minor flaw. If an eight-hour operation and an eight-day operation each have the same operation due (or start) date, their priorities are equal, but the eight-day operation actually should begin seven days sooner (or end seven days later). Such differences in processing times are accounted for when the least slack priority rule is used, but extra computations are required.

Slack may be loosely defined as demand time minus supply time. Operation slack is computed as follows:

$$\text{Slack} = \text{Demand (need) time} - \text{Supply (make) time} \qquad (13\text{–}1)$$

Or, equivalently:

$$\text{Slack} = \text{Time until operation due date} - \text{Operation lead time} \qquad (13\text{–}2)$$

where

$$\text{Time until operation due date} = \text{Operation due date} - \text{Today's date} \qquad (13\text{–}3)$$

$$\text{Operation lead time} = \text{Queue time} + \text{Processing time} \qquad (13\text{–}4)$$

$$\text{Processing time} = \text{Setup time} + \text{Run time} \qquad (13\text{–}5)$$

> A popular rearrangement of terms in the *slack* formula is: Critical ratio = Demand time / Supply time.

Alternatively:

$$\text{Operation lead time} = \text{Operation due date} - \text{Operation start date} \qquad (13\text{–}6)$$

The smaller the slack, the more urgent the job. Negative slack signifies a late condition: The operation is due for completion in less than planned operation lead time.

To demonstrate slack, let us assume that on day 101 four jobs are in queue at work center 16, which is the punch press center where metal is punched. Consider the data shown in Exhibit 13–9A (the first shop order, 9925, is from the QUIDCO example of Exhibit 13–3; recall that operation due dates are derived by back scheduling from the job due date). The slack for the four jobs is given in Exhibit 13–9B, which is roughly in the form of a daily priority report for work center 16. In the figure, slack values show that shop order 9925 is 4 days behind, 9938 and 9918 are each 2 days behind, and 9916 is 2 days ahead; the jobs should be run in work center 16 in that order.

Hot List and Other Rules.   The hot list is also known as a shortage list because it lists parts needed but unavailable for a current job. Hot-listed jobs get dispatched first at each work center. The other rules listed in Exhibit 13–8 are based on profitability, cost, preferred customer, and work center capacity. They are generally more complex than the timing-based rules (and should normally be used in conjunction with timing-based rules); elaboration on those kinds of rules is reserved for advanced studies.

> A hot-listed job getting priority *dispatching* at a single work center may also be a hot job being *expedited* (e.g., hand-carried) through many work centers.

Daily Priority Report.   The means of setting priorities is less important than the dispatching procedure. A proven procedure, perfected along with MRP, is the daily **priority report** (also called a dispatch list). A different priority report goes to each work center supervisor every day, only for jobs already in process, not those still in a planned-order state.

Centralized versus Decentralized Dispatching.   In some companies, production control department representatives are assigned to supervisors' offices. Their titles might be *dispatcher* or *shop scheduler*. The dispatcher does not just put higher-priority jobs ahead of lower-priority ones. The dispatcher may also handle blueprints, route sheets, service

Exhibit 13–9   Daily Priority Report, by Operation Slack, for Work Center 16

A.

Shop Order	Move/Queue Time	Punch Press Processing Time (Set up + Run)	Operation Due Date
9925	1 day	6.7 hours, or 1 day rounded	Day 99
9938	1 day	15.8 hours, or 2 days rounded	Day 102
9918	1 day	1.8 hours, or 1 day rounded	Day 101
9916	1 day	0.8 hours, or 1 day rounded	Day 105

B.

Shop Order	Demand Time (Due Date − Today)	Supply Time (Move/Queue + Processing)	Operation Slack
9925	99−101	1 + 1	−4
9938	102−101	1 + 2	−2
9918	101−101	1 + 1	−2
9916	105−101	1 + 1	+2

orders, job tickets, move tickets, inspection forms, tool orders, material issue forms, and completion forms. Those documents help get jobs started and account for their completion at each stage of their routing. Dispatchers on the scene can react quickly to delays. One reaction is to assign higher priority to the delayed job at the next work center. Others are to split a lot or reroute upstream jobs around serious sources of delay, such as absence of a key associate or a machine breakdown.

A few companies have a central dispatching group physically located away from front-line action. Why centralize? Consider this analogy. In an airport, decentralized air traffic control would amount to putting one air traffic controller on each runway. The controllers would try to communicate with one another via cellular phones. But the results would surely be suboptimal. The peak number of planes handled per hour would be small, or there would be frequent disasters. Thus, air traffic controllers (aircraft dispatchers) are centralized. That way they can coordinate tight scheduling and high peak volumes.

The same reasoning may apply in other businesses. Major reasons for centralized dispatching appear to be a need for tight scheduling with little margin for error during periods of surging demand volumes. Automobile assembly, shoe manufacturing, large-appliance manufacturing, and bank check and deposit processing may be among the better candidates for centralized dispatching.

We have considered a large number of activity control devices. Along with the many planning, scheduling, and expediting actions considered earlier in the chapter, these devices comprise a complex system that itself resists control. Efforts to simplify the system and make it easier to control are the next topic.

Simplification: Reduction of Variables

Criss-crossed flow paths, high error rates, piled-high in-baskets, bulging stock rooms of items not needed yet, shelves full of thick instruction manuals, frequent rescheduling, high overtime and undertime costs, poor on-time service rates, long lead times, and large backlogs: These are symptoms of overly complex job operations and high-cost, ineffective attempts to cope.

Assorted antidotes are available. We first consider ways to ease the related information processing burden, and then review an assortment of simplification methods discussed in other chapters.

Paperless and Visual Systems

Each of the planning and control topics addressed in this chapter puts more paperwork into the system. Will the product or client get lost under piles of paper? Sometimes it seems that way.

Communications and computer technology can be employed to create a paperless office or plant. A few such facilities already exist. Data-entry terminals in planning offices, display screens in work centers, bar codes on all parts containers or mail-distribution tubs, and bar code readers to track the work flow make it possible. The scheduling and activity control procedures may be just as described above. The difference is that job orders, priority reports, and other notices and files are called up on screens instead of from printed pages.

Another way to deal with paper is the visual office or plant. It is not hard to conceive of this for repetitive or continuous operations. No data screens are needed to tell people what to do when the same work units follow the same flow path (sometimes pulled by conveyors).

Can the scheduling and dispatching paper possibly be eliminated in a job shop? The answer is yes, at least partly. One documented case is the Hewlett-Packard 9000 computer workstation.[5] H-P calculates that the 9000 series can be produced in 6 million different configurations. All production is to fill customer orders, which are small and in diverse configurations. The H-P plant eliminated job orders, ceased using MRP on the shop floor, and adopted visual kanban. MRP is still used for exploding customer orders into components. The exploded customer order goes to final assembly and is also used in planning orders for purchased parts.

*P*RINCIPLE 16:

Cut transactions and reporting.

All printed circuit board assembly and major module assembly and testing are triggered visually. Very small amounts, often one unit, of each partially completed item are stored in slots or shelves on racks in the work centers. When a customer orders a certain configuration of the finished item, final assembly pulls major modules (keyboards, logic units, and power cords) from nearby shelves. That authorizes major module assembly to make one more of each module to refill the emptied shelf spaces. Module assemblers withdraw components, such as circuit boards, from nearby slots. The empty slots authorize test operators to pull untested circuit boards from one rack, test them, and place them in the other rack to fill the emptied slot. The visual authorization to make another item to fill a slot winds back through 11 production stages to the stockroom holding purchased items.

A few differences between visual and written work authorization are summarized in Exhibit 13–10. Note that the written system may include a job order, a pick list, and a priority report. The visual system may require an identification card in a slot, but that is fixed information, not transactions generated for each job; process instructions are also fixed information.

A final point is that often the visual system can be used for some but not all items and processes. For example, in aircraft production, it would make no sense to keep an extra huge wing in a shelf and then trigger production of the next wing when the shelf empties. A schedule, not an empty shelf, should authorize the production of a wing. The components that go into the wing are another story. Finished units of common struts, fabric

---

[5] See cases 2 and 3 in Richard J. Schonberger, *World Class Manufacturing Casebook: Implementing JIT and TQC* (New York: Free Press, 1987).

EXHIBIT 13–10   **Work Authorization in Job Operations**

	Visual	*Written*
Work in process	Exact small quantity located next to work center	Large shelf space in stockroom; may be full, partly full, or empty
Delivery	Empty slot tells associate to get next unprocessed unit from rack; cards identify units in rack spaces	Written job order is transformed into pick list; tells stockroom what items to pick and deliver to work centers
Dispatching	Emptiest slot is next job	Daily priority report tells work center the order of working on the jobs in queue
Process instructions	In a file at the work center	Part of work package accompanying the job order

pieces, cable lengths, wire assemblies, and other wing parts could be kept in kanban racks near the wing assembly area. Removal of a strut or other piece from a shelf may then visually authorize production of another unit to refill the shelf.

The visual system for job shops and offices is not yet in wide use, but its potential for application is almost limitless. It is a potent technique because it copes with the explosive growth of overhead costs, especially those of processing written transactions and of material handling and storage.

Other Antidotes

Complementing the shift toward simpler information processing are other complexity antidotes that have been discussed in other chapters. They are reviewed below in two groups, one general and the other specific to this chapter's topics:

General Simplifications.   These general items apply to all kinds of operations but are especially valuable in job and batch operations where complexity problems tend to be severe.

- Get focused: Strategically limit the variety of businesses per company, business unit, and site (Chapter 1).
- Reduce, simplify, and standardize designs for the line of goods and services (Chapter 3).
- Control processes at the source, rather than discovering mishaps downstream (Chapter 4).
- Stay tuned to the pulse of the market via comprehensive demand forecasting (Chapter 5).
- Employ a cross-functional master planning team to plan capacity and master schedules so that demand and supply are a reasonably close fit (Chapter 6).
- Adopt quick-response and just-in-time flow controls to remove sources of non-value-adding delay and stay close to the actual demand changes (Chapter 7).
- Cut to a few good supplier-partners (Chapter 8), thus shrinking purchasing complications.
- Adopt simple queue-limitation and kanban flow controls (Chapter 9), thereby avoiding a flood of order-control transactions.
- Cut job, lot, and batch sizes so that materials are ordered or produced based on current demand, thus avoiding problems of having too many of the wrong items and being out of the right ones (Chapter 10).

*C*ontrast

Getting the Hot Jobs Done

Expediting	Planning	Simplifying
• Expediter selects hot jobs from over-due list; uses lot splitting, overlapping, hand-carry, air freight, ''cannibaliza-tion'' of other jobs, and so forth, to push hot jobs through.	• MRP creates planned orders. • CRP identifies capacity shortfall. • Scheduling/rescheduling assigns dates. • Dispatching reprioritizes—latest jobs first.	• Quick setup so that hot jobs scarcely disrupt. • Cells process similar jobs with natural overlapping and few transactions.

Special Simplifications.   These items relate to lot splitting, rescheduling, and overlapping.

- Cut changeover and setup times (Chapter 10) so that lot splitting does not elevate costs.
- Keep physical resources in tip-top working condition (Chapter 16), thereby avoiding stoppages and rescheduling.
- Position facilities the way the work flows, thus avoiding long, jumbled flow paths (Chapter 17). A hot job then may go directly to the cell or flow line that is focused on similar items (goods, documents, or human services), where it may fit right in without special paperwork, setups, handling, or disruption. (Wherever cells are formed, overlapping is normal for every job.)
- Where there is flow distance to span (e.g., to and from a cell or in the absence of cells), downsize to lower-cost handling methods so that overlapping is still afford-able (Chapter 17). This final simplification may be illustrated with reference to forklift trucks and kanban on roller skates.

Forklift Trucks and Roller Skates

Forklift trucks are everywhere in industrial job shops. They can move loads of thousands of pounds. Since they can move very large loads, they do. Crates, pallets, and boxes are piled high, and the forklift moves the highly piled loads. In the late 1970s, Western visitors to Japan saw similar industrial job shops that made little use of forktrucks (except on receiving and shipping docks). In the 1980s, forktruck removal became popular sport in some companies.

The economics work as follows. Forktrucks, with their batteries and high battery-charging costs, are expensive. They require wide aisles, create safety hazards, and run into things and cause damage. If average transport loads are reduced, say, fivefold, simple wheeled carts will usually be strong enough. Wheeled carts moving one fifth of the former load sizes would have to make five times more trips. The total handling cost may be less, however, because of the eliminated direct and indirect costs of the forklifts. Thus, fork-truck removal may pay for itself even without the benefits of reduced delays and WIP inventories, which go down nearly fivefold as well.

Better yet, how about roller skates? That's the method of delivering small kanban quantities of parts to assembly cells at Sentrol, Inc. (see Exhibit 13–11). This producer of a premier line of sensors for business and home security (detection of glass breakage, motion, smoke, etc.) has fully implemented cells and kanban, which has driven average

$\mathscr{I}$nto $\mathscr{P}$ractice

Reducing Forklift Trucks at Emerson

William Rutledge, executive vice president of Emerson Electric Company, knew what to do about the firm's heavy use of forklift trucks and the piles of inventory they thrive on. At a company meeting in 1986, he told all his division presidents that henceforth corporate headquarters was charging a license fee for every new forklift: $5 for the first truck, $50 for the second, $500 for the third, and so on. The division presidents thought Rutledge was being facetious, but his point was clear!

EXHIBIT 13–11   Skater with Kanban Parts Containers, at Sentrol, Inc.

Left: Picking up empty container.
Middle: Emerging from stock room with full container.
Right: Dropping off full container.

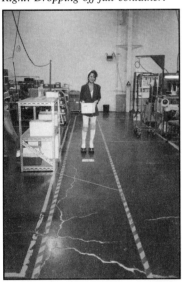

---

throughput times down from in excess of 10 weeks to about four hours. The perimeter of Sentrol's assembly floor is marked off with a painted pathway for the skater, who wheels around picking up empty kanban boxes, taking them to the adjacent parts storeroom, and skating back with full containers. While a forktruck driver or stock clerk pushing a trolley might make the rounds two or three times a day delivering large transfer quantities, Sentrol's skaters cover the entire floor several times per hour conveying small JIT quantities. Sentrol's skater position is highly sought after in the Portland, Oregon, area where the company is located.

In this chapter, we have examined a sophisticated, many-faceted system of managing complex job operations, a system perfected in North America, largely in the 1970s. We've

Reforming the Job Shop: An Example

also emphasized simplification, an approach that is highly attractive in view of the high costs and complexity of job operations. We end this chapter by elaborating upon that message via a real-life summary (see the accompanying box) of what can be done to improve a job shop. The message applies as well to job-oriented offices and, to some extent, to human service operations.

Into Practice

Reforming the Job Shop

In the summer of 1985 [Schlumberger's Houston downhole sensors (HDS) division] was struggling. Operations were costly, chaotic, and falling short of acceptable standards. Customers were dissatisfied. About 15 percent of the logging tools produced by HDS failed on final acceptance test. Most products were built to schedules established far in advance, but on-time delivery was no better than 70 percent. The average lead times exceeded 12 months. Senior management was also dissatisfied. Cost of sales was unacceptably high, and the plant was bulging with inventories. WIP alone averaged five months of output.

What explains the chronic and intractable problems afflicting job shops? The answer lies in the manufacturing philosophy. At HDS, most products were batched for final assembly and tested in lots that usually represented two or three months' requirements. Therefore, lead times on orders were at least two to three months (in reality much longer) even though many logging tools could be assembled and tested in two weeks.

So why batch? Because management wanted to be as efficient as possible, with efficiency defined as minimizing direct labor charges. Batching generated short-term savings in virtually every phase of the production process. Setup costs are a good example. Parts needed for final assembly must be "kitted" in a warehouse before arriving at the assembly area. Management believed that pulling kits in large lots, rather than as orders arrived, saved money. Batching also meant that workers had to learn how to assemble and test a product only once per batch. Batching minimized the unit costs of configuring test equipment and debugging completed products. Finally, moving products in large batches was combined with the use of queues to smooth work flows and adjust to ever-present parts shortages. Batching in effect, allowed all the factory's workers to be busy all the time.

In the long term, however, batching becomes a big obstacle to the very efficiencies it seeks to achieve. The long lead-time, large-lot, long-queue philosophy invariably re-

sults in split lots, broken setups, lost and defective parts, late deliveries, and large WIP. The results are visible in job-shops everywhere: the monthly shipments hockey stick, where a large volume of product leaves the factory at the end of each measurement period; relaxation of quality standards under pressure to make quotas; secret high-rework jobs hidden in WIP; ever-changing production priorities; and daily crises on the shop floor.

We believe the real solution lies in eliminating batching, smoothing, and artificial economies of scale, and organizing a job-shop that can quickly and efficiently "change over" from one product to another without incurring large delays and cost penalties.

HDS adopted such a production philosophy. It emphasizes shorter lead times (down from an average of three months to two weeks today), small to nonexistent queues, low inventories, and quick recognition and correction of defects.

Getting control over the shop floor has allowed us to slash overhead. In the summer of 1985, 520 of the division's 830 employees were salaried or indirect personnel. The overhead count now stands at 220 employees. The largest reductions came from three departments—quality control; shipping, receiving, and warehousing; and production control (expediters, dispatchers)—whose roles diminish as quality and on-time performance improves.

These dramatic results did not require large capital expenditures. The management team initially cut the capital budget by 50 percent; annual spending has since run at less than half of depreciation. Those results did not require sophisticated computer applications. In fact, we turned off our shop floor computer, adopted a manual floor-control approach, and canceled a $400,000 automation project.

Source: Adapted from James E. Ashton and Frank X. Cook, Jr., "Time to Reform Job-Shop Manufacturing," *Harvard Business Review,* March–April 1989, pp. 106–11. Used with permission.

Summary

Job and batch operations involve handling a diverse, changing mix of small orders and small customers. Managing job and service orders tends to require extensive scheduling, work center loading, expediting, reporting, and control. Extensive efforts to focus, simplify, become market-sensitive, and control process variables can avert many of the problems common in the job mode.

Job orders may subdivide into operations, each requiring a setup and each performed in a different work center. Scheduling at the operation level (work in queue at a work center) is called dispatching.

Because of variable queues, lead time to complete a job is often a question mark. The more congestion on the floor (e.g., WIP), the more uncertain the lead time. Schedulers can help by (1) controlling releases of orders (input control), and (2) employing the firm planned order feature of MRP in order to level work loads in gateway work centers. While on-demand services and stock replenishment may be forward scheduled, appointments and future orders (including those planned by MRP) are usually backward scheduled.

Appointments and scheduled jobs and operations should dovetail with schedules for operating resources: labor, equipment, tools, materials, and space. In services, it is sometimes helpful to display schedules on visual Gantt charts; Gantt control charts are used to plot status of work, especially in maintenance, construction, computer programming, and so forth.

Work center loading may include an extension of MRP, called capacity requirements planning (CRP), which adds planned orders to open orders, thus yielding more complete load reports. Schedulers can check the load report to see if scheduled jobs overload or underload the work center. A work center load report that is based only on open (released) orders gives little warning about over- or underloading.

Jobs are usually scheduled under an assumption of infinite capacity. While that is unrealistic, the infinite-capacity approach can work reasonably well in combination with priority controls: rearranging priorities of jobs as they queue up in the work center so that late jobs are processed first.

Hot jobs can be expedited. Expediting techniques include lot splitting, overlapped production, and hand carrying. The extra costs of those actions can be lessened by developing quick setup methods and shortening flow distances through creation of work cells.

There are several ways of setting priorities. A simple one is first come, first served, which is common in retailing and certain office and production work. For jobs having backward-scheduled due dates, earliest start (or due) date is a simple priority rule. Least slack also is popular.

When work flows are monitored by computer transactions, it is possible to produce a daily priority report, which advises the supervisor or dispatcher of the priorities of jobs present in the work center. Dispatchers sometimes work in a centralized office instead of in the workplace, especially where operations must be tightly coordinated.

Paperless work authorization is possible with computers. Visual kanban-like systems go a step further by eliminating the need for some written work authorizations and flow tracking.

Key Words

Solved Problems

Problem 1

The framing department has an order for 20-pound frames. The operations and standard times for producing one frame are:

Operation	Standard Time
Cut	4 hours
Weld	8 hours
Grind	3 hours
Finish	18 hours

a. If it is a hot job, how quickly (in eight-hour days) can it be completed allowing one extra day for material movement and delays?

b. The MRP system sets lead times for component parts by a formula: standard hours times five, plus two weeks, rounded upward to full weeks. What lead time does the MRP system use?

c. The above two answers are far apart, but both may be fairly realistic. Explain how a planned system can accommodate both.

Solution 1

a. Total work content $= 4 + 8 + 3 + 18 = 33$ standard hours
$= 4.125$ days, rounded up to 5 days
Total expedited lead time $= 5 + 1$ extra day
$= 6$ days

b. From part *a:*
Total hours $= 33$ hours
Then:
Lead time $= (33 \text{ hours} \times 5) + 2$ weeks
$= 165$ hours (or 4.125 weeks) $+ 2$ weeks
$= 6.125$, rounded up to 7 weeks

c. The MRP system must back schedule using normal time estimates. The result is a fairly realistic week of need, seven weeks prior to the week due for the frame order. It is nearly eight times greater than the expedite time of six days, which is to be expected since in conventional job shops work spends most of its total lead time in various kinds of delay. The few hot jobs interrupt the routine ones, causing the latter to be delayed still more. (While that situation has been normal in job-shops, simplified operations management systems are eliminating delays in some companies.)

Problem 2

Today is day 11 on the shop calendar, and three jobs are in work center 67, as shown in the following table:

Jobs in Work Center 67	Scheduled Operation Start Date	Scheduled Operation Due Date
A	12	18
B	8	16
C	13	17

Calculate operation slack for the three jobs. Arrange the jobs in priority order, and indicate which should be done first.

Solution 2

From Equations 13–1, 13–2, and 13–3:

Demand time = Operation due date − Today's date

Then:

Job	Demand Time Due − Today	Supply Time (Equation 13–6)	Operation Slack (Equation 13–2)
A	18 − 11 = 7	18 − 12 = 6	7 − 6 = +1
B	16 − 11 = 5	16 − 8 = 8	5 − 8 = −3
C	17 − 11 = 6	17 − 13 = 4	6 − 4 = +2
	First:	B	
	Second:	A	
	Third:	C	

For Further Reference

Books

Fitzsimmons, James A., and Robert S. Sullivan. *Service Operations Management*. New York: McGraw-Hill, 1982 (HD9980.5.F55).

Melnyk, Steven A.; Phillip L. Carter; David M. Dilts; and David M. Lyth. *Shop Floor Control*. Homewood, Ill.: Richard D. Irwin, 1985.

Plossl, G. W., and O. W. Wight. *Production and Inventory Control: Principles and Techniques*. Englewood Cliffs, N.J.: Prentice-Hall 1967 (HD55.P5).

Vollmann, Thomas E.; William L. Berry; and D. Clay Whybark. *Manufacturing Planning and Control*. 3d ed. Homewood, Ill.: Richard D. Irwin, 1992 (TS176.V63).

Wight, Oliver W. *Production and Inventory Management in the Computer Age*. Boston: CBI Publishing, 1974 (TS155.W533).

Periodicals/Societies

Decision Sciences (Decision Sciences Institute), an academic journal.

Production and Inventory Management (American Production and Inventory Control Society).

Journal Operations Management (American Production and Inventory Control Society), an academic journal.

Review Questions

1. Why is simplification relevant in managing job operations?
2. Distinguish among scheduling, dispatching, and loading.
3. What is the difference between a job and an operation?
4. Why is it hard to estimate production lead time accurately?
5. Why is it important to minimize work-in-process inventory?
6. Contrast backward and forward scheduling.
7. Explain how a due date for a shop order may be translated into finish dates for each operation in the job.
8. What are the uses of Gantt charts?
9. What is the difference between lot splitting and overlapped production?
10. What are some alternatives to expediting in services?
11. In what situations in capacity control would Principle 13, decrease the cycle interval, be useful?
12. How do CRP reports get produced, and what are they used for?

13. When work center workloads are calculated manually in a non-MRP system, why do they end up looking like the bar chart in Exhibit 13–6A; that is, why do the load in week 0 and the tapering-off pattern?

14. In MRP systems, infinite-capacity loading is usual. Does this make the MRP data invalid? Discuss.

15. How does the firm planned order help ensure that the right amount of work is released by the scheduler?

16. There are eight timing-based dispatching rules listed in Exhibit 13–8. How do the last five differ from the first three?

17. When is operation slack a useful priority rule?

18. Who receives the daily priority report (or dispatch list), and what is it used for?

19. When is it wise to do centralized dispatching?

20. Compare the paperless and visual systems.

Problems and Exercises

1. A manufacturer of stereo speakers produces five main types of high-quality speaker. The company considers itself a job shop. The single production line produces lots of each type of speaker on an irregular schedule. Price competition has been severe, and the company's profits have eroded. A conglomerate is buying the stereo manufacturer and intends to invest a considerable amount of cash to improve production control and cut production costs. What should the money be invested in?

2. An advertising agency has 12 departments. Every small ad job must pass through at least 6 of them, medium-sized ads through 9 of the departments, and large ads for major clients through all 12 departments. Typically, over 100 ad jobs (each a separate ad for a separate customer's product) are in process at any one time. Most are late, a contributing reason why the agency has lost a few long-standing clients. What should be done to improve on-time performance?

3. A scheduler at QUIDCO, Inc., is working up a schedule for making 20 of part number 0077AX. The inventory planner advises that the order be released this week, week of day 90, and that the order is due on the week of day 115, when it will be needed to go into a parent item. QUIDCO employs closed-loop MRP.
   a. How would the inventory planner have determined the week due and the week of release? If the inventory planner has determined these dates, doesn't that constitute rescheduling and eliminate the need for the scheduler to do anything? Discuss.
   b. The A in the part number signifies a costly item. For A items, the following rules are used for computing operation lead times:
      (1) Allow eight standard hours per day: round upward to whole (eight-hour) days.
      (2) Allow no time between operations. A items receive priority material handling.
      (3) Allow one day to inspect.
      (4) Release the job to the stockroom four days before it is to be started into production.
      (5) All dates are treated as end of the eight-hour day.
      Schedule a shop order for the item, assuming that the part goes through three operations plus inspection. You make up the setup times and operation times such that the schedule will fit between days 90 and 115. Explain.
   c. Compare the operation lead-time rules for part number 0077AX with the rules in Example 13–2 for part number 1005CX. Why should a more expensive item have different lead-time rules? (Hint: WIP has something to do with it.)
   d. A week passes. Inventory planning notifies scheduling that part number 0077AX is now due (to go into a parent item) in the week of day 120 instead of 115. The shop order, along with a planning package (blueprints, job tickets, etc.), has already been released. There is no need to issue new paperwork, because QUIDCO has a computer-produced

daily dispatch list for each work center. Least operation slack is the dispatching rule. The scheduler merely gets on a terminal and inputs updated scheduling information. Explain how that information would be used in generating dispatch lists. Also, explain how the dispatch lists serve the purpose of adjusting for the new due date.

4. The maintenance department has two renovation orders that are being scheduled. Order 1 requires these three jobs or tasks: 14 days of wiring, 7 days of drywall work, and 9 days of painting. Order 2 takes 5 days of drywall followed by 6 days of painting.
   a. Draw a Gantt chart showing the work loads (backlogs) for each of the three jobs (wiring, drywall, and paint).
   b. Draw a Gantt chart showing the two orders back scheduled, the first with completion due at the end of day 35 and the second due at the end of day 14.
   c. Draw a Gantt chart with the two orders forward scheduled. In what situation would forward scheduling for these three trades be useful?

5. Four jobs are on the desk of the scheduler for a firm's minor construction department. Each job begins with masonry, followed by carpentry and wiring. Work-order data are as follows:

Work Order	Estimated Task Time—Masonry	Estimated Task Time—Carpentry	Estimated Task Time—Wiring
58	2 weeks	3 weeks	1½ weeks
59	1 week	1½ weeks	1 week
60	3 weeks	2 weeks	3 weeks
61	5 weeks	½ week	1½ weeks

   a. Prepare a Gantt chart scheduling the four jobs through the three crafts (crafts are rows on your chart). Use first come, first served as the priority rule for scheduling (first *job* first—the whole job). Assume that a craft cannot divide its time between two work orders. How many weeks do the four jobs take?
   b. Repeat question *a,* but use the shortest-job processing time rule instead of first come, first served. Now how many weeks are required?
   c. Three weeks pass. The following progress is reported to the scheduler:
   Masonry completed on WO 58.
   Masonry not started on WO 59, 60 or 61.
   Carpentry half completed on WO 58.
   Show the progress on a Gantt control chart (using part *a* data).
   d. In this problem situation, each shop is fully loaded as the jobs are sequenced and scheduled. It is finite-capacity loading. What is there about minor construction work of this kind that makes scheduling and loading so uncomplicated (relative to job-lot parts fabrication)?

6. The following Gantt chart shows a scheduled project task and progress as of a given date:

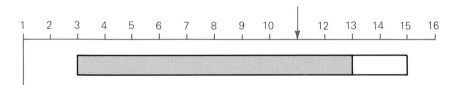

   a. What is the present date, and what is the percent of completion for the task? How many days ahead or behind schedule are shown?
   b. Redraw the chart as it will look tomorrow if the entire task is completed. How many days ahead or behind schedule does your chart represent?
   c. Saturdays and Sundays are not worked and are not identified on the chart. Explain how the dating system treats weekends (and holidays).

7. Open Air Furniture Company makes patio furniture. There are just three work centers: rough saw, finish saw, and assemble.

    Production control keeps track of total workloads for use in short-term scheduling and capacity management. Each week's component-parts orders are translated into machine-hours in rough saw and finish saw and into labor-hours in assembly. Current machine-hour and labor-hour loads are as follows:

	Rough Saw	Finish Saw	Assemble
Current week	270	470	410
Week 2	40	110	100
Week 3	—	40	50
Week 4	—	30	15
Weekly capacity	150	225	190

    a. Discuss probable reasons for the load pattern given for each work center.

    b. Is this the type of firm that is likely to rely heavily on expediting? Explain.

8. The following chart shows projected loads for one work center:

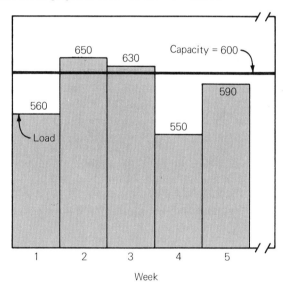

    a. What may the scheduler do to help correct the imbalance between load and capacity in some weeks? Discuss, including any limitations or difficulties in correcting the imbalance.

    b. How would the load report be produced?

9. On day 280, the daily priority report for the nickel-plating work center includes job number 2228. That job is due out of plating on day 279, and its planned run time is one day. If an additional day is allowed for move and queue time, what is the operation slack? Show your calculation. How should these calculated results be interpreted?

10. Jerrybuilt Machines, Inc., uses the least-operation-slack priority rule. On shop calendar day 62, the following shop orders will be in work center 30:

Shop Order	Move/Queue Allowance	Operation Time	Operation Due Date
889	2 days	3 days	68
916	2 days	1 day ·	64
901	2 days	1 day	69

Calculate the slack for each shop order, and arrange your calculated results in list form as they would appear on a daily dispatch list.

11. The following data apply to three shop orders that happen to end up in the same work center on day 120:

Shop Order	Preceding Work Center	Completion Date (Day Moved to Next Work Center)	Next (Current) Work Center	Queue Time plus Run Time in Work Center 17	Date Due Out of Work Center 17
300	28	119	17	122	3 days
310	14	117	17	123	2 days
290	13	118	17	121	1 day

Moves from one work center to another take virtually no time. Calculate operation slack for the three jobs, and arrange them in priority order, first to last.

12. On day 12, shop order number 222 is in the blanking work center; it requires two days in blanking (including all waits, setups, moves, etc.) and is due out of blanking on day 15. Also on day 12, shop order 333 is in the same work center; it requires three days in blanking and is due out on day 17. Finally, on day 12, shop order 444 is in the work center; it requires one day and is due out on day 12.

   Determine which order should be run first, which second, and which third. Calculate slack for each order to prove your answer. What is the meaning of the slack value you get for order 444?

13. An antenna manufacturer produces in lots. Part of the daily dispatch list on day 314 is shown below for the chrome-plating work center:

Shop Order	Part	Setup Time (Standard Hours)	Operation Time (Standard Hours)	Slack (Days)
910	AS65	0.5	3.5	−3
914	AS41	2.0	12.0	0
.				
.				
.				
885	AL88	4.5	10.0	+6

   a. If shop order 885 is as shown below, what is its operation slack at the plating operation on day 314 (a Friday)?

Shop Order 885, Part Number AL88, Quantity: 5 Loads

Operation	Setup Hours	Total Run Hours	Finish
Cut	1.0	6.0	320
Move			321
Chrome plate	4.5	10.0	323
Trim		8.0	324

   b. What rules for computing operation lead times can be detected from shop order 885?

   c. On day 315 (Monday morning), inventory planning notifies scheduling that the due date for part number AL88 is now day 319 instead of 324. The chrome-plating operation has not yet been done for the part. What is the new operation slack in the chrome-plating work center? Is shop order 885 now urgent?

    d. On day 315, where are shop orders 910 and 914 likely to be? Base your answer only on the above information.

    e. Assume that on day 316 the (partial) daily dispatch list is as follows:

Shop Order	Part Number	Setup Time (Standard Hours)	Operation Time (Standard Time)	Slack (Days)
898	AL26	1.5	4.0	−4
914	AS41	2.0	12.0	−1
885	AL88	4.5	10.0	−1

    Explain what has happened to yield this dispatch list.

    f. Will shop order 885 also appear on the daily dispatch list for the trim work center? Explain.

    g. Is this company likely to use centralized or decentralized dispatching? Explain.

14. For *a, b,* and *c,* explain the applicability and describe a suitable approach to (1) scheduling, (2) dispatching, including a priority control rule, and (3) expediting.

    a. Getting a driver's license, four stops: written test, driving test, photo, and payment of fee and receipt of license.

    b. Getting your car repaired at a large auto dealer: wheel alignment, electrical system, and installation of a new bumper.

    c. A manufacturer of a wide variety of models of metal office furniture, all models passing through four manufacturing areas: metal shop for cutting and forming the component parts, welding, painting, and final assembly.

15. A central sales office has seen its expediting (hand-carried orders) increase from 2 to 5 to over 10 percent in the last two years. Nonexpedited orders take at least a week to be processed. Suggest improvements in the priority and order-processing system.

16. The city planning department processes all requests for building and construction permits. The permit process, involving eight departments, has been unsatisfactory, and the mayor has appointed a new planning department administrator, who has stated her intention to install a computer system for logging and tracking the flow of all orders. The assistant administrator is arguing against the plan. She says it will be costly, add no value, and may not work. Elaborate upon her argument, including suggestions for an alternative approach.

MANAGING PROJECTS

14

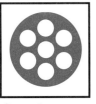

Human resources director: "Maybe someday everybody in this place will spend all of their time working in project teams."
Operations manager: "It's getting that way, all right. Half my associates are working for one of the project managers these days. And the rest are on improvement projects."
Marketing director: "Yes, when I started here, we sold the same models year after year. We hardly ever talked to people in other departments, much less joined project teams to launch new models or to team up on improvement projects."

The above exchange might be taking place, for example, at a manufacturer, a bank, an airline, or a ticket-selling firm. Its basis is modern phenomena: the collapsing of product/service life cycles, stemming from awareness of the strategic value of time-based competition (noted in Chapters 1 and 3), and the total quality management mandate for continuous improvement. Each new model introduction is a unique event—a project. Most continuous improvement endeavors (except small, simple improvement jobs) also are projects.

Project:
Large-scale, one-of-a-kind-endeavor; generally employs large amounts of diverse resources.

Project Management: Teamwork and Organization

The complex, unique nature of projects presents special management difficulties. By the 1980s, accelerated needs for new product/service and process improvement projects seemed overwhelming to the companies that were most attuned to the need for these projects.

But solutions to these difficulties began to appear, and many companies have been able to cut their project completion times by half and more. This permits pumping out many more projects in a given time period. In this chapter (the third on translating planned orders into outcomes), we consider, in order, five aspects of effective project management:

1. High-performance teamwork.
2. Project organization structures.
3. Information sharing.
4. Tools and techniques.
5. Combating project complexity.

The first three topics require only a few pages of discussion. On the other hand, project management tools and techniques are well developed and take up most of the chapter. The fifth topic provides a brief chapter conclusion.

Part of the formula for souped-up project management is to achieve high-performance teamwork. Specifically, project teams need to be multifunctional; they must, for urgent projects, work simultaneously rather than serially; and they must fully employ data-based quality improvement methods continually.

Simultaneous development was presented in Chapter 3, data-based quality improvement in Chapter 4, and multifunctional team processes throughout the book.

High-Performance Teamwork

Product development (Chapter 3) — overall plans for new and modified products/ services — includes project management, which is required to carry out the plans.

This brings us back to the gist of the chapter-opening conversation: more and more people spending more and more time in project work. That includes early and continuing involvement of people who formerly had late involvement or no involvement in new-product projects: suppliers; customers; quality specialists; equipment, tool, and materials people; front-line supervisors and associates; and others. Including these people greatly improves the quality of project outcomes, especially if they collect data on mishaps and hold team meetings to improve the process and prevent the mishaps from happening again, in this or future projects. Improved project quality is reflected by less project rework and scrap, in addition to speeding up project completion.

While broad representation on project teams is desirable, more people working more hours on a single project may not necessarily lead to quicker project completion time (see the accompanying box).

*𝒫*RINCIPLE 1:

Team up with next and final customer.

The diverse members of the project team may split their time and allegiance between the project and their functional organization unit. For example, an accountant may handle accounts receivable most of the time, but help the project team with cost estimating, as needed. Associates in operations may attend some project meetings to look for operational weaknesses of the proposed design, but spend most of their working hours on the front lines.

Project Organization Structures

Amount of time that people spend on projects versus working in their functional departments is partly determined by how people and functions are positioned in the organization. The extent of project emphasis in the organization structure can range from zero to total. Three degrees of project organization are shown in Exhibit 14–1, numbered 1 through 3; they are flanked by two nonproject forms, numbered 0 and 00. The five project organizational forms are explained below.

    0. *Pure functional organization.* In this structure there is no project activity; everyone in every functional department is engaged in ongoing operations. In some slow-to-change organizations, such as a government agency out of the

$$\mathcal{I}nto\ \mathcal{P}ractice$$

The More the Messier

Marvin Patterson, director of corporate engineering at Hewlett-Packard Company, offers evidence on the drawbacks of having too many people on a project team:

We observed this . . . in the completion of two projects sequentially. [The first was] a project requiring 127 new mechanical parts [and] six mechanical engineers over a period of three years. In a follow-up project, a low-cost roll of the same product, the task was to reduce the number of mechanical parts by two-thirds, thereby reducing the manufacturing costs. That job took 17 [mechanical engineers] four years. What happened? When we asked, the answer came back, "We had so many meetings, we had to talk so much to coordinate the design over 17 people, that the communications burden became onerous."

Source: Marvin L. Patterson with Sam Lightman, *Accelerating Innovation: Improving the Process of Product Development* (New York: Van Nostrand Reinhold, 1993), pp. 184–85 (TS176.P367).

public eye or a monopolistic business in a remote area, this lack of projects (other than occasional renovation and remodeling) may persist for years.

1. *Project coordinator.* This is the weakest approach to project management: a coordinator has a short-term assignment but no project budget or staff. The project coordinator's limited activities revolve around arranging meetings, working out schedules, and expediting. The effective coordinator tries to achieve teamwork by working closely with liaison people in the functional organization, where the real power rests.

2. *Product/commodity/brand manager or project engineer.* This second project form involves a career-track manager or engineer, sometimes with a small staff and limited budgetary authority. Responsibility is for an evolving product family (e.g., airplane upholstery), brand (e.g., Tide detergent), or succession of small engineering projects (e.g., civil engineering/construction). To be effective, the management or project engineering team must develop and work closely with a cohesive processing team of associates from the functional base, where most of the work is performed.

3. *Autonomous project management team.* Here the project manager has money to hire a full team out of the functional base (or outside the firm) to perform the work itself in its own space with its own equipment and other resources. The project manager is usually a high-level person who may even outrank the functional managers. Newer versions of this form of project management have been called "tiger" or "bandit" teams because of their aggressive, focused approach and disregard for practices standard in the rest of the firm. After completion of the project, the team disbands or its members join new project teams.

00. *New business unit.* Occasionally a super project is established as (or grows into) a separate division or business unit. In effect, it becomes a minicompany. As such, it may devolve into an ordinary functional organization, with no special project emphasis.

The three project management types in Exhibit 14–1 are general categories, not an exhaustive list. There are other ways to organize, staff, and fund projects, and many

EXHIBIT 14–1   Project Management Organization Structures

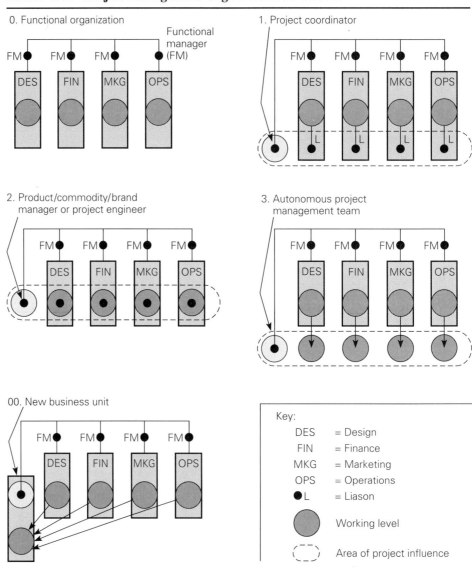

SOURCE: Adapted from Steven C. Wheelwright and Kim B. Clark, *Revolutionizing Product Development: Quantum Leaps in Speed, Efficiency, and Quality* (New York: The Free Press, 1992), p. 191 (HF5415.153.W44).

companies devise their own variations. See, for example, Chaparral Steel's three approaches (box), which are variants of the three project management forms in Exhibit 14–1.

Any form of project management can greatly benefit from high-performance teamwork. However, a weak project structure can make that teamwork more difficult. A very strong project structure, such as the autonomous form in Exhibit 14–1, might seem to be synonymous with a high degree of teamwork. Not so. That form has long been common in defense and aerospace; nevertheless, in most cases most of the work was divided up by functional specialty and processed slowly one stage at a time instead of simultaneously using cohesive teams. The influence of total quality management may be instrumental in correcting this weakness.

$\mathscr{I}$nto $\mathscr{P}$ractice

Three Types of Projects—Chaparral Steel

Wheelwright and Clark's research suggests that most companies force-fit a standard approach to all projects, which leads to underpowered big projects and overkilled small ones. Chaparral Steel (which appears often on lists of world-class companies) avoids these problems by having three different project management approaches:

- Incremental projects in the $100,000 to $200,000 cost range lasting about two months. These projects (40 or more likely to be in progress on average) are performed by functional subgroups and a lightweight project manager.
- Platform projects in the $500,000 to $1 million range requiring 12–24 months to complete. These projects

(three to five under way on average) are led by heavyweight project managers, who usually have moved from a department head position and will return to that position after project completion.

- Major advanced-development projects in the $3 million to $5 million expenditure range requiring 3–5 years to complete. These projects (usually only about two in progress at any given time) are led by one of seven general foremen.

SOURCE: Adapted from Steven C. Wheelwright and Kim B. Clark, *Revolutionizing Product Development: Quantum Leaps in Speed, Efficiency, and Quality* (New York: The Free Press, 1992), pp. 216–17 (HF5415.153.W44).

Project teams organized in any of the project management forms in Exhibit 14–1 may look outside the firm for team members. Outside teams could include fully staffed supplier or customer projects; for best results, the inside project group would want to establish cross-memberships with the outside project teams.

An excellent example of a company that gets maximum service from outside project teams is McDonald's Corporation. Out of a long string of McDonald's products that met its requirements for quality, speed, efficiency, production in a squeezed space, popularity, and profit, only one, the Quarter Pounder, was developed by an inside project team. All the rest were developed by franchised restaurant owners (the customers of McDonald's Corp.) and hard-charging, innovative suppliers.

One of McDonald's newer successes, Chicken McNuggets, was launched in 1980. The basic nuggets idea emerged after an inside project team had spent 10 years working toward a chicken product. But the nuggets still had to be developed. Bud Sweeney, an account executive at Gorton's (the frozen fish company) came to the rescue. On loan from Gorton's, Sweeney organized and led a chicken SWAT team (like a tiger team), which found help from several sources. Gorton's provided the unique tempura coating. McDonald's product development and quality assurance people handled specifications and test marketing. A chef on loan from a Chicago hotel came up with four dips. Keystone Foods, a frozen beef patty supplier, developed production lines to debone chicken and equipment to cut it into random-looking chunks. And Tyson Foods, a chicken processor, developed a special new breed of bird, called Mr. McDonald, that was almost twice the weight of an ordinary fryer, which made deboning easier.[1]

Members of the project team can do little without information, which may be likened to raw materials in a factory. However, sharing information goes against the grain of most

Information Sharing

---
[1] John F. Love, *McDonald's: Behind the Arches* (Toronto: Bantam Books, 1986).

*C*ontrast

Ownership of Information

Private Property	**Team Ownership**
Task-related information retained by the holder of the position in the holder's personal space. Experience and training belong to the individual.	Task-related information, experience, and training belong to the team and the company and should reside in files easily accessible by all team members.

---

people in Western cultures. The common individualistic attitude is, "My expertise, my experience, and my information is my strength, and I'll keep it for myself."

While no one wants to snuff out the Western spirit of individualism, which is a healthful source of innovation, neither do we want team members to withhold information from other team members. Information is power, and project teams with wide access to information, including each other's, are powerful and effective.

But what is the mechanism for pulling knowledge out of people's heads, personal files, desk drawers, and other hiding places? Can the Far East, where the culture is group oriented instead of individualistic, provide answers? Perhaps so. Funk details systematic procedures for information sharing at Mitsubishi Electric Company in Japan, based upon his two-year assignment working as a project engineer at that company.[2] Every scrap of information gleaned from visits to libraries, customers, trade shows, conferences, committee meetings, and so forth, is required to be written up and inserted into common files, fully cross-referenced. Newly hired engineers at Mitsubishi spend a good deal of their orientation period getting to know the filing system and the rules for its use.

*P*RINCIPLE 3:

Gain unified purpose via shared information.

Once such a system is established, it is easy for its users to identify anyone who fails to feed it. Peer pressure can shape behaviors for the common good.

At Mitsubishi, the information generally went into common file cabinets. The concept applies equally well to computer files. Patterson describes a project team at three geographically disbursed Hewlett-Packard sites: Waldbronn, Germany; Avondale, Pennsylvania; and Palo Alto, California. Each group was working on different parts of operating system software for an H-P analytical instrument:

> The Palo Alto group agreed to maintain the current version of the total operating system and make it remotely accessible to the other sites through a WAN [wide-area network]. The next version . . . would then . . . be made available for remote access. Within minutes both the Avondale and Waldbronn teams would have the current system running at their sites, and development could continue with all teams once again synchronized. This development effort progressed well and resulted in a successful product.
>
> In contrast, an earlier effort, before the age of WANs, attempted . . . the same thing through shipment of magnetic tapes. Shipment delays and time lost passing through customs hampered engineering efforts immensely. Engineers in the three sites were only rarely working with the

---

[2]Jeffrey L. Funk, "Case Study: Managing the Organizational Complexity of Applying CIM to Semiconductor Manufacturing in the Mitsubishi Electric Corporation," *Manufacturing Review,* March 1991, pp. 5–17.

same version of the operating system. Often as not, recently designed code would prove to be incompatible with operating system updates that had been two weeks or more in transit.[3]

The information sharing referred to so far is mainly what is used to create project outcomes: raw and semifinished information transformed by the project team into completed software, product designs, process specifications, architectural plans, and so forth. Besides this *operating information,* the project group must manage project *planning and control information,* our next topic.

Project Representation

The size and complexity of project operations translate into a sizable management planning and control task. Tailor-made for the job is a set of tools and techniques having the abbreviations CPM and PERT.

The **critical path method (CPM),** a project management tool, was developed by Catalytic Construction Company in 1957. Catalytic developed CPM as a method for improving planning and control of a project to construct a plant for Du Pont Corporation. CPM was credited with having saved time and money on that project, and today it is well known and widely used in the construction industry.

The **program evaluation and review technique (PERT)** was developed in 1958 by Booz Allen & Hamilton Inc., a large consulting firm, along with the U.S. Navy Special Projects Office. PERT was developed to provide more intensive management of the Polaris missile project. Polaris was one of the largest research and development projects ever undertaken. Nevertheless, it was completed in record time, about four years. PERT got much of the credit and soon was widely adopted in the R&D industry as a tool for intensive project management.

A few early differences between CPM and PERT have mostly disappeared, and it is convenient to think of PERT and CPM as being one and the same, going by the combined term PERT/CPM. The construction industry still calls it CPM, and R&D people, PERT; a few other terminological differences are noted later.

PERT/CPM begins with graphical models that represent (model or mimic) the project itself. These are the work breakdown structure and the network.

The **work breakdown structure** is for a project what the bill of materials is for a job. It is a representation of the building-block structure of the end product: major project modules, secondary components, and so on. To illustrate, we shall use a familiar example: home construction. (We'll make it a luxury home, since building ordinary houses is so routine as to be more like repetitive than project operations.)

Work Breakdown Structure

A work breakdown structure for building a house is shown in Exhibit 14–2. Part A is a preferred way to develop a work breakdown structure; the planning team breaks down the project into tangible products at levels 2 and 3. Part B is a process-oriented way to draw it that is not recommended. The process-oriented chart does not have tangible products whose completion may be assigned as a unit to a single manager or team. Carpentry, for example, is a process that results in several tangible products or parts: forms for footings, the house's frame, finished cabinets, and so forth. Painting, landscaping, and masonry also are found throughout the project and result in several products.

---

[3]Marvin L. Patterson, *Accelerating Innovation: Improving the Process of Product Development* (New York: Van Nostrand Reinhold, 1993), pp. 149–50 (TS176.P367).

EXHIBIT 14–2   **Work Breakdown Structures for a House-Building Project**

A. Recommended: Product-oriented work breakdown structure

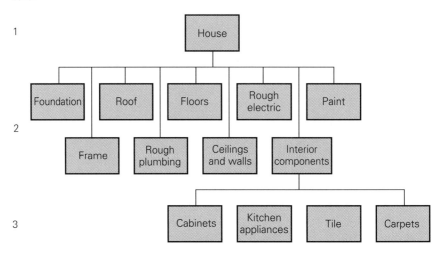

B. Not recommended: Process-oriented work breakdown structure

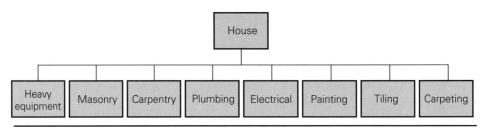

*P*RINCIPLE 1:

Know the customer.

When the project is delayed or resources are idled, painters can conveniently blame carpenters, and so forth. If managers supervise given parts of the project, instead of having foremen only for each craft or process, the managers may work to secure cooperation from the various crafts. The idea is to get each craft closely connected to a customer, the next craft, in a joint effort to complete a segment of the house correctly with no delays or wasted resources.

Network

A project consists of dozens, or even hundreds or thousands, of related tasks that must be performed in some sequence. PERT/CPM requires the sequence to be carefully defined in the form of a project **network** (see Exhibit 14–3). The starting and ending nodes are joined by a series of arrows and intermediate nodes that collectively reveal the sequence and relationships of the project tasks.

Networks facilitate project management in at least two ways. First, the immensity of most projects makes it hard to remember and visualize the day-to-day and task-level activities, but a computerized network model remembers with ease. Second, the network aids in managing a large project as a system, consisting of subprojects (subsystems), sub-subprojects, and so on. For example, two of the successive nodes in Exhibit 14–3 could represent the start and end nodes of a subproject, for which a separate, more detailed network could be drawn. Alternatively, the network in Exhibit 14–3 might represent one subproject in an even larger project.

EXHIBIT 14–3   **A PERT/CPM Network**

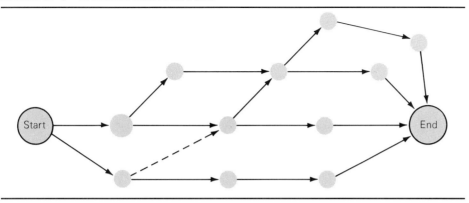

Although a good deal of attention is devoted to networks in this chapter, keep in mind that the network is only a tool. The project is being managed, not the network.

Phased PERT/CPM

Once the project team gets the PERT/CPM models built, members may use the models for the following: capacity planning, task sequencing, projecting completions, identifying most-critical tasks, simulating project change alternatives, scheduling, and controlling. These multiple uses of PERT/CPM tend to group into four phases of project management:

1. *Project planning and sequencing.* Activities in this phase resemble product/service design, process planning, and routing activities in repetitive and job operations.

2. *Time estimating and path analysis.* Time estimating for projects is like time estimating for job operations, but path analysis is unique to project management.

3. *Project scheduling.* Scheduling projects has some elements of both repetitive and job scheduling. But since a project is a single complex endeavor, schedulers must contend with many scheduling dependencies.

4. *Reporting and updating.* Treating the project as a single, large unit of work permits project managers to intensively control using the management-by-exception principle.

Management-by-exception:
Tightly manage what is straying off course—the exceptions—and ignore the rest.

When the team employs all four phases, PERT/CPM is more than just tools and techniques. It becomes a management system, with each of the four phases as subsystems. While most projects are not complex enough to warrant the expense of the full system treatment, very large scale projects often qualify. Each of the four subsystems is presented below.

In the first subsystem, the project management staff holds meetings with those who will be carrying out the project tasks. Together, in one round of meetings, they develop the work breakdown structure; from that, in a second round of meetings, they complete the network. Using the work breakdown structure of Exhibit 14–2 as our example, we'll proceed with the second round of meetings of the project staff and front-line construction people.

Project Planning and Sequencing

Exhibit 14–4   Translating Task Lists into Network Segments

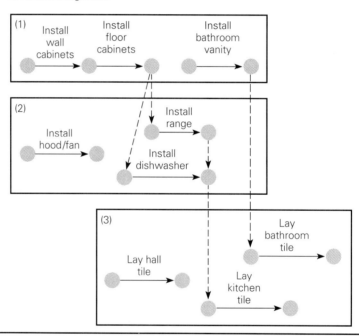

A. Task lists for project elements

Cabinets (1)	Kitchen appliances (2)	Tile (3)
Install kitchen wall cabinets	Install range	Lay kitchen tile
Install kitchen floor cabinets	Install dishwasher	Lay bathroom tile
Install bathroom vanity	Install hood/fan	Lay hall tile

B. Network segments

Source: Adapted from Fred Luthans, *Introduction to Management: A Contingency Approach* (Richard J. Schonberger, contributing author)(New York: McGraw-Hill, 1976), p. 88 (HD31.L86). Used with permission.

Task Lists, Network Segments, and Whole Networks.   Exhibit 14–4 shows how the project staff gets started on network development: Starting with one of the bottom-level elements of the work breakdown structure, they ask the front-line experts to make lists of tasks necessary to complete the element. Part A shows three of the project elements (cabinets, kitchen appliances, and tile) with tasks listed underneath each. Next step, part B, is to begin connecting the tasks into a logical sequence, forming a network segment. Kitchen wall cabinets go up early, since they are easier to install if the lower cabinets are not in the way. Floor cabinets are installed with gaps for the range and dishwasher, which are put in place next. Kitchen tile is laid after the kitchen cabinets and appliances have been installed; if laid sooner, the tile might not butt closely against the cabinets and appliances and also might get marred. Bathroom tile follows the bathroom vanity for the same reason. Since there appears to be no reason why the hood/fan and the hall tile should come either before or after the other tasks shown, the project staff temporarily draws them

Exhibit 14–5   **Network for House Construction**

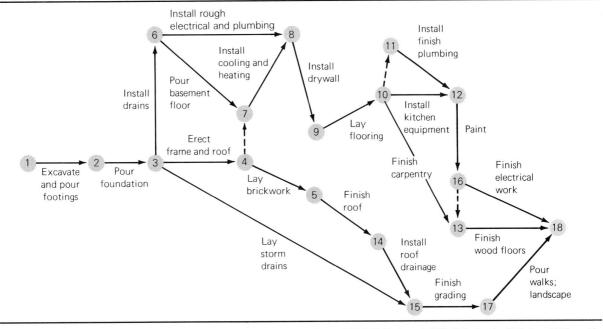

Source: Adapted from Jerome D. Wiest and Ferdinand K. Levy, *A Management Guide to PERT/CPM* (Englewood Cliffs, N.J.: Prentice-Hall, Inc., 1969), p. 16. Used with permission.

unlinked to other tasks. Later, when they put the full network together, they'll find the logical place in which to fit the hood/fan and hall tile.

The rectangles numbered 1, 2, and 3 in Figure 14–4B are not essential; they merely show craft groupings. Later, during scheduling, each craft may use Gantt charts to show when its project tasks occur. Note that it would serve no purpose to group all kitchen activities together, all bathroom activities together, and so forth; the kitchen is a room, but it is neither a product to be separately managed nor the responsibility of a separate craft. More important than the craft groupings in the rectangles are the dashed lines between the rectangles. They signify connections between the task of one craft and the task of the following craft.

Finally, the project staff combines the network segments into the full project network. Exhibit 14–5 is the result, except that, for study purposes, we've simplified it; for example, this house has no tile, carpets, or bathroom vanity. This completes the first subsystem. The project management staff has a reasonable representation of the sequence of project activities. It is a useful tool for coordinating and monitoring completions.

Networking Conventions.   A few rules and conventions of networking follow.

1. *One destination.* A PERT/CPM network (except segments) has only one start event and one end event. (In Exhibit 14–5, these are numbered 1 and 18.) To bring this about, all arrows must progress toward the end, and there can be no doubling back or loops.[4] Exhibit 14–6 shows those two no-no's. In large networks, it is common to make a few such errors inadvertently, for example, an arrowhead carelessly placed at the wrong end of a line. That results in event numbers going into wrong data fields on computer

---

[4]However, those two and other options are allowed in a PERT/CPM variation called GERT (graphical evaluation and review technique).

EXHIBIT 14–6   Networking Errors

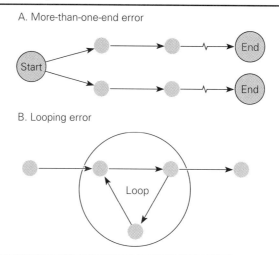

A. More-than-one-end error

B. Looping error

records, if the network plan is computerized. Most PERT/CPM computer packages detect such errors and print error messages.

2. *Event completion.* A network *event* stands for the completion of all activities leading into it. Further, in PERT/CPM logic no activity may begin at an event until all activities leading into that event have been completed. For example, consider event 8 in Exhibit 14–5, completion of rough electrical and plumbing, plus cooling and heating, presumably including an outdoor cooling compressor. We could question that network logic because it says that the next activity (after event 8), install drywall, depends on completion even of the outdoor compressor. In fact, the drywall is intended to cover up only the interior rough work. To reflect that intention, the segment of the network in the event 8 vicinity would need to be drawn differently, with activities relabeled.

Let us generalize to make an important point: Network logic should accurately reflect intended project-flow logic! Typically, managers who spend a little extra time and effort in network creation are rewarded during project implementation.

3. *Dummy activity.* A **dummy activity** is a dashed arrow; it takes no time and consumes no resources. Four of the five dummies in Exhibit 14–4 merely connect subnetworks. The project staff will probably omit them when the full network is drawn.

In Exhibit 14–5, two of the three dummies, 4–7 and 16–13, are necessary for project logic. Activity 4–7 is there to ensure that both 3–4 and 6–7 precede 7–8 but that only 3–4 precedes 4–5. The logic is as follows. We want cooling and heating to be installed on top of a basement floor (6–7) and through holes drilled in the frame (3–4). We want brickwork to go up against the frame (3–4), but it need not wait for a basement floor (6–7) to be poured. The dummy, 4–7, decouples the two merging and the two bursting activities to correctly show the logic. There is no other way to show it. Dummy activity 16–13 has the same purpose.

Dummy activity 10–11 exists only to avoid confusing the computer, if the network is computerized. The problem is that two different activities occur between events 10 and 12. In Exhibit 14–5 an extra event (11) creates a dummy activity, 10–11. This ensures that finish plumbing and kitchen equipment will have unique numbers. Three equivalent ways to do this are shown in Exhibit 14–7.

4. *Event numbering.* Most computer software for PERT/CPM does not require that event numbers go from smaller to larger. Larger to smaller (e.g., 16 to 13 in Exhibit

Event (node):
Point at which one or more activities (tasks) are completed, and, often, at which others are started; consumes no time or resources but merely marks a key point in time.

Activity (arrow):
Basic unit of work in a project.

PERT/CPM computer software identifies activities and their sequence by predecessor and successor event numbers, for example, dummy activity 10–11 goes *from* 10 *to* 11.

EXHIBIT 14–7   Use of a Dummy Activity

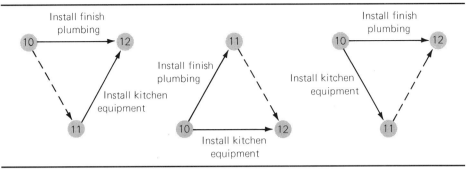

14–5) is all right, because the *from* event (16) is entered into the predecessor field in the computer record and the *to* event (13) into the successor field. Thus, the computer has no difficulty keeping the sequence straight.

5. *Level of detail.* Every activity in Exhibit 14–5 could be divided into subactivities. In addition to the burden that more activities impose, however, there is no need to plan for a level of detail beyond what a manager would want to control. On the other hand, there should be enough detail to show when one activity should precede another.

6. *Plan versus actual.* The network is only a plan; it is unlikely to be followed exactly. For example, maybe walks and landscapes will get poured (17–18 in Exhibit 14–5) before finish grading (15–17). Or maybe money will run out and finish grading will be cut from the project. Thus, the network is not an imperative, and it is not violated when not followed. The network is just a best estimate of how the project team expects to do the project. A best estimate is far better than no plan at all.

Networks are sometimes used even for small projects in small firms. This one is for a project under development at Bright Star, a 15-person company specializing in childrens' educational computer software.

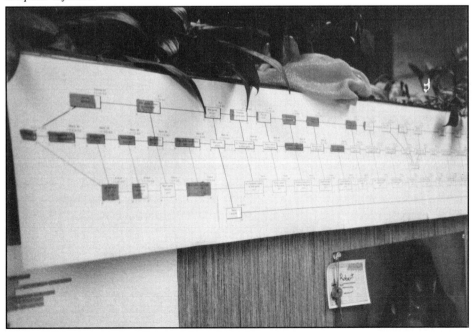

Exhibit 14–8   Events and Milestones

A. Event-oriented network

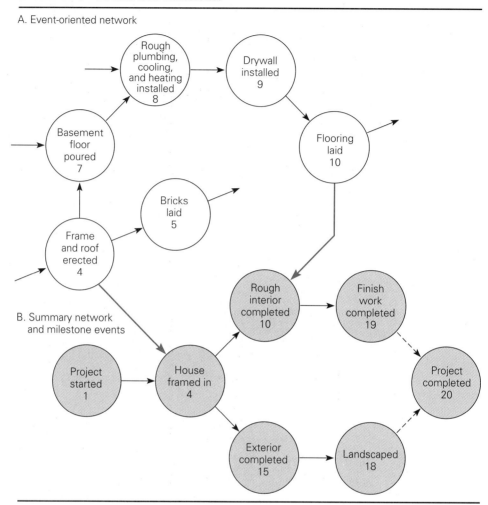

B. Summary network and milestone events

Events and Milestones.   Most of the network examples in this chapter are activity oriented. It is a form that front-line people can relate to, that is, it describes the work activities themselves. Upper managers are more interested in completions, or *events,* and an event-oriented network that they can use to review project completions. The project staff creates the event-oriented network from an activity-oriented network.

Exhibit 14–8 shows two forms of event-oriented networks. Exhibit 14–8A is a portion of the construction project example stated as an event-oriented network. Nodes are drawn large in order to hold event descriptions. Descriptions use present-tense verb forms in activity-oriented networks but past-tense forms in event-oriented networks. For example, "pour basement floor" becomes "basement floor poured" in Exhibit 14–8A. At merge points (nodes where two or more activities converge), the event description can get cumbersome. For example, event 8 is "rough plumbing, cooling, and heating installed."

Networks for big projects may include tens or even hundreds of thousands of events. Upper managers surely do not care to review the project event by event. Instead, it is common for project managers to create a summary network for upper managers. The

Also, activity-oriented networks in this chapter are activity-on-arrow (or on arc), in which the task is represented by the arrow (arc). Some people prefer activity-on-node networks, in which the node or circle represents the task, and the arrow just shows sequence.

summary network may be limited to certain key events, called **milestones.** As an example, events 4 and 10 in Exhibit 14–8B are shown to be a condensation of a five-event segment, events 4–7–8–9–10, from Exhibit 14–8A. The best way to construct a milestone chart is to make milestones out of events that signify the end of major project stages. In house construction, most people would think of completion of framing and completion of rough interior work as major stages; these are milestones 4 and 10 in Exhibit 14–8B.

Some sequential accuracy is lost in condensing a network. For example, milestone event 4 subsumes events 2 and 3 (from Exhibit 14–5). But in cutting out event 3, two branches of the tree at that point—branches 3–6 and 3–15—are unceremoniously chopped off, as shown in the following illustration. From an upper-management perspective, however, the inaccuracy is of little concern.

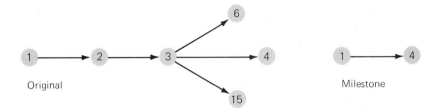

The second subsystem involves putting time estimates on each network activity so that the project management team can identify critical and slack paths through the network. Critical path activities warrant intensive management; slack path activities do not.

Time Estimating and Critical Path

Activity Times.   It is harder to accurately estimate times for projects than for repetitive and job operations because of project uncertainty and task variability. Engineered time standards are unlikely for project activities, except for those that tend to recur from project to project. Instead, the project manager obtains technical estimates from those in charge of each project activity.

Technical estimate: a type of historical, nonengineered (not carefully defined and timed) time standard; see Chapter 15.

The human tendency to pad time estimates in order to arrive at a more attainable goal is somewhat counteracted in construction projects. Typically, enough experience and historical data exist to keep estimators honest. Unfortunately, that is not the case with research and development projects.

R&D projects often include advanced, state-of-the-art activities; historical benchmark data are scarce. Because of this, PERT, the R&D-oriented half of PERT/CPM, was originally designed with a special statistically based routine. PERT project managers asked not for one activity time estimate but for three: a most likely, an optimistic, and a pessimistic estimate. Next, the three time estimates were converted into most likely times and variances, and the probability of completing any given event by a given date could be calculated.

The technical logic of the statistical procedure has been confounded in practice by human behavioral tendencies. First, for an activity never done before it is hard to pry one time estimate out of people, much less three. A request for three estimates may result in drawn-out discussion of the definitions of *most likely, optimistic,* and *pessimistic.* Second, the estimators for R&D activities often are scientists, engineers, and other professionals. They tend to be strong-willed and unafraid to withhold their cooperation. If pressed to provide three estimates, they may give meaningless ones such as 5–10–15 or 8–10–12.

For these reasons, the PERT three-time-estimating procedure has mostly fallen into disuse. Today, in both PERT and CPM, a single best estimate is the norm, where *best*

$$\mathcal{I}\text{nto } \mathcal{P}\text{ractice}$$

Turkey Time

John Battle, scion of an Old South political family and holder of a graduate degree in literature, was construction boss of the 62-story AT&T Gateway Tower in Seattle. "Estimates are done in heaven," says Battle. "The project is run in hell."

Battle likens the critical path to the turkey at a Thanksgiving dinner. Almost any other item on the menu can be done too soon, too late, or not at all, and its effect on the dinner will be marginal. But if the turkey gets delayed, so does dinner.

The critical elements on the path toward Gateway's completion included the digging and pouring of the foundation, erection of the frame, installation of the elevators, application of the granite and glass skin, and . . . the testing of all the electrical, mechanical and safety systems."

Source: Adapted from Terry McDermott, "High Rise: When a Tower Goes Up, Risk Is as Substantial as the Steel Itself," *Sunday Seattle Times and Post-Intelligencer,* March 25, 1990.

estimate is defined simply as how long the activity is expected to take under typical conditions and with normal resources.

Path Analysis.   The most time-consuming path is the **critical path.** The path is time-critical because a delay in completing any of its activities delays the whole project. We continue the house construction exercise to demonstrate path criticality.

The house construction network of Exhibit 14–5 is reproduced in Exhibit 14–9, with estimates for each activity added. Path durations are given below the network. Although this network is very small, for illustrative purposes, there are still 17 paths to add up. Computers are efficient at adding path times, and path analysis subroutines are basic in PERT/CPM software.

In the figure, path 12 is critical, at 34 days; it is shown in contrasting color in the network. Several other paths— 6, 7, 8, 9, 10, 11, 13, 14, and 15 —are nearly critical, at 31 to 33 days. The critical path and nearly critical path activities deserve close managerial attention. Other activities have slack or float time and need not be managed so closely. The more slack, the more flexibility managers have in scheduling activities.

Slack (slack time): The amount of time an activity may be delayed without delaying the project schedule; usually changes as the project progresses.

Activity Slack.   Calculating slack time by comparing the critical path with noncritical paths seems fairly simple, at least in the networks discussed thus far. However, it becomes tedious, even impossible, for larger, more realistic project networks. Consequently, a three-step algorithm has been developed for finding slack time.

First, we continue with our house construction example to gain an intuitive feel for the concept of slack, especially as it pertains to paths and activities. Second, we use the three-step algorithm to formally calculate slack for activities in a network segment.

In Exhibit 14–9, paths 7, 11, and 14 take 33 days, or 1 day less than the critical path. This means that relative to the critical path, paths 7, 11, and 14 contain a day of slack (in PERT lingo) or float (in CPM lingo). The day of slack applies not to the whole path but just to certain path activities. Consider path 7 first.

Path 7 is identical to critical path 12 except in the segment from event 3 to event 7. The critical path segment from 3 to 4 to 7 takes four days; the slack path segment from

Exhibit 14–9   Path Analysis

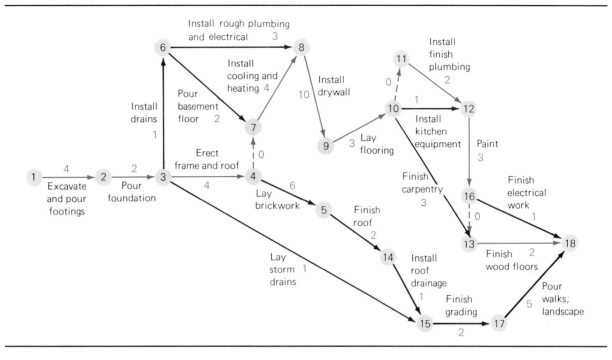

Path Number	Paths	Path Time	
1	1–2–3–6–8–9–10–11–12–16–18	29 days	
2	1–2–3–6–8–9–10–11–12–16–13–18	30	
3	1–2–3–6–8–9–10–12–16–18	28	
4	1–2–3–6–8–9–10–12–16–13–18	29	
5	1–2–3–6–8–9–10–13–18	28	
6	1–2–3–6–7–8–9–10–11–12–16–18	32	
7	1–2–3–6–7–8–9–10–11–12–16–13–18	33	Nearly critical
8	1–2–3–6–7–8–9–10–12–16–18	31	paths
9	1–2–3–6–7–8–9–10–12–16–13–18	31	
10	1–2–3–6–7–8–9–10–13–18	31	
11	1–2–3–4–7–8–9–10–11–12–16–18	33	
12	1–2–3–4–7–8–9–10–11–12–16–13–18	34 ◄———Critical path
13	1–2–3–4–7–8–9–10–12–16–18	32	
14	1–2–3–4–7–8–9–10–12–16–13–18	33	Nearly critical
15	1–2–3–4–7–8–9–10–13–18	32	paths
16	1–2–3–4–5–14–15–17–18	26	
17	1–2–3–15–17–18	14	

3 to 6 to 7 takes three days. Activities 3–6 and 6–7 are said to have one day of slack. This means that 3–6 or 6–7 (but not both) could be delayed by one day without affecting the planned project duration. By like reasoning, activity 16–18 on path 11 and activity 10–12 on path 14 have a day of slack.

Slack analysis is complicated when an activity is on more than one slack path segment. Activity 3–6, for example, is on slack path segments 3–6–7 and 3–6–8. Segment 3–6–8 takes four days as compared with eight days for critical path segment 3–4–7–8. It may seem that activities 3–6 and 6–8 have four days of slack and that either

Exhibit 14-10   Calculating Activity Slack—Summary Table

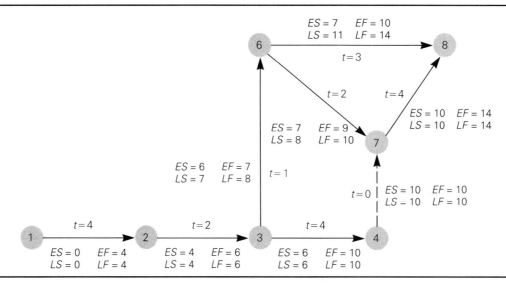

Activity	(LF − EF)	(LS − ES)	Slack	
1–2	(4 − 4)	(0 − 0)	0	Critical activity
2–3	(6 − 6)	(4 − 4)	0	Critical activity
3–4	(10 − 10)	(6 − 6)	0	Critical activity
3–6	(8 − 7)	(7 − 6)	1	
4–7	(10 − 10)	(10 − 10)	0	Critical activity
6–7	(10 − 9)	(8 − 7)	1	
6–8	(14 − 10)	(11 − 7)	4	
7–8	(14 − 14)	(10 − 10)	0	Critical activity

Critical path: 1–2–3–4–7–8
Critical path duration: 14 days

could be delayed four days without affecting the planned project duration. But we learned above that activity 3–6, on slack segment 3–6–7, may be delayed no more than one day. Slack on 3–6 is therefore one day, not four days; the larger value is rejected. Activity 6–8, however, does have four days of slack.

The formal calculation of slack time may, in three steps, now be demonstrated for the activities shown in Exhibit 14–10.

1. *Earliest start and earliest finish.* Each activity has an **earliest start (ES)** and an **earliest finish (EF)** time, expressed in days for our project. They are determined by a forward pass through the network. We begin with activity 1–2 and set its *ES* to zero, the start of the project. The *EF* for an activity is equal to its *ES* plus its duration, *t*. Thus, the *EF* for activity 1–2 is:

$$EF_{1-2} = ES_{1-2} + t_{1-2} = 0 + 4 = 4 \text{ (or day 4)}$$

The *ES* for each successive activity is equal to the largest *EF* of all predecessor activities. We see that node 2, the origin of activity 2–3, has but one predecessor: activity 1–2. Therefore, the *ES* for activity 2–3 is equal to the *EF* for activity 1–2 and has a value of 4. Continuing, we find the *EF* for activity 2–3 as follows:

$$EF_{2-3} = ES_{2-3} + t_{2-3} = 4 + 2 = 6$$

The remainder of the *ES* and *EF* values are shown in Exhibit 14–10. The largest *EF* (14 in this case) is taken as the project duration, which is also the duration of the critical path.

   2. *Latest start and latest finish.* Each network activity also has a **latest start (LS)** and a **latest finish (LF)** time, again expressed in days for our project. Values for *LS* and *LF* are found by a backward pass through the network. Beginning at node 8, we use the project duration ($EF_{7-8} = 14$) as the *LF* of all activities ending on node 8. Then we find the *LS* for each activity by subtracting its duration *(t)* from its *LF*. For example, the *LS* for activity 7–8 is:

$$LS_{7-8} = LF_{7-8} - t_{7-8} = 14 - 4 = 10 \text{ (or day 10)}$$

   And for activity 6–8:

$$LS_{6-8} = LF_{6-8} - t_{6-8} = 14 - 3 = 11$$

As we move backward through the network, each successive activity has its *LF* defined as the earliest *LS* of all activities that immediately follow. For example, the *LF* of activity 3–6 is 8, since 8 is the smaller of the *LS* values for activities 6–7 and 6–8. Exhibit 14–10 shows *LF* and *LS* values for the remaining activities.

   3. *Slack calculation.* Slack for each activity is simply $LS - ES$ or $LF - EF$.

Negative Slack.   If *LS* is less than *ES,* negative slack results. Negative slack means the activity is late. Not only is this possible, it is almost the norm, at least for critical path activities. It is so rare for projects to be on time that *The Wall Street Journal* published a front-page story some years ago with headlines proclaiming that a certain large construction project was completed on time. (The project was the domed stadium in Pontiac, Michigan, which also met targeted costs!)

   Suppose that in Exhibit 14–10 the due date had been day 11. For activity 7–8, for example, computations reveal:

$$LS_{7-8} = 11 - 4 = 7$$

$$\text{Slack}_{7-8} = LS_{7-8} - ES_{7-8} = 7 - 10 = -3 \text{ (negative slack)}$$

Each of the other critical path activities would have slack of -3 days, which means the project is three days late while still in the planning stage! Two clear options exist. First, the schedule could be relaxed—push out the due date to 14, for example—to avoid negative slack at the outset. Second, and often the case with large projects, the project could start out late with hopes of catching up.

Slack-Sort Computer Listing.   The most common PERT/CPM computer output is a slack-sort report of all project activities. Slack sort means sorting or listing activities in order of their degree of slack. Critical path activities have the least slack and therefore appear first; near-critical activities, usually from more than one path, appear next; and so on.

   Exhibit 14–11 illustrates this, again using the house-building example. Note that the top activities have negative slack and are most critical. Bottom-most activities are least critical; the last one, activity 3–15, has $+17$ days of slack, which means that it may be delayed 17 days without affecting the project due date.

   The slack-sorted computer listing helps a manager more than a network does. Indeed, most managers rely on this type of listing and never need to see a network.[5]

---

[5]Often the listing is event-oriented rather than activity-oriented; for example, instead of earliest- and latest-start activity times (*ES* and *LS*), there will be time-earliest and time-latest event times (T_E and T_L).

EXHIBIT 14-11   **Computer Listing for Path Analysis**

Slack-Sorted Activity Report

Activity Number	Description	Time	Earliest Start	Latest Start	Activity Slack	
1–2	Excavate, pour footings	4	0	−3	−3	⎫
2–3	Pour foundation	2	4	1	−3	⎪
3–4	Erect frame and roof	4	6	3	−3	⎪
4–7	Dummy	0	10	7	−3	⎬ Critical path
.	.	.	.	.	.	⎪
.	.	.	.	.	.	⎪
.	.	.	.	.	.	⎪
13–18	Lay flooring	2	32	29	−3	⎭
3–6	Install drains	1	6	4	−2	
6–7	Pour basement floor	2	7	5	−2	
10–12	Install kitchen equipment	1	27	25	−2	
16–18	Finish electrical work	1	32	30	−2	
10–13	Finish carpentry	3	27	26	−1	
.	.	.	.	.	.	
.	.	.	.	.	.	
.	.	.	.	.	.	
15–17	Finish grading	2	19	24	+5	
17–18	Pour walks and landscape	5	21	26	+5	
3–15	Lay storm drains	1	6	23	+17	

Project Scheduling

The time data generated in the second PERT/CPM phase is a required input for the third phase, project scheduling. The first step is to compare the projected project duration with allowable duration. If projected duration fails to meet company commitments, choices have to be made before the schedule is set in concrete. Company managers may consider spending more on resources to **crash** the network, literally buying some project time reduction. Managers will want to examine cost and time options, provided by the project management staff. Crashing and the time-cost trade-off procedure are explained next, followed by discussion of final project and work center scheduling.

Crashing and Time-Cost Trade-Offs.   If managers elect to spend more on resources to cut project time, they had better apply the extra resources to critical path activities since that path determines project completion time. As the critical path is crashed, new critical paths may emerge. The cost to further reduce the project duration may then involve extra resource costs to reduce activity times on multiple paths. The analysis can get complicated.

If resource costs are inconvenient to collect, the choice of which critical path activity to crash is not clear-cut. Crashing an early activity on the critical path may seem wise because the reduction will apply to other paths that could become critical later; but money spent early is gone. The opposite wait-and-see approach seems wise for another reason: Perhaps some critical path activities will be completed earlier than expected, thus averting the need to crash at all; but if that does not happen, late options for crashing may be few and costly.

When it is convenient to collect resource costs, the project team may employ time-cost trade-off analysis, which we explain using the small network and related data of Exhibit 14–12. The critical path is B–D–E, eight days long, at a cost of $390. Project managers need not accept this plan. They may want to spend more money for extra shifts,

EXHIBIT 14-12   Network and Time-Cost Data

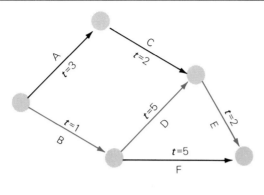

(critical path ——————→ is B–D–E at 8 days)

Activity	Normal Time	Normal Cost	Crash Time	Crash Cost	Cost per Day
A	3	$ 50	1	$100	$25
B	1	40	1	40	—
C	2	40	1	80	40
D	5	100	3	160	30
E	2	70	1	160	90
F	5	90	2	300	70
		$390			

SOURCE: Adapted from Fred Luthans, *Introduction to Management: A Contingency Approach* (Richard J. Schonberger, contributing author) (New York: McGraw-Hill, 1976), p. 378 (HD31.L86). Used with permission.

air freight, and so on, to reduce the time required to complete various tasks. For example, activity A costs $50 to do in three days (normal), $75 to do in two days (paying for overtime, perhaps), and $100 to do in one day (paying still more, perhaps for extra shifts).[6] The linear assumption, $25 for each day reduced, may be somewhat erroneous, but it is generally accurate enough for planning purposes.

The method of calculating average cost per day may be expressed as a formula:

$$\text{Cost per day} = \frac{\text{Crash cost} - \text{Normal cost}}{\text{Normal time} - \text{Crash time}} \qquad (14\text{--}1)$$

For activity A, the calculation is

$$\frac{\$100 - \$50}{3 \text{ days} - 1 \text{ day}} = \frac{\$50}{2 \text{ days}} = \$25 \text{ per day}$$

Cost per day for each of the other activities is calculated the same way. Activity B cannot be crashed and thus does not have a cost-per-day entry.

---

[6]The normal and crash costs are often engineers' or managers' estimates based on current known direct-labor and overhead rates; a careful cost accounting estimate may not be necessary. Also, the cost estimates may be incremental rather than full costs.

The question is: If it costs $390 to do the project in eight days, what would it cost to do it in seven? If we should pick the lowest total in the cost-per-day column, $25 for A, we would be wrong. Spending $25 more on A would reduce A from three to two days, but it would not affect the eight-day projection duration. A critical path activity—B, D, or E—must be selected. B is out because its crash time is no better than normal time. The choice between D and E favors D, at an extra cost of $30, as opposed to $90 for E. Thus, doing the project in seven days requires $30 more for a total cost of $420.

The next step is to investigate doing the project in six days. But the above reduction of D to four days results in two critical paths, B–D–E and A–C–E, both seven days long. Reducing the project duration to six days is possible by crashing A and D together at a cost of $55, D and C together at $70, or E alone at $90. The first option is cheapest; thus, it is selected, bringing the total project cost up to $475.

Next, try for five days. After the above step, all paths are critical at six days. The only choice (since B and D are already crashed to their minimum times) is to crash E and F by one day. The added cost is $160, with a total project cost of $635. No further time reductions are possible, since the B–D–E path is fully crashed.

If this were a construction project with a penalty of $100 for every day beyond a six-day project duration, alternative 3 below would look best since it has the lowest total cost, $475.

Alternative	Time	Construction Cost	Penalty Cost	Total Cost	
1	8 days	$390	$200	$590	
2	7	420	100	520	
3	6	475	0	475	← Minimum
4	5	635	0	635	

Time-cost trade-off analysis originated with the CPM people in the construction industry. It remains more suited for use in construction projects than in R&D efforts for at least two reasons. First, costs and times are easier to estimate in construction. Second, the frequent use of late penalties in construction projects serves as extra incentive for managers in construction to consider time-cost trade-off analysis.

In less-certain project environments (R&D, information systems, disaster relief, etc.) the need to crash projects is just as great as in construction. While the time-cost trade-off procedure is generally not appropriate (the cost uncertainty problem), there are several other approaches for crashing; discussion of them is reserved for the final section in the chapter.

Event Scheduling.   Event scheduling, the assigning of dates to events in the final network, follows selection of a time-cost alternative. Final activity times, with holidays and weekends considered, form the basis for event dates. An event-dating subroutine in PERT/CPM software accepts as input the planned date of the first event and computes the others. A typical listing shows time-earliest *(TE)* and time-latest *(TL)* to complete each event and event slack $(TL - TE)$.

A normal complication in project scheduling is meshing project schedules with work center schedules. Each subcontractor, department, or work center involved in a given project is likely to be in on other projects, jobs, and repetitive operations. Fitting work center activities into project networks and fitting project activities into work center schedules is a tricky balancing act.

Exhibit 14–13 illustrates this concern. The work center, a grading crew, has developed a Gantt chart showing three upcoming activities that are on the PERT/CPM networks

$\mathscr{I}$nto $\mathscr{P}$ractice

Bridging the Profit Gap

"At the rate of one a day, crews racing to rebuild the Mercer Island bridge have started sinking giant pontoon anchors weighing up to 300 tons each to the bottom of Lake Washington.

"Hundreds more workers at waterfront sites on Commencement Bay in Tacoma and on the Duwamish Waterway in Seattle are assembling the first pontoons, four of which are longer than a football field and so massive they'll have to be floated from their cradles on a high tide."

What's the rush? For General Construction Company and its partner, Rainier Steel Inc., the hurry is "about a $6

million bonus for finishing the job a year ahead of schedule. The state has agreed to pay the joint venture $18,500 a day for every day it finished early. . . . The bonus money 'is the majority of the profit on the project,' according to Scott McKellar, General Construction's vice president of operations."

SOURCE: Adapted from Mark Higgins, "Ready, Set, Build: Crews Race to Finish Bridge Ahead of Schedule," *Seattle Post-Intelligencer*, Monday, May 26, 1992.

EXHIBIT 14–13   Decomposition of Network Activities into Work Center Schedules

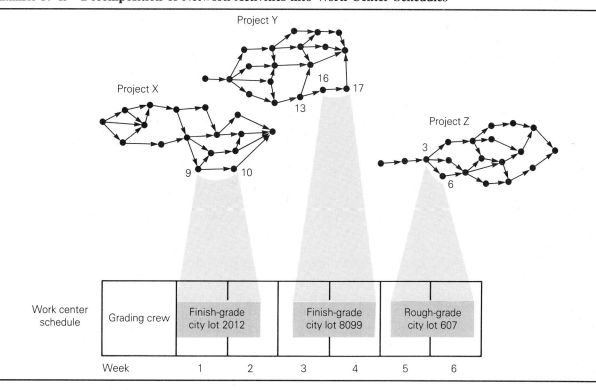

for three different projects. The activities are identified in their respective networks (the project managers' schedules) and on the work center schedule, which is the work center manager's concern. Consider activity 9–10 in project X, finish grading of city lot 2012. Obviously the project manager would like the grading crew on the job site at the right time. If activity 9–10 is a critical path activity, any delay on the grading crew's part will affect project X's completion. Any delay will also reflect negatively on the project X manager's performance, especially if late penalties are assessed.

The work center manager, on the other hand, strives for utilization of the work center's resources. After the grading of lot 2012, the work center manager might wish to proceed immediately to lot 8099 to avoid any work center idle time. The manager of project Y would probably have to veto the idea, however, if the predecessor activity for activity 16–17 (lot 8099 grading) has not been completed. Suppose the predecessor activity, shown as 13–16 in the project Y network, is removing a dead tree. Even the work center manager would agree with the project manager's logic: Grading simply cannot begin. Is the grading crew to remain idle for several work days?

Another common problem is when project schedules create demand for work crews to be in two places (perhaps on two projects, each with a different manager) at the same time. Suppose the manager of project Z decides to advance the schedule for activity 3–6, grading of city lot 607, by one week (five workdays). Obviously this will create a problem on the work center schedule during the fourth week. These kinds of conflicts are common and require compromise.

Reporting and Updating

Reporting and updating is the fourth and final subsystem. It extends PERT/CPM management beyond planning and scheduling and into the project control phase. PERT/CPM control revolves around periodic reports, which generally are issued every two weeks or monthly.

Exhibit 14–14 shows a typical reporting scheme. The partial network at the top of the figure divides into monthly reporting periods. At the end of each reporting period, event completion data go to the project management staff, who prepare them for entry into the computer. In Exhibit 14–14, the current month is February and February-planned events 1, 2, 3, 5, and 6 have been completed. A data-entry record is prepared for each; on the first record, for example, an 01 is placed in the event field and the completion date, 020491 for February 4, 1991, is entered in another field.

Event 4 was scheduled for February, but no notice of completion has been received. Instead, the project manager has received an activity reestimate notice. The first reestimate record shows the activity 03–04 (without the dash) in the key field, and places 21 (days), the new time estimate, in another field. The reestimate pertains to why event 4 has not been completed: event 3, completed on February 12, plus 21 days for activity 3–4, pushes the planned completion date for event 4 into March. Future activities may also be reestimated, as 08–10 has been in Exhibit 14–14.

With event completions and activity reestimates as inputs, the computer updates the PERT/CPM network. A new slack-sort report is produced, showing the new slack status of each activity. The report is like Exhibit 14–11, except that it gives start and due dates for events. The report tells all parties about the new project schedule for all events. Other reports may be printed, for example, a report listing activities by work center (or department or subcontractor); various resource, budget, and cost reports; and summary (milestone) reports for upper managers. Some of the reports get wide distribution, and in some firms those responsible for activities completed late must explain why.

Replanning is inherent to control. It is possible to rerun a time-cost trade-off analysis each month after the network has been updated, using event completion data and activity reestimates. Without this analysis, the computer will replan (reschedule) all events anyway, but without considering using more or less resources on given activities.

EXHIBIT 14-14   PERT/CPM Periodic Reporting

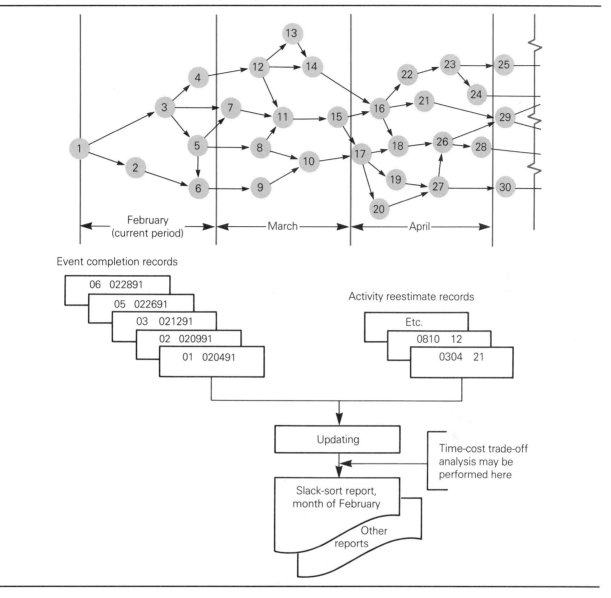

Another major type of replanning is altering the network. The project staff may add or subtract activities and may change the sequence. All that is required is adding, removing, or changing a few records. The ease of making such changes is a key asset of PERT/CPM, because project uncertainty demands planning flexibility.

Fitting PERT/CPM to the Situation

PERT/CPM is expensive. Fully computerized PERT/CPM may eat up an additional 2 or 3 percent of total project cost, because it is not a replacement for conventional management. Conventional forecasting, scheduling, inventory control, quality control, budgeting, and so forth, are still done in each functional area (e.g., department or work center). A project management group and PERT/CPM systems hardware and software are additional costs.

Some organizations have tried out and abandoned PERT/CPM because it seemed not to pay for itself. In some cases, the problem is in trying to apply fully computerized PERT/CPM to small-scale projects. Exhibit 14–15 reemphasizes a point partially made early in the chapter: PERT/CPM consists of distinct and separable subsystems. The exhibit further suggests that only projects that are grand in scope warrant the full PERT/CPM treatment. At the other extreme, projects of modest scope may justify the expense of only the first subsystem.

Project scope is expressed in Exhibit 14–15 in terms of four characteristics: size, uncertainty, urgency, and complexity. Size and urgency are self-explanatory. Project uncertainty is of two types:

1. Task uncertainty: doubts about what is to be done.
2. Time uncertainty: doubts about activity time estimates.

Similarly, complexity may be thought of in two ways:

1. Organizational complexity: many organizations involved in the project.
2. Activity complexity: many activities in progress at the same time.

To illustrate, consider the kinds of construction projects managed by a typical (for the United States) Army Corps of Engineers district: dams, man-made lakes, dredging, channel straightening, levees, bridges, and riverbank stabilization, to name a few. The district may have perhaps 100 projects in progress at a given time.

A project such as a major dam may be only moderately urgent and uncertain, but it is likely to be very large and complex. In sum, the project characteristics seem to be far enough to the right in Exhibit 14–15 to warrant full, computer-based PERT/CPM, including all four subsystems (four yeses in the exhibit). Without computer-based scheduling,

---

Exhibit 14–15   Matching PERT/CPM Subsystems to Project Scope

CONTINUUM OF PROJECT CHARACTERISTICS

Small ◄————— Size ————► Large
Low ◄————— Uncertainty ————► High
Low ◄————— Urgency ————► High
Low ◄————— Complexity ————► High

PERT/CPM subsystems				
1. Plan project and design network	Yes	Yes	Yes	Yes
2. Time estimation and path analysis	No	Yes	Yes	Yes
3. Network scheduling	No	No	Yes	Yes
4. Reporting and updating	No	No	No	Yes

reporting, and control, coordinating the many simultaneous activities of the numerous participating organizations might be chaotic.

Most bridge construction jobs are much smaller and less complex. For such intermediate-scope projects, the project engineer probably should design networks, conduct path analysis, and perhaps use a computer to schedule project events, which may include time-cost trade-off analysis (two or three yeses). But subsystem 4, reporting and updating, may not be warranted. It is the costliest subsystem to administer; it probably costs a lot more than subsystems 1, 2, and 3 combined. A typical bridge is not so urgent as to require the tight time controls of subsystem 4.

Channeling and riverbank stabilization projects are still less urgent and rarely are large, complex, or uncertain. The project engineer may expend a small amount of time, effort, and cost to accomplish subsystem 1, designing PERT/CPM networks (one yes, left column of the figure). The benefits (seeing who has to do what and in what order) are large for the modest cost. There seems little reason to perform path analysis and the other subsystems.

In R&D projects, the model seems equally valid. Designing a major aircraft, such as a B-1 bomber, is a project of massive scope and urgency as well, in view of the capital it ties up. Full PERT/CPM is easily justified. Redesign of a horizontal stabilizer for an existing aircraft, on the other hand, is a modest project; subsystem 1 may be sufficient.

While the logic of this situational approach to the use of PERT/CPM is clear, many managers have not followed it. Attempts to view PERT/CPM as a single indivisible system for use in every project result in disappointment. In such instances, the source of failure is not the PERT/CPM technique.

Continuous Improvement in Projects

The high degree of complexity and uncertainty inherent in project work is good reason for stressing continuous improvement in project management. In exploring this topic, we first take a closer look at the problem of chronic project lateness and then at a few measures to cope with it.

Network Simulation and the Always-Late Syndrome

Calculating critical paths is methodical and easily performed on a computer. Unfortunately, the method treats each path independently of all others. It fails to allow for time variation, which affects all event completion times and the total project duration. It is easy to prove by Monte Carlo simulation that the deterministic critical path time understates the likely project duration.[7] Exhibit 14–16 illustrates.

The exhibit presents the simplest possible project network: two activities occurring at the same time. (A single activity is a job; multiple activities going on simultaneously are a key distinguishing feature of a project.) In Exhibit 14–16A, both paths are critical at five days; thus, it is a five-day project. In Exhibit 14–16B, the mean or expected task time on each path is still five days. Yet, as the table shows, the simulated mean project duration is 8 percent greater at 5.4 days. In the table, the variability (four, five, and six days) is simulated by considering all time combinations and allowing equal chances for each time value on each path. For each combination the higher path time is the project duration, which pushes the expected (mean) project duration up to 5.4 days.

If more variability is added, the expected project duration increases further. For example, if the path time is 3, 4, 5, 6, or 7, each equally probable, expected duration by

[7] An explanation is given in A. R. Klingel, Jr., "Bias in PERT Project Completion Time Calculations for a Real Network," *Management Science* 13, no. 4 (December 1966), pp. B-194–201.

EXHIBIT 14–16   **Effects of Variable Activity Times on Project Duration**

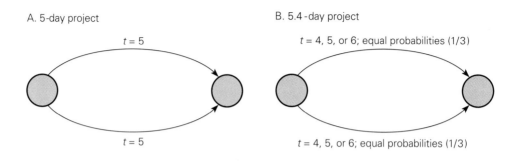

A. 5-day project

$t = 5$

$t = 5$

B. 5.4-day project

$t = 4, 5,$ or 6; equal probabilities (1/3)

$t = 4, 5,$ or 6; equal probabilities (1/3)

Possible Time Combinations

	Top Path	Bottom Path	Project Duration	
1	4	4	4	
2	4	5	5	
3	5	4	5	
4	5	5	5	
5	4	6	6	Mean $= 49/9 = 5.4$ days
6	5	6	6	
7	6	6	6	
8	6	5	6	
9	6	4	6	

simulation is 5.8 days, or 16 percent greater than the critical path time. If more paths are added, expected project duration also goes up. As a general rule, then, the fatter the network and the more variable the activity times, the more the project duration is in excess of the simple critical path time. This provides a mathematical explanation of why projects tend to be late.

Even though the critical path understates reality, it is widely used for the following reasons:

1. Path addition is cheaper to use than Monte Carlo simulation.
2. Path addition is simpler to understand than Monte Carlo simulation.
3. Activity time estimates are rough anyway, and there are diminishing returns in more rigorous analysis of rough data.
4. It is difficult to know what to do with simulated network data. How should it change project management?

Despite these reasons, managers should realize that critical path analysis does understate project reality. Caution is the key word in its use.

Combating Project Complexity

We have just proved by simulation that projects are likely to be late. Still, the project management staff can at least work toward reducing the lateness by controlling its causes. Basically, the causes have to do with unnecessary project complexity and uncertainty. The *unnecessary* category includes having the wrong size and type of project management team, and lack of information sharing (common files), topics discussed earlier in the chapter. A related set of complexity and uncertainty factors are high turnover of team members, poor communication, task unfamiliarity, and too many changes.

Project teams typically disband when the project ends. Team members scatter to the four winds, some joining new teams with new members and others returning to a functional home, such as the mortgage loan department or human resources department. Each time a new project is formed, it takes weeks or months for team members to become well enough acquainted to be able to work well together. Through at least the early project phases, communication is poor, even when the team is multifunctional and working concurrently. Since the skills of each team member are not fully known, members get placed in the wrong assignment, and later are moved one or more times in an effort to get a better matchup of needs and skills. Instability hampers effectiveness.

$\mathcal{P}$RINCIPLE 11:

Cut start-up time.

To avoid these common problems, some firms are keeping team members relatively intact from one project to the next. For example, Florida-based Harris Corp. does this in its government systems division. The division has established four project teams, each for a different series of its high-tech electronic products. Each team has a project manager, a project specialist, a material planner, a buyer, and a group of assemblers. The project manager and project specialist have complementary skills, one usually being an electrical engineer and the other a mechanical engineer. As one government contract winds down, the team gets started on the next contract, taking it from concept through production.

Two other key means of controlling causes of lateness are drawn from other chapters:

- *Total quality management*. Effective project management includes collection of data on mishaps, followed by improvement projects to develop solutions to prevent those mishaps on following projects. Every team member should be involved. Continuous improvement seems to be late in gaining a foothold in project management, even though project work is badly in need of it to combat uncertainty and lateness. A probable reason, ironically, is that since projects are usually late, team members resist taking time to collect data and concern themselves with future projects, another project team's problem. If project teams stayed somewhat intact from project to project, they would probably have more incentive to improve the process.

$\mathcal{P}$RINCIPLE 10:

Eliminate error and process variation.

- *Design-for-operations (DFO) guidelines* (from Chapter 3). These guidelines call for using standard, already proven designs. This reduces not only complexity but also project uncertainty. That is, with standard designs, project time estimates will have lower margins of error, which would make a simulated project completion time closer to the critical path time.

Summary

As product life cycles shrink and continuous improvement expands, more people will spend more time on new-product and improvement project teams. Getting projects done quickly and well requires compact, multifunctional teams working in the simultaneous mode.

Project leadership may range from a one-person project coordinator, to a small team respon sible for a succession of brands of small projects, to a fully-staffed, autonomous pure project management team with its own budgetary authority.

Some of the more effective project management taps the expertise of suppliers and customers, either by including them on internal project teams or by encouraging project work from outside the organization. Since project teams feed on information, every scrap of information—from team member investigation, training, or experience—should be filed and cross-referenced for easy access by other project associates. The Western tendency for individuals to horde information is an obstacle to be overcome.

Some project information may be organized for development and use in proven project planning and control models, specifically, the program management and review technique and the critical path method (PERT/CPM).

PERT and CPM are useful in the management of projects. Both are based on a sequence chart called a network.

PERT/CPM consists of four subsystems: designing the network, path analysis, scheduling, and reporting and updating. In designing the network, the project team begins with planning project goals; the project plan may be displayed as a work breakdown structure. Task lists are then created and arranged into networks. Networks are activity-oriented for lower managers and event-oriented for high-level managers.

The project manager may collect time estimates for each network activity. Activity times for each path through the network may be added up, and the sum for the most time-consuming path, called the critical path, is the estimated project duration. Path analysis also includes determining slack for each activity. Slack is the amount of time that an activity may be delayed without making the whole project late. Negative slack occurs often, especially on the critical path.

The project scheduling subsystem is aimed at determining due dates for each network event. If forward scheduling yields a late project completion time, certain activities may be crashed (cutting activity time). Crashing is done by spending more for resources, for example, overtime. Time-cost trade-off analysis yields combinations of project times and costs. One time-cost alternative is selected, and the selected times are the basis for scheduling network events. Finally, organizations having a role in more than one project must fit in the scheduled project tasks so that their capacities will be properly used.

The reporting and updating subsystem may come into play after the work begins. Reports are usually monthly or every two weeks. A basic report displays slack time for each activity; it lists most critical activities first, then next most critical activities, and so forth. The reports are valuable for replanning and rescheduling.

Each of the four PERT/CPM subsystems is more costly than its predecessor. All four should be used only if project size, uncertainty, urgency, and complexity are sufficient to justify the cost.

Projects are chronically late. Monte Carlo simulation of a project network will show that the deterministic critical path understates the likely project completion time, because activities taking more time than predicted become additive, rather than being counterbalanced by activities taking less time than predicted.

The complexity, uncertainty, and lateness tendencies of projects make them attractive candidates for continuous improvement and total quality management. Also, to combat complexity and uncertainty, project teams should, where possible, stay somewhat intact from project to project; and should employ standard designs with quality and timing already established.

Key Words

Solved Problems

Problem 1

If there is negative slack of three days on the upper path for the network shown:

    a. Will the project be completed on time?

    b. What is the slack on the lower path?

    c. Is there any need for crashing? Explain.

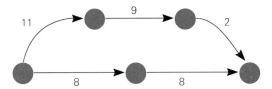

While the problem may be solved with the aid of *ES/EF/LS/LF* calculations, there is no need to do so for this uncomplicated network (it is uncomplicated in that the upper and lower paths each lead straight from first to last event with no interconnections). Further, avoiding the mechanical *ES/LS/EF/LF* tables forces us to think about what the critical path, the project schedule, and slack really mean.

Solution 1

a. Simple addition yields total duration on the two paths:

> Upper path: 11 + 9 + 2 = 22 days
> Lower path: 8 + 8 = 16 days

Since the lower path is less time-consuming, the upper is the critical path. And when there is negative slack on the critical path, that means the project is late, in this case, by 3 days.

b. Since slack on the upper path is −3 and its duration is 22 days, that means that the project's scheduled completion is in 19 days. Since the lower path takes 16 days, and 19 days are available in the schedule, slack on the lower path is +3 days.

c. The top path is late by 3 days and thus must be crashed by 3 days; the bottom path takes 3 days less than the schedule calls for and thus does not need crashing.

Exhibit 14–17 shows a project network with activity times given in weeks.

Problem 2

a. What are the paths in the network? What is the critical path? Its duration?

b. Compute the *ES*, *EF*, *LS*, and *LF* times and the slack for each activity.

c. Use the data in the time-cost information table to select appropriate time-cost alternatives for reducing the project duration by:
   (1) One week.
   (2) Two weeks.
   (3) Three weeks.

EXHIBIT 14–17   Example Project Network with Activity Times

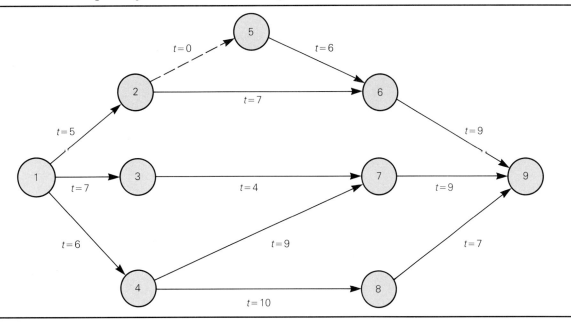

Solution 2

a. In this simple network, it is easy to identify all paths. (In more realistic networks, the task becomes impossible to accomplish without a computer.) Paths in this example network are:

1–2–5–6–9	20 weeks' duration	
1–2–6–9	21 weeks' duration	
1–3–7–9	20 weeks' duration	
1–4–7–9	24 weeks' duration	(critical path)
1–4–8–9	23 weeks' duration	

b. The following table contains the information requested in question *b:*

Activity	Duration (Weeks)	ES	EF	LS	LF	Slack
1–2	5	0	5	3	8	3
1–3	7	0	7	4	11	4
1–4	6	0	6	0	6	0*
2–5	0	5	5	9	9	4
2–6	7	5	12	8	15	3
3–7	4	7	11	11	15	4
4–7	9	6	15	6	15	0*
4–8	10	6	16	7	17	1
5–6	6	5	11	9	15	4
6–9	9	12	21	15	24	3
7–9	9	15	24	15	24	0*
8–9	7	16	23	17	24	1

NOTES: Activity 2–5 is a dummy, required to clarify the network because there are two separate activities between nodes 2 and 6.

Critical activities, marked with an * are determined through slack analysis. Recall that $LF - EF = LS - ES =$ Slack.

ES for activity 6–9 is the larger of the EF for 2–6 and the EF for 5–6. Of these values (12 and 11, respectively), 12 governs. The ES for activity 7–9 is determined in the same manner.

LF for activity 1–2 is the smaller of the LS for 2–5 and the LS for 2–6. Of these values, 9 and 8, 8 is used. The LF activity 1–4 is found by comparing the LS values for activities 4–7 and 4–8.

c. The time-cost information for the project is contained in the following table:

Activity	Normal Duration (Weeks)	Normal Cost ($)	Crash Duration (Weeks)	Crash Cost ($)	Crash Cost ($/Week)
1–2	5	800	3	1,100	150
1–3	7	950	3	2,150	300
1–4	6	600	4	1,400	400
2–5	0	—	0	—	—
2–6	7	1,100	5	1,500	200
3–7	4	750	4	750	—
4–7	9	1,600	8	1,800	200
4–8	10	1,000	9	1,300	300
5–6	6	1,300	4	2,200	450
6–9	9	2,000	8	2,500	500
7–9	9	1,500	7	2,000	250
8–9	7	900	5	1,600	350

(1) In order to achieve a one-week project time reduction, one of the critical activities (1−4, 4−7, and 7−9) must be crashed. Of the three, activity 4−7 has the lowest weekly crash cost, $200, and is therefore our selection.

(2) The two-week reduction cannot be found by considering only the *original* critical path. After 4−7 is crashed one week, there are *two* critical paths: 1−4−7−9 and 1−4−8−9. Also, note that 4−7 may not be crashed further. Since both (new) critical paths must be reduced in order to shorten the project, we might consider crashing 7−9 and 4−8 one week each. This costs $250 + $300 = $550, which is cheaper than the $600 cost of crashing 7−9 and 8−9.

Another alternative is to crash activity 1−4, which has the admirable effect of reducing time on both of our critical paths. While activity 1−4's crash cost seems high at $400, in this case it is a bargain, since it beats the $550 cost of crashing 7−9 and 4−8. Thus, our choice is to crash activity 1−4.

(3) Again look at activity 1−4. It may be crashed a second week for an additional $400. That should be done to obtain the desired three-week reduction in project duration.

For Further Reference

Books

Funk, Jeffrey L. *The Teamwork Advantage: An Inside Look at Japanese Product and Technology Development*. Cambridge, Mass.: Productivity Press, 1992 (HD66.F86).

Goodman, Louis J. *Project Planning and Management*. New York: Van Nostrand Reinhold, 1988 (HD69.P75G65).

Harris, Robert B. *Precedence and Arrow Networking Techniques for Construction*. New York: John Wiley & Sons, 1978 (TH438.H37).

Kerzner, Harold, and Hans Thamhain. *Project Management for Small and Medium Size Business*. New York: Van Nostrand Reinhold, 1984 (HD69.P75K491).

Meredith, Jack R., and Samuel J. Mantel Jr. *Project Management: A Managerial Approach*. New York: John Wiley & Sons, 1985.

Wiest, Jerome D., and Ferdinand K. Levy. *A Management Guide to PERT/CPM*. 2nd ed. Englewood Cliffs, N.J.: Prentice-Hall, 1977 (TS158.2.W53).

Periodicals/Societies

Journal of Operations Management (American Production and Inventory Control Society).

IIE Transactions (Institute of Industrial Engineers).

Project Management Quarterly (Project Management Institute); sometimes catalogued as a monograph series (HD69.P75p76) instead of a periodical.

Review Questions

1. Why should project teams not work in the serial mode?
2. Will the addition of more associates on the project team reduce the project completion time? Explain.
3. What type of project management organization and leadership is likely for management of a pharmaceutical company's line of headache remedies? Why?
4. In development projects, how can the ideas of suppliers and customers be effectively incorporated?
5. Private ownership is basic in our Western society. How might that right affect information needed by a project team?
6. Why is a process-oriented work breakdown structure not recommended?
7. How is a work breakdown structure translated into a PERT/CPM network?
8. Why must there be dummy activities in networks?

9. Why is the network an incorrect way to display activities (or tasks) occurring in repetitive production?

10. Why has the three-time-estimate (for each activity) procedure proved counter-productive?

11. Why might a project manager prepare both an activity-oriented and event-oriented network for the same project?

12. What is done with time estimates in PERT/CPM?

13. What is the purpose of path analysis in PERT/CPM?

14. What is a critical path?

15. Where and under what conditions is negative slack likely to occur?

16. For what is a slack-sort report used?

17. Why is it often sufficient for a project manager to develop a network but not carry the PERT/CPM technique any further?

18. What data are needed to perform time-cost trade-off analysis, and where are the data obtained?

19. In a time-cost trade-off analysis, why is it necessary to check to see which paths are critical after every change?

20. How are PERT/CPM data translated into scheduled jobs or tasks? Why might those scheduled task dates cause conflict for those who are to do the work?

21. Given the uncertainties inherent in R&D and construction projects, how can PERT/CPM adapt?

22. Why is PERT/CPM costly to administer?

23. Why is the deterministic critical path likely to understate the project duration?

24. How can project management teams combat project complexity and uncertainty?

Problems and Exercises

1. Which of the five organizational structures would be suitable for each of the following? Explain your answers.
   a. Putting on a world's fair.
   b. Remodeling a branch bank.
   c. New-car contracting for a major rental car agency.
   d. Dietary planning for Meals on Wheels (meals for the homebound elderly or disabled).
   e. A curb-and-gutter project in a city.

2. Contact a local construction company, information systems company (or department), public works agency, market research group, advertising agency, or research and development department (laboratory).
   a. Find out what form of project management is in dominant use and why.
   b. Find out if PERT/CPM is used, and which subsystems, and why.

3. Develop a product-oriented work breakdown structure for a nonconstruction project of your choice. (Examples are a market research project, a political campaign, a disaster-relief project, a research and development project, and a large-scale, computer-based information system development.) You may need to speculate about the nature of your chosen project if you have not had actual experience in a large project. In addition to drawing the work breakdown structure, explain the nature of your project. Show part of at least three levels on your structure.

4. The R&D group of Home Products Company (HOPROCO) is developing a prototype for a new, gasoline-powered lawn mower. The project is to be managed using PERT/CPM. Project activities include all design, manufacturing, and testing for the single prototype mower. The mower engine is to be designed and made by another firm, an engine manufacturer. All other major modules are to be designed and made by HOPROCO's employees.

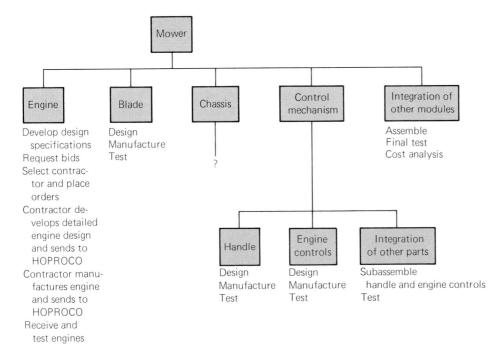

a. A partial work breakdown structure and task lists for the mower are shown in the exhibit. One module, the chassis, has not been broken down into major parts and task lists. Your assignment is to do this. You must decide, as best you can, what major parts the chassis would need to include. Then decide on tasks for each major part. Note that the work breakdown structure is product-oriented, except for an integration activity whenever there is a need to combine other modules or parts.

b. Some of the beginning and ending activities for the mower project are shown as a partial PERT/CPM network. Network activities are taken from the task lists in the work breakdown structure. Complete the network. (Note: Engine-design data are needed before certain HOPROCO tasks can begin. You must determine where this is the case and draw the network that way.)

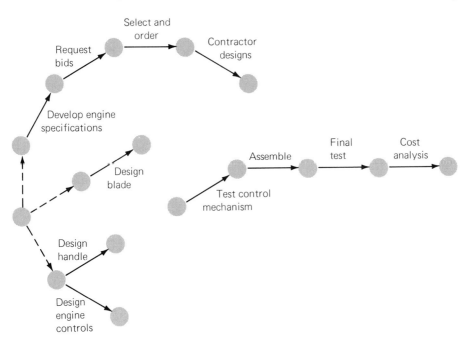

    c. Some of the dummy activities in your network are not needed. Redraw portions of the network to show elimination of all unnecessary dummy activities.

5. Explain the purpose of activity 16–13 in Exhibit 14–5.

6. You and several others have been appointed as a planning committee by the president of your social organization. Your committee has decided that in order to obtain additional funds for operating expenses, you will produce a play or a variety show. You have been asked to submit a plan for the next meeting. The plan is to include all the activities or tasks that will have to be accomplished up to the opening of the show. Publicity, tickets, printed programs, and so on, as well as staging for the production, should be part of the plan. The committee has already decided that the scenery will be constructed in a member's garage and that the costumes will be rented.

    To facilitate presentation of the plan, draw a network diagram of about 30 activities. Include brief descriptions of the activities.

7. A manufacturer of CD players buys disc magazines from outside contractors. A new contract is to be awarded for a new style of disc magazine. The company has developed an activity-on-node network for the disc magazine project. The accompanying network includes an initial contract for disc magazine development and a second contract (assuming that the disc magazine tests are OK) for production. Redraw the network in the activity-on-arrow form.

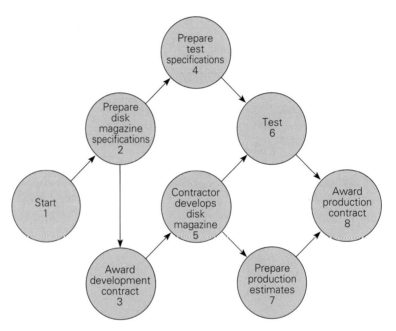

8. The manager for a project to develop a special antenna system is preparing a PERT-based project plan. Data for the plan are as follows:

Activity Number	Description	Expected Time (Days)
1–2	Design frame	4
1–3	Procure mechanism	5
2–4	Procure parts	1
3–4	Dummy	0
3–7	Determine repair requirements	4
4–6	Assemble	2
4–7	Hire maintenance crew	3
6–7	Test	1

 a. Draw the network.
 b. Compute and indicate the critical path.
 c. Compute slack times for all activities assuming that the project is scheduled for completion in the number of days on the critical path.
 d. Five working days have passed, and status data have been received, as follows:
   (1) Activity 1–2 was completed in five days.
   (2) Activity 1–3 was completed in four days.
   (3) Activity 4–6 has been reestimated at four days.
   Based on the data, recompute the critical path and slack on all of the remaining project activities. (Assume no change in scheduled project completion dates.)

9. Aeropa, Inc., has a contract to develop a guided missile. A PERT/CPM network and activity times are given in the following illustration. Times are in weeks.

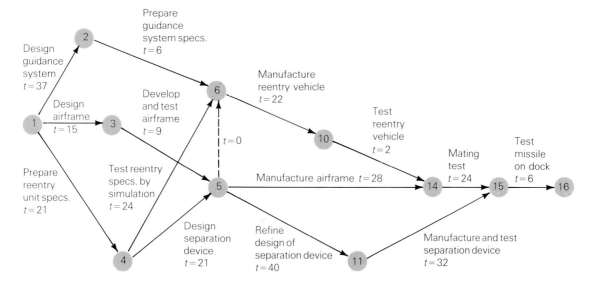

 a. Compute *ES, LS, EF, LF,* and slack for each activity. Assume that slack = 0 on the critical path. Identify the critical path activities and the critical path duration.
 b. Draw a condensed event-oriented network with only five milestone events. The five events should be designated as follows: 1. Start. 5. Shell specs completed. 6. Guidance specs completed. 14. Modules completed. 16. Missile tested.

  Put activity times on the arrows between your events. Compute *ES, LS, EF, LF,* and slack for each activity. Verify that the critical path duration is the same as in question *a.* What activity time goes on arrow 1–6? Explain the difficulty in deciding on a time for this activity.
 c. Assume the following project status at the end of week 50:

Activity	Actual Duration
1–2	39
1–3	17
1–4	20
2–6	7
3–5	9
4–5	28
4–6	20

No other activities have been completed.

Develop a slack-sorted activity report similar to Exhibit 14–11 for the project as of the end of week 50. What is the new projected project duration?

10. The following data have been collected for a certain project:

Activity		Normal		Crash	
Predecessor Event	*Successor Event*	*Time (Days)*	*Cost ($)*	*Time (Days)*	*Cost ($)*
1	2	6	250	5	360
2	3	2	300	1	480
2	4	1	100	1	100
2	5	7	270	6	470
3	4	2	120	1	200
4	5	5	200	1	440

   a. Draw the network.

   b. Compute and indicate the critical path and the normal project cost.

   c. Compute slack time for each activity in the network, using 12 days as the project due date.

   d. Perform time-cost trade-off analysis, crashing down to the minimum possible project duration. Display each time-cost alternative.

11. Normal and crash data for the accompanying network are given below. Compute all time-cost options. Which is best if there is a $40-per-day penalty for every day beyond a seven-day project duration?[8]

	Normal		Crash	
Activity	*Days*	*Cost*	*Days*	*Cost*
A	3	$ 50	2	$ 100
B	6	140	4	260
C	2	25	1	50
D	5	100	3	180
E	2	80	2	80
F	7	115	5	175
G	4	100	2	240
		$610		$1,085

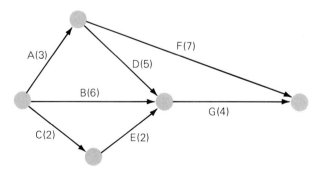

[8]Adapted from J. S. Sayer, J. E. Kelly, Jr., and M. R. Walker, "Critical Path Scheduling," *Factory,* July 1960.

12.   *a.* For the accompanying network, what is the critical path and expected project duration? What is the second most critical path and its duration?

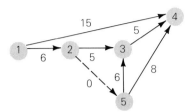

  b. What can the largest time value for activity 3–4 be to ensure that it is not a critical path activity? (Ignore the present time of five days for that activity in answering the question.)

13.   *a.* For the accompanying network, if there is a positive slack of +6 on the upper path, what is the slack on the lower path?
  b. If the slack is −4 on the upper path, what is the slack on the lower path?

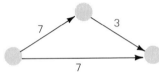

14.

  a. For the accompanying network, if there is slack of +5 on the lower path, what is the slack on the upper path?
  b. If there is slack of +1 on the upper path, what is the slack on the lower path?

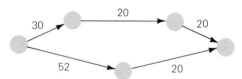

15.

| | **Normal** | | **Crash** | |
Activity	Time	Cost	Time	Cost
1–2	2	$10	1	$15
2–3	6	8	5	18
2–4	2	15	1	21
2–5	8	30	6	52
4–3	2	7	2	7
3–5	3	21	1	33
1–5	8	20	5	41

  a. For the accompanying time-and-cost table, what is the least costly way to reduce the project time by one day? (You may wish to draw the network for better visualization of the problem.)
  b. What is the least costly way to reduce the expected project duration (i.e., crash the project) by three days?

16.

| | Normal | | Crash | |
Activity	Time	Cost	Time	Cost
1–2	6	$100	5	$205
1–4	17	200	12	600
2–3	5	100	4	190
3–4	5	150	3	360
5–3	6	80	5	185
5–4	8	300	7	360

a. For the accompanying network and time-and-cost table, what is the least costly way to reduce (crash) the project by one day?

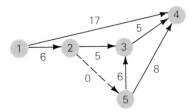

b. What is the fastest the project could be done if you used crash times?

17. A number of project types are listed below, ranging from small and simple to grand. As indicated in Exhibit 14–15, modest projects warrant only the first PERT/CPM subsystem, whereas grand projects justify all four subsystems; in-between projects warrant subsystems 1 and 2 or subsystems 1, 2 and 3. Decide which subsystems should apply for each project listed. Explain each.

  a. Computer selection and installation for company of 200 employees.
  b. Moving the computer facility for a large bank to a new building in a major city.
  c. Moving the computer facility (same size as the bank's) to a new building at a major university.
  d. Community project to attract new industry in three large, abandoned factory buildings (town of 10,000 people).
  e. Five-year overhaul of a nuclear submarine.
  f. Implementing MRP in a manufacturing company of 1,000 employees.
  g. New-product development and testing (including market research) for a major food company.
  h. Moving an army division from one closed-down post to a new one in another state.
  i. Planning a national sports championship event.
  j. Building a 500-room hotel in Lincoln, Nebraska.
  k. Building a 500-room hotel in Manhattan.

18. The accompanying network segments are all part of the same home construction project. Where is a dummy activity needed, and why?

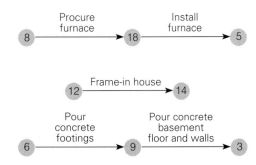

19. Exhibit 14–16 shows a simulation of a simple network with equally possible activity times of 4, 5, or 6. In discussing the figure, it was stated that expected project duration increases to 5.8 for the five equally probable activity times, 3, 4, 5, 6, and 7. Verify the figure 5.8.

20. A network consists of two activities that occur at the same time. Each is expected to take one, two, or three weeks to complete, and the probabilities of each possible time are ⅓, ⅓, and ⅓. What is the expected project duration based on the critical path? What is it based on PERT simulation?

21. A network consists of two activities that occur at the same time. Each is expected to take one or two months to complete, and the probabilities of each possible time are ½ and ½.

    a. What is the expected project duration based on the critical path? What is it based on PERT simulation?

    b. What would the expected project duration be using PERT simulation if the network had three instead of two activities, each with equally probable activity times of one or two months?

22. Develop an example of how each of the following tools of process improvement—fishbone chart, Pareto chart, check sheet—might be used in a construction project. Focus your examples on ways to reduce project uncertainty and lateness.

OM RESOURCES: MEASUREMENT, MANAGEMENT, AND IMPROVEMENT

Operations cannot occur without adequate resources. In fact, management of operating resources, the subject of Part V, is as important as management of the operations themselves.

In Chapter 15, we consider ways of measuring the productivity of resources. Chapter 16 addresses maintenance of physical resources, which in some businesses is a key to readiness and responsiveness to customer demands. Chapter 17 treats facilities positioning, which includes location of buildings and equipment, plus movement of materials or other resources to where they are needed. We conclude (Chapter 18) with a discussion of the relevance to your career of operations management, especially as practiced in superior organizations, and of the continuing evolution of operations management concepts and practices.

15   PRODUCTIVITY

Chapter Outline

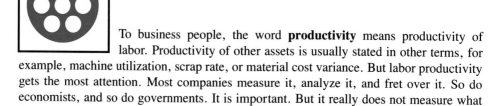

To business people, the word **productivity** means productivity of labor. Productivity of other assets is usually stated in other terms, for example, machine utilization, scrap rate, or material cost variance. But labor productivity gets the most attention. Most companies measure it, analyze it, and fret over it. So do economists, and so do governments. It is important. But it really does not measure what it purports to measure.

If labor productivity is low, that does not necessarily mean the labor resource is performing poorly. More likely, the management system is deficient. The system is failing to provide high-quality tools, timely information, equipment, materials, training, designs, technical support, strategic guidance, and proper motivational climate. The quality and productivity of the labor resource depends on many factors. A few of these are topics in this chapter, but most have to do with resources and processes discussed in each of the other chapters.

Thus, this chapter's scope is necessarily narrow. We'll look at common productivity concepts and measures, along with strengths, deficiencies, and evolving changes. Companies track productivity in output units, cost (money) units, and time units; they try to improve productivity through time, quality, method, and delay analysis, plus feedback on each of the measures. These productivity and motivational factors—output, cost, time, quality, method, delay, and feedback—are the main topics of the chapter.

Bottom Line for Operations Management

Michael Jordan, stellar guard of the Chicago Bulls, scores over 30 points a game, and dishes out plenty of assists, too. He's productive, per number of minutes played and, probably, per dollar that he's paid: a quality asset, a bottom-line player. Sports fans judge a basketball player's productivity according to these kinds of output units (points and assists) but are savvy enough also to weigh input units such as game minutes and salary. The National Basketball Association might prefer to judge "Air Jordan's" productivity in number of fans per game who come to see him and his team; the Bulls fill arenas all around the league.

Whether you consider the din of shouting fans, clanking factory machines, humming office equipment, or babbling customers, the bottom line for operations management is usually output units compared with input units. The measures are used for performance appraisal, recognition, reward, and motivation for continual improvement. Therefore, getting the units right is important to every department, team, and associate. Experts, such as cost and time analysts, have usually been in charge. Let's take a look at the measurement experts' handiwork: the classic cost-variance system.

Cost Variance

For years, best business practice has called for use of periodic cost variances as a control on productivity. The system sums up standard cost and actual cost for all work completed in a period. Standard cost represents the output of the period, what the output should cost using normal amounts of direct labor, materials, and so forth; the input is the actual cost: actual payroll, material, and other expenditures. Periodic reports, sent out to each operating manager, list cost variances. If actual cost is higher than standard cost, a negative cost variance results, and the pressure is on operations to do better.

Cost variance:
Standard cost minus actual cost.

More specifically, the cost-variance report is segmented into subcategories, including labor cost variance and material cost variance. A negative labor variance suggests that the direct-labor force should work more diligently; a negative material variance means it should work more carefully so as not to scrap so much material.

Misplaced Blame

The modern view is that far too much blame—for cost, scrap, rework, delays, and so forth—has been heaped on front-line employees. A century ago, when direct labor amounted to over 50 percent of operating cost on average, emphasis on labor variance made more sense. Today, overhead costs are commonly over five times the cost of direct labor. While a complete cost-variance system includes overhead cost, overhead includes too many diverse elements for an overhead variance to have much impact; managers therefore have fixed their attention on the labor variance data.

In manufacturing, direct labor now averages less than 15 percent of operating cost.

Contrast

Productivity

Old Productivity	**New Productivity**
Narrow, fractionated: On the output side, emphasis is on operations (rather than whole products). On the input side, focus is on direct-labor cost, charged to operations and departments (not to products or customers).	Broad, integrated: On the output side, focus is on whole products or subproducts. On the input side, all human resource and other operating costs are included and related to whole products or specific customers.

There are other reasons, besides the shrinking direct-labor cost component, for questioning the classic cost-variance measurement system. One is the realization that quality, not just output, is a key to competitive advantage. Another is the wholesale reorganization of resources (re-engineering) that has been taking place in many businesses: away from fragmented and toward product- or customer-focused. This paves the way to simpler, more meaningful measures of performance. A third is the blurring of job responsibilities: front-liners are assuming first responsibility for quality, good workplace organization, upkeep of equipment, data collection and diagnosis, problem solving, and, sometimes, interviewing and training new employees. Formerly, those activities were treated as indirect labor, supervision, and overhead.

Data Collection

Still another disadvantage of conventional productivity systems is the extensive data required to feed them. For example, some systems require data on when an associate starts and completes each different job, and commonly the associate works on several jobs every day; time not working (stoppages for lack of parts, breakdowns, etc.) thus can be deducted, which yields a refined measure of direct-labor productivity, or labor efficiency. To collect all that data, some companies have been persuaded to install data-entry terminals all over the operating area.

An alternative outlook favors lumping together all labor costs, not tracking labor job by job, or even separating direct labor from other payroll costs. As front-line associates team up with experts and managers, dividing lines blur, and so do the old labor cost categories. At a Westinghouse plant in North Carolina, employee pay is automatically charged to the miniplants each is assigned to (the plant had undergone reorganization into several product-focused miniplants); once a week, supervisors simply turn in an exception report noting any absenteeism or overtime hours.[1] The output of each miniplant is known, and so, without further data collection, is the miniplant's share of the payroll, in case a supervisor wants to determine a miniplant's productivity.

Simple, Effective Measures

While productivity measurement has often become cumbersome, costly, and ineffective, there are plenty of examples of simple, useful ones:

---

[1] S. S. Cherukuri, "Westinghouse Electric Corporation Asheville's Focused Factories Make a Difference—the 'Village' Concept," *Target*, Fall 1988, pp. 30–32.

• *Retailers.* An effective, widely used measure is sales per square foot. Stu Leonard's food stores and Circuit City electronic stores rate exceptionally high on this scale. Under this measure, store managers and sales associates become more attuned to customer needs—for example, for quality, quick service, and attentiveness—because these factors bring in business. On the other hand, if stores are rated on sales per salesperson, managers might tend to cut staff, resulting in declining service and, finally, less business.

• *Accounting, legal, and consultancy firms.* A common measure is billable hours (an hour of time billable to the client) per professional associate. This measure, again, reflects ability to attract customers. Moreover, it gives managers and professionals room to be real operations managers, that is, to weigh the value of different types of staffing, equipment, training, thoroughness, after-sale service, and so forth.

• *Manufacturers.* Harley-Davidson, the motorcycle manufacturer, is among the vanguard of producers shifting toward new, team-oriented productivity and quality measures. Two of the company's new measures are motorcycles per employee and total conversion cost per bike.[2] Formerly, like most other manufacturers, Harley computed productivity separately for each of its many work centers and departments. The new, simple, overall measures encourage these units to work together, and they support Harley's extensive efforts to eliminate inventories between departments and to merge the formerly separated processes into product-focused cells. Effects of these improvements show up clearly and directly in the new measures of performance for a whole motorcycle.

To summarize, these examples illustrate measures that are more effective, accurate, and simple:

• *Effective.* The newer measures are directed toward business activity, customers, and the products or services themselves. Older measures tend to measure resource activity instead of business activity, and functions rather than products and customer satisfaction.

• *Accurate.* The aim is to include not just direct labor but all operations and operating costs.

• *Simple.* Complex data collection, person by person, job by job, function by function, is out; using already available data is in.

Employees are likely to be supportive of measures that are truly customer-oriented, with simple-to-determine accuracy.

Controlling Causes of Cost

If companies abandon detailed cost measurements and substitute overall measures, such as Harley-Davidson's conversion cost per motorcycle, aren't there some risks? Won't it be all too easy for shirkers to escape detection, for poor performance to be hidden?

The answer to these questions is a multifaceted system of eliminating the *causes* of cost, poor quality, delays, and other wastes. A key element of cause reduction consists of teams of associates solving problems and displaying what they are doing and the results visually on large wall charts. The visual measurement data fall into three categories:

*P*RINCIPLE 16:

Cut reporting; control causes.

1. *Product, service, component, or customer specific.* Rework, returns, claims, scrap, mishaps, nonconformities, yield, on-time completions, lead time, flow distance, space, and idle inventory.

---

[2]John A. Saathoff, "Maintaining Excellence through Change," *Target,* Spring 1989, pp. 13–20.

2. *Process specific*. Process changeover and get-ready time, response ratios, check sheets, and control charts.

3. *Activities, recognition, rewards, celebration*. Present improvement projects, present training programs, completed projects, completed training, number of suggestions, appreciation letters from customers, awards won, plaques, photos of recognition ceremonies, and so forth.

Visual Controls[3]

This system is visual, located where the work is performed, usually owned by operating people, and up to date. Controlling causes in this way is, in the words of H. Thomas Johnson, "unlike the distant, often distorted financial echoes of those causes that appear in traditional cost and performance reports."[4] The full system of visual measures includes all of the factors listed in Chapter 1 (Exhibit 1–1) as "customer requirements," namely, quality, flexibility, service, cost, lead time, and variability.

Examples of the visual system are shown in the photographs in Exhibit 15–1, which come from Milliken & Co. Milliken, a large, privately held textile and chemical producer, has charts of these kinds throughout its offices and plants. This is one of the reasons why Milliken was a winner of the 1989 Baldrige National Quality Award.

The improvement charts have several purposes. If there really is progress, the people involved can take pride in the visible display of improvements.[5] Further, improvement trends silently call for more of the same, a motivational benefit. Finally, a good assortment of wall charts can be an excellent tool for communication among operations, support people, management, and visiting customers or suppliers. The charts may even help draw timid managers and others out of their offices to the source of problems. While it is not natural for a manager to carry a computer report to the floor to use in discussing problems, performance charts in the workplace are a natural focal point for discussion.

In the cause-control system, cost ceases to be used for controlling productivity. The on-the-spot visual signboard system controls the causes, and productivity improvement (as well as improvement in quality, lead time, etc.) follows.

That does not mean that costs are no longer measured; they are. Regulatory agencies require data such as the value of inventories and statements of profit and loss, but those reports require only a fraction of the data needed for a full-blown cost-variance system. The overall cost data needed for periodic profit and loss accounting (high-level score-keeping) will, of course, prove the value of the cause controls.

*P*RINCIPLE 14:

Record data at the workplace.

Improving the Old System

While the visual cause-control system appears to be the choice of leading-edge firms, many other companies are looking for ways to salvage some of their traditional productivity measures by correcting some of their weaknesses.

One weakness, the fixation on direct labor, is reduced when operators assume responsibility for quality, data collection, and other duties usually handled by large staffs of overhead people. More of the factors included in the productivity measures thus come under the control of operators, and the size of the overhead group and its cost shrink.

Another weakness, the focus on counting anything as output, even customer-rejected output, is greatly reduced when operations is successful in slashing lead times; this ties

---

[3]Visual management concept and examples are presented in Michel Grief, *The Visual Factory: Building Participation Through Shared Information*, Cambridge, Mass.: Productivity Press, 1991.

[4]H. Thomas Johnson, "A Blueprint for World-Class Management Accounting," *Management Accounting*, June 1988, pp. 23–30.

[5]A description of the use of visible performance graphs in a plant assembling minicomputers can be found in Richard C. Walleigh, "What's Your Excuse for Not Using JIT?" *Harvard Business Review*, March–April 1986, pp. 38–54.

EXHIBIT 15–1   Visual Management at Milliken and Company

Top: An "alcove of excellence" in a main trafficway.
Bottom: A "wall of fame," data and photos of award winners.

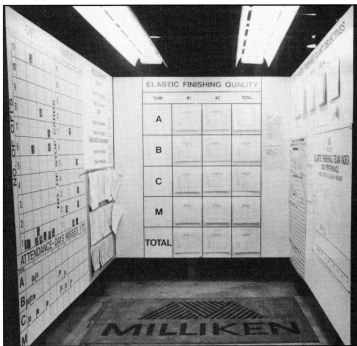

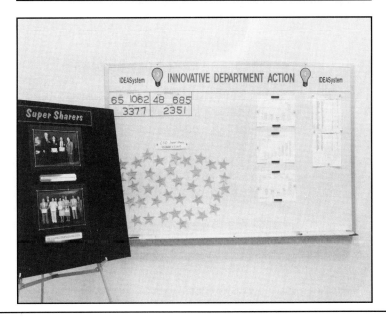

operations more closely in time to real customer demands. Related to this is the movement of people and equipment into product-focused groupings, which makes any measure of productivity more focused on what the customer is paying for.

Despite these improvements, the old productivity measures retain the weaknesses of being periodic, delayed, staff-directed, and not cause-oriented.

*Cost of Products
and Services*

Insurance Agent A: "How can the company be making money on these individual policies? Those clients are a pain in the neck to sell to, and a headache when they've got a claim."

Agent B: "Who cares, as long as you get your commission?"

This scenario repeats itself in nearly all large businesses, where costs are not easily tied to the actual service, customer, or product. While low-level people—managers and cost accountants, too—have long asked these kinds of questions, only recently has the truth emerged. And the truth often is that the low-volume specials (individual insurance policies, perhaps) are not profitable. They are not priced high enough to make money, because they are not assigned their fair share of company costs. By company costs we mean, especially, overhead costs, which, as noted, usually dwarf direct-labor costs. High-volume commodity items (e.g., group insurance policies), on the other hand, usually receive far more than their share of overhead cost. As a result, they are often overpriced or inaccurately judged to be financial losers.

By now, hundreds of articles and many books have noted this systematic bias in company costing systems. While cost accounting, pricing, and profit management are a bit beyond the scope of operations management studies, we nevertheless must note how the cost-bias problem can adversely affect OM decisions. Consider the following scenarios for a catering business:

- An improvement team of buyers, cooks, helpers, and drivers has come up with several productivity improvement ideas for high-volume catering customers (e.g., an airline), but at the same time a management group decides to abandon the high-volume business because the biased cost system falsely shows it to be losing money.

- Low-volume catering (weddings, etc.) actually is the money-losing business segment, but aided by biased costing, it looks profitable (in fact the sales manager for that segment has received a hefty pay hike). No one has had an incentive to improve it, service quality is barely adequate, and before long this segment is losing customers and money.

Costs are important, as well, for a few other common operations management activities, including evaluating process, method, and equipment alternatives, and making make-or-buy and offshore sourcing decisions.

According to one line of critical thought, several major businesses that American manufacturers abandoned as losers in the 1970s and early 1980s, such as commodity memory chips, actually may have been profitable.[6] Operations managers, not seeing any way to cut costs enough, would have been party to decisions to abandon such commodity product lines. (Companies in the world's largest mass market shedding highest, instead of lowest, volume products even sounds illogical.)

The bias in overhead cost allocation is directly addressed by **activity-based costing (ABC)** methods, which attempt to assign overhead costs to a product or service only where there is actual overhead activity related to the item. Briefly, in the ABC method a team, consisting of an accountant and representatives of an overhead activity such as scheduling or maintenance, is formed to search for simple activity cost drivers. For example, operating overhead costs could be allocated to a product based on a single driver, lead time. The reasoning is that if a product is in process for five days (lead time = 5), the product probably actually receives five days of overhead cost; if another

Cost, like dust, settles on items that move too slowly.

---

[6]H. Thomas Johnson, "Managing Costs: An Outmoded Philosophy," *Manufacturing Engineering,* May 1989, p. 44.

Contrast

A Fair Day's . . .

Nineteenth Century: A Fair Day's Grog

Manufacturer's notes:* "All hands drunk; Jacob Ventling hunting; molders all agree to quit work and went to the beach. Peter Cox very drunk and gone to bed."

Cigar manufacturer:* Men worked no more than two or three hours a day; spent the remainder in the beer saloon playing pinochle.

Twentieth Century: A Fair Day's Work

Standard methods and standard times provide a basis for uniform measurement of human performance and, therefore, control of it.

Twenty-First Century: A Fair Day's Improvement

Broad array of tools of data collection, analysis, problem solving, measurement, customer focus, teamwork, reward, and recognition make continuous improvement a normal part of everyone's job.

*Source: Shoshana Zuboff, *In the Age of the Smart Machine,* New York: Basic Books, 1988, p. 32.

---

product zips through in just one day, it is scarcely seen or handled by overhead people and therefore should receive proportionately less overhead cost—in this case, only one fifth as much.

Since its development in 1986, activity-based costing has spread quickly. It is widely valued for use in making critical operating and competitive decisions, which require accurate costs.

The same accuracy-enhanced cost data could also be used for correcting the inaccuracies in cost-variance reporting. Some believe, however, that the cost-variance system has outlived its usefulness. A number of other measures are available and are more effective and less costly to administer, so the reasoning goes. In the remainder of the chapter, some of these other performance measures and motivators are presented, starting with a few that date back to the beginnings of scientific management.

Productivity and Scientific Management

The first organized approach to improving the productivity of labor arose in the United States at the turn of the century from the work of the pioneers of scientific management, Frederick W. Taylor, Frank and Lillian Gilbreth, and others. Their approach was to standardize the labor element of production: standard methods and standard times. Nonstandard labor practices were simply too expensive and wasteful.

Scientific management (so named by U.S. Supreme Court Justice Louis Brandeis) was born in a period of transition and could be thought of as the last phase of the Industrial Revolution. Earlier phases concerned invention, mechanization, standardization of parts, division of labor, and the factory system. Machines and parts were standardized, and labor was divided into narrow specialties. Prior to scientific management, however, labor productivity was controlled more by supervisors' skill than by design. Taylor's and the Gilbreths' techniques for methods study (or motion study) and time study extended science into the realm of the line employee.

$\mathcal{I}$nto $\mathcal{P}$ractice

Taylorism: Boon or Bane?

Many business executives, consultants, and writers have blasted Taylorism recently. The basis for the criticism is Frederick W. Taylor's advocacy of specialist-managers.

The fairness of charging Taylor, who died in 1915, with today's sins of excessive specialization throughout business and government is uncertain. But there is no question about Taylor's central role in the development of methods study and time standards, which were the makings of the indus-

trial engineering profession. The methods study techniques have been absorbed into modern-day total quality management and continuous improvement, and thus are highly esteemed. Time standards have been misused and are reviled, but nevertheless they have a valued role in administering just-in-time operations, which require tight synchronization, scheduling, and timing.

Impact of Scientific Management

While putting the finishing touches on the Industrial Revolution, scientific management ushered in the beginnings of the modern manufacturing era. Since the United States was the birthplace of scientific management, it enjoyed the first benefits. Methods and standards programs spread rapidly in U.S. manufacturing firms between 1900 and 1950, which may help explain the phenomenal growth of industrial output in the United States in the first half of the century.

Methods and time standards programs are not limited to manufacturing. Beginning in the 1940s, they found their way into hospitals, food service, hotels, transportation, and other services. So carefully industrially engineered is the McDonald's hamburger that Levitt calls it "the technocratic hamburger."[7] By the early 1980s, the industrial engineering department at United Parcel Service (UPS) had grown to 3,000 people and "had so perfected manual package handling that UPS had the industry's lowest costs."[8] In many industries, it has been hard to compete without good methods design and labor standards.

Scientific management is not without its critics. Labor unions often have resisted time standards. Some believe that under work measurement a person is treated like a microcomputer memory chip. At the first sign of performance deterioration, the chip is discarded and replaced; it's just not cost effective to attempt to repair or recycle it. Often the ultimate plan is to replace the entire memory system, and even the computer itself, with faster memory and more powerful equipment.

Process Improvement and Productivity

Modern improvement tools, presented in Chapter 4, are a mixture of old and new: process flowcharting from the Taylor/Gilbreth era, plus several newer tools that originated in connection with quality improvement (see the 13 tools for process improvement, Exhibit 4–8). Here we take a second look, from a productivity angle.

Systematic productivity improvement, as developed by Taylor, the Gilbreths, and other pioneers of scientific management, involved **methods study,** with **flowcharting** at

---

[7]Theodore Levitt, "Production-Line Approach to Service," *Harvard Business Review,* September–October 1972, pp. 41–52.

[8]Peter Coy and Chuck Hawkins, "UPS: Up from the Stone Age," *Business Week,* June 15, 1992, p. 132.

EXHIBIT 15–2   Methods Study: Job and Process Improvement

Type	*Application*	*Flowchart*
Job level:		
Motion study	Manual task at work bench or desk	Left-and-right-hand time chart
Operator-machine analysis	Operator tending machines	Operator-machine time chart
Process level:	Mobile employee, product, or customer	Process flowchart

---

the core. Methods study always has been aimed at improving not only productivity but also safety and ease of performing the work. Making the work easier to do safely increasingly gets into issues of human physiology, stress, and bodily limitations, and has spawned a subfield of process improvement called **ergonomics.** Because of escalating worker's compensation and litigation costs, interest in ergonomics has never been higher.

Methods study takes place at the job level and at the process level. As Exhibit 15–2 shows, each application has a different set of before-and-after flowcharts.

One subdivision of job-level studies is **motion study,** which is limited to the work of an immobile employee at a desk or work bench. The analyst flowcharts what the left and right hands are doing. The other type of job-level study is for a mobile employee tending more than one machine; the analyst flowcharts both the person's and the machine's activities.

Both kinds of job-level analysis use standard flowcharting symbols (except for the decision diamond), and may also employ a flowcharting form with time units on the vertical. The flowcharting analysis steps are as follows:

- Flowchart the present method (*before* chart).
- Move, combine, or eliminate steps.
- Flowchart the proposed new method (*after* chart).
- Immediately determine the resulting productivity improvement by comparing cycle time on the *before* and *after* charts.

Job-level methods study is still valid, where it applies. However, it pertains to the productivity (and ergonomic conditions) of direct labor, but not overall productivity, including typically out-of-control overhead costs. Improvement teams may use process-level flowcharts in directly attacking the high overhead costs and wastes, along with some direct-labor wastes.

Unlike job-level flowcharts, process flowcharts do not have a time scale and thus do not readily reveal how much productivity improvement is achieved. If it is really important to know, a cost analyst could be called in to estimate and compare the costs of the old and new processes. Industrial engineers, who've used process flowcharts for decades, have rarely found it necessary to translate improvements into before and after costs. It is clear that productivity improves with the elimination of non-value-adding steps, which are visually portrayed by flowcharting symbols: arrow (transport), upside down triangle (storage), big D (delay), and square (inspection).

Though it may be unnecessary to determine degree of productivity gain for each improvement project, what about determining it for a whole organizational unit? That is our next topic.

> "A single case of carpal tunnel syndrome, a painful condition involving compression of the wrist's median nerve, costs up to $30,000. . . . Eliminating this type of ergonomics problem sometimes requires less than $1,000."
> Paula M. Noaker, "Ergonomics on Site," *Manufacturing Engineering,* June 1992, pp. 63–66.

Busy and Productive Resources

Walk into a drugstore when it is moderately busy, and what do you see? A clerk in the cameras and film department flitting back and forth taking care of three customers; one cashier up front ringing up a customer's purchases, and another cashier trying hard not to look idle and bored; customers bumping into each other in the cold remedies aisle while most other aisles are empty. The cameras and film clerk is busy, and working very efficiently as well. One cashier is busy, the other idle. The space around cold remedies is highly utilized, whereas most of the rest of the store isn't even justifying the power to keep the lights on.

We have identified some common, noncost ways of evaluating the productivity of various resources. Terms like *efficiency, busyness* and *idleness,* and *utilization* can be used loosely; they also have precise meanings and can be measured numerically. Examples follow, first for equipment and other nonhuman resources; then for people.

Machine Utilization   A general formula for **utilization** of labor or machines is:

$$\text{Utilization rate} = \frac{\text{Time in use}}{\text{Time available}} \qquad (15–1)$$

Machine utilization reports, expressing Equation 15–1 as a percentage, are common in larger companies. For some equipment, 40 hours (one shift operation) is used as available hours per week. Sometimes two or more shifts are the basis. Data for the reports sometimes can be collected automatically by timers in the machine, vehicle, conveyor line, or data terminal.

The machine utilization report has at least three purposes. First, it serves as a check on how well the plant and the company plan in advance for the right machine capacity. Second, trends in machine utilization suggest when more capacity will be needed so that equipment can be ordered in advance. Third, when the report shows decreasing utilization, that suggests the need for sales promotions aimed at generating more work for the unutilized capacity.

Exhibit 15–3 shows a machine utilized over 100 percent on a one-shift basis; that means the machine is run on overtime, extra shifts, or weekends, which may require payment of overtime wages. The company might have seen the trend months earlier so that another machine or a larger machine was put on order and is due in soon.

With today's mood of questioning virtually everything in operations management, the machine utilization report has come under fire. Harley Davidson has simply elimi nated machine utilization reports. Why? Because the reports can cover up certain faults

Exнıвıт 15–3   Machine Utilization Trend Report

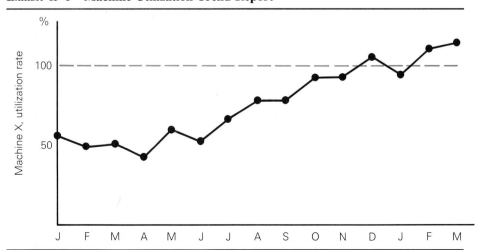

and result in treating symptoms, not real problems. The following are potential weaknesses in machine utilization reports or the way the reports are used:

- High utilization can be achieved by disposing of slow machines and running all jobs on new, fast machines. But old, slow machines are valuable when considering moving machines into cells or other focused zones within a building.
- Utilization may include bad time, such as production of scrap and rework, machine slowdowns, and setups or changeovers. If capacity is added when equipment is engaged in such ineffective activities, habits of accepting bad performance set it.
- High utilization may be achieved by running very large lots, which produce unneeded inventories and lengthen lead times.
- Utilization reports can encourage dabbling in peripheral products to keep machines busy; over time, the facility becomes unfocused.
- Utilization is usually measured in hours, when the real concern should be utilization of capital (return on investment).
- Finally, and perhaps most importantly, 100 percent utilization is not even desirable. For example, no computer center wants its mainframe to be 100 percent utilized because the effect would be long backlogs, interminable delays in getting jobs run, and squabbling for priority among anxious customers.

𝒫RINCIPLES 11 AND 13:

Cut flow time, inventory, and lot size.

Utilization of Space, Information, Materials, and Tools

Besides machine utilization, some firms, especially larger ones, measure and report on space utilization. The reports express space in use as a percentage of total space, which may be broken down by type of space or type of use. Colleges and universities generally report based on several room-use categories, which in the United States are specified by the Department of Education.

Use of information resources can also be measured. Typically the measure is frequency of use rather than percentage of time in use. For example, records and files may be archived based on a certain standard of use or nonuse and disposed of completely in the next phase of records/file control. (*Migration* is a common term for moving information from active storage to archives to disposal.) These are common techniques of records management.

Measures of materials utilization might include scrap, theft, deterioration, obsolescence, and misplacement, all of which hinder productive use of materials. Approximately the same utilization measures may be applied to tools.

Labor Utilization

For the labor resource, it is common to keep track of absences resulting from illness, jury duty, military duty, labor union activities, tardiness, and so forth. Each of these eats into productive time.

More specifically, the machine utilization formula, Equation 15–1, also works for the human resource.

Assume, for example, that a five-person office group spends 2,000 minutes at work on an assortment of 38 jobs (such as letters and reports) in an 8-hour day, which for five people is 2,400 minutes (8 × 60 × 5). The utilization rate, from Equation 15–1, is

$$\text{Utilization} = \frac{\text{Time working}}{\text{Time available for work}}$$
$$= \frac{2{,}000}{2{,}400} = 0.83, \text{ or 83 percent}$$

And what about the other 400 minutes of the 2,400-minute day? We should not be too quick to label it idleness. The five office associates might use that time for worthwhile activities such as cross-training or teaming up on improvement projects.

The utilization formula is simple, but it requires data on time working. An efficient, proven approach is to use work sampling.

Work Sampling

A **work-sampling** study yields data on percentage of idle or delay time.[9] Further, the study team can subdivide the idleness into categories, thereby showing process bottlenecks. Example 15–1 illustrates.

EXAMPLE 15–1   WORK SAMPLING—PATHOLOGY LAB

The director of Midtown Pathological Labs is concerned. Costs are going up rapidly; the staff has plenty to do, yet is often idled by assorted problems. The director decides to probe the sources of delay by conducting a one-week work-sampling study. Of special interest are lab equipment failures, supply shortages, delays waiting for instructions, excessive coffee breaks, and lab technicians absent from the work area. The director prepares a work-sampling data sheet that includes those five categories of delay (plus an *other* category); she also works up a schedule for taking 100 sample observations (20 per day).

The schedule and completed form are shown in Exhibit 15–4. The results, the staff not working 35 percent of the time, confirm the director's impression of serious delay problems. The breakdown into categories of delay yields insight into causes.

The management system can be blamed for the first 18 percent of nonworking time. Equipment failure (3 percent), supply shortages (6 percent), and wait for instructions (9 percent) are failures to provide technicians with resources for keeping busy.

The 13 percent of delay for coffee breaks is an employee problem. Authorized coffee breaks are a 15-minute morning break and a 15-minute afternoon break. This amounts to 30 minutes or, in percent of an 8-hour day:

$$\frac{30 \text{ min}}{8 \text{ hr.} \times 60 \text{ mins./hr.}} = 0.0625 \approx 6 \text{ percent}$$

The coffee-break abuses may be dealt with immediately. The data on resource shortages do not offer a solution, but they do tip off the director on where to look.

Besides delay statistics, work sampling yields the complement, utilization rate. As we have seen, utilization rate (65 percent in the example) means busyness—hours busy divided by hours available. But most of us are very busy at times and not so busy at others. To avoid bias, the analyst doing work sampling must take care to do the study in a representative time period, representative of average conditions, if that is the goal, or representative of very busy conditions if peak periods are being examined. (Ways of avoiding other types of bias, including insufficient sample size, can be found in basic industrial engineering books.)

Labor Efficiency

Human labor is a unique resource that is not merely utilized. Unlike the nonhuman kind (e.g., equipment and materials), the human resource has a will; it can choose to work at a normal pace or much faster or slower than that. Later, we shall see how to find out what normal, or standard, pace is. For now, we'll examine one of the uses of **standard time**—determining **labor efficiency,** which is done in one of two ways:

Standard time:
The time a person is expected to need to complete a task under normal conditions.

$$\text{Efficiency} = \frac{\text{Standard time per unit}}{\text{Actual time per unit}} \text{ or, simply, } \frac{\text{Standard time}}{\text{Actual time}} \tag{15–2}$$

---

[9]In fact, work sampling used to be *ratio delay,* a term coined by R. L. Morrow, an early U.S. user of the technique. (L. H. C. Tippett developed it in England in the 1920s.) Later, the editor of *Factory* magazine, recognizing its usefulness in time-standards as well as delay analysis, proposed the more general *work sampling*. See Ralph M. Barnes, *Work Sampling* (New York: John Wiley & Sons, 1957), pp. 8–10 (T60.T5B3).

EXHIBIT 15-4   Work-Sampling Data Sheets—Midtown Pathological Labs

SCHEDULE OF OBSERVATION TIMES

Mon.	Tues.	Wed.	Thurs.	Fri.

8:01
8:13
9:47
9:59
10:12
10:59
11:16
11:32

1:00
1:15
1:19
2:52
2:55
2:56
2:57
3:02
3:29
3:37
4:07
4:32

WORK-SAMPLING FORM

Category of activity	Observations (tallies)	Percentages
Working	⑥⑤	65%
Not working:		
• Equipment failure	/// ③	3%
• Supplies shortage	ⅢⅠ ⑥	6%
• Wait for instructions	Ⅲ //// ⑨	9%
• Coffee break	ⅢⅢ /// ⑬	13%
• Out of area	// ②	2%
• Other	// ②	2%
Total	100	100%

$$\text{Efficiency} = \frac{\text{Actual units per time period}}{\text{Standard units per time period}} \text{ or, simply, } \frac{\text{Actual units}}{\text{Standard units}} \quad (15\text{--}3)$$

Note that the two versions are mathematically equivalent; each is an inversion of the other.

Efficiency for Nonuniform and Uniform Products.   We may illustrate the formulas by returning to our five-person office team, which turned out 38 jobs yesterday. Assume that 34 is the standard output per day (for five people). According to Equation 15–3:

$$\text{Efficiency} = \frac{38 \text{ actual units/day}}{34 \text{ standard units/day}}$$
$$= 1.12, \text{ or } 112 \text{ percent}$$

To use Equation 15–2, the data must be converted to time per unit. Say that in their 2,400 minutes, the office staff actually spends 1,900 minutes at work on the 38 completed jobs. The other 500 minutes include coffee breaks, cleanup, improvement meetings, and time off for someone to visit a dentist. Then:

$$\text{Standard time} = \frac{1,900 \text{ minutes/day}}{34 \text{ standard units/day}}$$
$$= 55.8 \text{ minutes/unit}$$

$\mathcal{I}$nto $\mathcal{P}$ractice

Efficiency and Time Standards for Nonuniform Operations

Example: The U.S. Air Force Logistics Command, which operates very large job-shops for aircraft repair, compares accumulated standard times against accumulated clock hours for most of its repair-shop crews (and calculates efficiency using Equation 15–3). The reporting period of two weeks is long enough to include perhaps hundreds of task time standards.

Example: Most college libraries use computers to produce catalog cards. A cataloging aide with book in hand enters data about a new book at a terminal, and the data are transmitted to a central library cataloging service center. The center's computer database is searched to find (in the United States) a Library of Congress catalog number for the book. For the search to be successful, the cataloging aide

must enter the right data. This can be difficult, for example, for foreign-language books, musical compositions, and government documents.

Managers at one college library set a monthly standard rate (historical) of 300 books per cataloging aide. Aides deeply resented the standard rate because some aides arrived early in the morning in order to fill their carts with easy books, which allowed them to easily exceed 300 books per month. Other aides who liked the challenge of the tough books actually looked worse when the monthly report came out. The solution: distribute books to cataloging aides at random each morning. That way, each receives about the same variety of types of book over a period of months.

And:

$$\text{Actual time} = \frac{1,900 \text{ minutes/day}}{38 \text{ actual units/day}}$$
$$= 50.0 \text{ minutes/unit}$$

Then, by Equation 15–2:

$$\text{Efficiency} = \frac{55.8 \text{ minutes/unit}}{50.0 \text{ minutes/unit}}$$
$$= 1.12 \text{ or } 112 \text{ percent}$$

In this example, the 38 jobs (letters, reports, etc.) are not uniform. Thus, the standard time of 55.8 minutes represents an average job, but of course some jobs could take all day and others just a few minutes. With such a nonuniform product, an efficiency measure still can be meaningful, but only if it covers a sufficiently long time period, in which the mix of complex and simple jobs would tend to even out. One day and 38 jobs are not enough for a fair efficiency reading. Monthly reporting would be more acceptable.

The fairness issue is lessened when the production units are uniform, or nearly so, such as stuffing envelopes in a mass political mailing, and produced in quantity. A fair efficiency rating, using Equations 15–2 or 15–3, could even be turned out daily (although it is hard to think of reasons for doing so that often).

The matter of uniformity or type of output is itself a productivity measurement issue.

Measures of Output.   Measuring productive output is not always just a matter of counting envelopes or completed letters and reports. A few other output measures are commonly used in other kinds of operations. Exhibit 15–5 summarizes the three basic types of operation.

Exhibit 15-5 Output Measures, by Type of Operations

Type of Operation	Output Measures
Continuous or repetitive	Unit count
Job	Unit count (work center)
	Due dates met (job orders)
	Percent of completion
Project	Percent of completion
	Milestones completed on time
	Events completed on time

As the exhibit shows, in repetitive or continuous operations measuring output simply requires counting completed units that meet minimum quality standards. The count may be in units per day, and the unit of measurement may be pieces, gallons, yards, or numbers of clients. The count may be transformed into yield (good units completed divided by total units started) or variance from (amount short of) quantity scheduled.

In job production, output measurement can be costly and difficult. A parts order may be routed through multiple work centers, with output measured at each. As is shown in Exhibit 15-5, the measurement may include a unit count of clients or documents processed or parts successfully produced (not scrapped). Time of completion is also reported so priorities may be recomputed for upcoming work centers. Periodically, perhaps every two weeks, a report may summarize work moved out (after successful completion) as compared with work moved into each work center. Another report may show job-order due dates met, which measures the success for all the work centers put together. Due dates met is also a suitable output measure in simpler job operations involving perhaps only one unit and one work center. Examples are repairing a pair of shoes, papering the walls of a room, performing a lab test, and cooking a meal. Percent of completion is a suitable measure where processing time at a given work center is long (days or weeks) and the output is not readily countable. Examples are major overhauls and renovations.

Three kinds of output measures listed in Exhibit 15-5 for project operations are percent of completion, milestones completed on time, and events completed on time. Those measures are discussed in connection with project management and the PERT/CPM technique in Chapter 14.

Efficiency Compared with Cost Variance.   Labor efficiency reporting became popular in many manufacturing companies and some government and service organizations in the middle decades of this century. A bit later, some of the same organizations adopted cost-variance reporting; sometimes it replaced efficiency reporting, sometimes it was added on.

Cost variance (standard cost minus actual cost) goes two steps beyond labor efficiency.

1. Standard time, an input to the efficiency calculation, is multiplied by average wage to yield standard cost of direct labor.
2. Efficiency applies only to the labor resource; cost variance may include a labor variance, material variance, overhead variance, and price variances.

In a loose variation of the efficiency or cost-variance measure of productivity, standard time is historical. Say, for example, that a certain group of telephone ticketing agents average 3.5 minutes per transaction. But is that historical average, 3.5 minutes, representative of standard performance? Not if the agents are new and inexperienced, or seasoned and especially speedy. If agents are inexperienced, they would come out looking more efficient than they really are if efficiency is based on the 3.5 minutes standard. Still, even if imprecise, this kind of loose measure of productivity might, in some cases, point a problem solver in the right direction.

Later in the chapter, we examine differences between a real standard and a historical average; we also consider uses of time standards and measures of productivity and the precision required in developing them.

Productivity Reporting in Perspective

Reports on resource productivity tend to proliferate and get out of hand, sometimes to the point where as much is spent on reporting as on paying for the resources. For example, in a Tektronix plant producing portable oscilloscopes, a study revealed that the labor reporting (data entry, computer costs, error correction, etc.) was costing as much as the total payroll the labor reports were supposed to control! Needless to say, Tektronix canceled the labor reporting, which eliminated about 35,000 computer transactions per month.[10]

It is staff organizations, such as purchasing, human resources, and inventory control, that generate resource reports. They are input-oriented, and they exist only for serving line operations, which are output- and customer-oriented. But preservation, growth, and power instincts can conflict with the mandate to provide only the resources necessary for operations to use in serving customers. Those instincts tend to result in too much resource management and too many reports. When large organizations fall on hard times, regaining economic health may include cutting staff employees and many of their reports. The tens of thousands of jobs lost in the North American financial services industry in recent years serve as a reminder.

Thus far in this chapter, we have considered cost and noncost approaches to productivity management. Next we examine a key source of data for these approaches, namely, the time standard.

Time Standards and Their Uses

Work is simply a form of exertion. But a unit of work (such as a job, task, or project) is defined more specifically, including the time taken to perform it.

Sometimes work time is estimated in advance. For example, in a two-person operation, if person B must wait for person A to finish a job, B will want an advance estimate of how long A's job will take. A and B as an improvement team may want to time their operations as part of a process improvement project. Others may want time estimates in order to judge whether A and B can handle the work or need help (more staff). Still others may use these time estimates in preparing an estimate or bid. In addition, the existence of time estimates is likely to have motivational value—a target for A and B to shoot for.

To summarize, we have identified five purposes of time standards (time estimates): coordination and scheduling, process improvement, staffing, estimating and bidding, and motivation. In the remainder of this section, we examine these five topics.

Coordination and Scheduling

The primary use of time standards is in coordination and scheduling. Actually, by definition, a schedule is a time standard, with proper adjustments for efficiency and utiliza-

---

[10]Peter B. B. Turney and Bruce Anderson, ''Accounting for Continuous Improvement,'' *Sloan Management Review,* Winter 1989, pp. 37–47.

tion; that is, the time between the scheduled start and the scheduled finish of a task equals standard time (the time it should take under normal assumptions):

1. Adjusted downward for a fast employee or upward for a slow employee.
2. Adjusted downward for less than 100 percent labor utilization (i.e., for expected idleness).

Mathematically, scheduled output for a given time period is:

$$\text{Scheduled output} = \frac{\text{Efficiency} \times \text{Utilization}}{\text{Standard time per unit}} \qquad (15\text{--}4)$$

Or:

$$\text{Scheduled output} = \text{Standard units per time period} \\ \times \text{Efficiency} \times \text{Utilization} \qquad (15\text{--}5)$$

where (from Equation 15–1):

$$\text{Utilization} = \frac{\text{Time working}}{\text{Time available for work}}$$

A useful inversion of Equation 15–4 is:

$$\text{Scheduled time} = \frac{\text{Standard time per unit}}{\text{Efficiency} \times \text{Utilization}} \qquad (15\text{--}6)$$

As Equation 15–6 shows, as efficiency or utilization improve (denominator), scheduled time is reduced.

Where coordination demands are light, formal scheduling of work units may be unnecessary. But there is nearly always at least a vague time plan for starting and finishing an upcoming task. This plan is an implied time standard. For example, in the service sector implied time standards are at least in the back of people's minds for all work assignments. In factory work, however, a real (not implied) standard is often used, especially for repetitive production.

A second set of uses of time standards includes:

Analysis, Planning, and Motivation

- *Analysis of alternative methods and equipment.* Analysts may use time standards in estimating amount of labor required for each alternative.
- *Staffing.* Staff (labor) needed is the product of units forecast times standard time per unit. Labor budgeting goes a step further. Labor budget equals staff needed times average wage. (See Into Practice: Time Standards.)
- *Estimating and bidding.* The staff component of an estimate or bid is computed the same way as the staff budget. Accurate bidding is critical to profit and loss in the construction industry. Estimates or bids are also important in many kinds of services, such as medicine, law, consultancy, and automotive repair.
- *Motivation.* Without a deadline, people tend to put things off. A time standard acts like a deadline, helping to keep people motivated to meet the standard. A weakness of a time standard as a motivator is that it may not seem like a real need to employees. People are more likely to respond to a known, valid customer need date or quantity, which itself could be based on a time standard. The motivational value of a time standard also depends on whether people believe it is valid, which depends on the techniques used in developing the standard, our next topic.

Into Practice

Time Standards for Staffing Attorney's Offices

In one effort to set time standards on lawyers' tasks, the sole purpose was to straighten out a staffing mess. The lawyers worked in 36 program offices of the U.S. Department of the Interior, and it was hard to assign the proper number of lawyers to each office.

The department hired a consultant to help define work units and set standards. The basic work unit was a *matter* (not a case, because matters often did not result in cases). Fifty-nine varieties of matters were defined, and secretaries kept records on the time lawyers spent on each matter. The results were fairly consistent throughout the United States, and the average times served as historical (nonengineered) standards for use in staffing decisions; that is, in a given

office each matter could be forecast (by trend projection, etc.) and multiplied by standard time to yield labor-hours, which converted into staff needs.

Professional work like that of a lawyer is not only variable but often seen as something of an art and resistant to standardization. The lawyers in this example cooperated because the limited purpose, better staffing, was made clear. Probably there would have been no cooperation had the purpose been to judge efficiency or even to schedule lawyers' tasks.

SOURCE: Part of the consultant's story is told in Marvin E. Mundel, *Motion and Time Study: Improving Productivity,* 5th ed. (Englewood Cliffs, N.J.: Prentice-Hall, 1978), pp. 485–94 (T60.7.M86).

Time Standards Techniques

Exhibit 15–6 lists six ways of developing a time standard. The first four are engineered, which means rigorously developed to a high level of validity. The last two are nonengineered. In this section we consider the differences, go through the details for time study (the most prevalent technique), and briefly discuss the remaining five techniques.

Engineered and Nonengineered Standards

Four techniques may result in engineered time standards. Engineered standards are prepared at some expense following the scientific methods of the industrial engineer. The expense of an engineered time standard may be worthwhile if precision is needed, for example, in highly repetitive processes, where small gains add up fast. The following steps lead to an engineered standard:

1. Clearly specify the method.
2. Obtain time values via a proper sampling procedure or from validated tables.
3. Adjust for employee pace.
4. Include allowances for personal, rest, and delay time.

Each step adds precision. A precise time standard is associated with a known standard method (ideally an improved or engineered method). One way to get precise time values is to use direct observation and a proper sampling procedure; direct observation is avoided by use of a synthetic time value from validated tables. Where direct observation is used, the time value should be adjusted for employee pace, but validated tables for time values have built-in pace adjustments. Finally, the pace-adjusted time is further adjusted by adding reasonable allowances for employees' personal and rest time and for unavoidable delay.

Guesstimate:
Also known as WAG or SWAG, common abbreviations for slightly salty phrases some readers may be familiar with.

The nonengineered techniques, based on history or guesstimates, control for none of the above four factors of precision. (Even the first four techniques in Exhibit 15–6 are

EXHIBIT 15–6   **Techniques for Setting Time Standards**

Technique	*Source of Times*	*Timing Role of Analyst*
Engineered		
1. Time study	Stopwatch (or film)	Direct observation: Record times for several cycles of the task; judge and record pace.
2. Work sampling	Percent of study period busy at given task divided by number of units produced	Direct observation: Randomly check employee status; keep tallies of employee activities and pace; obtain production count.
3. Predetermined	Table lookup	Define task in basic body motions; look up time values in basic motion tables.
4. Standard data	Table lookup	Define task in small, common elements (e.g., pound nail); look up time value in standard-data tables.
Nonengineered		
5. Historical (statistical)	Past records on actual task times	Determine arithmetic mean and/or other useful statistics.
6. Technical estimate (guesstimate)	Experienced judgment	Experienced person estimates times, preferably after breaking task into operations.

worthy of the term *engineered* only if they are precisely developed following the four steps.) In the following discussions, we see how the steps apply for each technique.

The most direct approach to time standards is timing an employee who is performing the task. A stopwatch is the usual timing device, but motion picture film or videotape also works. **Time study** is best for shorter-cycle tasks. The cost of having an analyst at the worksite and timing a proper number of cycles of the task tends to rule out time study for longer-cycle tasks. The four time-study steps are explained next and illustrated in solved problem 3 in this chapter.

1. *Select task and define method.* There are choices to be made here. For example, packing and crating a large refrigeration unit consists of packing the unit into a carton, placing the carton on a pallet, building a wooden crate around the carton and pallet, stenciling, and steelstrapping. A single time study of the whole series of tasks is one possibility. Alternatively, analysts could separately time-study each major task, but each of those involves lesser tasks, which could be separately time studied. Pounding a single nail into a crate could be the task chosen for study.

Once the task has been chosen, the analyst defines the method and its elements. The definition must clearly specify the actions that constitute the start and the end of each element, which is how the analyst knows when to take each stopwatch reading.

2. *Cycle time.* Tools of the time-study analyst include a clipboard, a preprinted time-study data sheet, and a stopwatch. The watch is mounted on the clipboard. Before timing, the analyst observes for a while to be sure the operator is following the prescribed method.

In the timing phase, the analyst records a stopwatch reading for each element. Several cycles of the task should be timed so that effects of early or late readings can be averaged out. Multiple cycles also provide a better basis for judging pace and observing unavoidable delays and irregular activities. Comments on irregularities are entered in a remarks section on the data sheet.

The number of cycles to time could be calculated based on the statistical dispersion of individual element readings. However, most firms pay more attention to the cost of

Time Study

World War II was the heyday of film analysis. Almost anything that might help the war effort received funding.

multiple cycles than to the statistical dispersion of readings. For example, General Electric has established a table as a guide to the number of cycles.[11] The table calls for timing only 3 cycles if the cycle time is 40 minutes or more, but it calls for timing 200 cycles if the cycle time is as short as 0.1 minutes. Since 200 cycles at 0.1 minutes adds up to only 20 minutes of observer time, the 200-cycle study may cost less to do than the 3-cycle study of a 40-minute task.

The result of timing is an average **cycle time (CT),** a raw time value.

3. *Pace rating.* If the analyst times a slow person, the average cycle time will be excessive (*loose* is the term usually used); if a faster person is timed, the CT will be tight. To avoid loose or tight standards, the analyst judges the employee's pace during the study. The **pace rating** is then used mathematically to adjust CT to yield a **normal time.** This is called **leveling (normalizing).** The normal pace is 100 percent, a 125 percent pace is 25 percent faster, and so on.

Common benchmarks of normal (100 percent) pace:
• Hand motions: Deal four hands of 13 cards in 30 seconds.
• Walking, normal person, unloaded, level surface: three miles an hour.

Pace rating is the most judgmental part of setting time standards. But it need not be pure guesswork. Films are available from the American Management Association and other sources for training in pace rating. The films show a variety of factory and office tasks. The same task is shown at different speeds, and the viewer writes down the apparent pace for each speed. The projector is shut off, and the viewer's ratings are compared with an answer key. Correct answers have been decided upon by experts or measured by film speed.

Most people can become good enough at pace rating to be able to come within ± 5 percent of the correct ratings. It is easier to rate a person who is close to normal than one who is very slow or fast. Because of this, it is a good idea for the analyst to try to find a normal employee to observe in doing a time study (or work-sampling study). Sometimes pace rating is omitted by preselecting an employee who is performing at normal; the omission is illusory since the rating is done in the employee selection step.

4. *Personal, rest, and delay (PR&D).* The normalized time per unit is not the standard time. We can't expect a person to produce at that normal rate hour after hour without stopping. Personal time allowances (rest room, etc.) and rest allowances (e.g., coffee breaks) may be set by company policy or union contract. In industrial shops, the rest allowance may be for more than coffee; it may go as high as 50 percent for tasks performed in a freezer or near a furnace.

Strictly speaking, unavoidable delay, for example, difficulty in meeting tight tolerances or small variations in materials or equipment, is inherent in the method. Some companies also include certain delays that are beyond the method, such as unbalanced work flows, lack of work, or breakdowns. Unavoidable delays are sometimes determined by a work-sampling study in which occurrences of various types of delay are tallied.

The allowances are usually combined as a percentage, referred to as the **personal, rest, and delay (PR&D) allowance** (or PF&D, where *F* stands for "fatigue"). The combined allowance is then added to the normalized time, resulting in a standard time.

Work Sampling Standards

In Example 15–1 we looked at work sampling as a technique for determining labor utilization and delay rates. Work sampling for setting a time standard requires one extra piece of data: a production count, that is, a count of units produced or customers served during the study period. Cycle time (CT), then, is:

$$\text{Cycle time} = \frac{\text{Percent of time on task} \times \text{Total minutes in study period}}{\text{Production count}} \quad (15\text{–}7)$$

---

[11]Benjamin W. Niebel, *Motion and Time Study,* 9th ed. (Homewood, Ill.: Richard D. Irwin, 1993), p. 389; also see a more elaborate table from Westinghouse on the same page (T60.N54).

As in time study, the analyst transforms cycle time (CT) into standard time by normalizing for employee pace (rating factor, RF) and adding a PR&D allowance:

$$\text{Standard time} = \text{CT} \times \text{RF} \times (100 \text{ percent} + \text{PR\&D}) \qquad (15\text{--}8)$$

Solved problem 4 in this chapter shows work sampling applied to time standard determination. The problem also discusses some of the reservations that might arise in practical applications.

Predetermined time standards really are only partially predetermined. The predetermined part is the tables of time values for basic motions. The other part is properly selecting basic-motion time values in order to build a time standard for a larger task.

Predetermined Standards

Basic-motion tables were Frank Gilbreth's idea, but it took some 35 years of effort by many researchers to develop them, mostly through film analysis. The best-known tables are those of the MTM (Methods-Time Measurement) Association.[12] Our limited discussion focuses on **methods-time measurement (MTM).** MTM and other synthetic techniques have several advantages:

1. No need to time; the data are in tables.
2. No need to observe; the standard may be set before the job is ever performed and without disrupting the employee.
3. No need to rate pace; the time data in the table were normalized when the tables were created.

A disadvantage of MTM is the great amount of detail involved in building a standard from the tables. Basic MTM motions are tiny; motions are measured in *time measurement units (TMUs)*, and one TMU is only 0.0006 minutes. A 1.0-minute cycle time equals 1,667 TMUs. One MTM motion usually takes 10 to 20 TMUs; thus, about 80 to 160 basic motions would be identified in the 1.0-minute period. Although much training is required of the analyst to achieve that detail, MTM is perceived as a fair approach to time standards and is widely used.

Other predetermined time systems not requiring so much detail:
• Work-Factor.
• MODAPTS.

The MTM Association has developed tables for the following types of basic motions: reach; move; turn and apply pressure; grasp; position; release; disengage; eye travel and eye focus; body, leg, and foot motions; and simultaneous motions. Again, most times were developed by film analysis.

One of the tables, the reach table, is shown in Exhibit 15–7. From the table we see, for example, that reaching 16 inches to an ''object jumbled with other objects in a group so that search and select occur'' takes 17 TMUs. That motion, abbreviated as an *RC16* motion, takes about 0.01 minutes or less than a second.

In an MTM study, the analyst enters each motion on a simultaneous motion (SIMO) chart, which is a left-and-right-hand chart. The total TMUs on the chart are converted to minutes. The total is the rated (leveled) time, not the cycle time, because 100 percent pace is built into the tables. Add a PR&D allowance, and you have the standard time.

Standard-data standards, like predetermined (e.g., MTM) standards, are synthetically produced from tables. But standard-data tables are for larger units of work. An example is the flat-rate manuals used in the auto-repair industry.[13] Flat-rate tables list times for repair tasks such as ''replace points'' and ''change oil.''

Standard Data

---

[12]The tables were originally developed by H. B. Maynard and associates. See Harold B. Maynard. G. J. Stegemerten, and John L. Schwab, *Methods-Time Measurement* (New York: McGraw-Hill, 1948) (T60.T5M3).

[13]Auto manufacturers produce such tables for repairs on new cars. Flat-rate manuals for older cars, which take more time to repair, are available from independent companies. Best known are the Chilton manuals.

EXHIBIT 15–7   **Reach Table for MTM Analysis**

Length of Reach in Inches	Time in TMUs*				Hand in Motion (TMU)		Case and Description
	Case A	Case B	Case C or D	Case E	A	B	
¾ or less	2.0	2.0	2.0	2.0	1.6	1.6	A—Reach to object in a fixed loca-
1	2.5	2.5	3.6	2.4	2.3	2.3	tion or to object in other hand or on
2	4.0	4.0	5.9	3.8	3.5	2.7	which the other hand rests
3	5.3	5.3	7.3	5.3	4.5	3.6	
4	6.1	6.4	8.4	6.8	4.9	4.3	B—Reach to single object in loca-
5	6.5	7.8	9.4	7.4	5.3	5.0	tion that may vary slightly from
6	7.0	8.6	10.1	8.0	5.7	5.7	cycle to cycle
7	7.4	9.3	10.8	8.7	6.1	6.5	
8	7.9	10.1	11.5	9.3	6.5	7.2	C—Reach to object jumbled with
9	8.3	10.8	12.2	9.9	6.9	7.9	other objects in a group so that
10	8.7	11.5	12.9	10.5	7.3	8.6	search and select occur
12	9.6	12.9	14.2	11.8	8.1	10.1	
14	10.5	14.4	15.6	13.0	8.9	11.5	D—Reach to a very small object or
16	11.4	15.8	17.0	14.2	9.7	12.9	where accurate grasp is required
18	12.3	17.2	18.4	15.5	10.5	14.4	
20	13.1	18.6	19.8	16.7	11.3	15.8	E—Reach to indefinite position to
22	14.0	20.1	21.2	18.0	12.1	17.3	get hand in position for body bal-
24	14.9	21.5	22.5	19.2	12.9	18.8	ance, next motion, or out of way
26	15.8	22.9	23.9	20.4	13.7	20.2	
28	16.7	24.4	25.3	21.7	14.5	21.7	
30	17.5	25.8	26.7	22.9	15.3	23.2	

*One time measurement unit (TMU) represents 0.00001 hour.

SOURCE: MTM Association for Standards and Research. Copyrighted by the MTM Association for Standards and Research. No reprint permission without written consent from the MTM Association, 16-01 Broadway, Fair Lawn, New Jersey 07410.

If precise time study, word sampling, or MTM is the basis for the tables, the standard data may be considered to be engineered. It is normal for a firm to keep time standards on file, and it is just one more step to assemble standards from the files into standard-data tables. The next step is to assemble standard data for a whole trade or industry. This has been done in auto repair and other common trades, notably machining and maintenance trades.[14]

Variable working conditions and lack of common methods from firm to firm may compromise the built-in precision of standard data. Still, standard data are efficient in that they bring time standards down to the level of the planner, the supervisor, and the operator. Experts create the tables, but we all can use them.

Historical Standards and Technical Estimates

Nonengineered techniques—historical and technical estimates—are far more widely used than engineered techniques, and rightly so. Most of our work (or play) is variable, and the cost to measure it with precision is prohibitive. Still, explicit time estimates help improve management, and nonengineered techniques serve the purpose. Historical standards and technical estimates are simple to develop and need not be explained further.

---

[14]The standard-data tables come in several levels. Basic motions (e.g., MTM) are the most detailed level. Next come combinations of basic data (e.g., MTM Association's general-purpose data), such as a joint time for reach-grasp-release. Then come elemental standard data for common elements, like gauging and marking. Standard data for still larger units of work are at the level of whole tasks, such as those of auto repair mechanics or electricians.

$\mathcal{I}$nto $\mathcal{P}$ractice

Cracking the Electronic Whip

America's is a postindustrial service economy, runs the conventional wisdom, an economy wherein the product is information and work occurs in a clean, well-lighted place. It's the age of the telemarketer, the customer-service rep, and the flight reservationist—all of whom rely on computer technology to do their jobs. Abuse of workers in this new economy would seem unlikely, but it's here, with age-old cruelty. Twenty-six million employees nationwide, from telephone operators to elevator mechanics, have their work tracked electronically. For ten million of these men and women, computer-generated statistical evaluations are used to judge job performance and, it is held, to increase productivity. But the computer can't measure the physical and mental toll exacted by the stress of second-by-second surveillance.

Examples, from a supervisor's hand-written comments on a computer printout showing performance of one airline reservation agent:

- Agent is "reprimanded for taking 0.39 minutes" (about 23 seconds) "to complete her paperwork for each call."
- Agent's "percent utilization," 93.55 percent, is below this airline's 96.5 percent minimum standard. Agent must do better or will get a warning "or even unpaid suspension."
- Agent's UNM ("unmanned") time, "almost always time spent in the bathroom," adds up on the printout to 22 minutes—unacceptably high.
- Total number of calls handled, 79 for the day, is way below the airline's expectation of 150 to 200 calls a day. "Raw totals, and not customer needs, are what management is concerned with."

SOURCE: Adapted from Sharon Danann, "Cracking the Electronic Whip," *Harper's Magazine*, August 1990, pp. 58–59.

Humanity and Fairness Issues

Scientific management is a two-edged sword, one edge sharp and the other dull. The sharp edge raises productivity; the dull one leaves wounds and scars.

Employers have long sought solutions to the human problems associated with the application of methods and time standards. The most promising approaches, past and present, lie in putting variety and meaning back into the task or job. Closely related is the need to make sure that the reward system will recognize task differences and the many ways in which employees can serve their employers and customers. Those issues—tasks, jobs, customer service effects, and the reward system—are considered next.

The design of work and work systems has evolved through three phases. First was scientific management, which focuses on the task itself. Next came job design, which aims at improving the job and therefore the life of a jobholder. Today's approach, emphasized throughout this book, is on service to the next and final customer and related feelings of satisfaction by the server. A review of the three phases follows.

Tasks, Jobs, and Service to Customers

Tasks. Division of labor, performed scientifically using methods-study techniques, yields a well-engineered task. Consider the task of scraping food leavings off a stainless steel tray into a garbage can. Is that task also a job; that is, can the firm define it as a job and hire someone to do just that task over and over? The answer is yes. Such narrow tasks are sometimes treated as a whole job.

Jobs.   If all jobs were developed like the plate-scraping one, wouldn't work life be intolerable? A collection of concepts now called **job design** attempts to avoid such a fate for working people.

Best known among the job design ideas are job enlargement and job enrichment. Job enlargement dates back to the 1950s, when Thomas Watson, founder of IBM, promoted the effort out of his strong belief in providing people with meaningful work. Job enlargement means expanding the number of tasks included in a person's job, for example, cooking, serving, and scraping plates; it offers horizontal variety. Job enrichment, a later development with roots at Texas Instruments and AT&T, expands on the job enlargement idea. Enlargement means more tasks; enrichment means more meaningful, satisfying, and fulfilling tasks or responsibilities; for example, an enriched job may entail use of mental and interpersonal skills—scraping plates and teaming up with others to select new dishes, scrapers, and dishwashing equipment.

The liberating effects of enlargement/enrichment are not necessarily in conflict with the restrictions of prescribed methods and time standards. In fact, one could argue that without standards, an enlarged/enriched job might be poorly defined, exposing the employee to frustration and criticism. Existence of job standards offers a guidepath for avoiding problems, thereby offering more freedom for the associate to work on process improvements, which translate into still better job standards.

Customers, Internal and External

Enlargement and enrichment, as originally conceived, were oriented to the individual, not to the team and not to the next or final customer. The following will correct this deficiency:

- Ensure that enlargement is directed toward mastery of the jobs of fellow team members, that is, cross-training.
- Ensure that enrichment is customer-oriented. Specifically, this calls for associates to acquire the data collection, analysis, problem-solving, and teamwork skills and responsibilities required in total quality management.

*𝒫*RINCIPLE 7:

Cross-train for mastery of multiple skills.

An obstacle in the way of learning more skills is the job classification system, or work rules.

How could the Buick division of General Motors have turned itself around so dramatically, from among its sickest divisions in the mid-1980s to having car models in the Powers top-10 auto quality listing by 1990? Perhaps this had something to do with it: A cooperative agreement between Buick management and the United Auto Workers union that reduced the number of job classifications from hundreds to just three. Pay-for-skills, replacing the seniority pay system, also was part of the deal.[15] **Skill-based pay** fits with the new requirement for associates to master multiple skills. It is often palatable to the employee, union or nonunion, because the concern has shifted somewhat from job security to work-life security; each new skill mastered becomes another line on the employee's resume, should a resume be needed sometime.

Pay and Other Motivators

The concept of skill-based pay, also called pay-for-knowledge, emerged in connection with TQM and JIT: TQM calls for all employees to get involved in data collection, analysis, and improvement; assume process ownership; and take first responsibility for quality. Both TQM and just-in-time require that associates become cross-trained, able to move to where the work is, and fix things that go wrong on the spot; otherwise, there will be delays, and work will not get done just in time.

*𝒫*RINCIPLE 15:

Front-line teams: first line of attack on problems.

[15]Brian S. Moskal, "The Wizards of Buick City," *Industry Week,* May 7, 1990, pp. 22–27.

EXHIBIT 15-8   Concepts of Fair Pay

What Is Fair Pay?	*Who Subscribes to This?*
1. **Everyone paid the same.** Rationale: We are all created equal; we are all products of our environments and partners in society. Means: High minimum wage applied equally to all.	Organized labor Socialists
2. **Pay by the hour (or week, month, year).** Rationale: Though we are products of our environment, society's work must be done, and work is most easily measured in time units. Means: Have employees punch time clocks, and reprimand them for tardiness.	Supervisors (easy to figure out pay) Organized labor (employees like to "put in their time"—or their time and a half)
3. **Pay according to job content.** Rationale: It is not the person who should be paid but the position; "heavy" positions should be paid heavily, "light" positions lightly. Means: Job evaluation, using job ranking/classification, point plan, factor comparison.	Personnel managers (requires a large pay-and-classification staff) Bureaucrats (seems rational and impersonal; fits concept of rank or hierarchy)
4. **Pay according to output.** Rationale: Though we are products of our environment, society's work must be done, and work should be measured in output (not merely time on the job). Output efficiency is based on a count of actual units produced as compared to a standard. Means: Piecework, incentive pay, gain-sharing.	Industrial engineers Economists
5. **Pay according to supply and demand.** Rationale: Society's messiest jobs must be done too, and more pay for less desirable jobs is necessary to attract employees. Means: Let the labor market function (or list jobs needing to be done, and set pay according to willingness to do each job—The *Walden II* method)	Some economists (e.g., those advocating below-minimum wages for teenagers) B. F. Skinner (see his book *Walden II*)
6. **Pay for skills.** Rationale: Pay system should encourage learning so employees can take "ownership" of their processes, and can quickly fix problems. Means: Extra pay for passing tests of mastery of more skills and knowledge.	A growing number of some of the best-known companies

If associates assume all these new skills and duties, shouldn't they be paid more? Of course. It's only fair (though some companies cannot immediately afford it). This concept of fair pay (pay for skills) does not easily replace other fair-pay ideas, however. Exhibit 15–8 lists six popular views on fair pay, skill-based pay being the sixth.

Concepts of Fair Pay.   One concept of fair pay is that everyone should be paid the same; minimum-wage laws are a means of bringing that about. Pay by time worked is a second fair-pay concept, and a popular one. Pay by job content also seems fair, especially in large organizations where unequal pay for the same work would be a visible problem; evaluating job content has been a major function in larger human resources departments. A fourth concept of fair is pay based on output against standards, often called **incentive pay.** A pure incentive is simply a piece rate; for example, a berry picker's piece rate might be

$1 per bucket. But laws (such as the United States wage-and-hour laws) require that piece-rate earnings not fall below the minimum wage, based on hours worked.

Source: Reprinted with special permission of King Features Syndicate.

Another popular system is **measured daywork,** which is only nominally an incentive-pay system. In measured daywork, standard output serves as a target that trainers and supervisors help the employee attain. The employee who cannot attain it is moved to another position or advised to seek work elsewhere.

Reward and Recognition.   Pay, of course, is not the only effective motivator; it may not even be the strongest. To complete our discussion of productivity, we must note the impact of low-cost and no-cost rewards, recognition, celebration, and personal pride.

- *Suggestions.* Companies that win Baldrige or Deming quality awards generally have very high rates of employee suggestions. Until recently one suggestion per employee per year would have been impressive among Western companies. Now, a growing number of Western companies are in double digits, for example, Globe Metallurgical, winner of a 1988 Baldrige Quality Prize and a winner of a 1989 Shingo Prize. Moreover, at least one, Milliken & Co., 1989 Baldrige prize winner, has achieved the suggestion-rate level of top Japanese firms (see Exhibit 15–9), and Milliken showers praise and recognition upon everyone who contributes. While most firms pay something for even small suggestions, others bestow only praise and recognition, which has similar effects.

- *Personal, team, and group awards.* Companies are devising numerous awards to hclp sustain continuous improvement momentum: Friday afternoon pizza parties, cookouts, and keggers; a day off, with the supervisor filling in; next-to-the-door parking place; T-shirts, mugs, and plaques; theater or sports event tickets; dinner for two at a fancy restaurant; all-expense-paid trip to Hawaii; and trips for the whole team to a fine hotel to present its improvement at the annual management conference. While standard reinforcement theory does not distinguish particularly between private and public praise, today's leading companies tend toward a strong preference for making it public: wall charts, ceremonies, company and public news media, and so forth.

- *Meet the customer and supplier.* Superior companies, especially in North America, are sending their front-line employees to visit customers and suppliers, who are

Twenty-two finalist teams, pared from over 3,000 worldwide, gathered at the Marriott-O'Hare for Motorola's "Total Customer Satisfaction Team Competition." Using comedy, statistics, scatter diagrams, and fishbone charts, the teams presented their projects and top management manned the scoring tables.
Chicago Tribune, January 27, 1992

EXHIBIT 15–9   Employee Suggestion Rates for Selected Leading Companies

Company	Number of Suggestions	Number of Employees	Per Employee
Japanese*			
Tohoku Oki	734,044	881	833.2
Mazda	3,025,853	23,929	126.5
Fuji Electric	1,022,340	10,226	99.6
Matsushita	6,446,935	81,000	79.6
Canon	1,076,356	13,788	78.1
Hitachi	3,618,014	57,051	63.4
Toyota	2,648,710	55,578	47.6
Nippon Denso	1,393,745	48,849	38.5
North American			
Milliken, 1991			52.0

*Source: "The Power of Suggestions," Japan Human Relations Association, April 1988, cited in Min Basadur, "Managing Creativity: A Japanese Model," *The Executive*, May 1992, pp. 29–42.

sometimes out of state or even out of the country. Reorganization into cells has the effect of putting individuals into continuous contact with their next-process customer and prior-process supplier. Whether in the next state or at the next desk, being in contact with one's customer or supplier may offer the chance for genuine satisfaction; being denied this opportunity tends to reduce the possibilities for feeling real pride.

When the individual feels fairly paid, is justly praised in a public manner, and can personally see the impact of good work on the customer's face, the productivity loop is effectively complete.

Summary

Productivity is in a state of change, except for the basic components of measuring it: outputs compared with inputs. The traditions of productivity measurement date back to scientific management, which emerged at the turn of the century as a final phase of the Industrial Revolution. Its main ingredients are methods study, process design, and time standards.

One use of time standards is determination of standard labor cost, which when compared with actual labor cost yields labor variance. Labor variance, material variance, and total cost variance are the core of periodic accounting-based productivity measurement, which is entrenched in much of industry. A weakness has been too much emphasis on direct labor productivity; too much also on mere outputs, as opposed to meeting customers' needs.

Companies are addressing the weaknesses by moving resources into groups focused on whole products provided just in time with total quality, costing the outputs of the whole rather than the parts, putting up cause-control charts throughout the operating areas, and extensively training employees to become multiskilled problem solvers. Inasmuch as most operating costs become contained in the focused groups, complex operation-by-operation cost collection may no longer be needed.

To judge effectiveness, operations people need measures of results that are business-, customer-, and product-oriented, such as retail sales per square foot or total conversion cost per unit of output. The best ways to reduce costs are to control the causes of cost through cutting out wasteful delays and transactions, employing process controls, and motivating improvement teams by making improvement activities and results visible.

Still, good product cost information is needed in order to make good decisions, for example, on alternative processes or on make-versus-buy. Improvements in product costing are forthcoming through the use of activity-based costing techniques.

These new concepts of productivity management are still far from dominant. Traditional methods improvement and time standards are still in wide use and likely to continue to play several important roles. Current emphasis on total quality and process control breathes new life into one of the old techniques, process flowcharting, which may be done at the bench level, the operator-machine level, or the whole-process level.

Utilization rate (for equipment, labor, or other resources) is time-in-use over time available. A weakness is that this measure merely focuses on busyness, not on whether the resource is busy doing something that customers want. Work sampling studies can generate utilization data broken down by category of delay.

Labor efficiency goes beyond utilization; it gets at amount of output while working (speed), as compared with an output standard. Output measures themselves include unit counts; due dates, events, or milestones met; and percent of completion.

Time standards are necessary for coordinating and scheduling, analyzing operations, and motivating employees for improvement. Accurate time standards, for example, facilitate undercapacity labor scheduling, which allows time for important indirect work activities. Time standards also play key roles in determination of efficiency, utilization, and productivity values. They also may foster self-motivation among employees.

There are six basic techniques for setting time standards: stopwatch time study, work sampling, predetermined standards, standard-data time standards, historical standards, and technical estimates. Engineered (high-precision) standards require controls on methods, time measurement, employee pace, and allowances for personal, rest, and delay time.

Finally, care must be taken to ensure that productivity improvement does not dehumanize jobs, for this could lead to longer-term degradation of performance. Fortunately, an assortment of techniques that focus on meeting customer needs (e.g., JIT and TQM) also show promise for putting meaning back into people's work lives. For example, skill-based pay provides employees with new opportunities to develop, grow, and make themselves more valuable to present or future employers.

Key Words

Productivity 512	Cycle time (CT) 532
Cost variance 513	Pace rating 532
Activity-based costing (ABC) 518	Normal time 532
Methods study 520	Leveling (normalizing) 532
Flowcharting 520	Personal, rest, and delay (PR&D) 532
Ergonomics 521	Methods-time measurement (MTM) 533
Motion study 521	Standard data 533
Utilization 522	Job design 536
Work sampling 524	Skill-based pay 536
Standard time (time standard) 524	Incentive pay 537
Labor efficiency 524	Measured daywork 538
Time study 531	

Solved Problems

Problem 1

At Metro Gas and Electric, the productivity of each of five functional departments involved in billing (for power consumption and other sales to commercial, industrial, and residential customers) is reported monthly. The main measure in the report is cost variance, which is based on cost of billings processed as compared with standard cost. An improvement team has concluded that the variance system generally fails to lead to improved performance. What changes should they recommend?

The first step is to reengineer the five departments into a few focused cells; for example, separate cells for commercial, industrial, and residential customers—and perhaps separate cells for power usage and for other sales. That will contain most of the operating costs within each focused cell.

Other steps include posting cause-control charts in every cell, upgrading the skill levels of every employee (perhaps including pay for skills), and using activity-based costing to more accurately find the costs and track cost trends for processing bills in each cell.

Gate City Tire Company sells and installs tires, some by appointment and the rest to drop-in customers. Appointments are carefully scheduled so that (1) the customer may be told when the car will be ready and (2) installers are kept busy. The manager knows that under normal conditions a four-tire installation takes about 20 minutes. The time varies depending on the installer's speed (efficiency) and the delay (utilization) encountered. Gate City follows the concept of under-capacity scheduling: For an 8-hour paid shift, the company schedules 7.3 hours of tire installing.

During the 7.3 hours of assigned work, efficiency has been found to be 90 percent; it is low because the present crew lacks experience. Utilization, again during the 7.3 assigned hours, is 80 percent. Delays arise from tool breakdowns, parts shortages, special customer requests, and two authorized 15-minute coffee breaks; these, plus miscellaneous delays, account for the 20 percent nonutilization time.

Regardless of expected daily output, each daily job may be separately scheduled. For example, the third job of the day, a phoned appointment, is assigned to Jeff, who has been only 80 percent efficient. But the manager expects no delays for lack of materials, tool breakdowns, or other problems, and it is not near coffee-break time; thus, he expects utilization on this job to be 100 percent.

a. Calculate the current scheduled daily output.

b. What is the scheduled installation time of the third job of the day, assuming Jeff is given the job?

a. From Equation 15–5,

$$\text{Scheduled output} = \frac{7.3 \text{ hours} \times 60 \text{ minutes/hour}}{20 \text{ minutes/installation}} \times 90 \text{ percent efficiency}$$
$$\times 80 \text{ percent utilization} = 15.768, \text{ or approximately}$$
$$16 \text{ installations per day}$$

b. The scheduled installation time, from Equation 15–6 is:

$$\text{Scheduled time} = \frac{20 \text{ minutes/installation}}{80 \text{ percent} \times 100 \text{ percent}} = 25 \text{ minutes}$$

A proposed bolt-washer-nut assembly method was approved, and a time-study analyst was assigned to develop a time standard for the task. After observation, the analyst has reduced the task of four timable elements. Six cycles are timed[16] by the continuous stopwatch method, and each element is pace rated. Calculate the standard time.

The time-study data sheet is shown in Exhibit 15–10. The analyst reads the stopwatch in hundredths of a minute and does not insert decimal points until after the last computation. The stopwatch begins at zero and runs continuously for 7.55 minutes. The analyst enters continuous readings below the diagonal line, and then computes elemental times by successive subtraction.

Average cycle time (CT) is the sum of elemental times divided by 6; for element 2, CT is divided by 5 because one irregular elemental time was thrown out. The average goes below the diagonal line in the CT column. The analyst judges pace and enters pace ratings in the rating factor (RF) column, with decimal points not included. Normalized time (NT) equals CT times RF. The NT column adds up to 110, or 1.10 minutes per cycle.

---

[16]For a short-cycle task like bolt-washer-nut assembly, it would take less than an hour to time, say, 30 cycles, and this would improve reliability. The six-cycle example thus is less than ideal.

Exhibit 15–10   Time-Study Data Sheet—Bolt-Washer-Nut Assembly

Element	Cycles 1	2	3	4	5	6	CT	RF	NT	Remarks
1. Get bolts and place in fixture.	12 / 12	10 / 116	13 / 240	11 / 349	16 / 468	10 / 656	72 / 12	110	13.2	
2. Get washers and place on bolts.	14 / 26	16 / 132	15 / 255	14 / 363	93 / 561	14 / 670	73 / 14.6	100	14.6	5th cycle: Blew nose
3. Get nuts and assemble onto bolts.	75 / 101	86 / 218	77 / 332	82 / 445	79 / 640	78 / 748	477 / 79.5	95	75.5	
4. Drop assemblies down chutes.	05 / 106	09 / 227	06 / 338	07 / 452	06 / 646	07 / 755	40 / 6.7	100	6.7	

Calculations		
Total normalized time		110.0
× (PR&D allowance + 100%):		×111.25%
Standard time		122.375, or 1.22 minutes/unit

NOTE: CT is sometimes called the select time (ST); NT is sometimes called the leveled time (LT) or rated time (RT).

The analyst adds a PR&D allowance, which has been negotiated with the labor union. It provides 3 percent personal time (e.g., blow nose), two 15-minute rest (coffee) breaks, and 2 percent unavoidable delay allowance. (These are minimum allowances; the contract allows rest time to be set higher for highly fatiguing work, and the delay allowance may be set higher for tasks involving abnormal delays.)

The two 15-minute breaks convert to percentages of an 8-hour, or 480-minute, day by:

$$\frac{30 \text{ minutes}}{480 \text{ minutes}} = 0.0625, \text{ or } 6.25\%$$

$$\text{Total PR\&D allowance} = 3\% + 6.25\% + 2\%$$
$$= 11.25\%$$

In a final computation (using Equation 15–8) the analyst multiplies the total normalized time by the PR&D allowance of 11.25 percent plus 100 percent (which is mathematically the same as adding 11.25 percent of the total normalized time). The result is the standard time of 1.22 minutes per unit.

Problem 4

The director of Midtown Pathological Labs conducted a one-week work-sampling study of the lab staff. The results were that the staff was working 65 percent of the time. The director also tallied the type of work task observed. The lab performs two major types of analysis and a host of miscellaneous analyses. The director found that the 65 percent work time was divided as follows:

Serum-blood tests (standard tests) in chemistry lab	30%
Whole-blood tests (complete blood count) in hematology lab	25
Miscellaneous tests in either lab	10
Total work time	65%

There are two lab technicians in the chemistry lab and one in hematology.

At the end of the study, the director found that 48 serum tests and 32 whole-blood tests had been performed. Her estimates of operator pace are 90 percent for serum tests and 105 percent for whole-blood tests. Midtown uses a PR&D allowance of 13 percent.

With these data, calculate a time standard for both the serum test and the whole-blood test. Discuss the precision and fairness of the resulting standards and any effects on capacity planning.

Serum test: **Solution 4**

From Equation 15–7:

$$\text{Cycle time} = \frac{0.30 \times 5 \text{ days} \times 480 \text{ min./technician-day} \times 2 \text{ technicians}}{48 \text{ tests}}$$

$$= 30 \text{ minutes per test}$$

From Equation 15–8:

$$\text{Standard time} = \text{CT} \times \text{RF} \times (100 \text{ percent} + \text{PR\&D})$$
$$= 30 \times 90 \text{ percent} \times 113 \text{ percent}$$
$$= 30.51 \text{ minutes per test (per technician)}$$

Whole-blood test:

$$\text{Cycle time} = \frac{0.25 \times 5 \text{ days} \times 480 \text{ minutes/technician-day}}{32 \text{ tests}}$$

$$= 18.75 \text{ minutes}$$
$$\text{Standard time} = \text{CT} \times \text{RF} \times (100 \text{ percent} + \text{PR\&D})$$
$$= 18.75 \times 105 \text{ percent} \times 113 \text{ percent}$$
$$= 22.25 \text{ minutes per test}$$

Are these precise (engineered) time standards? The technicians in the chemistry lab don't think theirs is. They point out to the director that their method is to run the serum tests in batches and as a two-person team. There could be one or many samples in a batch, but the time to run a batch does not directly depend on the number of samples in it. The time standard for serum testing is imprecise, indeed, invalid, because the work-sampling study was not precise as to method.

The hematology technician has a milder objection: A mere 25 observations of the whole-blood testing were extrapolated into an assumed 600 minutes of testing time during the week. While the sample size seems rather small, the technician and the director decide that the standard time of 22.25 minutes per test is usable for short-term capacity adjustments. These include scheduling overtime, using part-time help, and subcontracting to other labs.

For example, on a given day, perhaps 30 blood samples will arrive and require testing in hematology. At 22.25 minutes per test, the workload is $22.25 \times 30 = 667.5$ minutes of testing. Since an 8-hour day is only 480 minutes, the director had better tell the technician to plan on some overtime that evening. Part-time help and subcontracting are other options.

For Further Reference

Books

Caruth, Donald L. *Work Measurement in Banking*. 2nd ed. Boston: Bankers Publishing, 1984 (HG1616.W6C37).

Kazarian, Edward A. *Work Analysis and Design for Hotels, Restaurants, and Institutions*. 2nd ed. Westport, Conn.: AVI Publications, 1979 (TX911.K36).

Konz, Stephan A. *Work Design: Industrial Ergonomics*. 2nd ed. Columbus, Ohio: Grid, 1983 (T60.8.K66).

Krick, Edward V. *Methods Engineering: Design and Measurement of Work Methods*. New York: John Wiley & Sons, 1962 (T56.K7).

Maynard, Harold B.; G. T. Stegemerten; and John L. Schwab. *Methods-Time Measurement*. New York: McGraw-Hill, 1948 (T60.T5M3).

Niebel, Benjamin W. *Motion and Time Study*. 9th ed. Homewood, Ill.: Richard D. Irwin, 1993 (T60.7.N54).

Salvendy, Gavriel. *Handbook of Human Factors*. New York: John Wiley & Sons, 1987.

Salvendy, Gavriel. *Handbook of Industrial Engineering*. 2d ed. New York: John Wiley & Sons, 1991.

Periodicals/Societies

Industrial Engineering (Institute of Industrial Engineering).

Journal of Systems Management (Association for Systems Management) (paperwork management and systems analysis).

Review Questions

1. What is the primary way of measuring productivity?
2. Why have some managers and accountants questioned the value of the cost-variance system?
3. What is meant by the phrase *control causes of cost?*
4. Explain the visual controls concept.
5. What operating decisions rely on product/service cost data? How can bias be avoided in arriving at those cost data?
6. In methods study, what information is included in a before-and-after comparison?
7. Which flowcharting symbols are used in each of the three types of methods study? Explain.
8. How do work sampling studies reveal deficiencies in the management system?
9. How can labor efficiency and utilization be allowed for in scheduling?
10. How can wages be based on time standards given minimum-wage laws?
11. When is a nonengineered time standard not good enough?
12. How can work-sampling data yield CT values?
13. Why isn't the CT the time standard?
14. Which of the PR&D factors are task dependent? Explain.
15. In what sense is pace rating unfair? Fair?
16. What is the difference between predetermined standards and standard data?
17. Why do employees tend to prefer synthetically set standards?
18. How can labor standards be fair if tasks are variable?
19. Is it fair to pay based on amount of work produced? Why or why not?
20. How can job enlargement/job enrichment be applied to enhance teamwork instead of being oriented to the individual?
21. How does skill-based pay help drive productivity improvement? What are some other good motivators?

Problems and Exercises

1. The president of Universal Service Corp. is concerned. His company is in serious financial trouble, even though its cost system (roughly the same system most other firms use) shows that labor costs have been going down significantly for months. How would you advise the president?
2. Name the four most important visual performance charts for control of causes in each of the following cases:
    a. A movie theater chain.
    b. A long-running play.
    c. A home-building construction company.
    d. A custom spray-painting plant.
3. Laws in many countries require division of company employees into management and labor, with different employment laws for each. For decision-making purposes, however, some companies have abolished these categories. Hewlett-Packard, for example, considers everyone overhead, with no separate category called direct labor.

    a. What is the effect of this practice on measuring labor productivity?

    b. Discuss the advantages and/or disadvantages of this practice.

4. Jim Talbot, supervisor at Florida Power and Light (first non-Japanese winner of Japan's Deming quality prize), has been quoted as saying, ''I can, literally, look at a wall and see what is going on in my department.''

    a. What does this statement suggest about the type of measures and controls in place in Talbot's department?

    b. Discuss what things should be on Mr. Talbot's walls for his visual system to be effective and complete.

5. Thumb's Tax Service has grown by 45 percent per year for the last three years, and now has 42 tax offices supported by a company headquarters of 13 people (tax specialists, computer programmers, marketers, etc.) along with a range of computer equipment. Thumb's profits, however, have been weak to nonexistent. Everyone suspects the reason is Thumb's costing, which leads to pricing in which difficult private and commercial clients pay an average of only 35 percent more than easy ones.

    a. What operating decisions at a tax service like Thumb's require good cost data? In your answer, explain what costs are needed.

    b. How can Thumb's management team resolve the costing problem?

6. At International Express Company, professionals and technicians from the industrial engineering (IE) department and the quality assurance (QA) department are engaged in a turf battle. The IE's are claiming that they are the experts in flowcharting and methods improvement and should retain that responsibility. The QA specialists are claiming they should now have the responsibility. Who is right? Explain.

7. Three key monthly reports reviewed by officers at Nanosoft Inc., a software development firm, are (1) utilization of Nanosoft's six copying machines; (2) utilization of labor, including clerical, machine operators, analysts, and programmers, based on work sampling studies covering a different office area each month; (3) utilization of books, reports, and documents in the Nanosoft library. Discuss the probable effectiveness of these reports. Should anything be changed in this reporting system? Explain.

8. The accompanying chart shows five days of actual on-the-job activities of a seamstress who sews decorator pillows together. (The quantity 10 minutes is used as the smallest time increment so that time values can be read off the chart easily.) You are to conduct a 50-observation work-sampling study, taking your observations from the chart instead of from on-site observation.

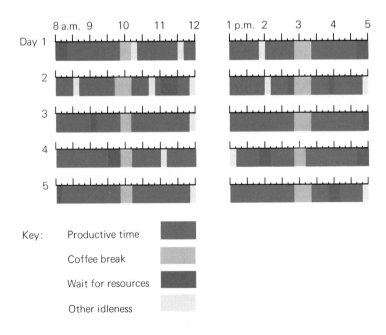

   a. As a first step in conducting the study, you will need a schedule of 50 random observation times. You will find a list of two-digit random numbers in Appendix C. Select 50 of those numbers, and devise a method of translating them into 50 clock times between 8:00 A.M. and 12:00 P.M. and between 1:00 and 5:00 P.M. for a 5-day study period. Show your 50 random numbers and 50 times.

   b. Develop a tally sheet and conduct the work-sampling study. The desired end result is percentage of time in four activity areas: productive time, coffee break, wait for resources, and other idleness.

   c. The unavoidable-delay component of the PR&D allowance is to be based on the wait-for-resources element of the work-sampling study in question *b*. The *rest* component is set at two 15-minute coffee breaks per day, and personal time is set by company policy at 5 percent. What is the total PR&D allowance?

   d. Explain the difference between the time allowed for coffee breaks and the time taken as revealed by the work-sampling data.

   e. During the five-day study period, the seamstress completed 760 pillows. You, the analyst, judged her pace during the study period. Your pace rating is 90 percent. Calculate the standard time. Express the standard in pieces per day (standard production rate).

   f. Discuss possible weaknesses or sources of bias in the work-sampling study. Is the time standard engineered?

   g. What should be the primary uses of this time standard? Explain.

   h. What, if any, steps would you take concerning quality?

   i. How would you change your results if only 720 pillows were acceptable?

9. A salesperson has an order for 1,000 candles in the shape of an athletic team's mascot. Production control assembles the following data from the candlemaking shop, to be used in setting a price (direct cost and overhead plus markup):

Cycle time	20,000 TMUs
Allowance for personal time and unavoidable delay	9%
Authorized break time	20 minutes per day

   Recent candlemaking statistics are:

Total clock hours for candlemakers	350 hours
Standard hours' worth of candles produced	380 hours

   a. What standard time should be used in computing standard cost?

   b. If there are two employees in candlemaking, how many hours should be scheduled for them to complete the order for the 1,000 special candles?

   c. Assume the candle order has been finished and took 190 hours to complete. What rate of efficiency did the crew attain?

10. The director of a social agency is preparing next year's budget. The agency's caseload averaged 42 clients per day last year, but it has been increasing at an annual rate of 15 percent. The director and caseworkers agree that it takes 3.5 hours on average to handle each client properly.

   a. How many caseworkers should be requested as the staff component of next year's budget assuming the 15 percent increase in caseload? Assume that caseworkers work an average 250 days per year (which allows for vacation days, sick days, etc.) at eight hours per workday.

   b. What kind of time standard is the agency using? Is there any way to improve this?

   c. What other reasonable uses exist for the time standard?

11. Assume your boss is supervisor of the packing and crating department and has just sent you the following memo: "The president wants all shops, including ours, covered by time standards.

I'd like you to do a preliminary study to see if reasonable time standards can be set for our type of work. Everything we pack is of a different size. So how can we have standard times?''

    a. Respond to the boss's memo.

    b. What technique for setting time standards is best for this type of work? Explain.

12. In an automobile plant, a time standards analyst finds that the average cycle time for mounting tires onto rims is 3.6 minutes. If the personal, rest, and delay allowance is 14 percent and the pace rating 105 percent, what is the standard time?

13. An MTM analyst predicts that installing a cord on a proposed new telephone set will take 4,250 TMUs.

    a. What is the standard time in minutes if the shop allows a 20 percent PR&D allowance?

    b. How can the analyst set a standard on a proposed telephone set? Doesn't the item have to actually exist? Discuss.

14. An employee in an electronics plant is using a lugging machine to attach a connector onto the end of a wire. (The machine automatically kicks the wire into a chute once the connector has been attached.) The following data are provided by a time-study analyst. Stopwatch readings are in hundredths of a minute and cumulative from element to element and cycle to cycle.

	Cycle				
Job Element	*1*	*2*	*3*	*4*	*Pace Rating*
Cut length of wire	21	48	74	103	100
Insert into lugger and press start button	30	58	86	112	90

    a. What is the standard time? Assume a personal time allowance of 5 percent, a delay allowance of 3 percent, and two 20-minute coffee breaks per eight-hour day.

    b. What would be the advantage in using methods-time-measurement (MTM) instead of stopwatch time study?

15. A work sampling study has been conducted for the job of spray-painting a set of parts. The job consists of mounting the parts on hangers, then spraying them. The PR&D allowance is 20 percent. The analyst's tally sheet is shown below:

Job: Spray painting	Time period: Five 8-hour days			
Activities Sampled	*Tallies*	*Total*	*Work Count*	*Pace Rating*
1. Mount	ᵀᴴᴸ ᵀᴴᴸ ᵀᴴᴸ ᵀᴴᴸ ᵀᴴᴸ ᵀᴴᴸ	30	20	110
2. Spray	ᵀᴴᴸ ᵀᴴᴸ ᵀᴴᴸ ᵀᴴᴸ ᵀᴴᴸ ᵀᴴᴸ ᵀᴴᴸ ᵀᴴᴸ ᵀᴴᴸ ᵀᴴᴸ	50	20	120
3. Nonwork	ᵀᴴᴸ ᵀᴴᴸ ᵀᴴᴸ ᵀᴴᴸ	20		
Total		100		

    a. What is the cycle time for each task?

    b. What is the rated time for each task?

    c. What is the standard time for each task?

    d. What is the value of the data on nonwork time? How could the data be improved to make them more useful?

16. A supervisor has done a work-sampling study of a subordinate, a clerk-typist. The purpose was to set time standards for typing letters and retrieving letters on file. Therefore, those two tasks were tallied on the work-sampling tally sheet, along with a miscellaneous category for all other clerk-typist activities. The complete tally sheet is as follows:

Subject: Typist Dates: November 29–December 10 (10 working days)		Tasks: Typing letters and retrieving letters on file Analyst: Clerical supervisor			
Activities Sampled	*Tallies*	*Total*	*Percentage*	*Work Count*	*Pace Rating*
1. Type letters	ℍℍℍℍℍℍℍℍ ℍℍℍℍℍℍℍℍ	80	40%	60	90
2. Retrieve letters	ℍℍℍℍℍℍ	30	15	150	80
3. Miscellaneous	ℍℍℍℍℍℍℍℍℍ ℍℍℍℍℍℍℍℍℍ	90	45	—	—
Totals		200	100%		

    a. PR&D allowance is 12 percent. Compute cycle time, rated time, and standard time for each task.

    b. Discuss the possible uses of these time standards.

    c. Comment on the fairness and/or validity of these time standards. Are they engineered?

17. Mailroom associates at an insurance company prepare all of the company's premiums and letters for mailing. A time study has been done on the job of enclosing premium statements in envelopes. Continuous stopwatch data are given below; the readings are in hundredths of minutes:

	Cycle							
Job Element	*1*	*2*	*3*	*4*	*5*	*6*	*7*	*Performance Rating*
Get two envelopes	11		55		105		151	105
Get and fold premium	22	41	65	83	116	135	162	115
Enclose in envelope and seal	29	48	73	97	123	143	169	95

    a. Develop a time standard and calculate standard output per 480-minute day, providing 15 percent for allowances.

    b. Assume that the premiums and letters are of various sizes and shapes. The get-and-fold element takes much longer if the item is large and requires several more folds than are needed if the item is small. Therefore, the time standard could be unfair to some of the associates it covers. Suggest some situations in which the standard would be unfair. Suggest some options for making it fair.

    c. Assume an irregular element: At every 25th envelope, an associate wraps 25 envelopes with a rubber band and places them in a box. This element was timed once, and the elemental time was 15 with a performance rating of 90. With this added factor, recompute the time standard and output from question *a*.

18. At Wabash Airways analysts have calculated that a flight attendant needs two minutes to fully serve a meal to a passenger on one of its aircraft; that is, the standard time is two attendant-minutes per meal.

    a. If two flight attendants are assigned to an aircraft with 80 passengers on board and serve all of them in a flight having one hour of serving time, what is their efficiency?

    b. If a new jumbo aircraft seats 600 passengers, how many flight attendants are needed for a flight with 100 minutes of serving time?

19. At the Transcona Plating Company, all metal-plating jobs are covered by time standards. Last week the company did 850 standard hours' worth of plating jobs. Total clock time for production employees was 1,000 hours that week, and their actual hours of direct labor (hours allocated to actual plating jobs) was 800.

    a. What is the efficiency rate?

    b. What is the utilization rate?

20. Following is a list of tasks on which time standards/estimates may be set. Suggest a suitable technique or techniques for setting a time standard for each task, and explain your choice.
   Mowing grass.
   Soldering connections in small electronic components.
   Drafting (design drawing).
   Typing and filing.
   Overhauling or adjusting carburetors.
   Cooking in fast-food restaurant.
   Computer programming.
   Installing auto bumpers on car assembly line.

21. "Equal pay for equal work" was the hot pay issue in an earlier era. Next came "Equal pay for comparable work." With which concept(s) of fair pay (from Exhibit 15–8) does the comparable-work idea seem most consistent? Explain.

CASE STUDY

LAND AND SKY WATERBED COMPANY

Land and Sky Waterbed Company of Lincoln, Nebraska, was the fourth largest waterbed company in the United States and the largest in the Midwest. Land and Sky (L&S) was founded in 1972 by two brothers, Ron and Lynn Larson. They remain as co-owner/managers. One of the brothers is responsible for research and development. (Outside R&D consultants are called on for assistance sometimes.)

The total work force, including office staff, is 67. The oldest employee is the vice president, Jim Wood, a psychology graduate in his mid-30s. Wood has played a major role in developing the scheduling, inventory, quality, and employee payment system at L&S.

The Product Line

L&S produces two lines of waterbed mattresses and liners in standard sizes (king, queen, double, super single, and twin). L&S also manufactures special made-to-order mattresses for other frame manufacturers. The Land and Sky label goes on the higher-quality gold and bronze bed sold exclusively to franchised dealers. L&S produces another brand called the Daymaker. It is sold without advertising as a commodity product. The Daymaker is available to any dealer.

A trade group for the waterbed industry has not yet achieved consensus on standard dimensions for king size, queen size, and so forth, for the soft-sided foam frame. Therefore, the L&S product line includes more than 60 sizes, built to order. Also, some customers make beds to their own dimensions before checking to see what mattress size they can readily obtain. L&S will accept special orders for such unusual sizes, but the price will be high and the order will take 30 days to be filled.

Case topics:
Self-discovery of JIT.
Make-to order JIT.
Off-line subassembly.
Pay for knowledge/multifunctional employees.
Pay incentive for quality.
Frequency of deliveries from key suppliers.
Evolving from a small to a large business.

SOURCE: Adapted from the *World Class Manufacturing Casebook: Implementing JIT and TQC*. Copyright © 1987 by Richard J. Schonberger. Reproduced by permission of The Free Press, a Division of Macmillan, Inc.

L&S also makes two kinds of soft-sided frames, which make a waterbed look like a conventional bed with box spring and ordinary mattress (''a waterbed that appeals to older people,'' according to Jim Wood). One kind is made of rigid foam and is cheap and easy to make. The other kind, L&S's own unique design, has a plastic rim built in and is called Naturalizer 2000; the rim keeps the foam from breaking down.

Competitive Climate

Since waterbed manufacturing is not highly technical and is quite labor-intensive, competitors spring up all over. Low-wage countries like Taiwan are becoming tough competitors.

L&S markets its product line throughout the United States and Canada. An Australian producer makes to L&S's specifications under a licensing agreement. (Jim Wood now wishes that L&S had set up its own Australian subsidiary, rather than licensing the Australian manufacturer.) The European market for waterbeds is still too small to bother with.

There are two main market outlets. The older outlet is the small waterbed retailer, many of whom tend to be less experienced in the ways of the business world and therefore unstable. Later waterbeds became popular enough for a second major market outlet to emerge: old-line furniture stores. The two market types place very different demands on the waterbed manufacturer. The small waterbed retailer wants instant delivery response.

L&S has developed a quick-response production system aimed at filling these orders faster than the competition. Most orders can be shipped within 48 hours, and same-day production and shipment is possible (but not cost-effective). Some inventory of finished waterbeds is kept in bonded public warehouses in different regions of the country, which further speeds up order filling in those regions.

One complicating factor is that a few retailers are unsophisticated in their ordering. For example, one retailer phoned in a large order specifying the quantity but not which models he wanted. When asked which models, he said, ''Just send about what I have ordered before.'' That was not of much help because prior orders had come in at different times for different models.

The old-line furniture stores order more conventionally. They plan orders carefully in advance and do not expect delivery right away, but do drive a hard bargain on price. In response to that price-conscious market, L&S has instituted procedures that tightly control material storage costs, labor costs, and costs of scrap and defects.

The Plant

L&S is in an industrial park, housed in three noncustom metal buildings arranged in a U-shaped configuration. Building 1, at one leg of the U, houses the sales and administrative offices with a shipping and receiving warehouse in the back. Building 2, forming the bottom of the U, is the main manufacturing and quality-check area. Building 3, the other leg of the U, is for fiber baffle production and assembly, liner production, and injection-molding and assembly of soft-sided frames. A parking lot in the center of the U is also used for vinyl storage.

Assembly

Producing the Waterbed.   *Vinyl processes.* The waterbed begins as a roll of vinyl. At first operation, an associate cuts it to size by hand. (A $20,000 cutting machine had been used, but it broke down often. It yielded too much scrap.) The next steps are to install valves and corner seam panels using special machines. Then the vinyl sheets go to machines that fuse the corners together by high-frequency radio waves. Last, the ends and sides are sealed (see Exhibit S15–1).

Baffle installation. High-quality waterbeds contain a fiber baffle that keeps the water from making waves when in use. Research and development at L&S has come up with a baffle made of polyurethane fiber that reduces the wave time from 25 to 3 seconds. L&S considers fusing of the side and end seams on the mattress especially important, and the best operators are assigned that operation. One outside observer watching the job estimated that the two operators were working at about 140 percent of normal pace.

EXHIBIT S15-1   **Sealing Ends and Sides**

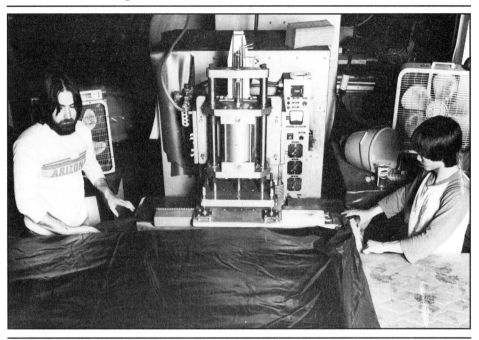

Responsiveness.   Total throughout time for these steps in making the waterbed is 35 minutes. The daily output is about 450 waterbed units.

One way that L&S holds down production lead time is by performing early stages of manufacture (such as cutting the vinyl, installing valves, and fusing corners) before knowing exactly what the model mix is. Later the same day, late-arriving orders are totaled by product type, and final model-mix instructions go out to the shop floor. Some of the options that are determined at the last minute are (1) the number that are to be top-of-the-line beds with fiber baffles and (2) the number that are to have the L&S label or the Daymaker commodity label.

> *Question 1.* In what sense do the assembly operations sound like just-in-time production? (No one at L&S had ever heard of JIT at the time of the case.) What JIT improvements do you suggest for assembly?

Subassemblies and Accessories

Baffles (a subassembly) and frames and liners (accessories) are scheduled so as to avoid stockouts. The items are made as follows:

> *Fiber baffles.* Baffles are machine-cut on the cutting machine originally bought for $20,000 to cut vinyl. Then holes are drilled around the edges of a stack of fiber sheets, and vinyl ties are threaded through the holes to hold the stack together for storage and transport (the idea for vinyl ties was developed after glue and plastic hooks failed).
>
> *Soft-sided frames.* Frames are injection-molded and assembled. L&S has patented a plastic rim insert, for which it spent $250,000 on research and development; the insert lends support and adds life to the foam in the frame.
>
> *Cardboard-reinforced bottom liner.* The bottom liners were developed by L&S to make it faster and easier for the customer to set up the waterbed (it cuts setup time by about 20 percent). The liners have been on the market for about seven months. Retailers love this feature because the liner is reusable, a good sales point. The bottom liners sell for $16 to $20 at retail.

Question 2. What could be done about subassembly and accessories manufacture to mold them into more of a JIT relationship with their customers (assembly and final pack and ship)?

Pay System

In July 1982, L&S converted from a straight hourly pay plan to a piece-rate system having the following features:

Base piece rate. The base piece rate depends on the assigned job (e.g., $0.20 per bed).

Achievement raise. An operator gets a 5 percent bonus on top of a base rate for each additional machine that the operator learns to run. A few operators have learned to run 10 or 12 machines and therefore get 50–60 percent more than the base piece rate. The bonus buys flexibility for the company. Typically an operator who can run just 2 or 3 machines averages $5–$7 per hour, while one who can run 12 machines might earn $9–$11 per hour. Jim Wood stated that other companies send people home when a machine is down; here ''we put them on another machine.''

Quality bonus. Operators get a bonus of 25 percent of total pay per period for zero errors. The bonus decreases for each error found: one or two errors, 20 percent; three errors, 15 percent; four errors, 10 percent; five errors, 5 percent, and six or more errors, 0 percent. The owners were initially dubious about the 25 percent bonus (Jim Wood's idea). Previously the bonus was 15 percent. Their feeling was, ''Why pay a large bonus for what the employees are supposed to do anyway?'' But they agreed to give the plan a try and were very pleased with the results. The error rate had been about 5 percent (5 out of 100 beds). It was down to about 0.5 percent by October. Some of the better operators were achieving zero error rates.

Error penalty. The operator has to pay a penalty of $0.65 for every error discovered by quality control inspectors. Errors are easily traced back to the operator responsible, because each operator has an employee number that is attached to the bed when the operator is working on it. If the operator notifies quality control of an error by marking it, then the penalty is only $0.25. Plans are in motion to make the penalty zero for an admitted error; that way there will be no temptation to try to sneak one by the inspector. Inspection is much more efficient and valid when operators mark their own errors.

Quality control (QC) does the bookkeeping for the entire piece-rate and quality incentive system. QC people record daily production and quality performance data for each employee. All information is maintained on the computer.

Labor Policies

Waterbeds are a somewhat seasonal product, which makes staffing difficult. The peak seasons are March-April-May and August-September-October. L&S will not build inventory just to keep operators busy. Competition from other waterbed manufacturers is fierce, especially the Taiwanese manufacturers of liners. A low-inventory policy is a competitive necessity. Therefore, in the slack season operators are laid off. Layoffs are strictly by productivity, not seniority.

Since bed materials are too large for one person to handle easily, operators usually work in pairs; pairings are generally by comparable skill levels. If one operator is tardy or absent, the partner must keep busy on lower-pay work and forgo the chance for piece-rate bonuses—a sacrifice that the operator is sure to complain about. Therefore, policies on absenteeism and tardiness are rigid: Absenteeism usually means automatic termination.

Question 3. In what ways does the pay and labor system stand in the way of, or further, quicker response?

Quality Control and Warranties

Quality control visually inspects each bed. Inspectors check surfaces for blemishes, check seams, check valves, and so forth. Once in a while the inspector will blow up a bed with air like a balloon in a more thorough leak check. Water is not used to test beds, because it leaves a residual odor.

If no blemishes or defects are found, L&S ships the bed to the retailer with a five-year warranty. Beds with a flaw are sold as blems at a lower cost with a three-year warranty.

Question 4. Critique the L&S approach to quality control.

Purchasing and Inventory Control

In the waterbed business, material costs are a good deal higher than payroll costs. Thus, materials are tightly controlled.

There are few manufacturers of vinyl, a key raw material, and vinyl suppliers require a 30-day lead time. Vinyl suppliers ship to L&S by a regular purchase-order schedule, and any schedule changes require about 30 to 60 days' advance notice. Therefore, demand forecasting is important for L&S. One of the owners does the forecasting, which is based on seasonal factors and past sales.

Other materials are reordered by a visual reorder-point method. When stock looks low based on the projected manufacturing schedule, an order is placed. The safety stock is typically about two and a half days' supply.

Average raw material inventory is typically two to three weeks' worth. In other words, inventory turns 20 times a year or more. That is partly a matter of necessity. Fiber must be stored indoors, but since it is bulky and there simply is not space to store more, it is maintained at a two-and-a-half-day inventory level. Fiber orders are delivered twice a week in semitrailer loads of 8,000 pounds.

The main purchased material is vinyl in large rolls. Since vinyl is waterproof and may be stored cheaply outdoors, L&S orders larger lots of vinyl than it does for other materials. Vinyl is received about three times a month, 40,000 pounds at a time.

Purchasing and traffic (shipping) are under the management of a single individual, Mr. Bergman. He buys from at least two sources, which provides protection in case one supplier should shut down, a serious matter, since L&S's inventories are kept so low. On occasion, purchased parts have been delayed to the point where vinyl rolls are gone; then the operators do what they can with scrap materials, after which they perform other duties or shut down and go home.

Finished goods are stored in the warehouse for a short time prior to loading onto an outbound truck.

A complete physical inventory of finished goods and raw materials is taken every four weeks.

Question 5. What are some ways to improve purchasing procedures?

Question 6. How can L&S protect itself from the miseries that plague most Western companies as they grow large?

16   MAINTAINING QUALITY OF PHYSICAL RESOURCES

Chapter Outline

Suppose one of the following occurs at your computer terminal at work:

- As you are working, your screen suddenly goes blank. When you call the control center you are told, "Sorry, the system failed again. We're fixing it now."
- As you log on one morning, a message warns you that the system will be shut down for a specified time period that day for periodic maintenance. This happens four or five times a month, seemingly at random and for varying lengths of downtime.
- During log-on, the system maintenance downtime schedule for the next several months is displayed, showing short downtime periods that occur on the same date and at the same time each month.

The three events describe different levels of performance and thus quality of service to customers. Quality is worst in the first example, and it improves as we move from one to another. In the third example, except for a short downtime maintenance period that occurs regularly and predictably, the network should be ready whenever you need to use it.

In Chapter 4, we learned that process performance depends on how well the process has been designed, built or installed, operated, and maintained. Here, we examine maintenance, whose goal is to keep operating resources in good working order and ready for use when needed. Part of meeting that goal is prevention: Stop trouble before it happens. Thus, a broad-based program of total preventive maintenance is essential.

Total Preventive Maintenance

Perhaps the classic image of a preventive maintenance reminder is the TV-commercial automobile mechanic who warns us to change our oil and oil filter regularly. By so doing, the ad implies, we will prevent engine damage and thus avoid costly repairs. A real mechanic would support the preventive benefits of regular oil changes, but would also remind us that we will need to replace tires and other worn parts and perhaps even to overhaul key components like the transmission if we wish to avoid breakdowns. Thus, the mechanic has summarized the three goals of **total preventive maintenance (TPM):**

Total productive maintenance is the term often used in manufacturing; we use total preventive maintenance, which is more type-of-business neutral.

- Regular preventive maintenance.
- Periodic replacement or overhauls.
- Intolerance for breakdowns.

As automobile owners or users, we are asked to buy in to the philosophy of TPM: Commit a little time and money for regular oil changes and less-frequent, but necessary, overhauls in order to prevent having to spend even greater amounts of time and money to repair a breakdown. By giving up a little, we gain a lot: a resource that remains in a high state of readiness.

Equipment that is ready for use when needed prevents many problems. When you're leaving the office to serve an important customer, for example, you have no time for a car that won't start. Too often, organizations act as though they fail to see the connection between effective maintenance and readiness.

Quality through Readiness

As the quality movement spread during the late 1980s and early 1990s, many industrial companies found themselves unable to remain competitive due to unreliable production equipment. Short on glamour and visibility, maintenance had often been first on the budget-cutter's list. Years of neglect had taken its toll: Bent shafts, broken-off adjustment cranks and knobs, stripped threads, worn bearings and seals, grime- and chip-clogged gears, and machine surfaces pocked from a thousand hammer blows made equipment incapable of meeting increasingly exacting customer requirements.

In offices (where human services rather than machine-intensive operations predominate), equipment maintenance may be less of a problem, but the need for readiness is just as intense. Consider how often customers wait for a service provider to find the proper form, or a pen, pencil, stapler, or other tool. Inability to find a needed resource due to a cluttered or poorly organized workplace is an obvious sign of poor maintenance. So too are scattered piles of repair parts and their identifying forms, broken fixtures, dirty equipment or work areas, and sloppy personal appearances. More subtly, overflowing in-baskets and disorganized files (even if hidden in cabinets, desks, or on computer disks) reflect poor maintenance too. Unavailable or improperly trained human resources can also be delay-causing culprits. In short, if it impedes timely and responsive high-quality customer service, it is a target for better maintenance.

Search time is delay time, which lengthens response time to the customer.

Thus, resource readiness is an overall indicator of the quality of a maintenance program. Next we consider measures reflecting the benefits of that readiness.

The payoff from a sound investment in maintenance (training as well as money) is often not immediately obvious; results might show up much later or appear elsewhere in the organization. Successful TPM results in faster and more dependable throughput times, higher productivity, improved quality of outputs, lower scheduling and control costs, increased health and safety, and lower operating costs (see Exhibit 16–1). Clearly, these

Maintenance Success Indicators

EXHIBIT 16–1   The Maintenance Payoff—General Indicators

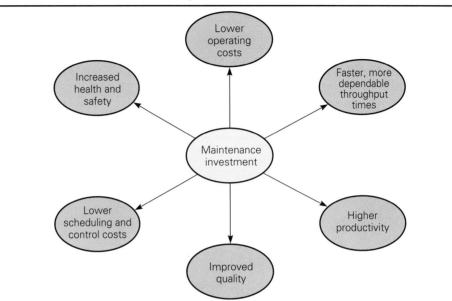

general-level payoffs should be viewed as team victories inasmuch as they stem from the efforts of people across the organization.

More specific indicators reveal that successful maintenance begins long before the wrench, mop, voltmeter, or dustcloth is applied. It begins in product and process planning and design. As Chapter 3 noted, the design teams are challenged to develop products and processes that are easier to build *and maintain*. As more people recognize the maintenance-quality connection, maintenance-oriented input on design teams increases, and maintenance parameters become important design goals in themselves. A few of these parameters are discussed below.

- **Maintainability** concerns the ease with which maintenance can be accomplished. It may reflect modular or standardized design, availability of repair parts or services, special skill requirements, and any of several popular quantitative indexes such as mean time between failures (*MTBF*) and mean time to repair (*MTTR*).
- **Mean time between failures (MTBF)** is the average time between failures of a repairable item, or the average time to the first failure of a nonrepairable item. MTBF is usually denoted by the Greek letter *mu (μ)*.
- **Mean time to repair (MTTR)** is the average time required to repair (or replace) assuming that appropriate parts and sufficient knowledge are available.
- **Availability** is the proportion of time a resource is ready for use. One version of availability (*A*) considers only designated operating time (excluding planned downtime for preventive maintenance, overhauls, etc.) and combines MTBF and MTTR:

$$A = \frac{MTBF}{MTBF + MTTR} \qquad (16\text{–}1)$$

- **Failure rate,** denoted by the Greek letter *lambda (λ)*, is the inverse of MTBF. That is, $\lambda = 1/\mu$.

- **Reliability** is the probability that an item will work over a given time period. Reliability (R) is calculated as follows:

$$R = e^{-\lambda t} \qquad (16\text{--}2)$$

where

R = Reliability, a value from 0 to 1.0
e = the base of natural logarithms (approximately 2.718)
λ = a constant failure rate
t = specified point in time

Examples 16–1 and 16–2 illustrate how these measures are used by teams to continuously improve customer service.

EXAMPLE 16–1   Ensuring Resource Availability

A redesign team is planning modifications to a line of its high-speed office photocopiers. A major customer's representative is on the team and has requested that every effort be made to provide an availability rating of at least 0.96. The historical MTBF for that line of photocopiers is 50 hours and the MTTR is 3 hours. What options might the team consider?

Solution:

Initial availability calculations reveal the magnitude of the problem. From equation 16–1:

$$A = \frac{50}{50 + 3} = 0.94$$

The customer has requested a higher availability than currently exists, so that problem must be addressed. Team members suggest two approaches: First, the team might try to achieve a higher MTBF rating by designing out failure-prone components. Suppose one design alternative could result in an MTBF of 60 hours. Application of Equation 16–1 reveals:

$$A = \frac{60}{60 + 3} = 0.95$$

Improvement is evident but more is needed. An alternative approach, suggested by team members who have operated and maintained the photocopiers, focuses on increased parts standardization and easier compartment access; their aim is a shorter repair time. Their estimates show a realistic value of two hours for MTTR. That, in turn, results in an availability rating of 50/52, or 0.96, the figure specified by the customer. Of course, the team ought to implement both changes, improving availability even more.

EXAMPLE 16–2   Battery Reliability

Woodlake Communication Services rents portable radios for use at outdoor events like cross-country runs and bike-a-thons. The standard radio batteries have a MTBF of 10 hours; failure occurs when battery charge is insufficient for effective communication. Organizers of an upcoming marathon have asked Woodlake personnel if their radios would last through the marathon that is expected to last 3 hours. How should Woodlake employees respond? Suppose Woodlake people can obtain an alternate (heavy duty) battery with an MTBF of 20 hours; how would its reliability compare with that of the standard battery? What other ideas might Woodlake employees suggest to these customers?

Solution:

First, Woodlake employees would want to determine the reliability of the standard battery. They would invert the MTBF to obtain λ, the constant failure rate:

$$\lambda = 1/MTBF = 1/10 = 0.1 \text{ failure per hour}$$

Then, from Equation 16–2, reliability is:

$$R = e^{-(0.1 \text{ failure/hr.})(3 \text{ hours})} = e^{-0.3} = 0.74$$

So Woodlake people could tell the marathon organizers that there is a 74 percent chance that any radio would last through the marathon. However, they should be careful to present that figure as an average; some batteries will last longer, some not as long.

To compare the alternate battery with the standard one, Woodlake associates could construct a simple graph of the two batteries' reliabilities. First, a brief table showing reliabilities at selected times might be prepared using Equation 16–2:

			Reliability Values			
Time (Hours)	1	2	3	4	5	6
Standard battery (MTBF = 10 hours)	0.90	0.82	0.74	0.67	0.61	0.55
Alternate battery (MTBF = 20 hours)	0.95	0.90	0.86	0.82	0.78	0.74

Exhibit 16–2A shows the reliability graphs for the two batteries as plotted using the data in the table. The time could be extended, of course, but the general downward progression shape would continue. Woodlake employees might suggest that if the customer is willing to rent extra batteries and change them at regular periods, say, every hour, radio reliability during the marathon will be approximately as shown in Exhibit 16–2B, assuming standard batteries are used.

Examples 16–1 and 16–2 introduce some key concepts about total preventive maintenance that we will develop further:

1. Maintenance success depends on other activities such as design. Design teams that recognize the operations impact of designed-in maintainability, availability, and reliability incorporate these and related parameters as goals for improvement, often acting on signals from customers included on those teams. (The La Victoria Foods example, page 560, illustrates.)

2. People who have operated and maintained equipment ought to be included on planning-and-design teams.

3. Customers, by learning to perform maintenance themselves, can affect the performance of their resources. Of course, for this to be possible, designers must consider owner- or operator-centered maintenance during the design phase (item 1).

Implementation of these TPM concepts depends on having people trained in proven methods and organized in ways that promote good maintenance habits. In the remainder of the chapter, we consider these related requirements.

EXHIBIT 16–2   **Battery Reliability Curves**

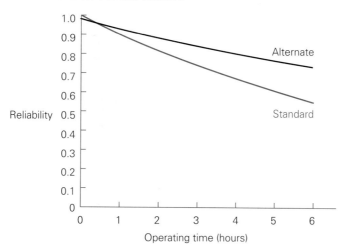

A. Standard versus alternate batteries

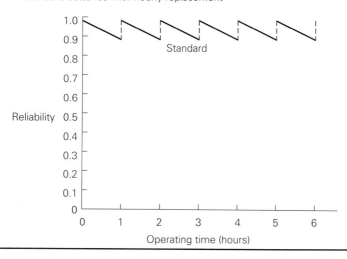

B. Standard batteries with hourly replacement

Maintenance Organization: People and Procedures

The centerpiece of total preventive maintenance is operator ownership backed up by special maintenance expertise to handle nonroutine problems. The wisdom of this approach becomes apparent as we consider traditional types of maintenance-related procedures in the following sections.

We classify maintenance operations into two general categories:

Types of
Maintenance

- *Periodic maintenance.* Periodic maintenance occurs at some regular interval (e.g., custodial activities are often performed daily). Of course, periodic maintenance

Into Practice

Maintainability at La Victoria Foods

"KISS—Keep It Simple Son—that is what I tell myself," grins Wes Guthrie, purchasing expediter at La Victoria Foods. The company's single plant, in Industry, California, produces salsas, jalapeños, nachos, and tomatillo entero.

"The simpler it is in a food plant, the better efficiency you have because there is less to break down. . . . When the chilis are here and when the tomatoes are here, we have to run. We cannot have breakdowns—none of this produce keeps."

Maintenance superintendent Andy Zamberlin notes that when he came to La Victoria 13 years before, the place was a nightmare. It had "too much complicated machinery such as stop/starts [switches], electric motors, and electric eyes that just did not run right." Some component was always breaking down and it often took hours to determine what had broken.

Zamberlin and his staff eliminated much of the assorted conventional electromechanical controls. Today, "almost all of La Victoria's equipment is run by PLC's [program-

mable logic controllers]. Several PLCs control the batching process. Some control the steam process, which is the 'breaking' or peeling of the tomatoes. Others control the fillers themselves. . . . These are programmed so that the drive motors are in step with the capping machines so they do not speed one up and slow one down." There are few parts on the food-processing equipment to break, and when a fault does occur, computers quickly identify the program.

But, as Guthrie points out, this kind of process control requires a good deal of human involvement. "We've got tomatoes of different sizes and textures. They might be mushy, they might be hard, they might not peel. . . . There are so many variables." He adds, "These PLCs have to be user-controllable. You program parameters, but the operator has to be able to control it."

Source: Adapted from Blake Svenson, "Keeping It Simple to Reduce Spoiled Efficiency in the Food Industry," *Industrial Engineering*, June 1992, pp. 29–32.

Periodic maintenance: Discretionary regular-interval maintenance aimed at forestalling breakdowns and ensuing work stoppages; sometimes is *preventive* periodic maintenance.

Irregular maintenance: Maintenance necessary because of a breakdown or a facility alteration.

forms the core of a preventive maintenance (PM) program. There are three popular versions of PM:

1. PM based on calendar or clock time—maintenance at regular intervals. An example is the hourly change of a filter on a clean-room's air conditioning unit.

2. PM based on time of usage, perhaps based on number of cycles. For example, change the cartridge in a laser printer after every 4,000 pages of print. This is often called **predictive maintenance;** the idea is to do maintenance before the predicted time of failure.

3. PM based on regular inspection. A maintenance requirement may be revealed by planned (perhaps daily or weekly) inspections. The U.S. Air Force refers to this as IRAN (*i*nspect and *r*epair *a*s *n*ecessary) maintenance.

- *Irregular maintenance.* This includes repairs, overhauls, irregular custodial work (e.g., cleaning up spills), irregular PM (e.g., prefailure replacement of components based on control chart deviations, tests, unusual equipment noises, etc.), installation and relocation of equipment, and minor construction.

Maintenance work has traditionally been assigned to associates housed in a central maintenance department, perhaps called plant or facilities maintenance, or (as in many hospitals) in a unit within the facilities engineering group. Typical types of maintenance associates include:

- *Millwrights*. These are skilled people who move and install equipment (e.g., in a mill), an irregular, hard-to-manage maintenance activity.
- *Repair technicians*. These are skilled, well-paid troubleshooters who have sharp diagnostic skills. Since they specialize in fixing problems, appropriate staffing levels are hard to predict.
- *Custodians*. Typically, these people are charged with housekeeping and perhaps minor repairs, light painting, and so forth. Staffing without costly idleness is fairly easy.
- *Preventive maintenance associates*. This category is hardest to define, for in addition to associates regularly scheduled for PM duties (perhaps on a special maintenance shift), available millwrights and repair personnel also perform PM duties, though typically at higher labor costs. The traditional idea was that skilled operators should not have to bother with chores like lubrication, nor should they be trained to clean equipment, change a filter or V-belt, and so forth. Let maintenance people do it.

Now that we have a basic grasp of what maintenance is supposed to do, we can consider how this might better be accomplished. Effective maintenance management focuses on:

1. Achieving the right mix of periodic and irregular maintenance. The last sections of this chapter, on group replacement and standby equipment, include ways to study that mix.
2. Improving planning, scheduling, and staffing of irregular maintenance, and improving the effectiveness of periodic maintenance.

Flexibility, regularity, and simplification—possible when maintenance becomes a front-line operator's responsibility—help to meet these ends.

The phrase *operator ownership* refers to the operators' believing that equipment condition is their responsibility and that maintenance, engineering, and outside service representatives are backups. This parallels the shift in responsibility for quality from quality professionals to front-line associates. TPM and TQM are cut from the same cloth. Exhibit 16–3 shows one manner of dispersing the maintenance function. As earlier chapters have noted, in the product- or customer-focused organization associates not only perform value-adding transformations, but they are also cross-trained to perform some of their own operations support. Maintenance specialists and other experts are often assigned to the group to provide on-the-spot training and technical support (see Exhibit 16–3).

The case for operator-centered maintenance is multifaceted. Front-line associates learn their equipment better, gain fuller control over their own processes, and take greater pride in their workplace when they assume cleanup tasks and responsibility for minor repairs. Repair time is also cut since there is less waiting around for someone from the maintenance shop to come and change a belt, for instance. Furthermore, the trend towards multiple, smaller, more mobile machines makes front-line associates less dependent on millwright availability; they can perform much of the relocation and installation themselves. Another approach is process fail-safing in which an operator who faces the same problem day after day will seek fail-safe ways to prevent that problem. Finally, work force scheduling is easier because maintenance can often be performed at times when scheduled work has been completed early; this is true, at least under JIT, which calls for associates to perform maintenance and other improvements rather than overproducing.

The backup role, however, is still important. While well-trained operators become the first line of defense against breakdowns, special expertise is needed to handle

Operators, Teams, and Functions

𝒫RINCIPLE 7:

Cross-train for mastery of multiple skills.

𝒫RINCIPLE 9:

Look for flexible, movable equipment.

Exhibit 16–3   Modern Maintenance Organization

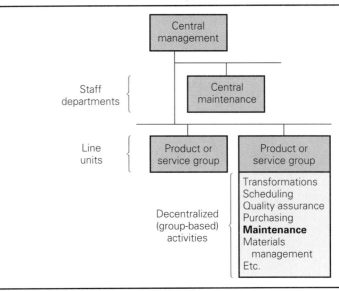

nonroutine trouble or direct focused maintenance-related training and other projects. That expertise might come from a central maintenance department or, especially in more recent years, from cross-functional teams dispersed throughout the organization.

Shifting primary maintenance responsibility to front-line associates doesn't put the maintenance department out of business; in fact, its responsibilities can become more focused and better defined. In addition to providing training and auditing of the TPM program, the maintenance department typically has plantwide responsibilities for buildings and grounds, utilities, environmental control, health and safety, facility design and improvement, and overall facility economics.

Increasingly, cross-functional teams trained to use a process approach are also contributing to better maintenance programs. Sometimes these teams begin as a quality circle and evolve, through team selection of projects, into a team focused on maintenance (one of the seven *M*s) improvements. Such a team at Action Technology, a Clinton, Illinois, division of Dart & Kraft Industries, decided to make safety concerns its prime target. The

*C*ontrast

Maintenance Responsibilities

Traditional Approach

- Maintenance is a functional support activity; operators rely on specialists (typically) in the central maintenance department for provision of custodial services, preventive and repair maintenance, and millwright work.

Operator Ownership/TPM Approach

- Front-line operators have first-level responsibility for maintenance in their workplaces.
- Specialists from a maintenance department or on cross-functional teams have back-up responsibility to handle especially difficult or unusual cases.

$\mathcal{I}$nto $\mathcal{P}$ractice

Maintenance Team with a Mission

Continual improvement, exceeding expectations, trouble-free operation, partnerships, long-term success: People at the Bayport Works, Texas, plant of Hoechst Celanese Corporation receive their motivation from those key business values and quality concepts. Preventive and predictive maintenance are acknowledged as top priorities, and a dedicated team of 14 has the primary mission of increasing equipment uptime.

The group is called the Bayport Works Reliability Team and was formed in 1989 "to identify and resolve root causes of problems that breed equipment downtime." Teamwork includes reliance on relationships with key suppliers. Commenting on a recent solution to excessive downtime with a gearbox, team leader Dave Gatling said: "We got the bear-

ings expertise from SKF, and we also called people in from Flender, the gearbox manufacturer, and from Mobil, which supplies our machine oil. You have to have total involvement if you're really going to get at all the aspects of a problem's root cause."

The team achieved its goal of a 25 percent increase in reliability in one plant, but has continued to improve machine operations throughout the facility. According to mechanical specialist Shawn Vail, "We've tackled a whole group of projects, and resolved problems that were costing up to $300,000 a year in maintenance costs and lost production."

SOURCE: Adapted from "Vibration Monitoring Increases Equipment Uptime," *Maintenance Technology,* July 1992, pp. 37–40.

feeling was that quality in the way things are done in the plant helped determine quality in products that left the plant. The team, after six months of operation, had implemented 22 major changes, most of them targeted maintenance improvements. In some cases, as the Into Practice box illustrates, these teams are empowered to call in the additional expertise of suppliers.

Operationally, each additional increment of PM tends to shift reliability upward toward 1.0, perfect reliability, just as replacing batteries more frequently improves radio reliability, as was shown in Example 16–2. Without PM, reliability deteriorates and failure becomes increasingly likely. A few companies are renowned for their intolerance of failures; Walt Disney Company is an example. Disney World in Florida has become a popular destination not only for vacationers but also for benchmarking teams wanting to study Disney's breakdown-intolerant maintenance program.

Dedicated Maintenance

Among the most ardent believers in PM, however, have been aircraft people, for in aircraft maintenance PM is everything; waiting for failure is unacceptable. The well-traveled B-52 is a good example of the PM concept. Even more remarkable is the 60-year-old DC-3; the military version, the C-47, is affectionately known as the "Gooney Bird." A few hundred of these venerable aircraft are still logging miles, thanks to good design and the thoroughness of PM practices.

Another company famed for its maintenance is United Parcel Service, which keeps most of its over-the-road and delivery vehicles operating and looking as good as new for 20 years or more (see Exhibit 16–4). A feature of the UPS program is dedicated mechanics and dedicated drivers. A driver operates the same vehicle every day, and a mechanic maintains the same group of vehicles. Many military aircraft maintenance

---

EXHIBIT 16–4   Maintenance at United Parcel Service

Exceptional maintenance of tractors, trailers, delivery trucks, planes, and sorting equipment is the basis for UPS's advertising slogan: ''The Tightest Ship in the Shipping Business.''

Photos reprinted courtesy of United Parcel Service.

𝒫RINCIPLE 6:

Organize resources into focused family groupings.

programs also use dedicated operator/mechanic programs; the names of both the pilot and the maintenance crew chief are painted on the aircraft. Both individuals proudly claim ownership and are responsible for the performance of the aircraft.

At UPS, mechanics work at night on delivery vehicles driven mostly during the day, but drivers and mechanics stay closely in touch. Drivers complete a post-trip vehicle inspection report every day, noting any problems. The mechanic goes to work on those problems that evening, and records completed work on the form. The driver uses the form in conducting a pretrip inspection every morning. Thank-yous and other personal comments between driver and mechanic are common. Similar interactions and documentation between pilots and maintenance crew chiefs have long been standard in military and (in some cases) commercial aircraft maintenance programs.

The interdependency of operator, machine, and mechanic keeps responsibilities focused and avoids blaming. In the more typical situation of changing mechanics and operators, any of the individuals can become lax, fail to keep good records, and leave problems for the next person or shift.

Clearly, a vital aspect of aircraft and UPS vehicle maintenance programs is thorough record keeping. Everything that happens to a vehicle or plane is recorded, every problem and every maintenance action. A complete history of engine, chassis, and all other major components is available.

Maintenance Records

Complete records permit computer calculation of failure rates, necessary for determining prefailure replacement schedules; mean times to repair, useful in scheduling maintenance people's time; and component reliabilities, which designers use to improve next-generation components.

As an added service to regular customers, some garages maintain computerized records of automobile maintenance. Customers are freed from some record-keeping worry, but the garage also benefits: Mechanics know when to call and suggest appointments, what parts are likely to need replacement, and what, if any, warranty time remains. Like aircraft and UPS vehicles, well-designed and well-maintained automobiles can have long operating lifetimes, and an automobile's value is enhanced if it is accompanied by a thorough set of maintenance records.

In Chapter 8, MRO (maintenance, repair, and operations) inventory was classified as a class B item, indicating that it is not typically among the most costly inventory (class A items), but that neither it is considered as part of the "trivial many" (class C items). In a TPM environment, with the focus on increased operator involvement and rapid response, location and care of MRO inventories deserve careful attention. Also, JIT operations avoids long distances. MRO inventory storage space must be close to the action and efficiently used.

Maintenance Inventories

It is common for even a medium-sized plant to have hundreds, even thousands, of MRO items, despite standardization and component part reduction programs. Many are like household hardware items we buy, small and available only in quantities of 10s or even 100s. Exhibit 16–5 shows how people at the Macomb, Illinois, plant of NTN Bearing Corporation solve the problem. Drawer cabinets (Exhibit 16–5A) consume less than half the space of shelving and facilitate storage of small items like brackets, sleeves, and pins (see Exhibit 16–5B). Adjacent part-location records and clear labeling on drawers make retrieval of even the most obscure item easy. The results? Lower MTTR values and less downtime.

When equipment runs day and night, people can't get at it to perform necessary maintenance and breakdowns follow. TPM calls for setting aside time each day for PM. Ford and Toyota go so far as to schedule minishifts for PM before and after production shifts. Companies that follow a pattern of two 4-hour maintenance shifts sandwiched between two 8-hour production shifts believe they get about the same amount of production as they would if they ran three production shifts in a 24-hour period. Even with massive equipment in such industries as paper making, sheet coating and extruding, and steel making, a daily maintenance shutdown usually makes sense.

PM Time

At one U.S. particle-board plant, the large mix-mold-bake-cool line was run 24 hours a day, 7 days a week, except for 1 hour of maintenance per week. For lack of regular PM, the line produced much scrap and defective particle board. When asked why there was no daily maintenance shutdown, the reply was, "We have startup problems." The general manager of several Brazilian particle-board plants heard that story and offered this comment: "We *do* shut down for maintenance every day, and we *don't* have startup problems." By having to face startup each day, they had learned how to make it an easy routine.

Perhaps a carryover from old accounting logic creates a tendency to want to run very expensive machines continuously. But the enlightened view asks, Don't our most expensive machines deserve our best care rather than our worst? This view is gaining ground in

EXHIBIT 16–5 The Little Parts—Managing MRO Items

A. Small-part storage drawer cabinets

B. Open storage cabinet drawer

SOURCE: Courtesy of NTN-Bower Corporation. Used with permission.

Exhibit 16-6   Probability of Failure over Component Operating Life

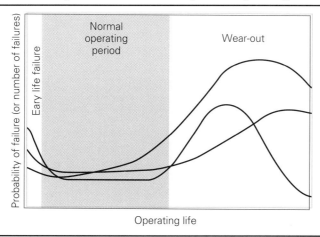

industry, especially as total quality and JIT successes show the importance of reliability, availability, and maintainability.

Maintenance Decisions: How Much Prevention?

Maintenance managers get paid to decide when to replace machines or components and *how much* spare or backup equipment to own. Whether the resources in question are repairable or must be replaced, the basic analyses of these problems is the same. Also, in both instances, it is helpful to understand failure patterns.

Exhibit 16-6 shows three examples of general failure probability patterns. Each might represent a different machine or component. Failure may be a sudden all-to-nothing event (such as cable snapping, bulb going out, etc.), or it might be defined as deterioration of performance to a preselected level (e.g., a battery dropping to 50 percent of its charge).

Failure Patterns
Failure patterns such as those shown in Exhibit 16-6 are referred to as bathtub curve patterns or graphs, due to their general shape.

The vertical axis is often probability, 0 to 1.0, or it may show the proportion or number of failures in a group of like items. Three horizontal (time) zones are defined in the figure. The first, the **early failure zone,** represents failures stemming from improper construction, or, if the pattern is for a repairable item, improper maintenance. For new items, preuse, or component ''burn-in'' before shipment, will reduce early failure for the customer. For example, Apple burns in its Macintosh computers for 24 hours prior to shipment. Sometimes component burn-in by suppliers is a quality requirement of electronics assemblers.

The next zone is normal operations, sometimes called steady-state operations. Failure probability is lowest here. Finally, surviving items enter the wear-out zone, where failure probability increases and may then fall sharply. Instability, however, is often the main characteristic. In the normal zone and the wearout zone, failure probability can sometimes be reduced by **derating,** that is, running equipment at less-than-full (rated) load or at better-than-normal conditions.

Where many components of the same type are in use, associates should consider group replacement rather than replacing individual items as they fail.

Group Replacement

Example 16–3 compares two policies on light bulb replacement. One is to allow light bulbs to last as long as they will before replacing them. In this policy, a few are early failures, a few more fail at random for various reasons, and the rest (probably the majority) fail in the wear-out zone.

In the second policy, bulbs are not left in their sockets long enough for wear-out. Instead, all bulbs are replaced at regular intervals (periodic maintenance) partway through their normal life expectancy. This second preventive policy, called **group replacement,** requires failure-rate data.

EXAMPLE 16–3   GROUP VERSUS INDIVIDUAL LIGHT BULB REPLACEMENT

At present, light bulbs in building C are replaced as they fail. Whoever notices a failure phones the trouble-call desk, maintenance department. The trouble-call dispatcher sends someone to change the light bulb. The average cost is $3.30 per bulb, including labor.

An alternative policy is to replace all building C bulbs at regular intervals (group replacement). For building C the group-replacement policy would cost $1 per bulb, including labor. There are 1,000 light bulbs in building C. Therefore each group replacement would cost $1,000. What replacement policy is optimal?

Solution:

When light bulb failure data are not given, we need to run an experiment. Place bulbs in 1,000 sockets in building C. It is impractical to let the building go dark, so the experimenters replace all failures during the experiment. The experimental results are shown in Exhibit 16–7.

It appears in Exhibit 16–7 that the experiment has been run long enough to achieve a nearly **steady state:** all new bulbs put in at the beginning of the year have been replaced and their replacements have been replaced, the mix of bulbs is now a more uniform mix of ages, and the steady-state failure rate is about 310 per month (a rough average of failures in recent months, e.g., in the last three months). Actually, there is no need to run the experiment long enough to achieve a steady state unless a new type of bulb is being used or the building is new. In an existing building the light bulb failure rate prior to the experiment would have been steady state.

Cost of present policy: The steady-state condition applies to the present replace-as-they-fail policy. Its cost is:

$$310 \text{ bulbs/month} \times \$3.30/\text{bulb} = \$1,023 \text{ per month}$$

Cost of group-replacement policy: The cost of group replacement every month is:

Group cost: 1,000 bulbs × $1.00/bulb = $1,000/month
Failure cost: 46 bulbs × $3.30/bulb =   152/month
Total cost   = $1,152/month

The cost of group replacement every two months is:

Group cost: $1,000/2 months
Failure cost: (46 + 150) × $3.30 =   647/2 months
Total cost   = $1,647/2 month = $ 823/month

EXHIBIT 16–7   Experimental Failure Data

Month	1	2	3	4	5	6	7	8	9	10	11	12
Failures during month	46	150	218	360	520	353	387	240	260	330	301	310

The cost of group replacement every three months is:

Group cost: $1,000/3 months
Failure cost: (46 + 150 + 218) × $3.30 = 1,366/3 months
Total cost   = $2,366/3 month = $ 789/month

The cost of group replacement every four months is:

Group cost: $1,000/4 months
Failure cost: (46 + 150 + 218 + 360) × $3.30 = 2,554/4 months
Total cost   = $3,554/4 month = $ 888/month

The costs have begun to turn upward; this suggests that we have found the optimum (lowest cost on a U-shaped cost curve). It is $789 per month for group replacement every three months. That beats the $1,023 per month for replacing the bulbs as they fail, so group replacement every three months is the optimum among the policies considered.

Does Example 16–3 explore all the issues in group replacement? It does not. What about the cost of interruptions for those components that fail? For light bulbs, the cost may be small. If the components were critical, the cost of interruptions would add a new layer of complexity to the problem. Common sense suggests, however, that where failures are costly, group replacement is even more attractive.

Standby Equipment Analysis

Sometimes the consequences of breakdowns are severe enough to justify spares or standby resources. Standbys provide comforting backup at some price, and they are an alternative to paying for high levels of maintenance in order to reduce breakdown chances.

When two or more components that can perform the same function are configured in *parallel*, the net effect is increased reliability. *Series* configurations, on the other hand, decrease reliability.

One computer manufacturer, Tandem Computers, has made a profitable market by making and selling a computer that has up to 16 processors operating in parallel. Their fault-tolerant computer appeals to customers for whom downtime is a crisis or even a life-threatening disaster. Tandem's largest market is in large fund transfers, as between the Federal Reserve and large banks. Shop-floor manufacturing uses are its second largest market, followed by monitoring hospital patients, power stations, and so forth.

When large numbers of identical machines exist, there is a simplified way to analyze standby policies. The method uses our knowledge about patterns of machine failure. Studies show that machine failures per unit of time are random variables that tend to follow the Poisson probability distribution. The shape of the Poisson is based on a mathematical function, and the complete shape can be developed by simply entering the mean number of failures per time unit into the Poisson general formula.

A characteristic shape of the distribution is shown in Exhibit 16–8. We see that there is some chance of zero failures per time unit (say, per day), but, of course, there can be no chance of negative failure per time unit. Poisson distributions rise to a peak probability and then taper off (are skewed) to the right. There is a 50 percent chance that in the given time period the number of failures will be less than the mean (2.5 per time unit in Exhibit 16–8) and also a 50 percent chance that the number of failures will exceed the mean.

Sometimes the merits of standby equipment may be judged by a cost analysis. Example 16–4 illustrates a type of cost analysis that employs the Poisson probability distribution.

EXAMPLE 16–4 STANDBY "SCOPES" AND POISSON-DISTRIBUTED FAILURES

A large electronics manufacturer does testing with scopes at each of 100 assembly and testing stations. When a scope breaks down, testing is halted at one station for one day (the time it takes to get the scope repaired). The company estimates the

---

Exhibit 16-8   Poisson Probability Distribution

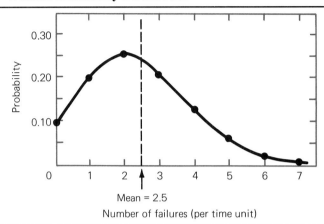

Mean = 2.5

Number of failures (per time unit)

---

cost of disruption and idleness at $100 for each day that a scope is down. That cost is $200 if two scopes are down, $300 if three scopes are down, and so forth. One way to avert the downtime cost is to keep spare scopes on hand. It costs about $50 per day to own and maintain each spare.

If scope breakdowns are random and average three per day, how many spare scopes should be maintained?

Solution:

The mean number of scope failures is known to be three per day. From that figure, the probabilities of any other number of failures per day can be calculated or looked up in a table or graph. The calculations (and tables and graphs) are based on the Poisson formula:

$$P(n) = \frac{e^{-\lambda}\lambda^n}{n!} \tag{16-3}$$

where

n = Number of failures per time unit
λ = Mean number of failures per time period = 3 scopes/day
e = 2.7183
$P(n)$ = Probability of n failures per time unit

For example, zero scope failures per day has the probability

$$P(0) = \frac{2.7183^{-3} \times 3^0}{0!} = \frac{1}{(1)(2.7183)^3} = \frac{1}{(20.086)} = 0.050$$

One scope failure per day has the probability:

$$P(1) = \frac{2.7183^{-3} \times 3^1}{1!} = \frac{3}{(1)(20.086)} = 0.150$$

Appendix B is an abbreviated table of *cumulative* Poisson probabilities. Find the *individual* probabilities by successive subtraction. For example, in the case of $\lambda = 3$ scopes per day, go to the row where $\lambda = 3.0$. Then, where $n = 0$, note that $P(0) = 0.050$. For $P(1)$, find 0.199 in the column where $n = 1$; subtract 0.050 from 0.199 and get 0.149, which (allowing for rounding error) is the same as the 0.150 that we obtained mathematically. Next, subtract 0.199 from 0.423 and get 0.224, which is $P(2)$; and so forth.

Calculating the optimal number of spare scopes requires a number of steps. Exhibit 16-9 simplifies the bookkeeping. The calculation procedure in the table

---

EXHIBIT 16–9   Calculating Optimal Number of Standby Machines—Tabular Approach

| Number of Spares | n: P(n): | Cost of Curtailed Scope Testing* | | | | | | | | Daily Cost of Curtailed Testing | Daily Cost of Spares | Total Cost per Day |
		0 0.050	1 0.150	2 0.224	3 0.224	4 0.168	5 0.101	6 0.050	7 0.022			
0		0	$100	$200	$300	$400	$500	$600	$700	$290.10	$ 0	$290.10
1			0	100	200	300	400	500	600	196.20	50	246.20
2				0	100	200	300	400	500	117.30	100	217.30
3					0	100	200	300	400	60.80	150	210.80←
4						0	100	200	300	26.70	200	226.70

*Based on $\lambda = 3$ failures per day.

---

follows the expected-value concept. For example, for the first row, zero spares, expected cost of failures is:

$$E_F = \$100(0.150) + \$200(0.224) + \$300(0.224) + \$400(0.168) + \$500(0.101) +$$
$$\$600(0.050) + \$700(0.022)$$
$$= \$15 + \$44.8 + \$67.2 + \$67.2 + \$50.5 + \$30.0 + \$15.4$$
$$= \$290.10$$

Calculate each row similarly. Stop when the total cost bottoms out and begins to rise. That identifies the optimal policy. In this case, it is to provide three spares at a total cost of $210.80 per day.

The standby and group-replacement methods have been around for many years, but we should be cautious about their apparent logic. The costs of downtime are many; some are not obvious or easy to measure, and estimating too low can yield a decision to allow the downtime. Today, managers increasingly are simply adopting the view that downtime is bad. In practice, that view translates into a policy of forcing downtime to decrease. That makes us look more favorably on group replacement and standby equipment.

Summary

Improved customer service increases the need for a responsive, comprehensive program of total preventive maintenance (TPM). The aims are threefold: regular preventive maintenance, periodic replacement and overhauls, and no breakdowns. The TPM contribution is resources ready for use.

Payoff from maintenance investment usually is not immediate but it typically shows up throughout an organization. Specific measures of maintenance program success include maintainability, availability, and reliability. Working in tandem with cross-functional design teams, front-line operators in product and service groups, supported when necessary by maintenance expertise, strive to increase mean time between failure (MTBF) and to decrease mean time to repair (MTTR), thus increasing resource availability. Preventive maintenance (PM), through component replacement or repair, serves to increase reliabilities.

There are two general classes of maintenance operations: periodic and irregular. Periodic maintenance occurs regularly and forms the core of PM programs, and PM is at the heart of TPM. Variations include PM that is a function of calendar or clock time, predictive maintenance based on time (or amount) of usage, and PM triggered by inspection. Irregular maintenance includes repairs, overhauls, and work performed as the result of a special test, unusual noise, and so forth.

The key to successful TPM is operator ownership, where the front-line associate assumes first-level responsibility for maintaining equipment and the workplace. Backup, for unusual or especially difficult jobs, is provided from a central maintenance department or from cross-functional teams dispersed throughout the organization. Advantages of such an approach include greater operator familiarity with equipment, better equipment care, faster repairs, process fail-safing, and a fuller utilization of work time—essential especially in JIT environments.

Dedicated maintenance, long a key part of aircraft care, is emerging in organizations outside the aircraft industry. United Parcel Service, for example, has a specific driver and mechanic permanently assigned to each of its vehicles. Successful PM depends on keeping good records, properly locating and storing maintenance-related inventories, and ensuring that sufficient time for PM is inserted into the schedule.

Maintenance managers have to decide how much prevention to buy. An understanding of equipment failure patterns can offer helpful insight. By deciding whether to perform group replacement, or by designating the amount of standby equipment to be owned, the manager is evaluating costs of downtime against expenses of extra prevention.

Key Words

Total preventive maintenance (TPM)	555	Periodic maintenance	560
Maintainability	556	Irregular maintenance	560
Mean time between failures (MTBF)	556	Predictive maintenance	560
Mean time to repair (MTTR)	556	Early failure zone	567
Availability	556	Derating	567
Failure rate	556	Group replacement	568
Reliability	557	Steady state	568

Solved Problems

Problem 1

Grittelbane Optics grinds special lenses for eyewear and for optical equipment used in medical and scientific laboratories. Almost without exception, once during each standard five-day (40-hour) workweek, the main grinder will get out of alignment. Grittelbane technicians call for a service representative to realign the grinder, a job that takes four hours on average. Company president Karl Grittelbane staunchly opposes having any of his employees perform PM: "That sort of thing is for repair people, we shouldn't waste our time on that, we've work to do." Karl's son Pete feels differently and has asked you to help convince his father.

Solution 1

One approach might begin by showing Karl the availability of the grinder. Using days as the time unit, $MTBF = 5$ and $MTTR = 0.5$. Then from equation 16–1:

$$A = \frac{MTBF}{MTBF + MTTR} = \frac{5}{5.5} = 0.91$$

We don't have access to cost data, but we must assume that the one-half day time of the service representative is costly. Also, we are unsure about what other work the Grittelbane employees do during the half day when the grinder is down. Finally, we ought to assume that any PM done by Grittelbane personnel would require training, from whom we aren't sure.

Knowing so little (although Pete may fill us in), can we help? Of course. The most interesting questions haven't been mentioned yet: Why is the grinder getting out of alignment? Is there a pattern? Same day each week? Same operator each time? Same operation being performed? Records would certainly help.

Problem 2

Betty's daughter will soon open her new advertising agency, and Betty is shopping for a small office gift to present when she visits the agency next week. At an office supply store, Betty finds an electric pencil sharpener she likes. A label on the box informs her that the sharpener has a mean time between failure (MTBF) of two years. A clerk who arrives to assist informs Betty that the MTBF figure means that after two years, there is a 50–50 chance that the sharpener will still be working. Is the clerk correct?

Solution 2

The value of the sharpener's reliability at a time period of two years is the issue. First compute the failure rate (we must assume that it is constant): $\lambda = 1/\mu$, or $\frac{1}{2}$ per year. Betty can now apply Equation 16–2:

$$R = e^{-\lambda t} = e^{-(\frac{1}{2})(2)} = e^{-(1)}$$
$$= 1/e = 1/2.718 = 0.368$$

So the clerk is incorrect. A common mistake is to assume that reliability at MTBF is one-half, or 50 percent. The correct value, however, is about 0.37, slightly over a one-third chance of successful operation.

Problem 3

A process control system contains 100 identical diodes, each costing $0.10. Electronic Service Providers, Inc. (ESP), which holds the maintenance contract for the control system, is searching for a low-cost replacement policy for the diodes, which are prone to failure. ESP has gathered its own failure data by starting up the control system with 100 new diodes and recording their operating lives; each failed diode was replaced during the data collection period. The data, collected over 5,000 hours of operation, are as follows:

Operating hours	500	1,000	1,500	2,000	2,500	3,000	3,500	4,000	4,500	5,000
Number of diodes replaced during period	18	10	8	10	37	49	54	56	57	53

ESP also has estimated that its labor and overhead cost to replace a single diode is $4.90, but is only $1.90 if all 100 are replaced at one time. What is the best replacement policy?

Solution 3

Replacing single diodes: The failure data show what appear to be steady-state conditions from about 3,500 hours on. The average failures replaced during steady state are 55 [(54 + 56 + 57 + 53)/4 = 55]. ESP calculates the cost, per 500 hours of operation, of replacing single diodes as:

55 diode failures per 500 hours × $5.00 = $275

Note: The cost of each failure, $5.00, is based on $0.10 for the diode plus $4.90 for labor and overhead.

Group replacement every 500 hours: Cost of replacing all 100 diodes every 500 hours, plus all failures during that 500 hours, is:

Group cost: 100 diodes × ($0.10 + $1.90) = $200
Failure cost: 18 failed diodes × $5.00 = $ 90
Total cost per 500 hours = $290

Group replacement every 1,000 hours:

Group cost: 100 diodes × ($0.10 + $1.90) = $200
Failure cost: (18 + 10) failed diodes × $5.00 = $140
Total cost for two 500-hour periods = $340
Cost per 500 hours = $340/2 = $170

Group replacement every 1,500 hours:

Group cost: 100 diodes × ($0.10 + $1.90) = $200
Failure cost: 36 failed diodes × $5.00 = $180
Total cost for three 500-hour periods = $380
Cost per 500 hours = $380/3 = $127

Group replacement every 2,000 hours:

Group cost: 100 diodes × ($0.10 + $1.90) = $200
Failure cost: 46 failed diodes × $5.00 = $230
Total cost for four 500-hour periods = $430
Cost per 500 hours = $430/4 = $108

Group replacement every 2,500 hours:

Group cost: 100 diodes × ($0.10 + $1.90) = $200
Failure cost: 83 failed diodes × $5.00 = $415
Total cost for five 500-hour periods = $615
Cost per 500 hours = $615/5 = $123

Since costs have begun to rise, it appears that the lowest-cost policy has been found: group replacement every 2,000 hours, plus replacement of any failures during that period. According to ESP's data, that policy's cost is about $108 per 500 hours, which is far better than the $275 cost for individual replacements.

Problem 4

Given:

Current number of units of an identical machine = 20
Cost to own and maintain a spare unit = $7 per hour
Mean number of failures per hour = 2

Cost of downtime:

$10 per hour for one unit out of service.

$30 per hour for two units out of service.

$60 per hour for three units out of service.

$100 per hour for four units out of service.

$150 per hour for five or more units out of service.

If breakdowns of the units are random, how many standby units should there be?

Solution 4

The following table aids in solution. To get the row of probabilities, $P(n)$, go to Appendix B. Use the row in which $\lambda = 2$ since the mean number of failures per hour is 2. The probability of zero failures, 0.135, is taken from the $n = 0$ column. The other probabilities require successive subtraction. For example, the 0.090 is obtained by subtracting the value in the $n = 3$ column from the value in the $n = 4$ column: $0.947 - 0.857 = 0.090$.

		Cost of Downtime								*Hourly*	*Hourly*	*Total*
Number of	*n:*	*0*	*1*	*2*	*3*	*4*	*5*	*6*	*7*	*Cost of*	*Cost of*	*Cost*
Standbys	*P(n):*	*0.135*	*0.271*	*0.271*	*0.180*	*0.090*	*0.036*	*0.012*	*0.004*	*Downtime*	*Standbys*	*per Hour*
0		0	$10	$30	$60	$100	$150	$150	$150	$38.44	$ 0.00	$38.44
1			0	10	30	60	100	150	150	19.51	7.00	26.51
2				0	10	30	60	100	150	8.46	14.00	22.46←
3					0	10	30	60	100	3.10	21.00	24.10

Sample cost calculation: For zero number of standbys, use the expected-value method to find the hourly cost of downtime: Multiply cost by probabilities across the entire row, from $n = 0$ to $n = 7$:

$$0.135(0) + 0.271(10) + 0.271(30) + 0.180(60) + 0.090(100)$$
$$+ 0.036(150) + 0.012(150) + 0.004(150) = \$38.44 \text{ per hour}$$

The optimum number of standbys is 2; that policy yields the lowest cost per hour, $22.46.

For Further Reference

Books

Cordero, S. T. *Maintenance Management Handbook*. Englewood Cliffs, N.J.: Fairmont Press, 1987.

Mobley, R. Keith. *An Introduction to Predictive Maintenance*. New York: Van Nostrand Reinhold, 1990 (TS192.M624).

Nakajima, Seiichi. *Introduction to TPM: Total Productive Maintenance*. Cambridge, Mass.: Productivity Press, 1988 (originally published in Japanese in 1984).

Tomlingson, Paul D. *Industrial Maintenance Management*. 8th ed. Chicago: McLean Hunter, 1989.

Wireman, Terry. *Total Productive Maintenance: An American Approach*. New York: Industrial Press, 1991.

Periodicals

AITPM Action Line (American Institute for Total Productive Maintenance).

Maintenance Technology.

Plant Engineering (includes plant maintenance).

Review Questions

1. What is total preventive maintenance?
2. How does a TPM program support total quality?
3. What is the role of cleanliness in the assessment of an overall maintenance program?
4. How does maintenance investment work for the organization? Where do benefits accrue?
5. Define the terms *maintainability, availability,* and *reliability.* Explain what customers would value about each.
6. What are the basic types of maintenance? Give examples of each.
7. What are the three popular versions of PM?
8. How might maintenance activity responsibility be assigned in a TPM-oriented company?
9. What is operator-centered maintenance? What are its advantages?
10. How do maintenance improvement teams augment other components of a TPM program?
11. What should be the role of a central maintenance department?
12. What is dedicated maintenance? How does it support the TPM idea?
13. What role do maintenance records play in TPM programs?
14. What is the controversy about making time in the schedule for maintenance?
15. What are early failures? How might burn-in or derating help with them?
16. Describe a bathtub curve. How is knowledge of it helpful in maintenance planning?
17. Where might one obtain failure probability data for individual components or products?
18. Group-replacement may occur every period, every two periods, every three, and so on. Why wouldn't the cost per period always be less the longer the interval between replacements?
19. How would an associate get the average number of failures per day (per week, etc.) in order to calculate the cost of replacing components as they fail?
20. What are the costs and savings of maintaining standby machines?

Problems and Exercises

1. To what extent do commercial semitrailer tractor drivers get involved in PM and repairs to their equipment? (You may need to interview someone.) Do you think their involvement is enough?

2. To what extent do copy machine operators get involved in cleaning and maintaining their own machines (clean glass, clean rollers, resupply with fluids and papers, etc.)? In repairing their machines? (You may need to interview someone.) Is their involvement adequate?

3. Every maintenance operation requires some degree of facilities analysis and planning. A number of maintenance operations are as follows:

   Replace ceramic tiles in a floor.

   Mop floors.

   Repair power outage.

   Change oil and grease equipment.

   Change extrusion heads (simply unscrew dirty one and screw on clean one) as they randomly clog up (in a factory full of plastics extrusion lines, each with an extrusion head to form the plastic).

   Replace drive belts, bearings, and so on as they fail (among large group of various machines on factory floor).

   Repaint walls.

   Maintain spare motors for bank of spinning machines.

   Remodel president's office.

   Repair shoes (shoe repair shop).
   a. Name one or more analysis techniques (if any) that apply to each maintenance operation.
   b. List the data inputs necessary for conducting the analysis. (Note: Some of the analysis methods are presented in other chapters.) Two completed examples follow:

Maintenance Operation	Analysis Technique	Data Inputs
Rearrange office equipment	Layout analysis (Chapter 17)	Flow data (types and volume) Relationship data
Prepare platform with utility hook-ups for new equipment	None	

4. With computers (microprocessors) now in common use as automobile control devices, they sometimes serve a preventive maintenance purpose. A dash panel could be used to input into a computer every maintenance operation performed on the car, and mileage data could be entered into the computer automatically. A screen could then recommend preventive maintenance whenever a program determines a need.
   a. To what extent is this idea in use right now? What are some obstacles in the way of implementing or improving on such a PM system?
   b. What are some important items of historical data that would need to be programmed into the auto's computer? Where would such data come from? Explain.
   c. Large numbers of nearly identical autos are sold, which provides a sizable potential database for gathering failure and wear-out data. For almost any type of factory machine there is a smaller potential data base; that is, there are far fewer copies of the same machine. Yet good factory PM is based on good failure records. How can good records be developed for factory machines?

5. Think of a consumer product that advertisers tout as being especially maintainable. Distinguish between the maintainability, availability, and reliability of the product.

6. Name two industries in which maintainability is especially important, and two in which it is especially unimportant. Discuss. What can maintenance managers do about the maintainability of the facilities in their firms?

7. Joe Black is head of the maintenance operations division of the plant engineering department at Wexco, Inc. Rumors have been flying around his division. The buzzing is regarding the company's plan to launch a new program called Operator Ownership. The program is aimed at

the problem of machine undependability and would place more responsibility for machine performance on the machine operators—a step backwards, in the minds of Black and his subordinates.

Part of the worry is that operator ownership is budget cutting (slashing the maintenance budget) in disguise, which equals losses of jobs in maintenance operations. Black also harbors natural concerns regarding losses of personal prestige and power.

Are those worries really justified? Discuss.

8. A security system timer controls lights, and other electrical components. The MTBF for the timer is advertised to be 2,000 hours. When should the operator or maintenance associate consider replacing the timer? Discuss your recommendations.

9. Equation 16–1 defined availability in terms of mean time between failure (MTBF) and mean time to repair (MTTR). To what extent are design teams responsible for these two parameters? To what extent are front-liners and maintenance associates responsible?

10. A control valve for a fuel supply system has an average failure rate of one failure per two years. Suppose the fuel supply system is to be used on an upcoming space mission that will last two weeks.

    a. Is this part of the vehicle safe enough? (Calculate value of reliability at mission end.)

    b. What might be done to improve reliability of this, or any other, component?

11. A design team at a test equipment provider has the following problem: A (potential) new customer wants the availability of any new computer testing units to be at least 0.99; that is a target for the team. Team members (maintenance personnel and the customer's operators) argue that, because of the need to recalibrate, a realistic figure for average repair time (should a breakdown occur in a test unit) is one hour. What options are open to the team?

12. There are 50 filter traps in the cooling system of a nuclear power plant. Monitor lights warn an attendant when a filter clogs up, and the attendant alerts the maintenance department. It costs $100 in labor and downtime to remove plates and clean out the filter. Maintenance can remove plates and clean out all 50 filters at the same time for a labor-and-downtime cost of $800.

    The maintenance department has collected some experimental data on filter-clogging frequencies. The experiment began with 50 clean traps and ran for 6,000 hours. Results are:

Operating hours	1,000	2,000	3,000	4,000	5,000	6,000
Number of clogged filters replaced during period	1	3	5	6	6	6

What is the optimal maintenance policy?

13. A refinery has 50 identical pumps installed in various places. Replacing the seal in the pump motor is a delicate task requiring a visit from a maintenance engineer of the pump company, in another city. The cost of the trip is $200. The cost of replacing one seal is $20. The refinery has used the 50 pumps for 10 quarters (2½ years), which is the amount of time the plant has been in service. Pump seals have been replaced as they failed. Following is the failure history for the 10 quarters:

Quarter	1	2	3	4	5	6	7	8	9	10
Seal failures	0	1	1	2	3	3	2	4	3	3

Analyze the merits of a group-replacement policy.

14. Duncan Aviation maintains a fleet of Lear jets. The fleet requires 30 identical jet engines installed in the planes. Spare engines are ready to go in Duncan's hangars in case of malfunction of an engine in one of the planes. The spares cost $500 a week to keep on hand. If a plane is idled for lack of a good engine, the cost (lost net revenue) is about $2,000 per week. If an average of two engines per week fail, what is the correct number of spares?

15. A refinery has 50 identical pumps installed in various places. When a pump fails, the product flow rate drops, but the refining continues. The estimated average cost of reduced flow rate when a pump is down is $1,000 per day. If a spare pump is on hand when one goes down, an associate can install the spare quickly enough so that flow-rate losses are negligible. It costs $60 per day to own and maintain one spare pump. The maintenance manager estimates that one pump per day fails on the average. How many spare pumps should be maintained?

16. Here are three situations in which standby machine analysis might be used. Comment on the suitability of standby analysis in each case.
    a. Spare fluorescent tubes in case one burns out in an auditorium.
    b. Spare memory cards (identical ones) in case one fails in one of a large number of microcomputers used in an electronic test equipment center.
    c. Spare pizza ovens in case one (of many) fails in a large take-out/eat-in pizza place.

17. Hewlett-Packard pays its janitors, guards, and food service associates the same wage as its product assembly people, yet the product assembly people have higher status. At one H-P division, the division manager intends to begin rotating assembly people into the lower-status positions, and vice versa. But she wonders how the assemblers will react when asked to "push a broom." From what you have learned about responsibility for maintenance, do you think this rotation plan is a step in the right direction? Explain. What else might be done?

18. Captain Henry Harrison has spent much of his career in navy shipyards. In the last 10 years, he has held three positions of authority over shops that build and repair ships. He has been a firm believer in conducting frequent inspections of shop facilities and is a stickler for having everything neat, clean, and painted. Some people think Captain Harrison spends too much time on this. What do you think?

 **CASE STUDY**

SWANBANK FROZEN FOODS

Swanbank is a major North American frozen food producer. Its Forbes, North Carolina, plant produces between 280,000 and 320,000 frozen dinners per day. Each year the schedule is cut back in the spring, in advance of reduced summer sales, and raised again in the fall.

In 1983 Jerry Hanks, plant manager at Forbes, inaugurated a just-in-time effort. Hank's JIT task force has progressed to goal setting, and one goal was to set a daily production rate for each product (type of dinner) and meet it everyday.

At that time, setting even a modest rate and hitting it daily was not remotely possible. The normal problems of undependable deliveries of ingredients and packaging materials could perhaps be resolved. Internal problems in food preparation, mixing, cooking, aluminum tray stamping, and material handling also seemed solvable. The big problems were in final assembly and packaging. This case study concerns only that stage of production.

Case topics:

Total preventive maintenance.	Buffer stock.
Just in time.	Crew staffing.
Linearity.	Shift scheduling.
Operator ownership.	Facility layout.
Breakdowns.	Job assignments/labor flexibility.
Failure rates.	Line changeover/cleanup.
Line speed (production rate).	Preventive maintenance.
Material handling.	Equipment design for operations.

Exhibit S16–1   Distribution of Durations of Stop Times

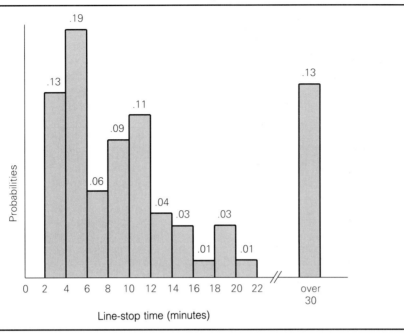

Fill and Pack

Final assembly and packaging consisted of three high-speed fill-and-pack lines located side by side in a large area stretching lengthwise from the main factory area through two plant additions. The lines were 600 to 850 feet long and conveyor driven. Filling nozzles, chutes, gravity drop devices, and mechanical pushers deposited cooked food items into aluminum tray compartments at early workstations along the line. Automatic cartoners, corrugated box packers, and palletizers were at the end of the line.

The lines were by no means fully automated. A crew of 50 to 60 people, classified as direct labor and supervision, tended a line. Their normal jobs were to load trays and kettles of cooked ingredients into hoppers. Their abnormal jobs were to keep production going manually whenever nozzles clogged up and jam-ups occurred on the line.

The company had always taken pride in the high speed at which its tray-filling lines were designed to run, about 270 trays per minute. However, with trays moving at that speed past many fill stations, through long and not always straight and level lengths of conveyor, and into temperamental cartoning and packing equipment, slight misalignments could result in spectacular jam-ups. Trays and their contents could fly into the air and quickly litter the floor and cover the equipment with gravy, peas, and apple cobbler. In such instances, the nearest line crew member would rush to hit the stop button. Then crew members would roll in trash barrels, push carts, and other apparatus so they could manually fill and forward stalled trays and dispose of ruined ones.

A line stop could also sometimes summon technicians from maintenance. Their job was to fix the cause. Often the cause was minor and fixable within a few minutes by a line supervisor or maintenance technician already present at lineside. Filling equipment was also frequently adjusted to correct for spilling of food portions into the wrong tray compartment, which tended to happen frequently because of the fast line speeds. Those adjustments often could be done on the fly.

Records kept by line supervisors revealed that the mean stoppage time per shift was 3 hours and the mean number of stops per shift was 26. Exhibit S16–1 is a distribution of the duration of stoppages per shift. The distribution summarizes a sample of stoppages over 50 shifts. It shows that the vast majority of stoppages were short; in fact, 58 percent were 12 minutes or less. Just 13 percent were over 30 minutes and these incorporated just one instance each of several different stoppage durations, such as 39, 41, . . . , 93, 171, . . . minutes. The longest stoppage in the 50 shifts sampled was 3 hours 17 minutes.

The high incidence of stoppages affected design of the line. Between each pair of fill stations, the conveyor length usually was long enough to hold a few dozen trays. Then, whenever the line stopped, the extra trays could be processed manually. Over the years, the conveyors lengthened as line speeds were increased.

When a line stoppage incident included under- or overfilling, spillover, or damaged containers, the bad product went into trash barrels. The average trash rate had been 5 percent.

Unfortunately, although the trash contained food, no one—company people, local charities, welfare agencies, or farm groups—could come up with an economical way to salvage the good food. The waste was bulldozed under at the local landfill. The average cost of one trashed unit was $0.38, of which $0.015 was container and packaging material (usually just an aluminum tray, since most stoppages came before cartoning).

Work Pace

When the line was running full speed, line crew members were not hard-pressed to keep up. Most people who watched the line would estimate that perhaps half the crew size, say, 30 people, could keep up with the line. With half a crew, each person would have to tend two geographically separated stations, but even with walk time from one to the next, it appeared that they should have been able to keep up; for example, dump a fresh kettle of gravy into a feeder tank, walk to the next station, load a tray of veal cutlets into the magazine of a feeder machine, walk back to gravy, and repeat.

Hanks summed up the crew size and work pace issue this way: "Half of the line crew are on hand because the equipment doesn't run right." Indeed, the leisurely pace of the line crew could swiftly change to frenzy, and it often did whenever the line stopped. Manual processing around the bottleneck was fast and furious. During longer stoppages, say, 20 minutes or more, line crews would run out of partially filled trays and then have to stop. They stayed idle until maintenance technicians and line supervisors could fix the problem and restart the line.

The unionized labor force was accustomed to this hurry-and-then-wait work life. Hanks and the JIT team anticipated the need for an education effort, but not big problems with labor, in the upcoming JIT conversion effort.

Work Shifts and Practices

Most of the year the Forbes plant operated five days a week with two work shifts per day. A 2½ hour changeover and cleanup shift followed each work shift. Product changes, chicken to beef or ravioli to lasagna, for example, generally occurred at the end of each shift. The shift schedule was as follows:

First work shift	5:30 A.M.–2:00 P.M.
Changeover/cleanup	2:00 P.M.–4:30 P.M.
Second work shift	4:30 P.M.–1:00 A.M.
Changeover/cleanup	1:00 A.M.–3:30 A.M.

Average line output per shift varied, depending partly on what product the line was producing. Some products, such as spaghetti dinners, were run at a slower speed than, say, fried shrimp dinners. The main cause of variable line output, however, was amount of line stoppage during a shift. Over one three-week period, output on line 3 was as shown in Exhibit S16–2.

Cleanup and Line Changeover

A five-person maintenance crew performed cleanups. About half the crew worked on disengaging filling equipment from the chain conveyor and reengaging equipment for use on the next

Exhibit S16–2   Output on Line 3 over Three-Week Period

Day	1	2	3	4	5	6	7	8	9	10	11	12	13	14	15
Output (000 trays packed)	95	102	123	100	87	103	57	85	113	103	68	107	60	102	108

shift. The other half began the task of shoveling, scraping, and push-brooming the litter of food and containers. Large piles went into garbage cans; smaller scatterings near the conveyor were pushed into a trough centered below the conveyor.

The crew started with fill-and-pack line 1, then went to line 2, then 3. As soon as line 1 was torn down and prep-cleaned, part of the crew, in rubber hip boots, began hosing down everything on that line. Hosing was in the direction of the central trough, where it drained into a filtering system. The filtered matter was recovered; it was containered and sold as feed to chicken growers.

As hosers moved to line 2, technicians wheeled the next set of filling machines to line 1 and attached and adjusted them for the next production run. The hose crew moved to line 3 and the setup technicians to line 2. Filling equipment to be used from one shift to the next stayed connected but was flushed in place. Hosing included detergent wash-down after the late shift but water only following the first shift.

As production lines started up, the maintenance crew moved to other areas. One remaining task was to completely flush and steam-clean the filling equipment just removed from the three lines. That was done in a separate steam room.

Equipment Maintenance

The filling machines were about 20 years old but had been ingeniously designed for quick and easy attach/detach from the rotary conveyor line shaft, and they were built to last. A strong corporate manufacturing engineering group (in another city) that had designed the equipment had dwindled to just a few people over the years.

The filling equipment in the steam room was cleaned—and that was all. There was no time for mechanical checking or other maintenance. In fact, throughout the Forbes plant there was a notable lack of preventive maintenance. Lines were lubricated daily by someone from maintenance, but not thoroughly. Old-timers recalled when there had been good PM in the Forbes plant and throughout the company, but PM programs had been pruned by company budget cutters. As PM dwindled, the plant's mode of operation evolved to, in Jerry Hanks's words, "run until it breaks."

The JIT task force was very much aware of the need to reinstall PM. The challenge was to do it without appreciably increasing payroll and other costs.

Discussion Questions

Question 1. Is the equipment maintenance problem severe? Support your answer with data and facts, if available. Consider possible causes of problems other than equipment troubles.

Question 2. What are the Forbes plant's three biggest problems, in rank order? Are they interrelated or mostly independent? Discuss.

Question 3. Devise a PM plan, including tasks, schedules, and labor needs, that will not appreciably raise costs. Discuss the benefits of the plan and its prospects for working.

17 FACILITIES POSITIONING

Facilities positioning: Location, layout, handling, and transportation planning.

Realtors say the three important factors in buying a house are location, location, and location. Our shopping patterns suggest the location of retail stores is similarly important. And transportation economics often make location a key success factor for wholesalers and manufacturers.

Location is one of the variables in facilities positioning, which also addresses what goes on inside and among facilities, including layout, handling, and transportation. We will consider these topics in this chapter, but first let's look at the strategic issues of positioning decisions.

Positioning Strategy

Positioning strategy helps answer the question, What facilities are needed? It ought to flow from and support overall business strategy. What do people in a firm want their own facilities to do? This is the lead-in question and answering it the first order of business.

Niche, Competencies, and Image

Care to do most of your wardrobe shopping from your home by catalog? Companies such as Spiegel, L. L. Bean, and Land's End are ready for your business. Their aim is to provide rapid-response, trouble-free home shopping service. A key facility need is a warehouse full of goods to ship. Saks Fifth Avenue, on the other hand, caters to the walk-in shopper with a hushed, nicely appointed decor. Its strategy is to operate a few fine stores and to retain a sense of exclusivity.

A carpeted showroom floor might be part of the desired image for a Porsche dealer, but it might be considered inappropriate at a dealership for construction or agricultural vehicles. Likewise, a health club catering to young people might build more aerobics and weight-training rooms, while a club seeking older members might favor pools and walking tracks. Remember the photographer from Chapter 6? If she elects not to do portrait work, she will not need studio facilities.

Thus, market niche, distinctive competencies, and desired image are determinants of facility needs. However, although retail-stage exchanges dominate the above examples, the facilities positioning issue encompasses the entire provider-customer chain.

When the using company does not have the needed facilities itself, it must rely on its suppliers. Furthermore, the company and its chain of suppliers and customers are collectively dependent on facilities in the infrastructure.

Exhibit 17–1 illustrates this dependency in the form of a facilities pyramid. Usually a company's own facilities are the first order of business, but failure of a supplier's facilities or infastructure problems can weaken the pyramid's base. To maintain a high level of customer service, a company might have to provide more facility support than anticipated. For example, firms that move plants into low-cost, perhaps rural, locations sometimes have to build roads, drill wells, or pay to expand sewer systems—public facilities. Lack of infrastructure is often a problem in less-developed countries, while crumbling infrastructure might be the concern in developed ones.

We can illustrate the facilities pyramid by considering a catalog shopping business like L. L. Bean. First, it needs its own facilities for processing orders. A mail-order business has its own warehousing and shipping facilities, and it might also have facilities to design, produce, and mail catalogs. But it probably would rely on suppliers' facilities for manufacturing of products advertised in its catalogs.

Beyond that, the mail-order business would have to rely considerably on public facilities, or infrastructure. Goods would arrive and be shipped via streets, highways, rails, bridges, airports, ports, and navigable waterways. Inadequate public water systems, sewage treatment plants, and flood-control facilities in the business's zone of operations could greatly increase costs for the mail-order house or any of its suppliers.

Let's summarize by drawing attention to the top of the pyramid in Exhibit 17–1: When a company answers the question What facilities are needed? it must include those required for planning and design, production, transportation, marketing, service, and the

*𝒫*RINCIPLE 6:

Organize resources to focus on a product, service, or customer family.

Facilities Along the Provider-Customer Chain

In partnering up with a supplier, it is important to certify that the supplier has the right facilities and that they are in good condition.

Exhibit 17–1   The Facilities Requirements Pyramid

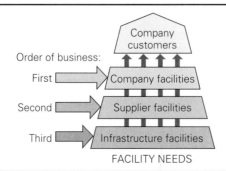

$\mathcal{I}$*nto* $\mathcal{P}$*ractice*

Is This Dublin or Montego Bay?

If you are a New Yorker who needs to get some program assistance from Quarterdeck Office Systems, the California-based software company, your early morning call will be answered in (where else?) Dublin, Ireland. Or if you plan on flying from Winnipeg to Salt Lake City, the toll-free number you call to make your reservation might be handled by an operator in Montego Bay, Jamaica. Telecommunications advances coupled with aggressive efforts by some nations to boost their educational systems have "put wings on everything from insurance work to engineering and computer programming."

Satellite dishes connect the United States to 3,500 Jamaicans in office parks, where they make airline reservations and process tickets, handle calls to toll-free numbers, and do data entry. Also, over 25,000 documents a day (such as credit card applications) are scanned in the United States and then transmitted to Jamaica for processing.

Beginning at 4:00 A.M., New York time, long before Californians are at work, calls to Quarterdeck are routed to Dublin, where Quarterdeck has its second phone-answering operation. At the same location, scores of multilingual employees handle inquiries from all over Europe. That would have been impossible until a few years ago when the Irish government spent billions to upgrade the country's phone system. The aim was to provide infrastructure needed to turn the island into a telecommunications service center.

SOURCE: Brian O'Reilly, "Your New Global Work Force," *Fortune*, December 14, 1992, pp. 52–66.

communications and information links that tie them all together and connect the company with its customers. Clearly, facilities-related decisions need cross-functional, team-based expertise, for the effects can extend throughout an organization and into its environment. Of those facilities-positioning decisions, however, the most far-reaching one is location.

Location

As the last century ended, daring individuals accomplished spectacular feats of travel, circling the globe in less than 70 days, making real the fiction of Jules Verne's 1872 classic, *Around the World in 80 Days*. As this century ends, the ordinary citizen could make the trip in less than 70 hours. Rather than guessing what lies another century ahead, we will simply note that it takes little time to move people or things from one spot on the globe to another. Communications advances are equally impressive. Satellites, microwave links, fiber-optic cables, and so on, make nearly immediate voice and facsimile transmission a global reality, as the box illustrates.

Location Economics   Any official of a city that has gained or lost a major plant or government facility will be able to point out the economic impact on the community. Location is far-reaching because where the jobs go, the money goes. Payrolls, along with the jobs and tax revenues generated as payrolls are spent, separate the haves among cities, states and nations, from the have-nots. Communities recognize this and keep increasing what they are willing to spend to attract businesses and jobs. According to Robert Reich, U.S. Secretary of Labor, "In 1980 Tennessee paid the equivalent of $11,000 per job to entice Nissan" to locate in the state, and "by 1986 Indiana had to spend $50,000 per job to induce Subaru-Isuzu to set up shop'' there. South Carolina's tab for bringing in BMW ''is the equivalent of about $100,000 per job.''[1]

Until recently, research and design and management jobs generally stayed in highly developed countries, and lower-skilled jobs were relegated to underdeveloped or emerging nations. But look at some recent examples of who's doing what:[2]

- Hewlett-Packard's new portable inkjet printer business is run from Singapore. The design, manufacture, and profit responsibility are all Singapore based.
- In the village of Fermoy, County Cork, Ireland, 150 Metropolitan Life Insurance Company employees analyze medical insurance claims to determine eligibility for reimbursement in the United States. The work requires knowledge of medicine, the American medical system, and the insurance business.
- In 1990, General Electric bought Tungsram, the Budapest, Hungary, light bulb manufacturer. In the bargain, GE got a work force that turned out to be among the world's best at designing and making advanced lighting systems.

New location economics seem to be emphasizing the human component. A more competitive and global work force has appeared, and work will continue to flow to wherever it can be performed best. Thus, managers responsible for making location decisions must rely on efficient yet comprehensive tools for rating alternative location possibilities.

One such rating system is in use at United Technologies, Inc., a large industrial corporation. The first of three steps is to comparatively rate the importance of a large number of location factors. Exhibit 17–2 is an abbreviated example (many more factors could be included in a location study).   *Rating Alternative Locations*

The figure shows that each of 14 factors (A through N) is compared with each other one; ratings are inserted on the matrix. Take, for example, the intersection of factors G and K, ''other technology-related companies in area'' and ''access to suppliers.'' The rating in the diamond-shaped box is 3G. Checking the ''importance'' scale, we see that 3 means ''medium preference,'' in this case, a medium preference of G over K.

The bottom row in Exhibit 17–2 contains total weighting raw scores. Those scores reflect type of facility. By studying the scores, we might be able to guess what kind of facility this matrix represents. Availability of higher education (F) is number one in importance; nearness to customer (C) and access to suppliers (K) are near the bottom. Could the facility be a design center?

Step 2 in United Technologies' system is to rate the locations under consideration against the location factors, A through N in this case. Exhibit 17–3A is a partial matrix (listing just 6 of the 14 factors) showing the results of this step for seven locations; in a real study real names rather than colors would be on the matrix. We see that location Red gets the highest rating, 10, on factor F, higher education. In fact, all of location Red's ratings (for the factors shown) are fairly high. But these are not the final ratings. A third stage is needed.

The third matrix, Exhibit 17–3B, combines ratings from the first and second steps. Location Red got 10 points for higher education, and higher education was rated 33 in importance; 10 times 33 is 330, which goes into the upper-left corner in Exhibit 17–3B. The rest of the matrix gets the same treatment, column totals are added, and total weighted

[1]Robert B. Reich, ''Toward a New Economic Development,'' *Industry Week,* October 5, 1992, pp. 37–44.
[2]Brian O'Reilly, ''Your New Global Workforce,'' *Fortune,* December 14, 1992, pp. 52–66.

EXHIBIT 17–2   Evaluation Matrix for Relative Weighting of Location Factors*

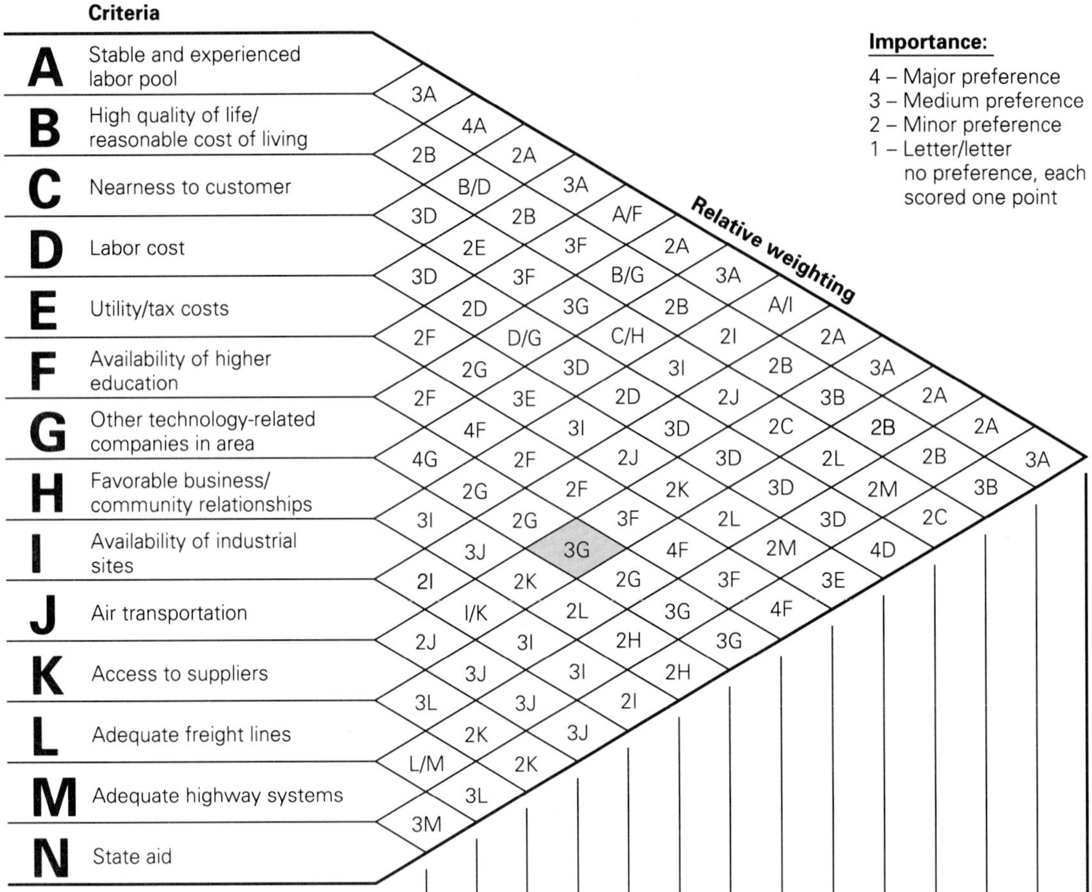

Criteria

A	Stable and experienced labor pool
B	High quality of life/reasonable cost of living
C	Nearness to customer
D	Labor cost
E	Utility/tax costs
F	Availability of higher education
G	Other technology-related companies in area
H	Favorable business/community relationships
I	Availability of industrial sites
J	Air transportation
K	Access to suppliers
L	Adequate freight lines
M	Adequate highway systems
N	State aid

Importance:
4 – Major preference
3 – Medium preference
2 – Minor preference
1 – Letter/letter
   no preference, each
   scored one point

Relative weighting

```
  3A
  4A
2B   2A
  B/D   3A
3D   2B   A/F
  2E   3F   2A
3D   3F   B/G   3A
  2D   3G   2B   A/I
2F   D/G   C/H   2I   2A
  2G   3D   3I   2B   3A
2F   3E   2D   2J   3B   2A
  4F   3I   3D   2C   2B   2A
4G   2F   2J   3D   2L   2B   3A
  2G   2F   2K   3D   2M   3B
3I   2G   3F   2L   3D   2C
  3J  [3G]  4F   2M   4D
2I   2K   2G   3F   3E
  I/K   2L   3G   4F
2J   3I   2H   3G
  3J   3I   2H
3L   3J   2I
  2K   3J
L/M   2K
  3L
3M
```

Factor letter	N	M	L	K	J	I	H	G	F	E	D	C	B	A
Total weighting raw score	0	8	13	9	18	23	5	26	33	8	31	5	20	31

*Not a comprehensive list.

SOURCE: Adapted from Eugene Bauchner, "Making the Most of Your Company's Resources," *Expansion Management*, 1989 Directory, pp. 20–25.

scores are compared. Location Purple is the winner with 1,227 points; locations Blue and Red are not far behind.

Intangibles, such as the whim of a CEO, could change the decision, or politics could intervene. In any case, systematic analysis is valuable because it reduces a lot of data to a few numbers, which can be used to influence the final decision. As we see next, however, gamesmanship also can figure into location strategies.

Preemptive Strategy

If you are a bridge player, you know that a preemptive bid is a very high opening bid made when one has few points. The purpose is to raise the stakes enough to discourage competitors from making their own bids, even though they may have more points. A similar

Exhibit 17–3 Rating Prospective Locations

A. Rating Locations by Factors

	Locations						
Factor	*Red*	*Yellow*	*Green*	*Orange*	*Blue*	*Purple*	*White*
F. Higher education	10	5	4	7	8	6	9
G. Other technology-related companies	6	5	4	7	8	9	10
A. Stable, experienced labor pool	6	5	4	7	8	9	7
D. Labor cost	9	6	7	4	8	10	5
E. Utility/tax cost	7	6	5	3	8	10	9
J. Air transportation	10	6	5	8	9	7	4

B. Weighted Location Scores

	Locations						
Factor	*Red*	*Yellow*	*Green*	*Orange*	*Blue*	*Purple*	*White*
F. Higher education (33)	330	165	132	231	264	198	297
G. Other technology companies (26)	156	130	104	182	208	234	260
A. Stable, experienced labor (31)	186	155	124	217	248	279	217
D. Labor cost (31)	279	186	217	124	248	310	155
E. Utility/tax cost (8)	56	48	40	24	64	80	72
J. Air transportation (18)	180	108	90	144	162	126	72
Total weighted score	1,187	792	707	922	1,194	1,227	1,073
Ranking	3	6	7	5	2	1	4

Source: Adapted from Eugene Bauchner, "Making the Most of Your Company's Resources," *Expansion Management*, 1989 Directory, pp. 20–25.

strategy occurs in locating businesses or adding production capacity. A grocery chain, hotel, or pizza franchise may decide to open its next facility in a sparsely populated location in the hope of discouraging competitors. Manufacturers also sometimes follow facility strategies aimed partly at deterring competition. Sometimes just an announcement (which itself can be a bluff) of an intent to add capacity somewhere may convince a competitor not to do likewise because overcapacity in the industry, with resulting lower profit expectations, might result. The practice is called a preemptive strategy in business and industry just as it is in the game of bridge.

Regardless of location, or even of the strategy used to make location decisions, deployment continues by looking inside facilities, at facility layout.

Layout

At precisely 12 noon, the entire insurance staff—nearly 500 clerks, technicians, and managers—piled their personal belongings on office chairs and said good-bye to fellow employees. Pushing the chairs along crowded corridors, crisscrossing and colliding at intersections, all 500 made their way to newly assigned work areas.[3]

That's the sound of moving day at Aid Association for Lutherans (AAL), an insurance company. But this moving day was different. Departments and sections weren't just

[3]John Hoerr, "Work Teams Can Rev Up Paper-Pushers, Too," *Business Week*, November 28, 1988, pp. 64–72.

Physical layout of facilities in a building entails decisions about organization of associates who use the facilities. In the broad sense, then, we are talking about organization of resources, not merely layout of facilities in space.

changing offices; the organization structure itself was on the chopping block. The 500 employees were shaken out into 15 focused teams in two tiers. The top tier is five groups, each serving insurance agents in a different region. Within each group are three bottom-tier teams of 20 to 30 people, one team for new policies, one for claims, and one for services.

We've noted the advantages of creating focused cells, flow lines, and teams throughout this book, and in Chapter 11, we introduced basic layout types and discussed their characteristics. That discussion focused more on what; here we concentrate more on how. First, however, we examine the effects of operating environment on layout and, perhaps more important, on re-layout.

Layout and Re-Layout

New facilities require new layouts. Existing facilities get out of date and require re-layout. Type of operating environment affects facility layout; we'll consider just four operating environments: mechanized production lines, labor-intensive production lines, job or batch production, and labor-intensive services.

1. In mechanized production lines, original layout planning had better be good because of the high cost of repositioning large machinery and related facilities. In a petrochemical plant, for example, the layout of tanks, chambers, valves, pipes, and other equipment is so much a part of the plant itself that major re-layout may never be feasible. In steel manufacturing the cost of major re-layout is also enormous, and steel plants may close rather than retool and re-layout to improve efficiency, meet pollution control regulations, and so on. Retooling of automated transfer lines in the auto industry is undertaken every few years, but the layout of retooled machines changes infrequently. In each of these examples, the initial layout choices restrict the firm's ability to respond to major changes in product line or technology for years to come.

2. Assembly lines (manual, not robotic) are less fixed. Assemblers and their tools are mobile. Thus, initial layout planning is not so critical; the focus is on re-layout, which has its own costs. These include costs of planning, line balancing, retraining, and rearranging benches, storage facilities, material handling aids, and large pieces of equipment.

3. Job and batch production often entails large machines and storage and handling aids. Re-layout may be attractive, however, because the equipment used tends to be general purpose, loosely coupled, and movable. A pump manufacturer in South Carolina has constructed a plant with very thick concrete floors so that heavy equipment can be moved anywhere. Exhibit 17–4 shows three versions of putting equipment on wheels for easy re-layout.

- Part A of the exhibit shows two large drill presses on casters, with detailed blowups of the casters and mountings themselves.

- Part B shows a combination assembly bench and material transport cart. It holds five cannisters in a plant producing self-contained breathing apparatus. The operation is laid out into several cells for assembly and test, and each cell provides floor space for one wheeled bench/cart.

- Part C shows a packing bench on wheels. It is used for packing the safety headgear shown in the background. Packers push the bench next to a machine printing customer logos on the caps or into aisles of a stockroom holding headgear so packing can take place there. Prior to development of the wheeled benches, conveyors were used to move headgear to a separate packing department.

These kinds of devices for flexible layout and re-layout are important; otherwise the ability to change and continually improve may be thwarted. Symptoms of the need include bottlenecks, backtracking, overcrowding, poor utilization of capacity (including

EXHIBIT 17–4   Equipment on Wheels

A. Machines on casters*

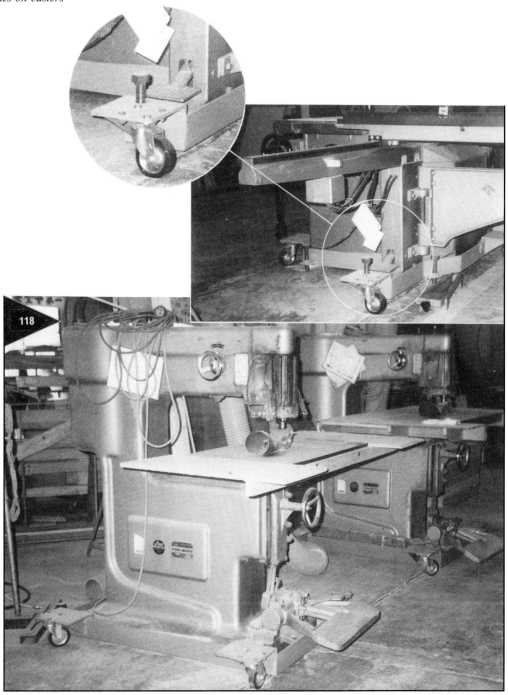

EXHIBIT 17–4   *(Continued)*

B. Assembly bench/cart for self-contained breathing apparatus at Mine Safety Appliance Co., Inc. Used with permission.
C. Wheeled packing benches for safety headgear at Mine Safety Appliance Co., Inc. Used with permission.

---

space), poor housekeeping, missed due dates, too much temporary storage, and a high or growing ratio of total lead time to actual work content.

4. Labor-intensive services undergo frequent re-layout. Office employees may begin to "wonder where my desk will be on Monday morning." The desk may be across town in newly rented office space. Physical obstacles are few; most offices can move overnight if telephone hookups can be arranged. With few physical problems, office re-layout commonly focuses on people and work climate, as the accompanying box illustrates.

$\mathcal{I}$nto $\mathcal{P}$ractice

Re-Layout: Employee-Centered Style

When Woodsmith, a Des Moines–based publisher of catalogs for do-it-yourself carpenters, recently redesigned its offices, CEO Donald Peshke chose to forgo the use of outside contractors and instead asked each of the 35-person staff to do his or her own area. Peshke's goal was not so much to save money as to save time.

Outside installers would have required over a week to break down the office's movable wall panels and modular furniture and transform the office. With a Friday evening kickoff pizza party, the Woodsmith staff launched the weekend stint, and by Monday morning had the walls redone, furniture installed, and equipment relocated.

With help from a local Herman Miller dealer, each employee had designed a layout for his or her work area, deciding where to locate work surfaces and position computers, file cabinets, and other equipment. Peshke explained: "Our approach was to get them involved in the design so they'd understand what couldn't be done. They accept limitations a lot better that way, instead of the boss saying, 'This is what you're going to live with, like it or not.' " But the best part of the whole experience, according to Peshke, "turned out to be the comraderie it developed."

SOURCE: Robert A. Mamis, "Employees as Contractors," *Inc.*, November 1992, p. 53.

Perhaps people and work climate should be central concerns in all layout and re-layout work. Certainly, many layout jobs are more complex than that faced by Woodsmith, yet human needs can be accommodated, for example, for specific interactions. We will see this in the next sections when we undertake a detailed layout-planning example.

In a complex layout situation, hundreds or thousands of jobs may be in progress at any given time. Repetitive, job, and project work may be included, with products and resources delivered to work centers via many routings.

Layout-Planning Steps

When routes are so diverse, how work areas are arranged in a building makes a difference. Dominant flow patterns from makers to customers are there among the apparent jumble of routings, and layout analysis helps to find those patterns.

One layout principle is to arrange work areas in the order of dominant flow. A goal is to get production or resources into, through, and out of each work center in minimum time at reasonable cost. The less time products/resources spend in the flow pattern, the less chance they have to collect labor and overhead charges and the faster the immediate and final customers are served.

Other factors besides flows may be important. If so, the nonflow factors (e.g., teamwork) may be combined with flow data. The combined data will suggest how close work areas should be to one another, and a rough layout can be developed. The next step is to determine the space requirements for a rough layout. The last step in layout planning is to fit the rough layout into the available space, that is, the proposed or existing building. Several layout plans can be developed for managers to choose from.

The layout planning steps just described are listed in Exhibit 17–5, along with planning aids usable in each step.

Example 17–1 demonstrates the layout planning steps. The method and some of the tools were developed by R. R. Muther, who calls the approach **systematic layout planning**

Layout Planning Example

EXHIBIT 17–5   Layout Planning—Steps and Possible Tools

Steps	*Possible Tools*
1. Analyze product (resource) flows.	Flow diagram From-to chart
2. Identify and include nonflow factors, where significant.	Activity-relationship (REL) chart Combined REL chart
3. Assess data and arrange work areas.	Activity arrangement diagram
4. Determine space arrangement plan.	Space relationship diagram
5. Fit space arrangement into available space.	Floor plan Detailed layout models

(SLP).[4] SLP, a practical approach, is widely referenced and used. Though developed in an earlier era, SLP works well in support of a modern, customer-oriented approach to layout.

EXAMPLE 17–1   LAYOUT PLANNING—GLOBE COUNTY OFFICES

Citizens' main contact with Globe County offices is in registering and licensing vehicles. Many people complain because the three county offices involved have not consolidated their services. On busy days there are waiting lines at all three offices. Many vehicle owners must visit all three, and it is common for a citizen to find out, after shuffling forward for awhile, that it is the wrong line.

The elected officials who run the three offices have decided to consolidate. Mr. Ross, a consultant, has been hired to conduct layout analysis using SLP.

Ross's analysis reveals that 12 activities are to be located in the available space, and that four of those have significant flows: three service counters, plus the office copier (see Exhibit 17–6). The space requirements are based on careful measurement of desks, files, and so forth, plus use of widely available industry space standards (e.g., 300 square feet per auto in a parking lot).

Flow analysis. For those four activities, Ross gathers flow data, which he enters on a from-to chart (which resembles the distance chart found on many road maps), as shown in Exhibit 17–7A. Numbers above the diagonal represent flows of patrons from one activity to another; numbers below the diagonal reflect backtracking by patrons who find themselves in the wrong office, and round trips to and from the copiers.

Exhibit 17–7B is a conversion chart, which Ross develops for displaying from-to data in order of descending flow volume. Ross then judgmentally inserts horizontal lines that divide the flow-volume bars into five zones, labeled A, E, I, O, and U, which are the standard SLP symbols for flow volume.

Nonflow factors. Next, Ross lists nonflow factors, such as the need for employees to be near their supervisor, and rates them using the same five vowel designators. He combines flow and nonflow factors on an activity relationship (REL) chart, as shown in Exhibit 17–8.

The REL chart is easy to interpret. The single A in the chart indicates that it is absolutely necessary for customer service people in the clerk and treasurer offices to be close together. Reasons are "work flow" (1), "employee sharing (between departments)" (3), and "share counter" (4). The same reasons apply to the E, for especially important, in the box connecting customer service counter people in the clerk and assessor office.

---

[4]Richard R. Muther, *Systematic Layout Planning* (Boston: Cahners, 1973), pp. 3-1–3-8 (TS178.M87).

Exhibit 17–6   Major Work Areas—County Offices

Activity	Space Requirements (square feet)
1. County assessor's office:	
a. Management	600
b. Motor vehicle—counter*	300
c. Motor vehicle—clerical	240
d. Assessors	960
2. County clerk's office:	
e. Management	840
f. Recording and filing—counter	240
g. Recording and filing—clerical	960
h. Motor vehicle—counter-clerical*	960
3. County treasurer's office:	
i. Management	420
j. Motor vehicle—counter-clerical*	1,600
4. Support areas:	
k. Mail and copier*	240
l. Conference room	160
Total	7,520

*Significant flows.

Source: This is adapted from a real case. Thanks go to Ross Greathouse of Greathouse-Flanders Associates, Lincoln, Nebraska, for providing original case data.

Activity arrangement. Now Ross converts the combined REL chart to an activity arrangement diagram, which shows the arrangement of all activities but without indicating requirements for space, utilities, halls, and so on (see Exhibit 17–9). In this diagram, number of lines between activities stands for flow volume: Four lines corresponds to an A rating on the REL chart, three lines stands for an E rating, and so forth. Distances between circles are set according to desired degree of closeness, as much as possible. Activities 2, 6, 8, and 10, at the core, are all service-counter activities, which earlier ratings showed should be placed close together.

Space arrangement. Ross's next-to-last chart, shown in Exhibit 17–10, includes the space data from Exhibit 17–6. The result is a diagram that is in the generally rectangular shape of the space into which the activities must fit; activity blocks are sized according to space needed. The space relationship diagram may be regarded as a rough layout.

Layout into available space. Finally, Ross is ready to draw some final layouts, complete with walls, halls, aisles, and other needed elements.

Exhibit 17–11 shows what Ross might have developed. Part A is an actual layout of the county office renovation that is the basis for this example. Part B shows the main feature of that layout, the shared counter. The layout was developed by an architectural firm (though the systematic layout planning process, as presented here, was not fully used) and approved and implemented by newly elected Lancaster County officials in Lincoln, Nebraska.

The Globe County Offices example is fairly simple. In large, complex layouts, analysis within each activity area could include the full SLP treatment, that is, all the SLP steps. In later steps, various two- and three-dimensional models (manual or computer graphic) can be manipulated to produce workable layout options. In the Globe County example, we also glossed over all the trial and error usually involved in the diagramming.

Some of the drudgery can be avoided by using computer software in the search phase of layout planning. One program, called CORELAP (computerized relationship layout   *Computer Assistance in Layout*

EXHIBIT 17–7   Flow Volume (People per Day)—County Offices

A. From-to chart

From	To	Clerk 1	Assessor 2	Treasurer 3	Copier 4	Totals 5
Motor vehicle counter— clerk	1		A 100	B 250	D 30	380
Motor vehicle counter— assessor	2	C 20		A 100	D 10	130
Motor vehicle counter— teasurer	3	C 40				40
Copier	4	D 30	D 10			40
Totals		90	90	350	40	590

Note: Types of product flow:

A   Patrons licensing newly purchased vehicles.

B   Patrons licensing same-owner vehicles.

C   Patrons to wrong office—backtrack to correct office.

D   Round trips to copier.

B. Conversion to vowel ratings on bar chart

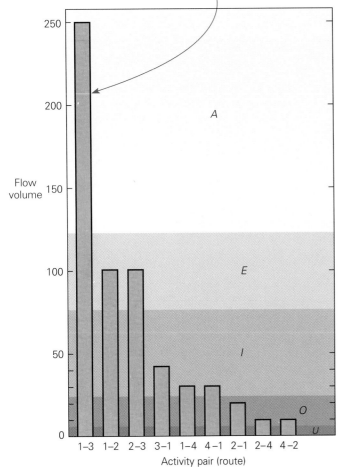

Key:

A   for *a*bnormally high flow

E   for *e*specially high flow

I   for *i*mportant flow

O   for *o*rdinary flow

U   for *u*nimportant moves of negligible flow volume

EXHIBIT 17–8 Combined Activity Relationship (REL) Chart—County Offices

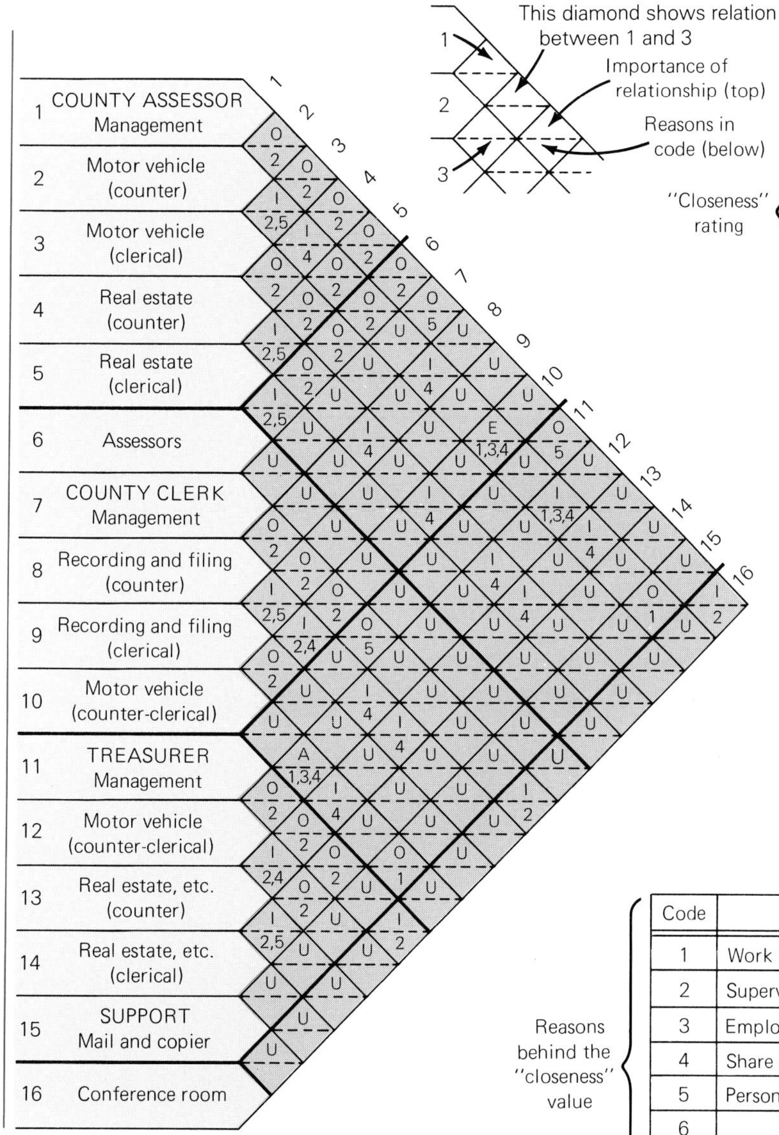

Value	Closeness	Number of ratings
A	Absolutely necessary	
E	Especially important	
I	Important	
O	Ordinary closeness OK	
U	Unimportant	
X	Not desirable	

Reasons behind the "closeness" value

Code	Reason
1	Work flow
2	Supervision
3	Employee sharing (between departments)
4	Share counter
5	Personal communication
6	
7	
8	
9	

SOURCE OF REL CHART FORM: Richard Muther and Associates, Kansas City, Missouri. Used with permission.

planning), uses closeness ratings from the REL chart (e.g., Exhibit 17–8) as inputs. It produces a single layout of rectangular-shaped departments; department lengths and widths are set forth in advance. The CORELAP algorithm maximizes common borders for closely related departments. CORELAP is flexible enough to be used for either office or plant layout.

A program called CRAFT (computerized relative allocation of facilities technique) requires an existing layout as an input. Its job is to improve the layout. CRAFT uses flow

EXHIBIT 17-9   Activity Arrangement Diagram—County Offices

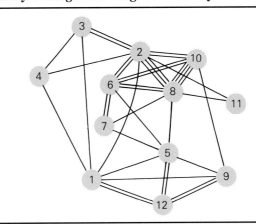

EXHIBIT 17-10   Space Relationship Diagram—County Offices

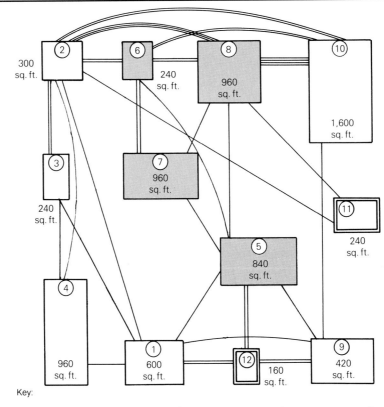

Key:

Numbers 2, 6, 8, and 10 are service-counter activities.	County assessor activities are 1-4.	County treasurer activities are 9-10.	County clerk activities are shaded.	Shared activities are double-bordered.

EXHIBIT 17–11   New Layout and Motor Vehicle Licensing Counter

A. Final layout—county offices

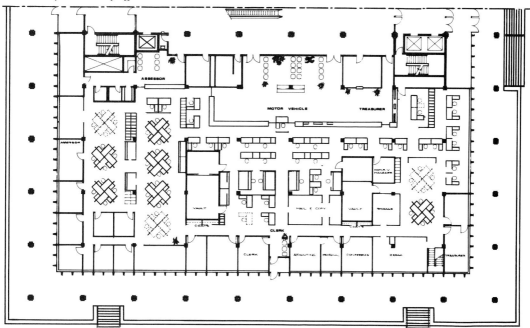

FIRST FLOOR SOUTH PLAN

B. Vehicle licensing counter shared by employees of the county assessor, clerk, and treasurer

$\mathcal{I}$nto $\mathcal{P}$ractice

Layout: Making Banks Look Like Stores

"Come see Chicago's newest architectural wonder," the advertisement proclaimed. The "wonder" is actually one of Citibank's new branches, unobtrusively placed on the ground floor of the USG Building in Chicago's Loop. Why all the fuss over a new branch bank? Layout.

When financial panics were more common, people were reluctant to let someone else guard their money. To win confidence, banks had to convey a trustworthy, solid image; massive stone and steel buildings with imposing granite counters and bars separating tellers from the public helped create the impression of security in customer's minds. Today, with banking an accepted way of life, security is largely a given, and bankers want their names associated with a new concept: service.

Increasingly, banks are being laid out like stores, though they resemble convenience stores more than top-of-the-line retailers. In the Citibank facility, for example, an employee in the "greeter station" directs customers to nearby areas for tellers, loan counselors, or investment sales personnel. The space is open, bars are gone, and signs promoting the bank's line of products and services are prominent.

The store concept is spreading throughout the banking industry. "We are a retailer of financial services," says Chuck Shoemaker, a senior vice president at First Chicago Corp. "I tell our employees we're no different from Marshall Field's, except they're selling shirts and ties and we're selling checking accounts and investment products."

SOURCE: Blair Kamin, "Edifice Exits: Banks Assume Retail Look," *Chicago Tribune*, Section 3, p. 1, November 12, 1992.

(from-to) data but not nonflow (REL-chart) data. Its main purpose is to minimize material-handling cost, which is a dominant concern in plant layout. CRAFT is usually not well suited for office layout, in which other matters besides work flow are important.[5]

Open Layouts

One of the special influences on office layout is the **open-office concept,** which became commonplace during the 1970s. The open-office idea eliminates many floor-to-ceiling walls and deemphasizes functional compartmentalization of people. One key advantage is that the open-office concept is more customer-friendly, especially in establishments that are trying to promote customer service. By opening up to customers, providers remove some of the mystery or secrecy from their operations. Banks are good examples, as the box illustrates.

Other advantages of open layouts are that they foster better employee communications and provide flexibility for easy re-layout. Modular office furniture and movable, partial-height partitions aid in achieving these goals.

Open offices in Japan, where the concept is deeply ingrained, often are truly wide open. North Americans, in contrast, have emphasized maintaining a degree of privacy and cutting noise. Interior designers use wall carpeting, sound-absorbent panels, acoustical screens, fabric-wrapped desktop risers, and free-standing padded partitions. Office landscaping (use of plants) is also commonplace.

Layout-planning expertise is also available from architectural firms and firms specializing in layout. Interior designers are likely to focus on appearance, atmosphere, light,

---

[5]Copies of the programs are available as follows: CORELAP from Engineering Management Associates of Boston, and CRAFT from the IBM Share Library System. Enhanced versions of these programs are announced frequently.

and acoustics, mostly in offices (especially offices in which the public is met frequently). Layout specialists are more engineering oriented and likely to direct their efforts to material-flow factors; they tend to work mostly on factory layouts, where function rather than appearance is the main concern. Architects are helpful for new construction or major remodeling.

Handling and Transportation

Transportation and handling systems add cost but not value, yet they are needed for work to move through operations and out into customers' hands. While layout concerns flow and nonflow factors, the flow factors are dominant in handling and transportation. In this section we examine handling concepts and analysis, and containerization, one of the techniques for reducing handling while goods are being moved.

A well-established practice that is supposed to hold down handling cost is the **unit-load concept.** The idea is simple: Avoid moving piece by piece; instead, accumulate enough pieces to move them as a unit load. Examples are truckloads and rail-car loads between plants, and a loaded pallet, skid, drum, tote box, hand truck, and carton within a facility.

Handling Concepts

The unit-load idea dominated thinking for years, but it is being questioned. The new idea is to avoid accumulating enough pieces to move them as a unit load; instead, try to move them piece by piece so there is no extra stock in a state of idleness and no delay for building up a load.

*P*RINCIPLE 13:

Decrease cycle interval and lot size.

Actually, the unit-load and piece-by-piece viewpoints can converge. If process layouts are broken up and work centers grouped into production cells or lines, handling distances collapse. Without distance to span, the economical unit-load size is pushed downward and may approach one piece.

*P*RINCIPLE 11:

Decrease flow distances.

Using several small, dispersed machines instead of a supermachine is a way to cut handling distances. Multiple small machines can be located close to where material comes from and goes to, that is, in a production line or cell.

*P*RINCIPLE 9:

Of course, there will always be some distances to span and therefore some handling costs. However, the fact that three OM principles are listed in this brief section should signal that handling is ripe with cost-saving opportunities. Careful analysis can often produce those savings.

Install multiple copies of small, simple machines.

Handling analysis requires two steps: (1) analyzing resource flows (materials and other resources that require handling, e.g., tools and mail), and (2) prescribing handling methods. If the first step is done well, the second is relatively easy.

Handling Analysis

Data collected on each product or resource can be plotted on a distance-quantity (DQ) chart or, if products/resources are dissimilar, on a distance intensity (DI) chart. Intensity of flow, a measure developed by Muther, equals quantity times transportability. Transportability is an artificial measure that may include size, density or bulk, shape, risk of damage, condition, and sometimes value of the given item.[6]

The DQ or DI chart helps show the types of handling methods needed. Exhibit 17–12 serves as a guide. Four quadrants are shown in the figure. A low-distance, high-volume product would plot in the first quadrant, which suggests complex handling equipment such as conveyors. Low-distance, low-volume calls for simple handling (second quadrant)

---

[6]A method for determining transportability may be found in Richard Muther, *Systematic Handling Analysis* (Management and Industrial Research Publications, 1969) (TS180.M8).

EXHIBIT 17–12   DQ or DI Chart Indicating Preferred Handling Methods

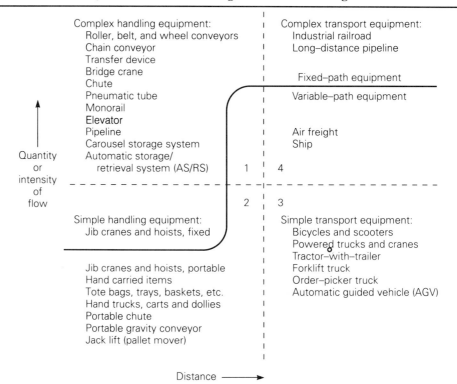

Complex handling equipment:
  Roller, belt, and wheel conveyors
  Chain conveyor
  Transfer device
  Bridge crane
  Chute
  Pneumatic tube
  Monorail
  Elevator
  Pipeline
  Carousel storage system
  Automatic storage/
      retrieval system (AS/RS)

Complex transport equipment:
  Industrial railroad
  Long–distance pipeline

Fixed–path equipment

Variable–path equipment

  Air freight
  Ship

Quantity
or
intensity
of
flow

1 | 4

2 | 3

Simple handling equipment:
  Jib cranes and hoists, fixed

  Jib cranes and hoists, portable
  Hand carried items
  Tote bags, trays, baskets, etc.
  Hand trucks, carts and dollies
  Portable chute
  Portable gravity conveyor
  Jack lift (pallet mover)

Simple transport equipment:
  Bicycles and scooters
  Powered trucks and cranes
  Tractor–with–trailer
  Forklift truck
  Order–picker truck
  Automatic guided vehicle (AGV)

Distance ⟶

such as hand-carry. High-distance, low-volume calls for simple transport equipment (any of the vehicle types in the third quadrant). High-distance, high-volume (fourth quadrant) suggests poor layout; handling distances are too great. If re-layout is impractical right away, the need is for complex transport equipment, such as a railroad.

The solid line cutting through the chart makes another distinction. Above the line are fixed-path types of handling equipment; below it are variable-path types. It is well to be cautious about investing in the fixed-path variety; it may be too costly to relocate or modify fixed equipment when needs change. It is common to enter a plant of average age and see unused remnants of an overhead conveyor or pneumatic tube system up in the rafters. Automatically guided vehicles and self-guiding order pickers, popularized in the 1960s, were something of a breakthrough. They have fixed-path advantages, but it is cheap to change their route: Simply paint a new white line on the floor for those that optically follow a line, or embed a new wire in the floor for those that sense a magnetic field generated by a current-carrying wire.

Some equipment has both handling and storage functions. One example is carousel systems, which are rotatable racks holding small parts, tools, documents, dry cleaning, and so forth. Another example, the automatic storage/retrieval system (AS/RS) consists of rows of racks with automated, perhaps computer-controlled, devices to put away and later select baskets or pallets of stock. Both types of equipment were widely installed in North America in the late 1970s and the 1980s. Recently, many companies have been figuring out ways to dismantle some of them; the racks conflict with the goal of avoiding storage. The AS/RS is fine in distribution centers, but when used for storing work-in-process inventories, it is usually a symptom of coordination problems. An exception is a

---

Exhibit 17-13   Mini AS/RS—Installed at Point of Use

Mini automatic storage/retrieval system being installed next to plastic-injection molding machine in South Korean factory. With mini AS/RS, the owner of the inventory is the machine operator, not a central stock room. Courtesy of Dorner Mfg. Corp., Hartland, Wisc.

---

newer type of "mini" AS/RS, which is small enough to be placed at the location where parts or tools are made or used (see Exhibit 17–13).

Forklift trucks are also losing favor as a means of handling in-process materials. If machines are close together, as in cells or product layout, materials may be moved by hand, conveyor, transfer device (transfer between adjacent stations), robot, or chute.

After the analyst identifies general types of handling equipment, it is time for detailed consideration of cost, reliability, maintainability, and adaptability. Vendors of material-handling equipment may help with the detailed design and then submit bids.

The equipment in quadrant 4 and some in quadrant 3 of Exhibit 17–12 serves a transportation as well as a handling function. Such equipment tends to be costly enough to warrant special cost analyses.

Container design, which once was haphazard, is critical for effective handling and transportation. The goals are to protect the goods, ensure exact counts, and simplify loading and unloading.

Containerization

The Automobile Industry Action Group's containerization task force has developed standard reusable collapsible containers for auto parts (see Exhibit 17–14), usable by competing suppliers and auto assembly plants. The containers avoid throw-away materials, especially cardboard, which cuts costs by a surprisingly large amount—over $50 per car already, according to the manager of one auto assembly plant. Other industries are also plunging into containerization, but mostly with each firm doing its own.

The new containers often are designed to hold an exact, easily verifiable quantity, perhaps through use of partitions or "egg-crate" molded bottoms or inserts. That helps solve a chronic problem. Outside suppliers would deliberately ship too much, hoping to be paid for the excess, or, where the supplier had a stock shortage, ship less than the

EXHIBIT 17–14   Reusable Collapsible Container

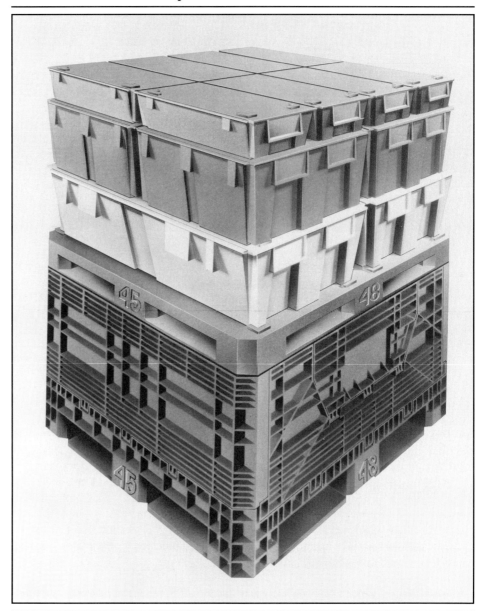

Courtesy Perstorp Xytec, Inc.

ordered quantity. Over- and undershipment led to costly delays to count every piece upon receipt and generated ill will. The new designs allow for counting containers, not pieces; or not counting at all, except on an audit basis. JIT makes containerization all the more necessary; it lowers inventories and available storage space to the point where receipt of too little or too much can't be tolerated.

On a larger scale, containerization includes semitrailers or large seagoing cargo boxes that can also move by rail or be trucked. Cargo boxes avoid costly handling of diverse small crates and boxes.

JIT shippers load the cargo boxes with small amounts of multiple components, called kits, rather than loading a huge lot of just one item into the box. Some North American plants use the transport-kit technique to receive just one day's supply of mixed parts every day from across an ocean.

Summary

The aim of facilities positioning is to improve customer service through management of facilities location, layout, handling, and transportation. The guiding strategy should support overall business strategy. A facility-positioning team's first order of business is to ensure that the company's own facilities support its market niche, special competencies, and image. A second concern is the facilities under control of suppliers, and infrastructure facility needs are a third concern.

The most far-reaching part of facilities positioning is the location decisions. Advances in transportation and telecommunications have included more of the world's labor force in modern, global commerce. Location economics—where the jobs go, the money goes—are mandating a higher emphasis on the readiness and willingness of the human component to carry out work.

Managers use alternative location rating models to help consider a broad set of factors such as labor, education, markets, taxes, supply sources, infrastructure, and transportation expense in location decisions. Various rating schemes are available to assist in reducing reams of location data to a ranking of each alternative location. A preemptive strategy is to announce pending capacity addition, seeking to deter competitors from taking similar actions.

Layout refers to facilities positioning within buildings, and re-layout is often necessary to restore facilities to a competitive, customer-serving status. Environment is a major determinant of what the layout ought to achieve.

Systematic layout planning (SLP) is a useful approach that usually begins with product and quantity analysis. From-to charts show flow volumes for products or resources that move in quantity; activity relationship charts address nonflow factors. The charted data are used to construct activity arrangement diagrams that lead to space relationship diagrams showing work area requirements for each activity. Finally, the activities are fit onto a floor plan, and the layout is complete. SLP may be partially computer assisted and is suitable for offices as well as plants. Interior design (furnishings, plants, acoustics, lighting, color, signs, fabrics, counters, landscapes, etc.) has become important in office layout. Thus, interior designers tend to rely more on art than on systematic layout analysis.

The primary aim of handling analysis is to reduce handling costs. Unit loading and sophisticated handling systems have been desirable, but modern thinking is that no handling is the best handling. Although this ideal is impossible, handling systems are being dismantled in favor of simpler methods for moving smaller lots over shorter distances. Layout improvement reduces the need for handling.

Systematic handling analysis starts with distance-quantity (or distance-intensity) data that suggest the type of handling equipment: simple or complex handling, simple or complex transport. Finally, specific handling equipment is selected. Variable-path equipment is more adaptable.

The use of standard containers with dividers to hold an exact quantity is increasing. Containerization reduces losses and amount of handling. The precise quantities per container eliminate time-consuming receiving counts and foster the precision called for in JIT purchasing.

Key Words

Facilities positioning   582

Systematic layout planning (SLP)   591

Open-office concept   598

Unit-load concept   599

Solved Problem

The five departments of a warehouse with their approximate square-footage requirements and activity relationships are as follows:

DEPARTMENT	AREA (square feet)	ACTIVITY RELATIONSHIPS
1. Materials scheduling	1,000	
2. Packaging and crating	1,500	E
3. Materials control supervisor	500	O A A E I
4. Shipping and receiving	3,000	I I O
5. Warehouse (storage)	6,000	A

TOTAL   12,000 square feet

a. Develop an activity arrangement diagram based on the REL chart data.

b. Develop a space relationship diagram for the five departmental areas.

c. Fit the five departments into a 100-foot by 150-foot building, and try to maintain 10-foot aisles between departments.

A. Activity arrangement diagram: *B.* Space relationship diagram:

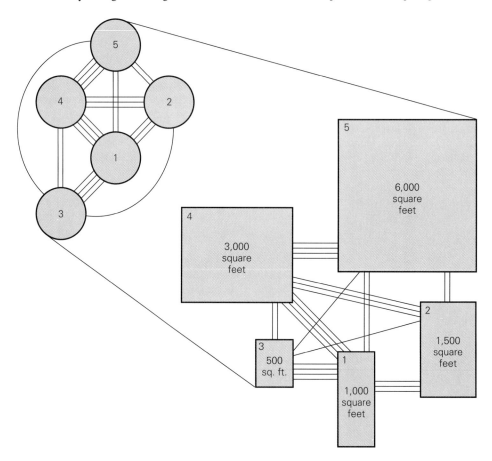

c. Following is a sample departmental layout in a 100-foot-by-150-foot building, maintaining 10-ft aisles. (Note: Department 1 has more space than required; all others have the required amount.)

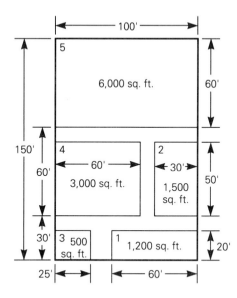

For Further Reference

Books

Apple, James M. *Plant Layout and Material Handling*. 3rd ed. New York: Ronald Press, 1977 (TS155.A58).

Coyle, John J.; Edward J. Bardi; and Joseph L. Cavinato. *Transportation*. 3rd ed. St. Paul, Minn.: West Publishing, 1990 (HE151.C88).

Hales, H. Lee. *Computer Aided Facilities Planning*. New York: Marcel Dekker, 1984 (TS177.H35).

Konz, Stephan A. *Facility Design*. New York: John Wiley & Sons, 1985 (TS177.K66).

Kulwiec, Raymond A., ed.-in-chief. *Materials Handling Handbook*. 2nd ed. New York: John Wiley & Sons, 1985 (TS180.M315).

Molnar, John. *Facilities Management Handbook*. New York: Van Nostrand Reinhold, 1983 (TH151.M59).

Steele, Fritz. *Making and Managing High-Quality Workplaces: An Organizational Ecology*. New York: Teachers College Press, 1986 (HF5547.2.S74)

Taff, Charles A. *Management of Physical Distribution and Transportation*. 7th ed. Homewood, Ill.: Richard D. Irwin, 1984.

Periodicals/Societies

Factory Management.

Industrial Engineering (Institute of Industrial Engineers).

Material Management Pacesetter (International Materials Management Society).

Modern Materials Handling.

Office.

Today's Office.

Review Questions

1. What is facilities positioning? Is the positioning process over after locations are chosen? Explain.

2. What three sets of facilities must positioning teams consider? Discuss each.

3. Identify factors that might be considered in location decisions.

4. What might a community, state, or nation do to attract business and industry? How do new location economics affect these efforts?

5. How might small, underdeveloped countries hope to benefit from global commerce?

6. Multiple variables could be important to facilities positioning teams. How might a team evaluate them all systematically?

7. What is a preemptive positioning strategy? How might such a strategy affect competition?

8. What is layout? How does layout affect customer service? Employee effectiveness?

9. How does office layout planning differ from plant layout planning?

10. What are some interior-design variables? How are they related to the concept of layout?

11. What is the origin of the data that go on the combined activity relationship chart?

12. How are degrees of closeness shown on the activity arrangement diagram? What determines sizes of blocks on the diagram?

13. How is the space relationship diagram converted to final layout?

14. What is the open-office concept? Is it desirable in all offices? Explain.

15. How is the handling system related to layout?

16. Is it a good idea to transport in unit loads? Explain.

17. What are the advantages of variable-path handling equipment?

18. Explain the role of containerization in modern operations management.

Problems and Exercises

1. Find out what you can about current location strategies for the following industries:

Carpeting.	Furniture.
Movie theaters.	Bottling.
Petroleum refining.	Electric power generation.
Boxing and packing materials.	Plastic molding.
Data entry.	Credit-rating services.

   a. How does the overall strategy serve various customers?

   b. Of the many variables that might affect location decisions, which seems to predominate?

2. Find out what you can about the U.S. Motor Carrier Deregulation Act of 1980. How has it affected handling or location strategies (or both) in North American industry? Discuss.

3. "Our approach to the labor union is to run from it." That is one auto parts executive's explanation of why they had nonunion plants in small, remote rural towns around the country. How do you think that strategy will be affected by the automakers' determination to get daily deliveries from their suppliers? Discuss.

4. Stuart Reeves, senior vice president for Dallas-based EDS, which manages information and technology, says:

   If you're hiring college types, there isn't a lot of difference among quality across nations. The difference among college graduates by countries is a lot less than the difference among day laborers and high schoolers. And there's a lot of pent-up talent out there.[7]

   a. If Mr. Reeves is correct, how might his assessment affect location decisions?

   b. If Mr. Reeves is correct, how would you use this information if you were a consultant retained to help an emerging nation become more attractive to foreign investors?

[7]Brian O'Reilly, "Your New Global Workforce," *Fortune,* December 14, 1992, pp. 52–66.

5. For each of the following types of industry, suggest which types of layout (process, product, cellular, fixed, and mixed) are likely to apply. Some types may have more than one likely type of layout. Explain your choices briefly.

Auto assembly.	Military physical exams.
Auto repair.	Small airplane manufacturing.
Shipbuilding.	Small airplane overhaul and repair.
Machine shop.	Large airplane overhaul and repair.
Cafeteria.	Shoe manufacturing.
Restaurant.	Shoe repair.
Medical clinic.	Central processing of insurance forms.
Hospital.	Packing and crating.

6. Draw a layout of a dentists' office (group practice with three dentists). Label the areas as to whether they are process, product, cellular, or fixed. Explain.

7. Develop an REL chart for a large discount or department store that you are familiar with. (You may need to visit the store for firsthand information.) Use the store's different departments as activities. Is the REL chart likely to be helpful in layout or re-layout of such a store? How about a flow diagram or a from-to chart? Explain.

8. Automatic Controls Corporation is building a new plant. Eight departments are involved. As part of a plant layout analysis, the activity relationships and square-footage needs for the departments are shown on the following combined REL chart (combined flow analysis and nonflow analysis):

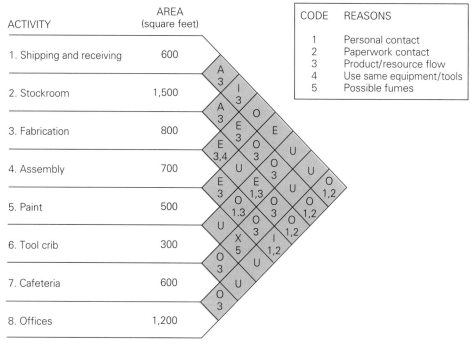

TOTAL	6,400 square feet

   a. Develop an activity arrangement diagram based on the REL chart data.

   b. Develop a space relationship diagram for the eight departmental areas.

   c. Fit the eight departments into a 100-foot-by-80-foot building in as close to an optimal layout as you can. Include aisles between departments on your layout.

   d. How necessary is the combined REL chart in this case? If it were not included in the analysis, what would the analysis steps be? Explain. (Hint: Note the pattern of reasons for relationships.)

9. Pharmaco, Inc., manufacturer of a drug line in liquid and tablet form, is considering moving to a new building. Layout planning is in process. The following data have been collected on material movements in the drug manufacturing process:[8]

	Unit Loads per Month	Move Distances (Feet) in Present Building
Raw-Material Movements		
Receiving to raw-material storage:		180
1. Powder in drums.	800	
2. Powder in sacks on pallets.	1,100	
3. Liquid in drums.	100	
4. Controlled substance (heroin) in cans in cartons.	10	
5. Empty bottles in cartons on pallets.	8,000	
6. Water piped into granulating and liquid mixing (gallons).	3,000	
In-Process Movements		
Raw-material storage to granulating:		410
7. Powder in drums.	800	
8. Powder in sacks.	1,000	
9. Controlled substance in cans.	50	
Raw-material storage to liquid mixing:		300
10. Powder in sacks.	100	
11. Liquid in drums.	100	
12. Controlled substance in cans.	10	
13. Granulating to tableting (granules in drums).	1,500	290
14. Tableting to fill and pack (tablets in tubs).	6,000	180
15. Liquid mixing to fill and pack (gallons piped).	4,000	370
16. Raw-material storage to fill and pack (empty bottles).	8,000	260
17. Fill and pack to finished storage (cartons of bottles and of tablet packs on pallets).	10,000	320

a. Convert the given flow-volume data to a vowel-rating scale; that is, identify which activity pairs (routes) should be rated A, E, I, O, and U.

b. Develop an activity arrangement diagram.

c. The layout planners see little need for a from-to chart or an REL chart. Explain why.

d. One option is to call off the move to the new building and update the material handling system in the present building. Develop a DQ chart using data for the present building. From your DQ chart, draw some conclusions about types of handling methods (equipment) that seem suitable for the present building.

10. The woodshop building of E-Z Window Company is undergoing major re-layout in order to reduce backtracking and decrease flow distances. A flow diagram of the frame-manufacturing operation and an REL chart for nonflow factors in the operation follow:

a. Construct a from-to chart based on flow diagram data. What is the meaning of the notation that quantities are in unit loads? Explain by referring to a few examples on the chart.

b. What proportion of total flow on your from-to chart represents backtracking? How does that proportion depend on your chosen order of listing activities on the chart? What does your chosen order of listing activities imply about the final layout arrangement?

[8]Problem adapted from materials developed for Material Handling Analysis, a course developed by Richard Muther & Associates and sponsored by the University of Kansas Extension Center, 1965.

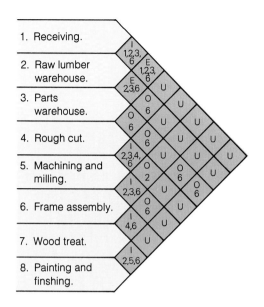

Code	Reason
1	Share records
2	Share employees
3	Share supervision
4	Share portable equipment (frame racks and saws)
5	Isolate together for reasons of fumes
6	Personal and paperwork coordination

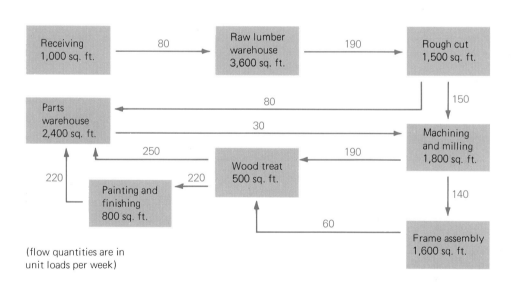

(flow quantities are in unit loads per week)

c. Convert the flow volume data in your from-to chart to a vowel-rating scale; that is, identify which activity pairs (routes) should be rated A, E, I, O, and U.

d. Combine your vowel-rating data representing flow volumes with the non-flow-factor vowel ratings on the REL chart. Express the result in a new, combined REL chart.

e. Convert your combined REL chart into an activity arrangement diagram.

f. Develop a space relationship diagram for the eight activity areas.

g. Fit the eight activity areas into a square building without allowances for aisles, and so on. Make your layout as nearly optimal as you can.

h. Based on distances between departments in your layout in question *g*, develop a DQ chart. From your DQ chart, draw some general conclusions about the types of handling methods (equipment) that seem suitable.

11. Acme Corporation has invested $5 million in storage and handling gear: $1 million in pallet racks, $1 million in an operatorless wire-guided vehicle delivery system, $1 million in carousel storage (three carousels), $1 million in an AS/RS, and $1 million in a transporter (moving parts from person to person in production cells and lines).

    Evaluate these five handling/storage systems. Rank them in worst-to-best order for a plant pursuing just-in-time production with continual improvement. Explain.

12. Examine the "Principles of Operations Management" (Exhibit 1–5). Which seem most directly affected by layout and re-layout decisions? Discuss.

13. We've seen how mobile furniture and equipment facilitate re-layout efforts. What about utilities? What innovations in utility design and installation support flexibility in layouts? A visit to an office products outlet or an interview with an office design professional may be helpful.

14. The chapter suggests that wise customers choose supplier partners that have facilities in good condition. Does it work in the other direction as well? Should suppliers be concerned about their customers' facilities? Discuss.

15. Company A has toxic-substance output as waste from some of its manufacturing processes. It disposes of those toxic wastes by transporting them to Company B's facilities and paying Company B a fee for proper disposal. Suppose Company B's facilities prove inadequate, and toxic waste escapes into the environment. Does Company A have a problem? Explain.

WHAT'S NEXT FOR YOU AND FOR OM?

18

Chapter Outline

People, Teams, Jobs, and Careers
    Employee Factor: OM Experience
    Employer Factors: Customer
    Service and Career Paths

Change
    Manufacturing in the Lead
    Services Close Behind

Quality of Work Life and the
Environment

Improvement Scenario
TQM in Less Developed Countries
Environmental and Labor
Protection

Currents and Countercurrents

First to Know

Case Study: Becoming World Class at
K2 Corporation

The first 17 chapters have focused on a few closely integrated new and evolving goals:

- Total quality.
- Data-based continuous improvement.
- Customer- and product-focused organization and measurement.
- Cross-functional teams.
- Streamlined, seamless flow of people, goods, and information.
- Flexibility.
- Simplicity.

However, despite their cohesiveness, these aims do not describe a single profession. Rather, they suggest that operations management includes an assortment of jobs and people, and that operations management is a part of every job. Coordinating that diversity is itself a major OM issue.

Furthermore, increasing acceptance of these core goals by those who set strategies for organizations is a clear signal that OM is in the midst of a period of evolution. In this final chapter we discuss the impact of contemporary OM on job diversity and people's careers, and the direction of change in how OM is practiced.

People, Teams, Jobs, and Careers

Whether you're seeking a position or are already working, you may have questions about the relevance of OM to your career. The following sections consider how all careers are a blend of employee and employer OM factors.

Employee Factor: OM Experience

If it hasn't already, your career will include considerable OM experience, which typically occurs in one of four ways: working in an OM department, providing offline OM support, serving on cross-functional teams, and participating in career-broadening assignments. (Of course, combinations of these factors are also possible.)

- *OM departments.* You may work in an operations department, managed by a vice president or director of operations, in a health care organization, welfare agency, military unit, information-processing firm, transportation company, or manufacturer. This is the operating end of the business—where products are made, campaigns are carried out, passengers and freight are moved, services are delivered, selling is done, information is processed, and so on.

- *OM support.* As we have seen, a lot of operations management takes place offline, before, while, and after operations themselves are performed. Examples include setting strategy and forecasting, designing and planning, buying and hiring, training and maintaining, scheduling and dispatching, locating and moving, and monitoring and controlling. Sometimes these activities are clearly in supporting roles, and sometimes distinctions between front-line and offline operations become blurred. What's important—for effective customer service—is that these activities blend seamlessly.

- *Cross-functional teams.* In nearly every chapter of this book, we have noted the growing reliance that competitive organizations place on cross-functional teams for solving problems and improving processes. The team may involve both professionals and front-line employees (see Exhibit 18–1). Regardless of your profession, your membership on such teams will involve you in operations management issues and improvement techniques presented in this text.

- *Career-broadening assignments.* If your career path begins in a non-OM specialty, you may gain OM experience by serving for a time in an operations department; the reverse also applies, of course.

Some companies have devised cross-careering policies that make career-broadening assignments easier and more attractive. For example:

- Becton Dickinson, a medical devices company, has initiated what it calls horizontal promotion, a promotion and pay increase for moving to another specialty, say, from accounting to purchasing or from order-entry to first-line supervision.

- Knighton Optical, a chain of retail optical shops with its own optical manufacturing plant, has cross-trained its accountants as opticians who can fit glasses for customers, and has trained its retail clerks to grind lenses and finish glasses in manufacturing.

- Calcomp, a maker of computer-driven plotters, moves senior development engineers to line supervisory positions.

- IBM has a long-standing tradition of repeatedly retraining people and moving them to alternative specialties.

Thus, whether you are based in operations or not, you should consider the value of broadening your understanding of other specialties. Increasingly, as the accompanying box illustrates, employers will be attracted to people who build breadth of skills. In fact,

EXHIBIT 18–1   Cross-functional Team—Bearing Manufacturer

Representatives from throughout the plant meet to solve problems at NTN-Bower's bearing plant in Macomb, Illinois.

Courtesy of NTN Bearing Corporation. Used with permission.

Into Practice

"Self-Reliance" Revisited

Over 150 years ago, Ralph Waldo Emerson wrote his classic essay, "Self Reliance." His theme, "trust thyself," is perhaps the best advice available today as individuals cope with new rules of employment. The future belongs to those who try to control their own destinies, who commit to a lifetime of learning. Richard Nelson Bolles (author of the job-hunter's bible, *What Color Is Your Parachute?*) advises everyone to inventory his or her skills, add to them every single year, and always have a ready answer to the question, What would you do if you lost your job tomorrow?

Experts agree that "the most employable people will be flexible folk who can move easily from one function to another, integrating diverse disciplines and perspectives." Competitive businesses know this. Although many have undergone significant downsizing, they are taking steps to ensure they keep the employees they want. There is also widespread agreement that after a period of perhaps painful demolition of outdated workplace structures and ideas, jobholders will have more respect, responsibility, challenge, and fun.

Anyone who wants to be retained should start adapting now. Abraham Zaleznik, psychoanalyst and professor emeritus at the Harvard business school, feels that "the theme of the dawning era is greater accountability on the part of individuals and corporations. He says that 'we're all up against a relentless, impersonal reality called the marketplace, which will reward those who do good jobs and punish those who don't.' "

SOURCE: Adapted from Stratford Sherman, "A Brave New Darwinian Workplace," *Fortune*, January 25, 1993, pp. 51–56.

in studying operations management, you have improved your preparation for a variety of careers, specialties, and professions.

Employer Factors:
Customer Service
and Career Paths

When employees participate in career-broadening experiences, employers also gain. An obvious example is work force flexibility. Flexibility breeds responsiveness, reducing the time customers must wait while providers get the right mix of human resources together. In addition, as Edward Lawler puts it, a "broad perspective helps employees to be innovative in improving operations. Thus, they become more effective in a quality circle, or any other problem-solving group."[1] Thus, for example, a buyer with receiving or stockroom experience will be not only a better buyer but also better able to work with receiving and stockroom associates on work-flow improvement projects. Similarly, a first-line supervisor who has taken orders from customers in an order-entry position will be more inclined to look outward, toward customers and overall business success, instead of inward.

*P*RINCIPLE 7:

Cross-train for mastery
of multiple skills.

Lawler makes the related point that since high-performance organizations have been flattening their organization structures, they need to create "new career tracks that do not depend on upward mobility" and that provide "a new 'nonlinear' way for people to grow and to succeed in their careers."[2]

The large baby-boom population exerts pressures in the same direction: many associates seeking few vertical advancement openings. Since the baby boomers will remain in the labor force for another two decades, employers will not soon escape from the need for policy changes such as horizontal promotions.

Moreover, human resource trends besides population cycles and employee cross-training will surely cause further changes in operations management and in management broadly. We will examine some of these forces and speculate on their effects in the remainder of this chapter.

Change

Change in operations management has been so extensive that many concepts treated in this book were unknown before the 1980s. The future is unpredictable, and the present, which contains the roots of future directions, is hard to assess. Even so, we can suggest at least a few desirable changes, such as changes that improve people's work lives, the environment, and standards of living. We would also like to see the benefits of today's best OM practices spreading from leading companies and industries to the rest, and we would like to see people in minimum-wage jobs and economically depressed countries helped by these practices as well.

Manufacturing in
the Lead

Most of the new concepts we have discussed originated in the manufacturing sector. Still, the majority of manufacturers retain older, less effective approaches and have not yet seriously embraced the new. Those that have done so set an impressive example that is hard to ignore. Ford Motor Company, for example, sold about the same number of vehicles in 1978 and 1988, but in 1988 they did it with half as many production associates. According to *The Wall Street Journal,* "Industry observers largely credit an employee involvement program [that Ford introduced] in the early 1980s."[3] That program

---

[1]Edward E. Lawler III, "Pay the Person, Not the Job," *Industry Week,* December 7, 1992, pp. 19–24.
[2]Ibid.
[3]Neal Templin, "Team Spirit: A Decisive Response to Crisis Brought Ford Enhanced Productivity," *The Wall Street Journal,* December 15, 1992.

EXHIBIT 18–2   Exploiting Gaps and Opportunities through Advanced Operations Management

Manufacturing:	Unprecedented OM-based advantages of superior companies may induce average companies to change.
Retailing:	OM-based quick-response and total quality partnerships may push other retailers to adapt.
Information services:	Adoption of remote processing (to tap special skills or low wages) may be followed by adoption of world-class operations management concepts to maintain a competitive edge.
Public service:	Lacking profit and sales targets, public servants may employ productivity targets as a way to have an impact, and total quality management might be the tool of choice.

---

has focused on the techniques of statistical process control, just-in-time, design for manufacture and assembly, and total preventive maintenance.

We believe that many manufacturers will adopt these techniques before too long because, simply, they will be noncompetitive without them. The specter of extinction can be a powerful stimulus. In addition, it is becoming easier for manufacturers to change and adapt, especially since the necessary information is so widely available. Quality councils have sprung up in many cities and regions, quality-related awards are publicized in the popular press, most of the 1,600-odd community and technical colleges in the United States and Canada offer subsidized instruction in statistical process control, and books and articles on quality and continuous improvement are flooding the market.

At one time, a good product (perhaps patented), a hard-to-copy technology, or superior marketing could make up for weak operations management. Moreover, weak OM usually was not so serious as to cause bankruptcy. Today, we think all that has changed: superior OM blends with superior design, marketing, accounting, supplier relations, human resource management, and business strategy as an essential component of success. Weak OM, on the other hand, tends to coincide with many other management weaknesses.

For these reasons, we may be approaching a golden age of manufacturing in which the majority of firms will improve their operations management dramatically. Those that don't will probably fail quickly, and their valuable assets will be acquired cheaply by strong companies. The wave of business mergers and acquisitions in the 1970s and early 1980s was driven mostly by financial objectives, but the new wave, if it occurs, should be aimed at creating successful companies through management excellence, with effective operations management leading the way.

Exhibit 18–2 summarizes these points for manufacturing and postulates similar developments in three service environments. In the next section we elaborate on those service-sector developments.

Services Close Behind

At the end of the 1980s, leading providers of a variety of services caught TQM fever. Although it is too early to make definitive evaluations (or suggest that a golden age of services is on the horizon), we can note two essential changes:

1. We had believed that many services, such as health care, sales, and teaching, were resistant to productivity improvement, and we had failed to realize how much rework, waste, delay, returns, and customer dissatisfaction is typically embedded in these services. We now realize that there is as much room for improvement in services as in manufacturing.

2. We also realize that most of the concepts and techniques of continuous improvement that have proven their worth in manufacturing also work well in services.

However, the pace of improvement in services may be mixed. Service organizations in highly competitive businesses may be forced to change quickly; more insulated organizations may be able to avoid this necessity for the time being. The following are examples of service businesses that are more competitively exposed:

Retailing.   The opening of Toys 'R' Us stores in Japan has sent shock waves through Japan's creaky distribution system. Japanese laws have been changed to accommodate high-volume, low-price retailers because consumers demanded it; many mom-and-pop toy shops are being put out of business. Wal-Mart has been doing the same thing in North America, forcing smaller retailers into niches or out of business.

*𝒫*RINCIPLE 13:

Operate at the customer's rate of use.

Toys 'R' Us and Wal-Mart are two very successful chain retailers. (Examples could also be cited from specialty goods and general merchandise.) A central element in their success formulas is partnering up with suppliers and freight carriers to minimize total inventories while still keeping the shelves stocked. These just-in-time partnerships eliminate intermediate warehousing and slash ordering and shipping transactions. In addition, project teams with members drawn from the retailer, freight carrier, producer, and even the producer's supplier are at work solving all sorts of intercompany problems.

The cover of *Business Week* for December 21, 1992, featured Wal-Mart, Toys 'R' Us, Home Depot, and Circuit City, along with the cover-story title, "Clout!" These retailers are using their power and influence to transform the supply chain and "revolutionizing the way consumer products are bought and sold." However, Sears, Roebuck & Co., along with Hudson Bay stores in Canada and Marks and Spencer in the United Kingdom, had equal clout in the pre-Wal-Mart era. They were famous for using it, too, for driving a hard bargain on price. But in that era, concepts such as JIT, supplier partnership, and cross-functional problem-solving teams were not taught and were largely unknown in Western enterprise.

*𝒫*RINCIPLE 6:

Organize chains of customers.

Today, these ideas are common knowledge. They have become part of the mainstream of operations management studies and are finding their way into textbooks in accounting, marketing, engineering, and other fields as well. Retailers achieve competitive advantage by using these techniques, and when a retailer has a blind spot, a knowledgeable supplier may take its just-in-time proposal to the retailer, pointing out ways to jointly cut costs and improve service. Milliken & Company's textile managers have taken such proposals not only to their customers in the apparel and upholstered furniture business and transport companies, but all the way to clothing and furniture retailers.

Many high-performance retail-supplier partnerships are partially founded on modern OM concepts, but the situation seems to be different in information services.

Information Services.   Increasingly, companies are farming out computer software development and heavy-duty data entry jobs to information service companies in India. Grocery chains fly sacks of merchandise coupons to Haiti for counting. Designers scattered around the globe jointly develop new products for Texas Instruments and the Gap. Omaha has become a center for telephone services such as airline reservations and credit checking. Satellite communications, E mail, global area networks, computer-aided design, rapid prototyping, air freight, and other technologies make these arrangements possible. Thus, the lowering of trade barriers that is occurring around the world is in some ways incidental; data and information already move from country to country without customs inspections.

So far, these out-sourcing arrangements do not appear to be based on total quality or continuous improvement. Just-in-time is not managed in; it simply seems to be a part of the technology. Management wants to harness special skills (e.g., pattern makers in Hong Kong, liquid-emitting diode designers in the Netherlands, or a neutral English accent for telephone answerers in Omaha), or to find useful skills at a very low wage (e.g., computer programmers in India).

Although any firm can use communications technology to out-source information services, it seems inevitable that firms will have to do more than just chase low wages or special skills to be competitive. Superior companies will gain an edge by employing OM-based techniques to improve quality and flexibility, eliminate waste, and continuously improve.

Public Services.   Denied the option of global out-sourcing, public agencies have even more reason to implement total quality management. TQM is now a dominant subject of employee training in public services. Results include, for example, substantial error reductions in the U.S. Internal Revenue Service, many times faster repair of city vehicles in Madison, Wisconsin, and elimination of chronic misplacement of X-rays in the San Diego Naval Hospital system.

Doubters may say that TQM in government is just a fad and that the government's customer is not clearly enough defined for customer-focused TQM to be effective. However, a more significant factor is that government has fewer ways to measure success than profit-making firms have, and this may be frustrating to dedicated public servants. If so, they may see TQM as a way to finally make a noticeable impact. Moreover, concepts that greatly improve an agency's ability to provide quick, accurate response and increase productivity may help make government service more personally fulfilling.

Quality of Work Life and the Environment

Personal fulfillment can be a powerful motivator, at least for those whose basic personal needs are taken care of. But what about people working at the minimum wage, in a clerical, fast-food, data entry, janitorial, or general labor capacity? To be competitive, their employers may deliberately encourage high turnover to reduce the pressure to grant pay raises. They may also offer mainly part-time work to avoid paying benefits, and call in extra part-timers to avoid paying overtime. Job-holders in these businesses may fall below the poverty line; be unable to pay for proper medical care, housing, and food; and have many unmet physiological and safety needs.

Here we refer to Abraham Maslow's hierarchy of needs: Physiological, safety, love, esteem, and, at the top, fulfillment.

Nevertheless, there may be a role for TQM in these businesses. Here is a possible scenario:

Improvement Scenario

- Burgers, Inc., launches a "world-class services" program via a two-day training course for every employee, including office support and managerial associates.
- Baseline performance measures, such as customer wait time, food and packaging waste, store cleanliness index, inventories, and invoice processing time, are plotted on large charts.
- Project teams, both spontaneous and assigned, are formed to improve performance, which is recorded on the wall charts. The teams capture and deal with root causes, then plot new points on the charts.
- Team members who are enthusiastic leaders, communicators, or innovators stand out. Supervisors and store managers don't want to lose these employees, so they are given more hours, benefits, and pay raises.
- The overall level of competence and motivation of the work force rises, and increasing numbers of associates rise up through the ranks to become supervisors, store managers, and executives. Other employees move on to other careers but with impressive problem-solving credentials.

*P*RINCIPLE 14:

Record quality, process, and problem data at the workplace.

- Better pay brings some of these standout associates up out of poverty, so that their physiological needs can be met. Burgers, Inc., values their continued employment, which meets their safety needs. These associates are in a better situation to pursue higher-level needs. Later on in life, some of these people may be at the level of high personal fulfillment, but meanwhile, they see learning, innovation, and continuous process improvement as a path out of poverty and a way to improve their credentials and résumés.

- Burgers, Inc., enjoys a reputation for the best quality and service in its industry at competitive prices. Though it offers pay raises, benefits, and security, the improvement teams drive out costly wastes so that its costs are no higher than those of its less capable competitors.

We cannot cite any Western companies that have adopted these measures sufficiently to show their merits. Although we think such measures make eminently good sense, it remains to be seen if this approach will come into wide use (or even become a competitive necessity in some businesses). Surprisingly, the best evidence for the viability of the scenario comes from less developed countries.

TQM in Less Developed Countries

The world will remain a tinder box of discontent if weak economic systems cannot be strengthened; the security of wealthy industrialized countries thus is tied to economic improvement in less developed countries. In previous chapters, we reviewed a few examples of companies in less developed countries that pay low wages (very low by Western standards) but still achieve world-class results:

- We noted the extensive implementation of TQM and JIT at Eicher Tractor Co. in India (Chapter 1).

- The Rio Bravo IV case study detailed the many JIT and continuous improvement achievements at a Packard Electric plant in Juarez, Mexico (Chapter 7).

In each case, company officers committed significant resources for employee training; TQM-literate managers and associates took it from there. There are many similar examples in less developed economies throughout South America and Asia. In many firms, world-class operations management and global competitiveness occur amid poverty, primitive infrastructure, stifling bureaucratic red tape, and unstable governments. The success formula should work at least as well in low-wage firms in developed countries, which face far fewer difficulties.

Environmental and Labor Protection

*P*RINCIPLE 7:

Continually invest in improved health, safety, and security.

Improvement teams will devote some of their time to job and environmental health and safety. They will do so in their own self-interest and because insurance policies and governmental regulations may require certain levels of protection. Environmental activists also press the issue and sometimes prove that strong safety and environmental policies pay. Companies known for their vigorous safety programs, such as Du Pont, have much lower workers' compensation payment rates.

International trade pacts also appear to be moving companies in this direction. For example, although the North American Free Trade Agreement will facilitate rapid growth of trade between Mexico and its northern neighbors, political leaders in the United States and Canada threaten restrictions unless Mexico upgrades and enforces antipollution and employment standards. The European Community is at least as firm about incorporating tough environmental and labor standards into its internal and external trade pacts. The United Nations also regularly debates these issues. Although international environmental and labor standards are being developed, implementation must occur at a much lower level. Front-line and cross-functional process improvement teams seem to be the natural instrument for implementation.

Currents and Countercurrents

Globalism affects operations management in many ways, but especially in the phenomenal growth of market size as trade barriers fall. A can of Coca Cola now is available almost everywhere, a potential market of over 5 billion people. But a few years ago, Coke was excluded from most of the Soviet bloc, China, and India. The company's business strategy is simple: build focused factories that produce economies of scale and meet its quality standards, and form supplier and distribution partnerships of all kinds. The eight success factors for process industries presented in Chapter 12 (Exhibit 12–2) set forth the operations management practices that carry out that strategy.

McDonald's, Gillette, Bank of America, Metropolitan Life, and other high-volume businesses may follow similar strategies. The vast world market offers relief from the limited strategy of just fighting Pepsi, Burger King, Schick, Citibank, and Prudential for local market share.

As these companies expand around the world, local companies are often swallowed up or go broke. For instance, James River Corp., a large American paper company, recently acquired joint ownership of 13 paper companies in 10 European countries. The European venture, called Jamont, then had the task of sorting out different countries' preferences. Regarding toilet tissue, the conventional wisdom said: "German-speaking countries . . . buy strength. The French want soft. And the Americans crave very soft."[4] But Jamont managers found that consumers want softness and strength regardless of nationality. Gradually, Jamont managers are developing similar world-class practices for all its plants: low quality-standards are raised, equipment is upgraded, and volume drives costs down. For example, all 13 plants formerly made their own deep-colored napkins, a time-consuming process involving costly dye changing. Now a single specialized Jamont plant in Finland makes deep-colored napkins for all 10 countries. Such opportunities arise from doing business in a mass market instead of a fractionated one.

*P*RINCIPLE 6:

Organize resources for product focus.

But there is a countercurrent: while the big get bigger and more specialized in new and massive markets, opportunities are growing for custom suppliers of speciality goods and services in those same mass markets. Unfortunately, however, while the Coca Colas and Citibanks of the world have always offered fairly good quality and high efficiency, most specialty companies have been woeful performers by today's standards. Customers may wait months, see promised delivery dates missed several times, and have little input or feedback; when the product or service is finally delivered, it's often wrong and needs to be redone. This description could apply to a printer, a tailor, a foundry, a bridge builder, a doctor, or a lawyer.

As noted in Chapter 11, providers of custom or specialty goods and services have *lower volumes* and *higher variety*, factors that partially explain their poor performance.

The eight-point list of Exhibit 12–2 summarizes world-class OM for the high-volume processor, but a world-class formula for the specialty company would be significantly longer and more complex. In fact, we have included ways to improve OM in almost every chapter, in part, because specialty operations are so complex and nonroutine. Modular design (Chapter 3), queue limitation (Chapter 9), quick-change flexibility (Chapter 10), total preventive maintenance (Chapter 16) and cells (Chapters 2 and 11) are just some of the concepts important to improving specialty operations.

---

[4]Janet Guyon, "A Joint-Venture Papermaker Casts Net Across Europe," *The Wall Street Journal,* December 12, 1992.

First to Know

In studying operations management, we have been exposed to several major evolutions in OM strategy. In about 1980, portions of Western industry awoke to the quality gap, and *quality as competitive advantage* became the dominant new strategy. A few years later, the focus was on *time-based competition,* then *globalization,* and lately, *flexibility.*

These ideas were developed as an integrated whole in certain pioneering books of the late 1970s and early 1980s, and they gained extra prominence after being blessed in prestigious business periodicals such as the *Harvard Business Review*. Moreover, each of these strategies tends to move like an avalanche through the adopting business, especially affecting operations management. People wonder, Is there more? If so, what's next?

We don't know. Rather than trying to guess, we would rather make this point: what's important is being the first to know and, therefore, having the first chance to implement and gain the advantage. It seems likely that the first to know will be organizations having strong benchmarking and competitive analysis, supplier and customer partnerships, a global presence, extensive continuous training, ethnic variety, and highly involved employees skilled at getting things done right the first time. In your own career, taking charge of building these first-to-know capabilities can be your best protection.

Summary

Operations management is in a period of renaissance, drawing upon diverse specialties, professions, and departments. A full OM career will include time in front-line operations and in a few OM support specialties as well. Each career step, however, should involve teaming up for problem solving with specialists in other career tracks. Flatter organization structures make horizontal movements attractive for people's careers and good for the firm's human resource development.

Organizations in all sectors are being competitively driven to implement total quality management, just in time, and related newer OM concepts.

- In manufacturing, these concepts have made weak companies strong. Visible examples (e.g., Ford Motor Co.) may help convince other manufacturers that they can no longer get by without wholesale changes in their operations management.

- In retailing, successful firms like Toys 'R' Us and Wal-Mart are forging quick-response, waste-eliminating partnerships with their supply chains. Manufacturers like Milliken & Co. are pressing for the same OM-based solutions with their chains of customers. Old-line retailers may have to adapt, retreat into niche retailing, or expire.

- In information services, technology allows you to locate a service center almost anywhere. Western companies are setting up operations in geographically remote areas, sometimes to tap special talents but often to cut wages. Since any firm may set up remote data services, gaining an edge may require using advanced OM concepts at the remote site.

- In nonprofit organizations, especially government, managers may be attracted to TQM-related ideas as a way to make an impact. Knowledge and training resources on how to do it are widely available and affordable.

It may seem that low-wage employees would be too concerned about their survival to worry about continuous improvement. However, if the employer provides the training and gets TQM going, some low-wage associates may be able to contribute innovative solutions that improve their employer's competitiveness. The employer may value this contribution sufficiently to begin treating the associate better, with better pay and job security. In this admittedly speculative scenario, low-wage employees see problem-solving skills and behaviors as a path upward, and act accordingly. There is preliminary evidence that this scenario has worked in low-wage countries.

A popular topic for improvement teams is improving their own job safety and health, in part because it is sensible to do so and in part in response to government regulations and environmentalist pressure. In addition, international trade pacts are including environmental standards for both pact members and outsiders. Global and political mandates to preserve the environment can be supported by TQM teams.

As trade barriers fall, superior companies (which often include advanced OM concepts in their success formulas) begin to tap massive new markets. High-volume producers or service providers standardize and adopt a short list of OM improvement concepts (see Exhibit 12–2). By contrast, specialty firms have a much more complex range of operations to manage and thus must employ a larger range of OM improvements (concepts found in nearly every chapter).

As operations management continues to evolve, companies—and OM associates—will want to be the first to know about the next development. The best ways of staying current include continuous benchmarking, training, global involvement, and participation on improvement projects with diverse other people.

For Further Reference

Books

Berry, Leonard L.; David R. Bennett; and Carter W. Brown. *Service Quality: A Profit Strategy for Financial Institutions*. Homewood, Ill.: Dow Jones–Irwin, 1989 (HG1616.C87B47).

Naisbitt, John, and Patricia Aburdene. *Megatrends 2000: Ten New Directions for the 1990s*. New York: Wm. Morrow, 1990 (HN59.2.N343).

Plossl, George W. *Managing in the New World of Manufacturing*. Englewood Cliffs, N.J.: Prentice-Hall, 1991 (HD9720.5.P56).

Porter, Michael E. *The Competitive Advantage of Nations*. New York: The Free Press, 1990 (HD3611.P654).

Schonberger, Richard J. *Building a Chain of Customers: Linking Business Functions to Create the World-Class Company*. New York: The Free Press, 1990 (HD58.9.S36).

Periodicals

Looking to the future is a popular activity. Many reputable business, economic, and scientific periodicals publish articles on it.

Review Questions

1. If you're employed in a job or profession other than operations, how can you put these operations management studies to use?

2. What socioeconomic trend is behind the development of what Becton Dickinson calls horizontal promotion?

3. Will TQM, JIT, and related concepts continue to expand in use in manufacturing companies? Explain.

4. Why are retailers like Wal-Mart and Circuit City so successful?

5. What can a manufacturer do to make its chain of customers, extending all the way to the retailer, more successful?

6. When remote partnerships for information services become established, can OM-related concepts play a useful role? If so, which concepts, and how?

7. Does TQM appeal to public servants? Explain.

8. Are people at the bottom level of Maslow's hierarchy of needs likely to take an interest in continuous improvement? Explain.

9. Is continuous improvement likely to interest low-wage people in less developed countries? Explain.

10. Governments and international bodies keep tightening environmental and labor standards. Will this cause affected companies' costs to rise, competitiveness to decline, and associates to resist? Explain.

11. Who will be best able to benefit from the enormous markets created by trade pacts? Explain.

12. How can you and your employer benefit from the continuing renaissance in operations management?

Problems and Exercises

1. If your family owned a store selling clothing, variety goods, or consumer electronics and a competitor like Home Depot or Circuit City opened a store in the same area, what would you advise your family to do? Explain.

2. Could medical opinions be delivered routinely from one country to another? If so, would TQM have any special value in such an arrangement? Answer the same question with regard to legal services and public accounting.

3. Bright Hope, Inc., operates a chain of private hospitals. A team of its managers benchmarked Wal-Mart and Toys 'R' Us, and all team members are excited about what they've learned. The next step is to develop a plan to implement the relevant parts of the Wal-Mart and Toys 'R' Us success formula. What should this plan consist of? Explain.

4. You serve meals in a university cafeteria, but with little enthusiasm for the work even though food service is your intended career. Your supervisor and upper managers are very receptive to suggestions. Develop an OM-based plan that will (*a*) make your present job more satisfying, (*b*) be received reasonably well by your front-line associates, (*c*) be welcomed by your bosses, and (*d*) be helpful to your career development.

5. In this chapter's speculations about future directions for operations management, little was said about emerging technologies. If you can, develop a logical scenario of significant OM changes that are based mainly on new technologies. If you think that technologies will have little impact, or that technological changes and effects are completely unpredictable, explain why.

 **CASE STUDY**

BECOMING WORLD-CLASS AT K2 CORPORATION

Scott Doss had just described the rapid progress he and his fellow maintenance technicians had made over the last three months in lowering setup times on the mold-presses used in forming ski bottoms. He went on to speculate on further improvements:

> Everyone on the team is looking ahead to the day when we can have a mold prestaged, maybe with removable plates—whatever—with molds already on; slide this one out and slide in the next one that's already been plugged in and preheated and is ready to go. What we've concentrated on, so far, are things where we don't have to remove the bolts—where we just change the profile. In the future basically anything is possible.

With faster mold changeovers, schedulers were starting to plan smaller lots that could be run more often with better response to the customer. Lot sizes on the presses had been weeks' or months' worth in the past, but Doss expressed the hope that "in the next couple of years, we get to the point where we could change day to day if we had to."

This case is based on research conducted by Richard J. Schonberger in August 1988.

Doss's employer is K2 Corporation, a manufacturer of high-quality snow skis. K2, which has been in the ski-manufacturing business for nearly three decades, became a subsidiary of Anthony Industries Co. in 1986. K2's main plant and headquarters is located on Vashon Island, across Puget Sound from Seattle. K2's current annual sales volume is $60 million, which is about 10 percent of the world market for skis. The company employs 500 people.

Spotlight on Manufacturing

In the fall of 1987, K2 hired consultant Peter Scontrino to study K2's compensation plan for hourly employees. At that time, about 35 percent of the company's hourly workers were paid on a piece-based incentive system. Mr. Scontrino learned that K2 managers favored extending that plan to cover more job classifications. Scontrino, however, believed that the company should shelve the incentive system and move toward a gain-sharing plan. He recommended Richard J. Schonberger's book, *World-Class Manufacturing,* as background reading for K2 managers.

Before long, the K2 management team had developed plans for its own "world-class manufacturing" system, which included gain-sharing, just-in-time production, total quality control, employee involvement, and total preventive maintenance. Implementation of the plan was swift, including the following improvements by late summer 1988:

- The former inventory of plastic top-edge strips was about 150,000 pieces, a 2½ weeks' supply. Still, with 22 different size/color combinations, it was common to be out of one that was needed. Now the inventory is about 20,000 and there are no stockouts. The machine operator runs a kanban quantity of 300 strips only when a green card is in one of the 22 slots in a nearby rack; otherwise the slot holds a red card. Material control people insert the green or red kanbans each morning based on how much of each part is on hand in the mold-press room. The operator, who has duties elsewhere, runs the strip cutter only when green cards are present. (The operator had to quit producing for six weeks while the large inventory was being whittled down.)

- The steel-edge crew (which bends and welds "cracked" steel to metal tail protectors to form a one-piece steel-edge assembly) has reduced its flow time from four days to six hours, its lot size from 450 to 150 pieces, and its inventory from 50 carts (20,000 pieces) to a maximum of 11 carts. The maximum is controlled by 11 kanban squares among the machines on the floor. Each operator has line-stop authority. Implementation was done in one day, but it took almost a week to work the steel inventory down by halting receipts from the local supplier (who provides the material already punched.)

- Setup time on mold-presses making K2's foam-core type of ski bottom has been reduced from 30 minutes to as little as 5 minutes.

- Setup time on mold-presses for K2's premier braided-fiber ski bottom has been reduced from two weeks to as little as 10 hours at zero capital cost. The setup reduction effort included providing each operator with a set of the right tools; rewiring electrical panels; checking first skis at the bench instead of in the lab; using uniform, easy-to-adjust, shorter bolts (requiring fewer turns); installing setting rails; using air equipment with Allen socket heads; putting T-handles on Allen wrenches; using stacked shims; and painting each machine as it was converted. Ten of the 50 presses were converted during summer 1988, with the rest due for conversion by year's end.

- In rough-base finishing, molded ski bottoms go through seven wet-sanders and four grinders, which had been grouped into three separate work centers; now they are merged into a flow line operated by an 11-person team. Formerly 60 to 90 carts (three or four weeks' worth) of skis were crammed into the rough-finishing room. Now carts come directly from molding for nearly immediate processing (no work orders); the buffer stock is about 10 carts, or three to four hours' worth, so feedback to molding on quality problems is fast. See the before and after photos in Exhibit S18–1.

- Lead time to produce a set of graphics (designs that go on the tops of the skis) has been cut from one week to one shift or less.

EXHIBIT S18–1   Skis in Rough Base Finishing at K2 Corp.

A. Three to four weeks' worth of skis—before world-class manufacturing emphasis.

B. Three to four hours' worth of skis—after world-class manufacturing emphasis.

- Changeover time on the five silk-screening lines has been reduced from 25 minutes to as little as 5 minutes.
- There used to be a queue of about 150 carts in front of the room housing the large piece of equipment (designed in-house) that joins ski tops to bottoms; it is now more like 7 carts (a typical cart holds 150 skis).
- Skis formerly spent about three weeks in finishing; now they zip through in one shift.
- Rework in finishing had been 50–60 percent; it is now down to about 0.5 percent. At the same time, attainable plant capacity has increased from under 2,000 good pairs per day to about 2,500 per day. The quality and capacity improvements occurred during the turmoil of hiring 100 new people and bringing them up to proper skill level.
- Inventory of the basic raw material (uniglass) has been reduced from $225,000 to $41,000.
- In 1986 there were 300 carts (about 50,000 skis) on the floor; now it is perhaps 20 carts.
- In many parts of the plant, work orders and completion reporting by bar-coding have been eliminated, along with sending material into stock and performing storekeeping on it. Jeff Bardsley, production and inventory control planner, states that he had been spending up to eight hours a day on the computer. ''Now I'm out on the floor, and I can see what the real problems are.'' Lead times on some items were reduced from three weeks to four days.
- At Vashon for meetings in August 1988, K2's sales representatives from all over the world were excited by what they saw in the factory. Some expressed the view that K2 is now the standard against which the best in the industry would have to be measured.

What's Next?

With such a string of impressive—and quick—accomplishments, a nagging notion in the back of some people's minds at K2 is, What's next? And how do we keep up the enthusiasm and create a sustained work culture of continual improvement?

Discussion Questions

Question 1. Is it reasonable for K2 people to expect much more improvement? Sustained improvement?

Question 2. Outline a strategic plan for operations management at K2 for the next five years.

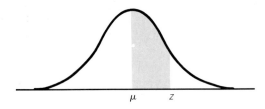

Example

The area between the mean (μ) and the point one standard deviation above the mean (z = 1.00) is 0.3413, or 34.13 percent of the total area under the curve. The area between z = − 1.00 and z = 1.00 is 0.3413 + 0.3413 = 0.6826.

TABLE A-1   Areas of Standard Normal Distribution

Z	0.00	0.01	0.02	0.03	0.04	0.05	0.06	0.07	0.08	0.09
0.0	0.0000	0.0040	0.0080	0.0120	0.0160	0.0199	0.0239	0.0279	0.0319	0.0359
0.1	0.0398	0.0438	0.0478	0.0517	0.0557	0.0596	0.0636	0.0675	0.0714	0.0753
0.2	0.0793	0.0832	0.0871	0.0910	0.0948	0.0987	0.1026	0.1064	0.1103	0.1141
0.3	0.1179	0.1217	0.1255	0.1293	0.1331	0.1368	0.1406	0.1443	0.1480	0.1517
0.4	0.1554	0.1591	0.1628	0.1664	0.1700	0.1736	0.1772	0.1808	0.1844	0.1879
0.5	0.1915	0.1950	0.1985	0.2019	0.2054	0.2088	0.2123	0.2157	0.2190	0.2224
0.6	0.2257	0.2291	0.2324	0.2357	0.2389	0.2422	0.2454	0.2486	0.2518	0.2549
0.7	0.2580	0.2612	0.2642	0.2673	0.2704	0.2734	0.2764	0.2794	0.2823	0.2852
0.8	0.2881	0.2910	0.2939	0.2967	0.2995	0.3023	0.3051	0.3078	0.3106	0.3133
0.9	0.3159	0.3186	0.3212	0.3238	0.3264	0.3289	0.3315	0.3340	0.3365	0.3389
1.0	0.3413	0.3438	0.3461	0.3485	0.3508	0.3531	0.3554	0.3577	0.3599	0.3621
1.1	0.3643	0.3665	0.3686	0.3708	0.3729	0.3749	0.3770	0.3790	0.3810	0.3830
1.2	0.3849	0.3869	0.3888	0.3907	0.3925	0.3944	0.3962	0.3980	0.3997	0.4015
1.3	0.4032	0.4049	0.4066	0.4082	0.4099	0.4115	0.4131	0.4147	0.4162	0.4177
1.4	0.4192	0.4207	0.4222	0.4236	0.4251	0.4265	0.4279	0.4292	0.4306	0.4319
1.5	0.4332	0.4345	0.4357	0.4370	0.4382	0.4394	0.4406	0.4418	0.4429	0.4441
1.6	0.4452	0.4463	0.4474	0.4484	0.4495	0.4505	0.4515	0.4525	0.4535	0.4545
1.7	0.4554	0.4564	0.4573	0.4582	0.4591	0.4599	0.4608	0.4616	0.4625	0.4633
1.8	0.4641	0.4649	0.4656	0.4664	0.4671	0.4678	0.4686	0.4693	0.4699	0.4706
1.9	0.4713	0.4719	0.4726	0.4732	0.4738	0.4744	0.4750	0.4756	0.4761	0.4767
2.0	0.4772	0.4778	0.4783	0.4788	0.4793	0.4798	0.4803	0.4808	0.4812	0.4817
2.1	0.4821	0.4826	0.4830	0.4834	0.4838	0.4842	0.4846	0.4850	0.4854	0.4857
2.2	0.4861	0.4864	0.4868	0.4871	0.4875	0.4878	0.4881	0.4884	0.4887	0.4890
2.3	0.4893	0.4896	0.4898	0.4901	0.4904	0.4906	0.4909	0.4911	0.4913	0.4916
2.4	0.4918	0.4920	0.4922	0.4925	0.4927	0.4929	0.4931	0.4932	0.4934	0.4936

TABLE A–1   Areas of Standard Normal Distribution—Continued

Z	0.00	0.01	0.02	0.03	0.04	0.05	0.06	0.07	0.08	0.09
2.5	0.4938	0.4940	0.4941	0.4943	0.4945	0.4946	0.4948	0.4949	0.4951	0.4952
2.6	0.4953	0.4955	0.4956	0.4957	0.4959	0.4960	0.4961	0.4962	0.4963	0.4964
2.7	0.4965	0.4966	0.4967	0.4968	0.4969	0.4970	0.4971	0.4972	0.4973	0.4974
2.8	0.4974	0.4975	0.4976	0.4977	0.4977	0.4978	0.4979	0.4979	0.4980	0.4981
2.9	0.4981	0.4982	0.4982	0.4983	0.4984	0.4984	0.4985	0.4985	0.4986	0.4986
3.0	0.4986	0.4987	0.4987	0.4988	0.4988	0.4989	0.4989	0.4989	0.4990	0.4990
3.1	0.4990	0.4991	0.4991	0.4991	0.4992	0.4992	0.4992	0.4992	0.4993	0.4993
3.2	0.4993	0.4993	0.4994	0.4994	0.4994	0.4994	0.4994	0.4995	0.4995	0.4995
3.3	0.4995	0.4995	0.4995	0.4996	0.4996	0.4996	0.4996	0.4996	0.4996	0.4997
3.4	0.4997	0.4997	0.4997	0.4997	0.4997	0.4997	0.4997	0.4997	0.4998	0.4998
3.5	0.4998	0.4998	0.4998	0.4998	0.4998	0.4998	0.4998	0.4998	0.4998	0.4998
3.6	0.4998	0.4998	0.4999	0.4999	0.4999	0.4999	0.4999	0.4999	0.4999	0.4999
3.7	0.4999	0.4999	0.4999	0.4999	0.4999	0.4999	0.4999	0.4999	0.4999	0.4999
3.8	0.4999	0.4999	0.4999	0.4999	0.4999	0.4999	0.4999	0.5000	0.5000	0.5000
3.9	0.5000	0.5000	0.5000	0.5000	0.5000	0.5000	0.5000	0.5000	0.5000	0.5000

APPENDIX B
THE POISSON DISTRIBUTION—CUMULATIVE PROBABILITIES

$$P(n) = \frac{e^{-\lambda}\lambda^n}{n!}$$

Where, for a given period of time,

λ = Mean number of events expected to occur
n = Actual number of events observed
$P(n)$ = Probability of observing exactly n events
e = Base of the natural logarithms, approximately 2.7183

Example

For $\lambda = 0.1$:

	Cumulative Probability
$P(0) = \dfrac{e^{-0.1}(0.1)^0}{0!} = 0.905$	0.905
$P(1) = \dfrac{e^{-0.1}(0.1)^1}{1!} = 0.090$	0.995
$P(2) = \dfrac{e^{-0.1}(0.1)^2}{2!} = 0.005$	1.000

TABLE B–1 The Poisson Distribution—Cumulative Probabilities

						P(n)					
λ	n = 0	1	2	3	4	5	6	7	8	9	10
0.02	0.980	1.000									
0.04	0.961	0.999	1.000								
0.06	0.942	0.998	1.000								
0.08	0.923	0.997	1.000								
0.10	0.905	0.995	1.000								
0.15	0.861	0.990	0.999	1.000							
0.20	0.819	0.982	0.999	1.000							
0.25	0.779	0.974	0.998	1.000							
0.30	0.741	0.963	0.996	1.000							
0.35	0.705	0.951	0.994	1.000							
0.40	0.670	0.938	0.992	0.999	1.000						
0.45	0.638	0.925	0.989	0.999	1.000						
0.50	0.607	0.910	0.986	0.998	1.000						
0.55	0.577	0.894	0.982	0.998	1.000						
0.60	0.549	0.878	0.977	0.997	1.000						
0.65	0.522	0.861	0.972	0.996	0.999	1.000					
0.70	0.497	0.844	0.966	0.994	0.999	1.000					
0.75	0.472	0.827	0.959	0.993	0.999	1.000					

TABLE B–1   The Poisson Distribution—Cumulative Probabilities

λ	n = 0	1	2	3	4	5	6	7	8	9	10
0.80	0.449	0.809	0.953	0.991	0.999	1.000					
0.85	0.427	0.791	0.945	0.989	0.998	1.000					
0.90	0.407	0.772	0.937	0.987	0.998	1.000					
0.95	0.387	0.754	0.929	0.984	0.997	1.000					
1.00	0.368	0.736	0.920	0.981	0.996	0.999	1.000				
1.1	0.333	0.699	0.900	0.974	0.995	0.999	1.000				
1.2	0.301	0.663	0.879	0.966	0.992	0.998	1.000				
1.3	0.273	0.627	0.857	0.957	0.989	0.998	1.000				
1.4	0.247	0.592	0.833	0.946	0.986	0.997	0.999	1.000			
1.5	0.223	0.558	0.809	0.934	0.981	0.996	0.999	1.000			
1.6	0.202	0.525	0.783	0.921	0.976	0.994	0.999	1.000			
1.7	0.183	0.493	0.757	0.907	0.970	0.992	0.998	1.000			
1.8	0.165	0.463	0.731	0.891	0.964	0.990	0.997	0.999	1.000		
1.9	0.150	0.434	0.704	0.875	0.956	0.987	0.997	0.999	1.000		
2.0	0.135	0.406	0.677	0.857	0.947	0.983	0.995	0.999	1.000		
2.2	0.111	0.355	0.623	0.819	0.928	0.975	0.993	0.998	1.000		
2.4	0.091	0.308	0.570	0.779	0.904	0.964	0.988	0.997	0.999	1.000	
2.6	0.074	0.267	0.518	0.736	0.877	0.951	0.983	0.995	0.999	1.000	
2.8	0.061	0.231	0.469	0.692	0.848	0.935	0.976	0.992	0.998	0.999	1.000
3.0	0.050	0.199	0.423	0.647	0.815	0.916	0.966	0.988	0.996	0.999	1.000
3.2	0.041	0.171	0.380	0.603	0.781	0.895	0.955	0.983	0.994	0.998	1.000
3.4	0.033	0.147	0.340	0.558	0.744	0.871	0.942	0.977	0.992	0.997	0.999
3.6	0.027	0.126	0.303	0.515	0.706	0.844	0.927	0.969	0.988	0.996	0.999
3.8	0.022	0.107	0.269	0.473	0.668	0.816	0.909	0.960	0.984	0.994	0.998
4.0	0.018	0.092	0.238	0.433	0.629	0.785	0.889	0.949	0.979	0.992	0.997
4.2	0.015	0.078	0.210	0.395	0.590	0.753	0.867	0.936	0.972	0.989	0.996
4.4	0.012	0.066	0.185	0.359	0.551	0.720	0.844	0.921	0.964	0.985	0.994
4.6	0.010	0.056	0.163	0.326	0.513	0.686	0.818	0.905	0.955	0.980	0.992
4.8	0.008	0.048	0.143	0.294	0.476	0.651	0.791	0.887	0.944	0.975	0.990
5.0	0.007	0.040	0.125	0.265	0.440	0.616	0.762	0.867	0.932	0.968	9.986
5.2	0.006	0.034	0.109	0.238	0.406	0.581	0.732	0.845	0.918	0.960	0.982
5.4	0.005	0.029	0.095	0.213	0.373	0.546	0.702	0.822	0.903	0.951	0.977
5.6	0.004	0.024	0.082	0.191	0.342	0.512	0.670	0.797	0.886	0.941	0.972
5.8	0.003	0.021	0.072	0.170	0.313	0.478	0.638	0.771	0.867	0.929	0.965
6.0	0.002	0.017	0.062	0.151	0.285	0.446	0.606	0.744	0.847	0.916	0.957
6.2	0.002	0.015	0.054	0.134	0.259	0.414	0.574	0.716	0.826	0.902	0.949
6.4	0.002	0.012	0.046	0.119	0.235	0.384	0.542	0.687	0.803	0.886	0.939
6.6	0.001	0.010	0.040	0.105	0.213	0.355	0.511	0.658	0.780	0.869	0.927
6.8	0.001	0.009	0.034	0.093	0.192	0.327	0.480	0.628	0.755	0.850	0.915
7.0	0.001	0.007	0.030	0.082	0.173	0.301	0.450	0.599	0.729	0.830	0.901
8.0	0.000	0.003	0.014	0.043	0.100	0.192	0.314	0.454	0.594	0.718	0.817
9.0	0.000	0.001	0.006	0.021	0.055	0.116	0.207	0.324	0.456	0.588	0.707
10.0	0.000	0.000	0.002	0.009	0.028	0.066	0.129	0.219	0.332	0.457	0.582

TABLE C–1   **Two-Digit Random Numbers—Uniform Distribution**

42	27	11	61	64	20
55	39	37	71	35	78
24	42	25	60	61	78
82	70	68	68	28	08
56	38	62	42	05	47
48	15	21	40	25	78
95	76	15	43	63	18
86	86	96	50	43	17
49	47	10	94	14	22
41	74	33	33	28	76
95	47	92	56	95	95
78	31	27	77	66	63
84	18	88	65	46	81
40	00	61	17	82	53
80	00	85	42	64	44
12	55	13	20	74	16
84	27	50	45	97	19
01	22	40	81	36	10
25	12	07	98	82	74
46	12	83	52	30	42
83	02	73	53	18	07
69	18	16	09	93	65
78	22	36	94	45	32
43	18	05	33	44	45
07	34	46	30	49	10
00	50	31	12	42	88
55	34	73	61	96	44
17	39	51	92	64	44
22	81	84	00	95	32
57	00	21	12	36	96
02	20	12	50	71	82
70	15	52	75	67	60
28	36	84	20	73	23
86	60	52	37	46	79
04	34	33	73	42	91
95	35	13	16	75	03
89	14	24	19	29	82
92	46	72	35	17	81
30	28	74	35	87	67
86	31	84	29	75	89
13	21	48	73	40	73
38	87	98	23	72	43
02	42	81	84	08	38
72	22	79	60	26	26
16	05	14	42	74	74
70	03	63	58	32	12
45	45	96	64	49	83
05	38	40	89	75	32
29	24	05	17	03	53
20	87	26	88	06	18

ANSWERS TO SELECTED PROBLEMS AND EXERCISES

Note to the student: Generally, the answers given here are "check" answers to about half of the problems and exercises, serving only to guide your thought process and solution procedures. Full rationales are not provided. Where multiple responses are sought, example responses are provided. Essay responses are omitted. A brief parenthetical identifier begins each item.

Chapter 1

2. (Distinctive competencies)
   - Holiday Inn: Dependability in price, accommodations, level of service.
   - U.S. Marines: Elite group, very selective.
   - Boeing: World leader in aircraft design, manufacture, and sales.
   - Procter & Gamble: Dominance in development and promotion of diversified product lines.

4. (Nonprofit organizations)
   Example: U.S. Postal Service:
   - Money: A traditional accounting function.
   - Design: New products/services such as 2nd-Day delivery, Express mail, and stamps-by-mail.
   - Demand: The postal service advertises, sets prices, conducts market research, and makes sales contracts with commercial customers.
   - Operations: Receiving, sorting, and delivering mail are primary operations activities.

6. (Cost and quality leadership) Examples include McDonalds, the North American farmer, Swatch watches, and Microsoft software.

8. (Western manufacturing) Western companies have been structured along functional specialties. Until recently, line people haven't been heard from. Solutions include cross-functional assignments, increasing line responsibilities (e.g., for problem solving, training, design, customer relationships) and placing fast-track employees in multifunctional teams or cells.

10. (Classic Wooden Toy Company) Generally, all of the implementation principles (numbers 5 through 16) serve to improve responsiveness. Specific examples include Principle 12 (cut setup and changeover times on woodworking equipment), Principle 11 (cut flow and wait time), Principle 16 (cut transactions and reporting) and Principle 7 (cross-train employees).

12. (John Deere) The up-to-date policy supports service to the customer. It directly supports Principle 7 and indi-

rectly supports others, especially Principles 1, 2, 7, and 15.

14. (Seagate) Principle 14 stresses recording and ownership of process data at the workplace to help ensure that line people get first crack at using that data for problem solving (Principle 15).

Chapter 2

2. (Zero defects) As you move down the list, pause to consider the potential effects of a mistake from each of the providers. None of us wants to be on the receiving end of defects. Our aim should be to avoid providing any. The last item helps pinpoint how that aim might be addressed now.

4. (Price versus quality) The perception that higher price denotes higher-quality service is the issue. Although challenged in recent years by numerous cost-effective, high-quality providers, that perception still permeates some sectors.

6. (PDCA cycle) Example for combating meeting tardiness and absenteeism:
   - Plan around attendance barriers by comparing members' schedules, and discuss causes.
   - Do implement a meeting schedule that is acceptable to all.
   - Check attendance and tardiness records.
   - Act by making the meeting schedule permanent or revising it if appropriate.

8. (Acme motor-generator set) It is an expense (arguably an investment) for quality and for productivity, better service, lower operating costs, and perhaps safety.

10. (Baldrige award winners) You will find considerable variation in post-Baldrige award performances from continued success to bankruptcy. Ability to meet the award's criteria over a certain time period is no guarantee of continuing success.

12. (Quality circles: hockey team and study group) Quality circles might work for the hockey team whose members coordinate plays, pass, feed, check, and assist for one another to improve overall performance. For the study group, the QC circle idea isn't so effective, to the extent that students go through the education experience as individuals. With curriculum redesign, however, greater QC circle possibilities exist.

14. (QC circles: basketball team and skiers) The QC circle could probably work well for the basketball team but not for the skiers. Skiers ski mainly as individuals.

Chapter 3

3. (McDonald's product development) Suppliers, customers, and McDonald's franchisees are responsible for originating many of McDonald's products. For example, Lou Groen, a Cincinnati-area franchisee, and Bud Sweeney of Gorton, a fish supplier, developed McDonald's fish sandwich. McDonald's first consideration is quality of ingredients.

5. (IBM's keyboard products) Design guidelines 2 (minimize part counts), 8 (one-way or layered assembly to enable use of cheap but precise robots), and 7 (eliminate screws for ease of joining).

7. (Role playing) Examples:
   - Dietician: Don't call for out-of-season fruits and vegetables.
   - Fashion designer: Don't produce designs that call for skins of rare or protected animals.
   - Architect: Don't specify nonstandard fixtures or unproven materials.
   - Portfolio manager: Don't advertise hard-to-get assets.

9. (Mazda)
   Designer unfamiliarity with customer desires (guideline 3), uncertain process capabilities (guideline 4), and fragile designs (guideline 10).

11. (QFD: hamburger container)
   The "roof" correlates each how with each other one. For example, ergonomics wouldn't correlate with biodegradability, but would correlate strongly with container design.

13. (Service design) Examples:
   a. Wedding consultants use checklists to avoid omitting asking the prospective bride and groom about important details.
   b. Electronic (television) express checkout from hotel rooms eliminates a return visit to the front desk in the lobby.
   c. A money fund account with check-writing privileges is offered by many investment brokerage firms.

15. (Robotic assembly)
   The second item, (*b*).

17. (Justify robot) Examples:
   - Cost: The expenses of buying the robot.
   - Benefit: Greater machining or assembly precision.

Chapter 4

2. (Food-processing company)
   a. Total tolerance band is 0.16 oz.; vendor's inherent capability (0.20 oz.) is not good enough, so don't buy.

b. No change. The vendor's problem is excess variation in process output; a change in location and process control can't change that fact.

c. Advise both to work together to determine and remove cause of excess variability.

4. (Plug-N-Go: Process capability)
   a. $C_{pk} = 0.833$.
   b. About 0.62 percent of the valve covers are out of spec.
   c. Two actions: First, always strive to reduce variation in process output; second, shift process downward toward target specification of 0.50 cm.

6. (Hypodermic needles)
   a. $UCL_{\bar{X}} = 27.96$ grams; $LCL_{\bar{X}} = 24.24$ grams; $UCL_R = 9.32$ grams; $LCL_R = 0.68$ grams.
   b. Create trial control charts, plot sample averages and ranges, test for process control. If in control, put process to use; if not, determine special causes, eliminate, and repeat trial control charts.
   c. R is below the *LCL,* so there is more process consistency than expected (out of control). Investigate to determine the cause and then try to replicate it permanently. Remember that being out of control is not necessarily bad, as shown in this case.

8. (Circuit current loss) Circuit current losses are lower than before, so some process improvement has occurred. The job is to find out why and make the improvement permanent. Most likely, factors of design, purchasing, production and/or training are responsible for the process output improvement. Pricing and marketing might incorporate improvement in advertising. Again, we see that being out of control sometimes is good news.

10. (OK-Mart & Electro Corp.)
   a. Center line on *p* chart is at 0.2%, the actual process average.
   b. Process improvements are needed; then sample again with new charts.

12. (Rescue Services Training, Ltd.)
   a. $\bar{c} = 4.2$ $UCL_c = 10.35$ $LCL_c = 0$
   b. The process is not in control.
   c. Example recommendation: As one of its initial steps, the training group should develop a check sheet (similar to the one shown in Solved Problem 3) that classifies errors. Recording during SERE training would then not only count mistakes but also reveal the most frequently occurring ones.

14. (Ajax) Assuming a normal process output distribution, the sketch should reveal that the distance from the process center ($\bar{\bar{X}}$) to the nearer specification limit is equal to six times the process standard deviation (σ).

16. (Pottery manufacturing) Process is out of control (inconsistent). Special causes of process variation need to

be identified and eliminated. Stop production if corrective action isn't immediately apparent.

18. (Orville's Popcorn: choice of control charting method) Variables charts, *X*-bar and *R,* are superior to attributes charts. Here, measurements can easily be taken, so variables charts are the proper choice.

20. (AmPen)

   a. Fishbone chart categorizes causes of error, alerts people to cause-effect relationships.

   b. Pareto chart shows relative importance of problems or defects; here, the impurity problem dramatically overshadows the others, and it should be the first problem attacked.

24. (Attributes and variables) Examples:

   • Telephone: Attributes: Does it ring? Does it convey sound? Variables: physical dimensions of components. The attributes are easy to evaluate; the physical dimensions would require some measurement equipment. Customers would find the attributes more meaningful and would assume the variables are suitable for assembly.

   • Dice: Attributes: Are the dots clearly visible? Are there any chips? Variables: distribution of weight. Again, the attributes are easily determined, but the weight distribution requires some precisely calibrated equipment.

   • Library reference services: Attributes: proportion of reference requests filled. Variables: time taken to fill requests. Here, both are easy to obtain. A simple charting system would suffice.

26. (Popcorn popper device) Place a sifter at the bottom of the popped-corn area and stir occasionally.

28. (Tolerance stackup) Example: Engine pistons and cylinders

Chapter 5

2. (Forecasting in organizational types) Examples: type 1, highway construction; type 2, air conditioning contractor; type 3, tractor manufacturer; type 4, small appliance manufacturer.

4. (County Hospital) Group totals: actual, 2,729; forecast, 2,580; error, +149, or 5.8 percent. Item error, 25.6 percent.

6. (Metro Auto Sales) Examples: Rolling forecast mode and group forecasting mode.

8. (Service part) MAD, 2.6; SD, 3.5; MAPE, 14.86.

10. (Computer logons) Both seasonality and trend. Approximately 13,500 logons.

12. (Public defender's office)

   a. A longer time span smooths the data more.

   b. June-centered moving average is 130. Index = 120/130 = 0.92.

c. True seasonality of caseload and best time span for forecasting.

14. (*BusinessWeek*) Both the production index and leading index are four-week moving averages.

17. (Huckleberry Farms)

   a. 501.5, applicable to next month.

   b. Nine months.

   c. 509.1, applicable to January of next year.

   d. $\alpha = 0.5$ is best of values tested.

   e. 3-quarter M.A. is 1,546; 3-year M.A. is 5,952; quarterly E.S. is 1,574; annual E.S. is 6,079.

18. (Seal-Fine Sash)

   a. 972, applicable to next quarter.

   b. Four quarters.

   c. 1,536, applicable to winter next year.

   d. $\alpha = 0.5$ is best of values tested.

20. (Smith's Kitchens)

   a. Rough association, lead time is about 18 months.

   b. $Y = 60.9 + 0.13X$.

   c. $r = 0.27$

22. (Acme Manufacturing)

   a. Approximately 35.

   b. New hires appear to lead by one month.

   c. $Y = 56.4 - 4.7X;$ next month is 38; two months away is 33.

   d. $r = 0.33$; $r = 0.86$

24. (Atlantic Envelope)

   a. Type of order determined the focus.

Chapter 6

2. (HP) Retraining and reassignment are major tools. That is easier when very talented people are hired in the first place. Aggressive development of new products and services ensures that there will be a place to go when older lines fade away.

6. (Bright Way) With a chase-demand strategy, Bright Way becomes more like its competitors. It would rely more on a transient work force for adjustable capacity, so there would be less need to plan capacity far ahead. New management problems would be in the labor area; hiring/firing, scheduling, and supervisor concerns.

8. (Windward Sportswear)

   a. Response may vary, depending on logic. Examples:

   • No. Demand surges above 130 per week in two of the five weeks, suggesting that customers won't be adequately served.

   • Yes. By assuming that overtime is used or additional capacity is available (say, from the director and other cross-trained associates), customers can be served.

b. Example response: Windward purchasers could staff at 130 per week and, with cross-training and flexible cell assignments, have a ready reserve of additional purchasing talent for weeks with heavy demand. In slower weeks, people have TQ circle meetings, train, and so forth.

c. Example: Streamline with flow lines focused on various types of PO's.

10. (Computer software)

- Recent standard: 1,400 packages/30 labor hours = 46.67 packages per hour.
- With new demand: 1,200 packages/46.67 packages per hour = 25.7 labor hours needed at full capacity.
- So at 90 percent undercapacity scheduling, assign 25.7/0.9 = 28.6 labor hours per day.

12. (Concrete Products, Inc.)

a. Have six operators and use shortened workweeks as needed. If contracts prevent that, use part-time personnel.

b. Have five operators and use overtime (or subcontracting if reliable concrete specialists can be found) as required.

14. (Gulf Tube and Pipe Company: production and capacity plans)

a. Chase demand (in millions of lineal feet):

Week	1	2	3	4
Production plan	5.5	5.3	4.9	4.1

b. Level-capacity:

Week	1	2	3	4
Production plan	4.9	4.9	4.9	4.9

c. Capacity plans (number of operators):

Week	1	2	3	4
Chase-demand	11.0	10.6	9.8	8.2
Level-capacity	9.8	9.8	9.8	9.8

d. Inventories absorb demand swings under level-capacity strategy and thus vary more.

18. (Gulf Tube and Pipe Company rough-cut capacity planning)

a. Dynacut capacity = 120,000 lineal feet/day × 5 day/week = 600,000 lineal feet/week. Possible actions: Overload of 80,000 lineal feet in week 2 and the underload of 130,000 lineal feet in week 3 sug-

gest shift of some work on the MPS from week 2 to week 3. For example, end-item 0845 could be split.

b. Tends toward chase-demand, though there isn't enough evidence to be sure.

20. (Piney Woods Furniture Company) Order calls for 1,000 cabinets, or 1,000/50 = 20 minimum order equivalents, due in week 6:

a. Cabinet order loads for load-profile weeks -4, -3, and -2 translate into MPS requirements (in cubic-yards) as follows: 800 for week 2, 200 for week 3, and 400 for week 4.

Added to other load yields, total kiln load is:

Week	1	2	3	4	5	6
Load (cubic yard-hours)	5,000	6,000	5,500	6,200	5,700	6,000

b. Week 4 shows a 200 cubic yard-hour overload.

c. Move the delivery date to week 5.

22. (Ceramic products)

$$
\begin{aligned}
\text{5th unit} &= 51.97 \text{ hours} \\
\text{10th unit} &= 48.85 \text{ hours} \\
\text{20th unit} &= 45.92 \text{ hours}
\end{aligned}
$$

Chapter 7

2. (Iota Company) Increase the risk. Raise the reorder point.

4. (Hewlett-Packard)

a. The computer transactions added no value to goods and services destined for customers. Excess documentation, like the work orders here, is a hidden cost associated with having inventories.

b. Student exercise.

6. (Ivy Memorial Hospital) Example items: Involve suppliers early; inform them of the QRP effort and explain the demand elements that will be "pulling the string" for hospital services and thus supplier goods and services. Next, try to separate those demands into independent and dependent items; they'll help determine how much lead time the hospital will be able to give suppliers. And, of course, all parties along the supply channels need to streamline processes.

8. (QRP examples)

a. The first three examples deal with retail supply; the fourth, the auto manufacturer, extends QRP to a durable goods producer.

b. Not right away (high cost); maybe later (e.g., for use in billing).

c. Fax initially since equipment is cheaper and more of the supplier-customer channel can join. Possibly EDI later between selected pairs (e.g., for financial purposes or for sharing MPS data for large end items).

10. (MRP, for an industrial thermostat producer) Lead time is still very bad.

12. (Queues at a campus testing service) Examples: Split large batch (say, from a large class) of papers into smaller transfer batches (between order-entry and scanner). Work during lull times to reduce setups, and perform preventive maintenance so that breakdowns are minimized.

14. (ABC Specialties, Inc.)
$T_{RM} = 6; T_{WIP} = 7; T_{FG} = 0.33; T_{TOT} = 3.33$

Chapter 8

2. (Auto repair service contract) General: Response should stress benefits of partnership relationship (e.g., you might keep maintenance records for vehicles, offer a pickup and delivery service, etc.)

4. (CalComp, Inc.) A design goal is fewer parts (see Chapter 3), but the other two items directly support principles of supplier-customer partnerships. All would serve to improve quality and delivery of incoming materials and thus help cut the plant's operating costs.

6. (Home Remodeling)
   a. Breakeven = 40 patios.

8. (Travel department)
   Breakeven is 2,353 tickets/year. Travel department should buy rather than make.

10. (ABC uses) Example: Make or buy analysis/decisions: A items, done by executive committee; B items, done by product or materials manager; C items, done by inventory planner.

12. (ABC classes)

Item Number	Dollar Usage Last Year	Class
030	$30,000	A
109	6,000	B
All others		C

14. (THIS Company) As conditions stand, loss of THIS Company's business could well be the death of the uniform supplier. One critical issue facing Adam, however, is time: THIS must be responsive to its customers; does Adam have enough time to bring the current uniform supplier up to quick-response partnership status?

16. (Organizational purchasing) Examples:
   b. The city is heavily involved in buying intangibles; examples include consultants' services and software.

c. Approved supplier lists: all except liquor wholesaler. Bid solicitation: city government and larger manufacturers (for selected items). Blanket orders: high-volume standard items going into fashions, home appliances, electric power, glass, plastics, computers, ships, aerospace.

18. (VA in JIT companies) JIT requires on-the-spot problem solving, including any design changes. For value analysis to be done on the fly, specifications should be held to a minimum, or focus just on performance specs.

20. (Jane Doe, standardization) Bad. A lack of standardization is shown.

Chapter 9

2. (Sentrol, Inc., telephone answering) Strategy is practical. Call arrival distributions suggest times to staff the telephone system with extra personnel, cross-trained in customer service, of course.

4. (X-ray machines)
   a. Push: Components are pushed onto final assembly.
   b. Convert to pull system, perhaps using kanban squares.

6. (Partial MRP data for FOQ) The fixed-order quantity is 160. Scheduled receipts are due in weeks 1 and 5, and a planned order release is scheduled for week 2.

10. (Tape dispenser)
   b. Planned order release schedule: Roll of tape, 5,000 in week 3 and 5,000 in week 6; Spool, 2,000 in week 1 and 5,000 in week 4.
   c. Planned receipts for rolls of tape are due in weeks 4 and 7, and for spools in weeks 3 and 6. Planned receipts do not become scheduled receipts, however, until orders are placed.

14. (Kitchen knives)
   a. Order 2,400 rivets in week 2.
   b. Order 2,400 blocks in week 3.
   c. Order 130 wood bars in week 3.

16. (Hospital safety stock factors) Example: for X-ray film, safety stock factors are high cost and obsolescence, so keep safety stock low. (But need rapid replenishment from medical supply company or other medical facilities in case of urgent high demand.)

18. (Brown Instrument Co. ROP)
   a. $ROP = 81.4$
   b. Both DLT and SS would increase.

20. (Service level and safety stock)
   a. SS = 51
   b. All three factors should lower the safety stock.

22. (Fuel oil ROP)

   a. About 3.75 orders per winter.

   b. $DLT = 3,000$ gallons; $SS = 3,400$ gallons

Chapter 10

2. (Restaurant changeovers) Examples: Sections are set up (changed over) to the new format while other sections continue to serve patrons having the current meal, and table setups (e.g., napkins folded, flowers put in vases, candles put in holders) are prepared in advance. Guideline 2 is illustrated.

4. (Die handling)

   a. Guidelines 3, 4, 5, and 6 are clear, others possible.

   b. Guidelines 7 and 8; more standardization and simplification.

6. (Lot-for-lot versus batch) Yes, the comparison also makes sense for processing when clients are people.

8. (Provincial government)

   a. $EOQ = 600$ boxes

   b. The EOQ is a zone that takes in the extra 10%. But OM principle 13 calls for seeking ways to justify smaller lots.

10. (Maple Tree Insurance)
   At $3.00, $EOQ = 258$ boxes (not feasible)
   At $2.60, $EOQ = 277$ boxes (feasible)

12. (Cannery) At $0.60, $EPQ = 3,266$ (feasible; total annual costs = $24,490); at $0.50, $EPQ = 3,577$ (not feasible). Total annual costs at order quantity of 4,000 are $20,450. The correct order quantity (4,000) will last about 1.2 months and is $2,000 worth.

14. (Print shop)

   a. $EMQ = 157,400$; 15.7 months

   b. $EOQ = 154,900$ (small difference since production rate is much larger than demand rate)

   c. $ROP = 1,000$ plus any desired safety stock

16. (Irrigation system)

   a. 3-inch $EMQ = 2,306$ pipe sections; 4-inch $EMQ = 2,246$ sections

   b. 3-inch $EMQ = 1,631$ pipe sections

20. (Federal Time Corporation)

   a. $EOQ = 6,532$ lenses

   b. Single-digit setup: Equip molding machines with tables to hold molds at usage height; use rollers or air cushions to make it easier to slide molds into position.

22. (Semiconductors in small lots) By always running in small lots; cut setup times to make that easier.

Chapter 11

2. (Operations management development) In repetitive operations, long runs of very nearly identical opera-

tions mean that OM development costs may be amortized over a large number of output units; thus, unit cost is smaller.

4. (Operations environments) Example: Construction crew foreman for builder of large, one-of-a-kind bridges. Project environment: industry is oligopolistic (few firms can handle such jobs) and each job is bid; volume is very low and each bridge is unique (high variety). Tools and equipment are flexible and include land-based and barge-mounted piling drivers, cranes, and other heavy construction equipment. Tools for steel and concrete placement and working are also required. Layout is fixed-position; the bridge stays put while people, materials, and equipment move around it.

6. (Golfers and sand wedges) The sand wedge golf club is special, but most golfers carry one. It is a commodity item. Professionals and other dedicated golfers, however, often have custom-made clubs.

8. (State University: *The Sound of Music*) Example response:

   a. Fixed-position layout; each site is unique, but equipment, the set, and other items are reused. Also, each performance is very nearly like the others, so there is repetition.

   b. If a different performance is given at each location, expect less repetitive operations; each performance would be a unique project.

   c. Streamlining can occur by focusing on some of the quick setup and quick changeover tools studied in earlier chapters.

10. (Corneal transplant) Typically performed in a job environment. Optic surgery has been streamlined in Russia; patients move along lines of surgeons, each performing part of the operation. Most of us would view surgery as a custom service.

Chapter 12

2. (Continuous versus repetitive processing) Examples:

   a. Soft drinks: Syrup processing (flavoring, sweetening, coloring, etc.) is continuous; bottling or canning is repetitive.

   b. Nursing care: Electronic monitoring of patient's heartbeat is continuous; hourly charting of temperature is repetitive.

4. (Detergent manufacturing)

   • Process design and capital investment; much automation and extensive process engineering.

   • Reliability of supply; firm, long-term contracts with suppliers and dependable transportation (e.g., an owned, or controlled pipeline).

6. (Synchronized mixed-model schedule) Not quite. Building A should strive for mixed-model schedules.

8. (Faiko Time Co.) Faiko should regularize mechanism assembly to about seven per day (for example, four of type A, two of B, and one of C); check demand every two weeks and adjust schedule as required. Enclosures are less amenable to regularizing. Still, perhaps there is dominant demand for one type and it should get regularized production.

10. (Line-balancing analysis) Time in minutes:

    a. Task time sum equals 100 minutes. Possible cycle time/number of stations pairs: 100/1, 50/2, 25/4, 20/5, 10/10, 5/20, 4/25, 2/50.

    b. The last three are not feasible since there are only 12 work elements. The first three are feasible only if multiple stages can be performed at a single workstation since two segments in the precedence diagram require five stages.

    c. With a cycle time of 20 minutes, a six-station solution would yield a balance delay of 17 percent.

12. (Worker's compensation claims office)

    a. Task time sum is 234 minutes. Possible cycle times/number of station pairs: 234/1, 117/2, 78/3, 39/6, 26/9, 18/13, 13/18, 9/26, 6/39, 3/78, 2/117.

    b. Not feasible: 1, 2, 3, 13, 18, 26, 39, 78, 117 stations.

    c. Five-station balance is better since its balance delay (10 percent) is less than the balance delay of the six-station solution (13 percent).

14. (Zeus, Inc., mixed models) Full cycle (10 minutes) production ratio L:M:S equals 1:2:4.

    a. Ten-minute cycle SMSMSLS challenges supplier to match it, possibly with simpler dedicated equipment.

    b. Supplier should slow down as Zeus slows down, and use excess labor for training and improvement projects.

    c. Zeus' schedule is too full. A policy of undercapacity scheduling is needed so targets can be met almost every day; for example, try L:M:S = 44:88:172 units per day.

16. (Heat treating mixed models) Mixed-model sequence is AAAB; five hours will be required.

18. (Typewriter table mixed model) Model ratio D:E:F:G equals 1:3:2:4. The most repetitive mixed-model sequence is GEFGEFGEDG, six times/day.

20. (Repetitive scheduling in bank) Yes, check and deposit processing are examples.

Chapter 13

2. (Advertising agency) Three examples: Create flow lines or cells dedicated to handling major categories of job types. Adopt queue-limitation and flow-control simplification, and, on a grander scale, consider focus-ing the business on a few types of jobs to reduce variety.

4. (Gantt charts) Student exercises.

6. (Gantt chart project task)

    a. Date is day 11. The task is 83 percent complete and is two days ahead of schedule.

    b. Chart should show three days ahead of schedule.

    c. Saturdays, Sundays, and holidays are skipped.

8. (Work center load imbalance)

    a. If the work center is a gateway, leveling techniques can be used, perhaps firm planned orders. In extreme cases, the master scheduler can be asked to adjust the MPS.

    b. Computer processes open order file, accumulating loads by time bucket for each work center. Next, the same thing is done for the planned orders via CRP software. The combination produces the load report.

10. (Jerrybuilt Machines, Inc.) The order list is:

    $$916 \text{ slack} = -1$$
    $$889 \text{ slack} = +1$$
    $$901 \text{ slack} = +4$$

12. (Blanking center—job priority list) The order list is:

    $$444 \text{ slack} = -1$$
    $$222 \text{ slack} = +1$$
    $$333 \text{ slack} = +2$$

14. (Applications) Example response: Getting a driver's license:

    • Scheduling: Walk-in, first come, first served, or by-appointment system

    • Dispatching: Queue control at each station, first come, first served.

    • Expediting: Probably limited need. However, if tests had been passed but applicant needed to leave for some reason (e.g., forgot checkbook), then applicant could move directly to the fourth station upon return.

Chapter 14

5. (Dummy activity) Dummy activity 16–13 assures that both 12–16 and 10–13 precede 13–18 but that only 12–16 precedes 16–18.

8. (Antenna system)

    b. Critical path: 1–3–7 = 9 days.

    c.
Activity	Slack
1–3	0
3–7	0
All others	1

    d. Critical path: 1–2–4–6–7 = 11.

10. (Network crashing)

    b. 1–2–3–4–5, 15 days; $1,240.

    c. May be crashed to 11 days at a project cost of $1,730.

12. (Path analysis)

    a. 1–2–5–3–4, 17 days.
       1–2–3–4, 16 days.

    b. Two days.

14. (Slack calculations)

    a. +7.

    b. −1.

16. (Time-cost trade-off analysis)

    a. To reduce by one day, $185 (hint: requires shortening two activities).

    b. Days = 13

18. (Dummy activity) Dummy needed from 3 to 12.

20. (Critical path and network simulation) Critical path time is 2 weeks; PERT simulation time is 2 4/9 weeks.

Chapter 15

2. (Visual performance charts)

    a. Queue length.

    b. Check sheet.

    c. Check sheet.

    d. Color-change time.

4. (Florida Power and Light) Operations-oriented measures appear on charts easily seen by all. Controls are suggested by the processes; associates monitor performance and act on results.

6. (International Express Company) Neither should have it. Promote front-line responsibility.

8. (Seamstress—Work sampling)

    f. Sample size is really too small. The standard is engineered, but not well done.

    g. Scheduling and staffing.

    h. Try undercapacity scheduling.

    i. Correct causes and re-do the work sampling study.

10. (Social service agency)

    a. 22 employees (rounded).

    b. Historical.

12. (Auto plant time standards) 3.6 × 1.14 × 1.05 = 4.31 minute/wheel

14. (Lugging machine standard time)

    a. S.T. = 0.314 minute/piece

    b. MTM data are already normalized, so pace rating is unnecessary.

16. (Typing work sampling) Assuming a 480-minute work day:

    a. Typing: C.T. = 32.00 minutes; R.T. = 28.80 minutes; S.T. = 32.26 minutes. Retrieving: C.T. = 4.80 minutes; R.T. = 3.84 minutes; S.T. = 4.30 minutes.

    b. Uses include staffing, scheduling, and evaluating equipment and methods.

    c. Yes, they are engineered. If biases (such as easy versus hard job assignments) are controlled, the standards could be used for personnel evaluation.

18. (Wabash Airways)

    a. Efficiency = 133 percent

    b. 12 attendants.

20. (Setting time standards) Examples:

    • Soldering connections: time study or predetermined standards.

    • Computer programmers: historical standards.

Chapter 16

2. (Copy machines) Operators do a considerable amount of maintenance and minor repair work; cleaning glass and rollers, adding toner and other fluids, and clearing paper jams. Major repairs and PM (usually predictive) are performed by service technicians, especially for large models.

4. (PM for automobiles)

    a. Considerable usage data exists. Obstacles center around getting owners to accept the maintenance recommendations.

    b. Wear-out and failure data for components and replacement parts would need to be input into car's computers at some regular interval, say, when new tires or filters are installed.

    c. Factory machines are usually operated intensively at rather uniform operating conditions (not the case for automobiles).

6. (Maintainability) Computers and projectors are examples of products that require a high degree of maintainability. Removable panels allow easy access to compartments where frequent repairs are needed (e.g., lamp compartment on projectors). Maintainability is less important where downtime costs are low, e.g., lawn and garden equipment and small kitchen appliances.

8. (Security system timer) For example, at 200 hours, the reliability of the timer is about 0.9. Depending on what is being secured, of course, that figure may be all the risk the user is willing to bear.

10. (Control valve for fuel supply system)

    a. At two weeks, $R = 0.98$.

    b. Reliability can be enhanced by redundancy, having a backup.

12. (Cooling system filter traps) Individual: Steady-state clogging rate is about six per 1,000 hours. Cleaning costs would be $100 × 6 = $600 per 1,000 hours. Group: Best policy is group replacement every 3,000 hours at a cost of $567 per 1,000 hours.

14. (Duncan Aviation) Best number of spares is three; cost is $1,938 per week. Remember that the Poisson distribution will yield engine breakdown probabilities.

16. (Standby machine analysis)

    a. Fluorescent tubes are not suitable; minor costs are involved.

    b. Memory cards are suitable; don't overstudy, just keep some spares.

    c. Pizza oven is not suitable; spare ovens aren't very practical.

18. (Captain Henry Harrison) The captain's approach is sound. A clean workplace reduces search time, prevents accidents, improves machine operation, and improves morale of personnel.

Chapter 17

2. (Motor carriers) JIT operations have caused more carriers to offer as-requested delivery times and other services. This willingness to serve customers' needs may slow the movement to locate supplier plants adjacent to customers.

4. (EDS hiring and location) If employers perceive equal talent is available around the globe, then the labor skill-factor ceases to be as important in location decisions.

5. (Layout types) Examples:

   • Auto assembly: product.

   • Shipbuilding: fixed position.

   • Shoe repair: process.

   • Hospital: mixed.

8. (Automatic Controls Corporation)

d. The combined REL chart is not very necessary. The large number of ''3 codes'' suggests that product/resource flow is the dominant factor. Proceed directly from the from-to chart to the activity-arrangement diagram.

10. (E-Z Window Company)

    a. Unit loads are ''natural move quantities.''

    b. About 1.9 percent represents backtracking.

11. (Acme Corporation)

Worst→	AS/RS
	Carousel
	Pallet racks
	Wire-guided system
Best→	Transporter

12. (Principles of Operations Management) Principles 6, 9, and 11.

14. (Supplier concern about customer facilities) Probably so. The customer's competitiveness depends on facilities.

Chapter 18

2. (Global medical opinions) Yes, and to some extent this is being done now. Language and communication network barriers are crumbling, making the task easier. TQM still has value; the provider-customer relationship still exists.

4. (University cafeteria) (Hint: Draw from the principles of operations management.) Consider, for example, Principles 6 and 9: Can you set up flow lines or cells dedicated to a family of meal types? Can you equip them?

ABC (inventory) analysis Materials classification system in which all stocked items are classified by annual dollar volume. The high-value A items receive close control; medium-value B items get intermediate control; low-value C items receive lowest priority.

Activity Basic unit of work in a project.

Activity-based costing (ABC) A method of costing whereby a job, product, or service is assigned overhead costs only if overhead activity is actually expended to support it; replaces the old methods of allocating overhead costs, typically in proportion to direct labor costs.

Activity-on-arrow network A PERT/CPM network form in which activities are shown as arrows.

Activity-on-node network A PERT/CPM network form in which activities are shown as nodes.

Adaptive smoothing Technique for automatic adjustment of time-series smoothing coefficients based on some function of forecast error, commonly the tracking signal.

Aggregate demand Long- and medium-range demand expressed in collective terms rather than broken down by type of product or service or specific model.

Aggregate demand forecast Forecast for whole-product or capacity groups; long- or medium-term focus.

Appointment book A master schedule for the provision of services; a statement of the services to be provided.

Approved supplier A supplier given preferential treatment in purchasing decisions by earning high ratings on quality, delivery, price, and service.

Attribute inspection Inspection requiring only a yes-no, pass-fail, or good-bad judgment.

Automatic storage and retrieval system (AS/RS) Automated equipment, such as racks, bins, forklifts, and computerized location records, collectively designed to hold and retrieve inventory.

Autonomous operations The assignment of all work on certain products to a single workstation; work is not passed from station to station.

Availability Proportion of time a resource is ready for use; time over which the proportion is determined may exclude planned time for maintenance.

Backflush A post-deduction method of accounting for component stock usage at the time of end-product completion. Uses

BOM explosion to identify quantity of components to deduct from inventory record balances.

Backlog Collection of orders awaiting processing.

Backorder An order accepted when stock is out; usually filled when stock arrives.

Backscheduling Subtracting lead time (or throughput time) from the due date to find the time to start processing or to place an order with a supplier; a basic MRP calculation.

Backward integration Setting up to provide goods or services formerly purchased; (sometimes) buying a supplier company, making it a subsidiary.

Backward scheduling See **Backscheduling.**

Balance delay Ratio of waiting or idle time to total available time per cycle in an assembly line.

Batch A large quantity (a lot) of a single item.

Batch processing A type of operations in which multiple units of a single item are treated as one processing unit (batch).

Benchmarking Investigating best practices anywhere in the world for a given process; basis for comparing benchmarked practice with that of one's own organization in order to inspire improvement.

Bill of labor Labor requirements (type and quantity) to produce a product or provide a service; analogous to a **BOM.**

Bill of materials (BOM) Product structure for an assembly; shows required components and their quantity at each level of fabrication and assembly.

Bill of materials (BOM) explosion Breaking down an order for end products into major, secondary, tertiary, and so forth, components for the purpose of finding gross requirements for all component items.

Blanket orders A contract covering purchase of relatively low-cost items for which there is continuous but varying need; specifies price and other matters, but delivery is usually triggered by simple release orders issued as required.

Bottleneck Workstation or facility for which demand exceeds service capacity; same as a constraint.

Buffer stock Inventory maintained to provide customer service in the face of demand and production uncertainty; also known as safety stock; see, also, **Offline buffer stock.**

Buying down Attempting to buy an item with historical price swings at a time when the price is down.

c chart (number-defective chart)   A process control chart for attributes based on the number of defective items in each sample.

Capacity control   Keeping work centers busy but not overloaded; takes place after work center loading and may include expediting.

Capacity planning   Planning for adjustable resources such as labor, equipment usage, and aggregate inventory, typically over a medium-term (a few weeks to about 18 months) planning horizon.

Capacity requirements planning (CRP)   A computer-based method of revealing work center loads; determines labor and machine resources needed to achieve planned outputs.

Capital cost   Cost (e.g., interest rate) of borrowing money; a component of **Inventory carrying cost.**

Carrying cost   The cost, above and beyond unit price, to carry or hold an inventory item in a state of idleness.

Catalog buying   Purchasing from current supplier catalogs; the common purchasing procedure, for example, for off-the-shelf maintenance, repair, and operating (MRO) items.

Cell   A linkage of maker-customer pairs, created by drawing people and machines from functional areas and placing them in the same work area to reduce movement distances, inventory, and throughput time and to improve coordination.

Cellular layout   A layout in which workstations and machines are arranged into cells that provide families of goods or services that follow similar flow paths; very similar to product layout.

Certification   Formal approval of a supplier as a source for purchased goods and services; typically bestowed after a supplier exhibits process control, design and delivery standards, and other desirable traits.

Changeover time   The time it takes to change the setup on a machine, production line, or process in order to produce a new product or service; the required time for start up; also called setup time.

Chase demand (strategy)   A capacity management strategy in which sufficient capacity is maintained to meet current demand; capacity levels chase (respond to) demand fluctuations.

Closed-loop MRP   An MRP system with feedback loops aimed at maintaining valid schedules; includes file control, rescheduling actions, and production activity control.

Commodity product   An undifferentiated product.

Common cause   Cause for common variation in process output (after specific or assignable causes have been removed).

Common variation   Variation remaining in process output after all special variation has been removed; may be thought of as the natural variation in a process that is in statistical control.

Competitive analysis   Thorough study (''reverse engineering'') of a competitor's product or service; aimed at generating usable ideas and for lowering complacency about competitors.

Complete physical inventory   An actual count of all inventory items.

Component item   An item that goes into the assembly of the parent item; for example, a bulb is a component of a flashlight.

Composition of demand   Refers to the varying degree of importance of each order in a group awaiting processing; of interest to a master planning committee, especially when demand exceeds capacity, so that more important demands (for preferred customers, or earning higher profit) can receive higher priority.

Computer-integrated manufacturing (CIM)   Computer assistance or direct control of manufacturing from product and process design to scheduling to production and material handling; may include FMS, CAD, and CAM.

Concurrency   Technique for reducing lead times in projects by doing design and production of later stages at the same time as, and coordinated with, earlier activities.

Continuous operations   Perpetual production of goods that flow; may include production of one batch after another.

Continuous process   See **Continuous operations.**

Correlation coefficient   A measure of the degree of association between two or more variables.

Cost variance   Productivity measure computed by subtracting actual costs of inputs from standard costs of outputs for a given operating unit or job.

Crash (crashing)   Reducing an activity's time by adding resources; crashing critical activities reduces project time.

Critical path   The path (activity sequence) through a project network that is estimated to consume the most time.

Critical path method (CPM)   A network-based project management technique initially used on construction projects; about the same as **PERT.**

Custom product   A highly differentiated, unique, special-purpose, or one-of-a-kind product.

Customer   The next process (where the work goes next); also, the end user or consumer.

Cycle counting   An inventory counting plan in which a small fraction of items are counted each day; an alternative to complete physical inventory.

Cycle interval   The time interval (minutes, hours, days, or weeks) between when a certain product or service is made or delivered until the next time it is made or delivered.

Cycle time (CT)   Raw average time for completion of one cycle or element of a repeating operation; may also be called *select time (ST)* in time study.

Cyclical pattern   Recurring pattern in a time series; generally, each occurrence spans several years.

Delayed differentiation   Retaining standard forms or parts further along the assembly sequence; waiting as long as possible to transform common- or general-purpose items into special-purpose parts.

Demand forecasting   Estimating future demand for goods and services.

Demand management Recognizing and managing all demands for products and services in accordance with the master plan.

Dependent demand Demand that results from demand for a parent item; for example, demand for mower blades is dependent on demand for mowers.

Derating Running a machine or production line at less than rated (maximum) capacity to forestall breakdowns, deteriorating quality, and early wear-out.

Design-build team Team consisting of product design and process development people, whose aim is a producible product design.

Design for operations (DFO) Concept of designing a product or service to be easy to produce or provide; a manufacturing version is design for manufacture and assembly (DFMA).

Design review A check on engineering designs to ensure satisfaction of customers' requirements and producibility.

Destructive testing Product inspection that destroys the product's usefulness, rendering it unfit for sale; may be used, for example, in inspecting a sample of flashbulbs.

Dispatcher A person whose responsibility is to release jobs into work centers or, sometimes, resources to jobs.

Distinctive competency A strength that sets an organization apart from its competition.

Distribution requirements planning (DRP) Incorporation of distribution requirements into master production schedules; requirements are based on actual forecast needs, not just shelf replacement.

Dummy activity A PERT/CPM network activity that consumes no time or resources; used to clarify a network diagram.

Earliest finish (EF) The earliest possible time when a project activity may be completed; *EF* equals *ES* plus activity duration (t).

Earliest start (ES) The earliest possible starting time for a project activity; if an activity has multiple predecessors, its *ES* is equal to the latest predecessors' *EF*.

Early-life failure Mortality upon startup for a component or product; often caused by improper assembly or rough handling.

Early supplier involvement A program for getting a supplier's personnel involved early in new development or changes affecting items the supplier provides.

Economic manufacturing quantity (EMQ) A variation of the EOQ model incorporating acquisition of a lot over the production time rather than all at once; applicable, for example, when goods are made rather than bought.

Economic order quantity (EOQ) The (fixed) quantity to be ordered in each order cycle that will minimize total inventory costs.

Efficiency Standard time divided by actual time or actual output (units) divided by standard output (units).

Engineering changes (ECs) Formal changes in product or process design that alter bills of materials, routing, or production technique.

Ergonomics Study of a work environment with emphasis on human physiological concerns; efforts to "fit the job to the person" are examples of ergonomics in practice.

Event Point signifying completion of one or more project activities and sometimes the beginning of others; consumes no time or resources but merely marks a point in time.

Expediting (Expediter) Actions aimed at pulling urgent jobs, purchases, or customers through more quickly; expediters also called parts chasers.

Exponential smoothing A form of weighted moving average forecasting that uses a smoothing coefficient to assign an aged weight to each period of historical data.

Facilitator An individual with overall responsibility for formation, training, and leadership of improvement teams.

Facilities Plant and equipment that are generally fixed and unalterable for months to years.

Fail-safing Designing a process to be incapable of *(a)* allowing an error to be passed on to the next process, or *(b)* allowing an error at all.

Failure rate Average number of failures in a given time period; the inverse of **Mean time between failures.**

Finite-capacity planning Workload planning methods that consider the limited (finite) capacity of workstations and assign work accordingly.

Firm planned order An MRP tool for overriding the automatic rescheduling feature of MRP; useful for getting a job into a gateway work center at a convenient time, even if different from the calculated order due date.

Fishbone chart A chart resembling the skeleton of a fish in which the spine bone represents the major cause of quality problems and connecting bones, contributing causes; reveals cause-effect linkages. (Also known as cause-effect diagram and Ishikawa diagram.)

Fixed-position layout A facility layout in which the product is kept in one place and facilities come to it; examples include construction and production of very large items.

Flexible manufacturing cell (FMC) Cluster of machines capable of producing a whole part or family of parts.

Flexible manufacturing system (FMS) Machine workcell controlled by a local micro- or minicomputer and assisted by one or more robots; produces a whole part or family of parts.

Flowcharts A family of charts showing work sequence; used in data collection and analysis in an improvement study.

Focus forecasting A form of simulation-based forecasting; involves selection of the most accurate of several forecasting models as the basis for the next forecast.

Focused factory   Concept that stresses doing one or a few things well at a given plant.

Forecast error   For a given time period, actual demand minus forecast demand.

Forward scheduling   Beginning with current date or expected start date, adding throughput (lead) time, thus arriving at a scheduled order completion date.

Gain-sharing   An incentive pay system in which everyone receives a share of the value of productivity increases.

Gantt control chart   A chart used to control certain types of jobs with stable priorities, for example, renovation and major maintenance.

Gantt scheduling chart   A widely used scheduling chart, with horizontal rows representing jobs or resources to be scheduled and vertical divisions representing time periods.

Gross requirements   The total amount of each component needed to produce the ordered quantity of the parent item.

Group-based capacity planning   Creating aggregate capacity plans with product and service groups or families as core requirement components and a cross-trained labor force available for assignment.

Group replacement   Replacing a whole set of components, whether bad or not, at planned intervals; an alternative to a replace-as-they-fail policy.

Hedging   A form of purchasing that offers some protection from price changes; applies especially to commodities and includes trading on futures markets.

Holding cost   An element of carrying cost; generally associated with stockroom costs, insurance, inventory taxes, and damage or shrinkage during storage.

House of quality   Name given to the basic QFD matrix, which includes a house-like roof showing correlations between process factors. See also **Quality function deployment.**

Idleness rate   Percentage of time that a facility is idle; computed as 1 minus the utilization rate.

Incentive pay   Pay based on work output; in its purest form, a piece rate.

Independent demand   Demand for items that do not go into parent items; generally, independent demand is forecast and dependent demand is calculated.

Infinite-capacity loading   Scheduling jobs without regard for resulting work center loads. See also **Infinite-capacity planning.**

Infinite-capacity planning   A work load planning system that assumes the availability of resources required to provide needed parts and services and assigns work accordingly; relies on an activity control subroutine to adjust priorities when bottlenecks arise.

Input control   Control of work releases to gateway or bottleneck work centers.

Inventory carrying cost   See **Carrying cost.**

Inventory turnover   Annual cost of goods sold divided by value of average inventory.

Irregular maintenance   Unscheduled repairs, machine installations (millwright work), and minor construction.

Item demand   Demand broken down into specific types or models of products or services.

Item master file   An inventory file containing records for each component and assembly; holds on-hand balances, planning factors, and independent demand data.

Job   A task of limited size and complexity, usually resulting in something tangible; the whole work activity required to fill a service order or produce a component.

Job design   The function of fitting tasks together to form a job that can be assigned to a person; emphasis is on creating useful jobs that people can and want to do; job enlargement, job enrichment, and cross-training are associated with theories of job design.

Job operations   Intermittent processing, frequently one at a time; characterized by extreme variation in output and process; type of operations in a job shop.

Just-in-time (JIT) operations   A system of managing operations with little or no delay time or idle inventories between one process and the next.

Kanban   A communication or signal from the user to the maker (or supplier) for more work; from the Japanese word for "card" or "visible record"; a queue-limitation device.

Latest finish (LF)   The latest possible completion time for a project activity to avoid project delay; if the activity has multiple successor activities, its *LF* equals the successors' earliest *LS*.

Latest start (LS)   The latest possible starting time for a project activity to avoid project delay; $LS = LF - $ Activity duration (t).

Lead time   See **Throughput time.**

Leading indicator   A variable that correlates with demand one or more periods later, giving some signal of magnitude and direction of pending demand change.

Learning curve   Graphical representation of the economy of scale concept: greater volume yields lower unit cost; the curve plots resource consumption as a function of lot quantity.

Level-by-level MRP processing   The MRP way of calculating planned order release quantities and dates, top (zero) level of the BOM first, then subsequent lower levels; ensures complete capture of all requirements.

Level capacity (strategy)   A capacity management strategy that seeks to retain a stable or constant amount of capacity, especially labor.

Leveling (normalizing)   In setting time standards, adjusting the raw cycle time to reflect the pace (level of effort) of the person observed, which yields the leveled (normalized) time.

Line balancing   A procedure for dividing tasks evenly among employees or workstations in a product or cellular layout; also known as assembly-line balancing.

Linear output   Production of the same quantity each time period; also may mean meeting a variable schedule every day.

Linearity index   A measure of the success in attaining targeted production or processing quantities; mathematically, it is 100 percent minus the mean percent deviation from scheduled production quantity.

Load leveling   Scheduler's attempt to release a mix of orders that neither overloads nor underloads work centers.

Load profile   Future work center capacity requirements for open and planned orders.

Loading (load, workload)   Assigning workload to a work center.

Lot   Large purchase or production quantity of the same item; often has its own identifying number.

Lot-for-lot   The simplest approach to lot sizing; the exact order quantity required by the parent item or ordered by the customer.

Lot size   Quantity of an item produced, serviced, or transported at one time.

Lot sizing   Planning order quantities.

Lot splitting   Splitting a lot quantity into more than one sublot, traditionally for expediting reasons: stop (split up) a current lot already on a machine so a hot job can replace it. Under JIT, lot splitting is fairly normal practice (not expediting), especially if a lot can be split among several of the same type of machine or workstation.

Lumpy workload (demand)   Highly variable pattern of workload (demand).

Maintainability   Features that make equipment or products easy to maintain.

Manufacturability   See **Producibility.**

Manufacturing resource planning (MRPII)   A comprehensive planning and control system that uses the master production schedule as a basis for scheduling capacity, shipments, tool changes, design work, and cash flow.

Master planning   Broadly, matching aggregate demand with capacity; narrowly, steering the firm's capacity toward actual item demands that materialize over time.

Master production schedule (MPS)   Master schedule for product-oriented company.

Master schedule   A statement of what the firm plans to produce (products) and/or provide (services), broken down by product model or service type.

Material requirements planning (MRP)   A computer-based system of planning orders to meet the requirements of an MPS, and of tracking inventory flows.

Mean absolute deviation (MAD)   A measure of forecast model accuracy; the sum of absolute values of forecast errors over a number of periods divided by the number of periods.

Mean absolute percent error (MAPE)   Measure of forecast model accuracy; the average of the absolute error to demand ratio over a number of periods converted to a percentage.

Mean time between failures   Average time elapsing between failure of a repairable item, or average time to first failure of a nonrepairable item; the inverse of **Failure rate.**

Mean time to repair   Average time to effect repair or replacement.

Measured daywork (MDW) system   A nominal incentive-wage system in which standard output serves as a target for an employee.

Methods study   Procedure for improving the way work is done; follows the scientific method of inquiry.

Methods-time-measurement (MTM)   Procedure for developing synthetic time standards by referring to tables of standards for basic motions.

Milestone   A key event in a project; one type of upper management–oriented network consists solely of milestone events.

Mixed-model assembly lines   Assembly lines on which more than one model of a product is made.

Mixed-model production (mixed-model assembly)   Production schedule that is repetitive in short cycles; conducive to supplying some of each needed model each day closely in line with customer requirements.

Model   A likeness (mental, graphic, mathematical, or procedural) of a reality.

Motion study   Methods improvement approach focusing on basic hand and body motions called **Therbligs.**

Moving average   In forecasting, the mean or average of a given number of the most recent demand amounts, which becomes the forecast for the next (first future) period; the procedure repeats each period by dropping the oldest, and adding the newest, demand.

Multiple regression/correlation   A mathematical model allowing for investigation of a number of causal variables in order to determine their simultaneous effect on a predicted variable such as demand.

Negotiation   A form of purchasing without competitive bidding, typically in a stable supply situation; usually applies to high-dollar-volume items produced to a buyer's specs.

Net requirement   For an item, its gross requirement minus current or projected stock on hand.

Netting   A procedure for determining the net requirement for an item; a basic MRP calculation.

Normal time   Time for accomplishment of a work task after the cycle time has been adjusted to reflect pace rating. See also **Pace rating.**

Numerically controlled (NC) machine   A machine that performs tasks in response to pre-programmed digital instructions (numeric codes) on punched tape or in a computer program.

Offline buffer stock   Buffer stock that is kept out of active storage and handling; its purpose is to provide low-cost protection against infrequent, unpredictable process stoppages or surges in demand without consuming throughput time.

Open-office concept   An office arrangement plan that eliminates most floor-to-ceiling walls; stresses use of modular furniture and movable, partial-height partitions; and deemphasizes compartmentalization of people.

Open order   An order that has been placed but not completed.

Operation   Part of a job; one step or task that requires a new setup, often at a different work center.

Operations   The operating end of the business, where resources are transformed into goods and services.

Operations management   Direction and control of operations; includes self-management, expert management, team management, and formal manager management; aims are improvement of transformations and allied processes.

Order entry   Organizational acceptance of an order into the order-processing system; includes credit checks, customer documentation, translation into production terms, stock queries, and order number assignment.

Order promising   Making a commitment to a customer to ship or deliver an order.

Out-sourcing   Finding an outside source of a good or service, instead of making or providing it internally.

Overlapped production   Condition in which a lot is in production at two or more work centers at the same time, typically because some of the lot is rushed forward on a hot basis; normal practice within work cells.

p chart (percent-defective chart)   A process control chart for attributes, which shows the proportion or fraction defective in each sample.

Pace rating   Judging the pace of the subject of a time-standards study, where 100 percent is considered normal; yields a factor used in normalizing or leveling the raw cycle time.

Parent item   For a component, its next higher level assembly; the part into which a component goes.

Pareto chart   A chart showing items in any population grouped by category from most to least frequently occurring; useful in categorizing data in order to set priorities for process improvement.

Pay for skills   Remuneration system in which employees are paid more for acquiring additional skills and greater knowledge; also known as skill-based pay, or pay for knowledge.

Periodic maintenance   Regularly scheduled custodial services and preventive maintenance.

Perpetual inventory system   A system in which every issue from inventory triggers a check of on-hand stock to see if the reorder point has been reached.

Personal, rest, and delay (PR&D) allowance   Amount of time added to normal time to yield standard time; accommodates personal needs and unavoidable delay when setting time standards.

Planned order (planned order release)   Anticipated order placement; indicated by item, date, and quantity.

Planning horizon   Period of time covered by a certain type of plan; for example, a long-range forecast might, in a certain kind of business, have a planning horizon of five years.

Preautomation   What must be done to the work space to make the work possible for a machine to do; basically concentrates on close, exact positioning.

Precedence diagram   A chart showing a repetitive job broken into sequenced flow lines; used in assembly-line balancing.

Precontrol chart   A quality-monitoring chart composed of three colored zones that encompass specification (not control) limits; measures of quality are plotted, and the zones they fall into tell the operator what action to take.

Predictive maintenance   Maintenance in advance of failure or wear out, based on predicted life of the component to be maintained.

Preventive maintenance (PM)   Any actions, including adjustments, replacements, and basic cleanliness, that forestall equipment failure; may be based on calendar time, time of usage, or faults revealed in an inspection.

Priority report   A (typically) daily list of job priorities sent to a work center; also called a dispatch list.

Process   A unique set of interrelated elements that act together to determine performance; categories from which the specific elements are taken include labor, materials, methods, machines, measurement, maintenance, and management.

Process capability   In general, a statement of the ability of process output to meet specifications; inherent capability is the width (approximately six standard deviations) of the distribution of process output.

Process control   A condition signifying that all special or assignable variation has been removed from process output; only common or chance variation remains; also known as statistical control.

Process control chart   Statistical control chart on which to record samples of measured process outputs; the purpose is to note whether the process is statistically stable or changing, so that adjustments can be made as needed.

Process flowchart   See **Flowcharts.**

Process industry   An industry that produces goods that flow, pour, or mix together; also called continuous-flow process industry.

Process (functional) layout   A layout type in which similar facilities and functions are grouped together in one place, usually meaning that all people working in these functional areas are also grouped together.

Process lot   A number of units treated as one lot for processing; may be subdivided or combined with other lots into a different sized transfer lot for handling and transport.

Producible or **producibility**   Easy to make without error and undue cost with present or planned equipment and people; a desirable product design characteristic; also, manufacturability or operability.

Product layout   A type of layout in which facilities are placed along product flow lines, with the customer (next process) next to the provider.

Product planning   Developing lines of goods and services.

Product structure   See **Bill of materials (BOM).**

Production activity control   Keeping work on schedule on the shop floor, using progress information (feedback), which is compared with schedules; sometimes employs daily priority report, which gives priority based on relative lateness.

Production control   Directing or regulating the flow of work through the production cycle, from purchase of materials to delivery of finished items; flow control. A production control department may include operations planning, scheduling, dispatching, and expediting.

Production line   Multiple sequential processes arranged into one grand process to produce a product or narrow family of products.

Production/operations management (POM)   See **Operations management.**

Production plan   Total planned production, or production rate; unspecific as to product model or type of service.

Production rate   Pace of production output, expressed in units per time period.

Productivity   In general, output divided by input; in various forms, may apply to labor, materials, or other resources.

Program evaluation and review technique (PERT)   A network-based project management technique originally developed for R&D projects; about the same as CPM.

Progressive operations   Production in which material being worked on is passed from workstation to workstation; alternative to autonomous production.

Project   A large-scale, one-of-a-kind endeavor; generally employs large amounts of diverse resources.

Project manager   A manager or management team having responsibility for a project, not a function; various project manager types include project manager, commodity manager, project coordinator, project engineer, and brand manager, each having a different degree of authority over the project.

Pull system   A system in which the user pulls work from the maker or provider by some kind of signal (called kanban); pull signals should be issued at rate of actual usage.

Push system   A system in which the maker pushes work forward into storage or onto the next process with little regard for rate of use; rate of pushing out the work often is preset by schedule.

Quality assurance   In general, the activities associated with making sure that the customer receives quality goods and services; often, the name given to a department charged with carrying out these responsibilities.

Quality characteristic   A process performance (output) property of a product or service deemed important enough to control.

Quality control circle (quality circle)   A small work group that meets periodically to discuss ways to improve quality, productivity, or the work environment.

Quality cost   Costs of preventing defects, checking process output, and paying for the results of defective output; more broadly, the loss to society of any deviation from target.

Quality function deployment (QFD)   Matrix-based procedure for displaying customers' requirements, processes for meeting them, and competitors' versus one's own company's capabilities on each process; basic QFD matrix may be supplemented with other, more detailed process matrices. See also **House of quality.**

Queue limiter (queue limitation)   Device that places an upper limit on number of units waiting (or time waiting) for processing. See also **Kanban.**

Quick response program (QRP)   System of linking final retail sales with production and shipping schedules back through the chain of supply; usually employs point-of-sale scanning plus electronic communication and may employ direct shipment from a factory, thus avoiding distribution warehousing.

R chart (ranges chart)   A process control chart for variables; shows range of each sample, that is, within-sample variation.

Random events   In a time series, patternless occurrences, such as jumps or drops in demand, for which there is no apparent cause.

Regularized schedule   A schedule in which certain items are produced at regular intervals.

Reliability   Probability that an item will work at a given time.

Reorder point (ROP) Quantity of on-hand inventory that serves as a trigger for placing an order for more.

Repetitive operations Producing the same item or providing the same service over and over.

Requisition An internal request to have something purchased; usually goes to a purchasing department, which uses it in preparing a purchase order.

Rescheduling notice A notice (usually from an MRP system) that an order for a component part needs to be rescheduled; stems from a change in due dates or quantities for one or more parent items.

Residual inventory Inventory left over when an order is canceled or reduced in quantity.

Resource requirements planning (RRP) A gross check to see if items in the master schedule will overload a scarce resource; also known as rough-cut capacity planning on the trial master schedule.

Response-ratio analysis A method for measuring idle work in work centers by using ratios of lead time to work content, process speed to use rate, and pieces to workstations or operators; process improvements are reflected in smaller ratios.

Rolling forecast A forecast that is redone at intervals, typically dropping oldest data and replacing it with most recent data.

Rough-cut capacity planning Conversion of an operations plan into capacity needs for key resources; the purpose is to evaluate a plan before trying to implement it.

Routings Path from work center to work center that work follows in its transformation into a finished item or complete service; standard routings may be kept in records.

Run diagram A running plot of measurements of some process or quality characteristic, piece by piece as a process continues.

Scatter (correlation) diagram A plot of effects (e.g., quality changes) against experimental changes in process inputs.

Seasonal index Ratio of demand for a particular season to demand for the average season.

Seasonality (seasonal variation) Recurring pattern in a time series; occurring within one year and repeating annually.

Service level Percentage of orders filled from stock on hand.

Setup time See **Changeover time.**

Shop calendar A scheduling calendar with workdays as sequentially numbered days; sometimes numbered 000 to 999.

Simultaneous engineering Inclusion of supplier, process, and manufacturing engineers early in product design stages; aims for shorter lead times, better quality, and better coordination; concurrent design.

Slack (slack time) The amount of time an activity may be delayed without delaying the project schedule; usually changes as the project progresses.

Social loss (of bad quality) A concept introduced by Genichi Taguchi stating that there is a cost imparted to society whenever process output deviates from the target.

Soliciting competitive bids Inviting prospective suppliers to bid (offer a price) on a contract to provide goods or services according to specifications.

Special cause variation A type of variation in process output that can be traced to a specific cause such as a fault or malfunction, removal of which removes the variation.

Specification Process output description commonly in two parts: the target (nominal) and the tolerances.

Speculation (speculative) buying Purchasing to get an attractive price rather than because of need.

Standard data Tables of time-standard values used to construct synthetic standards.

Standard deviation (SD) A measure of dispersion in a distribution; equal to the square root of the variance; in forecasting, defined as the square root of the mean-square error.

Standard time The time a person is expected to take to complete a task; the normal time plus an allowance factor.

Standardization Settling on a few, rather than many, variations of a given part, product, or service.

Statistical process control (SPC) Collection of process analysis techniques including process flowchart, Pareto analysis, fishbone chart, run diagram, control chart, and scatter diagram.

Stockkeeping unit (SKU) An item of inventory at a particular geographic location. For example, if six packs of canned Classic Coca Cola are in a special display near the checkout counters and also stocked with the other soft drinks, that constitutes two SKU's.

Stockout Failure to deliver from stock upon receipt of a customer order.

Strategy A basic type of plan with far-reaching effects; a foundation for more specific plans.

Streamlined operations Steady-flow operations with few delays, stops, starts, or storages.

Synchronized schedules (synchronized processing) Processing with schedules in which the timing of delivery or production of a component is meshed with the use rate of the parent item.

Systematic layout planning (SLP) A multistep approach to layout planning based on flow and relationship data.

Systems contract A contract with a supplier for a defined set of items, often allowing orders to be placed by line managers without going through the purchasing department.

Theory of constraints Approach to operations that attempts to schedule and feed work so as to maximize work flow rate (and therefore cash flow as well) through bottlenecks and constraints.

Therbligs   The 17 basic units of work motion, first set forth by Frank and Lillian Gilbreth; examples include grasp, move, release, select, and position.

Throughput time   Elapsed time, including all delays, to transform resources into goods or services; same as **lead time.**

Time fence   A point on a company's planning horizon that separates the firm portion (typically, the near future) from the tentative portion (more distant future).

Time measurement unit (TMU)   A time unit in MTM analysis: 1 TMU = 0.0006 minutes, or 0.00001 hours.

Time-phased order point (TPOP)   A subset of MRP for handling independent demand items.

Time series   A sequential set of observations of a variable taken at regular intervals over time.

Time standard   See **Standard time.**

Time study   A direct approach for obtaining the cycle time to be used in setting a time standard; obtained by stopwatch or film analysis.

Tolerance stackup   See **Variation stackup.**

Total preventive maintenance (TPM)   A full agenda of procedures that improve dependability of equipment, with emphasis on maintaining equipment before it breaks down; bestows primary responsibility for PM on equipment operator.

Total quality (TQ)   Comprehensive management approach to ensure quality throughout an organization; includes planning and design, supplier and user/processor interface, self-inspection for control, and continual improvement in customer service through process monitoring and feedback; places primary responsibility for quality at the source (i.e., the maker or provider).

Total quality control (TQC)   See **Total quality.**

Total quality management (TQM)   See **Total quality.**

Tracking signal   Typically, the cumulative deviation in a time series divided by the MAD; used as a limit to trigger adjustment in smoothing coefficients in adaptive smoothing models.

Transfer lot   A number of units treated as one lot for transport; may be larger or smaller than lots sized for processing (**process lots**).

Trend   A long-term shift, positive or negative, in the value of a time series; also known as slope.

Undercapacity (labor) scheduling   Scheduling labor output at less than full capacity; allows schedule to be met on most days and allows times for operators to work on quality and maintenance.

Unit load concept   A concept calling for accumulation of enough pieces to make a "full load" before moving any pieces.

Utilization   Ratio of time in use to time available.

Value-adding activities   Activities in which value is added to the resource undergoing transformation; does not include non-value-adding transactions, inspections, handling, delays, and so on.

Value analysis   Examination of existing product design specifications with the aim of lowering cost; typically centered in the purchasing department.

Value engineering   Same as **value analysis,** but typically centered in the engineering organization.

Variables inspection   A test in which measurements of an output (quality) characteristic are taken.

Variation stackup   The output that results when two or more components at extreme edges within tolerance (specification) limits are assembled or mixed together; often the result is an assembly, batch, or service that performs poorly or is out of specification limits.

Work breakdown structure (WBS)   Product-oriented list and definition of major modules and secondary components in a project.

Workcell   See **Cell.**

Work content time   Time required to make a complete assembly or perform a job; usually the sum of the times of all tasks needed.

Work in process (WIP)   Partly completed work that is either waiting between processes or is in process.

$\overline{X}$ chart (averages chart)   A process control chart for variables inspection showing the sample averages for a number of samples or subgroups and thus revealing between-sample variations.

Zero defects (ZD)   Proposed as the proper goal of a quality program; an alternative to the past practice of setting an acceptable quality (defect) level.